SOCIOBIOLOGY AND PSYCHOLOGY:
Ideas, Issues and Applications

SOCIOBIOLOGY AND PSYCHOLOGY:
Ideas, Issues and Applications

Edited by

CHARLES CRAWFORD
Simon Fraser University

MARTIN SMITH
Brock University

DENNIS KREBS
Simon Fraser University

IEA LAWRENCE ERLBAUM ASSOCIATES, PUBLISHERS
1987   Hillsdale, New Jersey   London

Lawrence Erlbaum Associates, Inc. Publishers
365 Broadway
Hillsdale, New Jersey 07642

Library of Congress Cataloging-in-Publication Data
Sociobiology and psychology.

  Includes bibliographies and indexes.
  1. Psychology. 2. Sociobiology. 3. Genetic
psychology. I. Crawford, Charles (Charles B.)
II. Smith, Martin (Martin S.) III. Krebs, Dennis.
BF57.S62   1987   304.5   87-6783
ISBN 0-89859-580-0

Printed in the United States of America
10 9 8 7 6 5 4 3 2

Contents

Preface

Sociobiology is the scientific study of the biological basis of social behaviors. As a synthesis of ideas from behavioral ecology, population genetics, ethology, comparative psychology and behavior genetics, sociobiology offers the opportunity of integrating ideas from biology into the social sciences and even into the humanities. Some believe that its eventual impact may be as great as that of psychoanalysis and behaviorism.

Psychology spans that part of the social sciences extending from sociology through social psychology, personality theory, learning, perception, motivation, developmental psychology and comparative and physiological psychology to the biological disciplines of ethology, genetics and neurophysiology. Since each of these subdisciplines of psychology has at least some roots in biology, psychology is ideally situated to assist in the integration of evolutionary thinking into the social sciences. Furthermore, psychology has had long and explicit associations with the biological sciences. Psychologists have been conducting animal and physiological research and attempting to generalize from animals to humans for almost a hundred years. The quantitative style of reasoning used by evolutionary theorists, ecologists and population geneticists is shared by psychology. The statistical models of test theory, for example, are similar to those used by quantitative geneticists.

Sophisticated explanations of behavior require an understanding of both its adaptive significance and the proximate mechanisms producing it. An understanding of how animals learn, perceive, and are motivated is required in order to put these explanations together. Psychology is the discipline that has been most concerned with providing these explanations. It has, therefore, an important role to play in developing integrative explanations of behavior.

Furthermore, the discipline of psychology needs a "re-animation" of its biological roots. Current psychological thinking about social behavior is dominated by social learning, Piagetian and psychodynamic theory. Few of the proponents of these theories have made a serious attempt to integrate ideas from modern biology into their thinking, at least partly because psychologists are generally unaware of recent advances in evolutionary theory. Contemporary psychology is having trouble constructing a comprehensive view of human nature, and an infusion of biological concepts could invigorate the discipline.

The aim of the editors was to compile a volume that would facilitate the integration of evolutionary thinking into psychology and the other social sciences by communicating some of the major *ideas, issues* and *applications* of sociobiology that are relevant to psychology. The book is intended to be intelligible to senior psychology undergraduates, but should also be useful to the professional psychologist desiring an introduction to an exciting new way of thinking about psychological problems.

Although most of the chapters deal with the authors' own work, they were written specifically for this book. The treatment is meant to be thorough, but nontechnical. The editors have attempted to maintain a consistent level of sophistication throughout the chapters. It should be possible to use this volume in senior undergraduate and graduate courses in human sociobiology, social development, behavioral biology and psychology. Anthropologists, biologists and sociologists may also find it useful.

This volume grew out of a two-year institute on sociobiology sponsored by a Programs of Distinction grant from Simon Fraser University. Many of the articles in it developed from presentations sponsored by this institute. Others were commissioned by the editors because the topics seem particularly interesting to psychologists or because many psychologists appeared to be uninformed about critical ideas.

Charles Crawford
Martin Smith
Dennis Krebs

ACKNOWLEDGMENTS

The authors wish to acknowledge the generous support of Simon Fraser University, which made this book possible. Many of the chapter authors participated in a two-year lecture series on psychology and sociobiology sponsored by a Simon Fraser University Programs of Distinction Project Grant. The university also provided funds for construction of the index and for proofreading.

Contributors

David M. Buss
Department of Psychology
University of Michigan
Ann Arbor, Michigan

Denys de Catanzaro
Department of Psychology
McMaster University
Hamilton, Ontario, Canada, L8S 4K1

Charles B. Crawford
Department of Psychology
Simon Fraser University
Burnaby, British Columbia, V5A 1S6

Martin Daly
Department of Psychology
Hamilton, Ontario, L8S 4K1

Robert Fagen
School of Fisheries and Science
University of Alaska
Juneau, Alaska, 99801

John L. Fuller
Department of Psychology
State University of New York at
Binghamton
Binghamton, New York

Dennis Krebs
Department of Psychology
Simon Fraser University
Burnaby, British Columbia, V5A 1S6

Katherine M. Noonan
609 Kains Road
Albany, California 94706

Richard H. Porter
John F. Kennedy Centre for Research on
Education and Human Development
Vanderbilt University
Nashville, Tennessee, 73203

Michael Ruse
Departments of History and Philosophy
University of Guelph
Guelph, Ontario, N1G 2W1

Irwin Silverman
Department of Psychology
York University
Downsview, Ontario M3J 1P3

Martin S. Smith
Department of Psychology
Brock University
St. Catherines, Ontario, L2S 3A1

Donald Symons
Department of Anthropology
University of California
Santa Barbara, California, 93106

Nancy Wilson Thornhill
Department of Anthropology
University of New Mexico
Albuquerque, N.M., U.S.A. 87131

Randy Thornhill
Department of Biology
The University of New Mexico
Albuquerque, New Mexico, 87131

Margo Wilson
Department of Psychology
McMaster University
Hamilton, Ontario, L8S 4K1

Pierre L. van den Berghe
Department of Sociology
University of Washington
Seattle, Washington, 98195

SOCIOBIOLOGY AND PSYCHOLOGY:
Ideas, Issues and Applications

I
IDEAS

One of the problems that psychologists encounter when they consider E. O. Wilson's definition of sociobiology as "The systematic study of the biological basis of all social behavior" is that they associate the word biology with brain physiology, hormones, nerve impulses and other proximate biological mechanisms. However, biology, as used by sociobiologists, refers to the modern synthetic theory of evolution, which is a synthesis of natural selection and modern genetics. When used in this sense biology may have ramifications not only for the social sciences, but also for the humanities.

The first section of the book introduces readers to contemporary evolutionary thinking and to some fundamental sociobiological concepts. Chapters 1 and 2 deal with the theory of evolution. In the first chapter Charles Crawford, who was originally trained in psychology and statistics, introduces several key sociobiological concepts, illustrates how they can be used by psychologists, and explores how an evolutionary perspective can be of value to psychologists. In the following chapter an entomologist and evolutionary ecologist, Katherine Noonan, provides a primer of evolutionary theory for psychologists. Together these two chapters provide an overview of evolutionary theory and some general suggestions regarding its relevance to understanding human behavior.

Sociobiology is a controversial discipline and the validity of applying ideas from the modern synthetic theory of evolution to

1

human behavior has been questioned. Michael Ruse, a philosopher of science, addresses some of these controversies in Chapter 3. He argues that although sociobiology has a long ways to go before it becomes as solid a science as quantum mechanics, or even molecular biology, it does provide a vital new way of understanding human nature.

The paradox of altruism lies at the heart of sociobiology and its relation to psychology. The Ideas section concludes with an essay on the psychology and biology of altruism by Dennis Krebs. He is a theoretical social psychologist who has found sociobiological theory useful as one of a number of paradigms that integrate and organize our ideas about altruism and other social behaviors.

We hope that the four essays in this section will aid psychologists in applying and critically evaluating the use of evolutionary thinking by psychologists and other life scientists. There are conceptual issues involved in the integration of psychology and sociobiology that are particularly important. Some of these are considered in the second section of the book.

1

Sociobiology: Of What Value to Psychology?

Charles Crawford
Simon Fraser University

> *Man with all his noble qualities, with sympathy that feels for the most debased, with benevolence which extends not only to other men but to the humblest of living creature, with his god-like intellect which has penetrated into the movements and constitution of the solar system—with all these exalted powers—still bears in his bodily frame the indelible stamp of his lowly origin.*
> —Charles Darwin in *The Descent of Man, 1871*

Most psychologists would find little to object to in Darwin's words. Many would undoubtedly stand up and argue that the theory of evolution is the explanation of the origin of life that should be taught in school. But suppose the phrase "bodily frame" was interpreted as Darwin surely intended, as meaning that man's behavior as well as his physical structure "still bears the indelible stamp of his lowly origin," how many psychologists would then defend it? Controversy has raged around Edward O. Wilson, Richard Alexander and other sociobiologists because they have been forcefully arguing that we cannot fully understand human nature until we explore its biological roots and how they affect our actions.

Sociobiology is the systematic study of the biological basis of all social behaviors. Its explanatory tools are provided by the modern synthetic theory of evolution which is a synthesis of natural selection and genetics. Ecology, ethology, comparative psychology, population biology, and behavioral genetics are its supporting sciences. The evolutionary significance of altruistic, cooperative, parental, mating, aggressive, territorial, and communicative behaviors is particularly intriguing to sociobiologists.

3

Sociobiological concepts have been used to help explain a wide variety of animal behaviors including: the evolution of sterile castes in insects (Hamilton, 1964), alarm calling in birds and rodents (Barash, 1982; Hoogland, 1981, 1983; Sherman, 1980), "rape" in waterfowl and other animals (Barash, 1977; McKinney, Derrickson, & Mineau, 1983; Thornhill, 1980), "prostitution" in tropical hummingbirds (Wolf, 1975), "jealousy" in birds (Barash, 1976; Erickson & Zenone, 1976; Rissman, 1983), clutch size in birds (Darwin, 1859; Lack, 1968; Ricklefs, 1977), infanticide in langurs, lions, and rodents (Bertram, 1975; Hausfater & Hrdy, 1984; Hrdy, 1979; McLean, 1983) and induced abortion in rodents and feral horses (Berger, 1983; Bruce, 1960). Biologists, psychologists, anthropologists and sociologists have used its principles to help explain human helping behavior and altruism (Alexander, 1974, 1979; Axelrod & Hamilton, 1981; Chagnon & Irons, 1979; Krebs & Miller, 1985; Trivers, 1971), cooperation (Alexander, 1974, 1979; Trivers, 1971, 1985), the avoidance of incest (Shepher, 1983; van den Berghe, 1983), child abuse (Daly & Wilson, 1980), homicide (Daly & Wilson, 1982), rape (Shields & Shields, 1983; Thornhill & Thornhill, 1983), suicide and self-destructive behavior (de Catanzaro, 1980), war (Alcock, 1984; Shaw, 1985), male sexual jealousy (Daly, Wilson, & Weghorst, 1982), grand parental investment (Smith, 1982; Turke & Betzig, 1985), bequest behavior (Smith, Kish, & Crawford, 1984) and competition, sometimes involving war, rape and resource allocation (Betzig, 1986; Chagnon & Irons, 1979).

Over a thousand articles and several dozen books on evolution and human behavior have appeared during the last 10 years. Journals such as *Animal Behavior, The American Naturalist,* and *The Journal of Theoretical Biology* have been publishing extensions of its concepts and new applications of its principles for some time. Five new sociobiology journals have recently been founded. Of these, *Ethology and Sociobiology, Behavioral Ecology and Sociobiology,* and the *Journal of Biological and Social Structures* are probably of most interest to psychologists interested in the study of human behavior.

PSYCHOLOGICAL RESISTANCE TO EVOLUTIONARY THEORY

Early psychologists such as Freud, William James and the Chicago Functionalists embraced Darwinism with enthusiasm. During the past half century, however, a major activity of psychologists has been "de-biologizing" the discipline. Social learning theory, cognitive theory, what might be called third generation psychoanalysis, and politically liberal approaches to the amelioration of social problems currently dominate mainstream academic psychology. These approaches focus on nurture, not nature, in attempting to understand human behavior.

There are both political and technical reasons why psychologists have resisted incorporating ideas from the theory of evolution into their thinking. Those who desired scientific justification for predatory business ethics, social inequality, the existing social order, racism and imperialism used the ideas of "the struggle for existence" and "the survival of the fittest" to support their causes. In a talk to a Sunday School class, John D. Rockefeller stated:

> The growth of a large business is merely a survival of the fittest . . . it is merely the working out of a law of nature and a law of God. (Allen, 1975, p. 260)

Later Adolf Hitler wrote:

> If we did not respect the law of nature, imposing our will by the right of the stronger, a day would come when the wild animals would again devour us—then the insects would eat the wild animals, and finally nothing would exist on earth except the microbes. (Trever-Roper, 1953, p. 39)

The fact that the theory of evolution was used to justify such views provides a heavy burden for those wishing to use the theory of evolution to help understand human behavior.

However, the primary reason why the theory of evolution has been used by psychologists merely as a convenient framework for integrating apparently diverse ideas, or as a last resort when standard psychological explanations failed, is that until recently it did not provide a set of constructs useful for formulating explanations of particular human and animal behaviors. The development of concepts such as inclusive fitness, parental investment, evolutionary stable strategies, reciprocal altruism, and life history theory are revolutionizing the study of animal behavior. The purpose of this volume is to explain the use of such concepts to psychologists and explore their value for constructing explanations of important human behaviors.

An example illustrating the difference between traditional evolutionary theory and current theory may be instructive. Patry (1983), writing in the *American Psychologist* argued that evolutionary theory is of limited value in formulating hypotheses about developmental processes since they must be based on the disputed notion that ontogeny recapitulates phylogeny. However, it is the modern theory of "the evolution of life histories" (Gadgil & Bossert, 1970; Hamilton, 1966; Stearns, 1976; Williams, 1957, 1966) not the obsolete idea of "ontogeny recapitulating phylogeny" that may be of use to developmental psychologists. These theorists argue that the developmental time table of organisms is a trait shaped by natural selection and that "key life history traits are brood size, size of young, the age distribution of reproductive effort, the interaction of reproductive effort with adult mortality and the variation of these traits among individual's progeny" (Stearns, 1976, p. 3). In chapter 9 Martin Smith discusses how an understanding of life history theory and other sociobiological concepts may help developmental psychologists integrate the psychological and biological study of development as well as aid them in formulating specific developmental hypotheses.

THE THEORY OF EVOLUTION

Sociobiologists are interested in adaptation. According to Dunbar (1982) an adaptation is ''an attribute that permits the possessor to accomplish those immediate objectives that it must achieve in order to survive and reproduce successfully'' (p. 12). Any anatomical structure, physiological process or behavior pattern that contributes to an individual's ability to survive and reproduce is said to be adaptive. Although we are accustomed to thinking of the teeth of lions, the hooves of horses and the hands of humans as adaptations, we are less inclined to regard the cub-killing behavior of male lions (Schaller, 1972), stallion-induced abortion in feral horses (Berger, 1983), and love in humans (Barash, 1979) as behaviors that may have evolved through natural selection to promote reproductive fitness.

The notion of adaptation appears again and again throughout this book. Williams (1966), in one of the most influential books on evolution written since Darwin, argued that it is a special and onerous concept, that principles for distinguishing adaptations from beneficial effects are not well developed, and therefore should only be used with care. A brief discussion of some of the problems associated with determining if a behavior can be said to be an adaptation appears later in this chapter.

Let us take a brief look at Darwin's theory of evolution in order to prepare ourselves for considering its value to psychologists. There are two complementary ways of describing evolution. The first, which follows directly from Darwin's work focuses on the adaptations themselves, and the ecological pressures responsible for their formation. It can be explained in terms of the following ''assumptions and inferences'':

Assumption 1: All species are capable of over-producing offspring.
Assumption 2: The size of populations of individuals tends to remain relatively stable over time.
Assumption 3: Resources for supporting individuals are limited.
Inference 1: A struggle for existence among individuals ensues.
Assumption 4: Individuals differ in their ability to survive and reproduce.
Assumption 5: At least some individual variation in this ability is heritable.
Inference 2: Differential contribution of offspring to the next generation by individuals of different genotypes, which is by definition natural selection, occurs.
Inference 3: Through many generations evolution of traits that are more adaptive than others will occur through natural selection.

Some aspect of the environment, a change in climate, the arrival of a new competitor for food, poses a problem for an organism. A solution, thicker fur, a taste for a different food, an adaptation, is needed. The assumptions and inferences described above indicate how evolution by natural selection provides the solution. The actual adaptation that evolves is limited by previously existing adaptations, called preadaptations, and shaped by the ecological pressure that posed the problem. Thus an adaptation is often "jerry-rigged" from a limited set of components rather than the work of an ideal engineer (Gould, 1982).

This view might be called the phenotypic view of evolution as the focus is on the anatomical structures, physiological process or the behavior patterns that are the solution to the problem faced by the organism. Although at least some of the phenotypic variation must be heritable genetic concepts are not explicitly required. It is possible, however, to describe evolution by natural selection in terms of changes in gene frequencies caused by mutation, selection, migration, genetic drift, and other processes. This more quantitative approach is often favored by sociobiologists because it enables them to construct precise models of evolutionary processes that may be tested through experimental research, field studies or computer simulation.

Psychologists and other social scientists who may have been taught the more traditional view of evolutionary theory sometimes have difficulty relating the more quantitative, modern view, to behavior. The two descriptions are complementary and together make up the modern synthetic theory of evolution. In chapter 2 Katherine Noonan, who is a biologist, attempts to explain the modern synthesis to psychologists. Michael Ruse, a philosopher of science, examines, in chapter 3, its viability for answering questions about human behavior.

Several points must be emphasized before turning our attention to the relevance of the theory of evolution for psychology. First, inference 1 does not imply that the struggle for existence must be "red in tooth and claw." Differential production or survival of offspring by genetically different members of the population is the basis of evolution by natural selection. Animals use a variety of subtle and not so subtle strategies for competing with conspecifics. For example, juvenile Florida scrub jays apparently increase their fitness by deferring reproduction in order to assist their parents raise an additional brood of siblings (Woolfenden & Fitzpatrick, 1984). In "The geometry of the selfish herd" Hamilton (1971) suggests that individual animals in aggregations may position themselves in such a way that their risk of predation relative to others in the aggregation is minimized.

Second, assumptions 4 and 5 require only that a small proportion of the observed variation in a trait is due to genetic differences among individuals in the population for natural selection to affect the trait. Evolving traits do not depend on genetic preprogramming! If the ontogeny of a trait is influenced by environmental factors, biologists refer to it as a *facultative trait* and the genes involved in its ontogeny as *facultative genes*. The white crowned sparrow, for example, must hear an adult male sparrow sing while it is a nestling and itself sing as a juvenile if it is to sing a complete song as an adult (Konishi, 1965). Moreover, the young sparrow does not, and indeed cannot, learn the song of another species. Apparently this developmental process ensures that the species' song is learned, but that it can be adjusted to local dialects.

Nor do these assumptions deny genotype-environment interactions. If two different facultative genes bias development in different directions depending on the nature of the environment in which the development occurs, then a genotype-environment interaction is said to have occurred. Some of the best examples come from the study of the effects of early experience on adult behavior. Cooper and Zubek (1958) reared Tryon's "maze bright" and "maze dull" rats in enriched and impoverished environments. The enriched environment had no effect on the "bright" rats, but it improved the performance of the "dull" rats. The impoverished environment had little effect on the "dull" rats, but it had an very detrimental effect on the performance of the "bright" rats. Natural selection has produced facultative traits and genotype-environment interactions because they contribute to fitness!

Evolution does not have a purpose or a goal. Although some organisms such as killer whales and sharks appear to be ideally adapted to their circumstances, in comparison with others such as the whooping crane or the California condor that are on the endangered species list, they cannot be said to have evolved to some ideal state of "whaleness" or "sharkness." The introduction of a predator or a change in the physical conditions of their environment could threaten their existence. Evolution is a purely mechanical process: phenotypes that pass on many genes through their offspring and relatives are fit, those that pass on few genes are less fit. Organisms are not evolving to some ideal state. Humans may not be evolving toward the gods!

Finally, it must be emphasized that studying the evolutionary significance of behaviors, whether they are human or animal behaviors, does not require the assumption that evolution is currently occurring, or that behaviors studied are currently adaptive. The only assumption required is that adaptations that evolved to solve problems encountered in the past may affect current behavior in some way. The perspective, that human behavior should be influenced by a history of natural selection, is most clearly developed in the work of Alexander (1979) and Chagnon and Irons (1979) and their students. It is reflected in many of the chapters in the final section of this book.

EVOLUTION AND PSYCHOLOGY

Let us consider some of the benefits that psychology can obtain from a serious study of evolution and how it works.

Clarifying the relationship
between humans and animals

The fact that a very large proportion of intergenerational behavioral change in humans is due to cultural and environmental change has led many social scientists to conclude that our evolutionary past is of little consequence in understanding our current behavior (Washburn, 1978). However, if we believe that human beings are an evolved species, as do the contributors to this volume, the question of whether adaptations contributing to survival and reproduction in the remote past affect our behavior in some way demands scientific attention.

Evolutionary theory tells us that species are related in the sense that more recent species evolved from earlier species. Therefore, we should not be too surprised to find the presence of some traits that were once considered uniquely human in animals. For example, the fact that chimpanzees can be taught a few words is not surprising from an evolutionary perspective, nor is the fact that complex social hierarchies exist within many primate groups. Similarly, we should not be surprised to find some traits within ourselves that reflect adaptations evolved by our primate ancestors. Behaviors such as rape, induced abortion, and infanticide, which if judged by current human standards are clearly immoral, have apparently evolved independently several times. Is it possible that some of our less pleasant human traits have a basis in our evolutionary past? Randy and Nancy Thornhill's chapter on human rape (chapter 11), Martin Daly and Margo Wilson's chapter on family violence (chapter 12) and Denys de Catanzaro's chapter on suicide and self-destructive behavior (chapter 13) are relevant to this point.

An homology is any similarity between two species that can be explained by their descent from a common ancestor (Dewsbury, 1978). The wings of birds and bats are said to be homologous as forelegs since their evolution can be traced to forelegs in a common reptile ancestor. Early ethologists such as Konrad Lorenz believed that identifying behavioral homologies was important for understanding the evolution of behavior. Researchers who study the behavior of nonhuman primates in an attempt to illuminate some aspect of human behavior often share this view.

However, understanding the evolutionary significance of a behavior does not depend on tracing its origin. Nor does it depend on studying analogies, similarities in structures and behaviors in two or more species due to their response to similar ecological pressures, rather than to their common ancestry. For example, Thornhill and Thornhill (chapter 11) discuss the evolutionary significance of "rape" in scorpionflies and humans. Their analysis suggests some similarities between the evolution of this behavior in the two species. However, they do not claim that human rape is analogous to scorpionfly rape, or that understanding scorpionfly rape helps explain human rape. They are merely applying the same theory, the theory of evolution, to the behavior of the two species. Its use does not depend on drawing analogies between them.

There are at least four approaches for studying the evolutionary significance of behaviors. The *historical* method involves reconstructing the evolutionary history of the behavior. Since the results of behavior rarely fossilize, looking for "behavioral homologies" is unlikely to elucidate the evolution of a particular human behavioral adaptation.

The *comparative* method relies on comparing species with similar ancestry, but living in different environments and/or comparing species with different ancestries, but living in similar environments. There are several reasons why this method is difficult to use in the study of human behavioral adaptations. The nearest common ancestor of humans and the other great apes (organutans, chimpanzees and gorillas) lived from 6 to 10 million years ago. The difference between human behavior and that of the other great apes is so pronounced that the validity of comparisons is questionable. Moreover, since behavior does not fossilize, comparisons must be made on the basis of the artifacts of behavior such as tools. Although this method has been used by primatologists such as Sarah Hrdy (1981), it is difficult to apply to the fine grained behaviors that are of interest to psychologists.

The *evaluative* method involves determining the value of the behavior in promoting reproductive fitness. This method was used by Tinbergen (1963a) when he showed that egg shell removal by black headed gulls reduces predation of chicks. There are at least two reasons why it is difficult to use in the study of human behavior. Its strongest form requires experimental manipulations that may be unethical. Moreover, its use requires that the behavior in question is currently adaptive. Thus it cannot be applied to behaviors which may have been adaptive in prehistorical times, but are no longer adaptive for individuals living in modern industrial societies.

The *predictive* method which involves setting up coherent sets of hypotheses derived from evolutionary theory and then testing them using various techniques has the most promise for studying the evolutionary significance of human behaviors. It was this approach that Thornhill and Thornhill (1983) used in their evolutionary analysis of human rape. This approach is reflected in many of the chapters in part III.

Provides a Critical Perspective
for Analyzing Conceptions of Human Nature

We have all realized that the theory of evolution eliminates the necessity of using "gods" and "souls" for explaining behavior. Its use, however, is not limited to the extirpation of nonscientific concepts. The brief discussion of "behaving for the good of the group or species" and "intrafamily conflict" that follows illustrates how an understanding of evolutionary theory may help psychologists develop a more critical attitude toward the concepts they employ for explaining behavior.

Laymen as well as psychologists and other social scientists often assume that there is a tendency for organisms to behave for the good of group in which they reside or the species to which they belong. Two examples taken from recent issues of the *American Psychologist* illustrate this assumption:

> The modern biological evolutionary theory is based on the dual process of mutations of genes and increased transmission via the gene pool of the genes *from which the species profits the most,* . . . [emphasis added] (Patry, 1983, p. 1027)

Later, in the same year, Miller (1983) wrote:

> In other words, although it is the individual organism that lives by growing and maintaining itself, it does this in the context of a group of closely related and interbreeding organisms. *It is this local population, or deme, and its gene pool that is the entity which ultimately must struggle against disorder in order to survive* . . . But sexual reproduction has inherent risks. It means bringing together the germ cells (sperm and ova) from two separate individuals in a way and with a frequency *that ensures maintenance of the deme.* [emphasis added] (p. 1198)

Both authors assume what biologist Wynne-Edwards (1962) assumed when he argued that selection acts on groups rather than on individuals.

Although a number of models of group selection have been proposed, they have usually foundered on the problem of "cheating" (Maynard Smith, 1976; Williams, 1966). Suppose that groups were made up of individuals who sacrifice some of their reproductive fitness for the good of other group members. An individual possessing a mutation that programmed it to accept, or enabled it to learn to accept, but not to reciprocate, helping behavior would leave more offspring than altruistic individuals in the group. Groups made up of individuals acting for the good of the group or species would be undermined by mutation from within and by immigration from without. A more thorough discussion of the problems of group selection is given by Katherine Noonan in chapter 2. The inadequacies of theories of group selection cast a shadow of doubt on psychological theories that implicitly assume that individuals behave for the common good of the group.

A major step in resolving the paradox created by these arguments and the fact that altruism exists in many species of animals and may even exist in plants (Trivers, 1985) was made when Hamilton (1964) showed that the behavior of an individual can affect the passage of its genes into future generations in two ways: (1) directly through its offspring, and (2) indirectly through offspring that relatives are able to rear *because they are helped by the individual.* Thus, nepotism, helping behavior directed toward relatives, can evolve through natural selection.

Hamilton's broadened notion of fitness, known as inclusive fitness, is one of the most powerful concepts that sociobiology has to offer the social sciences for understanding helping and conflict behavior and will appear again and again throughout this volume. It focuses attention on genetic relatedness, mechanisms for recognizing relatives, and the behavioral consequences of genetic kinship. Richard Porter discusses kin recognition, its functions and mediating mechanisms (chapter 7); Katherine Noonan provides a more technical discussion of the concept and the difficulties in employing it in her primer on evolution (chapter 2); and Dennis Krebs explains its role in understanding altruism (chapter 4). Some of its ramifications for suicide and self-destructive behavior are described by Denys de Catanzaro in chapter 13.

Many of us like to think of the family in a romantic light: as a harmonious group of loving individuals cooperating to bring happiness to one another. This view has led many individuals to oppose divorce, abortion, and the division of children between parents after a marriage breakup. Trivers (1974) provided a more realistic view of the family when he showed how Hamilton's (1964) concept of inclusive fitness can be used to explain why parents, offspring, and siblings can be shaped by natural selection to disagree on how much assistance each should give and receive, and hence why a certain amount of conflict can be expected within families.

Assume that parents, offspring, and siblings are shaped by natural selection to behave in such a way that their actions maximize their respective inclusive fitnesses: the number of genes replicated in subsequent generations through behavior directed to their descendants and the descendants of their relatives. Now an individual shares one-half its genes with its offspring and only one-quarter with its sibling's offspring. Therefore, siblings that seek an unequal share of their parent's resources may have greater fitness than those that behave in a more equitable fashion. But parents are equally related to all their offspring and should be selected to resist this conflict. Sibling rivalry and parental desires to reduce it are no surprise to sociobiologists.

A similar argument can be made to explain not only why natural selection might shape parents and offspring to disagree on the age at which parental care is terminated, but also on the amount of parental care provided. Weaning aggression and anxiety as well as parental offspring conflict are expected if ontogeny is viewed from an evolutionary perspective (Trivers, 1974). Psychologists use concepts such as "sibling rivalry" to explain intrafamily conflicts, sometimes implying that such conflicts are "unnatural." Understanding and dealing with family conflicts may be easier once we realize that both helping and conflict behavior are to be expected within the family. Trivers' ideas are important for anyone interested in the behavior of the members of animal and human families. Martin Daly's and Margo Wilson's discussion on family violence in chapter 12 and Martin Smith's chapter on sociobiology and developmental psychology give some indication of how psychologists might use them.

Focuses Attention on the Behavior of Individuals

Darwin (1871) observed that behavior probably changes before the physiological structures mediating it. Thus, an attempt at using tools likely produces selection pressure for the evolution of hands and brains. The idea is that the function of an organ changes as a function of changes in the physical environment and the behaviors of the other organisms living in it. The structural changes are an accommodation to the functional changes. Behavior is the evolutionary pacemaker (Wilson, 1975).

Since natural selection acts primarily on individuals rather than on groups, the behavior of individuals, which provides the data on which most current research and theorizing in psychology is based, must be of great importance in understanding evolution in general and the evolution of human nature in particular. Anthropologists, sociologists, and other social scientists have a place in elucidating human nature. The role of psychologists, with their focus on the behavior of individuals, is crucial in this endeavor. It is a role that they have been reluctant to fill.

Focuses Attention on Emotion

The function of behavior in an evolutionary context is simply to keep the organism alive and well long enough to reproduce successfully. If the presence of an environmental event, such as an empty stomach, a predator, an infant requiring care, the loss of a prospective mate to a rival, a need for assistance, or an indication that a helped individual may not reciprocate, impinges on the inclusive fitness of an organism, then becoming aroused, evaluating the situation, and taking some kind of action is adaptive. Psychologists use the concepts of emotion, motivation, and cognition to explain the resulting actions.

An understanding of cognition helps us understand how organisms evaluate events and plan strategies for dealing with them. The concept of motivation can be used to explain how energy is mobilized and directed. However, it is the emotions, those states of psychological and physiological arousal, that are derived from problems ''solved'' during our millions of years of evolution that guide the present development of human behavior.

For sociobiologists the cortex is the servant of the hypothalamus (Wilson, 1975). This view requires that psychologists focus their attention on the interplay of emotions and cognition. The issue of emotion is relevant to the material in many of the following behaviors: to reciprocal altruism and other helping behaviors (chapter 4), to child abuse and infanticide (chapter 12), to suicide and self-destructive behavior (chapter 13), to incest (chapters 15 and 16), to rape (chapter 11) and to mate choice (chapter 14).

Focuses Attention on the Costs and Benefits of Learning

Psychologists often assume that more facultative behaviors are somehow more adaptive than those whose development is less facultative and that species possessing a large repertoire of learning abilities are better equipped for survival than those with fewer learning abilities. Sociobiologists realize, however, that learning is no exception to the rule that all adaptations have costs as well as benefits.

If there is a highly predictable relationship between a stimulus and an inclusive fitness enhancing response such as avoiding a predator, finding a mating partner or caring for offspring, then relatively tight genetic control of the development of the response may be adaptive. Moreover, such a system may have fewer neurophysiological and energetic requirements than one mediating more complex learning. If, however, stimuli similar to, but not requiring the response, can trigger it, then the response may be made in inappropriate circumstances. For example, some of the parasites of insects mimic the food soliciting behavior of their host's young and thereby obtain food and shelter. Human motion sickness may be the result of an adaptation for expelling toxic foods from the stomach (Alcock, 1984). Again, if a response depends on specific stimuli, then its possessor may have difficulty dealing with new or changing environments. In either case its fitness will suffer.

The flexibility and adaptability made possible by learning are well known. Its costs are often unappreciated. Delicate and energetically costly neurophysiology may be required. Fitness reducing information may be acquired as when a Norway rat or a human being learns to avoid an edible food because on first contact it was tainted or associated with a tainted food. Conspecifics and members of other species may exploit learning abilities. Humans and other animals practice deception by providing false information for others to learn (Alexander, 1974)). Given the costs and benefits associated with genetic involvement in development it is unlikely that any species, including *Homo sapiens,* is completely free of biological constraints on at least some of its learning abilities. More precisely, for learning to evolve individuals must learn adaptive things, therefore, there must be constraints on what can be learned. Both the capacities and the constraints are a product of evolutionary history (Alexander, 1979).

Lumsden and Wilson (1981, 1983) have elaborated this view. They consider three ways of transmitting culture from one member of a society to another: pure genetic transmission, pure cultural transmission, and gene-culture transmission, and they argue that a species with pure cultural transmission would evolve toward a culture based on gene-culture transmission. Moreover, the speed of the evolution is a function of the number of options available to individuals. Their argument is based on the premise that if the environment of a developing organism is varied and complex, biological guidelines for what is learned are adaptive. The human species with its vast array of cultural alternatives would thus evolve to a state where biological constraints affected learning. The *tabula rasa* state would not evolve.

Some type of restricted development must be involved in the acquisition of at least some human traits. They provide evidence that brother-sister incest avoidance, the learning of color vocabularies, infant preferences for object shapes and arrangements, the development of facial recognition, infant taste preferences, anxiety in the presence of strangers, and the acquisition of phobias are mediated by "secondary epigenetic rules" which are genetically influenced regularities during development that affect perceptual, emotional and cognitive development (Lumsden & Wilson, 1981).

Most chapter authors do not specifically deal with the proximate mechanisms for acquiring behaviors. However, some type of semirestricted development is implicit in the writings of most authors and are of particular importance in Robert Fagen's chapter on play (chapter 10) and van den Berghe's and the Thornhills' chapters on incest (chapters 15 and 16). In chapter 5 Donald Symons provides a provocative discussion of the subject that will interest psychologists, philosophers and anthropologists. "What genes can do," the subject of chapter 6 by John Fuller, is also relevant to this controversial issue.

Focuses Attention on Individual and Group Differences

Race, sex, and other group differences and individual differences in intelligence, personality, and achievement have fascinated psychology throughout this century. The notion that environmental differences are primarily, if not solely, responsible for these perturbing inequalities is widely accepted. An evolutionary perspective may require us to confront some unpleasant issues. Genetic diversity is essential to the theory of evolution because without it evolution could not occur. Therefore, if humans evolved through evolution by natural selection, a great deal of human diversity must have existed in the past and may still exist.

Even closely related strains and subspecies of animals may display genetically conditioned differences in behavioral traits (Fuller & Thompson, 1978; Plomin, deFries, & McClearn, 1980) These strains and subspecies exist because subgroups have inhabited slightly different ecological niches for considerable periods of time. The ecological niches that different "racial" groups inhabit differ to some extent. Human beings, for example, live in areas as diverse as the high arctic and the equator. They inhabit areas from sea level to areas thousands of feet above sea level. They exist in small nomadic groups and in large cities that have endured for thousands of years. These niches have produced strains of humans that differ in many anatomical and physiological traits. Similarly, some strains of human beings with concomitant genetically conditioned behavioral differences may exist. Doctrines built on the assumption that political equality requires that individual differences in behavioral traits are not genetically conditioned must somehow come to terms with this diversity. Psychologists can help with this task by integrating the study of differential psychology and ethics. Irwin Silverman provides an interesting discussion of race, racism and race relations in chapter 8.

The existence of group differences among humans does not imply that one strain is socially superior to another. It is essential to distinguish biological fitness from social standing. Michelangelo, Isaac Newton, and Leonardo da Vinci had zero reproductive fitness since they apparently did not leave offspring. However, their social standing is beyond question.

Darwin's theory of sexual selection predicts the existence of sex differences in behavior. Females are often a limiting resource for males since they usually put more time and energy into producing gametes, nurturing zygotes, and rearing young than do males. Darwin identified two kinds of male competition for access to this resource. In intrasexual selection, males compete with each other for access to females. The result is selection pressure for increased physical size, organs of threat, aggressiveness and dominance in males, and sexual dimorphism in these traits. Male elephant seals, for example, compete vigorously for access to females. They are about 60% larger than females and much heavier. Some males may have as many as 100 females in their harems.

Males may also compete with each other in terms of features that are attractive to females. This type of selection is referred to as epigamic selection, or intersexual selection, and is the result of female choice. The tail of the peacock provides the classic example. These two processes are assumed to reinforce each other since females who ''choose'' strong, dominant or large males will have sons exhibiting these traits who will therefore attract many mates and provide more grandchildren for their mothers (Fisher, 1930). Some of the implications of the theory of sexual selection for human mate choice are discussed by David Buss in chapter 14.

The greater male, than female, variance in human reproductive success and the sexual dimorphism present in the physical characteristics of humans suggests that we, too, are a sexually selected species and therefore that some genetically based differences in behavior related to sex may exist. But evolutionary theory also tells us that males and females are equal in a biological sense. Fisher (1930) proved that, if individuals in a species have one parent of each sex, it then follows that the amount of parental investment put into each sex must be equal at the time offspring become independent of their parents. An example may help to clarify this point.

Suppose that a female costs two units of time and energy to rear to independence while a male requires only one unit of similar investment to reach the same point in development. Let us further suppose that a mother has 100 units of time and energy available to rear offspring. If she invests in an equal number of males and females, her 100 units of parental care will produce 33.3 (33.3 females × 2 care units) females and 33.3 (33.3 males × one care unit) males or 66.6 offspring. On average, each of the 33.3 males and 33.3 females give her the same number of grandchildren since each grandchild *must have one parent of each sex.* Our hypothetical female might expect 66.6 × 66.6 = 4435.56 grandchildren.

Now consider another hypothetical female in the same population. She puts two units of investment into each of 25 females and one unit into each of 50 males. The same 100 units of parental care now bring 25 daughters and 50 sons to independence. Each of the sons and and daughters will give her on average the same number of grand offspring. Such a "wise" female can expect 75 × 75 = 5625 grandchildren. Thus, natural selection will produce an equilibrium sex ratio that is inversely proportional to the investment in males and females: the cost of males × the proportion of males = the cost of females × the proportion of females. It follows that if the sex ratio for a species is 50:50, the cost of rearing the sexes to the point of independence from their parents must be the same.

However, the fact that they are biologically equal and receive equal investment does not mean that they are biologically identical or that the patterns of investment in males and females are identical. Males, for example, may require more food while females may require more protection from predators. Moreover, the theory applies to the population. It is possible that particular individuals or members of subgroups may bias their investment toward one sex or the other.

Sex allocation theory is concerned with how an individual can maximize its fitness by partitioning its investment between its male and female reproductive function (Charnov, 1982). In species that remain male or female throughout their entire lives it focuses on how investment is parceled between male and female offspring. Fisher's (1930) theory assumes that parents do not have information on the possible reproductive success of their offspring and that competition between relatives is no more common than competition between other randomly chosen members of the population (Hamilton, 1967). Sociobiologists are currently doing some very interesting work on the nature of sex allocation when these assumptions do not hold. Although space to review this work is not available, a brief discussion of Trivers and Willard's (1973) ideas may stimulate the thinking of psychologists.

Suppose the females of a species have approximately the same number of offspring. However, some males of this hypothetical species leave many offspring because their physical condition and/or social status enables them to compete successfully for many females. Other males leave few progeny because they lack these attributes. A female of such a species could improve her reproductive fitness if she had "knowledge" of the likely reproductive success of her offspring. If she can produce strong and/or dominant offspring she will be more fit if she allocates more investment to her male progeny since they will likely give her many grandchildren. However, if she cannot produce such offspring she will be more fit if she allocates more investment to daughters since, in our hypothetical species, differences in their reproductive success are less dependent on differences in their physical condition or social status. Variance in reproductive success of males is greater than that of females in many animal species, including humans, which suggests that sex allocation may occur in these animals.

The sex ratio of progeny is usually used as the measure of allocated parental investment. Trivers and Willard (1973) were able to find considerable support for their theory in pigs, sheep, mink, seals, deer, and humans. A striking piece of evidence in support of it is McClure's (1981) finding that when lactating wood rats are put on a food restricted diet, they selectively eliminate the males from their litters. Recently Wright and Crawford (1985) reported evidence suggesting that dietary stress can induce mice to alter the sex ratio of their progeny during gestation. Clutton-Brock and Albon (1982) discuss theories of parental investment in male and female offspring and review evidence from mammals bearing on them.

Evidence that Trivers' and Willard's theory may apply to humans is accumulating. Tentative evidence suggests that parental ability to invest in offspring may influence the sex of offspring (Clutton-Brock & Albon, 1982). There is better evidence that humans invest differentially in their offspring during the rearing process. Dickemann (1979), Voland (1984, 1986) and Boone (in press) have found support for Alexander's (1974) suggestion that in highly stratified societies male biased sex ratios would be produced among high status parents by female infanticide, abuse and neglect. There is also evidence that individuals bequeath wealth to their male and female relatives as a function of the status of those making the wills (Boone, in press; Dickemann, 1979; Smith, Kish, & Crawford, 1984; van den Berghe & Mesher, 1980). Betzig (1986) provides strong support for the theory of Trivers and Willard from a large cross-cultural sample.

Psychologists, who are more interested in patterns of differential investment that may be involved in the production of sex differences in behavior than in the sex ratio, may be especially interested in a recent study by Betzig and Turke (1986). They studied parent-child associations in Ifaluk, a small Pacific atoll 400 miles south of the island of Guam, and found that although the sex ratio does not differ among high- and low-status parents, higher status parents spent more time with sons while lower status parents spent more time with daughters. These results support the findings of the studies of bequest behavior mentioned above and should be of considerable interest to anyone interested in the development of sex differences in personality, abilities, and sex roles.

Since the time of Darwin evolutionary biologists have focused their attention on males and male-male competition. The theory of sexual selection and the observed sexual dimorphism that it explained led many to conclude that males are at the cutting edge of evolutionary change. However, the nature and extent of female-female competition is becoming a topic of major importance to evolutionary ecologists (Hrdy, 1981; Wasser, 1983). One of the tasks of psychology can be to help explore the differences that exist between males and females and how they develop.

We have seen that if each individual has one parent of each sex, it follows that natural selection adjusts the sex ratio so that the average investment in males equals the average investment in females (Fisher, 1930). Thus, if the sex ratio is 50:50 the average investment in males and females must be the same for the population. If competence depends on parental investment then the average level of competence of males and females must be the same. In this context competence refers to any trait related to the enhancement of inclusive fitness. Traits that come to mind are the ability to acquire a mate, to breed successfully, to rear offspring, to detect predators, to acquire food, to learn a skill such as hunting, gathering, growing vegetables, to recognize relatives, to detect liars, to cooperate with others, etc. It is difficult to think of a trait that is not in some way related to inclusive fitness.

The theory of sexual selection, however, suggests that the patterns of investment in males and females, and hence the patterns of competence of males and females, may differ. Moreover, the patterns of investment in the two sexes may differ as a function of the social status, health, and resources of the investors.

Evolution as a Model of Change

Psychologists should understand the details of the theory of evolution because evolution is one of our best models of change in general; not only organic change in species, but changes in individuals and societies. Skinner (1966) uses an evolutionary model in understanding the acquisition of operant behaviors. Two population geneticists have recently proposed an evolutionary theory of cultural transmission (Cavalli-Sforza & Feldman, 1981). Their model, it must be emphasized, differs considerably from the Darwinian model of change in that it does not assume cumulative genetic change and does not recognize the importance of a history of natural selection of alternative alleles. As such it stands as a weak alternative to the Darwinian model assumed by all contributors to this book.

Evolutionary theory cannot be used to predict the ultimate fate of a species since major changes in future environments cannot always be known. However, a knowledge of the principles of microevolution and the evolutionary history of a species may provide insights into how future environments could affect a species. The evolutionary model has influenced thinking in disciplines ranging from sociology through literature to astronomy. Psychologists cannot afford to be unaware of the details of how such a powerful model for explaining change works.

Focuses Attention on Ecology

Evolutionary theory focuses attention on the interaction of organisms with their environment, where environment includes both the physical environment and the actions and products of other organisms living in it. It is important to realize that even though a trait has evolutionary significance, this does not mean that it cannot be affected by ecological conditions. When animals engage in destructive behavior such as infanticide they may do it because of the ecological circumstances under which they are living. For example, research in my laboratory suggests that if a female lactating mouse is put on a restricted diet, she will recycle her litter by killing her pups and eating them. However, mice that are given an adequate diet and adequate living conditions do not kill their young. Thus, infanticide in mice may be under environmental control because mice have adaptations that enable them to deal with the varying environments that they may encounter.

Psychologists occasionally argue that if the development of a trait has a strong genetic bias it should appear in a similar form in all cultures. This belief is incorrect. Biological adaptations enable organisms to respond to contingencies posed by their environment; they do not isolate them from it. As such they often involve conditional strategies; the strategy employed depending on the state of the environment in which the organism resides or develops.

Two examples from the animal literature illustrate this approach. Male scorpionflies have three mating strategies. They present a dead insect to a female and copulate with her as she eats it. They may generate a salivary mass and present it to the female as a nuptial gift. Or they may attempt to copulate forcibly with a female if the first two strategies are unavailable to them. Thornhill (1980) has shown that all three strategies are available to adult males and that the one employed depends on the male's success in male-male competition. Even dominant, successful males can be turned into vigorous forced copulators if their resources are restricted.

All male digger bees have the potential for two reproductive strategies: they may grow large and compete for females by digging them out of the ground and defending them from other males or they may grow less and compete for females by scrambling for them as members of hovering aggregations of males (Thornhill & Alcock, 1983). The strategy employed apparently depends on the amount of provisions that the female places in the nest when laying.

Scorpionflies might be said to employ concurrently contingent strategies since the mating strategy employed depends on the male's current relations with his physical environment and the other organisms in it. The mating strategies of digger bees, on the other hand, are developmentally contingent in that the strategy employed depends on the ecology in which development occurred.

Draper and Harpending (1982) have attempted to use this approach to explain the effects of father absence on human intellectual and emotional development. They argue that the type of family environment that a child experiences before the age of five affects the reproductive strategy he or she pursues in later life. The low father involvement child is "preparing" for life in a society in which males compete frequently for access to a number of females and do not form enduring bonds or provide much investment in their offspring. The high father involvement child, on the other hand, is developing attributes that will enable it to maximize its reproductive success in a society where males form long lasting relationships with a single female and provide a high level of investment in their offspring.

An ecological perspective suggests that it is likely, for example, that identical twins reared in different environments might develop somewhat different personalities. Moreover, the fact that they did develop different personalities cannot necessarily be interpreted as implying that genetic factors are unimportant in the development of the differences. The particular traits developed should, however, be related to reproductive success in the environment in which development occurred, or if environmental conditions have recently changed, to reproductive success in the environment of the organism's ancestral population. The theory of evolution requires that we take an ecological perspective, that we focus on understanding our relationships with our natural environment and the other organisms living in it. Although all chapter authors take such a perspective it is, perhaps, most evident in the work on rape and incest (chapters 11 and 17) by Randy and Nancy Thornhill.

Enriches our Repertoire of Explanatory Concepts

Evolutionary biologists have developed many new concepts for the analysis of social behavior in animals. The concept of inclusive fitness which has had immense impact on our understanding of the evolution of social behavior has been briefly discussed. Two others, *parental investment* and *evolutionary stable strategy,* can help illustrate the value of such concepts for psychologists.

When psychologists think of parental care they usually consider provision of food, provision of shelter, protection from predators, etc. Trivers (1972) provides a more abstract conception. He defines parental investment as the "behavior of a parent toward its offspring that increases the chances of that offspring's survival (and hence reproductive success) at the cost of the parent's investment in other offspring" (p. 139). That is, the cost of rearing current offspring is expressed in terms of the reduced number of future offspring that can be reared because of the current investment. Biologists have used this concept in constructing models of parent offspring conflict, parental allocation of resources to male and female offspring, mating systems and sex differences in parental care (Trivers, 1985). It could be useful for understanding human parental behavior. For example, Zajonc's (1983) confluence model, which uses child spacing to explain birth order effects on intelligence, may be a special case of the theory of parental investment.

Another concept from evolutionary biology that may be useful to psychologists is Maynard Smith's (1974) notion of an *evolutionary stable strategy.* An optimal strategy is one that would provide the greatest benefit to everyone if it were adopted by all members of a population. Dawkins (1976) illustrates this strategy in the following way. Suppose there are two fighting strategies possible in a given population, a "dove" strategy, in which each participant threatens the other until one backs down, and a "hawk" strategy, in which the participants fight until death or serious injury declares one the winner. It would seem that the best, or optimal, strategy possible for the population to adopt would be to act like a dove when encountering a conflict situation. Thus serious injury could be avoided all around. However, a group of individuals employing this strategy could be invaded by an individual playing a hawk strategy. A single hawk in a population employing a dove strategy would decrease the fitness of the less aggressive doves while dramatically increasing its own fitness. Thus a dove strategy is not evolutionarily stable as it is prone to invasion by immigrant or mutant hawks. Similarly, the hawk strategy may not be stable because a group whose members employ it could be invaded by individuals using a "retaliatory" strategy, or a strategy in which an individual acts like a dove until seriously threatened, then retaliates with hawk-like behavior. This conditional retaliatory strategy appears to be the most successful strategy, or in other words, an evolutionary stable strategy. An evolutionary stable strategy, therefore, is a behavioral policy that, although not ideal, cannot be bettered if it is adapted by a large proportion of the population (Maynard Smith, 1974). Although this concept was devised for genetic analysis its use does not require that it be applied strictly to genetic traits. For example, true altruism among individuals and free trade among nations may not be evolutionarily stable.

Broadens Our Understanding of the Causes of Behavior

Probably the most important reason why psychologists should attend to evolutionary theory is that it enables us to obtain a deeper understanding of behavior. In order to make this point it is necessary to explain the distinction between *proximate* and *ultimate* causation. Proximate causation refers to the immediate factors responsible for the production of a particular response (Tinbergen, 1963b; Wilson, 1975). Internal physiology, previous experience, and environmental stimuli are all examples of proximate causes. They are the causes that most psychologists, sociologists, anthropologists, and structural biologists consider when developing explanations.

Proximate causes must be clearly distinguished from the ultimate causes, the conditions of the environment that render certain traits adaptive and others nonadaptive (Wilson, 1975). Adaptive traits are maintained in the population through natural selection while the nonadaptive ones are eliminated by it.

An example may help clarify this distinction. Consider the question, "Why do ground squirrels hibernate?" The proximate explanation is that current climatic conditions trigger physiological mechanisms which cause hibernation to take place. The ultimate explanation is that they evolved (and may still be evolving) in an ecology that made physiological mechanisms mediating hibernation adaptive. Thus, climate, predator pressure, etc., all on an evolutionary time scale, are the ultimate causes of chipmunk hibernation.

Psychologists often confuse the notions of distal and ultimate. For psychologists describing a stimulus as distal implies that the object or event in question is out in the environment, at a distance from the organism, and describing a stimulus as proximal implies that it is closer to the actual behavior of the organism. For example, in a recent discussion of factors affecting children's IQ's Scarr (1985) treated mother's IQ and education as distal causes and mother's positive discipline and positive control as proximate causes. Since *ultimate* in an evolutionary sense implies interpreting environmental factors in terms of their significance in producing adaptations, a distal cause, such as a mother's IQ, is an ultimate cause of behavior to the extent that it is considered an environmental factor that is influencing the adaptations that children have evolved, or are evolving.

A discussion of Trivers' (1985) explanation of the cause of the excess in male over female mortality and Zuckerman's (Zuckerman, Buchsbaum, & Murphy, 1980) work on sensation seeking may provide further insight into the importance of considering ultimate causation when developing explanations of behaviors that are of interest to psychologists. In a wide variety of species, including humans, from many orders of animals, more males than females die at all ages because of disease, trauma and stress, and murder. Trivers (1985) summarizes the following evidence against the prevailing view that the differential mortality is due to the unguarded X chromosome in males that exposes them, more than females, to deleterious recessive genes on the X chromosome. Animals such as fish and birds where males are XX still exhibit excess male mortality when they direct their efforts into seeking additional copulations rather than providing parental care for their offspring. Increasing the number of mutations on the X chromosome by irradiation does not increase the differential male mortality. Studies of castrated animals indicate that it is the male hormones, not the X chromosome, that is the source of the excess male mortality. These hormones apparently predispose males to develop the kind of physiology, anatomy and behavior that exposes them to risk. Thus, depending on the level of analysis, either hormones or risky mechanisms and behavior they mediate are the proximate cause of the excess male mortality.

But what are the ultimate causes of the differential male mortality? Recall that in sexually selected species males compete among themselves for access to females because females are a limiting resource for males. Some males may be considerably more successful in this competition for matings than others. Now imagine, as does Trivers (1985), that in the evolution of male competitive behaviors, males are trading mortality before reproduction for increased reproductive success during the period of reproduction. Thus, a male trait that causes a one-half reduction in survival prior to reproduction, but more than doubles the reproductive success of those who do survive to mate, can spread by natural selection. Males could be selected to divert growth from the immune system to the growth of muscles, organs of threat or displays!

The factors determining the extent to which females are a limiting resource for males are: (1) the resources invested in the construction of a gamete (females usually invest more in each gamete), (2) any additional post zygotic parental effort per offspring (females usually make the larger investment), (3) any effort or resources (dowries and bride prices in humans and the nuptial gifts that are provided by some male insects) exchanged for a mating that limit the ability to compete for additional mates (Thornhill & Alcock, 1983). These are the ultimate causes of the excess in male over female mortality.

Proximate explanations tell us how a behavior occurs and ultimate explanations tell us why it occurs. The above example illustrates that both levels of explanation are required for a full understanding of a behavior and therefore that evolutionary theory, physiology or psychology by itself, cannot provide a complete understanding of behavior. However, it also illustrates that it is possible to provide insights into behavior without considering the physiological and biochemical factors involved in its development.

Perceptive readers will no doubt have noted that although the three causes mentioned above are ultimate causes, they are not the most ultimate causes. The most ultimate explanation of sex differences in mortality and sensation seeking are the conditions in the ancestral environment of a species that favored sexual dimorphism in gamete size, parental care and mating behavior. However, the variables mentioned above are those that sociobiologists would use in constructing an evolutionary model of sensation seeking.

It would be possible, for example, to develop a model of risk taking behavior in males and females based on the ultimate variables mentioned above. The model should predict sex differences in risk taking behavior across a variety of species without the necessity of considering the details of physiology and biochemistry. If we assume that the members of a species have evolved a number of concurrently contingent, or facultatively contingent, strategies for maximizing their inclusive fitness, it should also be possible to construct a model to predict individual differences in risk taking behavior within a species. It would include measures of variables such as physical size, social status, and resources controlled, that are useful to males in attaining matings. Males lacking these attributes should be higher risk takers and should show higher excess male mortality over both males who possess these attributes and females.

Biologically oriented psychologists often attempt to increase our understanding of behavior by correlating behavioral measures with physiological and biochemical measures. For example, Zuckerman, Buchsbaum, and Murphy (1980) have developed a measure of sensation seeking which correlates with risk taking in a number of situations and is also related to sexual experience, interest in new situations, experience with drugs, social dominance, sociability, playfulness, manic-depressive tendencies and psychopathy. There are marked sex differences in sensation seeking, with males receiving the higher scores. Scores decline with age starting at age 16. His measure of sensation seeking is correlated with strength of initial orienting reflex, augmenting versus reducing of the average evoked brain potential, gonadal hormones and the enzyme monoamine oxidase.

In behavioral research, such as that on sensation seeking, it is often difficult to determine which behavioral and biological correlates of the behavior should be considered causes and which should be considered effects of the behavior of interest. This distinction is particularly important if changing the behavior is of interest. A consideration of the ultimate causes of the behavior may be helpful in distinguishing the causes and effects. For example, a consideration of the ultimate causes of sensation seeking suggests that it is a common element in behaviors that males perform in attempts to achieve social status and acquire resources that were necessary for obtaining mates in ancestral populations of humans. If this line of reasoning is followed then gonadal hormones rather than strength of initial orienting reflex, augmenting versus reducing of the average evoked brain potential or monoamine oxidase are likely to be an important proximate biological cause of sensation seeking. The ultimate cause analysis further suggests that if behaviors related to sensation seeking are to be changed then early training of social and technical skills required for achieving social status and obtaining resources or reducing the importance of these in obtaining mates should be the treatment of choice.

Finally, psychologists currently prefer explanations using proximate rather than distal variables (Scarr, 1985). Sensation seeking, for example, is apparently a concept derived from inspection and analysis of several types of observational data. Currently many psychological constructs are developed in this manner. As such, as explanatory constructs, they are close to the observational data. Although such concepts have an intuitive and common sense appeal and may function reasonably well as predictors within a narrow context, they lack generality. If psychologists desire to develop theories of behavior that are not situation and population specific then they must seek constructs that have greater generality.

The problem in developing psychological theories incorporating more general constructs is that, in contrast to the natural sciences that can call on theories such as classical mechanics, the theory of relativity or the theory of evolution for guiding the search for explanatory ideas, psychology does not have any framework for guiding its search. One of the purposes of this book is to try and show how the modern synthetic theory of evolution can be used to help develop more general and hence more powerful explanatory theories of behavior. Using this theory sociobiologists have developed a variety of concepts such as inclusive fitness (Hamilton, 1964), parental investment (Trivers, 1972) and evolutionary stable strategies (Maynard Smith, 1974). A consideration of the ultimate causes of behavior may enrich psychology. That is the hope of the contributors to this book and the reason for producing it.

CONCLUSIONS

Since the behavior of individuals is the "evolutionary pacemaker," psychology, which is the study of the behavior of individuals, must be a key discipline for understanding the process of evolution in general and the evolution of human nature in particular. Moreover, an understanding of evolutionary thinking can provide a critical perspective on psychological theorizing as well as a rich source of ideas for developing alternative explanations for behaviors that cannot readily be explained using current psychological theories.

A serious study of evolution focuses attention on the existence of individual and group differences. Psychologists have an important role to play in helping humanity come to terms with ethics and individual and group differences.

Although most psychologists realize that learning has costs, benefits, and constraints and that an understanding of emotion is important, a study of evolution focuses attention on the importance of these ideas. An evolutionary perspective also emphasizes the importance of ecology, the study of the interaction of organisms with their physical environment and the other organisms in it. It can thus broaden our understanding of the process of adaptation.

The theory of evolution provides one of the most important models of change and has provided a model of change for several disciplines. Although it cannot tell us the ultimate fate of humanity, it can help us understand the process of change and provide many insights into where we are going. However, the most important benefit to accrue to psychologists from a study of evolution is that it can broaden our understanding of the causes of behavior and help relate psychology to the other social and life sciences and possibly even to the humanities.

REFERENCES

Alcock, J. (1984). *Animal behavior: An evolutionary approach* (3rd ed.). Sunderland, MA: Sinauer Associates.

Allen, J. (1975). *Life science in the twentieth century.* New York: Wiley.

Alexander, R. D. (1974). The evolution of social behavior. *Annual Review of Ecology and Systematics, 5,* 324–383.

Alexander, R. D. (1979). *Darwinism and human affairs.* Seattle: University of Washington Press.

Axelrod, R., & Hamilton, W. D. (1981). The evolution of cooperation. *Science, 211,* 1390–1396.

Barash, D. P. (1976). Male response to apparent female adultery in the mountain bluebird (*Sialia currucoides*): An evolutionary interpretation. *American Naturalist, 110,* 1097–1101.

Barash, D. P. (1977). Sociobiology of rape in mallards (*Anas platyrhynchos*): Responses of the mated male. *Science, 197,* 788–789.

Barash, D. P. (1979). *The whisperings within.* London: Penguin.

Barash, D. P. (1982). *Sociobiology and behavior.* New York: Elsevier.

Berger, J. (1983). Induced abortion and social factors in wild horses. *Nature, 303,* 59.

Bertram, B. C. R. (1975). Social factors influencing reproduction. *Journal of Zoology, 177,* 463–482.

Betzig, L. L. (1986). *Despotism and differential reproduction: A Darwinian view of history.* Hawthorne, NY: Aldine.

Betzig, L L., & Turke, P. W. (1986). Parental investment by sex on Ifaluk. *Ethology and Sociobiology*, 7, 29–37.

Boone, J. L. (in press). Parental investment and elite family structure in preindustrial states: A case study in late medieval-early modern Portuguese geneologies. *American Anthropologist*.

Bruce, H. M. (1960). A block to pregnancy in the mouse caused by the proximity of strange males. *Journal of Reproduction and Fertility*, 1, 96–103.

Cavalli-Sforza, L. L., & Feldman, M. W. (1981). *Cultural transmission and evolution: A quantitative approach*. New Jersey: Princeton University Press.

Chagnon, N. A., & Irons, N. (Eds.). (1979) *Evolutionary biology and human social behavior: An anthropological perspective*. North Scituate, MA: Duxbury Press.

Charnov, E. L. (1982). *The theory of sex allocation*. New Jersey: Princeton University Press.

Clutton-Brock, T. H., & Albon, H. D. (1982). Parental investment in male and female offspring in mammals. In King's College Sociology Group (Ed.), *Current problems in sociobiology*. London: Cambridge University Press.

Cooper, R. M., & Zubek, J. L. (1958). Effects of enriched and restricted early environment on the learning ability of bright and dull rats. *Canadian Journal of Psychology*, 12, 159–164.

Daly, M., & Wilson, M. (1980). Discriminative parental solicitude: A biological perspective. *Journal of Marriage & the Family*, 42, 277–288.

Daly, M., & Wilson, M. (1982). Homicide and kinship. *American Anthropologist*, 84, 372–378.

Daly, M., & Wilson, M. (1983). *Sex, evolution, and behavior* (2nd ed.). Boston, MA: Prindle, Weber & Schmidt.

Daly, M., Wilson, M., & Weghorst, S. J. (1982). Male sexual jealousy. *Ethology and Sociobiology*, 3, 11–27.

Darwin, C. (1859). *On the origin of the species by means of natural selection, or, the preservation of favored races in the struggle for life*. London: John Murray.

Darwin, C. (1871). *The descent of man, and selection in relation to sex* (1887 edition). New York: D. Appleton and Co.

Dawkins, R. (1976). *The selfish gene*. New York: Oxford University Press.

de Catanzaro D. (1980). Human suicide: A biological perspective. *The Behavioral and Brain Sciences*, 3, 265–290.

Dewsbury, D. (1978). *Comparative animal behavior*. New York: McGraw-Hill.

Dickemann, M. (1979). Female infanticide, reproductive strategies, and social stratification: A preliminary model. In N. A. Chagnon & W. Irons (Eds.), *Evolutionary biology and human social behavior: An anthropological perspective* (pp. 255–273). North Scituate, MA: Duxbury.

Draper, P., & Harpending, H. (1982). Father absence and reproductive stretegy: An evolutionary perspective. *Journal of Anthropological Research*, 38, 255–273.

Dunbar, R. I. M. (1982). Adaptation, fitness and the evolutionary tautology. In Kings College Sociobiology Group (Eds.), *Current problems in sociobiology* (pp. 9–29). Cambridge: Cambridge University Press.

Erikson, C. J., & Zenone, P. G. (1976). Courtship differences in male ring doves: Avoidance of cuckoldry? *Science*, 192, 1353–1354.

Fisher, R. A. (1930). *The genetical theory of natural selection*. Oxford: Clarendon Press.

Fuller, J. L., & Thompson, W. R. (1978). *Foundations of behavior genetics*. St. Louis, MO: Mosby.

Gadgil, M., & Bossert, W. H. (1970). Life historical consequences of natural selection. *American Naturalist*, 104, 1–24.

Gould, S. J. (1982). *The panda's thumb: More reflections in natural history*. New York: Norton.

Hamilton, W. D. (1964). The genetical evolution of social behavior. I, II. *Journal of Theoretical Biology*, 7, 7–52.

Hamilton, W. D. (1966). The moulding of senescence by natural selection. *Journal of Theoretical Biology*, 12, 12–45.

Hamilton, W. D. (1967). Extraordinary sex ratios. *Science, 156*, 477–488.

Hamilton, W. D. (1971). Geometry of the selfish herd. *Journal of Theoretical Biology, 31*, 295–311.

Hausfater, G., & Hrdy, S. (1984). *Infanticide: Comparative and evolutionary perspectives.* New York: Aldine.

Hoogland, J. L. (1981). Prairie dogs avoid extreme inbreeding. *Science, 215*, 1639–1641.

Hoogland, J. L. (1983). Nepotism and alarm calling in the black-tailed prairie dog (*Cynomys indovicianus*). *Animal Behavior, 31*(2), 472.

Hrdy, S. B. (1979). Infanticide among animals: A review, classification, and examination of the implications for the reproductive strategies of females. *Ethology and Sociobiology, 1*, 13–40.

Hrdy, S. (1981). *The woman that never evolved.* Cambridge, MA: Harvard University Press.

Konishi, M. (1965). The role of auditory feedback in the control of vocalization in the white-crowned sparrow. *Zeitschrift fur Tierpsychologie, 22*, 770–783.

Krebs, D., Miller, D. (1985). Altruism and aggression. In G. Lindzay & E. Aronson (Eds.), *Handbook of social psychology* (3rd. ed.). New York: Addison-Wesley.

Lack, D. (1968). *Ecological adaptations for breeding in birds.* London: Methuen.

Lorenz, K. Z. (1966). *On aggression.* New York: Harcourt Brace Jovanovich.

Lumsden, C. J., & Wilson, E. O. (1981). *Genes, mind and culture: The coevolutionary process.* Cambridge, MA: Harvard University press.

Lumsden, C. J., & Wilson, E. O. (1983). *Promethean fire: Reflections on the origin of mind.* Cambridge, MA: Harvard University Press.

Maynard Smith, J. (1974). The theory of games and the evolution of animal conflicts. *Journal of Theoretical Biology, 47*, 209–221.

Maynard Smith, J. (1976). Group selection. *Quarterly Review of Biology, 51*, 277–283.

McClure, P. A. (1981). Sex biased litter reduction in food restricted woods rats (*Neotoma floridana*). *Science, 211*, 1058–1060.

McKinney, F., Derrickson, S. R., & Mineau, P. (1983). Forced copulation in waterfowl. *Behavior, 86*, 250–294.

McFalls, J. (1979). *Psychopathology and subfecundity.* Orlando, FL: Academic Press.

McLean, I. G. (1983). Paternal behavior and killing of young in Arctic ground squirrels. *Animal Behavior, 31*, 32.

Miller, W. B. (1983). Chance, choice and the future of reproduction. *American Psychologist, 38*, 1198–1205.

Patry, J. L. (1983). Evolution and "evolutionary behaviorism". *American Psychologist, 38*, 1026–1028.

Plomin, R., DeFries, J. C., & McClearn, G. E. (1980). *Behavioral genetics: A primer.* San Francisco: Freeman.

Ricklefs, R. E. (1977). A note on the evolution of clutch size in altricial birds. In B. Stonehouse & C. M. Perrins (Eds.), *Evolutionary Ecology* (pp. 193–214). London: Macillan.

Rissman, E. F. (1983). Detection of cuckoldry in ring doves. *Animal Behavior, 31*, 449–456.

Scarr, S. (1985). Constructing psychology: Making facts and fables for our times. *American Psychologist, 40*, 499–512.

Schaller, G. B. (1972). *The Serengeti lion: A study of predator-prey relations.* Chicago: University of Chicago Press.

Shaw, R. P. (1985). Humanity's propensity for warfare: a sociobiological perspective. *Canadian Review of Sociology and Anthropology, 22*, 158–183.

Shepher, J. (1983). *Incest: A biosocial view.* Orlando, FL: Academic Press.

Sherman, P. W. (1980). The limits of ground squirrel nepotism. In G. W. Barlow & J. Silverberg (Eds.), *Sociobiology: Beyond nature/nurture?* Boulder, CO: Westview Press.

Skinner, B. F. (1966). The phylogeny and ontogeny of behavior. *Science, 157*, 1205–1213.

Shields, W. M., & Shields, L. M. (1983). Forcible rape: An evolutionary perspective. *Ethology and Sociobiology, 4,* 115–136.

Smith, M. S. (1982, August). *Grandparenting as kin investment.* Paper presented at the annual meeting of the International Society for Human Ethology, Atlanta.

Smith, M. S., Kish, B. J., & Crawford, C. B. (1984, August). *Inheritance of wealth as human kin investment.* Paper presented at Animal Behavior Society meeting, Cheney, Washington.

Stearns, S. C. (1976). Life-history tactics: A review of the ideas. *Quarterly Review of Biology, 51,* 3–47.

Thornhill, R. (1980). Rape in *Panorpa* scorpionflies and a general rape hypothesis. *Animal Behavior, 28,* 52–59.

Thornhill, R., & Alcock, J., (1983). *The evolution of insect mating systems.* Cambridge, MA: Harvard University Press.

Thornhill, R., & Thornhill, N. W. (1983). Human rape: An evolutionary analysis. *Ethology and Sociobiology, 4,* 137–173.

Tinbergen, N. (1963a). The shell menace. *Natural History, 77,* 28–35.

Tinbergen, N. (1963b). On aims and methods of ethology. *Zeitschrift fur Tierpsychologie, 20,* 410–429.

Trever-Roper, H. R. (Ed.). (1953). *Hitler's table talk.* London: Weidenfeld & Nicolson.

Trivers, R. L. (1971). The evolution of reciprocal altruism. *Quarterly Review of Biology, 46,* 35–57.

Trivers, R. L. (1972). Parental investment and sexual selection. In B. Campbell (Ed.), *Sexual selection and the descent of man 1871–1971.* Chicago: Aldine.

Trivers, R. L. (1974). Parent-offspring conflict. *American Zoologist, 14,* 249–264.

Trivers, R. (1985). *Social evolution.* Menlo Park, CA: The Benjamin/Cummings Publishing company.

Trivers, R. L., & Willard, D. E. (1973). Natural selection of parental ability to vary the sex ratio of offspring. *Science, 179,* 90–92.

Turke, P. W., & Betzig, L. L. (1985). Those who can do: Wealth, status, and reproductive success on Ifaluk. *Ethology and Sociobiology, 6,* 79–87.

van den Berghe, P. (1983). Human inbreeding avoidance: Culture in nature. *The Behavioral and Brain Sciences, 6,* 91–125.

van den Berghe, P. L., & Mesher, G. (1980).Royal incest and inclusive fitness. *American Ethnologist, 7,* 300–317.

Voland, E. (1984). Human sex-ratio manipulation: Historical data from a German parish. *Journal of Human Evolution, 13,* 99–107.

Voland, E. (1986). Parental investment and reproductive potential: A study of a German parish. In L. L. Betzig, M. Bogerhoff Mulder, & P. Turke (Eds.), *Human reproductive behavior.* London: Cambridge University Press.

Washburn, S. L. (1978). Human behavior and the behavior of other animals. *American Psychologist, 33,* 405–418.

Wasser, S. K. (1983). *Social behavior of female vertebrates.* Orlando, FL: Academic Press.

Williams, G. C. (1957). Pleiotropy, natural selection, and the evolution of senescence. *Evolution, 11,* 398–411.

Williams, G. C. (1966). *Adaptation and natural selection: A critique of some current evolutionary thought.* New Jersey: Princeton University Press.

Wilson, E. O. (1975). *Sociobiology: The new synthesis.* Cambridge, MA: Harvard University Press.

Wittenberger, J. F. (1981). *Animal social behavior.* Boston: Duxbury Press.

Wolf, L. L. (1975). Prostitution behavior in a tropical hummingbird. *Condor, 77,* 140–144.

Woolfenden, G. E., & Fitzpatrick, J. W. (1984). *The Florida scrub jay: Demography of a cooperative-breeding bird.* New Jersey: Princeton University Press.

Wright, S. L., & Crawford, C. B. (1985). *Maternal manipulation of the sex ratio in mice (Mus musculus) during gestation.* Manuscript submitted for publication.

Wynne-Edwards, V. C. (1962). *Animal dispersion in relation to social behavior.* Edinburgh: Oliver & Boyd.

Zajonc, R. M. (1983). Validating the confluence model. *Psychological Bulletin, 92,* 457–480.

Zuckerman, M., Buchsbaum, M., & Murphy, D. (1980). Sensation seeking and its biological correlates. *Psychological Bulletin, 88,* 187–214.

2 Evolution: A Primer for Psychologists

Katharine M. Noonan
Albany, California

INTRODUCTION

What does human evolutionary history have to do with modern psychological issues such as sex role differences, homosexuality, child development, and mid-life crises? Despite the conviction of early psychologists that human behavior must be viewed in a biological context, it was not until the mid-1960s that this question could be answered in anything but vague generalities. The insights that made more specific answers possible came from biologists attempting to understand animal behavior and the evolutionary processes which shaped it (Alexander, 1971, 1974, 1975, 1977a, 1977b, 1978a, 1978b, 1979a, 1979b, 1979c, 1979d, 1979e; Alexander & Tinkle, 1968; Hamilton, 1963, 1964, 1966, 1967, 1971, 1972, 1975; Maynard Smith, 1964, 1966; Trivers, 1971, 1972, 1974; Williams, 1957, 1966a, 1966b). In the progress of human sociobiology, as in any science, there have been a good many partial, glib, and even wrong answers. Yet, as indicated by the contributions to this volume, and others (e.g., Alexander & Tinkle, 1981; Barash, 1977, 1979; Chagnon & Irons, 1979; Daly & Wilson, 1978), psychologists and other social scientists have increasingly found evolutionary theory to be a powerful tool in analyzing human behavior. This article strives to show why an understanding of the process of evolution is important, even essential, to psychologists working in the present and to provide the basic ideas needed to apply it to modern psychological problems.

The new developments in evolutionary theory in the past 2 decades have sparked both intense enthusiasm and bitter controversy among students of human behavior (Caplan, 1978). To biologists, the corollaries to Darwin's original theory offered increased precision in formulating hypotheses and increased power to test them (Alcock, 1975; Alexander, 1971–79; Alexander & Tinkle, 1968; Daly & Wilson, 1978; Dawkins, 1976, 1979, 1982; Ghiselin, 1969; Hamilton, 1963–1975; Krebs & Davies, 1984; Williams, 1966a; Wilson, 1975, 1978). They truly revolutionized the collection, analysis, and interpretation of data in the fields of animal behavior and ecology (and increasingly in anthropology and psychology). To many social scientists, however, the new approach to human behavior attributed a false simplicity and determinism, and raised the specter of pernicious social idealogies such as social Darwinism, sexism, and racism (For discussion, see Alexander, 1977a, 1979; Caplan, 1978; Sahlins, 1976). Some argued that the basic assumptions of the evolutionary model were not met with regard to human behavior, and that the theory was fundamentally untestable. Much has been published on this subject (see Caplan, 1978; Ruse, 1982, this volume). It seems likely that the acceptance of evolutionary theory by the social sciences has been slowed as much by misunderstanding of its elements and their workings as by interdisciplinary rivalries, wild hypothesizing by biologists and irrational resistances to self-knowledge. Here I introduce the terminology and basic assumptions of Darwinian theory, then address some of the subtheories of special relevance to human social behavior. Along the way I hope to clarify points of common misunderstanding between biologists and social scientists in talking about human behavior.

Outside biology, evolution often means the study of extinct forms or the change in morphology of species over geological time spans. Evolution certainly encompasses these subjects, but modern evolutionary theory has become a powerful paradigm because of its emphasis on understanding the processes of evolutionary change which appear to be universal to life and to allow predictions to be made and tested from theory.

Evolutionary biology and the social sciences have traditionally looked for explanations of behavior at different levels of causality. Social scientists concerned themselves with the immediate physiological, experiential, and environmental causes of behavior (called proximate mechanisms by biologists). Evolutionists, on the other hand concerned themselves with the selective pressures underlying the evolution and maintenance of behaviors (called ultimate causes, because proximate mechanisms are frequently evolved responses to selection). The two kinds of explanation are not exclusive of one another. The current challenge facing behavioral scientists is to explore the extent to which our increasingly detailed understanding of how natural selection operates can shed light on the proximate mechanisms of interest to social scientists. The hope that they might stems from the reasonable expectation that the process of evolution by natural selection is reflected in its products.

In 1859, Charles Darwin provided the first rational explanation of how evolution occurred. His theory of evolution by natural selection offered a simple and general hypothesis which could be tested by making observations of the natural world. Darwin himself presented abundant evidence supporting predictions from the theory—evidence which convinced leading scientists of the day. Supporting evidence continues to accumulate from all areas of biology so that today the theory of evolution by natural selection stands both as theory and as fact (Alexander, 1971, 1974, 1978a, 1979a, 1979b, 1979c, 1979d, 1979e, Ruse; 1982, this volume; Williams, 1966a). There are no reasonable alternatives for explaining the characteristics of life.

The modern theory of evolution retains the essential outline of Darwin's original theory, but has incorporated a more detailed understanding of inheritance, including the concept of the gene and the mechanics of gene transmission from generation to generation. The basic elements of Darwin's theory—*evolution, inheritance, natural selection, mutation,* and *reproductive isolation*—have been recast in terms of population genetics. The result has been called the *modern synthetic theory* (Huxley, 1942). In order to understand the basics of the theory and its potential bearing upon understanding humans, it is necessary to define some terms and examine the process of evolution more closely.

THE MODERN SYNTHETIC THEORY

Although evolution is reflected in the changing characteristics, or *phenotypes,* of individuals over time, it is the *population* to which individuals belong which undergoes the permanent, cumulative change of interest here. A *population* is a collection of individuals of a species living in the same place at the same time. The members of a population are linked genetically with one another by the possibility of interbreeding. Genes from separate individuals recombine during sexual reproduction. As a result, members of a population are linked genetically with one another in varying degrees through common ancestors.

At conception, individuals inherit two copies of every kind of gene (e.g., the gene for eye color), one from each parent. Copies which differ in genetic codings are called *alleles* of one another (the phenotypic effect of the difference may be large or minimal). When an individual forms sex cells (eggs or sperm), genes from both parents mix together in new combinations. In this way children may inherit genes from all four grandparents.

The genes carried by individuals of a population at any time can be thought of as a *gene pool,* or reservoir of genes from which the hereditary make-up of future generations will be drawn. In each generation, genes mix with a small subset of the population gene pool. Over many generations, however, they recombine more extensively within the gene pool.

An individual can carry only two alleles of any gene, but more alleles of that gene may exist in the gene pool carried by different individuals. The proportionate representation of an allele in the gene pool is called its *allele frequency.* The set of copies carried by an individual (e.g., AA, Aa, or aa) is called its *genotype* at that locus. The particular set of alleles for all of the kinds of genes in the organism is referred to as the individual's whole genotype. The proportionate representation of a genotype in the gene pool is called its *genotype frequency*. Because all of the genes cooperate during individual development, the particular genotype carried by an individual can be crucial in determining its reproductive success and hence its contribution to the gene pool of the next generation. Individual genotypes, however, are broken up each generation through sexual reproduction and recombination, leaving the gene or allele as the stable unit of inheritance between generations. It passes intact through different individuals from generation to generation (Alexander, 1971, 1974; Dawkins, 1976; Dobzhansky, 1970; Williams, 1966a; Wilson & Bossert, 1971).

Evolution can now be defined as the change in allele frequencies over time within the population. Accounting for evolution then becomes a matter of identifying the means by which alleles fluctuate in frequency, enter, and disappear from population gene pools.

PROCESSES OF EVOLUTIONARY CHANGE

Population biologists identify four processes which bring about changes in allele frequencies (Dobzhansky, 1970; Wilson & Bossert, 1971). They are: *mutation, migration, genetic drift* (or chance events), and *natural selection. Mutations* are changes in the genetic material. They sometimes happen spontaneously, but can be induced by chemicals or radiation (Drake, Glickman, & Ripley, 1983). Naturally occuring radiation has probably been the most important cause of mutations throughout the history of life. The effects mutations have on the functions of affected genes can be major or almost insignificant. If mutations occur in sperm or eggs, they can be passed to offspring and thus alter allele frequencies in the population. The movement of individuals into or out of populations (*migration*) is another potential cause of change in allele frequencies. *Genetic drift* encompasses a variety of chance events which may lead to the loss of alleles from the gene pool. For example, a disproportionate number of individuals carrying one allele may be killed in a disaster such as a flood or a fire. The random recombination of genes during meiosis and conception may result in fluctuation in allele frequencies and the loss of low frequency alleles.

The fourth evolutionary process is natural selection. *Natural selection* can be defined simply as differential reproduction. Attributes common to all living things give them the capacity to evolve by natural selection. These are:

1. Inheritance. Offspring resemble their parents. (Alleles can be passed intact, in terms of the information they carry, from generation to generation.)

2. Mutation. (The genetic material changes occasionally, and the changes are heritable, giving rise to heritable variation.)

3. Differential reproduction. (Not all individuals reproduce equally.)

4. Isolation. (All genetic lines are not able to interbreed freely. External barriers or intrinsic ones stand in the way of genetic recombination between some of them.)

Some alleles by their phenotypic effects allow their bearers to outreproduce their contemporaries. These alleles are passed on to the next generation in a higher frequency than their alternatives. Alleles which confer more reproductive advantage therefore accumulate in the gene pool (their allele frequency rises). Alleles which do not disappear. In this way, natural selection tends to reduce the variation on which it operates. If the selective environment is consistent, allele frequencies eventually reach an equilibrium at which no net change occurs. Superior alleles will have replaced their alternatives (or have become fixed) and inferior alleles will be represented only in low frequencies attributable to new mutations or migration. Thus, paradoxically, although natural selection requires genetic variation to produce evolutionary change, an intensely selected population may show little genetic variation.

It is worth noting that some selective environments favor the maintenance of allelic variation. Sometimes heterozygotes, or individuals bearing two different alleles, reproduce better than either homozygote, or individuals bearing like copies of either allele. This is called heterozygous advantage. The human sickle-cell anemia allele, reproductively lethal as a homozygote, is the classic example. As a hererozygote with the normal allele, it confers resistance to malaria (Allison, 1954), and so is maintained in significant frequencies in malaria-ridden environments of Africa and the Mediterranean.

Frequency-dependent selection is another circumstance which can maintain variation by favoring alleles when they are rare and disfavoring them when they are common. Frequency-dependent selection has drawn attention recently in the study of social behavior under the auspices of evolutionarily stable strategies (ESS's) (Maynard Smith & Price, 1973; Parker, 1984). For example, the success of "hawk" and "dove" strategies (Maynard Smith & Price, 1973) depends on the frequencies of hawk and dove phenotypes in the population. Variations in selection pressures over time (e.g., seasons; Sheppard, 1967; Dobzhansky, 1970) and variation in selection regimes from place to place in a species' range also contribute to the maintenance of allelic variation (Sheppard, 1967).

Natural selection is sometimes called "survival of the fittest," but it could be described more accurately as the *genetic* survival of the fittest. Individuals do not survive forever, and it appears from the wide range of senescence patterns in organisms that individual survival has not even been maximized during evolution (Hamilton, 1966; Lamb, 1977; Williams, 1957). Genes, on the other hand, are potentially immortal through faithful replication during individual reproduction. As Dawkins (1976,1982) puts it, individuals are vehicles to immortality for the genes they carry.

Natural selection is simply differential reproduction, but the reasons for differences in reproductive success among individuals can be complicated. They involve every aspect of the life cycle. For example, natural selection can result from differences in infant mortality as well as adult mortality, from differences in the number of children born to parents, from differences in the ability of individuals to be good parents, and even differences in the ability of individuals to be good grandparents. In a complicated social environment, differential reproduction may result from differences in the ability of individuals to cooperate effectively with others, as well as from differences in their ability to compete directly.

The selective value of alleles depends on many features of the environment in which they occur (Williams, 1966a). It depends on all the levels of environment which influence their expression during individual development—the genetic and physiological background within the organism as well as the individual's social and ecological surroundings. Moreover, selection is specific to the particular environment. Alter the environment naturally or artificially, and the direction of selection may reverse itself. Ultimately, the allele's fate depends on the presence or absence of superior competing alleles in the gene pool.

Isolation proved to be a key concept in the development of evolutionary theory, because of its role in the formation of new species. The origin of species was the problem which led Darwin to his discovery of the mechanism of evolutionary change. A *species* may be defined as a collection of populations whose gene pools are connected by interbreeding among them (Dobzhansky, 1970). (The definition excludes populations which interbreed only under novel circumstances in laboratories or zoos.) The formation of new species involves the separation of gene pools by extrinsic or intrinsic barriers to interbreeding. Extrinsic barriers are usually physical impediments to movement of individuals from one population to another, for example, oceans, deserts, and mountain ranges. If individuals cannot meet, they cannot mate. Intrinsic barriers include behavioral differences that prevent individuals of different populations from meeting or from mating if they meet. They also include physiological mechanisms by which development and reproduction of hybrids break down. Accounting for the evolution of intrinsic barriers to interbreeding constitutes the central problem in explaining the origin of two or more new species from an ancestral one.

As ship naturalist on a voyage around the world, Darwin made observations on the distribution of species. He noted that fossils found in a region tended to resemble existing species in that region, and that island species tended to resemble species on the nearest mainland. These observations supported the idea that species changed and occasionally gave rise to new species. Darwin was also struck by the high proportion of species inhabiting remote islands which were unique to those islands. This suggested to him that isolation was an important condition for the origin of species. Isolation alone, however, could not explain the permanent separation of gene pools. What prevented populations from reuniting genetically after some periods of isolation? Darwin proposed that natural selection acting differently on isolated populations of a species sometimes led to genetic differences which made interbreeding disadvantageous for the individuals concerned when the populations came into contact again. In this way, natural selection, in combination with isolation, could account for the generation of new species, as well as for evolutionary changes within species over time.

WHY NATURAL SELECTION IS THE DRIVING FORCE OF EVOLUTION

The four evolutionary processes (mutation, migration, genetic drift, and natural selection) all occur in natural populations. Their action has been documented again and again by observation and by experiment (Dobzhansky, 1970; Ford, 1971; Ghiselin, 1969; Maynard Smith, 1966; Sheppard, 1967). Their relative importance in directing the course of evolution was hotly debated in the 1920s and 1930s, and the issue continues to have important implications for the kind of beings humans evolved to be. In judging their importance, we should consider both their efficiency in producing changes in gene frequencies and also how well they account for the most striking characteristic of living things, *adaptation*.

Throughout the living world, the structure, physiology, and behavior of organisms seem designed almost purposefully and in intricate ways for survival and reproduction. These seemingly purposeful traits are called *adaptations*. They can be simple and obvious, such as the shape of a bird's bill in relation to its food, or complex and subtle, such as the dances by which honeybee foragers communicate the location and richness of food sources to their nestmates, or the aggressive mimicry practiced by female fireflies, which lure males of other species close with species-specific mating signals only to capture and eat them (Lloyd, 1975). Adaptations function at all stages of the life cycle. They include traits that develop only in response to certain environmental circumstances, for example, physiological acclimatization or learning, as well as traits that always develop in the range of environments the species inhabits (Williams, 1966a). Adaptations such as arms and legs or complex behavior patterns involve the interaction of sets of genes with the environment and with themselves at various levels during development. The process or processes responsible for evolution must therefore be able to accumulate complexes of genes capable of working together harmoniously to enhance survival and reproduction in a particular way.

These observations allow us to eliminate all but one of the possible causes of evolution as being responsible for the direction of evolutionary change. Mutation can be ruled out because the direction of mutation is unrelated to the survival and reproductive interests of the organism; an allele does not increase its likelihood of mutating to a new form no matter how advantageous that new form might be. For this reason, mutation cannot account for adaptation. It is especially unlikely to account for the accumulation of adaptive complexes of genes which underlie most adaptations. In fact, most mutations are harmful to organisms. This is in part because they disrupt the activity of organized sets of genes. Mutation rates are low enough that the effects of mutation on allele frequencies are easily outweighed by the action of other processes. It is reasonable to think that the low rate of mutation is itself an adaptation in view of the generally deleterious effects mutations have (Williams, 1966a). Mutation, however, does provide a source of new variation in the gene pools of populations.

Similarly, migration is unlikely to produce the accumulation of genes performing a particular function that is characteristic of adaptations. The rates of immigration and emigration vary widely for different populations of organisms, but are not necessarily correlated with the rate of evolution. The third evolutionary process, genetic drift, influences allele frequencies significantly only in very small populations. Its effects are therefore usually minor compared to the effects of other processes.

Only natural selection can account for both the observed rates of evolution and adaptation. The early population geneticists, Fisher (1930), Haldane (1932), and Wright (1945), showed mathematically that natural selection acting at intensities observed in nature could overcome the effects of other processes acting on allele frequencies. Artificially reversing the direction of selection effectively reversed the direction of evolution.

Natural selection is uniquely capable of producing adaptation. It saves those alleles which in their particular genetic, physiological, ecological, and cultural environments served reproduction better than their alternatives. It acts simultaneously on alleles of every type of gene in the organism. Because genes from different individuals can recombine through sexual reproduction, favorable alleles of different genes scattered throughout the population can be brought together in single individuals after several generations to produce adaptive complexes of genes. The increase in frequency of each favorable allele makes their combination in one individual more and more likely. Finally, there is a direct relationship between the alleles saved and spread by natural selection and the survival and reproductive interests of the individual in the immediate situation in which selection occurs.

The last sentence raises an important point. Natural selection does not prepare organisms for the future—unless the future environment is essentially like the past one. It simply favors the most reproductive variants in the situation at hand (Williams, 1966a). The apparent purposefulness of adaptations merely reflects the accumulation of genes that have been reproductively successful in the past. If the environment changes, adaptive features may become useless or disadvantageous. Or, they may remain adaptive but for a different reason. Imperfect or awkward adaptations (at least in relation to conceivable ones) often can be traced to selection building upon structures or patterns advantageous in previous environments (see Williams, 1966a). Evolutionary biologists have fallen into the habit of using teleological language to express the purposeful appearance of evolved traits. Behavior patterns are described as strategies Anthropomorphic terms such as altruism and selfishness are applied that seem to imply an anticipation of future events (as well as conscious thought). If an evolutionary argument cannot be restated in a nonteleological form, however, it is not consistent with Darwinian theory. For example, one might say that bull elephant seals are over twice as large as elephant seal cows in order to compete effectively for mates on crowded beaches. This seems to suggest that large size in bulls evolved to fill a future need. The statement could be rephrased, however, to eliminate teleology. Large size in bulls evolved because larger males consistently excluded smaller ones from mating so that alleles favoring large size in males accumulated in elephant seal gene pools.

Recently, paleontologists Eldredge and Gould (Eldredge & Gould, 1972; Gould & Eldredge, 1977) have argued that the gradual change envisioned by Darwin probably occurs infrequently. They propose that the course of evolution is more appropriately described by long periods of equilibrium, during which selection maintains the status quo (stabilizing selection) punctuated by short, catastrophic periods during which selection promotes radical change (directional selection). Unfortunately, their theory of punctuated equilibria has been presented as an alternative to Darwinian selection (see Dawkins, 1982, for an in-depth discussion of this controversy). It is not a competing theory of evolution, but rather an hypothesis about the temporal patterning of selective events. Although Darwin (1859) emphasized that gradual changes could bring about significant evolutionary changes over many generations, there is no reason under the theory to expect that selection has been uniform or that brief periods of intense selection could not be important in directing evolutionary change. The punctuated equilibrium theory has been coupled with the idea of selection among species rather than individuals or genes. The relative power such selection can be expected to have is discussed below (see also Alexander & Borgia, 1978; Leigh, 1977; Lewontin, 1970; Williams, 1966a; Wright, 1945).

UNITS OF SELECTION

One thing Darwin failed to specify was the unit of life that selection acted upon most effectively—survival of the fittest what? The fittest species? population? group? individual? or gene? Selection at the different levels potentially conflicts. For example, the survival and expansion of populations or species might often benefit from some kind of intrinsic population regulation practiced by member individuals so that they do not outstrip their food supply (Wynne-Edwards, 1962). Such self-restraint would run counter to selection, or reproductive competition, among individuals (Williams, 1966a). The imprecision in Darwin's theory led to difficulties in constructing hypotheses that could be falsified, because adaptation could be attributed to any convenient level. Then in 1966,

George Williams (1966a) published a landmark critique of the use of the concept of adaptation in biology, arguing persuasively that selection could be expected to be effective generally at levels no higher than the individual.

Both individuals and groups (higher level units from populations to eco-systems) are subject to the four processes, (inheritance, mutation, selection, and isolation), which make evolution by natural selection possible. Group selection, however, is almost always less effective than individual selection in producing evolutionary change (Williams, 1966a; Wright, 1945). Natural selection works by accumulating hereditary elements of the unit under selection which serve that unit's reproduction best. Its effectiveness is limited by the rate at which those elements change due to other causes (the slower they change by mutation, migration, or genetic drift, the more effective selection will be), and by the rate at which the units experience selective events (the more frequent and intense the more effective). It was argued earlier that mutation, migration, and genetic drift are generally ineffective in opposing selection at the individual level. In other words, genes selected for their contributions to individual reproduction can accumulate with little erosion due to other causes. The hereditary elements of groups, however, be they genes or culture patterns or species or ecological assemblages, are subject to change resulting from the selection among their constituent individuals as well as to change resulting from mutation, migration, and drift (e.g., genetically or physically unequal divisions of the group). In addition, selective events occur more frequently among individuals than among groups. If selection acts in opposite directions on the two levels, it is likely that the hereditary elements favorable to the group will be selected out by individual selection *before* they can be accumulated by the differential survival and reproduction of groups (Alexander & Borgia, 1978; Williams, 1966a).

Recently, Dawkins (1976,1982) and his colleagues have argued vigorously that selection is most effective at the gene rather than the individual level. The differences between the two views are subtle because genes have evolved to reproduce themselves in groups (the individual genotype). What happens when individual and genic level selection oppose one another is obviously an important focus of research and theory in evolutionary biology. Nevertheless, individual versus genic level selection is not fairly regarded as a major rift in evolutionary theory. As Dawkins (1982) puts it, "The selfish organism, and the selfish gene with its extended phenotype, are two views of the same Necker Cube (visual illusion) . . . I am not saying that the selfish organism view is necessarily wrong, but my argument, in its strong form, is that it is looking at the matter the wrong way up" (p. 6). I have adopted the perspective of the selfish organism in this chapter because I suspect it might be easier to envision for someone unfamiliar with selectionist thinking and because I am so far convinced that selection has been relatively powerful on the groups of genes we call genotypes. I refer the reader to Dawkins' books, and to works by Alexander (1974,1979e),

Leigh (1977), and Alexander and Borgia (1978) for a lively discussion of this issue.

WHAT ORGANISMS HAVE EVOLVED TO BE

Understanding the process of evolution leads one inevitably to a sweeping general hypothesis: that all organisms, including humans, have been forged by natural selection into reproductive machines geared to outreproduce their conspecifics and to do nothing else which might detract from that purpose. Individual organisms, then, like alleles, are in reproductive competition with one another. An individual's reproductive success, compared with that of all other individuals in the population, is its *relative fitness*. It can be measured by the number of children the individual rears to reproductive maturity, or by the numbers of its grandchildren. Natural selection tends to maximize fitness.

It follows from evolutionary theory that all traits of organisms, as well, should be *reproductively* selfish, i.e., they should evolve so as to promote the survival and increase of their bearer's genes over those of all competing individuals. As discussed earlier, this view differs in a crucial way from the popular one in which selection favors the survival of the species (at individual expense if need be). Of course, adaptations which benefit individuals often benefit the species as well. For example, development of resistance to malaria, aside from improving individual reproductive success, might allow human populations to grow and occupy otherwise uninhabitable areas. Where the genetic interests of individuals and the species conflict, however, reproductively selfish individuals will outreproduce individuals which put the survival of the species before their own survival and the survival of their genetic lines. For example, suppose that a population could maximize its growth if males and females mated monogamously and both parents participated in rearing offspring. At the same time some males were able to monopolize sexual access to several females so that they left many more descendants than either monogamous males or males left without mates. Selection among individuals would rapidly favor males that selfishly took multiple mates at the expense of other males, and even at the expense of their own mates receiving less help in parenting, over males which took only one mate in the interests of population or species success.

Alleles permitting reproductive altruism should be short-lived in gene pools. This implies a test of evolutionary theory as well as a general hypothesis about organisms which can be used to analyze their attributes. On this point, Darwin said, his entire theory could be disproved. For, if it could be shown that a characteristic of any organism had evolved solely for the reproductive good of another species, or a genetic competitor of the same species (Alexander, 1971), it could not have evolved by natural selection (Darwin, 1859, p. 201). Ruse

(1982, this volume) discusses in depth the challenges that have been raised to evolution by natural selection as a testable scientific theory. I will deal with a few of them here.

First, it is sometimes argued that evolutionary theory explains nothing because one can propose an adaptive explanation for everything. Darwin's claim of universality indicates that this is not so. One can envision findings that would falsify the theory, namely, an instance in which a trait has evolved expressly because it benefits the reproduction of a genetic competitor. That none has been conclusively demonstrated supports the theory's power and effectiveness. There is no problem for the theory if multiple or conflicting hypotheses can be developed concerning the adaptive function of particular traits. Careful observations and imaginative experiments should be able to establish which is likely to be correct.

Second, it has been argued that evolutionary theory is untestable in regard to behavior and human behavior particularly because specific genes for the behaviors of interest have not been identified. The implication is that unless the specific mechanism of inheritance is known, behavior should not be considered to be influenced by genes. This objection makes no biological sense. Behavioral geneticists have shown that specific genes do influence some behaviors and that behavior responds to artificial selection as do other polygenic traits (traits influenced by large numbers of genes) (Fuller, this volume). There is no reason to think that behavior is different from other kinds of traits in relation to genetic influence.

All traits, including behavior, are products of gene-environment interactions (Hinde, 1968; Fuller, this volume). When observed behavior correlates with patterns of selection, and fortuitous reasons can be ruled out, evolutionary theory is tested and supported.

Finally, some critics have argued that evolutionary theorists promote the false expectation that organisms should be perfectly adapted to their environments (a view labeled Panglossianism by Gould and Lewontin, 1979). Perfection, however, is not predicted by evolutionary theory. We have already discussed how selection adapts organisms for past environments. New adaptations must build upon existing adaptations at every step.

The expectation of perfection is often applied by nonevolutionists to features of organisms which contribute to survival and reproduction in a particular way, as the eye does in vision or the limbs in locomotion. Different functions are not likely to be maximized simultaneously, however. Their performance is refined by natural selection only as a byproduct of the refinement of the whole individual as a reproductive machine. The important point is that costs as well as benefits must be weighed in the evolution of any trait, and the currency in the balance is genetic reproduction.

Increasingly, biologists are becoming aware that the fitness of individuals depends on the phenotypes displayed by other members of the population with which the individual interacts. Fitness, in other words, is often frequency-dependent. Nowhere is this more likely to be true than with the behavior patterns of complex social species. Maynard Smith introduced the concept of an evolutionarily stable strategy (or ESS) to describe the equilibrium distribution of traits or behaviors in such situations (see Maynard Smith & Price, 1973; Parker, 1984). He argued that at equilibrium, more than one trait may be maintained, but that no alternative could spread at the expense of another because its advantage was frequency-dependent. Thus, an evolutionarily stable strategy does not necessarily win, or outreproduce, in every interaction, but, averaging over all encounters, it does as well or better than any other variant. It is important to note that the ESS model, like other evolutionary models (Alexander, 1975, 1977a), does not rule out flexibility or multiple strategies on the part of individuals. It describes a pattern of behaviors that will be stable against invasion by other variants.

NEPOTISM, RECIPROCITY, AND INCLUSIVE-FITNESS-MAXIMIZING

Animal behavior generally fits a model of reproductive selfishness. Individuals compete openly for food, shelter, and mates. Human behavior, too, is marked by competition at every level of interaction. Within families, children compete for the attention of their parents. Within social groups, families compete for position, power and wealth (Chagnon, 1979a; Irons, 1979a, 1979b; Dickemann, 1979, 1981). Nations compete among themselves for the sources of wealth and influence. Yet, interactions between animals are sometimes positive beyond the nurturing behavior one might expect between parent and offspring. For example, birds and mammals in large aggregations often give alarm calls when they see a predator, thus perhaps calling the predator's attention to themselves while warning competitors of danger (Sherman, 1977; Williams, 1966a). Interactions among members of human social groups frequently involve cooperation and occasionally behavior which seems truly altruistic (i.e., benefits the reproduction of a genetic competitor at some expense to the individual's own reproduction).

If natural selection is sufficient to explain the evolution of behavior in humans and other animals, then these apparently altruistic acts must fall into one of three categories:

1. mistakes—accidents which occur rarely and are being selected out,

2. behaviors which had a reproductive function in previous environments but are now disadvantageous, or

3. behaviors which appear altruistic, but which have a hidden reproductive advantage.

The first two cases no doubt account for some examples of altruistic behavior in both humans and animals. Many instances of supposed altruism, however, can be shown to have a nonobvious reproductive function. They differ from most reproductively selfish behaviors only in that the genetic gain is indirect rather than direct.

In 1964, W.D. Hamilton suggested a possible indirect benefit of altruistic behavior which had broad applicability especially in group-living species. He argued that, just as parental care is reproductively selfish because it promotes the survival of the parent's genes, altruism toward nondescendent genetic relatives could be favored by natural selection. Help directed toward genetic relatives is referred to as *nepotism*. The selective pressures favoring such help are called *kin selection* (Hamilton, 1964; Maynard Smith, 1964). Alleles specifying helping behavior at the expense of individual reproduction might spread if the helping behavior promoted enough copies of the allele carried in other individuals. An offspring shares exactly one half of its genes with its parent. Siblings on average share one half of their genes, full cousins share one eighth, and so on. The probability that an individual shares an allele identical by descent from a common ancestor with another individual is called the *coefficient of relationship* between them. Hamilton (1964) predicted that: "The social behavior of a species evolves in such a way that in each distinct behaviour-evoking situation the individual will seem to value his neighbor's fitness against his own according to the coefficients of relationship appropriate to that situation" (p. 19). Hamilton's work revolutionized the study of social behavior in biology. It meant that researchers had to identify not only individuals (Williams, 1966a), but their genetic relatives as well, and to estimate the effects of behaviors on the reproduction of all.

Hamilton redefined fitness to include an individual's effects upon genes carried by its genetic relatives. This he called *inclusive fitness*. Note that inclusive fitness includes only that reproduction which is the direct result of the individual's own effort. It is not simply the summed reproduction of the individual and his collection of relatives devalued by their coefficients of relationship with him (Dawkins, 1976, 1979, 1982; Grafen, 1982; West Eberhard, 1975). Only the genetic gains which follow from the helping efforts of the individual will consistently bias selection over many generations in favor of the alleles responsible for that helping behavior. This excludes reproduction realized because of help from relatives and the reproduction of relatives achieved without the individual's help. In human terms, this means that an individual's inclusive fitness is not enhanced, for example, by the reproductive bonanza achieved by a nephew who becomes a rock star (without the individual's help) and inseminates many females, or by the beneficence of a rich aunt which allows him to rear a large family (although the aunt's inclusive fitness might well be enhanced).

A second reproductive benefit may sometimes be gained by apparently altruistic behavior. R.L. Trivers (1971) pointed out that helping behavior might evolve between genetically unrelated individuals if (a) the benefit of the act to the recipient was greater than its cost to the performer, (b) there were sufficient opportunities for help to be reciprocated, and (c) cheaters (individuals accepting but not giving help) could be identified and discriminated against in social interactions. Trivers called such help *reciprocal altruism*. The conditions for reciprocal altruism to evolve appear to be widespread (Alexander & Borgia, 1979; Axelrod & Hamilton, 1981). They are likely to have prevailed during most of human evolution, and reciprocity appears to be most highly developed among humans (Alexander, 1977b, 1979c; Trivers, 1971). Note that the genetic pay-off for nepotism is through the reproduction of other related individuals. The pay-off for reciprocal altruism may be to the performer's own reproduction, or to his relatives' reproduction. The individual returning the help may be the recipient of help (direct reciprocity) or another member of the social group (indirect reciprocity); indirect reciprocity is likely to evolve only where helping is supported by collectively enforced rewards for helping and punishments for failing to help (Alexander 1978b, 1979e). There is no expectation of return with nepotism, but reciprocal altruism will evolve only when altruism is reliably matched with received help.

Alexander (1974) called attention to a third circumstance in which altruistic behavior is likely to evolve: *parental manipulation*. He argued that parents may evolve to manipulate the behavior of offspring under their influence so as to maximize the parent's reproduction even at the expense of the offspring's inclusive fitness. Parents are usually able to get their way when conflicts of interest with their offspring arise because they are more powerful, their offspring are dependent on further parental attention, and selfish offspring stand to lose reproductively as adults when they become parents of selfish broods. Dawkins (1976,1982), Blick (1977), Alexander and Borgia (1978), and Alexander (1979e) discuss when conflicts of interest are likely to be resolved in favor of offspring and when they are likely to be resolved in favor of parents.

BEHAVIOR AND EVOLUTION

Most people have no difficulty accepting that their anatomy and physiology are products of evolution by natural selection. Many, on the other hand, find it hard to fit behavior, and particularly learned social behavior, into the evolutionary framework. Their reluctance usually stems from an understandable confusion about the relationship between behavior and heredity. Behavior has traditionally been classified into two kinds—instinctual and learned. Instincts were supposed to be uninfluenced by experience during development, while learned behaviors were thought of as liberated from genetic control and determined entirely by the learning situations encountered during development. In order to evolve by natural selection, traits must be heritable. Yet, it is clear that complex human behaviors, the sort that concern most psychologists and other social scientists, are not determined in any rigid or obvious way by genes. Certainly, people are not usually conscious of trying to maximize their reproductive success. Behavior need not be conscious, however, to be favored by selection. It has even been suggested that humans have evolved a basic unwillingness to view their own behavior as adaptive, i.e., evolved because it enhanced individual reproduction (Alexander, 1971–1979; Alexander & Noonan, 1979; Burley, 1979; Trivers, 1971). I will discuss how natural selection may have shaped our self-awareness and tendencies toward self-deception later. First, however, I will consider the extreme instinctualist and environmentalist views of behavior in general.

Both extreme viewpoints neglect an important fact about the development of any trait. Development involves the interaction of both genes and the environment. To say that a trait is genetically determined is really to express ignorance about the environmental factors necessary for its development. To say that a trait is environmentally determined is to ignore the contribution of the genes to the structures which respond to the environment (Alexander, 1975; Hinde, 1968). Organisms tend to extract from learning situations information which assists them in survival and reproduction (Garcia et al., 1974; Shettlesworth, 1984). Their ability to do so depends on the capabilities of their sensory receptor systems, and on emotions and sensations felt in response to the environmental stimuli perceived. These capabilities and responses are programed into the organism by gene-environment interactions during development. What is inherited, then, is not the specific information learned, but the ability to learn the right thing in the learning situations usually encountered during development.

The confusion about learning and inheritance is partly understandable because behavior is connected to gene activity in more intricate and indirect ways than any other aspect of the organism. Genes code for specific proteins, which, in turn, function as structural components of organisms and as enzymes, catalysts which facilitate and control all the chemical reactions which go on in the organism. Anatomy and physiology represent constellations of proteins and products of protein-catalysed reactions interacting in complex ways to perform life functions. In no case can physiologists or anatomists trace the development of a complete system back to the functioning of particular genes. It is clear, however, that these systems rest on the products of gene activity and are therefore influenced by heredity. In a perhaps less obvious way, behavior, too, rests on the products of gene activity. Behavior springs from anatomy and physiology. It builds upon all the levels of organization from the cell upward and mediates their interaction with the external environment.

Thus, behavior is furthest from the genes, in terms of the individual's development and function. At the same time, it may be said to be closest to the action of natural selection (Alexander, 1971, 1975). If individuals are vehicles for the transmission of their genes, then behavior is the last phenotypic buffer between those genes and the selecting environment. The reproductive effects of the body's biochemistry, anatomy, and physiology can be and usually are modified by some aspect of behavior. For example, an individual facing temperatures below its physiological tolerance can seek shelter, put on clothes, or migrate to a more favorable climate and thus avoid selective death. On the other hand, a perfectly viable specimen might come to a reproductive dead end if it fails to behave appropriately at a key moment (e.g., during courtship).

Because natural selection acts so directly upon behavior, analyzing behavior in terms of its effects on fitness has important advantages. Even the most complex behaviors can be approached in this way. Because of the intense action of natural selection, the effect of behavior on the reproductive success of the organism may be more predictable than the exact physiological mechanism used to produce the behavior. The evolutionary approach thus affords an efficient way of extending our knowledge about behavior and our ability to predict it before the physiological mechanisms underlying it are known (Alexander, 1975).

It is worth mentioning here some special problems in using evolutionary theory to understand humans. First, we humans have changed our environment radically from the one in which we evolved for most of our history as a species. In particular, we have increased enormously the size and complexity of our social groups. These changes, facilitated by our capacity for culture, have happened so quickly that they most likely have outpaced the evolution of reproductively appropriate behaviors in many cases (Alexander, 1971, 1974, 1977a, 1977b, 1979a, 1979e; Barash, 1979; Bigelow, 1969; Symons, 1979; Wilson, 1975, 1978). Our behavior may make more sense if we think of its reproductive consequences in the kinds of environments we lived in for most of our history. The elaborate learned behavior characteristic of humans may be especially vulnerable to novel environments because it depends upon many environmental cues being connected with reproduction in particular ways.

The selective pressures that shaped human behavior appear to be especially complex, involving extensive nepotism, reciprocity, and parental influence as well as the possibility of significant group selection. All of these must be taken into account in formulating hypotheses. Our extensive self-knowledge, no doubt an advantage in a complicated social environment, makes it difficult to make genuine predictions about behavior. In addition, constructing and testing hypotheses about human behavior from evolutionary theory is made more challenging by the fact that few closely related species have survived with which to compare ourselves.

HOW UNDERSTANDING THE PROCESS
OF EVOLUTION CAN HELP IN DEVELOPING
HYPOTHESES ABOUT HUMAN BEHAVIOR

To return to the opening question of this article, what does the process of evolution mean for understanding human behavior and the psychological issues of today? Perhaps it is wise to begin with what the process of evolution does *not* mean. It is unlikely, first of all, to supply easy answers about how to solve practical problems. Practical problems often involve selective compromises within the individual's reproductive strategy or conflicts of (reproductive) interests between individuals. Although evolutionary theory may help us to sort out what those compromises and interests are in a detail never before possible, the conflicts will still remain. Solving practical problems, in addition, may require some insights into the specific developmental mechanisms underlying behavior, which selection theory can approach only obliquely. This is because selection itself acts indirectly on those proximate mechanisms through their net effects on individual inclusive fitness. It is difficult to predict those mechanisms from a knowledge of selection pressures because all that matters, in terms of selection, is that the appropriate response be produced at the right time and in a cost-effective manner.

Second, evolutionary theory cannot describe biological limits of human behavior. Evolutionary theory builds upon the fact that behavior, and all other traits, are products of gene-environment interactions during development. In novel environments, new ranges of human behavior are likely to emerge. Evolutionary theory is likely to be predictive of human behavior in the past, and in other environments similar to the ones in which we evolve. It is not necessarily predictive about the future. It has been argued, intriguingly, that a key element of the environment relevant to human behavior is the awareness, or lack of awareness, of our own inclusive-fitness-maximizing goals (Alexander, 1974, 1979). Finally, as discussed extensively in the recent literature (Alexander, 1974–79; Caplan, 1978; Ruse, 1982, this volume), evolutionary theory is irrelevent to questions of what ought to be.

What evolutionary theory does mean is that we have a new perspective on what lifetimes are about, at least what they evolved to be about (inclusive-fitness-maximizing). It means that explanations which ignore the genetic interests of interactants are unlikely to be as correct or as complete as ones which do. This seems true even when proponents of hypotheses are unaware of the fine points of current theory. For example, Bowlby (1969) revolutionized the study of mother-infant relationships by focusing on the survival benefit of attachment for infants, rather than attempting to account for the bond by proximate mechanisms alone (the satisfaction of the primary hunger drive). His theory emphasized survival, rather than reproduction. Nevertheless, it offered improved insight into why attachment develops at particular ages, persists beyond suckling and early dependence on the mother, and, given consistent proximity and interaction, may be maintained despite abusive treatment by the object of attachment. A consideration of the genetic interests of the infant and its mother promises a fuller understanding yet (Porter & Laney, 1980). It suggests why the infant forms an attachment to a particular person (the one whose genetic interests are likely to be closest to its own) rather than turning to any convenient adult. Attachment may also serve to channel learning via imitation, identification, and teaching so that the infant and child attends to individuals who share most closely his reproductive interests.

Similarly, attempts to understand male-female relationships in terms of sex drives, needs for intimacy, or pair-bonding, have fallen short of predicting the variation in attitudes and actions of men and women (Symons, 1979). By using evolutionary theory to delineate circumstances in which the interests of the two sexes are differed as well as ones in which they coincided, Donald Symons (1979) was able to propose and test many nonobvious hypotheses about human sexuality.

Evolutionary theory implies that the human brain is first and foremost a reproductive organ, attuned to the reproductively relevant cues in the environment and functioning to integrate the conflicting demands of selection so as to direct behavior in a way which maximizes inclusive fitness. If we wish to understand what the brain is doing, evolutionary theory suggests that it will pay to try to understand how selection acts—at different stages of the life cycle, on males and females, on parents and their offspring, and on relations between kin and strangers. During the past 2 decades, evolutionary biologists have addressed these issues in a series of subtheories under the general theory of evolution by natural selection. Other chapters in this book show how these subtheories have been used to generate testable hypotheses about human behavior. In the final section of this chapter, I shall briefly introduce several which are particularly relevant to human behavior.

SIX EVOLUTIONARY THEORIES INDISPENSIBLE TO PSYCHOLOGISTS (AND OTHER SOCIAL SCIENTISTS)

1. *Hamilton's Theory of Inclusive-Fitness Maximizing.* As we have seen, this theory argues that individuals are vehicles evolved to further the replication of the genes they carry by assisting copies of these genes in offspring and nondescendent relatives. It means that behavior is likely to be understood only when its probable effects on the full array of genetic relatives' fitnesses are taken into account as well as its effects upon the individual's own survival and reproduction (Chagnon, 1979b). It suggests hidden pay-offs for behaviors which at first may seem self-destructive, e.g., heroism (Fisher, 1930) or infanticide (Daly & Wilson, 1981; this volume). It suggests that the behavior of individuals with many opportunities for helping relatives might differ significantly from that of individuals without relatives to help (see Thornhill, this volume; Flinn, 1981).

2. *Group-living.* Humans live in groups wherever they occur, and were no doubt group-living from the start. Groups formed and persisted because their individual members outreproduced their solitary competitors. Alexander (1974)

called attention to the fact that group-living is not automatically advantageous. In fact, it has several automatic disadvantages and only a limited number of possible specific benefits. This suggests that social behavior should be viewed as a compromise between advantages and disadvantages, rather than a pure advantage. The specific benefits of group-living for humans may have been common defense against predators, cooperation in hunting big game, or protection against human enemies. Whatever they were, group-living profoundly influenced all subsequent selection on human behavior (Alexander, 1971, 1979e; Bigelow, 1969).

Group-living automatically intensifies all kinds of competition for the resources of reproduction, including food and mates. The value of protecting and nurturing juveniles in the face of this competition may have been a key factor in the evolution of increased paternal care during human evolution (Alexander & Noonan, 1979), and in the evolution of menopause (Alexander, 1971, 1974; Alexander & Noonan, 1979; Benshoof & Thornhill, 1979; Hamilton, 1966; Strassmann, 1981). It may be related to the evolution of concealed ovulation by women and its influences upon human mating systems. Group-living secondarily set up conditions for nepotism and reciprocity to flourish. Parental influences, too, could extend beyond the parent's own lifetime through group rules (a form of indirect reciprocity) (Alexander, 1979b). The complication of reproductive competition by group living and the value of learning its intricacies in a specific social context no doubt were prime factors in offsetting the disadvantage of lengthening juvenile life in humans.

If group-living was a prerequisite for reproduction during human evolution, then the importance of group-effectiveness and the threat of expulsion would have placed limits on how directly individual competition could be expressed. Sensitivity to others and eagerness to win their approval and admiration would have been reproductive assets. In turn, such attitudes on the part of individuals would have been rewarded by group members who shared a real reproductive interest in the group's survival and success. Throughout human history, then, individuals could increase their reproductive success indirectly by helping to preserve the social group without which they could not reproduce at all. Judging when to identify wholeheartedly with the group and when to pursue selfish interests at the group's expense must have been critical lifetime concerns of individuals. In fact, some evolutionists (Alexander, 1971, 1974; Trivers, 1971) argue that, as people became more adept at detecting and discouraging social cheaters, an unconsciousness of competitive functions may have been favored. Individuals who lacked an awareness of their dual reproductive strategy may have been able to cut a finer line between advantageous cooperation and competition.

The evolutionary scenario described above involves simultaneous selection on the group and individuals levels. Interestingly, humans may be one of the few species for which group selection has played any significant role in shaping social behavior. The small, intensely competitive bands of closely related individuals in which early humans probably lived exemplify the population structure most favorable to group selection (Wright, 1945). The hypothesis that humans evolved their complex social behavior in the context of intense inter-group competition is expanded upon in writings of Bigelow (1968), and Alexander (1971, 1974). While opposed strongly by many social scientists, this model poses an important question not yet answered satisfactorily in any other way: what were the powerful, uniquely human selective forces which made cooperation on the group level increasingly more important during human evolution?

In connection with group-living, it is appropriate briefly to consider culture as a biological adaptation. Social scientists sometimes say that man adapts to his environment culturally rather than biologically through changes in allele frequencies. This view ignores the unarguably biological basis of culture, the extraordinarily large and specialized human brain. Culture is the product of human brains. It depends not only on the brain's ability to generate ideas, attitudes, symbols, and technology which form the content of culture, but on its ability to absorb that knowledge and to select among its competing elements during development. During human evolution, culture became an increasingly important element of the social environment in which selection of individuals took place. Culture and its underlying brain structure therefore evolved together.

Certain features of cultural transmission admittedly make it seem unrelated to biological evolution (Alexander, 1979a, 1979e; Durham, 1979; Flinn & Alexander, 1982). An individual's contribution to culture affects the reproductive success of the whole group, not simply its own genetic line. Contributing to culture may be advantageous, however, both because it strengthens the group and is rewarded by the group. Moreover, individuals cannot contribute to culture at will. Ideas pass into the culture only by proving useful directly or indirectly to other members of the social group.

Cultural differences, specifically in technology, have been the deciding factor in the outcome of competition between social groups time and time again in modern history. Although genetic changes probably take place during these episodes, it is difficult to relate them to the evolution of culture or of the capacity for culture. In other words, genetic differences do not seem to be the reason for one group's outcompeting another. Members of the losing group interbreed with members of the winning one and after a few generations, their descendants are culturally indistinguishable from the general population. This may tempt one to conclude that episodes of intergroup conflict have had no influence on the evolution of culture in humans. It must be remembered, however, that these clashes have a long evolutionary history. One cannot deny that culture contributes immensely to the effectiveness of groups. If human history involved the repeated replacement of one group by another, with culture the deciding factor, then selection acting at both individual and group levels could have refined the human capacity for culture to a very high level. One would therefore not expect to find gross differences among existing groups in their capacity for culture. However, accidents of history could easily produce gross differences in the specific content of existing cultures, and such differences could lead to the pattern of social competition without obviously related genetic change which appears to occur today.

3. *Patterns of effort over lifetimes.*

Whole lifetimes evolve to maximize genetic reproduction, but the ways this end is pursued (effort) vary predictably from birth to death (Gadgil & Bossert, 1970; Stearns, 1977; Williams, 1966b). The kinds of trade-offs or choices individuals struggle with at one level or another can also be expected to vary in parallel. Early reproduction is usually favored by selection, other things being equal, but most organisms delay reproduction in order to realize a greater benefit from a period of concentrated growth and development (somatic effort). At reproductive maturity, effort turns toward securing a mate or mates (mating effort) and, sometimes, toward parental effort and other forms of nepotism (Lack, 1968; Low, 1978; Williams, 1966a, 1966b).

The amount of resources, time, and energy individuals have to spend is finite. Effort spent securing a mate, for example, detracts from what might have been spent on parental care. Individuals may be expected to direct effort in ways which maximize their lifetime inclusive fitness. Patterns of effort can be predicted to vary with the intensity of sexual competition, confidence of parenthood (how certain an adult is that an offspring is really his/hers), the value of parental care, and the probability of future reproduction (Alexander & Borgia, 1979; Trivers, 1972). This theory has relevance for understanding child development (Smith, this volume; Alexander & Low, 1984; Low, 1986), sex rules, mid-life crises, and many kinds of individual conflicts.

Senescence is a predictable phenomenon which shapes patterns of reproductive effort. Williams (1957) and Hamilton (1966) show that senescence is the inevitable result of reproductive competition among individuals. According to their argument, genes can have their major effects (good or bad) at different times in the life cycle. A good effect early in life will have more impact on fitness than one later in life for two reasons. First, it affects more of the total lifetime reproduction. Second, because it affects more individuals (fewer will have died off for reasons other than senescence), an early beneficial effect will be exposed to positive selection more often than a late one. It follows that a strong positive effect early in life might compensate for a bad effect later on. Williams (1957) and Hamilton (1966) argue that senescence evolves as a byproduct of the selection of alleles with such mixed effects. Once senescence evolves, the probability of reproduction late in life diminishes, and fewer individuals survive to advanced ages, paving the way for the selection of even more alleles with good effects early and bad effects late in life. Species which experience high mortality for other reasons can be expected to evolve to senesce more rapidly than those which suffer lower extrinsic mortality. The same can be said of differences between the sexes within species. The importance of giving parental care over extended periods tends to slow the evolution of senescence by increasing the value of survival later in life. This too, can vary between species and between the sexes within species. The fact of senescence may have led to the evolution of menopause in human females. The probability of surviving to produce and rear another offspring may have fallen predictably such that females gained by stopping production of new offspring and concentrating their parental effort on offspring already produced. Because males potentially can produce offspring without investing parentally, such a physiological shutdown of sperm production would not be favored. Thus, senescence theory relates to psychological issues of sex differences, mid-life crises, and aging.

4. *Sexual Selection and Parental Investment.* Selection acts differently on males and females in regard to mating competition and the value of giving parental care (Darwin, 1871; Bateman, 1948; Trivers, 1974; Williams, 1975). Females are generally confident of who their offspring are, and have evolved to invest heavily in individual offspring (Alexander & Borgia, 1979; Trivers, 1971; Williams, 1975). Female reproductive success is almost always limited by the amount of resources females have to invest in offspring. On the other hand, males are generally less confident of parenthood. One male can inseminate many females and male reproductive success is usually limited by the number of matings a male achieves. Even in species where males typically invest in their offspring, the possibility of reproducing by inseminating females without further investment tends to favor a mixed strategy of pair-bonding and philandering by males (Trivers, 1972). Thus, females become a limiting resource for males, and sexual competition generally is more intense among males than among females (Bateman, 1948; Daly & Wilson, 1978; Williams, 1975).

The intensity of sexual selection varies among species and between the sexes within species. It can be quantified by the difference in variance of reproductive success between males and females. The mating effort of males goes to subduing rivals and to convincing females to accept them as mates. Their gaudy advertisements and elaborate adaptations for fighting or otherwise outmanoeuvering competing males are products of sexual selection (Darwin, 1871; Fisher, 1930). Being a male has been described as a high risk, high stakes strategy.

Females usually *know* who their offspring are, but males, especially in species with internal fertilization and long gestation periods, are less certain. This means that females are selected more strongly than males do invest parentally in particular offspring. Because females invest more in each offspring, they are usually more discriminating in their choice of mates. Where males to invest parentally, as in humans, one would expect mechanisms to evolve to promote confidence of paternity (e.g., sexual jealousy on the part of males, modesty on the part of females hoping to secure paternal care for their offspring). In some human societies, certain males are able to be highly parental, and females compete intensely for the limited number of high quality mates (Dickemann, 1979). The tendency of females to ornament themselves was shown by Low (1979) to vary with the intensity of such competition.

A whole array of traits is associated with greater sexual competitiveness in males in a wide range of organisms (Alexander, Hoogland, Howard, Noonan, & Sherman, 1979). These include greater size and gaudiness, relative frailty in development throughout life, shorter lifespans due to senescence, risk-taking, and extrinsic causes of mortality, and tendencies on the part of parents to invest more per individual male offspring compared to females. Sexual selection theory has obvious relevence for understanding sexual behavior (Symons, 1979), relations between spouses, the development and rearing of male and female children (Alexander & Low, 1984; Low, 1986; Trivers & Willard, 1973), sex roles (Alexander, 1979d; Daly & Wilson, 1978; Symons, 1979; Wilson, 1978), and mid-life shifts in strategies of males and females (see Alexander, 1979c, 1979d; Hrdy, 1981; Symons, 1979; Wilson, 1978).

5. *Reciprocity and the Evolution of Self-Deception.*   Reciprocity has already been introduced, together with nepotism, as one of two pervasive principles underlying human social relationships. Trivers (1971) and Alexander (1974) argue that, as a consequence of a long history of reciprocal altruism, humans have evolved sophisticated abilities to deceive one another in social interactions without detection and to spot very subtle degrees of cheating in associates. They hypothesize that an unawareness and even denial of one's own competitive goals may have been favored by selection by allowing individuals to cheat more effectively by not betraying themselves "by the subtle signs of self-knowledge" (Trivers, 1976). As Trivers (1976) puts it, ". . . the conventional view that natural selection favors nervous systems which produce ever more accurate images of the world must be a very naive view of mental evolution." Here evolutionary theory suggests a revolutionary way to view psychodynamics and the structure of mental life (Ghiselin, 1974; Leak & Christopher, 1982; Krebs & Dawkins, 1984; Symons, 1979, this volume; Trivers, 1971, 1976). It suggests that the stream of consciousness functions more directly to evaluate the fitness costs and benefits of alternative, even hypothetical courses of action (though not consciously in those terms) (Alexander, 1979e; Symons, 1979; Thornhill & Thornhill, 1983). It suggests that pleasure will be attached to those activities which tend to maximize individual inclusive fitness, and that where pleasures conflict, the criterion of choice (at conscious or unconscious levels) will be maximizing lifetime reproductive sucess in the environments of our history.

As Trivers pointed out, human individuals compete in a complex web of near and distant kin. The pursuit of pleasure is likely to have inclusive fitness repercussions, both through effects on relatives and effects upon reciprocal relations. To the extent that deception allows individuals to maximize their gains in reciprocal interactions, unconsciousness of grossly self-serving motives would be favored, especially when they compromise the reproductive success of individuals with whom one interacts over extended periods of time. Thus the "id" of Freudian psychology, locus of "animalistic" motivations, and "operating on the pleasure principle" does not have cognitive capabilities (Leak & Christopher, 1982). Because being detected as a social cheater would sharply curtail future benefits from reciprocity, individuals should be selected to closely monitor the success of their deception, perhaps through testing by sending and reading of subtle signals (Alexander, 1979e; Trivers, 1971). Evolutionary theory further suggests that, as fitness is relative, individual striving should frequently conflict with the interests of other individuals and that satisfaction or pleasure should often be relative to the success of social competitors (Alexander, 1978b, 1979e).

6. *Parent-Offspring Conflict.*   Alexander (1974) and Trivers (1974) point out that the reproductive interests of parents and offspring are not identical, and this fact influences the evolution of relations between them. Parents gain by providing parental care which maximizes their lifetime inclusive fitness, whereas individual offspring value their own inclusive fitnesses above that of their siblings and are selected to strive for more than their *share*. To what extent this conflict of interest erupts into behavioral conflicts has been the subject of considerable discussion. It appears that, for several reasons mentioned earlier, parents are more likely than offspring to realize their optima in most circumstances, however, they can only respond to the appearance of selfish traits in their offspring by evolving mechanisms for suppressing them.

Another context for the evolution of behavioral conflict between individuals, such as parents and offspring, whose reproductive interests are closely allied, was suggested by Alexander (1974). He argued that parents and offspring may be privy to different kinds of information the synthesis of which was important in maximizing the fitness value of an interaction. For example, weaning conflict might be viewed as a process whereby infants inform parents of their need for further suckling (ability to convert milk profitably, from the mother's viewpoint, into future reproduction), and mothers integrate this information with their own physiological state to settle upon an optimal course of action.

CONCLUSION

These theories are but a small sample of specific arguments elaborated from Darwin's original theory which apply directly to understanding what human behavior is about and why it varies as it does. The articles which follow in this volume illustrate how they can be used to generate testable hypotheses. Many areas of inquiry into human behavior are waiting to be interpreted in this light. I hope that this primer makes the point that the processes of evolution and their implications for the present cannot reasonably be ignored by any modern researcher in the social sciences.

ACKNOWLEDGMENTS

I thank my doctoral chairman, R. D. Alexander, for many years of inspiring teaching and for sharing with me his original ideas represented throughout this article. R. M. Nesse made helpful comments on the manuscript. E. Burnstein, M. A. Morris, and M. W. Plunkett provided valuable discussions.

REFERENCES

Alcock, L. (1975). *Animal behavior: An evolutionary approach.* Sunderland, MA: Sinauer.

Alexander, R. D. (1971). The search for an evolutionary philosophy of man. *Proceedings of the Royal Society of Victoria, Melbourne, 84,* 99–120.

Alexander, R. D. (1974). The evolution of social behavior. *Annual Review of Ecology and Systematics,5,* 325–383.

Alexander, R. D. (1975). The search for a general theory of behavior. *Behavioral Science, 20,* 77–100.

Alexander, R. D. (1977a). Evolution, human behavior, and determinism. *Proceedings of the Biennial Meeting of the Philosophy of Science Association (1976), 2,* 3–21.

Alexander, R. D. (1977b). Natural Selection and the analysis of human sociality. In C. E. Goulden (Ed.), *Changing scenes in the natural sciences: 1776–1976* (pp. 283–337). Bicentennial Symposium Monograph, Philadelphia Academy of Sciences, Special Publication 12.

Alexander, R. D. (1978a). Evolution, creation, and biology teaching. *American Biology Teacher, 40,* 91–107.

Alexander, R. D. (1978b). Natural selection and societal laws. In T. Engelhardt & D. Callahan (Eds.), *The foundations of ethics and its relationship to science. Volume 3, Morals, science, and society* (pp. 138–182). Hastings-on-Hudson, New York: Hastings Institute.

Alexander, R. D. (1979a). Evolution and culture. In N. A. Chagnon & W. G. Irons (Eds.), *Evolutionary biology and Human Social behavior: An anthropological perspective* (pp. 59–78). North Scituate, MA: Duxbury Press.

Alexander, R. D. (1979b). Natural selection and social exchange. In R. L. Burgess & T. L. Hudson (Eds.), *Social exchange in developing relationships.* New York: Academic Press.

Alexander, R. D. (1979c). Sexuality and sociality in humans and other primates. In A. Katchadourian (Ed.), *Human sexuality: A comparative and developmental perspective (pp. 81–97). Berkeley: University of California Press.*

Alexander, R. D. (1979d). Human sexuality and evolutionary models. In A. Katchadourian (Ed.), Human sexuality: A comparative and developmental perspective (pp. 107–112). Berkeley: University of California Press.

Alexander, R. D. (1979e). *Darwinism and human affairs.* Seattle: University of Washington Press.

Alexander, R. D., & Borgia, G. (1978). Group selection, altruism, and levels of organization of life. *Annual Review of Ecology and Systematics, 9,* 449–474.

Alexander, R. D., & Borgia, G. (1979). On the origin and basis of the male-female phenomenon. In M. F. & N. Blum (Eds.), *Sexual selection and reproductive competition in insects* (pp. 417–440). New York: Academic Press.

Alexander, R. D., Hoogland, J. L., Howard, R. D., Noonan, K. M., & Sherman, P. W. (1979). Sexual dimorphisms and breeding systems in pinnipeds, primates, ungulates, and humans. In N. A. Chagnon & W. G. Irons (Eds.), *Evolutionary biology: An anthropological perspective* (pp. 402–435). North Scituate, MA: Duxbury Press.

Alexander, R. D., & Low, B. S. (1984). *Evolutionary theory and the study of child development.* Unpublished manuscript, The University of Michigan, Ann Arbor, MI.

Alexander, R. D., & Noonan, K. M. (1979). Concealment of ovulation, parental care, and human social evolution. In N. A. Chagnon & W. G. Irons (Eds.), *Evolutionary biology and social behavior: An anthropological perspective* (pp. 436–453). North Scituate, MA: Duxbury Press.

Alexander, R. D., & Tinkle, D. W. (1968). Review of *On aggression* by Konrad Lorenz and *The territorial imperative* by Robert Ardrey. *Bioscience, 18,* 245–248.

Alexander, R. D., & Tinkle, D. W. (1981). *Natural selection and social behavior: Recent research and new theory.* New York: Chiron Press.

Allison, A. C. (1954). Notes on sickle-cell polymorphism. *Annals of Human Genetics, 19,* 39–57.

Axelrod, R., & Hamilton, W. D. (1981). The evolution of cooperation. *Science, 211,* 1390–1396.

Barash, D. P. (1977). *Sociobiology and behavior.* New York: Elsevier.

Barash, D. P. (1979). *The whisperings within.* New York: Harper & Row.

Bateman, A. J. (1948). Intrasexual selection in *Drosophila. Heredity, 2,* 349–368.

Benshoof, L., & Thornhill, R. (1979). The evolution of monogamy and concealed ovulation in humans. *Journal of Social and Biological Structures, 2,* 95–106.

Bigelow, R. S. (1969). *The dawn warriors: Man's evolution toward peace.* Boston: Little, Brown.

Blick, J. (1977). Selection for traits which lower individual reproduction. *Journal of Theoretical Biology, 67,* 597–601. Academic Press.

Bowlby, J. (1969) *Attachment and loss, Volume 1, Attachment.* London: Hogarth.

Burley, N. (1979). The evolution of concealed ovulation. *American Naturalist, 114,* 835–858.

Caplan, A. L. (1978). *The sociobology debate.* New York: Harper & Row.

Chagnon, N. A. (1979a). Is reproductive success equal in egalitarian societies? In N. A. Chagnan & W. B. Irons (Eds.), *Evolutionary biology and human social behavior: An anthropological perspective* (pp. 371–401). North Scituate, MA: Duxbury Press.

Chagnon, N. A. (1979b). Mate competition, favoring close kin, and village fissioning among the Yanamamo Indians. In N. A. Chagnon & W. G. Irons (Eds.), *Evolutionary biology and human social behavior: An anthropological perspective* (pp. 86–131). North Scituate, MA: Duxbury Press.

Chagnon, N. A., & Irons, W. G. (1979). *Evolutionary biology and human social behavior: An anthropological perspective.* North Scituate, MA: Duxbury Press.

Daly, M., & Wilson, M. (1978). *Sex, evolution, and behavior.* North Scituate, MA: Duxbury Press.

Daly, M., & Wilson, M. (1981). Abuse and neglect of children in evolutionary perspective. In R. D. Alexander & D. W. Tinkle (Eds.), *Natural selection and social behavior: Recent research and new theory.* New York: Chiron Press.

Darwin, C. D. (1859). *On the origin of species.* A facsimile of the first edition with an introduction by Ernst Mayr, published in 1967. Cambridge, MA: Harvard University Press.

Darwin, C. D. (1871). *The descent of man and selection in relation to sex.* New York: Appleton.

Dawkins, R. (1976). *The selfish gene.* New York: Oxford University Press.

Dawkins, R. (1979). Twelve misunderstandings of kin selection. *Zeitschrift fur Tierpsychologie, 51,* 184–200.

Dawkins, R. (1982). *The extended phenotype.* Oxford, England: W. H. Freeman.

Dickemann, M. (1979). The reproductive structure of stratified human societies: A preliminary model. In N. A. Chagnon & W. G. Irons (Eds.), *Evolutionary biology and human social behavior: An anthropological perspective* (pp. 321–367). North Scituate, MA: Duxbury Press.

Dickemann, M. (1981). Parental confidence and dowry competition: A biocultural analysis of purdah. In R. D. Alexander & D. W. Tinkle (Eds.), *Natural selection and social behavior: Recent research and new theory.* New York: Chiron.

Dobzhansky, T. (1970). *Genetics of the evolutionary process.* New York: Columbia University Press.

Drake, J. W., Glickman, B. W., & Ripley, L. S. (1983). Updating the theory of mutation. *American Scientist 71,* 621–630.

Durham, W. H. (1979). Toward a coevolutionary theory of human biology and culture. In N. A. Chagnon & W. G. Irons (Eds.), *Evolutionary biology and human social behavior: An anthropological perspective* (pp. 39–58). North Scituate, MA: Duxbury Press.

Eldredge, N., & Gould, S. J. (1972). Punctuated equilibria: An alternative to phyletic gradualism. In T. J. M. Schapf (Ed.) *Models in Paleobiology* (pp. 82–115). San Francisco: Freeman Cooper.

Fisher, R. A. (1930). *The genetic theory of natural selection.* (2nd ed., 1958). New York, Dover.

Flinn, M. V. (1981). Human family structure and mating-marriage systems: An evolutionary biological analysis. In R. D. Alexander & D. W. Tinkle (Eds.), *Natural selection and social behavior: Recent research and new theory.* New York: Chiron Press.

Flinn, M. V., & Alexander R. D. (1982). Culture theory: The developing synthesis from biology. *Human Ecology, 10,* 383–400.

Ford, E. B. (1971). Ecological genetics. (3rd ed.). London: Chapman & Hall.

Gadgil, M., & Bossert, W. H. (1970). *Life historical consequences of natural selection. American Naturalist, 104,* 1–24.

Garcia, J., Hankins, W. G. & Rusiniak, K. W. (1974). Behavior regulation of the milieu interne in man and rat. *Science,* 185, 824–831.

Ghiselin, M. T. (1969). *The triumph of the Darwinian method.* Berkeley: University of California Press.

Gould, S. J., & Eldredge, N. (1977). Punctuated equilibria: The tempo and mode of evolution reconsidered. *Paleobiology, 3,* 115–151.

Gould, S. J., & Lewontin, R. (1979). The spandrels of San Marco and the Panglossian paradigm: A critique of the adaptationist programme. *Proceedings of the Royal Society of London, 205,* 581–598.

Grafen, A. (1982). How not to measure inclusive fitness. *Nature, 298,* 425–426.

Haldane, J. B. S. (1932). *The causes of evolution.* London: Longmans, Green. (Reprinted, 1966, Cornell University Press).

Hamilton, W. D. (1964). The genetical evolution of social behavior, I, II. *Journal of Theoretical Biology, 7,* 1–52.

Hamilton, W. D. (1966). The moulding of senescence by natural selection. *Journal of Theoretical Biology, 12,* 12–45.

Hamilton, W. D. (1967). Extraordinary sex ratios. *Science, 156,* 477–488.

Hamilton, W. D. (1971). Geometry for selfish herd. *Journal of Theoretical Biology, 31,* 295–311.

Hamilton, W. D. (1972). Altruism and related phenomena, mainly in the social insects. *Annual Review of Ecology and Systematics, 3,* 191–323.

Hamilton, W. D. (1975). Innate social aptitudes of man: An approach from evolutionary genetics. In R. Fox (Ed.), *Biosocial anthropology* (pp. 133–155). New York: Wiley.

Hinde, R. A. (1968). Dichotomies in the study of development. In J. M. Thoday & A. S. Parkes (Eds.), *Genetics and environmental influences on behavior.* Edinburgh: Oliver & Boyd.

Hrdy, S. B. (1981). *The woman that never evolved.* Cambridge, MA: Harvard University Press.

Huxley, J. (1942). *Evolution: The modern synthesis.* London: Allen & Unwin.

Irons, W. G. (1979a). Investment and primary social dyads. In N. A. Chagnon & W. G. Irons (Eds.), *Evolutionary biology and human social behavior: An anthropological perspective* (pp. 181–213). North Scituate, MA: Duxbury Press.

Irons, W. G. (1979b). Natural selection, adaptation, and human social behavior. In N. A. Chagnon

& W. G. Irons (Eds.), *Evolutionary biology and human social behavior: An anthropological perspective* (pp. 4–39). North Scituate, MA: Duxbury Press.

Krebs, J. R., & Davies, N. B. (Eds.). (1984). *Behavioural ecology: An evolutionary approach.* Oxford: Blackwell.

Krebs, J. R., & Dawkins, R. (1984). Animal signals: Mind-reading and manipulation. In J. R. Krebs & N. B. Davies (Eds.), *Behavioural ecology: An evolutionary approach* (pp. 380–402). Oxford: Blackwell.

Lack, D. (1968). *Ecological adaptations for breeding in birds.* London: Methuen.

Lamb, M. J. (1977). *The biology of aging.* New York: Wiley.

Leak, G. K., & Christopher, S. B. (1982). Freudian psycho-analysis and sociobiology. A synthesis. *American Psychologist, 37,* 313–322.

Leigh, E. (1977). How does natural selection reconcile individual advantage with the good of the group? *Proceedings of the National Academy of Sciences, 74,* 4542–4546.

Lewontin, R. C. (1970). The units of selection. *Annual Review of Ecology and Systematics, 1,* 1–18.

Lloyd, J. E. (1975). Aggressive mimicry in *Photuris:* Signal repertoires by femmes fatales. *Science, 187,* 452–453.

Low, B. S. (1978). Environmental uncertainty and the parental strategies of marsupials and placentals. *American Naturalist, 112,* 197–213.

Low, B. S. (1979). Sexual selection and human ornamentation. In N. A. Chagnon & W. G. Irons (Eds.), *Evolutionary biology and human social behavior: An anthropological perspective* (pp. 462–486). North Scituate, MA: Duxbury Press.

Low, B. S. (1986). *Cross-cultural patterns in the training of children: An evolutionary perspective.* Unpublished manuscript. The University of Michigan.

Maynard Smith, J. (1964). Group selection and kin selection. *Nature, 201,* 1145–1147.

Maynard Smith, J. (1966). *The theory of evolution.* Baltimore, MD: Penguin Books.

Maynard Smith, J., & Price, G. R. (1973). The logic of animal conflict. *Nature, 246,* 15–18.

Parker, G. A. (1984). Evolutionarily stable strategies. In J. R. Krebs & N. B. Davies (Eds.), 2nd edition, *Behavioural ecology: An evolutionary approach* (pp. 30–61). Oxford, England: Blackwell Scientific Publications.

Porter, R. H., & Laney, M. D. (1980). Attachment theory and the concept of inclusive fitness. *Merrill-Palmer Quarterly, 28,* 35–51.

Ruse, M. (1982). *Darwinism defended.* Reading, MA: Addison-Wesley.

Sahlins, M. D. (1976). *The use and abuse of biology: An anthropological critique of sociobiology.* Ann Arbor: The University of Michigan Press.

Sheppard, P. M. (1967). *Natural selection and heredity.* London: Hutchinson.

Sherman, P. W. (1977). Nepotism and the evolution of alarm calls. *Science, 197,* 1246–1253.

Shettlesworth, S. J. (1984). Learning and behavioural ecology. In J. R. Krebs & N. B. Davies (Eds.), *Behavioral ecology: An evolutionary approach* (pp. 170–200). Oxford: Blackwell.

Stearns, S. C. (1977). The evolution of life history traits: A critique of the theory and a review of the data. *Annual Review of Ecology and Systematics, 8,* 145–171.

Strassmann, B. I. (1981). Sexual selection, paternal care, and concealed ovulation in humans. *Ethology and Sociobiology, 2*(1), 31–40.

Symons, D. (1979). *The evolution of human sexuality.* New York: Oxford University Press.

Thornhill, R., & Thornhill, N. W. (1983). Human rape: An evolutionary analysis. *Ethology and Sociobiology, 4,* 137–173.

Trivers, R. L. (1971). The evolution of reciprocal altruism. *Quarterly Review of Biology, 46,* 35–57.

Trivers, R. L. (1972). Parental investment and sexual selection. In B. Campbell (Eds.), *Sexual selection and the descent of man* (pp. 134–179). Chicago: Aldine.

Trivers, R. L. (1974). Parent-offspring conflict. *American Zoologist, 14,* 249–265.

Trivers, R. L. (1976). Foreword to R. Dawkins, *The selfish gene* (pp. v-vii). Oxford: Oxford University Press.

Trivers, R. L., & Willard, D. E. (1973). Natural selection of parental ability to vary the sex ratio of offspring. *Science, 179,* 90–92.

West Eberhard, M. J. (1975). The evolution of social behavior by kin selection. *Quarterly Review of Biology, 50,* 1–33.

Williams, G. C. (1957). Pleiotropy, natural selection, and the evolution of senescence. *Evolution,* 11, 398–411.

Williams, G. C. (1966a). *Adaptation and natural selection.* New Jersey: Princeton University Press.

Williams, G. C. (1966b). Natural selection, the costs of reproduction, and a refinement of Lack's principle. *American Naturalist, 100,* 687–690.

Williams, G. C. (1975). *Sex and evolution.* New Jersey: Princeton University Press.

Wilson, E. O. (1975). *Sociobiology: The new synthesis.* Cambridge, MA: Harvard University Press.

Wilson, E. O. (1978). *On human nature.* Cambridge, MA: Harvard University Press.

Wilson, E. O., & Bossert, W. H. (1971). *A primer of population biology.* Stamford, CT: Sinauer.

Wright, S. (1945). Tempo and mode in evolution: A critical review. *Ecology, 26,* 415–419.

Wynne-Edwards, V. C. (1962). *Animal dispersion in relation to social behaviour.* Edinburgh: Oliver & Boyd.

3 Sociobiology and Knowledge: Is Evolutionary Epistemology a Viable Option?

Michael Ruse
University of Guelph

> *Camus said that the only serious philosophical question is suicide. That is wrong even in the strict sense intended. The biologist, who is concerned with questions of physiology and evolutionary history, realizes that self-knowledge is constrained and shaped by the emotional control centers in the hypothalamus and limbic system of the brain. These centers flood our consciousness with all the emotions—hate, love, guilt, fear, and others—that are consulted by ethical philosophers who wish to intuit the standards of good and evil. What, we are then compelled to ask, made the hypothalamus and limbic system? They evolved by natural selection. That simple biological statement must be pursued to explain ethics and ethical philosophers, if not epistemology and epistemologists, at all depths.*
> —(The opening lines of E. O. Wilson's, *Sociobiology: The New Synthesis.*)

I want to consider the relevance of biology for one of the major problems of philosophy, and a problem which worries students in other disciplines, particularly psychology. What do we know of the external world? A number of scientists and philosophers argue that evolutionary theory throws fresh vital light on these central concerns of "epistemology" (Campbell, 1974; Lorenz, 1962; Plotkin, 1982). I believe that many claims of this kind are ill-founded. Nevertheless, recent advances in evolutionary studies, particularly those concerned with the evolution of social behavior—so-called "sociobiology"—may well open up a fruitful interchange between biology and philosophy. Indeed, we in philosophy may be on the verge of a revolution as important for us in the 20th

61

century as was Darwin's original revolution important for philosophy in the 19th century (Darwin, 1859, 1871).

Clearly, if we are going to consider knowledge, we are going to focus (primarily if not exclusively) on our own species. It is human beings who have knowledge, or who think they do. In other words, we are going to have to consider evolution, as it applies to *Homo sapiens*.

This involves no great conceptual leap. The assumption has always been that Darwinism applies to humans, as well as to other organisms. But clearly, if we're going to think seriously about knowledge, we're going to have to move beyond thinking of humans simply as physical beings. The physical organs of sensation—eyes, ears, and so forth—are clearly crucial to knowledge. But there is more than these involved. Knowledge is part and parcel of our awareness and response to the external world, including here our physical selves and our fellow humans.

In other words, if we are going to get to grips at all with knowledge from an evolutionary perspective, we are going to have to think of some types of knowledge as *adaptations*. Moreover, it must be as adaptations which enable humans to deal with, and respond to, their environment. Essentially, then, we are going to have to fit knowledge into the sphere of human activity, considered as part of our human heritage.

Until recently, any suggestions that we might have to do something like this would have had to remain as little more than suggestions. But things are changing rapidly on the scientific scene. Today, we can perhaps make some real progress in relating knowledge to our biology, throwing light on some of the traditional philosophical queries. Before turning to the question of knowledge as an adaptation, however, let us consider the rationale for viewing knowledge from a biological perspective.

I do not claim that human sociobiology is a well-established, polished theory. It certainly is not. But, in outline, it is an attractive hypothesis. It accounts for a lot of facts, and it opens up many prospects of new research. One cannot really ask more of it than that, at this stage. (Psychologically and sociologically, it has the marks that Thomas Kuhn [1970] identifies with "paradigms." However, given that it is the extension of an already-existing theory—Darwinism— whether the term "paradigm" properly applies is a nice point (see Ruse, 1979b; 1982b.)

This all being so, I suggest it is certainly worth our while seeing if human sociobiology can help us in our inquiry about the nature of knowledge. There is no reason why philosophers, any more than active scientists, should wait until a discipline becomes engraven on tablets of stone, before they take note of it. Indeed, if the application of human sociobiology to knowledge finds a response in traditional philosophical analyses, this might be added reason for taking sociobiology seriously.

RESPONSE TO CRITICISMS: IDEOLOGY

Before we turn to our primary task, it is unfortunately necessary to clear the ground a little. It is rare for a new science to emerge without controversy, and it is surely impossible for a new science dealing with humans to emerge without debate. Certainly, this has been the fate of human sociobiology. It has been damned by a varied range of individuals and groups—Marxists, feminists, social scientists, and others (including some of my fellow philosophers).

To be honest, I think most of the criticisms are more deserving of sociological understanding than philosophical or scientific refutation. Certainly, those very people who are loudest in their condemnation of sociobiology tend to be those very people who see it as a personal threat. Should sociobiology be successful, will this mean the end of feminist aspirations? Should sociobiology be successful, will this mean the end of departments of social science? (See Geertz, 1980; Sahlins, 1976.)

Nevertheless, let us take the objections as serious. Philosophy based on bad science is bad philosophy. Although I cannot speak to all criticisms, I suggest that they really do not strangle human sociobiology at birth. No doubt human sociobiologists have not always been as wise as they might have been; but this is far from saying that the subject itself if a total pseudo-science and sham.

First, there is the cry that sociobiology is ideologically offensive. It is simply right-wing rhetoric dressed up as science, and is demeaning of all minority or otherwise disadvantaged groups, such as blacks or women or homosexuals. The claim that the genes control our behavior is no more than Nazi propaganda brought up to date (Allen et al., 1975, 1976, 1977).

In response, I suggest that this is simply not true (Ruse, 1979b). There is, for instance, absolutely no necessary suggestion in human sociobiology that any one group or race or whatever is going to be less intelligent or otherwise capable than any other. Nor is it argued that humans are rigorously programmed by their genes. Biologists always think of the world as being a result of the interaction between the innate and the environmental (Ayala & Kiger, 1980). And this holds for humans (Bodmer & Cavalli-Sforza, 1976; Levitan & Montagu, 1977). Height is clearly partially a function of the genes—tall people tend to have tall children. But good nutrition in childhood is also an important factor. The same is true of behavior and abilities. Intelligence may be a function of the genes (sociobiologists think it is), but good or bad schooling also has a crucial effect. (For more on sociobiology and the intelligence question, see my remarks in Ruse, 1979b, 1982a.)

What about the charge of sexism? Sociobiologists certainly believe that a number of sex differences in human behavior may be the result of evolution. But does this mean that there is a deliberate bias—an unjustified prejudice—against females in sociobiology? This is a different matter, and I doubt it can be substantiated (Ruse, 1981a). There's certainly no implication that women are less intelligent, or otherwise less well equipped than men. Nor is there implication that women are less important. Sociobiology preaches the equality of the sexes. And sociobiology does not say one cannot change things. If intercourse means women are liable to get pregnant, then there is a selective value on women being careful. But, if you remove the threat—as can be done through efficient contraception—then the reason for the coyness vanishes. This is precisely what has occurred in the West in the past quarter-century. In the 1950s, nice girls said "No!" Now they have fewer reasons to do so—and they often don't!

One final point, on this whole charge of the putatively ideologically offensive nature of human sociobiology. For obvious reasons, people still feel the threat of Hitler and the Nazis hanging over any suggestions that biology might be an important factor in the human makeup. But to refuse to take any such idea seriously because Hitler endorsed a perverted version is to give the fiend a power beyond the grave. There is no necessary connection between Hitler and sociobiology. Indeed, in the 1920s it was the Russian communists who thought humans a function of their biology: In Germany at the time, they were all pushing environmentalism (Graham, 1981). To condemn sociobiology because of Hitler is akin to condemning straight roads because Hitler built the *Autobahnen*. (The analogy is stronger than you might think. The *Autobahn* was a crucial part of the Nazi world-plan. Hitler wasn't aesthetically attracted to straight roads for their own sake. Hitler wanted efficient ways of transferring military equipment and men around Germany.)

RESPONSE TO CRITICISMS: PSEUDO-SCIENCE

Let's move on to a second common objection against human sociobiology, namely, that it is not really a genuine science. Usually, the complaint is made that it fails the Popperian test of falsifiability or some such thing. Thus, supposedly, sociobiology is little more than a quasi- science (Allen et al., 1977; Lewontin 1977). It is a metaphysical wolf masquerading as a scientific lamb. (I'm never quite sure why it is, but when scientists want to condemn something as second-rate, they usually end up calling it "philosophical.")

A lot of ink has been spilt in recent years about precisely what it means to call something "scientific." Indeed, there are some who would argue that you really can't draw such a distinction. Standards change and are fluid. People pursue their interests regardless of boundaries. After all, a person who is working on models of the brain doesn't keep stopping and saying: "Am I doing psychology now, or philosophy, or pure mathematics, or computer science, or whatever?"

My own feeling, however, is that you really can point to some areas of genuine science, like physics, and some areas which simply don't qualify, like Creationism (Ruse, 1982a, 1982c, 1982d). But I do think that one has to be very careful not to try to make a decision just by picking out one or two isolated bits of a system, and then arguing that all hangs on them. If something is a genuine science, then it must be judged as such as a whole—and the same goes for rejection (Ruse, 1979b). After all, there are lots of parts of physics which are very tenuous, taken in isolation—what nonsense to say something can be both wave and particle at the same time—but these parts are seen to be perfectly good, when taken in the overall context.

This all holds very much for judgments about human sociobiology. Critics frequently take just one rather speculative piece of sociobiological hypothesizing, and then generalize. But this isn't fair. Human sociobiology is a new subject, and expectantly people try out all sorts of wild ideas. Could it be, for instance, that homosexuality is a function of kin selection? Perhaps an idea like this will work. Perhaps it won't. At the moment, there's precious little evidence one way or the other. But this is not to say sociobiology is bad or pseudo-science. Indeed, it is just the kind of thing that Popper endorses. Throw up lots of conjectures, and then see if you can knock them down. (For reviews of sociobiological thinking on homosexuality, see Ruse, 1981b; Weinrich, 1976; Wilson, 1978.)

Sociobiology must be judged as a whole. And this means that one simply has to make reference to the whole of evolutionary biology. Sociobiology does not stand alone. Rather, it is part and parcel of the whole neo-Darwinian synthesis. In every respect, it is the attempt to apply the Darwinian synthesis to human behavior and understanding. However, once this is seen, then things are rather altered. Evolutionary biology is indeed a genuine science, judged by any criteria you might like to name (Ruse, 1973). The evolutionary effect of natural selection working on genes is about as close to scientific fact as it is possible to be. That the hand and the eye are adaptations brought about by Darwinian causes is freely accepted by all who are prepared to accept a scientific explanation at all (Lewontin, 1978).

I will not labor the point. Darwinian evolutionary biology is a genuine science. Sociobiology, including human sociobiology, is an extension of Darwinism. Admittedly, it is new, and only an uncritical enthusiast would pretend that it is well-established science. But, inasmuch as it is an extension of Darwinism—which it is—there seems no reason to deny its genuine scientific status. To argue otherwise is to apply standards that you would probably not apply in physics. And this is unfair.

RESPONSE TO CRITICISMS: REDUCTIONISM

Let me mention one final criticism made against human sociobiology. It is sometimes claimed that the trouble with human sociobiology is that it is unduly "reductionistic" (Lewontin, 1977; Allen et al., 1977; Rose, 1982). Part of the trouble here is to know precisely what is meant by "reductionistic," for whatever else it is clearly not a good thing. Presumably, however, at least part of what is meant is that sociobiology tries to replace or otherwise exclude the conventional social sciences. Somehow it is felt that sociobiology tries to deny or negate our essential humanity. Free will is excluded, and all is attributed to a blind determinism. Humans are no more than epiphenomena on causally programmed genes.

Again it is easy to understand how this criticism arises, and only the insensitive could feel no sympathy for it. It you have spent your whole life working on desperately difficult problems, you will hardly welcome aliens from biology who promise to put all right with a few swift moves of the genes. But, notwithstanding the brash ignorance sociobiologists have sometimes shown, worries in this direction are really mistaken. It cannot be overemphasized that the one thing sociobiology will *not* do is make the conventional social sciences redundant.

To the contrary: Sociobiology provides a background—an overall framework—in which one can hope to locate specific social science analyses and explanations. But these specific analyses are crucial. Take as an example something sociobiologists hold as a paradigm of the effects of evolution on human behaviors and attitudes: incest taboos. Why is it that humans who, generally, are obsessed by sex, fail to copulate or otherwise relate sexually to those most freely available, namely close relatives like siblings? Sociobiologists argue that there is a very good reason. Close inbreeding leads to horrendous deleterious genetic effects. Hence, there has been strong selection against it. Humans are therefore inclined to look outside the family for sexual partners (Alexander, 1979; Wilson, 1978). This thesis is, of course, a fresh version of the thesis first proposed in the 19th century by Westermarck (1891).

But how are the incest barriers set up? Here, sociobiology says nothing. It is enough that they are there. At this point we have to turn to conventional social science for answers. And, fortunately, such answers do seem to be forthcoming (Shepher, 1979; van den Berghe, 1979). In particular, there is good sociological and anthropological evidence that close relationships at life's early stages leads to a kind of negative imprinting. The person with whom one shared a potty as a toddler can never be regarded as a potential mate after adolescence. In other words, one does not have (as it were) a gene for incest avoidance. One does, however, have a genetic makeup which makes one susceptible to negative imprinting in childhood. Puzzling out this fact—how the genes translate into action—is an essential part of the overall work of understanding human attitudes towards incest. And since it is the work of the social scientist, not the biologist, fears of redundancy or elimination are obviously unfounded. (For a somewhat different, but still biologically sympathetic account of incest barriers, see Fox, 1980.)

Sociobiology certainly claims that the social sciences on their own cannot achieve a full understanding of humankind. But this is not to say that the conventional social sciences have no role to play in the understanding of human-kind. There is work enough for all. Panic reactions against "reductionism" are misplaced.

Enough by way of apology. We have considered—and put down—sufficient objections to warrant taking human sociobiology seriously. And this means that we can now turn again to our main query about the nature of human knowledge. Specifically, what light does human sociobiology throw upon it? Was Wilson right (in the opening passage to *Sociobiology* quoted at the beginning of this essay) in claiming that sociobiology holds all of the answers to human knowledge? Is sociobiology the key to an adequate epistemology?

KNOWLEDGE AS BIOLOGICALLY ADAPTIVE

We are going to consider knowledge in the light of modern biology, in particular, in the light of sociobiology. Let us concentrate on scientific knowledge, although I am sure that any interesting results can be extended to the rest of human knowledge, including practical knowledge (like morality). Fairly obviously, from a sociobiological perspective, the key move is going to be the taking of science as adaptive. By this, I don't mean *adaptive* in any metaphorical sense, but in a literal biological sense. The suggestion has to be that the human being with scientific knowledge is better able to survive and reproduce than the human without it.

Prima facie, this is not that adventurous a move to make. On the positive side, there are good reasons for thinking that science would be, generally, adaptive. Science leads to applied subjects like technology and medicine, and these have obviously led to improved human living conditions, and to improved reproductive chances. Science is an important facet of human culture, and a key player in the team that makes humans so (biologically) successful.

On the negative side, despite having assumed that science is adaptive, one can side-step or answer some of the obvious queries. For instance, nagging philosophical worries about the status of the "mental"—to which science clearly belongs in some sense—and the mental's relationship to the physical, need not impede an initial inquiry. One may believe in some sort of monism (that mental and physical are essentially one), or one may believe in some sort of dualism (that mental and physical are essentially different). However, at first it is enough merely to acknowledge the obvious intimate connection between science and the human organs on which it depends—brain parts, organs of sensation, and so forth. All we need note in a preliminary inquiry is that the adaptiveness of the human parts on which it depends are parallel questions, or perhaps even the same question.

Moreover, sociobiology has an obvious counter to the objection that science bids fair to outrun its mandate, for, through its applications to nuclear technology, science may destroy us all in the near future. No evolutionist denies the possibility of extinction or that adaptations fail, or even that adaptations of today may prove counterproductive tomorrow. Extinction is, in fact, the ultimate fate we should expect for humans. Additionally, remember, sociobiology emphasizes the fact that selection is *not* for the good of the species. It is for the good of the individual, and perhaps indirectly for those around the individual. This means that evolution can be very "short-sighted." Someone might get hold of some aspect of science and technology, then use it for his own immediate gain, despite disasterous consequences for the species. An obvious example which springs to mind starts with improved child care and ends with the horrendous long-term effects on population numbers.

Let's grant, then, that there is at least some case for presuming scientific knowledge to be biologically adaptive. Even if this were an entirely reasonable position to take, and even if the evidence pointed to a tight connection between science and biology (a point we get to in a moment), what exactly would this mean? Philosophers and others ask some difficult questions about knowledge, and even if one cannot give the secure answers that a preevolutionist might give, it is incumbent upon one to address the issues. Fortunately, subject to some qualifications to be added later, one can already make some strong replies to the most difficult of questions.

First, and most definitely, if one thinks that knowledge is biologically adaptive, then one is committed to some sort of *realist* position. One just has to think that there is some sort of world "out there" that knowledge is about. The whole idea behind Darwinism is that the organism responds to the external world—we are what we are and we have what we have because this enables us to get on in the world. In other words, some sort of idealism, where everything is just in the human imagination, is ruled out of court. (*Idealism* means many things to many people, so I am not saying that other forms of idealism couldn't capture what I call *realism*.) (For more on realism see Boyd, 1981; Smart, 1963; van Fraassen, 1980.)

Second, what about the question of *truth,* meaning the correspondence of what we believe or sense with what is "out there"? Clearly, the Darwinian has no guarantee that the information sent out by the world and the information received or processed by humans is one and the same (Lewontin, 1982). Indeed, this is probably the last thing one would expect. An organism uses the external information to its own advantage. There are strong selective advantages to a very processed reception of information.

Indeed, by the very nature of the case this is precisely what one expects. Humans work through their five senses, and the information received is a function of the senses. The sky is not blue in itself, but "blue-as-seen-by-us-through-our-human-eyes." Of course, this is something long appreciated by pre-Darwinian philosophers (Locke, 1975). "Secondary qualities," like color, are a function of our senses. But it is usually claimed that "primary qualities," like shape and size, are independent of our sensing. I would just like to say that (along with some pre-Darwinian philosophers like Berkeley) I am nothing like as sure (Berkeley, 1963).

Consider the following: Many animals do not sense as we do, but rather through "pheremones," that is through chemical information. As E. O. Wilson (1975) points out, this is an incredibly efficient way of communicating, and certainly could provide enough input for organisms like humans.

> The amount of potential information that might be encoded in this manner is surprisingly high. Under two special circumstances, when transmission occurs in still air over a distance of the order of a centimeter or less, or when it is accomplished in a steady, moderate wind, modulation is not only practicable but highly efficient. Under extremely favorable conditions, a perfectly designed system could transmit on the order or 10,000 bits of information a second, an astonishingly high figure considering that only one substance is involved. Under more realistic circumstances, say for example in a steady 400-centimeters-per-second wind over a distance of 10 meters, the maximum potential rate of information transfer is still quite high—over 100 bits a second, or enough to transfer the equivalent of 20 words of English text per second at 5.5 bits per word. For every pheromone released independently, the same amount of capacity could be added to the channel capacity. (p. 233)

Yet, if our primary sense were chemical, using pheromones, would we have the awareness of size and shape in the way(s) that we have now? I suggest it would be fairly drastically altered (Ruse, 1984).

What I'm suggesting therefore is realism, but with a very human element in what we sense. But before we move on, note that I'm not just suggesting a subjective morass, where anything goes. Apart from anything else, we have epistemic stability between humans. We all have the same evolutionary background. With obvious qualifications, red for me is red for you, and chemical sensations are barred for me as they are for you. (The qualifications, for instance color blindness, are a lot easier to explain if you posit evolution, than if you posit the creative interference of a good god.)

Moreover, continuing with the theme of stability, note that between species, even between species using different kinds of senses, it seems more reasonable to say that we are responding in different ways to the same thing, than to say we are responding to different things. Animals using pheromones don't just sail gladly through objects which we humans regard as solid. We sense the objects in different ways, but it seems correct to say that they are the same object.

Nor should it be thought that we are positing a mysterious world out there, for ever unknowable, and rather frightening, a real world beyond our senses. This is to mix up metaphors. This fear is rather like saying that here we have a coffin, and although we can never open it, the sounds and smells and groans from within suggest an awesome interior. The interior is only awesome because, in principle, we know what it would be like to open up the coffin and to find a maggoty zombie within. But the picture the evolutionist is sketching has no interior to the coffin: an interior which could itself in principle be sensed. The coffin exterior is all there is. Objects present themselves to us as sensed by us, and that is all there is to it. (Atoms and the like are similarly sensed indirectly through instruments. I'm not saying we can't discover the makeup of a microscopic object.)

Hence, what I am arguing *qua* Darwinian evolutionary biologist, is that there is a reality, but that what we know of it comes through our evolved organs. Thus, how we sense reality is necessarily a function of that evolution. (In spirit, I am obviously much in tune with Piaget [1967], although my biological starting point is rather different.)

THE PROBLEMS WITH CULTURE

At this point, we have to backtrack a little. The assumption has been that knowledge, specifically scientific knowledge, is biologically adaptive. But, although this may be true in a broad sense, we cannot just leave matters at that. As noted, science is part of what we would broadly regard as culture. And this being so, there are some problems which have to be faced.

Culture is certainly part of humankind's general biology, and as such is properly considered adaptive. We've looked at some reasons for this in the specific case of science. But culture is a strange adaptation. On the one hand, it is a great deal more powerful than conventional adaptations. There, as we've seen, you have to wait on random mutations. Moreover, any good *ideas* (i.e., favorable mutations) have to work through the generations, as they are passed on and collected by the normal processes of reproduction. If I have a favorable mutation, I cannot give it directly to my siblings or anyone else. Favorable mutations can only be passed on to descendents, and even then they are subject to the vagaries of the reproductive process. (For instance, only one half of one's genes are given to offspring, so a favorable mutation may not even be transmitted.)

In the case of culture, however, both of these restrictions are broken—or more properly, transcended. New ideas can be produced as needed—that was why the traditional evolutionary epistemology analogy broke down. And, one adult can pass on ideas straight to another adult. Whether this transition may be quite as free and easy as sometimes assumed may be doubted. As Thomas Kuhn (1970) points out, mature scientists are frequently not that receptive to new ideas. And you can see why. Selection would not have favored too much inquisitiveness and susceptibility in adult proto-humans. Nevertheless, the transmission of cultural information is not restricted to the usual modes of inheritance.

Because culture rises above the usual biological mechanisms (although culture is still part of biology), its power and rate of change is much higher than that of usual biological processes. You cannot turn an arm into a wing in one or two generations, but you can turn a heathen into a Christian. And you can have the whole rise and fall of the Roman Empire in less time than it would take to make a new human species.

However, with the power of culture comes another major difference between culture and the rest of biology. The tight links between organic features and adaptive advantages are loosened. Even the strict Darwinian must admit this. Rapid change means one can throw up lots of different elements: elements which don't subsequently get incorporated into the species' genotype—and which don't have to. So long as the basic pattern works, you can tolerate a certain amount of "junk" or "adaptive noise." Therefore, details of culture are just not likely to be tied tightly to biological demands.

And this qualification obviously applies particularly in the case of science. Science itself may be broadly adaptive—just the basic stuff of science certainly comes through our evolved senses—but particular scientific theories or hypotheses are not tied tightly to biological needs.

Indeed, how could one think otherwise? Some of the greatest names in science have died childless, whereas some of the biggest charlatans have had large families. There is certainly no immediate connection between the endorsing of what posterity judges to be a good scientific idea and reproductive success. Nor is there immediate connection between the endorsement of a bad idea and reproductive failure. To be receptive to science, and to live in a culture which is scientific, helps you biologically. But the details of specific theories are not (at least not usually and directly) of great biological value.

THE STANDARDS OF SCIENCE

What does this mean? Does one therefore have to remain with vague generalities? Can one say more than that science in some general sense is adaptive? I think one can. Science is not just a collection of ideas, or just a collection of chunks of information gathered through the senses. One has hypotheses and theories which attempt to make understandable and useful the information of the senses. But hypotheses and theories are not just things which can be formulated randomly. A scientist cannot just do anything at all that he or she likes with the data of the senses. To the contrary, there are all sorts of rules and conventions which scientists must obey. For instance, scientific speculations have to conform to the laws of mathematics. You can't just flagrantly break with the rules of arithmetic and geometry and so forth. Even if unusual mathematics, like non-Euclidean geometries, are used, rigorous standards have still to be met (Hempel, 1966; Nagel, 1961).

Again, science has to conform to strong standards about causality. Indeed, one might almost go so far as to say that this lies at the crux of the scientific method. Science attempts to understand through the bringing of events beneath law, that is to say, unbroken regularity. When you can see how one thing follows from another, because *this is the way the world works,* then you are well on the way to scientific understanding. And when your laws are causal laws, your job is just about done. (For details of this in one great scientific revolution, see Ruse, 1979a.)

What I am arguing, therefore, is that there are certain rules or standards which we set upon scientific understanding, particularly upon good scientific understanding. Moreover, if we modify or abandon any of them it is usually because we want to preserve even more fundamental rules (Hanson, 1958). Thus, in quantum mechanics, we give up demands for the usual find of causality, because by so doing we can preserve certain demands on consistency and the like: demands which we hold even dearer. How do we deal with something which is apparently both a wave and a particle? To say that it is both involves contradiction. Hence, thanks to Heisenberg's Uncertainty Principle, we refuse to countenance questions which might require affirmations of simultaneous wave/particle natures.

I am certainly not claiming that all of the rules or standards of science are of exactly the same kind, or that they are all equally explicitly understood by the practicing scientist. Certainly some of the standards are well known to all. Everyone knows that you must obey mathematics, for example. Other rules are followed instinctively by scientists, and made explicit (if at all) only by those reflecting on science, like philosophers. I refer here to something like a consilience. Generally, scientists are driven to unite different paths of theory, beneath one or a few all-encompassing premises. We have seen how this happened in Darwinian evolutionary biology: but it occurs throughout science—from Newtonian physics to plate techtonics geology (Ruse, 1982e). Darwin, in fact, was conscious of his methodology. Not all scientists are. But, aware or not, the ideal of a consilience is a major guide for scientists.

I am sure you can predict what I am going to argue now: Although the specific details of a scientific theory may not be directly linked to adaptive advantage, these rules or standards are. Simply put, the human or proto-human who thought that $2 + 2 = 4$ rather than $2 + 2 = 5$; who thought that fire causes burning and not orgasm; and who thought that similarities might indicate an underlying common cause rather than coincidence, tended to be better suited for life's struggles than the human or proto-human who did not.

In other words, there is an adaptive advantage in seeing and interpreting the world in certain ways—mathematically, causally, and so forth. These interpretations then in turn mold our science. Hence, the dictates of *biological* advantage run right through the way science is done, and reflect themselves in the finished product.

The kind of point I am making has been put well by the philosopher Elliott Sober (1981), in a first-class discussion of the evolution of human rationality.

Sober asks why it is that we take seriously (consider "rational") the "straight rule" of induction:

(SR) If n/m of the observed As have been B, infer that n/m of the remaining As are B.

Sober comments as follows:

We might imagine that (SR) is so fundamental to the construction of beliefs about the world that it could not be learned: rather, it is something the possession of which is required for any learning at all to take place. The problem, then, will be to explain how (SR) could have been selected for. We can easily imagine situations in which (SR) contributed to survival in a way that the following rule, that of counterinduction, would not have:

(CI) If n/m of the observed As are B, infer that 1—n/m of the remaining As are B.

Counter-induction recommends that we infer that the sampled individuals are precisely *non*representative of the rest of the population from which they are drawn. Although the inductive rule (SR) isn't infallible, it is not implausible to think that it has historically been more reliable than (CI), and that, because of this, (SR) confers a selection advantage. (p. 101)

This is precisely what I argue.

EPIGENETIC RULES

What I am offering is a thoroughly Darwinian perspective on human scientific knowledge. If you have significant doubts about human sociobiology, then you will have significant doubts about what I am claiming. Sociobiologists argue that the key to the understanding of human beings—in all aspects—is Darwinian advantage, and this is precisely what I argue in science. I claim that there is a real world out there, but that the way in which we humans deal with it—both in sensation and in the organization of this basic sensory information—must be understood in terms of *literal* biological adaptive advantage.

Surely, if indeed what I claim is truly sociobiological, then we might expect that professional sociobiologists have themselves been thinking along lines I've just been sketching. At this point, I must confess that I have been less than candid with the reader, for such a view of knowledge is precisely what some sociobiologists are endorsing: They argue that the organs of sense and the brain have evolved, in just such a way that we interpret the world so as to maximize advantage to us as organisms in the world.

Most exciting and pertinently, let me refer to some of the recent thoughts of

E. O. Wilson, as he has expressed them with his coworker Charles Lumsden, in their recent book, *Genes, Mind, and Culture* (1981; see also Lumsden & Wilson, 1983). They argue for a picture of humans which involves what they call a "coevolutionary process," where genes and culture interact with each other, alterations at one level bringing about alterations at the other level, and *vice versa*.

The key concept is that of an *epigenetic* rule, which refers to a way in which humans receive and process information from the outside world. It is worth quoting in full their introductory comments on these rules.

> The key element in the theory of gene-culture coevolution is the role of the epigenetic rules in culturgen choice. [A culturgen is a unit of culture.]
>
> Existing information on cognition is most efficiently organized with reference to gene-culture theory by classifying the epigenetic rules into two classes that occur sequentially within the nervous system. *Primary epigenetic rules* are the more automatic processes that lead from sensory filtering to perception. Their consequences are the least subject to variation due to learning and other higher cortical processes. For example, the cones of the retina and the internuncial neurons of the lateral geniculate nucleus are constructed so as to facilitate a perception of four basic colors. The *secondary epigenetic rules* act on color and all other information displayed in the perceptual fields. They include the evaluation of perception through the processes of memory, emotional response, and decision making through which individuals are predisposed to use certain culturgens in preference to others. (Lumsden & Wilson, 1981, p. 36)

This, of course, is just the way in which I have analysed scientific knowledge. The primary epigenetic rules deal with the initial sensations. The secondary epigenetic rules deal with the ways in which we process the sensory information. And the sorts of things that Lumsden and Wilson have in mind for the secondary rules are precisely those rules and standards I identified as the rules and standards of good science. In short, the picture I am sketching of scientific knowledge is just that being paraded at the forefront of contemporary sociobiology.

SYNTHETIC "A PRIORI"

Let me conclude this discussion by switching back for a moment to more traditional modes of thought, specifically those of conventional philosophy. I have been arguing for a modern biological perspective on scientific knowledge. Indeed, I would go so far as to argue that, unless one takes modern sociobiological thought very seriously indeed, one fails to see the true nature of knowledge. In this sense, I am a full-blooded "evolutionary epistemologist." Nevertheless, very rarely is it the case that philosophical positions are entirely new. One can usually find important links with the past, even if earlier thinkers' visions were necessarily somewhat limited (by their lack of full scientific knowledge). Truly, Whitehead once quipped that the history of philosophy is a series of footnotes to Plato.

Without going quite this far back, as a number of recent thinkers have noted, the sociobiological approach to knowledge is in fact the completion of the epistemological program started by the great pre-evolutionary philosophers, David Hume and Immanuel Kant. (See particularly Lorenz, 1962. In fairness to Popper, I must note that he too has aired such ideas, although he has not developed such a position in Popper [1962, pp. 47–48]. Campbell [1974] has full details.)

It was Hume (1740) who pointed out that much which we take for granted simply cannot be read off directly from nature. For instance, we do not see causes "out there." The fire burns on this occasion, but there is nothing in nature to say that it *must* always burn. Any notions of causal necessity have to have some other origin. This, of course, is precisely what a sociobiologically inspired epistemology claims. The external world does not present, on a platter, those rules by which we order experience.

Kant then took up the challenge set by Hume, solving it by arguing that the mind interprets the world in certain set ways—according to principles of mathematics, principles of causality, and so forth (Kant, 1929, 1949). In the very acts of sensing and of thinking, we give structure and form to our experiences. We see things as governed by mathematics, as governed by causality, and the like.

Kant spoke of claims about mathematics and causality and so forth as being "synthetic a priori." They are "synthetic" in that they are not logically required truths. It could be that the fire fails to burn. On the other hand, they are "a priori" meaning they are views that we impose on the world, rather than read from it. They are conditions of thinking.

The sociobiological approach to knowledge clearly picks up where Kant leaves off. What Kant regards as synthetic a priori claims are what the sociobiologist regards likewise as claims involving human interpretations of experience: Specifically, they are claims interpreted via what Lumsden and Wilson speak of as secondary epigenetic rules. The Kantian and the sociobiologist both take Hume's problem seriously, and both offer the same answer: Knowledge is not given, but is a function of the way humans respond to and think about the world. Moreover, Kantians and sociobiologist overlap on what interpretations they think humans make of the world: mathematics, causality, and the like.

This is not to say that there is no difference between traditional Kantian and sociobiologist. Kant thought we think in the way we do because this is the only way in which rational thought can occur. The sociobiologist would not be as certain. What is a priori for the individual is a posteriori for the species. We think in the way that we do, because of evolutionary advantage. Things presumably could have been otherwise, at least to an extent. (This is why the sociobiologist is untroubled by the standard criticism against Kant, namely that modern science shows many things Kant thought necessary are not really necessary (Körner, 1955). Sociobiology does not claim anything is absolute for all time. Indeed, as pointed out, one would expect jettison or suspension of some rules, were other more fundamental ones at stake. (I suspect also that the sociobiologist can speak to the Quine [1953] worries about whether one can properly make an analytic/synthetic distinction. As you'll see in a moment, the sociobiologist makes *necessity* rather less absolute than a Kantian would. Interestingly, Quine has endorsed a position much as I am arguing for [see Quine, 1969; Ruse, 1984.])

Nevertheless, for all the differences, it must be emphasized that those differences between Kantian and sociobiologist are more theoretical than practical. If you asked the Kantian what justification he (she) would have for making claims about mathematics and causality, ultimately he (she) would say that the denial is *inconceivable*. One just can't imagine what a world would be like where $2 + 2 = 5$. And this surely is the reply also of the sociobiologist.

If you object that now the ultimate standard is evolutionary expediency, and that everything is thus *relative,* then there are two responses. First, everything is not relative in the sense of *relative to a certain limited group of human beings,* which is one sense in which we usually understand the term relative. We are all the same species, and the inconceivability of $2 + 2 = 5$ to a Chinese man is just that of the inconceivability of an Englishman. Second, the simple fact of the matter is that whatever may be the *true* state of affairs, as far as we are concerned, the denial of mathematics and causality and so forth is inconceivable. And that is all we can say on the matter. Literally!

But note that, because the denial of something is inconceivable, it does not follow that that which is being denied is a reasonable alternative option—if only we could think of it. Inasmuch as we can think about the world, it is the way we can think about it—a tautology, but not without some force. We can't think of other options, but this is no cause for concern or for thinking that we are thereby limited.

And this fact surely answers a criticism of circularity, which you may think lurking. You may accept everything I've said, but feel worried. My whole position depends on the truth of claims about natural selection—and it is the very status of claims of this kind that I've been considering. This is true, but the circularity—if such there be—can be countered. Allow that the whole argument does depend on natural selection. But supposing that the world is not law-bound (as we suppose when we invoke selection) is inconceivable. And that is enough of a counterargument. My whole case could be wrong because natural selection does not operate in the way I suppose. However, if you grant that natural selection is a good theory, as best we can tell, it simply isn't reasonable to worry about other options which we humans just can't think about. The unpleasant truth is that Hume and Kant and Darwin have shown us that there is no hope of a direct line to absolute truth. Anything we achieve is bound by our human faculties. But, as there was no reason to fear a mysterious unknown, beyond our senses, so there is no reason to fear a mysterious unknown—with different mathematics and causality—beyond our intellect. For all that I disagree with Popper, he was surely right in thinking that the quest for absolute nonhuman truth is hopeless, and he was equally right in thinking this no cause for concern (Popper, 1959, 1962).

CONCLUSION

Human sociobiology has far to go before it can claim to be as solid a science as quantum mechanics, or even molecular biology. But, even in its present primitive state, it commands our attention. The critical arrows fired against it fail to penetrate to vital organs. As science, it bears full promise of a vital new way of understanding human nature. For this reason, it must be studied by those of us— whether we be professional philosophers or not—who would understand human knowledge, including scientific knowledge. (Perhaps morality also. See Murphy, 1982.)

What I have argued in this essay is that, thus employed, sociobiology leads to renewed insights into the nature of that most crucial of human products: natural science. Thanks to sociobiology, we are able to pick up the work of the great pre-evolutionary philosophers and to carry it to fruition.

ACKNOWLEDGMENT

This essay was written during a time of support by the John Simon Guggenheim Memorial Foundation.

REFERENCES

Alexander, R. (1979). *Darwinism and human affairs.* Seattle: University of Washington Press.
Allen, E. et al. (1975). Letter to editor. *New York Review of Books, 22*(18), 43–44.
Allen, E. et al. (1976). Sociobiology: Another biological determinism. *BioScience, 26,* 182–186.
Allen, E. et al. (1977). Sociobiology: A new biological determinism. In Sociobiology Study Group of Boston (Ed.), *Biology as a social weapon.* Minneapolis: Burgess.
Ayala, F., & Kiger J., (1980). *Modern genetics.* Reading, MA: Addison-Wesley.
Berkeley, G. (1963). *Works on vision.* Indianapolis: Library of Liberal Arts.
Bodmer, W., & L. Cavalli-Sforza (1976). *Genetics, evolution, and man.* San Francisco: Freeman.
Boyd, R. (1981). Scientific realism and naturalistic epistemology. In P. Asquith & R. Giere (Eds.), *PSA 1980,* East Lansing, MI: Philosophy of Science Association, *2,* 613–662.
Campbell, D. T. (1974). Evolutionary epistemology. In P. A. Schilpp (Ed.), *The philosophy of Karl Popper.* LaSalle, IL: Open Court Publishing, Vol. 1, pp. 413–463.
Darwin, C. (1859). *On the origin of species by means of natural selection.* London: Murray.
Darwin, C. (1871). *Descent of man.* London: Murray.

Fox, R. (1980). *The red lamp of incest*. New York: Dutton.

Geertz, C. (1980). Sociosexology. *New York Review of Books, 26*, January 24, 3–4.

Graham, L. R. (1981). *Between science and values*. New York: Columbia University Press.

Hanson, N. R. (1958). *Patterns of discovery*. Cambridge: Cambridge University Press.

Hempel, C. (1966). *Philosophy of natural science*. Englewood Cliffs, NJ: Prentice-Hall.

Hume, D. (1740). *Treatise of human nature*. London: John Noon.

Kant, I. (1929). *Critique of pure reason* (trans. N. Kemp-Smith). London: Macmillan.

Kant I. (1949). *Critique of practical reason* (trans. L. W. Beck). Chicago: Chicago University Press.

Körner, S. (1955). *Kant*. Harmondsworth: Penguin.

Kuhn, T. S. (1970). *The structure of scientific revolutions* (2nd ed.). Chicago: University of Chicago Press.

Levitan. M., & Montagu, A. (1977). *Textbook of human genetics* (2nd ed.). New York: Oxford University Press.

Lewontin, R. C. (1977). Sociobiology—a caricature of Darwinism. In F. Suppe & P. Asquith (Eds.), *PSA 1976*. Lansing, MI: PSA, *2*, 22–31.

Lewontin, R. C. (1978). Adaptation. *Scientific American, 239*(3) 212–230.

Lewontin, R. C. (1982). Organism and environment. In H. C. Plotkin (Ed.), *Learning, development, and culture* (pp. 151–170). Chichester: Wiley.

Locke, J. (1975). *An essay concerning human understanding*. In P. H. Nidditch (Ed.). New York: Oxford University Press.

Lorenz, K. (1962). Kant's doctrine of the priori in the light of contemporary biology. *General Systems, 7*, 23–35.

Lumsden, C. J., & Wilson, E. O. (1981). *Genes, mind and culture: The coevolutionary process*, Cambridge, MA: Harvard University Press.

Lumsden, C. J., & Wilson, E. O. (1983). *Promethean fire*. Cambridge, MA: Harvard University Press.

Murphy, J. G. (1982). *Evolution, morality, and the meaning of life*. Totowa, NJ: Rowman and Littlefield.

Nagel, E. (1961). *The structure of science*. New York: Harcourt, Brace, and World.

Piaget, J. (1967). *Biologie et connaissance*. Paris: Gallimard).

Plotkin, H. C. (1982). *Learning, development, and culture: essays in evolutionary epistemology*. Chichester: Wiley.

Popper, K. R. (1959). *The logic of scientific discovery*. London: Hutchinson.

Popper, K. R. (1962). *Conjectures and refutations*. New York: Basic Books.

Quine, W. (Ed). (1953). Two dogmas of empiricism. In *From a logical point of view*. Cambridge, MA: Harvard University Press.

Quine W. (1969). Natural kinds. In *ontological relativity and Other essays*. New York: Columbia University Press.

Rose, S. (1982). *Towards a liberatory biology*. London: Allison and Busby.

Ruse, M. (1973). *The philosophy of biology*. London: Hutchinson.

Ruse, M. (1979a). *The Darwinian revolution: Science red in tooth and claw*. Chicago: University of Chicago Press.

Ruse, M. (1979b). *Sociobiology: Sense or nonsense?* Dordrecht: Reidel.

Ruse, M. (1981a). *Is science sexist?* Dordrecht: Reidel.

Ruse, M. (1981b). Are there gay genes? Sociobiology and homosexuality. *Journal of Homosexuality, 6*(4), 5–34.

Ruse, M. (1982a). *Darwinism defended: A guide to the evolution controversies*. Reading, MA: Addison-Wesley.

Ruse, M. (1982b). Is human sociobiology a new paradigm? *Philosophical Forum, 13*, 119–43.

Ruse, M. (1982c). The Arkansas creation trial 1981: Is there a message for us all? *The History and Social Science Teacher, 18,* 23–8.

Ruse, M. (1982d). Darwin's legacy. In R. Chapman (Ed.), *Charles Darwin: A centennial commemorative.* Wellington, N.Z.: Nova Pacifica.

Ruse, M. (1982e). The revolution in geology. In P. Asquith (Ed.), *PSA 1978, 2.*

Ruse, M. (1984). Is rape wrong in Andromeda: philosophical reflections on extra-terrestrial life. In E. Regis (Ed.), *The search for extra-terrestrial intelligence.* New York: Cambridge University Press.

Sahlins, M. (1976). *The use and abuse of biology.* Ann Arbor: University of Michigan Press.

Shepher, J. (1979). *Incest, the biosocial view.* Cambridge, MA: Harvard University Press.

Smart, J. J. C. (1963). *Philosophy and scientific realism.* London: Routledge and Kegan Paul.

Sober, E. (1981). The evolution of rationality. *Synthese, 46,* 95–120.

van den Berghe, P. (1979). *Human family systems: An evolutionary view.* New York: Elsevier.

van Fraassen, B. C. (1980). *The scientific image.* Oxford: Clarendon Press.

Weinrich, J. D. (1976). Human Reproductive Strategy. I. *Environmental predictability and reproductive strategy: Effects of social class and race.* II. *Homosexuality and non-reproduction: Some evolutionary models.* Unpublished doctoral thesis, Harvard University.

Westermarck, E. (1891). *The history of human marriage.* London: Macmillan.

Wilson, E. O. (1975). *Sociobiology: The new synthesis.* Cambridge, MA: Harvard University Press.

Wilson, E. O. (1978). *On human nature.* Cambridge, MA: Harvard University Press.

4 The Challenge of Altruism in Biology and Psychology

Dennis Krebs
Simon Fraser University

Virtually everyone has engaged in arguments about the role of altruism in human nature at one time or another, and philosophers have debated the issue for centuries. Whether cast at a cocktail party or dignified by a philosopher's pen, such arguments tend to assume a common form. Those who believe that humans are altruistic support their position by adducing examples of apparent acts of altruism. Soldiers smothering grenades, people rushing into burning buildings to save children, and Mother Theresa are common stock. Those who believe that humans are not altruistic respond by showing how such acts could stem from selfish motives and reap hidden rewards. The soldier may have cracked under pressure; he may have thought that he would get to the grenade before it went off; or he may have been attempting to promote a better place for himself in another world. As such arguments progress, it usually becomes apparent that there is considerable ambiguity about what, exactly, altruism is, and how the occurrence of altruistic behaviors can be established.

How, then, should altruism be defined? It is helpful to recognize that altruism is a construct that is used by different people to refer to different types of behavior. No one has a franchise on the meaning of the term. At a semantic level, it is futile to argue about whose definition is correct. It is more useful to assume that there are different types of altruism—different behaviors that parade under the same banner—and establish clearly which type is being considered in the issue at hand.

On virtually all definitions, altruism refers to behavior that benefits another ("alter") at some cost to the helper. Differences in definitions relate primarily to two factors—the relative emphasis on the intentions underlying a behavior and its consequences, and the amount of benefit an act may reap and remain altruistic. For example, altruism may be defined as (a) behavior that has the consequence of benefiting another, (b) behavior based on the intention to help another, whether or not it produces a beneficial effect, or (c) behavior that meets both criteria—helping behavior motivated by the intention to help another. Research on social cognition indicates that most people base their attributions of altruism on both the intention underlying an act and its consequences, with most altruism attributed to intentional acts that produce great benefit (see Krebs, 1970, 1982). As concerns benefits for the helper, altruism may refer to (a) behavior that benefits another regardless of the gain to the helper, (b) behavior that confers more benefit on the recipient than on the helper, (c) behavior that benefits a recipient at a net loss to the helper, or (d) helping behavior that is completely selfless, reaping no rewards. Although there may be differences among people in the level of sacrifice they believe is necessary in order for an act to qualify as altruistic, most people would agree that, all else equal, the greater the sacrifice, the more altruistic the act.

Although altruism may be defined in a variety of ways, it is controversial and theoretically significant only when defined in certain ways (see Krebs & Wispé, 1974). Some types of altruism are easy to explain, whereas other types are exceedingly difficult. Altruism is controversial and significant when defined in ways that constitute a challenge to what must certainly be the most powerful and pervasive principle of behavior in the biological and social sciences, namely that behavior is reinforced by its consequences: behaviors that produce gains to their perpetrators prevail, and behaviors that produce losses become extinct. This principle finds its most popular form in the principle of reinforcement in psychology and in the principle of natural selection in biology. Altruism, defined as behavior that violates these principles, presents a challenge to the theories based on them. The purpose of this chapter is to review the responses that biologists and psychologists have made to the challenge of altruism in their respective fields, and to examine what each discipline can learn from the other.

THE CHALLENGE OF ALTRUISM IN BIOLOGY

The central assumption of Darwin's theory of evolution is that individuals who inherit the types of characteristics that maximize their chances of surviving and reproducing leave more offspring (who inherit their "adaptive" characteristics) than those who are less "fit." In Darwinian theory, "fitness" means "reproductive fitness," which is assessed in terms of the number of offspring (and offspring's offspring, etc.) that individuals leave by their efforts (see Noonan, this volume). Through the process of natural selection, fitness-enhancing characteristics come to characterize the nature of the species. Although Darwin was not always consistent about the unit of natural selection—what is selected—his theory is based on the assumption that the unit of selection is the individual (see Williams, 1966).

If altruism is defined as behavior that enhances the net fitness of another individual at a net reduction in the fitness of the helper (we will call this type of altruism *individual altruism*), then it should not evolve according to Darwin's principle of natural selection. In the extreme case, individuals who inherit characteristics that dispose them to sacrifice their lives for the sake of others would be less likely to survive and reproduce other individuals with such altruistic characteristics than those who were more selfish. Therefore, altruistic characteristics would diminish and die in the species. Similarly, characteristics that render individuals sterile, dispose them to commit suicide before they reproduce, make them sexually abstinent, or dispose them toward homosexuality should not evolve through natural selection. If, by refraining from reproduction, individuals enhance the net fitness of others and reduce their own net fitness (because, for example, they make scarce resources such as food or mates more available for others), then behaviors that cause individuals to refrain from reproduction qualify as instances of individual altruism.

On the face of it then, according to Darwin's theory, no species should be altruistic by nature. However, we don't have to look very hard to find species that appear to practice individual altruism on a routine basis. Ethnocentric intuitions notwithstanding, humans do not provide the most compelling evidence for altruism. Rather, the strongest evidence is evinced by social insects such as bees, wasps, ants and termites. Worker castes in these species devote themselves entirely to the service of their queen; and the soldier castes of these species routinely sacrifice their lives in defense of their fellows. In addition, these paragons of altruism are sterile. Alluding to "the neuters or sterile females in insect-communities," Darwin (1859) wrote that they presented "one special difficulty, which at first appeared to me insuperable, and actually fatal to the whole theory." Although the idea of altruistic ants may seem preposterous to some because it offends their definition of altruism, by whatever name, in whatever species, behaviors that enhance the net fitness of others and reduce the net fitness of the benefactor constitute a challenge to the principle of natural selection. If this type of behavior has evolved in ants, then there either must be a route to altruism through natural selection or an exception to the principle.

There are two approaches that one can take in responding to the challenge that apparent incidents of individual altruism entail for Darwin's theory of evolution—establishing that behaviors that seem altruistic do not meet the criteria of individual altruism because they enhance the fitness of their perpetrators in some subtle way, or by revising and refining Darwin's theory in a way that enables it to account for the exceptions. We first examine helping behaviors that seem altruistic but in fact are not because they enhance the individual fitness of those who practice them, then turn to helping behaviors that meet the criteria of individual altruism and have precipitated refinements in Darwinian theory.

NONALTRUISTIC HELPING BEHAVIORS

Incidental Helping

Individuals in many species routinely behave in ways that enhance the fitness of other members of their species, but behaviors that enhance the fitness of others may not present any problem for Darwinian theory because they may enhance the fitness of the individuals who emit them even more. Consider alarm calling for example. In some species individuals who see a predator warn their conspecifies of the danger. Birds cry out, deer bark, and gazelles stot, or jump high in the air. Alarm calling seems altruistic because it draws attention to the alarm caller, and thus appears to jeopardize his or her fitness. However, on close examination, the benefits of alarm calling may outweigh its costs, disqualifying it as an instance of individual altruism. When a bird emits an alarm call, the other birds in the flock take flight, thereby making the alarm caller less conspicuous and less vulnerable to the predator (Charnov & Krebs, 1974; Hamilton, 1964). Stotting may discourage predators by demonstrating the stotter's strength, by showing the predator that the stotter is aware of his or her presence (Woodland, Jaafar, & Knight, 1980), and by enabling the stotter to check out the possibility of an ambush (Pitcher, 1979). In order to determine whether helping behaviors such as alarm calling are altruistic, we must determine their effects on the fitness of the individuals who engage in them and the fitness of the others. How often are alarm callers killed or injured relative to those who do not call out? How many offspring do they leave behind relative to those who do not give warnings? If it turns out that alarm calling enhances the fitness of alarm callers, the behavior poses no problem for Darwinian theory.

Cooperation and Reciprocity

Individuals in many species also help one another for their mutual benefit. Wolves assist one another kill large prey. Bison group together for mutual defense. Pairs of male manakin birds help one another perform integrated courtship rituals that enhance each of their chances of obtaining a mate. Cooperative behaviors such as these do not pose a problem for Darwinian theory because they enhance the fitness of their perpetrators.

Reciprocity is an especially significant form of cooperation. In an early and influential article entitled "The evolution of reciprocal altruism," the sociobiologist Robert Trivers (1971) explained the evolution of a wide array of helping behaviors by showing how they could reap compensatory returns at some future time. Trivers showed that it pays off for individuals to render assistance to others when the costs are low if in so doing they increase the probability that they will receive help of greater value at some future time. Alexander (1979) distinguishes between direct reciprocity, where the recipient of help repays the debt, and indirect reciprocity, where individuals other than the recipient, including society at large, repay the debt. Since the publication of Trivers' article, investigators have observed reciprocal helping in nonhuman species, most notably baboons (Dunbar, 1980; Packer, 1977).

Trivers (1971) listed six conditions that should favor the evolution of "reciprocal altruism" (1) long life span, (2) low rate of dispersal, (3) high degree of mutual dependence, (4) long parental care, (5) the ability to assist conspecifics in combat, and (6) flexible dominance hierarchies. In addition, suggested Trivers, reciprocal altruism should be favored in species capable of recognizing one another and remembering previous encounters. In short, reciprocity should be particularly adaptive in K-selected, intelligent, closely knit, social species such as our own.

Reciprocity is based on trust, whether consciously experienced or not; and trust can be violated. Therefore, systems of reciprocity are vulnerable to cheating. Unless there is some check against cheating, it is in an individual's best genetic interest to induce others to assist him or her under the assumption that he or she will repay the assistance, then to default on the obligation. So, according to Trivers, checks against cheating should evolve. Trivers suggests that emotions such as moralistic anger toward cheaters, gratitude toward benefactors, sympathy for individuals in need of help, and guilt in recipients who fail to reciprocate evolve to support systems of reciprocity.

It is interesting to note that from a sociobiological perspective the disposition to behave morally (in this case honoring trust and abiding by the principle of reciprocity) should be a provisional and even reluctant inclination. Individuals should not be genetically disposed to reciprocate in situations in which they will not be held accountable. Indeed, dispositions to feign reciprocity and the emotions that support it—to appear to abide by the principle so as to reap the benefits from it while escaping the costs—might well be expected to evolve, along with dispositions that enable individuals to catch cheaters, and so on (Alexander, 1974). Campbell (1983) has suggested that the "criterion images" that have evolved in humans to enable them to identify transgressions in others are significantly stronger than those that have evolved to help individuals identify transgressions in themselves. Other investigators have made cases for the adaptiveness of self-deception (Alexander, 1974, 1979; Lockhard, 1980; Trivers, 1985).

The evolution of systems of reciprocity is governed by the adaptiveness of reciprocity relative to other alternatives. As it turns out, some systems, for example "tit for tat" reciprocity, may pay off very well for the individuals who employ them. For example, in a computor simulation contest employing a prisoner's dilemma format—a two party game—Axelrod & Hamilton (1981) found that this strategy could not be beaten.

Once in place, tit for tat reciprocity is an evolutionarily stable strategy (Maynard-Smith & Price, 1973); and there is no problem in explaining how it is maintained. But how could such a system originate? This turns out to be a difficult question. If we assume that the original system with which a species begins is selfish individualism (see Axelrod, 1984), how could a system of reciprocity replace it? What would cause an individual to make an initial altruistic response; and what would induce the recipient of it to reciprocate? We might imagine a mutant altruist making an initial altruistic response and a mutant recipient reciprocating, but researchers who have worked out the mathematics of the matter have found that a small number of reciprocators is not enough to break into a system of selfish individualism (Axelrod, 1984). In order for a system of tit for tat reciprocity to displace a system of selfish individualism, a relatively large cluster of individuals must employ the tit for tat strategy; otherwise, the probability of receiving help after helping is too low. Therefore in order to explain the evolution of reciprocity, we must explain how a cluster of individuals could acquire the disposition to behave altruistically, which brings us back to our focal concern.

Trivers called reciprocal helping "altruism," but it does not meet our criteria of individual altruism because it enhances the fitness of helpers. Although initial acts of helping and subsequent acts of reciprocity may meet the criteria of individual altruism when considered out of context as though they were the only behaviors of concern, isolated acts of altruism do not violate the principle of natural selection because isolated acts are not selected. General characteristics, dispositions, and behavioral strategies are selected. Therefore, it is the types of general dispositions or behavioral strategies that reduce an individual's fitness to which we must attend. Reciprocity is best viewed as a special form of cooperation, and cooperation is best viewed as a special form of selfishness. Individuals perform a service for another (i.e., they emit a behavior that reduces their net fitness relative to the net fitness of another at that moment), but the benefits they confer are payed back some time in the future with interest, robbing the original act of its altruism.

Forced Helping and Tactical Helping

Circumstances sometimes permit only Hobson's choices: the only alternatives available to individuals are undesirable. In some cases the least of the evils (the least fitness reducing option) involves helping another. In the extreme case, an individual may be forced to choose between helping and dying. In other cases, individuals may elect to help another in order to pave the way for or to create a situation that will enable them to foster their own fitness. For example, an individual may help an older, dominant male protect his harum until he becomes powerful enough to overthrow him and mate with his "wives."

Forced helping and tactical helping are like helping that is reinforced through reciprocity. They meet the conditions for altruism when considered out of context, in and of themselves, but when examined in a broader perspective, they turn out to be self-interested. A substantial portion of the apparently altruistic behavior of individuals in some species turns out to be part of a long term selfish strategy—behavioral investments that pay off in the end.

To summarize, when certain types of helping are viewed out of context—removed from the system of which they are a part—they seem altruistic: Individuals behave in ways that enhance the immediate fitness of others at an immediate cost to their own fitness. However, the sacrifices involved in the helping behaviors are little different from the costs in calories individuals make to move food to their mouths—they pay off in the long run. A lesson that emerges from a consideration of forced helping, tactical helping, and reciprocity is that acts of helping always should be viewed in the context of the systems of which they are a part. The function of a behavior can be discerned only by determining its ultimate effect on the individuals who display it. Needless to say, it is extremely difficult to determine the ultimate effect of behavioral strategies in most instances.

Manipulated Helping

The Darwinian perspective leads us to expect a potential conflict between individuals in which it is in each actor's best interest to evoke altruistic behavior from others, but to resist their attempts to evoke it from him or her. As a result, we would expect characteristics to evolve in individuals designed both to evoke altruistic behavior from others and to resist others' attempts to evoke altruism from them. There are many examples in the animal kingdom of individuals being manipulated into helping others at a net cost to their own fitness (see Ridley & Dawkins, 1981). Consider the behaviors of some species of birds, for example. Our word cuckold means, literally, cuckooed. It is derived from the behavior of cuckoo birds who deposit their eggs in the nests of other birds who nurture them as though they were their own. The behavior of birds who raise the offspring of cuckoos seems altruistic—it enhances the reproductive fitness of the cuckoo at a net cost to their own reproductive fitness. Although we can safely assume that the foster parents do not intend to behave altruistically—they are manipulated into it by cuckoos—, the effect of their behavior is altruistic nonetheless.

Most kinds of manipulation are based on false promise. Manipulated individuals behave in ways that they assume will enhance their own fitness (or, if this subjective attribution is inappropriate, that usually enhance their fitness), but the behavior produces an "unintended" effect (enhancement of the fitness of another). Helping evoked through manipulation often involves the failure to discriminate between a stimulus that enhances one's fitness (one's own eggs in a nest) and a stimulus that enhances the fitness of another (the eggs of a cuckoo).

Natural selection is neither perfect nor precise. It works on rules of thumb and probabilities (see Dawkins, 1982). If, on balance, a behavioral strategy produces a greater gain in fitness than an alternative, it should be favored by selection, even though it occasionally gives rise to fitness-reducing (altruistic) errors. For example, if the only alternatives available to individuals are to nurture the eggs in their nests or to abandon them, and if they do not possess the ability to determine whether the eggs are their own or not, then it may well be in their best evolutionary interest to nurture all eggs in their nests, because, on balance, this strategy will pay off (enhance their reproductive fitness) more than any alternative. This point applies even in cases where maladaptive overgeneralizations prove lethal for some individuals. Ridley and Dawkins (1981) give the example of fish that are seduced by the "lures" on angler fish that look like worms. The fish are engaging in a behavior (approaching stimuli that have the form of a worm) that, on balance, pays off for them. The strategy—their intent if you will—is unequivocally selfish. The effect of this selfish strategy may, however, be to enhance the fitness of a predator, thereby giving rise to behaviors that are altruistic in consequence.

Susceptability to manipulation is, in a sense, an evolutionary mistake. Whether it is corrected through natural selection or not depends on how serious a mistake it is and on the ability of the species susceptible to it to evolve an antedote. If an environment contained a small number of angler fish masquerading as worms, and if there were little or no genetic difference between fish seduced by the angler fish and fish not seduced, there would be little basis for a discriminating adaptation to evolve in the victims. If, on the other hand, a large proportion of fish with relatively poor genetically based discriminatory abilities (compared to other members of their species) fell victim to the mimic, these fish (and with them the lethal vulnerability) would be expected to become extinct. Of course, natural selection also could affect the predator species, producing increasingly effective lures, which, in turn, may mediate the selection of greater discriminatory powers in the prey, and so on. As discussed by Dawkins (1982), however, an "arms race" (escalation of manipulative adaptations in a predatory species and antedotes in the prey) would be expected to develop only in certain cases: "fundamental asymmetries . . . will see to it that many arms races reach a stable state in which animals on one side permanently work for the benefit of animals on the other side, and to their own detriment" (p. 80).

The examples that we have been considering involve individuals from different species. The issue becomes more complicated when the individuals under consideration are from the same species because altruism-evoking and altruism resisting tendencies may evolve in the same individuals. The optimal strategy for an individual would be to employ highly effective altruism-evoking and highly effective altruism-resisting mechanisms, but this strategy could not become evolutionarily stable in the sense outlined by Maynard-Smith (1976) (see Noonan, this volume) because individuals practicing it would flood the population, leaving no one from whom to evoke altruism. The expected result of selection on such strategies would be a dynamic equilibrium of moderately effective counterbalancing combinations that pay off for most individuals most of the time.

Ridley and Dawkins (1981) argue that helping evoked through manipulation qualifies as altruism because it reduces the net reproductive fitness of the helper at a net gain to the reproductive fitness of the recipient. In our view, the degree of altruism involved in helping evoked through manipulation depends on the nature of the disposition rendering individuals susceptible to manipulation. If a disposition or behavioral strategy rendering individuals susceptible to manipulation were to evolve in a species (call it gullibility), then the behaviors that follow from this disposition or strategy might well qualify as altruistic. However, if the helping behaviors displayed by individuals stem from a strategy that, on balance, enhances the fitness of those who practice it, then the behaviors seem best construed as investments similar to the helping involved in reciprocal, tactical, and forced helping. The foster parents who nurture the eggs of the cuckoo are enhancing the fitness of the cuckoo at a cost to their own fitness, but the *strategy* or program governing their behavior (for example "nurture all eggs in your nest") may well be selfish—on balance it enhances the fitness of those who practice it.

In summary, many species behave in ways that contribute to the fitness of others but the helping behaviors they display are a means to an end—maximizing their own fitness. Incidental, reciprocal, forced, tactical, and manipulated helping do not constitute violations of the principle of natural selection. The behavioral strategies of which they are a part are selfish strategies that evolved because they maximized the net fitness of those who employed them. Darwinian theory has no difficulty countering the challenge they entail.

We turn now to an examination of two evolutionary routes to altruism that cannot be accounted for by Darwinian theory in its classic form. As indicated earlier, Darwin focused on individuals as the unit of selection, leading to a definition of fitness in terms of the number of offspring (i.e., individuals) a propagator contributed to the population, and leading to a definition of altruism based on sacrifices in individual fitness and contributions to the individual fitness of others. Both of the routes to which we now turn are based on alternative units of selection. In the first case, altruism is alleged to evolve through the selection of groups, and in the second, altruism is alleged to evolve through the selection of genes.

THE EVOLUTION OF ALTRUISM THROUGH GROUP SELECTION

In 1962, in an influential book, Wynne Edwards assembled a wide array of evidence in support of the thesis that animals who live in groups are attentive to the density of their populations, and when their numbers reach a level where they jeopardize the availability of resources, some of their members refrain from reproducing. This thesis departed significantly from Darwinian theory because it implied that individuals may behave in ways that reduce their net individual fitness for the good of other members of their species—i.e., they may behave altruistically. Wynne Edwards recognized that his thesis appeared to contradict the principle of natural selection, but, undaunted, set out to explain how altruistic restraint could evolve. He pointed out that in many species individuals cohabit in discrete interdependent groups. Indeed, in some species, what looks like an individual may be a group of organisms. Therefore, argued Wynne Edwards, groups rather than individuals may be selected, and altruism may evolve because groups that contain individual altruists fare better in intergroup competition than groups that do not.

As ingenious as Wynne Edwards' arguments may be, there is a potentially lethal limitation to the idea that altruism can evolve through group selection, namely variation in the tendency of individuals *within* groups to behave altruistically. In the process of prevailing over selfish groups, the more altruistic individuals within altruistic groups would be expected to die out and the more selfish would be expected to increase in number. Thus, the group selection of altruism would be opposed by the individual selection of selfishness.

The implications of the natural conflict between the good of the individual and the good of the group is a familiar one in the social sciences. How does between-group selection for altruism fare in the conflict with within-group selection for selfishness? There are two ways in which biologists have attempted to answer this question—by constructing theoretical models that specify the conditions under which altruism could evolve through group selection, and by adducing cases where it ostensibly has. Although a consensus on the issue has not been reached, most experts agree that although altruism could evolve through group selection—that is to say, it is a logical possibility—the conditions that would have to pertain for it to evolve are so extraordinary as to make it exceedingly unlikely (see Alexander & Borgia, 1978; Barash, 1982; Dawkins, 1982; Maynard-Smith, 1976). Computor simulations indicate that under virtually all conditions, individual selection out-paces group selection (see Boorman & Levitt, 1980). There are several reasons for this but the most basic is that the selection of individuals virtually always occurs more quickly than the selection of groups. Groups of altruists would have to prevail over groups of selfish individualists at a faster rate than the selfish individualists within the groups prevailed over their more altruistic associates in order for altruism to evolve through group selection. In addition, group selection requires (a) that the presence of altruistic individuals in groups produces a significant increase in the fitness of the groups (i.e., in their ability to reproduce), (b) that little genetic exchange occur between altruistic and selfish groups, and (c) that altruistic individuals in altruistic groups reproduce fast enough to leave altruistic offspring in new groups before they perish (see Noonan, this volume).

Trait Group Selection

The area that encompasses the breeding population of a species is called a deme. Most models of group selection make what seem like an innocent assumption—

that individuals within a deme are assorted randomly—but this assumption is not valid for humans and other species that form "trait groups" within their demes. Trait groups consist of individuals who live in encompassed regions in demes, and join together for various periods of time, often to their mutual advantage. Families and extended families are one type of trait group.

D. S. Wilson (1979, 1980) explores the implications for the evolution of altruism of assuming (a) that individuals form trait groups that differ in proportion of altruists, (b) that these trait groups stay together long enough for the individuals in them to reap the advantages of their altruism relative to more selfish groups, and (c) that at some later time the progeny from altruistic groups breed with the progeny from more selfish groups. Wilson's model is really rather ingenious. Imagine that there are two trait groups with 20 individuals in each, one composed mainly of altruists and the other composed mainly of selfish individualists. Let's say that the altruistic group contains 15 altruists and 5 selfish individualists, and that the selfish group contains 5 altruists and 15 selfish individualists. Note that in the population as a whole the proportion of altruists and selfish individuals is equal: 50/50. Two opposing forces work on these groups. Individual selection reduces the number of altruists relative to the number of selfish individuals within each group; but, because of the disadvantages of living in a selfish group, the mortality rate of the selfish group is much higher than that of the altruistic group. So, after some period of time, say 5 individuals are eliminated from the altruistic group—4 altruists (who, by definition are more vulnerable than their selfish cohorts) and 1 selfish individualist. Because of the disadvantages of selfishness, the selfish group fares less well—15 individuals are eliminated—and, within the selfish group, the altruists fare more poorly than the selfish individualists: 4 of the 5 altruists are eliminated (80%), compared to 11 out of 15 selfish individualists (73%). Now calculate the proportion of altruists who have survived in the population as a whole (i.e., the two trait groups combined). Even though altruism is selected against within each trait group, it is selected for in the deme as a whole. A total of 12 altruists survive, compared to 8 selfish individualists, which produces an increase in the proportion of altruists in the population—from 50% to 60%. It should be noted that increasing the proportion of altruists in the deme will not lead to the evolution of altruism unless the individuals in the trait groups mix—otherwise the proportion of altruists relative to selfish individualists would continue to decrease within each group until the altruists were eliminated entirely.

In D. S. Wilson's model, altruistic behavior produces a decrease in the relative fitness of altruistic individuals within trait groups through individual selection (altruists produce fewer progeny than nonaltruists, whatever the absolute number of progeny), but because the absolute number of progeny produced by surviving altruists in altruistic trait groups is greater than the absolute number of progeny produced by selfish individuals in selfish trait groups, the relative fitness of the altruists increases in the deme as a whole through group selection. D. S. Wilson labels the type of altruism that can evolve through the process he describes "weak altruism" because it does not entail an increase in the relative fitness of the altruist within the trait group.

In summary, although it is theoretically possible for a "weak" form of altruism to evolve through trait group selection, the conditions necessary for this process to occur are so special that we would not expect it to mediate the evolution of altruism in many (if any) species.

THE EVOLUTION OF ALTRUISM THROUGH KIN SELECTION

When Darwin published his theory of evolution, he did not know about genes. All he knew was that individuals who possessed adaptive characteristics tended to leave more individuals like themselves in future generations than individuals who possessed less adaptive characteristics. We now know that the mechanism through which this is accomplished is genetic transmission. The way in which Darwin assessed fitness was to count the number of offspring produced by an individual (or perhaps more exactly, the number of offsprings' offspring, etc.). If Darwin had known about genes, he might have defined fitness differently—as the number of genes (or, more exactly, replicas of genes) that an individual leaves in future generations. For most purposes, it doesn't matter whether you calculate an individual's reproductive success in terms of numbers of offspring or number of genes (see Grafen, 1982). The most direct way for individuals to propagate their genes is to produce offspring, so the two measures are highly correlated. However, producing offspring is not the only way for individuals to get their genes into subsequent generations because offspring are not the only individuals who carry replicas of individuals' genes. Individuals also share genes with their brothers and sisters, nieces and nephews, aunts and uncles. Thus, to quote Hamilton (1964):

> for a gene to receive positive selection it is not necessarily enough that it should increase the fitness of its bearer above the average if this tends to be done at the heavy expense of related individuals, because relatives, on account of their common ancestry, tend to carry replicas of the same gene; and conversely that a gene may receive positive selection even though disadvantageous to its bearers if it causes them to confer sufficiently large advantages on relatives. (p. 17)

The positive selection of genes disadvantageous to their bearers relates to the evolution of altruism, and in his 1964 paper Hamilton mapped out a route to the evolution of altruism based on the idea that individuals may enhance their fitness by helping their relatives. Hamilton argued that individual altruism, defined as behavior that reduces the Darwinian fitness (reproductive success) of an individual while enhancing the reproductive success of another, will evolve whenever k < 1/r, where k is the ratio of recipient benefit to altruist cost, and r is the coefficient of genetic relatedness between altruist and recipient. In view of the significance of Hamilton's formula, it is worth examining each factor in detail.

Relatedness

The reason why relatedness is important in Hamilton's formula is because the coefficient of relatedness between two individuals is equivalent to the probability that they share a gene for altruism, not because they share a high proportion of other, nonaltruistic genes. By some measures, all humans share more than 99% of their genes, and, indeed, there is 98% genetic overlap between chimpanzees and humans (see Plomin, Defries, & McClearn 1980, for the particulars of such calculations and the controversy surrounding them). Shared genes are not significant in Hamilton's theory except inasmuch as the proportion of genes shared by two individuals reflects the probability that each shares a gene for altruism. Kinship would become epiphenomenal if there were a more direct way for altruistic individuals to identify those who possessed replicas of their altruistic genes.

Recognition alleles.   Why, then, talk roughly and probabilistically about kin at all? Why not talk simply about alleles that possess the ability to recognize replicas of themselves in others—"recognition alleles?" The implications of this possibility are explored by Rushton, Russell, and Wells (1984) in what they call "genetic similarity theory." These authors suggest that "rather than merely protecting kin at the expense of strangers, organisms have a tendency to detect other genetically similar organisms and to exhibit altruistic behavior toward these "strangers" as well as toward [their] own relatives." (p. 181)

The possibility that a genetically based ability to recognize genetic similarity in others could evolve and mediate favorable and unfavorable discriminations has far-reaching implications. The weight of expert opinion, however, does not favor it. Hamilton considered the possibility in his 1964 paper, and concluded that it was improbable. Naming the phenomenon "the green beard effect" (referring to the evolution of a gene capable of producing a distinguishing characteristic such as a green beard; the ability to detect it in others, and the tendency to treat those who possess it altruistically), Dawkins (1976) and others (see Johnson, 1986) also have concluded that it is unlikely. Porter considers the issue in the present volume.

In addition to the implausibility of the evolution of recognition alleles for altruism, Rushton et al.'s theory has been criticized by Mealey (1985) for confusing the *proportion* of shared genes and the *probability* of a shared gene for altruism: "Altruistic behavior . . . is contingent solely on the likelihood that another shares this particular allele at a particular locus, not an overall genetic or phenotypic similarity." (p. 573)

Recognizing relatives.   Concluding that altruistic alleles are unable to recognize replicas of themselves in others does not put an end to the issue of discrimination in the evolution of altruism. If altruism is to evolve through the mechanism identified by Hamilton, individuals must somehow discriminate between relatives and nonrelatives. Porter (this volume) reviews research on the mechanisms underlying kin recognition. In addition to recognition alleles, three main mechanisms mediating preferential treatment of relatives have been suggested. These mechanisms can be viewed as genetically based programs containing the following general commands: (1) "help all individuals who possess a phenotypic characteristic that matches one possessed by you (or by one or more of your relatives)" (phenotype-matching), (2) "help all individuals with whom you have had a particular type of association" (association-based preference), and (3) "help all individuals who occupy a particular spatial location" (location-based preference).

As described by Porter (this volume) several species appear to discriminate between relatives and nonrelatives on the basis of phenotypic characteristics such as odor. Phenotype matching is different from allele recognition because it involves a learned rather than genetically based association. Individuals learn to identify a distinguishing aspect of their own phenotype (or of the phenotype of close relatives), and they treat those who possess it preferentially. However, as pointed out by Blaustein (1983), in order to establish that a behavior is mediated by phenotype matching and not by allele recognition, an investigator would have to deprive an animal of the opportunity to learn the aspect of its phenotype in question without disrupting its ability to recognize it—a condition that has not been met in any study to date.

Individuals in several species have been found to distinguish between relatives and nonrelatives on the basis of early associations, for example, extending preferential treatment to littermates or imprinting on their parents during a critical period (Holmes & Sherman, 1982). Similarly, individuals in many species, especially birds, have been found to distinguish between relatives and nonrelatives on the basis of their presence in spatial locations such as nests. In natural circumstances, the individuals who receive the preferential treatment on the basis of these programs are virtually always kin.

It is safe to assume that the programs mediating preferential treatment to kin payed off in inclusive fitness in the evolutionary history of the animals that employ them. Indeed, there is compelling evidence showing that when such programs would not work (spatial location for colony dwellers, for example) they do not evolve, or that additional discriminatory mechanisms evolve (see Porter, this volume). This does not, however, mean that such programs are foolproof or exact. Programs that worked in past environments may not work in present environments. Extraordinary circumstances (such as biologists rearranging nests, litters or phenotypic characteristics) may induce individuals to make

mistakes. The fallibility of such programs pave the way for the types of manipulations employed by cuckoos and other manipulators.

To summarize, in order to maximize one's inclusive fitness through kin
selection, an animal must direct its assistance toward its relatives. The mechanisms that mediate behavioral discriminations between kin and nonkin are probably based on cues correlated with kinship rather than kinship itself.

Benefit to Recipient

The benefits of an altruistic act are reckoned in terms of fitness. They may be
obvious, such as assistance that saves another's life, helping another reproduce,
or rearing another's offspring; or they may be subtle, such as moving over so
another can gain access to some resource. Four points need to be made about
benefits. First, the extent to which an act benefits an individual depends on the
individual's need. Sharing food with someone who is starving contributes more
to his or her fitness than sharing food with someone who is sated. Second, in
evolutionary terms, it is not really the amount of assistance that counts, it is the
ultimate effect of the assistance on the recipient's inclusive fitness. From this
perspective, helping individuals who are likely to produce many offspring is
more altruistic than rendering exactly the same assistance to those who are less
likely to reproduce. Third, the benefits in question are net benefits—benefits
minus costs. Imagine an incident in which one individual gives another a portion
of his food. At the same time as this act provides needed nourishment, it might
draw a predator's attention to the recipient, thereby endangering the recipient's
life. Finally, "altruistic" acts often affect individuals other than the recipient,
and thus may feed back on the fitness of the helper. For example, providing an
individual with nourishment may make him strong enough to kill a predator,
thereby enhancing the helper's inclusive fitness. Strictly speaking, we would
have to calculate the net benefit to everyone affected by an act, including the
helper, in order to obtain an accurate estimate of the benefit factor in Hamilton's
formula, although, as demonstrated by Grafen (1982) number of offspring supplies an adequate estimate in virtually all species.

Costs to Altruist

Like benefits, costs are often difficult to reckon. The ultimate measure of cost
must assess the net effect of an act on an individual's inclusive fitness. The costs
of life-threatening acts are obvious, but any act that requires energy—throwing a
life-preserver to a drowning person for example, can be viewed as exacting some
small reduction in fitness. Some acts, of course, are more costly to some individuals than to others; therefore, it is harder for some individuals to render
assistance than it is for others. However, the more costly an act, the more

altruistic it is. Exactly the same act—helping fight off a predator, for example, may be significantly more altruistic when perpetrated by a small, weak ally than by someone who is sure to win. Similarly, because individuals who are senescent may have less to lose in terms of inclusive fitness than those who are in their reproductive prime, the extent to which their behaviors can be costly (in terms of their inclusive fitness) may be limited.

1/r

The greater the degree of relatedness, the smaller the fraction $1/r$. Thus, the greater the degree of relatedness, the smaller the ratio of recipient benefits to benefactor costs need be in order for altruism to evolve. This means that individuals will be disposed to render benefits that supercede the costs to them to those to whom they are closely related, but not to those to whom they are distantly related.

The principles of kin selection and inclusive fitness maximization invite us to view individuals in terms of the probability that they share genes identical by descent. Viewing individuals in this way gives rise to an interesting perspective on human nature and social relations. Although different individuals possess distinct bodies, they are, to varying degrees, identical at a genetic level. An evolutionary analysis suggests that when we help our relatives and others who share replicas of our genes, we are, in effect, helping our (genetic) selves; and when we harm our relatives, we are harming ourselves. This perspective has both positive and negative implications. On the positive side, it suggests that individuals need not be individualistically selfish by nature. On the negative side, it suggests that individuals may inherit dispositions that cause them to discriminate between others in terms of how closely related they are (or seem to be) to themselves.

To summarize, individuals may sacrifice themselves for other individuals without sacrificing the genes that mediate such altruism if the individuals they help possess replicas of the genes. While altruistic at the individual or Darwinian level of analysis, such behaviors are selfish at the genetic level (Dawkins, 1976). In effect, selfish genes induce individuals to behave altruistically toward those who possess replicas of them as a way of propagating themselves.

THE EVOLUTION OF ALTRUISM
IN THE HUMAN SPECIES

The primary question of concern here relates to the evolution of altruism in the human species, and thus, to the role of altruism in human nature. Could altruism have evolved in humans, and if so, how? In order to answer this question, we must examine what is known about the early history of the species and ask how plausible it is that the conditions necessary for the evolution of altruism could have prevailed.

We are a K-selected species that invests heavily in a small number of offspring: Human offspring have long periods of gestation, remain dependent on their parents for many years, and require a great deal of care. Humans pairbond, sometimes for life, and are attentive to the bonds of kinship. Early humans probably lived in bands of extended families similar to the !Kung Bushmen, interacting with other bands, at least for the purpose of outbreeding. Their social structure undoubtedly involved a division of labor, probably with females specializing in child-rearing and food-gathering, and males traveling in bands to hunt. Our ancestors almost surely shared food. We know that from 1 1/2 to 2 million years ago, they engaged in the cooperative hunting of large game (see Leaky & Lewin, 1977; Lovejoy, 1981; and Lumsden & Wilson, 1983, for documentation of these inferences and for additional references).

Cooperation and Reciprocity

There can be no question about the adaptiveness of cooperation and reciprocity in the lives of our ancestors. To quote Leaky and Lewin (1977):

> Throughout our recent evolutionary history, particularly since the rise of a hunting way of life, there must have been extreme selective pressures in favor of our ability to cooperate as a group: organized food gathering and hunts are successful only if each member of the band knows his task and joins in with the activity of his fellows. The degree of selective identification was so strong, and the period over which it operated was so extended, that it can hardly have failed to have become embedded to some degree in our genetic makeup.

The conditions that favor the evolution of reciprocity—long life span, low rate of dispersal, high degree of mutual dependence, long parental care, the ability to assist conspecifics in combat, and flexible dominance hierarchies (Trivers, 1971) were characteristic of early humans. But cooperation and reciprocity are not altruistic, and the origin of systems of reciprocity remains to be explained.

Individual Altruism

Group selection supplies a route to altruism, but it seems implausible that our ancestors would have met the rather extraordinary conditions necessary for it to occur (see Alexander & Borgia, 1978 for elaborations of and a review of evidence in support of this argument).

The most promising route to altruism in the human species is by way of kin selection. The sacrifice of parents for their offspring is the clearest manifestation, but assistance to more distant relatives also would be expected to pay off in inclusive fitness in groups of people living in extended families. We know that conerns about kinship are significant in all preliterate societies, even if kinship discriminations do not correspond exactly to degree of biological relatedness (Chagon & Irons, 1979). It seems plausible that early humans employed spatial location, association, and phenotype matching to discriminate between kin and nonkin, and that, in the environment in which they lived, these mechanisms worked well enough to foster the evolution of individual (nepotistic) altruism.

Kin selection also may have paved the way for the origin of reciprocity. In their analysis of the tit for tat system, Axelrod and Hamilton (1981) note that:

> Recalculation of the payoff matrix in such a way that an individual has a part interest in the partner's gain (that is, reckoning payoffs in terms of inclusive fitness) can often eliminate the inequalities . . . in which case cooperation becomes uncon- ditionally favored [over selfish individualism] . . . it is possible to imagine that the benefits of cooperation . . . can begin to be harvested by groups of closely-related individuals. (p. 1399)

Once there is a significant large cluster of individuals (i.e., kin) employing a system such as tit for tat reciprocity there is no problem explaining how it permeates the system (i.e., spreads to nonrelatives). It is sort of a "try it, you'll like it" phenomenon. Tit for tat reciprocity pays off better that selfish indi- vidualism when enough people practice it to enable it to work.

As pointed out by Alexander and Borgia (1978) and Alexander (1979) kin selection and reciprocity may have been closely connected among early humans. Indeed, the reciprocal relations of people currently living in the types of small bands that humans apparently formed early in their evolutionary history typically occur almost exclusively among relatives (see Wiessner, 1977, for the !Kung Bushmen, and Chagnon, 1979, for the Yanomamo). Alexander (1979) argues that nepotism and reciprocity almost always occur together, and points out that each involves an investment. In nepotism, individuals invest in the reproductive success of their relatives; in reciprocity, individuals "lend" others fitness-en- hancing resources in the expectation that they will be repaid with interest at some later date. Alexander suggests that, in effect, our ancestors were most likely to have covered their bets by engaging in reciprocity with relatives, picking up gains in inclusive fitness when their investments didn't pay off.

Genetic Altruism

While kin selection supplies a plausible mechanism for the evolution of altruism toward relatives in the human species, it does not supply a route to individual altruism toward nonrelatives (and, therefore, to *genetic altruism*—altruism not reinforced by inclusive fitness maximization). Or does it? Circumstances have changed since the dispositions mediating altruism evolved in our ancestors. In particular, people who live in proximity to us, with whom we associate, and who are phenotypically similar are not as likely to be related to us as they were in the past. If the evolved disposition to discriminate between kin and nonkin is based on spatial location, association, and phenotype-matching, it would be expected, in effect, to misfire in most parts of the modern world, making us inclined to help individuals who possess the types of characteristics possessed by relatives in our evolutionary past—characteristics such as ingroup membership, familiarity, and phenotypic similarity. If this were the case, modern humans might be altruistic by nature and by mistake. We might possess the disposition to assist individuals who possess characteristics similar to the relatives we were reinforced genetically for helping in our evolutionary past even though such behavior no longer has the same genetic (inclusive fitness maximizing) payoff that originally enabled it to evolve. In effect, the genetically "selfish" disposition to enhance one's inclusive fitness by helping one's relatives is fooled into altruism when it is evoked by those who resemble them.

How plausible is the idea that humans are genetically disposed to help individuals who live in the types of locations, form the types of associations, and possess the types of phenotypic characteristics possessed by kin in the past? Little social psychological research on prosocial behavior has been informed by the principle of kin selection or has attempted to test predictions derived from it; however, the results from several areas of inquiry are consistent with the idea that correlates of genetic relatedness evoke altruistic behavior. Consider, for example, research on familiarity, ingroup status, and similarity.

Familiarity. Familiarity is highly associated with kinship status and propinquity in preliterate societies. In one anthropological study, Hames (1979) found an almost perfect positive correlation between degree of relatedness and the frequency with which individuals interact with one another. Social psychological research has shown that *mere exposure* to another, even by way of repeatedly shown photographs, enhances the other's attractiveness (Zajonc, 1980), and increases the probability of him or her receiving help (Baer, Goldman, & Juhnke, 1977; Lindskold, Forte, Haabe, & Schmidt, 1977). Mcaulay (1975) found that familiarity may override likeability as a determinant of helping. Obviously, the effect of familiarity is dependent on the type of past experience people have with others: Positive experiences increase the probability of prosocial behavior, and negative experiences reduce it (see Baron, 1971). Equally obviously, familiarity is a necessary condition for most systems of reciprocity.

Favoring those who are familiar is one thing. Persecuting those who are unfamiliar is another. Biologists and psychologists have found that many species seem negatively disposed toward strangers. As put so dramatically by Ardrey (1970): "However the animosity for a stranger is expressed, whether through attack or avoidance, xenophobia is there, and it is as if throughout the animals world invisible curtains hang between the familiar and the strange" (p. 15).

According to E. O. Wilson (1975) "This xenophobic principle has been documented in virtually every group of animals displaying higher forms of social organization" (p. 249).

Ingroup Status.   Members of extended families apparently formed ingroups in our evolutionary past. A spate of social psychological research has found that people favor members of groups with which they are identified. Feldman (1968) and Hornstein, Fisch, & Holmes (1968) for example, have found that people are more willing to help compatriots than to help foreigners; and a large number of studies have found that people favor members of one-shot experimental groups to which they have been arbitrarily assigned (Tajfel, Billig, Bundy, & Flammont, 1971). Although members of most of the groups studied by social psychologists are not related genetically, the evidence suggests that group members identify with one another in a brotherly and sisterly way. Billig and Tajfel (1973) and Allen and Wilder (1975) report that ingroup nepotism is intensified when group members are led to believe that they are similar to one another.

Hornstein (1978) has developed a theory of "promotive tension" that features the significance of ingroup identification. Hornstein reviews evidence that indicates that "in some circumstances human beings experience others as 'we,' not as 'they.'" When this happens, one individual's plight may become a source of tension for another. Seeking relief from this vicariously experienced tension, the other may help the person with whom he or she is identified complete a task or reach a goal, especially if the person is in close proximity. "Through a formation of 'we,' self-interest is fused together with a concern for others, and the basis of promotive tension and selfless behavior is born" (p. 189). From a biological perspective, we would expect the sense of we-ness to have a genetic base. It also is the case, of course, that members of ingroups establish reciprocal relations, making it difficult to identify the source of the helping behavior they display (and its status as altruistic).

Familiarity and ingroup status are related to kin recognition processes based on spatial location and association. Genetic programs disposing individuals who lived in bands of extended families to help those who lived close to them, who were members of their group, and who were familiar would be expected to have maximized their inclusive fitness, and, therefore, to have mediated the evolution of nepotistic altruism. In our present environment, these programs would be expected to mediate altruism toward friends and acquaintances.

Similarity.   Phenotype matching may extend the domain of recipients even further. There is a great deal of evidence that modern humans show preferences for individuals who are similar to them in a variety of ways. In an interesting series of studies, Porter (this volume) has found that mothers and newborn babies prefer one another's odors, suggesting that olfactory cues serve as the basis for phenotype matching. A spate of research has found that various sources of similarity are positively associated with interpersonal attraction (Bersheid &

Walster, 1978) and helping behavior (see Hoffman, 1981; and Krebs & Miller, 1985, for reviews).

It is well-established that humans practice assortative mating (see Rushton et al., 1985 for a review). Rushton et al. (1985) present evidence that individuals are more likely to base their preferences for mates on highly heritable sources of similarity than on sources of similarity that are more environmentally based. These reviewers argue that this evidence supports the theory that individuals inherit the ability to detect genetic similarity in others and to treat them preferentially, but Rushton et al. (1985) allow that preferential treatment of those who are genetically similar may be based on other mechanisms.

In view of the theoretical significance of similarity in the evolution of altruism, it is surprising that it has captured so little attention from researchers. Many sources of similarity are positively correlated with familiarity and propinquity, and many are environmentally induced. Others, however, especially those that stem from inherited physical characteristics, may be independent from other associations. Are individuals disposed to help strangers who look like them or who look like their relatives, and if so how is this disposition acquired? The answer to this question has obvious implications for ethnic relations.

Ethnic Relations.   Physical characteristics such as skin color, shape of nose, type of hair, and style of dress are associated with ethnic heritage. So also are correlates of relatedness such as ingroup status and familiarity. Rushton et al. (1985) have suggested that, contrary to our moral ideals, we may be genetically predisposed to favor those who are ethnically similar. The results of research on the relationship between ethnic similarity and prosocial behavior are inconsistent. Some studies have failed to find any differences in assistance to members of the same vs. different races (Farra, Zinser, & Bailey, 1978, Wispé & Freshley, 1971); some studies have found more cross-race than same-race helping (Dutton, 1971; Dutton & Lake, 1973; Katz, Glass, Lucido, & Farber, 1979); and some studies have found more same-race than cross-race helping (Bryan & Test, 1967; Benson, Karabenick, & Lerner, 1976; Clark, 1974; Gaertner & Bickman, 1971). Attempts to disentangle the contradictory findings have indicated that while individuals may be disposed to discriminate in favor of members of their own race, this disposition may not be translated into behavior: (1) when the costs of helping are minimal, (2) when recipients are from the same location, (3) when the request for help is related to a worthy goal, and (4) when discriminating against members of different races is costly (see Gaertner & Dovidio, 1977; Katz, Cohen, & Glass, 1975; Wegner & Crano, 1975; Wispe & Freshley, 1971). Studies have found that racial discrimination is often masked, but may seep out in subtle and disguised ways. For example, Weitz (1972) found that nonverbal, but not overt, behavior correlated with racial prejudice; and Goodstadt (1971) found that prejudiced individuals may behave prosocially toward members of minority groups in order to maintain a nonbigoted public image.

Silverman (this volume) examines racism from a sociobiological perspective and concludes that "whatever small gains have accrued to inclusive fitness by fixed responses, based on similarity, to extrafamilial others, would have been lost to the advantages of the capacity to form situationally optimal alliances." It is important to recognize that the focus of Silverman's analysis is on *intergroup conflict,* not *interindividual altruism.* The dynamics of conflict and aggression between groups may be different from the dynamics of altruism and nepotism between individuals. Indeed, in reviewing research on ingroup solidarity in minimal social situations, Brewer (1979) found substantial evidence for favoritism toward ingroup members, but little evidence in support of antagonism toward outgroup members. Whether inclusive fitness is (or more exactly, was) maximized more by favoring those from one's ethnic group or through some other strategy is an open question. Silverman (this volume) suggests that favoring ingroup members was adaptive during most of our evolutionary history, but was selected out during the past 10,000 years when we made the transition from "small intra- and inter-related bands to larger heterogeneous groupings." Ten thousand years seems like too short a time span for such a major evolutionary change to have occurred in humans, but the point that the benefits of flexible strategies should outweigh the benefits of ethnic nepotism seems well taken.

It is important to note that however disposed we may be biologically to favor members of our own ethnic groups, there is nothing in sociobiological theory that negates the possibility that individuals will feel disposed to behave prosocially toward strangers and members of different ethnic groups (or to behave aggressively toward relatives and members of ingroups) when such behavior enhances their inclusive fitness (or, more exactly, when did so in their evolutionary past).

By way of summary, several strands of social psychological research are consistent with the idea that humans are genetically predisposed to enhance the fitness of unrelated individuals who possess the types of characteristics that were associated with kinship in our evolutionary past, even though this anachronistic disposition may not pay off in their present environment. If this is the case humans may help others without any return, and, therefore, engage in behavior that is genuinely altruistic.

THE CHALLENGE OF ALTRUISM IN PSYCHOLOGY

By and large, advances in the biological study of altruism have not had much impact on psychological research on prosocial behavior. The main reason why sociobiological ideas have been neglected probably relates to a preference among psychologists for accounting for human behavior in terms of learning and environmental factors rather than in terms of heredity. Consider, for example, the conclusions reached by the authors of two psychological volumes on prosocial behavior:

> What humankind inherits is the potential or possibility of learning a wide variety of social behaviors. But what is actually learned depends on the social situation. Socially adaptive cooperative and altruistic behaviors are the products of social learning and not biological evolution. (Mussen & Eisenberg-berg, 1977, p. 45)

> Whatever the extent to which organisms possess the genetic potential to learn to respond prosocially to other organisms, the most useful and reasonable approach is to explore the social origins of prosocial reactivity, individual differences as the consequences of opportunities for learning, and the determination of prosocial behavior by the individual characteristics that developed and the social conditions that exist. (Staub, 1978, p. 38)

The conception of human nature that fits most easily with most psychological theories and with the implicit ideas of the average person is that humans are inherently selfish, but, unlike other animals, they may be taught to behave altruistically. This "original sin" assumption lies at the base of psychoanalytic theory, reinforcement theories of learning, virtually all theories of motivation (see Cofer & Appley, 1964), and Judeo-Christian religious dogma (see Krebs & Miller, 1985). This assumption was stated clearly in 1975 by Donald Campbell in a Presidential address to the American Psychological Association: "Social evolution has had to counter individual selfish tendencies which biological evolution has continued to select as a result of . . . genetic competition" (p. 1115). I have attempted to show how altruistic dispositions could have evolved biologically in the human species. I would now like to turn to the other side of the original sin conception of human nature and examine the evidence supporting the assumption that altruism has been instilled in humans through nurture.

Although the discipline of psychology is not encompassed by any one overriding theory, it is dominated implicitly and explicitly by an overriding principle of learning—a principle that has been called by names such as hedonism, the law of effect, the pleasure principle, and the principle of reinforcement. This principle dictates that organisms tend to repeat (i.e., learn) behaviors that pay off psychologically, and to suppress behaviors that do not. It lies at the foundation of psychological theories as diverse as psychoanalysis and operant learning theory (see Campbell, 1972; Gelfand and Hartmann, 1982; Krebs & Miller, 1985). If altruism is defined on a psychological plane as behavior that violates the principle of reinforcement, it creates a challenge in psychology similar to the challenge that it creates in biology: How can it prevail in the absence of reinforcement?

While biologists have faced the challenge of altruism face on, psychologists have tended to skirt it. So firmly entrenched in psychology is the principle of reinforcement that some psychologists believe that defining altruism in a way that contradicts it entails defining altruism "out of existence": "If a satisfied feeling afterwards is characteristic of all motives, then it cannot be used as the defining criterion of a particular class of motives (e.g., egoistic motives)." (Hoffman, 1981, p. 134): "Our social learning orientation caused us to doubt the utility of definitions of altruism that excluded the possibility of external reinforcement . . ." (Gelfand & Hartmann, 1982, p. 168).

The relatively few psychologists who have attempted to meet the challenge of altruism have tended to take a tact similar to that taken by sociobiologists. They have shown how behavior that seems altruistic actually is controlled by subtle reinforcers. For example, psychologists have shown how helping behavior that is reinforced through reciprocity can prevail without immediate reinforcement in much the same way that sociobiologists have shown how "reciprocal altruism" can evolve (see Krebs & Miller, 1985). Psychologists such as Goldiamond (1968), Aronfreed (1968), and Gelfand & Hartmann (1982) have shown how helping behaviors that seem altruistic may turn out, on close examination, to reap hidden gains. Gelfand & Hartmann demonstrate that people are prone to attribute their helping behavior to altruistic motives even though it is controlled by external reinforcement. Interestingly, these investigators report that this tendency does not extend to the helping behavior of others, which tends to be attributed to external forces and to be denied the label of altruism.

The most significant attempts to resolve the paradox of altruism in psychology have involved an appeal to the construct of empathy. Because of the relevance of these attempts to biological theory and research, it is worth considering them in some detail.

The Psychology of Empathy and Altruism

What shared genes are to the biology of altruism, empathy is to the psychology of altruism. In the same way that genes connect people physically, empathy connects them emotionally. When we empathize with people, we react as though we were they. Sociobiologists suggest that altruistic dispositions evolve when they foster the propogation of shared genes. Psychologists suggest that individuals are motivated to help others when it enhances their shared affective state.

The idea that empathy mediates altruism has a long history in philosophy and the social sciences. It was discussed by Adam Smith and David Hume in the 18th century, and considered at length by social philosophers such as Mill and Spencer in the 19th century. The first psychologist to offer empirical support for the idea was the social learning theorist Justin Aronfreed. Defining empathy as "a person's affective response to the expressive behavioral cues of another person's affective experience," Aronfreed (1979, p. 107) accounted for both the origin of empathy and the capacity of empathic reactions to give rise to altruistic behaviors in terms of conditioning. According to Aronfreed, children learn to feel bad when others feel bad and they learn to feel good when others feel good early in their lives because the affective experiences of others serve as conditioned stimuli which, through association, come to evoke similar affective responses.

Consider a common example. A mother ignores or chastizes her child when the mother is upset. Through repeated association, signs of distress in the mother evoke a conditioned distress response ("empathy") in the child. Once the association between the affective state of the child and the affective state of the mother is established, the child may learn to reduce his or her own vicariously experienced distress (or enhance his or her vicariously experienced pleasure) by doing things that relieve the mother's distress (or increase her pleasure).

In the same way that several of the routes to altruism offered by biologists turned out on examination not to entail a violation of the principle of natural selection, and, therefore, not to qualify as altruistic, the psychological route outlined by Aronfreed turns out not to entail a violation of the principle of reinforcement. Aronfreed (1972) is explicit on this point:

> the fact that an act has no directly rewarding external consequences for the actor does not imply that the act functions entirely without reinforcing consequences. . .
> We would do better to assume that altruistic acts are indeed governed by the affective value of their anticipated outcomes, and that they often do have reinforcing consequences for the person who carries them out." (p. 105)

In order to establish that empathy mediates *altruism* (as opposed to helping behavior), an investigator must establish (1) that the potential helper experiences an affective state that is empathic in nature, (2) that the empathic state gives rise to helping behavior, and (3) that the helping behavior is altruistic. In 1975, Martin Hoffman introduced a model of empathy and altruism synthesizing research in support of these three conditions—a model he elaborated in several subsequent publications.

Evidence for Empathy.   Hoffman (1982) defines empathy as "a vicarious affective response to others: that is, an affective response appropriate to someone else's situation rather than one's own" (p. 128). He describes six modes of empathic arousal that vary "in degree of perceptual and cognitive involvement, type of eliciting stimulus . . . , and amount and kind of past experience required" (p. 44). The first, an "early precursor of empathy," is the reactive cry of the newborn. One- and 2-day-old infants cry in response to another infant's cry, but not in response to equally loud nonhuman sounds or computor-simulated infant cries. The second is a mode based on classical conditioning—the type of empathy investigated by Aronfreed (1970). The third mode is called "direct association." In it, cues of pain and pleasure in others "evoke associations with the observer's own past pain or pleasure." The forth mode, "objective motor mimicry," involves, for example, increased lip activity in observers watching a person who stutters. The fifth mode involves the type of symbolic association experienced by people reading a letter from a friend who is unhappy; and the final mode involves role-taking.

Although Hoffman makes a theoretical distinction between six modes of empathic arousal, most of the empirical work he adduces in support of his model does not. Hoffman accepts evidence (a) that observers experience elevated levels of physiological arousal when exposed to cues of pain or distress in others, (b) that there is a correlation between the intensity of the pain cues and the level of such arousal, and (c) that the arousal diminishes when the others' distress is relieved as evidence that the arousal is empathic in nature.

The psychological evidence is strong and consistent in support of the assumption that both human and nonhuman subjects undergo an affective experience when they observe a conspecific in distress or in a distressful situation (see Krebs, 1971, 1975; Piliavin et al., 1981; and Stotland et al., 1978 for reviews). Further, as documented by Piliavin et al. (1981, pp. 60–62) the amount of arousal experienced by people exposed to an emergency is positively correlated with the severity and clarity of the emergency, the degree of their involvement with the victim, and the amount of distress displayed by the victim. But is this arousal empathic?

In order to establish that a response is empathic, an investigator must establish that it is vicarious—i.e., that an observer is reacting as though he or she were another or in another's situation—not a direct response to physical stimuli emanating either from the affective experience of the other (e.g., screams) or from the situation. In addition, an investigator must establish that the vicarious reaction is similar in kind to the affective experience of the person who is observed. If a victim is feeling upset, the observer must feel upset, not sorry; if the victim is feeling fearful, the observer must feel fearful, not angry about the victim's plight or guilty about his or her responsibility for it. Psychophysiological research has shown that people make affective responses to small changes in stimulation. Indeed, even attending to an event may evoke changes in physiological arousal (an "orienting response"). In a recent review of the literature, Greene & Osborne (1985) concluded that few studies have satisfied the conditions for vicarious instigation. Fewer still, if any, have met the conditions for empathy (see Berger, 1962).

The exact nature of the arousal experienced by people who observe others in distress or in a difficult situation may seem somewhat academic but it relates integrally to the question of whether the resulting helping behavior is egoistic or altruistic in nature.

The Relationship between Empathy and Helping Behavior.   In support of the idea that some kinds of helping behavior, especially bystander intervention in emergencies, are mediated by empathic reactions, Hoffman adduces the following evidence: (a) people frequently help others who show signs of distress, (b) there is a correlation between level of arousal in observers and the speed and probability of subsequent helping, and (c) physiological arousal diminishes after others are helped. Hoffman (1981) concludes that "It is difficult to explain these results except to assume that empathic arousal serves as a motive for the helping action" (p. 131).

Although a large number of studies have found a positive correlation between the affective reactions of observers and both the probability and speed of helping (see Piliavin et al., 1981), the relationship is not unconditional. Hoffman (1981) himself points out that empathic arousal may at times be "so intense as to direct the observer's attention to him- or herself rather than to the victim, with a resulting decrease in the likelihood of an altruistic response" (p. 133). In addition, research has shown that optimally aroused bystanders help others only under certain conditions, namely when the costs for helping (e.g., expenditures of effort, exposure to danger, susceptability to embarrassment) are low, and the costs for not helping (either "personal costs" such as public censure or self-blame, or "empathy costs" such as a continuation of an unpleasant state of vicariously-experienced arousal) are high (see Piliavin et al., 1981).

The Nature of Empathic Motivation.   The most straightforward interpretation of the motivation underlying empathically induced helping is that it is egoistic in nature—the function of helping is to relieve vicariously experienced distress; and, indeed, some researchers in the area endorse this interpretation (see Piliavin et al., 1981). However, defining altruism as "behavior that promotes the welfare of others without conscious regard for one's own self-interest" (p. 124), Hoffman (1981) disagrees, insisting that empathically mediated helping is altruistic. He gives two reasons: (1) Although the *consequence* of helping may be to reduce the helper's vicarious distress, there is evidence that the conscious *intention* of helpers is to relieve the distress of another, and (2) Because all motives are accompanied by a feeling of satisfaction, a feeling of satisfaction cannot be used as a basis for distinguishing between egoistic and altruistic motives.

The arguments offered by Hoffman in support of the idea that the motivation underlying empathically induced helping is altruistic are not strong. To suggest that definitions of altruism that disallow the reinforcement associated with "a satisfied feeling afterwards" are impossibly strict because all motives produce a satisfied feeling misses the point. Altruism is paradoxical in psychology precisely because it appears to violate the principle of reinforcement. The suggestion that the motivation underlying behavior should be defined in terms of the goal of the behavior or the intention of the actor and not the consequences of the behavior is consistent with the intuitions of the average person and the orientation of many psychologists. However, the empirical evidence adduced by Hoffman in support of it is not strong, and, in any event, it fails to supply a resolution of the paradox of altruism.

To my knowledge only one group of psychologists, Batson et al., have taken a significant step toward identifying the nature of motivation underlying empathically mediated altruism. Batson et al. (1981) suggest that the arousal experienced by individuals who observe another in distress may assume two qualitatively different forms: personal distress (shock, alarm, disgust, fear) and empathic concern (compassion, warmth, concern, softheartedness). According to these investigators, the former emotional state gives rise to egoistic motivation—to reduce personal distress as an end in itself; and the latter emotional state gives rise to altruistic motivation—to reduce the distress of the other as an end in itself. Batson et al. supply evidence to support the assumption that observers experience both personal distress and empathic concern in response to distress in others. In addition, they report positive correlations between degree of empathic concern, but not personal distress, and helping behavior. They also show that in cases where subjects are induced to misattribute arousal evoked by the distress of another to an extraneous source such as a placebo (Coke, Batson, & McDavis, 1978), or noise (Harris & Huang, 1973), they are disinclined to help.

In view of the fact that both egoistic and altruistic motives may be satisfied by helping (i.e., helping may allay both personal distress and empathic concern), it is difficult to determine which motive gave rise to helping behavior in a given situation. In an attempt to identify the motivational basis of helping behavior, Batson et al. (1981) reasoned that when the motivation to help originates from the personal distress evoked by the plight of another, observers should help only when they are not able to relieve the distress by escaping from the situation. In cases where the motivation to help originates from empathic concern, however, observers should be equally likely to help in situations where it is easy and difficult to escape. In support of these hypotheses these investigators found that subjects experiencing personal distress helped a victim only when it was difficult to escape from the experimental situation (i.e., when helping was the easiest way to relieve their own distress), but subjects experiencing empathic concern helped regardless.

The ideas advanced by Batson et al. constitute one of the only attempts to distinguish between egoistic and altruistic motives. It is unclear, however, why Batson et al. chose to label the emotional state that gives rise to altruism "empathic concern." Feelings described as "compassionate," "warmth," and "softheartedness" would seem more appropriately characterized as sympathy. Batson et al. (1981) define empathy somewhat idiocyncratically (as "an emotional response elicited by and congruent with the perceived welfare of someone else"), and acknowledge that "congruent emotion elicited by witnessing another in distress in a helping situation could appropriately be called sympathy instead of empathy" (p. 170).

It is interesting to note that, by and large, psychologists have chosen to focus on the relationship between empathy and altruism, not on the relationship between sympathy and altruism (see Wispé, 1986). It seems unlikely that the paradox of altruism will ever be resolved through appeals to empathy except by definitional finesse because reductions in empathic distress and elevations in empathic pleasure are reinforcing to potential helpers. The route to altruism through sympathy may prove more tenable. Sympathy may well be a more intrinsically altruistic state than empathy, involving as it does feeling bad about the condition or circumstances of *another* rather than experiencing another's emotional state as one's *own*. Hoffman (1981) is attentive to this possibility. He speculates that empathic feelings undergo several transformations as infants develop and as they acquire the ability to make increasingly clear distinctions between themselves and others; and that at an advanced stage:

> their own empathic distress, which is a parallel response—a more or less exact replication of the victim's actual feelings of distress—may be transformed at least in part into a more reciprocal feeling of concern for the victim, that is, they continue to respond in a purely empathic, quasiegoistic manner—to feel uncomfortable and highly distressed themselves—but they also experience a feeling of compassion or what I call sympathetic distress for the victim along with a conscious desire to help because they feel sorry for him or her and not just to relieve their own empathic distress. (p. 51)

By way of summary, I have suggested that most psychologists have skirted the paradox of altruism; that the few who have attempted to resolve it have attributed altruistic behavior to empathic reactions; and that sympathetic reactions may supply a more adequate basis than empathy for an intrinsically altruistic motive. The evidence suggests that observers may undergo an affective experience that includes both feelings of personal distress and sympathetic concern when they encounter another who needs help, and feelings of sympathetic concern may motivate people to help even when they do not believe that helping will relieve their personal distress. Whether or not sympathetic helping entails a violation of the principle of reinforcement, and, thus, resolves the paradox of altruism, remains, however, an open question.

Virtually all psychological research on vicarious instigation and empathy has been conducted within the framework of learning theory. Hoffman (1981) makes a notable departure from this tradition. He suggests that both altruistic behaviors and empathic reactions have a "constitutional" basis. In drawing together support for this idea, Hoffman explicitly sets out to "show that psychology may supplement biology in helping to throw light on a central issue in the sociobiological literature—whether altruism is a part of human nature." (p. 121)

THE BIOLOGICAL BASIS OF ALTRUISM AND EMPATHY

Hoffman (1981) opens his case for the biological basis of altruism by appealing to sociobiological theory. On his interpretation, "the concept of inclusive fitness, which encompasses kin selection, reciprocal altruism, and probably also group selection . . . makes a good case for biological altruism'' (p. 124). Hoffman recognizes that the case he builds for the evolution of altruism may seem limited, ''since the donor's own genes ultimately benefit,'' but argues that because total organisms are selected, it does not make sense to define altruism at the genetic level.

Hoffman offers four kinds of behavioral evidence for biologically based altruism: (1) that people frequently help others in our society, (2) that a great deal of the helping is performed by people whose need for approval is not strong, in situations in which approval would not be expected, (3) that helping behavior often occurs almost immediately, (''If altruistic action at times reflects a true biologically-based motive, we would therefore expect to find instances in which altruistic action has a more or less automatic quality'' (p. 126)), and (4) that signs of relief in others appear to reinforce helping behaviors. Hoffman appropriately recognizes that this behavioral evidence is ''by no means conclusive.''

Having made his case for biologically based altruism, Hoffman asks ''what mechanism underlies altruistic action?'' (p. 127). He suggests that natural selection ''requires an altruistic response system that is reliable and yet also flexible,'' and goes on to argue that ''what therefore must have been acquired . . . is a predisposition or motive to help that, although biologically based, is nevertheless amenable to control by perceptual or cognitive processes'' (p. 128). He suggests that automatic helping responses such as those displayed by the social insects would not be adaptive in the human species; rather, what must have evolved was a mediator that is sensitive to perceptual cues relevant to degree of relatedness and cognitive considerations such as the costs and benefits of helping. (Note the apparent contradiction between the idea that ''natural selection requires a response system that is reliable and flexible'' and the idea that responses that are ''involuntary and automatic'' are biologically based.)

Hoffman (1981) contends that empathy meets these requirements, and supports this contention with three types of evidence: (a) ''people of all ages respond empathically to another person in distress'' (p. 128), (b) such ''empathic'' responses have an involuntary and automatic element, and (c) that there is a neural basis for empathy in the limbic system (MacLean, 1973). In discussing specific modes of empathic arousal, Hoffman suggests that the reactive cry of the newborn may be innate, and that objective motor mimicry and empathy based on classical conditioning ''have the earmarks of species-wide responses'' (p. 130). (''Although the focus here is on conditioning, which is a learning mechanism, the empathic response that results is involuntary and virtually automatic'' (p. 130)).

The case made by Hoffman for the biological basis of empathy seems confused. Empathy is construed as both a flexible mechanism and a reflexive response; it is unclear which of the six modes of empathic arousal Hoffman is discussing; and the evidence he presents in support of the universality of the response is weak. Moreover, it is unclear what Hoffman means by "biologically based," "species-wide," "constitutional," and "possibly innate."

There is good reason to assume that empathic reactions are adaptive and heritable, even if the mechanism underlying them involves learning. Whether people inherit the disposition to feel distressed when others are distressed (and to feel good when others feel good) or whether they inherit the capacity to learn such reactions early in their lives doesn't really matter for the purpose of most analyses. Empathy seems adaptive, not only for the reason given by Hoffman (that it mediates inclusive fitness-enhancing altruistic behavior), but also for at least three other reasons. First, experiencing the affective state of another vicariously supplies potentially valuable information ("He is frightened, there must be danger." "She is angry, I better be careful." "He is happy, now is a good time to ask for a favor."). Second, it induces a state of arousal that may facilitate appropriate action. And third, as suggested by Leak & Christopher (1982), "individuals with [empathic] predispositions would be more likley than their non-feeling counterparts to offer aid under certain circumstances, thus enhancing their status in the reciprocal altruism network and consequently improving their own fitness through an increased probability of receiving favors in return" (p. 81).

In a more empirical vein, recent research on individual differences offers support for the idea that empathy is heritable. In a study in which a self-report measure of empathy was given to monozygotic and dizygotic twins, Matthews, Batson, Horn, and Rosenman (1981) obtained a heritability coefficient of .72. In another study Rushton et al. (1986) compared the responses of a sample of 206 monozygotic and 277 dizygotic twins to Mehrabian and Epstein's (1972) measure of emotional empathy. The intraclass correlation was .54 for monozygotic and .20 for dizygotic twins, producing a heritability estimate of .68. Unfortunately, the validity of self-report measures of empathy is uncertain, and no studies have assessed the heritability of psychophysiological measures of empathy.

It is possible that biological research demonstrating that various kinds of phenotypic similarity evoke altruistic responses and psychological research indicating that empathic and sympathetic reactions mediate altruistic behaviors may converge, helping to resolve the paradox of altruism. Several studies have found that perception of similarity evokes empathic reactions (Batson ct al., 1981; Feshbach & Row, 1968; Krebs, 1975). Indeed, perception of similarity may be a precondition for empathy (see Stotland et al., 1978). Interestingly, in one study Klein (1971) found that ethnic similarity, but not similarity of attitudes or interest, evoked empathy in young girls. Empathy may serve as a proximal (psychological) mechanism intervening between phenotype matching and altruism. It may constitute the affective correlate of the sense of "we-ness" identified by Hornstein, Piliavin et al., and others as a determinant of prosocial behavior.

Impuslive Helping

An evaluation of the idea that genetically based empathic reactions mediate altruistic behavior would not be complete without consideration of an anomalous set of findings from research on emergency intervention. Most research on helping in emergencies indicates that bystanders weigh the costs and benefits of intervening, and that the result of this "hedonic calculus" determines whether they help or not (Piliavin et al., 1981). This evidence leads us to expect individuals to be least likely to help in life-threatening (high-cost) situations—an expectation consistent with Hoffman's (1981) contention that "inclusive fitness . . . requires that people be disposed to help others in distress but be capable of making some kind of assessment wherein the degree of kinship and the benefits vs. cost of helping or not helping are considered" (p. 128). In the early years of research on bystander intervention, studies generally supported the hedonic calculus model; however, later studies occasionally reported an anomalous result: bystanders would intervene almost reflexively, whether they were alone or in a crowd, apparently oblivious to the costs and consequences for themselves. Indeed, in some situations, such as when an individual appeared to have been electrocuted, bystanders behaved in an irrational way, grabbing the victim even though, had the emergency been real, they would have endangered their own lives (Clark & Word, 1974).

As the number of studies finding such "impulsive" helping grew, it became clear that it was evoked in situations involving clear, realistic, and imposing emergencies, and that it was facilitated when the intervener had prior experience with the victim. Piliavin et al. note that "not coincidentally, the same factors that facilitate impulsive helping—clarity, reality, involvement with the victim— have also been demonstrated to be related to greater levels of bystander arousal" (p. 238). These investigators conclude that the dynamics of impulsive helping are qualitatively different from the dynamics of other kinds of bystander intervention. They suggest that when individuals encounter an emergency that they cannot avoid, they become flooded with intense arousal. This arousal produces a narrowing of attention (Easterbrook, 1959) directed toward the plight of the victim. "Cost considerations become peripheral and not attended to" (p. 239), and observers help reflexively. Piliavin et al. (1981) speculate that "there may be an evolutionary basis for . . . impulsive helping" (p. 180).

As indicated earlier, Hoffman appears to posit two contradictory mechanisms underlying empathy—a flexible mechanism sensitive to inclusive fitness considerations, and a "reflexive" mechanism that is not. Perhaps humans inherit dispositions that mediate both mechanisms. The first, flexible, mechanisms may give rise to empathically or sympathetically mediated altruism; and the second, reflexive, mechanism may give rise to impulsive helping. The emotional reactions of impulsive helpers do not seem vicarious in nature. Indeed, observers may intervene impulsively to help someone who is oblivious to the danger he or she is in.

Evidence on impulsive helping suggests that although humans may not be capable of learning to behave altruistically (when altruism is defined in a way that entails a violation of the principle of reinforcement), they may be genetically disposed to engage in impulsive acts of helping. The reflexiveness of impulsive helping would be expected to be adaptive in situations requiring immediate reactions, and, in spite of its obvious costs, the disposition to engage in it may have been reinforced through kin selection in our early evolutionary history. The finding that prior experience with a victim facilitates impulsive helping is consistent with evidence on familiarity in support of the possibility that impulsive helping is an anachronistic anomaly.

SUMMARY

Altruism presents a challenge to the principle of natural selection in Darwin's theory of evolution and to the principle of reinforcement in psychology. Biologists have responded to the challenge of altruism by making refinements in the units of selection in evolutionary theory—refinements that have stimulated research and fostered the growth of sociobiology. Psychologists have tended to skirt the challenge of altruism, but there are some notable exceptions. Empathy has been adduced as a proximal mechanism mediating altruistic behavior, but no one has, as yet, established that the motivation underlying empathically mediated helping is altruistic. Sympathy may have a closer connection to altruism than empathy. Empathy appears to give rise to relatively slow and considered helping responses, but people sometimes help impulsively, apparently without reflection and concern for their own welfare. Both empathic and impulsive helping may have been adaptive in the early evolutionary history of the species, and, therefore, may have evolved through kin selection.

REFERENCES

Alexander, R. D. (1974). The evolution of social behavior. *Annual Review of Ecology and Systematics, 5,* 325–383.

Alexander, R. D., & Borgia, G. (1978). Group selection, altruism and the level of organization of life. *Annual Review of Ecology and Systematics, 9,* 449–474.

Alexander, R. D. (1979). *Darwinism and human affairs.* Seattle: University of Washington Press.

Allen, V. L., & Wilder, D. A. (1975). Categorization, belief similarity, and intergroup discrimination. *Journal of Personality and Social Psychology, 32,* 971–977.

Ardrey, R. (1970). *The social contract.* New York: Atheneum.

Aronfreed, J. (1968). *Conduct and conscience: The socialization of internalized control over behavior.* Orlando, FL: Academic Press.

Aronfreed, J. (1972). The socialization of altruistic and sympathic behavior: Some theoretical and experimental analyses. In J. Macaulay & L. Berkowitz (Eds.), *Altruism and helping behavior*. Orlando, FL: Academic Press.

Axelrod, R. (1984). *The evolution of cooperation*. New York: Basic Books.

Axelrod, R., & Hamilton, W. D. (1981). The evolution of cooperation. *Science, 211*, 1390–1396.

Baer, R., Goldman, M., & Juhnke, R. (1977). Factors affecting prosocial behavior. *Journal of Social Psychology, 103*, 209–216.

Barash, D. P. (1982). *Sociobiology and behavior* (2nd Ed.). New York: Elsevier.

Baron, R. A. (1971). Behavioral effects of interpersonal attraction: Compliance with requests from liked and disliked others. *Psychonomic Science, 25*, 325–326.

Batson, C. D., Duncan, B., Ackerman, P., Buckley, T., & Birch, K. (1981). Is empathic emotion a source of altruistic motivation? *Journal of Personality and Social Psychology, 40*, 290–302.

Benson, P. K., Karabenick, S. A., & Lerner, R. M. (1976). Pretty pleases: The effects of physical attractiveness, race, and sex on receiving help. *Journal of Experimental Social Psychology, 12*, 409–415.

Berger, S. M. (1962). Conditioning through vicarious instigation. *Psychological Review, 69*, 450–466.

Bersheid, E., & Walster, E. (1978). *Interpersonal attraction* (2nd Ed.). Reading, MA: Addison-Wesley.

Billig, M., & Tajfel, H. (1973). Social categorization and similarity in intergroup behavior. *European Journal of Social Psychology, 3*, 27–52.

Blaustein, A. R. (1983). Kin recognition mechanisms; phenotype matching or recognition alleles? *American Naturalist, 121,*749–754.

Boorman, S. A., & Levitt, P. R. (1980). *The genetics of altruism*. Orlando, FL: Academic Press.

Brewer, M. B. (1979). In-group bias in the minimal intergroup situation: A cognitive-motivational analysis. *Psychological Bulletin, 86*, 307–324.

Bryan, J. H., & Test, M. J. (1967). Models and helping: Naturalistic studies in aiding behavior. *Journal of Personality and Social Psychology, 6*, 400–407.

Campbell, D. T. (1972). On the genetics of altruism and the counter-hedonic components in human culture. *Journal of Social Issues, 28*, 21–37.

Campbell, D. T. (1975). On the conflict between biological and social evolution and between psychology and moral tradition. *American Psychologist, 30*, 1103–1126.

Campbell, D. T. (1983). The two distinct routes beyond kin selection to ultrasociality: Implications for the humanities and social sciences. In D. L. Bridgeman (Ed.), *The nature of prosocial behavior*. Orlando, FL: Academic Press.

Chagnon, N. (1979). Mate competition, favoring close kin and village fissioning among the Yanomamo Indians. In N. Chagnon & W. Irons (Eds.), *Evolutionary biology and human social behavior*. No. Scituate, MA.

Chagnon, N., & Irons, W., (Eds.). (1979). *Evolutionary biology and human social behavior*. No. Scituate, MA.

Charnov, E., & Krebs, J. R. (1974). The evolution of alarm calls: Altruism or manipulation? *American Naturalist, 109*, 107–112.

Clark, R. D., III. (1974). Effects of sex and race on helping behavior in a nonreactive setting. *Representative Research in Social Psychology, 5*, 1–6.

Clark, R. D., III, & Word, L. E. (1974). Where is the apathetic bystander? Situational characteristics of the emergency. *Journal of Personality and Social Psychology, 29*, 279–287.

Cofer, C., & Appley, M. (1964). *Motivation: Theory and research*. New York: Wiley.

Coke, J. S., Batson, C. D., & McDavis, K. (1978). Empathic mediation of helping: A two-stage model. *Journal of Personality and Social Psychology, 36*, 752–766.

Darwin, C. (1859). *On the origin of species by means of natural selection*. London: John Murray.

Dawkins, R. (1976). *The selfish gene*. London: Oxford University Press.

Dawkins, R. (1982). *The extended phenotype: The gene as the unit of selection.* San Francisco: W. H. Freeman.

Dunbar, R. (1980). Determinants and evolutionary consequences of dominance among female Gelade baboons. *Behavioral Ecology and Sociobiology, 7,* 253–265.

Dutton, D. G. (1971). Reactions of restauranteurs to blacks and whites violating restaurant dress requirements. *Canadian Journal of Behavioral Science, 3,* 298–302.

Dutton, D. G., & Lake, R. A. (1973). Threat of own prejudice and reverse discrimination in interracial situations. *Journal of Personality and Social Psychology, 28,* 94–100.

Easterbrook, J. A. (1959). The effect of emotion on cue utilization and the organization of behavior. *Psychological Review, 66,* 183–201.

Emswiller, T., Deaux, K., & Willits, J. E. (1971). Similarity, sex, and requests for small favors. *Journal of Applied Social Psychology, 1,* 284–291.

Farra, J. D., Zinser, O., & Bailey, R. C. (1978). Effects of I-E of donor and race and locus of cause of failure of recipient on helping behavior. *Journal of Social Psychology, 106,* 73–81.

Feldman, R. E. (1968). Response to compatriot and foreigners who seek assistance. *Journal of Personality and Social Psychology, 10,* 202–214.

Feshback, N. D., & Roe, K. (1968). Empathy in 6- and 7-year-olds. *Child Development, 39,* 133–145.

Gaertner, S. L., & Bickman, L. (1971). Effects of race on the elicitation of helping behavior: The wrong number technique. *Journal of Personality and Social Psychology, 20,* 218–222.

Gaertner, S. L., & Dovidio, J. F. (1977). The subtlety of white racism, arousal, and helping behavior. *Journal of Personality and Social Psychology, 35,* 691–707.

Gelfand, D. M., & Hartmann, D. P. (1982). Response consequences and attributions· Two contributors to prosocial behavior. In N. Eisenberg (Ed.), *The development of prosocial behavior.* Orlando, FL: Academic Press.

Goldiamond, I. (1968). Moral behavior: A functional analysis. *Psychology Today, 2,* 31–34.

Goodstadt, M. S. (1971). Helping and refusal to help: A test of balance and reactance theories. *Journal of Experimental Social Psychology, 7*(6), 610–622.

Grafen, A. (1982). How not to measure inclusive fitness. *Nature, 298,* 425–426.

Graves, N. B., & Graves, T. D. (1983). The cultural context of prosocial development: An ecological model. In D. L. Bridgeman (Ed.), *The nature of prosocial behavior.* Orlando, FL: Academic Press.

Green, G., & Osborne, J. G. (1985). Does vicarious instigation produce support for observational learning theories? A critical review. *Psychological Bulletin, 97,* 3–17.

Hames, R. (1979). Relatedness and interaction among the Ye'Kwana: A preliminary analysis. In N. Chagnon & W. Irons (Eds.), *Evolutionary biology and human social behaviors.* No. Scituate, MA.

Hamilton, W. D. (1964). The genetical evolution of social behavior: I and II. *Journal of Theoretical Biology, 7,* 1–52.

Harris, M. B., & Baudin, H. (1973). The language of altruism: The effects of language, dress, and ethnic group. *Journal of Social Psychology, 91,* 37–41.

Harris, M. B., & Huang, L. C. (1973). Competence and helping. *Journal of Social Psychology, 89,* 203–210.

Hoffman, M. L. (1975). Altruistic behavior and the parent-child relationship. *Journal of Personality and Social Psychology, 31,* 937–943.

Hoffman, M. L. (1981). Is altruism part of human nature? *Journal of Personality and Social Psychology, 40,* 121–137.

Holmes, W., & Sherman, P. W. (1982). Kin recognition in animals. *American Scientist, 71,* 46–55.

Hornstein, H. A. (1978). Promotive tension and prosocial behavior: A Lewinian analysis. In L.

Wispe (Ed.), *Altruism, sympathy, and helping: Psychological and sociological principles*. Orlando, FL: Academic Press.

Hornstein, H. A., Fisch, E., & Holmes, M. (1968). Influence of a model's feelings about his behavior and his relevance as a comparison on other observers' helping behavior. *Journal of Personality and Social Psychology, 10,* 222–226.

Johnson, G. R. (1986). Kin selection, socialization, and patriotism: An integrated theory. *Politics and Life Sciences, 4*(2), 127–153.

Katz, I., Cohen, S., & Glass, D. (1975). Some determinants of cross-racial helping behavior. *Journal of Personality and Social Psychology, 32,* 964–970.

Katz, I., Glass, D. C., Lucido, D. & Farber, J. (1979). Harm-doing and victim's racial or orthopedic stigma as determinants of helping behavior. *Journal of Personality, 47,* 340–364.

Klein, R. (1971). Some factors influencing empathy in six and seven year old children varying in ethnic background. *Dissertation Abstracts, 31,* 3960A. (University Microfilms No. 71-3862).

Krebs, D. L. (1970). Altruism—an examination of the concept and a review of the literature. *Psychological Bulletin, 73,* 258–302.

Krebs, D. L. (1971). Infrahuman altruism. *Psychological Bulletin, 76,* 410–414.

Krebs, D. L. (1975). Empathy and altruism. *Journal of Personality and Social Psychology, 32,* 1134–1146.

Krebs, D. L. (1982). Psychological approaches to altruism: An evaluation. *Ethics, 92,* 447–458.

Krebs, D., & Miller, D. (1985). Altruism and aggression. In G. Lindzey & E. Aronson (Eds.), *Handbook of social psychology* (3rd Ed.), (pp. 1–71.) New York: Addison-Wesley.

Krebs, D. L., & Wispé, L. (1974). On defining altruism. *Journal of Social Issues, 30,* 194–199.

Leak, G., & Christopher, S. (1982). Empathy from an evolutionary perspective. *Journal for the Theory of Social Behavior, 12,* 79–82.

Leaky, R. E., & Lewis, R. (1977). *Origins.* New York: Dutton.

Lewontin, R. C. (1970). Sociobiology as an adaptationist program. *Behavioral Science, 24,* 5–14.

Lightcap, J. L., Kurland, J. A., & Burgess, R. L. (1982). Child abuse: A test of some predictions from evoluationary theory. *Ethol. Sociobiology, 3,* 61–67.

Lindskold, S., Forte, R. A., Haabe, C. S., & Schmidt, D. K. (1977). The effects of directness of face-to-face requests and sex of solicitor on street corner donations. *Journal of Social Psychology, 101,* 45–51.

Lockard, J. S. (1980). Speculations on the adaptive significance of self deception. In J. S. Lockard (Ed.), *The evolution of human social behavior.* New York: Elsevier.

Lovejoy, C. O. (1981). The origin of man. *Science, 211,* 341–350.

Lumsden, C. J., & Wilson, E. O. (1983). *Promethean fire: Reflections on the origin of mind.* Cambridge: Harvard University Press.

Macaulay, J. R. (1975). Familiarity, attraction and charity. *Journal of Social Psychology, 95,* 27–37.

Matthews, K. A., Batson, C. D., Horn, J., & Rosenman, R. H. (1981). Principles in his nature which interest him in the fortune of others. . . . The heritability of empathic concern for others. *Journal of Personality, 49,* 237–247.

Maynard Smith, J. (1976). Group selection. *Quarterly Review of Biology, 51,* 277–283.

Maynard Smith, J., & Price, G. R. (1973). The logic of animal conflict. *Nature, 246,* 15–18.

MacLean, P. D. (1973). *A triune concept of the brain and behavior.* Canada: University of Toronto Press.

Mealey, L. (1985). Comment on genetic similarity theory. *Behavior Genetics, 15,* 571–574.

Mehrabian, A., & Epstein, N. (1972). A measure of emotional empathy. *Journal of Personality, 40,* 525–543.

Mussen, P., & Eisenberg-berg, N. (1977). *Roots of caring, sharing, and helping.* San Francisco: Freeman.

Packer, C. (1977). Reciprocal altruism in Papio anubis. *Nature, 265,* 441–443.

Piliavin, J. A., Dovidio, J. F., Gaertner, S. L., & Clark, R. D. III. (1981). *Emergency intervention*. Orlando, FL: Academic Press.

Pitcher, T. (1979). He who hesitates lives. Is stotting antiambush behavior? *American Naturalist, 113*, 453–456.

Plomin, R., Defries, J., & McClearn, J. (1980). *Behavioral genetics: A primer*. San Francisco: Freeman.

Raymond, B. J., & Unger, R. K. (1972). "The apparel oft proclaims the man": Cooperation with deviant and conventional youths. *Journal of Social Psychology, 87*, 75–82.

Ridley, M., & Dawkins, R. (1981). The natural selection of altruism. In J. P. Rushton & R. M. Sorrentino (Eds.), *Altruism and helping behavior*. Hillsdale, NJ: Lawrence Erlbaum Associates.

Rubin, Z. (1973). *Liking and loving: An invitation to social psychology*. New York: Holt, Rinehart and Winston.

Rushton, P. J. (1982). Moral cognition, behaviorism, and social learning theory. *Ethics, 92*(3) 459–467.

Rushton, J. P., Fulker, D. W., Neale, M. C., Nias, D. K. B., & Eysenck, H. J. (1985). Altruism and aggression: Individual differences are substantially heritable. *Journal of Personality and Social Psychology, 50*, 1192–1198.

Rushton, J. P. & Russell, R. J. H. (1985). Genetic similarity theory: A reply to Mealy and new evidence. *Behavior Genetics, 15*, 575–582.

Rushton, J. P., Russell, R. J. H., & Wells, P. A. (1984). Genetic similarity theory: Beyond kin selection. *Behavior Genetics, 14*(3), 179–193.

Russell, R. J. H., Rushton, J. P., & Wells, P. A. (1984). Sociobiology, personality and genetic similarity detection. In J. R. Royce & L. P. Mos (Eds.), *Annals of Theoretical Psychology, Vol. 2*. New York: Plenum Press.

Staub, E. (1978). *Positive social behavior and morality* (Vol. 1). Orlando, FL: Academic Press.

Stotland, E., Mathews, K. E., Sherman, S. E., Hanson, R. O., & Richardson, B. Z. (1978). *Empathy, fantasy, and helping*. Sage Library of Social Research, 65.

Tajfel, H., Billig, M. G., Bundy, R. P., & Flament, C. (1971). Social categorization and intergroup behavior. *European Journal of Social Psychology, 1*, 149–178.

Thiessen, D. D., & Gregg, B. (1980). Human assortative mating and genetic equilibrium: An evolutionary perspective. *Ethol. Sociobiology, 1*, 111–140.

Trivers, R. L. (1971). The evolution of reciprocal altruism. *Quarterly Review of Biology, 46*, 35–57.

Trivers, R. (1985). *Social evolution*. New York: Benjamin-Cummings.

van den Berghe, P. L. (1983). Human inbreeding avoidance: Culture in nature. *Behav. Brain Science, 6*, 91–123.

Wegner, D. M., & Crano, W. D. (1975). Racial factors in helping behavior: An unobtrusive field experiment. *Journal of Personality and Social Psychology, 32*(5), 901–905.

Weitz, S. (1972). Attitude, voice, and behavior. A repressed affect model of interracial interaction. *Journal of Personality and Social Psychology, 24*, 14–21.

Whiting, B. B. (1983). The genesis of prosocial behavior. In D. L. Bridgeman (Ed.), *The nature of prosocial behavior*. Orlando, FL: Academic Press.

Wiessner, P. (1977). *Hxaro: A regional system of reciprocity among the !Kung San for reducing risk*. Unpublished doctoral dissertation. University of Michigan.

Williams, G. C. (1966). *Adaption and natural selection*. New Jersey: Princeton University Press.

Wilson, D. S. (1979). Structured demes and trait-group variation. *American Naturalist, 113*, 606–610.

Wilson, D. S. (1980). *The selection of populations and communities*. Mento Park, CA: Benjamin Cummings.

Wilson, E. O. (1975). *Sociobiology: The new synthesis*. Cambridge, MA: Belknap Press.

Wispé, L. (1986). The distinction between sympathy and empathy: To call forth a concept, a word is needed. *Journal of Personality and Social Psychology, 50*(2), 314–321.

Wispé, L. G., & Freshley, H. B. (1971). Race, sex and sympathetic helping behavior: The broken bag caper. *Journal of Personality and Social Psychology, 17*(1), 59–65.

Woodland, D., Jaafar, Z., & Knight, M. L. (1980). The "pursuit deterrent" function of alarm signals. *American Naturalist, 115,* 748–753.

Wynne Edwards, W. C. (1962). *Animal dispersion in relation to social behavior.* New York: Hafner.

Zajonc, R. B. (1980). Feeling and thinking. Preferences need no inferences. *American Psychologist, 35,* 151–175.

II ISSUES

In the first chapter in this section the anthropologist Donald Symons argues that Darwinism can do more than merely rule out certain views of the mind: it can guide research, prevent certain kinds of errors, inspire new questions, and call attention to aspects of the mind that are normally too mundane or uniform to be noticed. Specifically, it can lead us to anticipate a brain/mind comprising numerous, specific, complex mechanisms rather than simple, general mechanisms of association or symbol manipulation, and may be especially useful in guiding research on the mechanisms of feeling. In the second chapter in this section John Fuller, one of the founders of the discipline of behavior genetics, points out that sociobiologists are interested in the differences between species and the environmental pressures that shaped them, while behavior geneticists are interested in the role of genetic and environmental differences in producing individual differences within species. He goes on to discuss some behavior genetic concepts and their importance for sociobiologists.

Kinship and how it is involved in the evolution of social behavior lies at the core of sociobiology. If organisms are to direct their helping behavior preferentially toward relatives that may carry some of their genes, then mechanisms for recognizing relatives must have evolved. Since genes for automatic relative recognition are unlikely to evolve through natural selection, some type of social learning is likely involved in relative recognition. In Chapter 7, Richard Porter, a comparative/developmental psychologist, discusses recent work on the recognition of relatives and some of its implications for sociobiologists and psychologists.

Some critics have claimed that sociobiological thinking necessarily leads to classism, sexism and racism. Social psychologist Irwin Silverman provides some interesting insights into the latter issue in the concluding essay in this section. He argues that pragmatism and flexibility in the formation of human alliances, rather than perceived genetic communality, are more likely to characterize the human species.

5 If We're All Darwinians, What's the Fuss About?

Donald Symons
University of California, Santa Barbara

Organisms have teleological organization. When we speak of the *process* of photosynthesis, the visual *system*, a reflex *mechanism*, or the *functions* of the liver we manifestly assume that organisms—including human beings—are goal-directed, purposeful entities comprising organized parts with their own goals or purposes. Since Darwin's theory of adaptation through natural selection is "the only workable theory we have to explain the organized complexity of life" (Dawkins 1982, p. 35), these goal-directed mechanisms—*qua* mechanisms—were necessarily designed by natural selection. If, in Dawkins' words, we are all Darwinians, and if we all hold an interactional view of development, why have attempts to examine human feeling, thought and action in evolutionary perspective been so controversial? I argue that what really underlies this controversy has not been confronted: the nature of the mechanisms that comprise the human mind.

Two decades ago George Williams (1966) asked rhetorically: "Is it not reasonable to anticipate that our understanding of the human mind would be aided greatly by knowing the purpose for which it was designed?" (p. 16). Obviously Williams did not mean to imply the tautology that by knowing the mind's purpose we would be aided in understanding its purpose; he meant to imply that we would be aided in understanding its nature. This essay is a meditation on Williams' question.

SPECIES-TYPICAL MECHANISMS

Evolutionary explanations are often said to suffer from reductionism, genetic determinism, and adaptationism. Gould and Lewontin (1979) and Lewontin (1979), for example, criticize what they call the "adaptationist program" in

121

evolutionary biology which entails, they say, dividing organisms into arbitrary traits, each of which is *explained* as the perfect adaptive solution to some problem. But organisms are integrated entities, they argue, not collections of discrete parts, and many things constrain the achievement of perfection.[1]

Evolutionists typically reply that, while they may be reductionists, they are not genetic determinists and they are aware of constraints on perfection. Every trait, they say, is the product of the interaction of genes and environments: To ask whether the genes or the environment is more important in determining a trait is like asking whether the height or the width is more important in determining the area of a rectangle. What their critics fail to grasp, say the evolutionists, is the logical distinction between the proximate and the ultimate causes of a species-typical trait. Proximate causes have to do with development, physiology, and stimulus control, ultimate causes with adaptation and evolutionary history. We are interested, say the evolutionists, in ultimate, not proximate, causes, in the trait's evolution and function, not in whether or not it is learned.

It is my thesis, however, that what really underlies most of these debates is an implicit disagreement about the nature of the species-typical traits that comprise a given phenotype. When no such disagreement exists, questions of reductionism, genetic determinism, adaptationism, and proximate versus ultimate causation rarely arise at all. Consider the following (presumably) noncontroversial species-typical trait: Each time a human being swallows his larynx rises. The evolutionist might argue that this mechanism's function is to shut off the passage to the lungs, thereby reducing the likelihood of choking to death. The mechanism was produced (and is maintained) by natural selection because individuals who choke to death bear (and bore) fewer than average offspring, and progeny tend to resemble their parents.

It seems most unlikely that this interpretation will be thought to suffer from undue reductionism or genetic determinism, from ignoring "social factors" or neglecting "environmental inputs." Neither is it likely to be criticized on the grounds of excessive adaptationism. The fact that a human body is an integrated entity apparently does not preclude its being considered to be—to some interesting extent—a collection of interacting parts: The problem with arbitrary traits seems to be not in the traits but in the arbitrariness. Nor does an attribution of function necessarily imply perfection. We all know that the rise of the larynx does not inevitably prevent choking (that's why the word *choking* exists).

The human swallowing mechanism may be imperfect because, for example, it is somehow better adapted to the foods of times past than to the present, because it was pieced together by selection from whatever material was available (not designed by an engineer from scratch), because theoretically desirable mutations did not happen to occur, or because the larynx's role in voice production some-

---

[1]As has often been noted, in their own research Gould and Lewontin typically have been well within adaptationist tradition.

how compromises its role in swallowing (see Dawkins, 1982, for an excellent discussion of constraints on perfection).

Surely the reason the rise of the larynx is not controversial is that everyone— evolutionist and physiologist, naturist and nurturist, layman and scientist—intuitively perceives it to be a *nonarbitrary* trait, an example of a "natural kind." By picking it out one carves nature at a joint. The referents of the terms *swallows*, *larynx* and *rises* are unambiguous, and equally unambiguous is the mechanism's function.

Now contrast this mechanism with another species-typical trait, the redness of human arterial blood. Evolutionists do not offer adaptive explanations for redness, physiologists do not study how redness works in the body, and developmentalists do not consider the ontogeny of redness to be an interesting question. Why? Apparently we intuitively perceive the redness of arterial blood to be an *arbitrary* trait; by picking it out we fail to carve nature at a joint. Redness, of course, has proximate causes (everything does): the chemical natures of oxygen and hemoglobin and the nature of human color vision. But it has no ultimate cause because redness per se was never *specifically* selected for; it is simply a functionless byproduct of other adaptations. In fact, an organism could be divided into traits in an infinite number of ways, and the overwhelming majority of such arbitrarily demarcated traits would have no ultimate cause or function. To characterize a trait nonarbitrarily is to make assumptions about function. One picks out the rise of the larynx, but not the redness of arterial blood, as a natural subject for physiological, developmental or evolutionary analysis precisely because one intuitively perceives in the former, but not in the latter, a goal-directed mechanism amidst the blooming, buzzing confusion of organic flux.[2]

In an important sense, therefore, the distinction between proximate and ultimate causation is less clear-cut than is generally imagined. Questions about the physiology and development of the rise of the larynx, which appear to be purely proximate, imply the existence of a goal-directed mechanism, a mechanism which can be described teleologically without reference to evolution or natural selection. Indeed, it is precisely the *possibility* of discovering a biological mechanism that was *not* designed by natural selection that makes Darwin's theory of adaptation nontautological and, hence, falsifiable (see Alexander, 1975; Darwin, 1859; Williams, 1966; and, especially, Dunbar, 1982). But, at present, there is no known designer of such mechanisms other than natural selection, and the essence

---

[2]Human intuition has proved to be a powerful tool for analyzing the structure and function— i.e., the anatomy and physiology—of adult organisms. Part of the reason may be that natural selection and human beings often create similar mechanisms: the lens of an eye/the lens of a camera; a heart/a mechanical pump; the camouflage of an insect/the camouflage of a soldier; and so forth. Intuition seems to be much less useful for analyzing ontogenetic processes, perhaps because organisms are never constructed the way human beings construct things. In fact, the notion that there is such a thing as "ontogeny," which is somehow distinct from "physiology," may have to do less with the nature of organisms than with the nature of the human mind.

of natural selection is the differential survival of alternative alleles. So just by picking out the-rise-of-the-larynx-during-swallowing as a mechanism one implies something about function (the avoidance of choking), about ultimate causation (the differential reproductive success of chokers and nonchokers in ancestral populations, in the absence of a plausible alternative theory of ultimate causation) and, hence, about genes (the ultimate beneficiaries of this mechanism).

While all this might seem to imply an important role for the evolutionist in describing or characterizing goal-directed, species-typical mechanisms, note that in the case of the rise of the larynx the evolutionist actually contributes nothing. Human intuition, not selectional thinking, is responsible for picking out this mechanism. By the same token, the evolutionist is unlikely to dream up an adaptive story to account for the redness of arterial blood: He intuitively perceives that redness is an artifact. The problem of identifying nonarbitrary traits confronts all students of living things, not just evolutionists, and, unfortunately, there are no hard and fast solutions to this problem when intuition is inadequate. It is in these cases that the evolutionary perspective can sometimes help to stimulate and guide our thinking.

THE USES OF DARWINISM

Darwin's discovery of the creative process responsible for adaptive design answered one of the Great Questions: What is life? It is a question almost as monumental as, Why is there something rather than nothing? and, What is mind? And yet, after more than a century, Darwinism seems to have had little influence on such life sciences as physiology and even less influence on the social and behavioral sciences. One possible explanation is implicit in the example of the rise of the larynx: It's simply not clear that the Darwinian student of the physiology of swallowing has any special advantage over his colleague who believes the swallowing mechanisms to be the handiwork of God. Another possible explanation is that the knowledge that organisms have been designed by natural selection does not—at first glance—seem to constrain their natures. After all, the incredible diversity of living things that did evolve obviously could evolve, and a still more incredible diversity presumably could have evolved had mutational and selectional circumstances happened to have been different.

First glances, however, can be misleading. Darwin's theory of adaptation through natural selection does constrain what can evolve and is, to this extent, predictive. Mechanisms in one species designed exclusively to promote the welfare of another species (Darwin, 1859, p. 201) or in an individual designed exclusively to promote the welfare of a conspecific reproductive competitor (Alexander, 1975, p. 82), for example, are ruled out by Darwin's theory. The reason Darwinists tend to harp on these predictions is that, elementary though they may be, they often appear not to have been understood. The hypotheses that rattlesnakes have rattles for our benefit rather than their own, or that monkeys harass a copulating male in their group in order to direct his aggression away from his sexual partner and thereby assist him in fertilizing her (both of which actually have been proposed) are worse than no hypotheses at all. The current bull market in Darwinism may be in part the result of the growing realization that some theories in the social and behavioral sciences are surely wrong because they imply the existence of mechanisms that could not have arisen through natural selection. Darwinism rules out, for example, species-typical mechanisms designed to promote the survival of species, gene pools, groups, societies, cultures or collective representations.

But even within the realm of the apparently possible, Darwinism can provide strong, if not absolute, predictions. For example, Darwin (1871) wrote that "promiscuous [random] intercourse in a state of nature is extremely improbable" (p. 362). Not impossible, just extremely improbable. Why? Presumably because it is extremely difficult to imagine how millions of years could have passed without the chance occurrence of individuals who enjoyed greater than average reproductive success by virtue of possessing inheritable tendencies to exercise prudent selectivity in their choice of mates. For similar reasons, I argued (Symons, 1979) that men and women almost certainly differ in some of the brain mechanisms that underpin sexual feeling, thought, and action. For millions of years ancestral males and females must have encountered very different reproductive opportunities and constraints. Because mutation was constantly generating variation it is almost impossible to visualize circumstances in which selection would have failed to produce divergent male and female sexualities.

The notion of *prediction* grades insensibly into the notion of *expectation*. If it were demonstrated that the function of rattlesnake rattles is to promote human rather than rattlesnake reproduction, Darwin's theory of adaptation would be refuted. If it were demonstrated that mating in some species is completely random, Darwin's theory would not be refuted, though the demonstration would be surprising. But even weaker expectations can lead to interesting research. For example, it is reasonable to suppose that parents who are capable of biasing the sex of their offspring (prior to birth) to fit particular ecological circumstances will enjoy greater than average reproductive success. That Williams (1979) was unable to find evidence for such adaptations in vertebrates in no way diminishes the power of Darwinism to sharpen our thinking about functional mechanisms and to guide our research. Naturally, our expectations and hunches won't always pan out; but selectional thinking can be a source of inspiration. For example, Hames (1979) demonstrated that among the Ye'Kwana Indians of Southern Venezuela degree of genetic relatedness is a much better predictor of the frequency of interaction between individuals than Ye'Kwana (or our own) kin terms are. Although this interesting finding is not, in my opinion, even an *expected*, much less a *predicted*, result of Darwinian theory, it nevertheless was made only because Hames was inspired to analyze his data in a nontraditional way by recent progress in evolutionary genetics.

DARWINISM AND PSYCHOLOGY

All psychological theories, including the most extreme empiricist/associationist ones, assume that the mind has structure. No one imagines that a pile of bricks, a bowl of oatmeal, or a blank slate will ever perceive, think, learn, or act, even if given every advantage. And all psychological theories assume this structure to be goal-directed: The mind comprises *mechanisms*. Since the only known creative process capable of producing such mechanisms is natural selection, Darwinism has at least one obvious implication for psychology: Hypothesized psychological mechanisms must be realizable via natural selection. Very few psychological theories, however, seem to imply the existence of mechanisms manifestly incompatible with Darwinian evolution. The creative potential of natural selection is so vast, and our understanding of the human mind is so slight, that such entirely different creatures as a Skinnerian human being, a Piagetian human being, and a Chomskyan human being, and such diverse theoretical positions as structuralism (Laughlin & d'Aquili, 1974) and behaviorism (Pulliam & Dunford, 1980) have been thought to be reconciliable with Darwinism.

Thus, if Darwinism's only contribution to psychology was to rule out the manifestly impossible, this contribution would be slight. I believe, however, that Darwinism can do more than merely rule out certain views of the mind: It can provide grounds for favoring some views over others and it can guide hypothesis formation and help us to decide which of the infinite number of questions we might ask about the mind are the ones most likely to bear scientific fruit.

Perhaps the central issue in psychology is whether the mechanisms of the mind are few, general, and simple, on the one hand, or numerous, specific, and complex, on the other. It is no accident that Darwinists tend, at least implicitly, to hold the latter view. Selectional thinking focuses attention on *goals:* The mind is, in some utterly mysterious way, an aspect of the brain, and the brain has been designed by selection *to do specific things.* An organism that does different kinds of things must solve different kinds of problems. There is no more reason to anticipate that all problems can be solved by one general-purpose mental mechanism than there is to anticipate that all physiological processes can be the result of one general-purpose organ. An adaptational view of the brain/mind thus implies that higher organisms—especially human beings—are endowed with many specialized mental mechanisms and that different species are endowed with different mechanisms. As Fodor (1980) puts it:

> . . . in all other species cognitive capacities are molded by selection pressures as Darwin taught us to expect. A truly *general* intelligence (a cognitive capacity fit to discover just *any* truths there are) would be a biological anomaly and an evolutionary enigma . . .
>
> The reasonable assumption, in any event is that human beings have an ethology,

just as other species do; that the morphology of our cognitive capacities reflects our specific (in both senses) modes of adaptation. Of course, we are in some respects uniquely badly situated to elucidate its structure . . . *From in here* it looks as though we're fit to think whatever thoughts there are to think . . . it *would,* of course, precisely because we *are* in here. But there is surely good reason to suppose that this is hubris bred of an epistemological illusion. No doubt spiders think that webs exhaust the options. (p. 333)

A Darwinian view of the mind also implies that at least some human mental mechanisms are exceedingly stable and complex, since human behavior is exceedingly flexible. This implication has not been widely appreciated; in fact, many writers seem to believe that behavioral flexibility somehow implies the existence of simple, amorphous mental structures. There is a litany in the literature of anthropology that goes something like this: Human beings have no nature because the essence of the human adaptation is plasticity, which makes possible rapid behavioral adjustments to environmental variations. This litany, however, has the matter backwards: Extreme behavioral plasticity implies extreme mental complexity and stability; that is, an elaborate human nature. Behavioral plasticity for its own sake would be worse than useless, random variation suicide. During the course of evolutionary history the more plastic hominid behavior became the more complex the neural machinery must have become to channel this plasticity into adaptive action.

Thus, when Gould (1983) writes that human beings are different from other creatures "as a result of enormous flexibility based on the complexity of an oversized brain and the potentially cultural and nongenetic basis of adaptive behaviors" (p. 243), although he is doubtless in some sense right, he begs all the interesting psychological questions. The greater the variety of possible adaptive behaviors the greater the variety of possible maladaptive behaviors (Symons, 1979, pp. 307–308). What psychological mechanisms make the former more likely? What Gould (like many others who argue in the same vein) fails to come to grips with is that the answer must lie somewhere in the *complexity.* This fundamental, though generally unappreciated, point has been addressed in rather different ways by different evolutionists.

Lorenz (1973), for example, notes that a random phenotypic modification resulting from some environmental change stands no greater chance of being adaptive than a mutation does. "If in response to a specific influence an adaptive modification regularly occurs, one can be virtually certain that this specific modifiability is the result of an earlier process of natural selection" (p. 64).

> . . . the ontogenetic realization of the most appropriate option among those offered by the open programme is an adaptive process.
>   The fact that the open programme acquires and retains information in this way

must not lead us to overlook that it requires for this purpose not less, but more genetic information than that required for a closed programme. . . . All learning ability is based on open programmes which presupposes the presence not of less but of more information in the genome than do so-called innate behaviour patterns. (p. 65)

*   *   *   *

If one part of a behavioral system can be considerably modified by learning, one is bound to assume that other parts are sufficiently resistant to modification to ensure that the learning of the variable parts is carried out. (p. 89)

Midgley (1978) argues that behavioral flexibility entails the existence of stable mechanisms of desire: "The more adaptable a creature is, the more directions it can go in. So it has more, not less, need for definite tastes to guide it. *What replaces closed instincts, therefore, is not just cleverness, but strong, innate general desires and interests*" (p. 332). I shall argue that this should be amended to strong *specific* desires and interests.

While all this might seem to imply an important role for the Darwinist in psychology, as it happens, the view that the human mind comprises many, specific, complex mechanisms is already being argued forcefully without recourse to Darwinism. Chomsky (1980), for example, outlines

. . . the prospects for assimilating the study of human intelligence and its products to the natural sciences through the investigation of cognitive structures, understood as systems of rules and representations that can be regarded as "mental organs." These mental structures serve as the vehicles for the exercise of various capacities. They develop in the mind on the basis of an innate endowment that permits the growth of rich and highly articulated structures along an intrinsically determined course under the triggering and partially shaping effect of experience which fixes parameters in an intricate system of predetermined form. It is argued that the mind is modular in character, with a diversity of cognitive structures, each with its specific properties and principles. Knowledge of language, of the behavior of objects, and much else crucially involves these mental structures, and is thus not characterizable in terms of capacities, dispositions, or practical abilities, nor is it necessarily grounded in experience in the standard sense of this term. (p. 1)[3]

Chomsky's argument is partly an empirical one, especially with respect to his own research on the "language organ," and partly a common-sensical analogy with other bodily organs. It is no more reasonable to expect structural or func-

---

[3]Chomsky refers, of course, to the experience of the individual. This knowledge is grounded in the cumulative experience of the lineage. As Lorenz (1962:25) puts it: "Our categories and forms of perception, fixed prior to individual experience, are adapted to the external world for exactly the same reasons as the hoof of the horse is already adapted to the ground of the steppe before the horse is born and the fin of the fish is adapted to the water before the fish hatches." (Also see Lorenz 1973; Campbell 1974; and Fox, 1980.)

tional similarities between two cognitive systems than it is to expect such similarities between, say, the visual system and the liver.

Fodor (1983), refining this line of argument, presents the case for a rebirth of faculty psychology:

> FACULTY PSYCHOLOGY is getting to be respectable again after centuries of hanging around with phrenologists and other dubious types. By faculty psychology I mean, roughly, the view that many fundamentally different kinds of psychological mechanisms must be postulated in order to explain the facts of mental life. Faculty psychology takes seriously the apparent heterogeneity of the mental and is impressed by such prima facie differences as between, say, sensation and perception, volition and cognition, learning and remembering, or language and thought. Since, according to faculty psychologists, the mental causation of behavior typically involves the simultaneous activity of a variety of distinct psychological mechanisms, the best research strategy would seem to be divide and conquer: first study the intrinsic characteristics of each of the presumed faculties, then study the ways in which they interact. Viewed from the faculty psychologist's perspective, overt, observable behavior is an interaction effect par excellence.

Fodor argues that some, but not all, faculties can be regarded as *modules*. Nonmodular faculties are central processes that operate *horizontally,* across content domains, accessing all *input systems* and functioning to *fix belief.* They include the sorts of mental phenomena we refer to in everyday, common-sense psychology as thought and problem solving. Almost nothing is known about these faculties and Fodor suspects that little ever will be known about them.

Modular, or *vertical,* faculties, on the other hand, are "domain-specific, innately specified, hardwired, autonomous, and not assembled" (p. 37). The clearest instances of modules are to be found in input systems, which comprise highly specialized mechanisms. "Candidates might include, in the case of vision, mechanisms for color perception, for the analysis of shape, and for the analysis of three-dimensional spatial relations. They might also include quite narrowly, task-specific 'higher level' systems concerned with the visual guidance of bodily motions or with the recognition of faces by conspecifics" (p. 47). Most current cognitive science is the science of input systems.

Fodor outlines a number of features that input systems seem to share. For example, their operation is *mandatory:* One can't help hearing a word (in a language one knows) as a word, or seeing a visual array as objects in three-dimensional space, or feeling what one runs one's finger over as the surface of an object. Input systems also are to some extent encapsulated from *higher level* information. If one presses one's eyeball with a finger, the world will appear to move despite the fact that one knows that this movement is illusory.

Although Fodor's analysis of the mind is not informed by Darwinism, it is hard to fault it on that ground. Just as Darwinism was not needed to detect a functional mechanism in the rise of the larynx, so it does not seem to be needed to pick out the functionally significant features of input systems. The visual system, for example, contains mechanisms that maintain constancies of size, color, shape, and so forth in the face of continuously varying distal stimulation; our perceptions are thus immensely more accurate representations of the world than the projections on our retinas are. Natural selection designed these mechanisms, but that fact does not seem to add much to our understanding of them. The adaptive advantage of, say, not perceiving the world as moving every time one moves one's eyes is as obvious as the adaptive advantage of raising one's larynx every time one swallows. In fact, cognitive psychologists and philosophers regularly refer whimsically to God as the artificer of mental mechanisms without, apparently, impeding their abilities to argue about the nature of these mechanisms.

The reason that cognitive psychologists have not found it necessary to be serious about the question of the artificer is that, although they refer occasionally to the *goals* or *utilities* of organisms, they have not been much interested in exactly what these goals or utilities are. This may be a consequence of the emphases in cognitive science on language and input systems. In the case of the *language organ,* it is not even clear what the goal of the mechanism *itself* is. Its goal is often assumed to be communication, but, as Chomsky has often pointed out, it may have been designed for certain kinds of thinking, and communication may be derived. And in the case of input systems, the goals of the component mechanisms are so intuitively obvious that it is possible to study these mechanisms without considering higher-level goals at all. No matter what a person does, he's bound to do it better if his visual system contains perceptual-constancy mechanisms than if it doesn't.

The question "Why do people do anything?" cannot be addressed without making assumptions about the artificer of psychological mechanisms; but if an acceptable answer is a common-sensical "Because they're hungry," or "Because they're frightened," it won't matter much that the artificer is natural selection. Selectional thinking sheds little light on perceptual-constancy mechanisms because an *ideal* design for such a mechanism probably would be the same whether the mechanism's ultimate goal was to promote the survival of genes, individual human bodies, or *Homo sapiens;* for precisely the same reason, selectional thinking sheds little light on organismic goals as vague as *not being hungry* or *not being frightened.* It is only when *it really matters* that the brain/mind was designed to promote the survival of genes—and not, say, to promote, the survival of bodies, the perpetuation of species, the stability of ecosystems, the welfare of societies, or the glory of God—that psychology is likely to benefit significantly from Darwin's view of life.

THE MECHANISMS OF FEELING

In Robert Penn Warren's novel *All The King's Men,* the hero, Jack Burden, sets himself the task of getting the goods on a certain judge. He begins to sleuth by asking himself: "For what reason, barring Original Sin, is a man most likely to step over the line?'' And he answers: ''Ambition, love, fear, money.''[4] While not a complete catalogue of human motives, this list does call attention to two aspects of the psyche. First, our goals, desires, tastes, and hungers are not nearly as protean as are the means we have developed to achieve, fulfill, indulge, and satisfy them. As Will Durant remarked, ''We repeatedly enlarge our instrumentalities without improving our purposes.'' And second, most human desires are by nature competitive. ''Let each man sound himself within,'' wrote Montaigne, ''and he will find that our private wishes are for the most part born and nourished at the expense of others.'' Darwinism's most significant contribution to psychology may lie in its potential to shed light on these goals, wishes, purposes and desires—these mechanisms of feeling that motivate human action.

One advantage the Darwinist brings to the study of feeling is that his imagination is not likely to be limited by the legacies of empiricism and associationism. Our astonishingly accurate perceptions are grounded in complex, specialized mechanisms, and the Darwinist anticipates no less complexity or specialization in the mechanisms of feeling. Common-sense has proved to be a reliable guide to reasoning about the design of perceptual mechanisms—presumably because human perceptions of the world can be compared to the more sophisticated representations of the world that are made possible by measuring devices—but what constitutes an ideal design for a mechanism of feeling? From where will hypotheses come about the nature of desire? I shall argue that the most fertile hypotheses are likely to come from imaginations informed by Darwinism.

Another advantage the Darwinist brings to the study of feeling is that his imagination is not likely to be limited by the traditional wisdom, which can be traced to the very roots of Western thought, that there is a unity and a harmony in nature. Since the only known creative evolutionary process is differential reproduction, the Darwinist expects organisms to have goals that can be achieved only at one another's expense, and thus he is unlikely to dissipate his resources in vain attempts to explain away the evidence for competition. The Darwinist's advantage in this respect may be negligible in the study of perceptual mechanisms, since one organism's success in representing the world accurately, or usefully, is not predicated upon another organism's failure; but there would appear to be more scope for the Darwinist in the study of desire, since the wish for, say, high status for oneself is the wish for others to fail to achieve their status goals. (This may be why mechanisms underpinning such things as status-striving are often described as ''Darwinian'' and mechanisms underpinning such things as perception are not; in reality, of course, all mechanisms are equally ''Darwinian.'')

The Darwinist's third advantage is that his imagination is inevitably informed by the knowledge that the human mind is designed to deal with environments that, in some respects, no longer exist. This may not be especially significant in

---

[4]Not stepping over the line, following the rules, pursuing the good opinion of others presumably is an alternative route to status, love, money and the elimination of fear.

the study of perceptual mechanisms, which provide as accurate representations of automobiles as they do of saber-toothed tigers, but the details of some of the mechanisms of feeling can be understood only as adaptations to a world quite different from our own.

Perhaps these general remarks can be clarified with a couple of examples. I have argued (Symons, 1979, in press) that several specialized, and somewhat sexually dimorphic, mechanisms underpin our feelings of sexual attraction. There is neither the room nor the necessity to detail this argument here, but perhaps the reader can get enough of its flavor to advance the present discussion by imagining that a heretofore unknown tribal people, the Bongo-Bongos, is discovered living in darkest wherever. Now, we would surely be astonished to find that the Bongo-Bongos perceive the world as moving whenever they move their eyes, and if my claim for the existence of specialized mechanisms of sexual attraction is valid, we should be just as astonished if we cannot predict with reasonable accuracy Bongo-Bongo standards of sexual attractiveness. I predict that a randomly selected Bongo-Bongo man's ideal sexual partner will have the following characteristics:

1. She will be newly nubile (that is, she will just recently have begun ovulatory menstrual cycles), approximately 17-years-of-age.

2. She will evidence signs of good health, especially unblemished skin.

3. In most features, such as height, she will fall near the midpoint of the female Bongo-Bongo population distribution. Her face will be the sort of composite one would get by superimposing photographs of faces of many newly nubile Bongo-Bongo women on a single photographic plate.

4. Her skin will be a bit lighter than the female average (see van den Berghe & Frost, 1986).

5. She will possess whatever physical features and accouterments happen to be reliably associated with high status among the Bongo-Bongos.

6. She will have stored at least 144,000 calories in the form of body fat.

7. She will be a woman with whom the man in question has never had sexual intercourse.

8. She will not be a woman with whom the man in question was raised as a child (see Shepher, 1983).

(See Symons, 1979, and in press for a detailed discussion and for the woman's point of view on male attractiveness.)

Underlying these predictions is a logic of *mate value*. For most sexually reproducing animal species, all conspecifics of the other sex are not equally valuable as mates, hence selection has designed diverse mechanisms to detect the best mates. Such mechanisms, insofar as they are known, appear to be highly specialized, and I know of no reason to expect *Homo sapiens* to be in this respect exceptional. Each of the characteristics listed above (with the possible exception of skin color) can be accounted for in a straightforward fashion in terms of mate value (see Symons, 1979, in press; and Shepher, 1983).

Note that my hypothesis about the psychology of sexual attraction is not in itself a hypothesis about nonhuman animals, ancestral hominids, or the nature of the evolutionary process. Even if it were to turn out that chimpanzees do not possess specialized mechanisms of sexual attraction, that ancestral hominids were monogamous fugitives from a Norman Rockwell painting, or that human beings evolved from tree frogs, artificially selected by astronauts from outer space, my hypothesis could still be correct. Conversely, even if it were to turn out that everything I believe to be true of nonhuman animals, early hominids, and natural selection is, in fact, true, I could still be completely wrong about the psychology of sexual attraction.

The point is this: Although my thinking about human sexuality has been strongly influenced by Darwinism, my predictions are not correctly regarded as "predictions from modern evolutionary theory." My hypotheses about the psychology of sexual attraction had many influences, including ethnographies, studies of nonhuman animal behavior, works of fiction, psychological research on sexual attraction, everyday life, introspection, the arguments of writers as diverse as Konrad Lorenz and Jerry Fodor, and, of course, Darwin's view of life. But Darwinism, in and of itself, does not generate predictions about what will evolve. The most straightforward prediction I could have made, based on simple reproductive logic and the study of nonhuman animals, would have been that Bongo Bongo men will be able to detect when women are ovulating and will find ovulating women most sexually attractive. Such adaptations have been looked for in the human male and have never been found, hence this was not one of my predictions.

My hypothesis is about the nature of one small aspect of the human mind and, as such, must survive or perish on its own merits, in competition with other psychological hypotheses. I know of no other hypothesis about the nature of sexual attraction that is even remotely comparable in the specificity of its predictions, hence the only available views with which mine can be compared are those that ascribe feelings of sexual attraction to such things as *learning, culture,* and *socialization.* From the standpoint of psychology, what such views seem to boil down to is the (usually tacit) assumption that specialized mechanisms of sexual attraction do not exist at all, that sexual attraction is somehow the result of generalized mechanisms of association or symbol manipulation. If such views imply anything about Bongo-Bongo sexual tastes, it is that these tastes cannot be predicted in advance by me or by anyone else. The gauntlet is down, and the matter can be tested empirically.

Orians' (1980) work on the sentiments that underpin human habitat preferences is another example of the usefulness of Darwinism in the study of feeling.

Human beings, according to Orians, have a species-typical emotional response to a specific type of landscape, the savannah: ". . . we enjoy being in savannah vegetation, prefer to avoid both closed forests and open plains, will pay more for land giving us the impression of being a savannah, mold recreational environments to be more like savannahs, and develop varieties of ornamental plants that converge on the shapes of tropical savannahs" (p. 64). Orians supports his "savannah hypothesis" with evidence as diverse as real estate prices, journal records of early explorers' emotional responses to new regions, and world-wide similarities in the way vegetation is manipulated for purely esthetic reasons in yards and parks. Orians does not claim that the savannah-detecting-and-preferring mechanism is the sole determinant of human feelings about habitats: He also suspects the existence of a mechanism that promotes attachment to a habitat in which one is raised. Nevertheless, Orians is able to derive a remarkably specific set of predictions for testing the savannah hypothesis.

Just as a logic of *mate value* underlies my sexual attraction hypothesis, a logic of *habitat value* underlies the savannah hypothesis. Orians (1980) notes that most animal species possess mechanisms designed by natural selection to detect and prefer habitats optimal for reproductive success, that the majority of human evolution occurred on the savannahs of Africa, and that human beings require certain habitat features to achieve optimal reproduction. "Our responses are exactly as would be predicted from [an] analysis of habitat quality combined with the assumption that positive responses to habitats are a major proximate factor in making decisions about settling" (p. 61).

But the savannah hypothesis, like my views on sexual attraction, is in essence a *psychological* hypothesis, which could have been formalized without reference to or knowledge of nonhuman animals, human evolution, or natural selection. It must stand or fall on its own merits, whether or not Orians is right about the power of habitat selection theory and the nature of hominid habitats in times past. On the other hand, it is surely more than a coincidence that Orians is an evolutionary biologist and an expert in habitat selection theory. It seems most unlikely that the savannah hypothesis would have been formalized by someone who was not already disposed to conceive the human mind as comprising specialized mechanisms which were designed in specific sorts of Pleistocene environments by natural selection.

CONCLUSIONS

In one sense, I have suggested a very modest role for Darwinism in psychology: a source of inspiration. As Lloyd (1979) points out, a conclusion reached by the Darwinian imagination, "as to what should or should not be, is not final or binding on nature" (p. 18). In another sense, however, Darwinism's contribution to the social and behavioral sciences may turn out to be substantial. Darwinism, Lloyd continues, "merely provides a guide and prevents certain kinds of errors, raises suspicions of certain explanations or observations, suggests lines of research to be followed, and provides a sound criterion for recognizing significant observations on natural phenomena" (p. 18). Because they have developed almost entirely innocent of Darwinism, the social and behavioral sciences have committed certain kinds of errors, put forward certain suspect explanations, failed to pursue certain lines of research, and, by and large, lacked a sound criterion for recognizing significant observations.

The notion that the human brain/mind is enormously complex and comprises a diverse array of specialized mechanisms accords well with common-sense psychology, the neurosciences, and certain schools of academic psychology, such as linguistics, but it is profoundly at odds with some of the major theoretical currents in the social and behavioral sciences. Three different strategies have been adopted in the social and behavioral sciences to avoid the messiness of the human mind: (a) supraindividual entities or systems, such as society and culture, with needs of their own have been imagined to exist *sui generis* and to cause human action; (b) behavior rather than psyche has been taken as the subject matter; and (c) the mind has been assumed to comprise mechanisms of association or symbol manipulation which are too simple and generalized to require much analysis. My concern here is less to re-open the cases against social behavioral science theories (see, e.g., Lindblom & Cohen, 1979, Murdock, 1972, Rosenberg, 1980, Ziman, 1978) than to note that the Darwinian wagon may be in danger of being hitched to a meteor shower.

Many recent evolutionary perspectives on human affairs are astonishingly ecumenical: they treat genetic evolution and cultural evolution as separate, interacting systems; they purport to explain human behavior rather than human psyche; and, wherever possible, they claim compatibility with learning theory. On the one hand, this strategy of conciliation undoubtedly has led to a wider acceptance of evolutionary views than would otherwise be the case; on the other hand, however, it has led Darwinists down virtually every theoretical blind alley in the social and behavioral sciences.

Supraindividual Entities

Anthropologist G. P. Murdock (1972) argues that reified supraindividual entities, such as "sociocultural system," when used to explain rather than to describe, have more in common with myth than with science. The controversies surrounding these concepts are, according to Murdock, much like debates among competing religious sects. Murdock's argument seems eminently congenial to Darwinism. Since the only known creative evolutionary process is natural selection, no species-typical adaptations exist *for the sake of* groups or abstractions.

Certain mechanisms of the human mind may make it possible for human beings to be, to some extent, merely passive vehicles whereby abstract representations perpetuate themselves, but from the standpoint of natural selection this possibility is a cost and not a benefit. In *The Selfish Gene* (1976), Richard Dawkins outlines one of the best known claims for the existence of a "unit of information," the "meme," residing within human brains, which, like a gene, manipulates phenotypes to promote its own survival. In *The Extended Phenotype* (1982), however, Dawkins lists seven differences between "meme evolution" and gene evolution, and concludes: "These differences may prove sufficient to render the analogy with genetic natural selection worthless or even positively misleading" (p. 112). See Daly (1982) and Flinn and Alexander (1982) for cogent criticisms of recent arguments that genetic evolution and cultural evolution are separate, interacting systems.

Behavior

According to Washburn (1976), the phrase "cultural evolution" replaces the less pretentious "history" in the social and behavioral sciences, despite the fact that the analogy with organic evolution breaks down at virtually every possible point, because "evolution is a *magic word*" (p. 353) connoting the overwhelming importance of materialism. "Behavior" is, I believe, another magic word, and for precisely the same reason, despite decades of seemingly incontrovertible arguments that regularities in human behavior can be captured only with mentalistic concepts, not with behavioral ones (e.g., Pylyshyn, 1980).

Imagine a future computer capable of continuously recording the precise magnitude and timing of every contraction of every muscle in a person's body as well as the person's precise position and deployment in space. This computer's printout would be the ultimate behavioral record, and tiny parts of it might actually be of use in a few fields—for example, in the study of species-typical facial expressions and locomotor patterns—but for the overwhelming majority of issues in the study of human affairs such an infinitely variable, largely idiosyncratic record would be utterly worthless. Generalizations about human sexual preferences, for example, would not be expressible from such a record; in fact, categories such as "sexual" (except for a few species-typical consummatory patterns) and concepts such as "preference" would not even exist.

Human action not only cannot be *explained,* it cannot even be *described* without referring—albeit implicitly—to the mind and its goals. The point is *not* that we should pay more attention to what people think and feel than to what they do. It is rather that whenever our descriptions and categorizations of what people do are based on *effects* or *intentions* (which is virtually always), we are necessarily using mentalistic concepts. Evolutionists rightly assume that the mind has been designed by selection via mind's effects on behavior; nevertheless, their hypotheses about human affairs are ineluctably psychological.

General Mechanisms

It is obvious from everyday life that human beings learn a good deal about the nature of the world and about how to do various things. It is less obvious, however, that *learning theory* has enhanced our understanding of learning, in its ordinary, everyday usage. Certainly there appears to be scant justification for the assumption that a few association mechanisms underpin the varied phenomena we lump together, in ordinary usage, as learning, and such notions as *constraints* on learning and *propensities* to learn will not salvage associationism if it is fundamentally wrong. The learning theorist's view of life and Darwin's view of life are implicitly at odds, and Darwinists propitiate behaviorists at their peril.

A few examples from the study of human sexuality may help to make this point clear. My contention (Symons, 1979) that a male-female difference exists in the significance of partner variety for sexual attraction was disputed by McGuinness (1980) on the grounds that "habituation is a fundamental neural process" which necessarily produces declining arousal with familiarity in both sexes. If McGuinness should turn out to be right about the nature of human sexual attraction it will not be because human feelings can be predicted on the basis of some fundamental neural process. In McGuinness' account an actual neural process, habituation, becomes a metaphor for boredom. The problem with this metaphor is that it also explains why koalas become bored eating eucalyptus leaves (Symons, 1980).

A Second Example. I argued (Symons, 1979) that if one adopted Williams' (1966) dictum that adaptation is a special and onerous concept that should be used only when it really is necessary, and that adaptation can be recognized in the precision, economy, efficiency and complexity with which goals are achieved, then existing evidence is insufficient to warrant the conclusion that the human female's capacity for orgasm is an adaptation. This argument was disputed by at least three critics (see Symons 1980, p. 208) on the grounds that the very irregularity of female orgasm itself constitutes evidence for adaptation, since, according to operant learning theory, irregularly reinforced behaviors are more persistent than behaviors that are invariably reinforced. My response (Symons, 1980, p. 208) was, first, to note that if women always had orgasms during intercourse no one would ever have concluded on the grounds of failure to conform to operant theory that female orgasm is not an adaptation. Second, I imagined two women, Helen and Aphrodite. Helen has an orgasm only occasionally, Aphrodite has one every time she makes love. Does operant theory predict that Helen will initiate intercourse more often than Aphrodite does? It predicts nothing of the sort. Quite apart from the matter of exceedingly dubious analogies (sexual intercourse/bar-pressing, orgasm/food pellet), operant theory predicts only that Helen might be more likely than Aphrodite to continue initiating intercourse in the absence of orgasm. Since Aphrodite always has an orgasm, however, what she might do if she didn't is irrelevant.

A Final Example.   Fox (1980) argues, on the basis of considerable empirical evidence, that childhood propinquity promotes subsequent sexual indifference. But then, on the basis of essentially no evidence at all, he appeals to *learning theory* to explain this phenomenon: children's play allegedly generates intense sexual excitement, which, since it is rarely consummated, ultimately results in pain and frustration (pp. 24–25). The essential point is not that available evidence is all against this explanation, which it is (Shepher, 1983), but rather that this small blot on one of the most important discussions of brother-sister incest ever written is wholly gratuitous: an adaptive mechanism specifying a rule such as "don't lust after your childhood playmates" is just the sort of specialization Darwinism leads us to anticipate. Fox's appeal to the general mechanisms imagined in learning theory—which Robinson (1979) notes is not really theory at all but rather "loose federations of fact, opinion, polemic, and habit" (p. 12)—is especially incongruous coming, as it does, only a few pages after he has expressed the hope for a better science of human affairs than exists "now amidst the ruins of behaviorist psychology, functionalist sociology, and cultural anthropology" (p. ix).

For all their differences, theories that purport to explain human affairs in terms of *learning, socialization, culture,* and so on seem to have one thing in common: They assume that a few generalized brain/mind mechanisms of association or symbol manipulation underpin human action. If, as Darwinism leads us to expect, the human brain/mind actually comprises many specialized mechanisms, certain theoretical stances within the social and behavioral sciences must be flawed. Yet many evolutionists, apparently hoping to accommodate every theoretical position in the social and behavioral sciences, try to maintain an Olympian detachment from potentially divisive questions of human psychology. If one reads between the lines of the Darwinists' accounts of human affairs, however, one usually senses specialized psychological mechanisms at work, hence these accounts tend to provoke strong remarks from the social and behavioral scientists whose theoretical oxen are gored, despite the Darwinists' protestations of benign intentions toward all oxen.

Consider the following imaginary but realistic example. The Darwinist anthropologist T. A. Claw has discovered that the Bongo-Bongos practice infanticide while their neighbors the Yawnomamo (the bored people) do not. Claw accounts for these data as follows: Human beings do not have an instinct to commit infanticide, nor do the Bongo-Bongos and the Yawnomamo differ genetically; rather, infanticide is a "facultative adaptation." The Bongo-Bongos practice it because it is adaptive in their particular ecological circumstances, the Yawnomamo do not practice it because not practicing it is adaptive in their, somewhat different, circumstances. Claw's Swedish colleague Bjorn Free, however, contends that infanticide is the product of cultural conditioning, not biology. This contention causes Claw to rend his garments and to wonder aloud how the Frees of this world can be so obtuse as to fail to comprehend such simple concepts as "facultative adaptation" and "ultimate causation." "I'm talking about the *ultimate* cause of infanticide," says Claw, "not its *proximate* cause. Nothing about my hypothesis implies that infanticide isn't learned." This placates Free a bit, though he continues to harbor vague misgivings.

I think that Free's misgivings are well-founded. Just by picking out "infanticide" and certain aspects of the Bongo-Bongos' environment in his characterization of the adaptation, Claw implies the existence of some sort of specialized mechanism(s) "for" infant-killing, mechanism(s) shaped by natural selection in ancestral populations because individuals who killed infants in certain circumstances (but not in others) enjoyed greater than average reproductive success and passed on their facultative infanticidal ways. But when Free argues that infanticide is the product of cultural conditioning he implies that it is underpinned by unspecialized mechanisms, mechanisms which influence many or all aspects of human activities and have nothing specifically to do with infanticide at all. In other words, if Free is correct, infanticide is not an appropriate "trait" for causual analysis, and Claw has failed to carve nature at a joint: Infanticide is no more an adaptation than is the redness of arterial blood, and killing or not-killing infants in ancestral populations had no more influence on the design of the mechanisms that underpin Bongo-Bongo infanticide than did chosing or not chosing certain mates, settling or not settling in certain habitats, et cetera.

That Free's assumptions about the mind are almost surely wrong does not mean that Claw's hypothesis is right. I would argue, in fact, that although Claw's data are certainly intriguing and suggestive, he has not yet stated his hypothesis with sufficient precision. An adaptive hypothesis is, in essence, a hypothesis that some specific aspect of the phenotype—structure, behavior or psyche—has been shaped by natural selection to serve some specific function. But Claw's *infanticide* hypothesis does not specify *any* aspect of the phenotype: It merely asserts that in a certain range of environmental circumstances people are likely either to do or to omit to do any of an infinite number of things which have nothing in common except that they increase the probability of an infant's death.

I trust that no one seriously imagines that human beings have a species-typical behavioral pattern (analogous, say, to smiling or crying) designed specifically to kill infants in certain circumstances. I also trust that no one knows enough about the human brain to even guess at the neurology of infanticide. Therefore, the infanticide-as-adaptation hypothesis must be, in essence, a psychological hypothesis, presumably about the mechanisms of feeling. If the Bongo-Bongos kill infants merely because of (the interaction of) *general* emotional goals, *general* mechanisms of problem-solving, foresight, and so forth, and mechanisms specifying[5] such *general* rules as, "do traditional things," then it is not infanticide but rather these *general* mechanisms of emotion and cognition that are the adaptations, regardless of infanticide's effect on reproductive success.

Claw's hypothesis is, as he says, about ultimate causes, but it is about the ultimate causes of (brain/mind) mechanisms that have not heretofore been dreamt of in our psychologies. A species-typical psychological mechanism that specifies a rule such as "feel X for your infant in circumstance A and Y in circumstance B" is a mechanism that is far too specialized to be accommodated by any existing view of the mind, including the explicit theories of academic psychology, the implicit psychological theories that underpin the social sciences, and, indeed, the ordinary, everyday psychological theories of common sense. Claw is thus quite wrong when he says, "Nothing in my hypothesis implies that infanticide isn't learned." By ordinary usages of the word *learned* that is just what he is implying: At the core of every notion of *learning* is the implication of nonspecialization. If infanticide is *learned* it is the relevant unspecialized learning mechanism, and not infanticide, that was shaped by selection. Because this mechanism is unspecialized, it can be expected to be imperfectly designed to achieve any particular goal, such as infanticide. To support his hypothesis, Claw needs to present evidence for design; that is, evidence that infant killing is achieved with a sufficient degree of precision, economy, efficiency, and complexity to rule out the operation of unspecialized mechanisms and/or chance (see, e.g., Elwood & Ostermeyer 1984, p. 384). Data on reproductive differentials are neither necessary nor sufficient to demonstrate adaptation (see Williams, 1966).

It thus would be meaningless to characterize Claw's account of infanticide as *biological* and Free's account as *cultural:* Both accounts are ultimately psychological; and both accounts are wedded to the extraordinary belief that a science of human affairs is possible in the absence of a science of the human mind.

In summary, the essence of a modern Darwinian view of life is that organisms—including human beings—have been designed by natural selection to promote the survival of genes. Thus Darwinism's most important role in the study of human affairs inheres in its potential for illuminating design; that is, human nature. This contribution most often may be negligible. If a Darwinist interrupts a lecture on the physiology of swallowing to point out that the goal of the rise of the larynx is, ultimately, to promote gene survival, his interruption will rightly be viewed merely as annoying pedantry. In other cases, however, especially in the study of feeling, the Darwinist may have an important contribution to make, and this contribution will be the result of unabashed psychological

---

[5]The phrase ". . . mechanisms specifying . . ." is shorthand for ". . . mechanisms that act *as if* they specify . . ." In other words, I am simply trying to characterize a mechanism, not to describe how the brain/mind actually works. Specifically, I do not mean to imply that the brain/mind is in any sense analogous to a digital computer.

reductionism and *a special kind of* "genetic determinism." Reductionism has been an ingredient in all important scientific discoveries and surely ought not to be cause for embarrassment. And although the genes and the environment jointly determine the phenotype (Oyama, 1981, 1982, 1986), the teleological mechanisms that comprise the phenotype exist *for the sake of* gene survival, not *for the sake of* environmental survival, if current understandings of natural selection are approximately correct.

A science in which phenotypes were not conceived as comprising goal-directed mechanisms would not contain a term for anything that is picked out on *functional* grounds, which includes virtually every term used in physiology. Neither would it contain any notion of *adaptation,* since the adaptive fit between organism and environment is not specifiable in physical or chemical terms: It is a *functional* fit. In fact, such a science would not distinguish conceptually between living and nonliving matter. Perhaps such a science will one day be done by some sort of science-doing robot, but it is unlikely to be accessible, or of interest, to human beings.

Darwinian students of human affairs, in their professional capacities, tend to emphasize human nature because studying human nature is what Darwinists do best. Most ordinary human concerns, however, are about human differences: A disinterested observer may find two middle-aged women barely distinguishable, but there will be all the difference in the world to me if one of them happens to be my mother. Chomsky's assurances that human beings possess a species-typical "language organ" will be of little consolation to an American who finds himself in China, unable to understand a single word. An executive in the cosmetics industry is likely to be concerned primarily with enhancing her position in her company and enhancing her company's position vis à vis other companies; she is unlikely to need a Darwinian analysis of human nature to restrain her from bringing out a line of cosmetics designed to exaggerate wrinkles and mimic the effects of ringworm.

Darwinism's concern with human nature, in my opinion, tends to make it minimally relevant to social policy decisions. Social policy exists because human beings satisfy their wishes in part at one another's expense. Human affairs can change dramatically, human wishes cannot, and "it is the changing aspects that are often pertinent to social problems and their solutions" (Lindblom & Cohen, 1979, p. 52). Perhaps in part because they hope to influence social policy, social and behavioral scientists seem to be more interested, professionally, in human differences than in human nature. This was brought home to me recently when I addressed a plenary session of the annual meeting of the Society for the Scientific Study of Sex. The theme of my talk was that a Darwinian view of life can be useful to sex researchers even if they have no special interest in adaptation or evolution. It occurred to me to illustrate this point with some examples from papers being delivered at the meeting; but as I looked through the program, I had to admit that Darwinism didn't seem relevant to most of the topics therein. The reason, I suspect, is that sex research is designed largely to solve problems, not to illuminate human nature. Most of the papers were either clinical, aimed at alleviating sexual dysfunction and misery, or addressed to some social problem, aimed, for example, at assessing the effects of pornography on men's anger toward women.[6]

It is not the business of Darwinism to dash people's hopes for less suffering and more happiness with gloomy pronouncements about the intransigence of human nature. Neither the Darwinist nor anyone else can predict the limits of human invention. As Gould (1980) points out:

> Natural selection may build an organ 'for' a specific function or group of functions. But this 'purpose' need not fully specify the capacity of that organ. Objects designed for definite purposes can, as a result of their structural complexity, perform, many other tasks as well . . . Our large brains may have originated 'for' some set of necessary skills in gathering food, socializing, or whatever; but these skills do not exhaust the limits of what such a complex machine can do. (p. 57)

It is the business of Darwinism, however, to emphasize that human inventiveness is made possible by the richness and complexity of human nature. A human being has more scope than an amoeba has precisely because a human being has more nature than an amoeba has:

> Consider again the question whether cognitive functions are both diverse and determined in considerable detail by a rich innate endowment. If the answer is positive, for some organism, that organism is fortunate indeed. It can then live in a rich and complex world of understanding shared with others similarly endowed, extending far beyond limited and varying experience. Were it not for this endowment, individuals would grow into mental amoeboids, unlike one another, each merely reflecting the limited and impoverished environment in which he or she develops, lacking entirely the finely articulated and refined cognitive organs that make possible rich and creative mental life that is characteristic of all individuals not seriously impaired by individual or social pathology—though, once again, we must bear in mind that the very same intrinsic factors that permit these achievements also impose severe limits on the states that can be attained: to put it differently, that there is an inseparable connection between the scope and limits of human knowledge. (Chomsky, 1980, p. 4)

Every hypothesis about human affairs necessarily entails assumptions about human nature (Gordon, 1978). By taking as their subject matters *culture, learn-*

---

[6]This problem-solving bent may sometimes skew social and behavioral science theories in directions theorists regard as optimistic. An optimistic bias not only can put a scientist in the questionable company of those shamans, witch doctors, politicians, psychics, preachers, human potentialists, self-help book writers, and faith healers who exploit ignorance, misery, fear and hope, but also, ironically, can jeopardize problem solving. In the long run, human suffering is not ameliorated by optimism but by knowledge.

ing, behavior, and so forth, social and behavioral scientists have allowed themselves to avoid making their assumptions about human nature explicit; but the assumptions exist nonetheless, and, in most cases, seem to be that the brain/mind comprises a few general mechanisms of association or symbol manipulation. The accumulating empirical evidence is uniformly against this view. For example, Ornstein and Thompson (1984) conclude their review of the incredibly complex, specialized, species-typical neural mechanisms that underpin our experience of seeing as follows: "There is a very ancient debate about how we see the world. Do we learn to see it as we do, or is it given? The scientific answer seems more and more to be that it is given—determined by the extraordinary architecture of the visual cortex. However, normal visual experience is critically important to the normal growth and development of this architecture" (p. 57).[7]

Complex, specialized, species-typical brain/mind mechanisms are precisely what a Darwinian view of life should lead us to anticipate, and, in fact, are what Darwinists imply when they hypothesize that acts as specific as infanticide represent adaptation.[8] Yet instead of acknowledging this, and attempting to make their assumptions explicit, many Darwinists evade potentially divisive questions of human nature by phrasing their hypotheses in the friendly terms of *culture, learning,* and *behavior,* and by emphasizing the distinction between ultimate and proximate causation. Thus evolutionary interpretations of human feeling, thought, and action remain intensely controversial although everyone professes evolutionism and developmental interactionism: The controversy, in the final analysis, is about human nature. No commitment to the proposition that the genes and the environment jointly determine the phenotype during ontogeny, however frequently, intensely, and sincerely made, can make these controversies go away if they are not really about ontogeny at all but about the nature of the phenotype.

The potential contribution of Darwinism to psychology does not lie merely in assigning ultimate causes to psychological mechanisms. Rather, as the opening quotation from Williams implies, Darwinism can aid our understanding of the mind: It guides research, prevents certain kinds of errors, inspires new questions, and calls attention to aspects of the mind that are normally too mundane or

---

[7]Human intervention can modify this architecture only by degrading or decomposing it, by turning it, in some degree, into organic "mush." With currently available techniques, the specialized edge-detecting cells in the human visual cortex can easily be prevented from developing normally; some future technology may be able to rehabilitate abnormal, dysfunctional cells; but it seems much less likely that any technology will be able to "improve" normal cells or transform them into cells with some other function. Only selection can do that. This is the level at which human nature truly can be said to be intransigent.

[8]Ironically, Darwinists, whose hypotheses about human beings almost invariably imply the existence of a richly detailed and specialized psyche, often express these hypotheses in terms so vague and flabby as to be virtually devoid of psychological content (e.g., "bonding").

uniform to be noticed (see, e.g., Barkow, 1984; Buss & Barnes, 1986; Cosmides, n.d.; Daly & Wilson, 1984). Even such a modest contribution to the formidable task of understanding the most complex thing in the known universe, the human brain/mind, surely will be welcome.

ACKNOWLEDGMENTS

I am very grateful to D. E. Brown, David Buss, Henry James, Susan Oyama and George Williams for their comments on earlier drafts of this essay.

REFERENCES

Alexander, R. D. (1975). The search for a general theory of behavior. *Behavioral Science, 20,* 77–100.

Barkow, J. H. (1984). The distance between genes and culture. *Journal of Anthropological Research, 40,* 367–379.

Buss, D. M., & Barnes, M. (1986). Preferences in human mate selection. *Journal of Personality and Social Psychology, 50,* 559–570.

Campbell, D. T. (1974). Evolutionary epistemology. In P. A. Schilpp (Ed.), *The philosophy of Karl Popper* (pp. 413–463). La Salle, IL: Open Court.

Chomsky, N. (1980). Rules and representations. *The Behavioral and Brain Sciences, 3,* 1–15.

Cosmides, L. (n.d.). Has natural selection shaped how humans reason?

Daly, M. (1982). Some caveats about cultural transmission models. *Human Ecology, 10,* 401–408.

Daly, M., & Wilson, M. (1984). A sociobiological analysis of human infanticide. In G. Hausfater & S. B. Hrdy (Eds.), *Infanticide: Comparative and evolutionary perspectives* (pp. 487–502). New York: Aldine.

Darwin, C. (1859). *On the origin of species by means of natural selection, or the preservation of favoured races in the struggle for life.* London: Watts and Co.

Darwin, C. (1871). *The descent of man and selection in relation to sex.* London: John Murray.

Dawkins, R. (1976). *The selfish gene.* Oxford: Oxford University Press.

Dawkins, R. (1982). *The extended phenotype: The gene as the unit of selection.* San Francisco: Freeman.

Dunbar, R. I. M. (1982). Adaptation, fitness and the evolutionary tautology. In King's College Sociobiology Group, Cambridge (Ed.), *Current problems in sociobiology* (pp. 9–28). New York: Cambridge University Press.

Elwood, R. W., & Ostermeyer, M. C. (1984). Infanticide by male and female Mongolian gerbils: Ontogeny, causation, and function. In G. Hausfater & S. B. Hrdy (Eds.), *Infanticide: Comparative and evolutionary perspectives* (pp. 367–386). New York: Aldine.

Flinn, M. V., & Alexander, R. D. (1982). Culture theory: The developing synthesis from biology. *Human Ecology, 10,* 383–400.

Fodor, J. A. (1980). Reply to Putnam. In *Language and learning: The debate between Jean Piaget and Noam Chomsky* (pp. 325–334). Cambridge, MA: Harvard University Press.

Fodor, J. A. (1983). *The modularity of mind: An essay on faculty psychology.* Cambridge, MA: MIT Press.

Fox, R. (1980). *The red lamp of incest.* New York: Dutton.

Gordon, M. M. (1978). *Human nature, class, and ethnicity.* New York: Oxford University Press.

Gould, S. J. (1977). *Ever since Darwin: Reflections in natural history.* New York: Norton.

Gould, S. J. (1980). *The panda's thumb.* New York: Norton.

Gould, S. J. (1983). *Hen's teeth and horse's toes.* New York: Norton.

Gould, S. J., & Lewontin, R. C. (1979). The spandrels of San Marco and the Panglossian paradigm: A critique of the adaptationist programme. *Proceedings of the Royal Society of London B, 205,* 581–598.

Hames, R. B. (1979). Relatedness and interaction among the Ye'Kwana: A preliminary analysis. In N. A. Chagnon & W. Irons (Eds.), *Evolutionary biology and human social behavior: An anthropological perspective* (pp. 239–249). North Scituate, MA: Duxbury Press.

Laughlin, C. D., Jr., & d'Aquili, E. G. (1974). *Biogenetic structuralism.* New York: Columbia University Press.

Lewontin, R. C. (1979). Sociobiology as an adaptationist program. *Behavioral Science, 24,* 5–14.

Lindblom, C. E., & Cohen, D. K. (1979). *Usable knowledge: Social science and social problem solving.* New Haven: Yale University Press.

Lloyd, J. E. (1979). Mating behavior and natural selection. The *Florida Entomologist, 62,* 17–34.

Lorenz, K. (1962). Kant's doctrine of the a priori in the light of contemporary biology. In L. Von Bertalanffy & A. Rapoport (Eds.), *General Systems, Yearbook of the Society for General Systems Research* (Vol. 7, pp. 23–35). New York: Society for General Systems Research.

Lorenz, K. (1973). *Behind the mirror: A search for a natural history of human knowledge.* New York: Harcourt Brace Jovanovich.

McGuinness, D. (1980). Male and female choice in human sexuality. *The Behavioral and Brain Sciences, 3,* 194–195.

Midgley, M. (1978). *Beast and man: The roots of human nature.* Ithaca, NY: Cornell University Press.

Murdock, G. P. (1972). Anthropology's mythology. *Proceedings of the Royal Anthropological Institute of Great Britain and Ireland for 1971,* pp. 17–24.

Ornstein, R., & Thompson, R. F. (1984). *The amazing brain.* Boston: Houghton Mifflin.

Orians, G. (1980). Habitat selection: General theory and applications to human behavior. In J. S. Lockard (Ed.), *The Evolution of Human Social Behavior* (pp. 49–66). New York: Elsevier.

Oyama, S. (1981). What does the phenocopy copy? *Psychological Reports, 48,* 571–581.

Oyama, S. (1982). A reformulation of the idea of maturation. In P. P. G. Bateson & P. H. Klopfer (Eds.), *Perspectives in ethology 5* (pp. 101–131). New York: Plenum.

Oyama, S. (1986). *The ontogeny of information: Developmental systems and evolution.* New York: Cambridge University Press.

Pulliam, H. R., & Dunford, C. (1980). *Programmed to learn: An essay on the evolution of culture.* New York: Columbia University Press.

Pylyshyn, Z. (1980). Computation and cognition: Issues in the foundation of cognitive science. *The Behavioral and Brain Sciences, 3,* 111–132.

Robinson, D. N. (1979). *Systems of modern psychology: A critical sketch.* New York: Columbia University Press.

Rosenberg, A. (1980). *Sociobiology and the preemption of social science.* Baltimore: Johns Hopkins University Press.

Shepher, J. (1983). *Incest: A biosocial view.* Orlando, FL: Academic Press.

Symons, D. (1979). *The evolution of human sexuality.* New York: Oxford University Press.

Symons, D. (1980). The evolution of human sexuality revisited. *The Behavioral and Brain Sciences, 3,* 203–211.

Symons, D. (in press). The evolutionary approach: Can Darwin's view of life shed light on human sexuality. In J. Geer & W. O'Donohue (Eds.), *Approaches and paradigms in human sexuality.* New York: Plenum Press.

van den Berghe, P. L., & Frost, P. (1986). Skin color preference, sexual dimorphism, and sexual selection: a case of gene-culture co-evolution? *Ethnic and Racial Studies, 9,* 87–113.

Washburn, S. L. (1976). Comment on D. T. Campbell's 'On the conflicts between biological and social evolution and between psychology and moral tradition.' *American Psychologist, 31,* 353–355.

Williams, G. C. (1966). *Adaptation and natural selection.* Princeton, NJ: Princeton University Press.

Williams, G. C. (1979). The question of adaptive sex ratio in outcrossed vertebrates. *Proceedings of the Royal Society of London B, 205,* 567–580.

Ziman, J. (1978). *Reliable knowledge: An exploration of the grounds for belief in science.* Cambridge: Cambridge University Press.

6 What Can Genes Do?

John L. Fuller
State University of New York at Binghamton

It is likely that some persons attribute more importance to genes than most behavior geneticists do. For them, Ben's quick temper was inherited from his grandfather, and Lucy's artistic talent from her Aunt Mabel. True, children do tend to resemble their parents physically and in IQ scores, and a large body of research supports the thesis that such similarities are heritable. Some early investigators of the inheritance of behavioral characteristics were convinced that their own social or ethnic group owed its dominance to superior genes. Immigration laws were based on this assumption and some eugenicists urged sterilization of mentally deficient persons in order to improve the quality of the human species.

These extreme views are no longer held by scientists interested in the genetics of behavior. However, the nature-nurture issue has not disappeared even among scientists, and it is unlikely to do so (Fuller, 1982). What should disappear is the idea that nature and nurture (or genes and environment) are opposing forces. A more acceptable view is that the course of an individual's life is guided by interactions between his or her genotype and the physical and social environments. In interactive systems the effects of environment on individuals vary with their genotypes. Likewise, identical genotypes do not ensure identical phenotypes. Neither do identical environments.

GENETIC APPROACHES TO BEHAVIOR

The rediscovery of Mendel's research on the inheritance of color and form in garden peas led to the concepts of genes, chromosomes, dominance and recessivity. For a time there appeared to be a contradiction between the Mendelian

147

particulate approach to the inheritance of alternative characters such as pigmentation, and biometrical analysis of quantitative characters such as size. It was soon demonstrated that biometrics and mendelism were compatible as it was demonstrated that quantitative variation in a character could be explained by summation of the effects of multiple genes. Some alleles could enhance and others reduce characters such as height, weight, and various behavioral traits.

Both Mendelian and quantitative genetics play an important role in artificial selection for desired qualities in domesticated animals and plants. Individuals with the characteristics desired by a breeder are mated; others leave no descendants. For Darwin artificial selection was a model for natural selection, the difference being that natural selection was for the benefit of the species; artificial selection for the benefit of the breeder. Evolution by natural selection is now universally accepted by biologists, although there are still disagreements on the mechanisms. Ethologists tend to emphasize selection of individuals (e.g., Williams, 1966), but some biologists believe that group selection is also important, particularly when small populations are separated by physical barriers. Most evolutionists think of evolution as the selection of alleles rather than individuals. The argument is that it is genes that are faithfully replicated, not genotypes (e.g., Dawkins, 1976). (Actually, gene mutations in gametes are an exception. Most such mutations are deleterious to their owners, but some hopeful ones become a part of evolution.) Genotypes can be replicated by cloning or by close brother-sister mating. The outcome of such inbreeding cannot be predicted completely but it has produced inbred lines that differ reliably in behavior, and have proved to be useful for researchers.

The Nature of Genes.   The chemical composition and helical structure of genes was only discovered in 1953 by Watson and Crick. Thirty years later it is possible to write the chemical formula of many genes, and manipulate them so that they can be transferred from one species to another. We ascribe no sense of purpose to a gene any more than we do to a die that stamps out pennies. A gene is merely a complex molecule capable of processing raw materials in a specific way, and of synthesizing duplicates of itself. The importance of replication is basic for geneticists. Many of our genes are copies of those that originated before humans or even mammals existed. Some may have originated during our own life span, the result of radiation or chemical factors changing the structure of our inherited genes.

From one point of view this chapter could end here. Biochemistry has reduced gene action to the provision of information for the synthesis of polypeptides via RNA. An organism, of course, is more than a random collection of miscellaneous molecules. It is an integrated system of cells, tissues, and organs whose development is guided by genes. At appropriate points during development genes are turned on and off (Britten & Davidson, 1969, 1971; Davidson & Britten, 1973). In a mature organism, except for the reproductive cells, only a part of the total genotype is active within any one cell. The orderliness of development depends on the exchange of information among a class of genes known as regulators. These have been investigated primarily in simple organisms, but they must also be essential for the orderly assemblage of cells, tissues, and organs. It is tempting to compare a genotype with a computer program that enables a robot to construct additional similar robots from a store of parts. However, the analogy is not helpful for understanding the relation of genes to behavior.

GENES, BEHAVIOR, AND EVOLUTION

The origins of life on our planet have not yet been explained. Despite progress in biochemistry not even a primitive, unicellular organism has been synthesized from inorganic, or even organic, compounds. Once reproducing organisms appeared, their characteristics were transmitted via molecules of DNA or in some viruses by RNA. Increases in diversity are almost universally attributed to natural selection. For all organisms with which psychologists are concerned DNA functions to transmit information from one generation to another, with RNA acting as a link between DNA (genes) and the polypeptides that play so important a role in physical development. Random mutation of genes occurred constantly (and still does) because of radiation, temperature changes, and contact with mutagenic chemicals. Some of these mutations enabled their possessors to move into new habitats; others led to the extinction of their bearers. The variety of organisms can be ascribed to the diversity of terrestrial and aquatic environments that were available. Naturalists are well aware that the survival of a species depends on the degree to which its members can find a suitable environment. This does not mean that natural selection has produced optimal adaptations, although ethologists are sometimes accused of accepting an "adaptational fallacy" (Gould, 1980; Lewontin, 1979). Obviously organisms must be adapted to their environment in order to survive and reproduce, but there need not be a designer (Dawkins, 1982).

Behavior must have played an important role in evolution from the very beginning of life on earth. Mutations that led to better utilization of an environment would tend to increase. Changes in motor skills and sensory capacity that are based on the nervous system were important. Detailed changes in the nervous system left no fossils, but the evolution of brain size in vertebrates has been deduced from the cranium. Natural selection worked on the fate of any gene-related innovation whether it modified a carnivore's dentition to make it a more efficient killer, or a neural change that enabled it to stalk quietly and strike quickly. This is what Skinner (1981) calls "selection by consequences." He notes many similarities between operant conditioning and natural selection. In the operant situation an individual confronted with a new problem makes varied responses from a number of possible alternatives. Rewarded responses increase in frequency; non-rewarded ones decrease. As applied to the evolutionary process genes mutate and gene combinations are regularly reshuffled in meiosis and mating. Some gene combinations increase the ability of their owner to leave more than the average number of descendants. It should be noted here that natural selection has had an effect on operant learning (Shettleworth, 1972). All stimuli are not created equal as elicitors of a conditioned response. It is not far fetched to argue that the behavioral consequences of a genetic innovation are the major agents of natural selection, and that structural changes are selected primarily on their behavioral effects (Alexander, 1974).

A Classification of Phenotypes.
Just as a genotype is an individual's collection of genes, its phenotype is its total observable qualities. The word is also used in a specific sense to name characteristics ranging from the molecular structure of a protein to performance on psychological tests. In the first instance it is sometimes possible to deduce the structure of the gene that guides the synthesis of that protein. There is no such relation between a gene and a behavior, because behavior always involves interactions among structures that have different ontogenetic histories. Genes can be matched with polypeptides, but not for complex structures and functions. Some alleles produce syndromes such as phenylpyruvic dementia. If not treated the individual is mentally and physically retarded. The consequences of a double dose of an allele that cannot deal with phenylalanine go far beyond the chemical imbalance. Mental and physical development is seriously affected. Fortunately in this particular situation physicians can prescribe a low phenylalanine diet that ameliorates the consequences of the genetic defect. In such circumstances human intervention changes an individual's phenotype without altering the genotype. The day may come when gene therapy involving incorporation of genes into a deficient genome will compensate for such inherited deficiences, but I doubt that it will become a major boon to the human species. For the time being, at least, we must get along with the genes given us by our parents, and phenotypes that come with them.

I have proposed a classification of phenotypes based on the criteria by which they are recognized (Fuller, 1979). The following scheme is essentially the same, but nomenclature has been changed for etymological consistency. A *phene* is any identifiable component of an individual's total phenotype. *Somatophenes* are based on physical characteristics and include two classes: *chemophenes* defined by their molecular structure, and *morphenes* identified as physical structures of complex composition and form. Finger-ridge count, number of digits, and brain size are examples. *Physiophenes* are functions such as blood pressure, brain waves, and secretion rates that may correlate with behavior, but are of primary interest to physiologists rather than psychologists. *Ethophenes* are behavioral characteristics that can be measured quantitatively by a qualified observer. (I originally called these *ostensible psychophenes*.) *Psychophenes* are attributes or traits that are inferred from correlations among ethophenes that have common features. (I originally called these *inferred psychophenes.*) The response time of a rat to a signal paired with shock is an ethophene. Using this value as a measure of emotionality implies that the rat can be ranked as high or low on a trait that is involved in other stressful situations. The response may be different depending on the stress and the available responses, but emotional subjects will react consistently in a variety of situations. When we record the number of correct responses on an intelligence test we are reporting an ethophene. When we convert this to an IQ score we are inferring that there is a trait of intelligence.

The purpose of this classification is not to add more terms to an already overloaded vocabulary, but to recognize the variability of the genotype-phenotype relationship; specific and direct for chemophenes, multiple and indirect for ethophenes and psychophenes. As one moves from chemophenes to psychophenes the contribution of the environment to the phenotype becomes more significant. The environment is always important—a hemoglobin gene cannot produce hemoglobin in the absence of iron—and it is also critical in the development of ethophenes and psychophenes. Any answer to the question of "what do genes do?" requires knowledge of the environment in which an organism develops and lives. The complexities of development and the complexities of the polygenic systems that are involved in producing the sensory, neural, and hormonal systems assure that behavior genetics will always be a "softer" science than most areas of genetics. For psychology, however, and perhaps also for evolutionary theory, the contribution of genes to behavioral differences and uniformities is very important.

BEHAVIOR GENETICS: AN OVERVIEW

Behavior genetics has been recognized as a discipline for less than 30 years, although the inheritance of psychological traits had attracted interest in the mid-19th century. And long before the scientific era animal breeders selected domestic animals for temperament and skills: dogs for sheep herding or tracking game; horses for hauling carts and for racing. Fuller and Thompson (1960) summarized the field in its emergent phase. More recent general accounts include Ehrman & Parsons (1981), Fuller & Thompson, (1978), and Plomin, DeFries, & McClearn (1980). Over 50 edited collections of symposia, solicited chapters, and monographs on particular issues have appeared. The genetics of behavior along with sociobiology is an expanding area of research and discussion. Although both of these disciplines involve genes their objectives differ. Sociobiology, the main theme of this volume, is primarily interested in the "ultimate" causation of social behavior and organization. To achieve this purpose sociobiologists try to reconstruct the evolution of behavior through population genetics and concepts such as inclusive fitness, and reciprocal altruism. Male and female differences in mating behavior are attributed to their relative investments in reproduction. Parental care, when it exists, is explained as an adaptation to increase the likelihood that parental genes will be passed on. The prevalence of monogamous mating in birds is attributed to the advantage of dual parenting when food must be gathered and brought to immature nestlings. The rarity of monogamy in mammals arises from the fact that in most species a lactating female can provide for her offspring without aid, thus allowing her mate to further his inclusive fitness by seeking other females (Trivers, 1972; Williams, 1966). General accounts of sociobiological theory can be found in Barash (1977), Clutton-Brock and Harvey (1978), and Wilson (1975).

Sociobiologists have not been particularly involved with identifying the genes that modify behavior, discovering physiological pathways between genes and behavior, or explaining individual behavioral differences within a species. Behavior geneticists are concerned with such problems, and with genotype-environmental interactions from fertilization, through development, and finally to aging and death. It is possible to do good work in either of the two disciplines without much regard for the other. Both employ a similar body of knowledge about genes and behavior. Both are in a sense reductionist, but neither advocates complete genetic or environmental determinism, although they have been charged with such beliefs. I believe, however, that more intercommunication between the two disciplines would benefit both. Before pointing to specifics it is useful to discuss briefly the branches of genetics that have been applied to the study of behavior.

Objectives of Behavior Genetics.   Geneticists investigate genetic influences on behavior in a variety of ways. One of the most familiar is the calculation of the *heritability* of characters in a specified population. A second objective is the determination of the genetic locus or chromosome associated with a heritable behavioral characteristic. A third is the analysis of interactions between genotypes and environments. With animals this is done by observing the behavioral effects of varying environments on the behavior of individuals from different selected or inbred strains. With humans it is impossible to control either the genetic or environmental variable experimentally, but some information can be gathered using degrees of relationship to estimate genetic similarity, and life-history data to evaluate the environment. Although there is interest in the role of behavior as a factor in evolution (Wilson, 1975, p. 13) it is difficult to test hypotheses experimentally. Behavior leaves few fossils beyond footprints, and the genotypes of extinct species are lost forever. Perhaps the best evidence for Wilson's thesis is the success in prehistoric times of selection for behavioral traits (many of them social) in domestic animals, and recently in laboratory species such as rats, mice, and drosophila.

Experimental behavior genetics is restricted to nonhuman animals. Drosophila and house mice are favorite subjects because their genes and chromosomes are well studied; they are adapted to laboratory rearing, and many selected lines are available. Rats, dogs, domestic fowl, and even paramecia are among other species that have received attention. Human behavior genetics must rely on comparisons of monozygotic and dizygotic twins, natural and adopted children in the same family, and correlations among individuals with differing degrees of relationship. Obviously Nature's "experiments" with humans are not designed to test genetic hypotheses rigorously. One must rely on consistency of the results of carefully designed studies in a wide variety of situations. Despite limitations to an experimental approach to human behavior genetics we now have a large body of evidence supporting the thesis that genes are responsible for a significant part of behavioral variation in our own species.

The variability of human behavior, particularly social behavior, poses problems for both behavior genetics and sociobiology. One can find credible explanations based on genetic selection for the prevalence of monogamy in perching birds and its absence in mammalian herbivores, but it is difficult to explain the variety of human marriage arrangements by gene selection. Nevertheless Van den Berghe (1979) has made a case for reconciling the variety of human family systems with sociobiological theory. Humans have evolved a complex nervous system that is programmed by experience and the consequences of an individual's actions. Even the most radical advocate of genetic determination of behavior acknowledges that much of human behavior is shaped by cultural surroundings and individual experience. This kind of learned adaptation to an environment is frequently found in animals also but to a lesser degree (Morse, 1981).

METHODS IN BEHAVIOR GENETICS

This section describes in simplified terms the methods of genetics that are most relevant to behavior. For more detailed accounts of techniques and their results see Ehrman & Parsons (1981), Fuller & Thompson (1978), Plomin, DeFries, & McClearn (1980), and Hay (1985).

Mendelian and Chromosomal Genetics.   The Mendelian approach to behavior genetics concentrates on the identification of loci that affect behavior. Many behavioral anomalies are associated with homozygosity of recessive genes. Such genes are usually rare in natural populations, but can be maintained readily in laboratory animals. Waltzing mice and human phenylketonuria are familiar examples. Other disorders such as Huntington's chorea are associated with a single dominant gene. This disease, which causes severe degeneration of the nervous system in middle age, persists because its symptoms are often not recognized before the affected person has reproduced. The number of identifiable heritable syndromes affecting the nervous and endocrine systems and thereby affecting behavior is constantly growing, as new mutations occur and existing ones are identified.

Chromosomal anomalies also have behavioral effects. The most common of these is Down's syndrome with a frequency of about 1% in children born to women over 40. It is caused by an extra chromosome 21 that was transmitted when the pair failed to separate during meiosis. Thus, the alternate name of trisomy-21. A rare form of Down's syndrome occurs when chromosome 21 is attached to another large chromosome. A woman bearing this translocation has a high risk of bearing a Down child at any age.

Although sociobiology is based on a genetic theory of natural selection, and genes and chromosomes are the fundamental units of genetics, sociobiologists make little use of gene catalogs and chromosome maps. They seem to accept the hypothesis that genes affect behavior, and that mutations are the agents for inducing change in behavior. But while they postulate genes for altruism or aggression, they make little attempt to locate these genes on a particular chromosome nor to identify their biochemical effects. Behavior geneticists, when dealing with differences in emotional, social, and cognitive behaviors generally fall back on statistical analysis of the results of tests rather than gene analysis. Genetic counselors and physicians do use the genic and chromosomal approach for dealing with clearly defined pathologies. There is now some interaction between behavior geneticists and neuropsychologists.

Biochemical Genetics.   A gene is an organized section of DNA (deoxyribonucleic acid) that codes for the structure of a polypeptide. Small polypeptides often serve as neurotransmitters or modulators. Larger ones are proteins with structural, motor, and other vital functions. The fields known as psychiatric genetics (Motulsky & Omenn, 1975) and psychopharmacogenetics (Horowitz & Dudek, 1983) seek to find a biochemical basis for susceptibility to psychoses and drug addictions. Although ethical and logistic problems limit research on humans there is strong evidence that chemical factors play an important role in these serious disorders. In animals experiments have clearly demonstrated genetic differences in behavioral and physiological responses to opiates and alcohol (Horowitz & Dudek, 1983). Whereas earlier animal research concentrated on genetic differences in the enzymes that participate in the metabolism of these substances, attention is now being given also to possible heritable variation in neurotransmitters.

Heritable variation in catecholamines and adrenal steroids have been linked with schizophrenia and depressive disorders. An introduction to this field is available in a collection of review papers dealing with biological factors in mental disorders (Fieve, Rosenthal, & Brill, 1975). Biochemical genetics is a lively area of research with behavioral connotations, but it has played little role in sociobiology. Perhaps it will eventually. Variations in sexual behavior, caretaking, and aggression are important aspects of social behavior, and hormones and neurotransmitters are important influences in such behavior. For the moment, however, the reduction of differences in social behavior to biochemistry is limited, and may remain so.

Quantitative Genetics and Heritability.   Many of the behaviors studied by geneticists vary quantitatively. There is no sharp line separating maze-bright and maze-dull rats, nor aggressive and peaceful humans. Selective breeding in animals has clearly shown that quantitative traits can be altered by mating like with like. Classic examples are selection of rats for maze-brightness (Tryon, 1940) and open-field activity and emotionality (Broadhurst, 1960). But, long before there was a science of genetics, breeds of horses and dogs were selected for specialized behavioral characteristics that made them more useful to humans.

I shall consider here how allele frequencies and dominance relationships affect the distribution of phenotypes in a random-breeding population, and the correlation of phenotypes in relatives. These are the factors that enter into the concept we call heritability. The following section is greatly simplified, but it covers the basic principles. Consider a phenotype, Stature (S) that is influenced by alleles at a locus, Height, with two alleles, H and h. Each H allele increases S by one inch; an h decreases S by the same amount. When the frequencies of H and h are equal the frequencies of the genotypes are: HH (.25); Hh, (.50); and hh (.25). Their phenotypes are HH, $(S + 2)$; Hh, (S); and hh, $(S - 2)$. The mean value of the phenotype is S. This is an example of additive gene action. When gene frequencies are the same, but additive gene action is replaced by complete dominance of H over h, the relation of phenotype to genotype changes. Now the phenotypes are: HH, $(S + 2)$; Hh, $(S + 2)$; and hh, $(S - 2)$. Although gene frequencies are the same as in the additive example, the average Stature of the group is substantially higher.

Changes in allele frequencies also affect the distribution of phenotypes. Using the additive model consider a population where the frequency of H is .75, and of h, .25. Now the frequencies of the three genotypes are: HH, (.5625); Hh, (.3750); and hh, (.0625). When mating continues at random, and environmental factors remain the same, genotypic frequencies will be stable from generation to generation. Phenotypic frequencies will also tend to be stable, but environmental factors can cause differences. The increase of human stature in the industrial nations over the past century is due more to better nutrition and medical care than to genetic selection.

Heritability is a widely used term in quantitative genetics that is often misinterpreted by nongeneticists. It is not a fixed attribute of a phenotype such as intelligence or emotionality. Instead it varies with the genetic composition of the population and environment in which it is measured. In general, heritability will be lower in a population of genetically similar individuals, and higher in a genetically heterogeneous group. It can be formally defined as the proportion of phenotypic variance of a character attributable to additive gene differences in a specified population. Heritability in the narrow sense deals only with the sum of additive factors as discrete loci. Broad heritability is higher and includes the effects of dominance at heterozygous loci, and interactions among different loci. Broad heritability overstates the potential for changing phenotypes by selection.

Heritability is estimated by measuring the regression of phenotypic scores of offspring on the scores of their parents. It turns out that in a simple additive system with random mating each parental combination contributes its own phenotypic as well as its genetic characters to the next generation. In a dominance system this is not so. For example an *Hh* by *Hh* mating (both phenotypically tall) will, on the average, produce 1/4 *hh* offspring with below normal height. In such a situation parent-offspring correlations are reduced, and heritability decreased. Geneticists consider that dominance of an allele indicates that it has been selected to pass on characters of benefit to its owners with only one rather than two fitness enhancing genes.

So many techniques have been developed for the estimation of heritabilities that it is impractical to describe them here. In humans, correlations between parents and offspring, comparisons of pair similarity in monozygotic and dizygotic twins, and correlations between natural and adopted children are best known. All of these have problems but, in general, the methods produce similar results. In animals similar procedures can be used with a much greater degree of control in both genotypes and environmental history. Behavioral heritabilities can be calculated from the results of selection from a genetically heterogeneous base stock. The availability of a large number of genetically homogeneous strains in some species allows interstrain crosses, backcrosses of hybrids to parents, and specialized procedures such as diallel and triple-test crosses. (For information on methods see the general sources already mentioned and consult recent issues of journals such as *Behavior Genetics.*)

Reiterating the fact that heritability is an estimate of the contribution of additive genic affects to the variance of a specific phenotype in a defined population in a particular environment, it is clear that it is a statistical concept and not a constant like molecular weight. Even in animal research where genotypes, environments, and behavioral phenotypes can be controlled, respected workers still argue about the legitamacy of their assumptions (Drewek & Broadhurst, 1983; Whitney, McClearn, & DeFries, 1982). For the most part, however, differing measures of heritability are in general agreement. The same is generally true with recent estimates of heritabilities in human populations. Erlenmeyer-Kimling and Jarvik (1963) collated the results of many studies on the heritability of intelligence, and showed that the means of these were close to that predicted by genetic theory. One would expect that there would be considerable variability among different populations and different tests. Not all scientists agree with the conclusion that intelligence is heritable, and strong objections have been raised (Feldman & Lewontin, 1975; Kamin, 1974; Layzer, 1974). It should be noted that none of these individuals has worked in the field of behavior genetics. They are, however, competent scientists in related fields. For a sympathetic, but still critical, appraisal of the heritability of human intelligence see Scarr & Carter-Saltzman (1983). Rejectors of the heritability hypothesis of intelligence are on the nurture side of the long lasting nature-nurture controversy. Others have presented evidence against the extreme environmentalist theory of differences in intelligence (e.g., Erlenmeyer-Kimling, 1972).

I have written elsewhere that the nature-nurture issue is not a pseudo-problem, nor a clash between incompatible explanations (Fuller, 1982). Variations in behavior cannot be explained by reducing them to differences in an individuals genotype, or to details of environmental history. A more sensible view is that these two sources of information are jointly responsible for the state of the neural machinery that organizes behavior, and determines responses to external and internal stimuli.

Threshold Characters.   Many physical and behavioral characteristics are neither inherited in a Mendelian manner nor distributed along a continuum. Cleft palate and some psychiatric disorders are examples in which individuals can be classified as impaired or normal. The general explanation of such traits is that numerous genes are involved and that their combined effects determine the degree of susceptibility to environmental stressors. In the cleft palate case an embryo at the high end of the susceptibility distribution has a high risk of malformation even in a normal pregnancy; at the other end the fetus can tolerate considerable stress and develop normally. Similarly, identical twins may be discordant for schizophrenia, even though their genotypes are the same. The diasthesis-stress theory is widely accepted by many workers in the field of psychiatry (Gottesman & Shields, 1972). Actually it is difficult to determine whether a threshold is regulated by a polygenic system in which many loci participate, or by a single locus with several alleles. As an example Elston and Campbell (1970) favored a single locus hypothesis for schizophrenia, but admitted that the evidence was not conclusive. Kidd and Cavalli-Sforza (1973) favored a polygenic hypothesis, but could not disprove the single-locus explanation. The matter could probably be settled by planned genetic experiments if schizophrenia was a disorder of mice, but it may never be resolved in humans.

As an example the genetics of audiogenic seizures in mice has been widely studied. When subjected to a strong, high-pitched sound many young mice run wildly about their enclosure and in a few seconds go into a clonic or tonic seizure. The phenotype is similar to some forms of human epilepsy. There are marked differences in risk, ranging from near zero to nearly 100%, related to genotype and age. Early investigators emphasized single or two-locus explanations for these differences; others favored a polygenic threshold model (Fuller, Easler, & Smith, 1950). Thirty years later Seyfried, Yu, and Glazer (1980) using recombinant inbred strains found that the genes relevant to susceptibility were distributed among several chromosomes. My personal belief is that most of the behavioral characteristics studied by psychologists and sociobiologists are affected by numerous genes and that interactions among these genes influence an organism's sensitivity to its environment and regulate the level of its response. It would be too strong to state that every locus affects every behavior, but reasonable to conclude that every locus has effects that influence a number of phenotypic characters (somatophenes, ethophenes, or psychophenes), and that every phene (possibly omitting chemophenes) is the product of a number of genes.

Population Genetics.   Population genetics deals with the frequency and distribution of alleles within a population. The account here is greatly simplified and can be supplemented by the general texts already cited and, for those who wish to go further, by *The Genetics of Human Populations* (Cavalli-Sforza & Bodmer, 1971). A good starting point is the Hardy-Weinberg equilibrium. We assume a large, random-mating population in which the frequency of allele A is p and of a is q ($q = 1 - p$). The probabilities of the three genotypes at this locus are: AA, p^2; Aa, $2pq$; and aa, q^2. Assuming a large population, equal fertility in the three genotypes, and equal probability of survival of offspring, the values of p and q, and the frequencies of the three genotypes will remain stable indefinitely aside from random fluctuations. In the real world deviations from these assumptions are common and probably universal, but Hardy-Weinberg is still useful as an explanation of the stability found in populations.

For our purposes the most important deviation is assortative mating in which individuals mate preferentially rather than randomly. For the most part like tends to mate with like so that the proportion of homozygotes, AA and aa increases. Assortative mating is found in Drosophila (Petit & Ehrman, 1969); snow geese (Cooke, Finney, & Rockwell, 1976); mice (Yanai & McClearn, 1973), and humans (Eckland, 1968; Vandenberg, 1972). Assortative mating is generally based on phenotypes and generally acts on genotype rather than gene frequencies. If any genotype, say aa, regularly decreases the reproductive success of its bearers the frequency of allele a will decrease relative to allele A. Suppose that aa individuals are sterile. When a is common it will decrease rapidly, but as it becomes rare the value of q is so small that the elimination of a by selection is countered by the occurence of new mutations from A to a. At equilibrium the rate of mutation $m = 2q$.

Real populations do not behave as simply as these models, but the models do provide insight into the mechanisms of natural and artificial selection. Somehow, over time, additions and deletions of genes from the genotypes of the past have led to speciation. We tend to think of evolution as moving toward forms of higher complexity of behavior and increased "intelligence," but evolution does not always work that way. Many parasitic worms evolved from free living ancestors. Although they are specialized for their parasitic life, we would scarcely think of them as more advanced than their ancestors. In other lines of descent there has been a trend toward greater complexity and flexibility of behavior, and with it an increase in the amount of DNA in the genome.

Sociobiology assumes that the evolutionary process was essentially like the selection process now practiced by humans with their domestic animals, but guided by impersonal natural selection rather than by the objectives of humans to better their own welfare. In seeking "ultimate explanations" of the social behavior of humans and other animals it falls back on population genetics to account for their evolution from ancestral forms. Unfortunately behavior leaves few fossils and its evolution cannot be traced as readily as the evolution of structure. This has not dissuaded a number of biologists, and a few psychologists and anthropologists, from trying to explain present-day behavior, particularly social relationships, by invoking the concept of evolution by natural selection. For these individuals there is a basic human nature that has been shaped by an impersonal selective process over the past million years or so.

Developmental Genetics. Although a fertilized ovum contains the instructions for the development of a mature organism it requires a benign environment and a source of energy. Development involves cell division (except for unicellular forms, which are of minor interest to psychologists), functional and structural differentiation, and integration of these processes to produce tissues, organs, and finally an individual. In this process the totipotent zygote is replaced by a community of heterogeneous cell types, each with a specialized and restricted function. In humans erythopoetic cells generate blood corpuscles throughout life, and Leydig cells produce testosterone. Both have descended from the same pluripotent cell. Cell and organ differentiation involve an orderly process of selective activation and inactivation of genes in what looks like a preprogrammed process.

The orderliness of normal development implies an overall program that coordinates cellular changes as though directed by a program, but the source of this program has not been identified. A start has been made with a theory of activation and inactivation in various tissues (Britten & Davidson, 1969; Davidson & Britten, 1973), but the integrative mechanisms that operate from fertilization until maturity are not well understood. It is clear that maturation in a species varies adaptively among species. Chicks can run about and forage for themselves soon after hatching. Young housemice open their eyes 11–14 days after birth and become truly mobile during the third week. Human infants must be fed and protected for several years in order to survive. Evolutionary theory postulates that these sequences are gene-regulated and the product of natural selection. Over the life span of an individual the genetic contribution to its behavior changes in a manner that maximizes the likelihood of that individual's genes being passed on to its descendants. A good example is the finding that low activity in infant mice is dominant over high activity: in adults the opposite is found (Henderson, 1978). Remaining quietly in the nest is adaptive for helpless infants; exploratory activity is needed by older individuals. For a simple organism with high fecundity all that is necessary for survival and reproduction is a program for responding correctly to a small set of stimuli. A small set of reflexive responses will do the job. In unpredictable and complex environments a better way is to incorporate a decision-making program into the nervous system that integrates information from the environment before responding. A program of this sort will change over time as the individual and its environment also change.

Mayr (1974) divided behavioral programs in two classes: open and closed. Closed programs are carried out regardless of experiential history and result in the "fixed action patterns" of classical ethology. Open programs are strongly influenced by experience, and some of the programming may be possible only during a critical or sensitive period (Scott, 1962). An opposing view holds that behavioral development is a continuous process and that critical periods have no real status (Schneirla & Rosenblatt, 1963). My own view is that there is a continuity between sharp breaks in development (e.g., insect metamorphosis) and the gradual appearance of more and more complex motor skills and social attributes in most vertebrates. Bateson (1979) expresses his opinion well in these words: "Wholesale reorganization of behavior can occur as the ecology of the animal changes with age . . . So the experiences that exert . . . a profound effect on behaviour at one stage may fail totally to carry over into adulthood." At the extremes it is possible to distinguish between closed programs such as suckling in the human infant, and open programs such as the acquisition of a grammar and vocabulary that begins early in life and persists throughout life. Programs differ greatly depending on the rules of the language. Openess to programming is a relative concept. Children acquire skills in several languages more readily than adults, but it not impossible for adults to become competent in a new language if they are sufficiently motivated.

EMPIRICAL STUDIES

To this point I have emphasized the techniques of behavior genetics, their uses and their limitations. This section provides a sample of experiments that demonstrate correlations between genes and behavioral differences. These examples feature animal studies because controlled experiments with humans are not feasible. This does not mean that the genetics of human behavior cannot be studied with profit. Much good work is being done with family, twin, and adoption methods. The results of these studies clearly demonstrate that genes have significant influence on personality and cognitive functions, but a discussion of them would require another chapter.

I shall begin with a scientist who never heard of genes, let alone DNA, or techniques for measuring heritability. Charles Darwin used "inherited changes of habit or instinct in domesticated animals" as the major support for his theory of natural selection. With respect to dogs he wrote: "Young pointers . . . will sometimes point . . . the very first time they are taken out; retrieving is certainly to some extent inherited by retrievers; and a tendency to run round, instead of at, a flock of sheep by shepherd dogs." "Domestic instincts . . . are far less fixed than natural instincts, but they have been acted on by far less rigorous selection" (Darwin, 1859/1927). As additional evidence for the importance of heredity he wrote: "These domestic instincts, when they are tested by crossing, resemble natural instincts . . . and for a long period exhibit traces of the instincts of either parent."

Domestication. More than a century later, aided by a new understanding of genetics, Scott and Fuller (1965) reported the results of a 10-year study comparing five breeds of dogs on formal tests of emotional reactivity, socialization, trainability, and problem solving. Significant differences among breeds were found in all areas. In problem solving, breeds differed depending on the nature of the problem and the responses required, but there was no evidence of differences in general intelligence. A cross between the two most different breeds yielded hybrids that were intermediate to the parents on many social and learning measures. For the most part the results confirmed the opinions of dog breeders and owners, and were compatible with Darwin's inferences from field observations. Although the concept of instinct is now out of fashion something like it seems to be passed on by genes. It should also be noted that Scott and Fuller also carried out experiments demonstrating that experience (or lack of it) at certain stages of development, had important influence on later behavior. They noted that genetic contributions to differences in behavior did not imply genetic determinism.

It is interesting that most animals that have been domesticated come from a few taxonomic groups (Hale, 1969). These include Bovids (sheep, goats, etc.), Galliformes (chickens, turkeys), and Carnivora (cats, canines). Favorable preexisting characteristics for domestication of a species are large social groups, hierarchically organized with male dominance, and promiscuous mating. Also important is the capacity for cross-species bonding at a young age (particularly important in house pets), and adaptability to a variety of foods and environments.

Domesticated animals generally are protected from the rigors of exposure to severe environments, and their social contacts with conspecifics are often restricted. It is commonly believed that social and survival skills of domesticated animals have degenerated through disuse. This belief may not be justified. Albino rats, exposed to outdoor living during a severe winter, coped with its problems in the same way as wild rats (Boice, 1981). The albinos maintained a stable population, constructed burrows, and behaved like wild rats. Feral domestic rats are practically identical to wild rats in social behavior (Boice, 1981). Price (1969) carried out a similar experiment comparing wild and semidomesticated deer mice. He concluded that the domestication process should not affect behaviors unrelated to characters that are subject to selection. If a character has a radically different relation to fitness in conditions of captivity and the wild, and if there is genetic variance for that character, selection will occur. If there is insufficient genetic variance in a wild population domestication must await a suitable mutation.

A comparison of mating displays in mallard ducks (*Anas platyrhyncos*) and closely related, long time domesticated, Peking ducks is of particular interest since it pertains to highly stylized behavior patterns. Miller (1977) placed Peking ducks in a natural environment and gave them an opportunity to perform the courtship rituals characteristic of mallards. Pekings differ physically from mallards in a number of ways that would seem to cause difficulties in performing complex displays. They are heavier, flightless, and have lost the striking sexual-plumage dimorphism of mallards. Nevertheless they performed all the species-typical displays in the same sequences that are characteristic of mallards. Miller concluded that there is no justification for the view that domestication leads to degeneration of social behavior patterns. He ascribes their usual nonoccurence in Pekings to the barrenness of the environments in which they are usually reared.

In summary, a good case can be made for the hypothesis that the genetic substrate for behavior is stable, and that the behavioral changes that accompany domestication are largely attributable to environment. Disuse of a particular skill because of the lack of opportunity to display it need not imply the loss of the capacity for its appearance in suitable circumstances. If this hypothesis is true, and if it applies to modern humans, its implications are at least amusing, and either disquieting or reassuring to those of us who speculate on the future of our species.

Behavioral Selection in Laboratory Animals.   The classic example of genetic selection for a behavioral characteristic in a laboratory is Tryon's work on "maze-brightness" in rats. Summaries of his numerous papers are found in most elementary psychology texts, and in Tryon (1940). Selection for high- and low-error scores in a 17-unit maze was successful, and hybrids between the "bright" and "dull" lines scored at an intermediate level. Tryon and his associates tested the generality of problem learning ability by comparing bright and dull rats on different problems. They found that maze-running ability was specific to the situation on which selection had been based. Tryon concluded that: "Maze learning is specific. The doctrine of alleged 'general ability' supported by many psychologists has not been substantiated in rats."

Another long-term selection program using rats was based on the measurement of "emotionality" by the amount of defecation when subjects were placed is a brightly illuminated, unfamiliar open-field (Broadhurst, 1960). Two lines, designated as the Maudsley reactive (MR), and Maudsley nonreactive (MNR) were produced. They have been widely used in experiments by Broadhurst, his students, and many others. In a review of the results of 280 studies with these lines, Broadhurst (1975) concluded that the MR and MNR lines differed significantly on a variety of behavioral, psychophysiological, psychopharmacological, and psychoendocrinological measures. In most of these studies the differences between the lines were in the direction predicted from the concept of a general trait of emotional reactivity. In a minority of experiments the results were ambiguous or contrary to the Broadhurst hypothesis. See Fuller and Thompson (1978) for a discussion of criticisms of the generality of a trait of emotionality. Regardless of disputes over the generality of Broadhurst's emotionality concept, it is clear that genetic selection can produce large heritable differences in response to stressful situations.

The high-activity and low-activity mice selected by DeFries and his collaborators react differently in a number of situations that involve placement in an open field (DeFries, Gervais, & Thomas, 1978; DeFries, Wilson, & McClearn, 1970). In confining situations and in exercise wheels the lines do not differ in activity. After 30 generations there is no overlap of activity scores in the open field between the two lines. Much of the difference was attributed to the albino gene (c) that was fixed in the low-activity line, and almost eliminated in the high-activity line (DeFries, Gervais, & Thomas, 1978). The active and inactive open-field lines showed no differences in rate of avoidance learning, nor in amount of running in a wheel. Inactive mice were slower in traversing a Lashley III maze, but were equal to Actives in error scores (Streng, 1974). As in other selection experiments some behaviors were unchanged. Others, not specifically selected, moved in a direction that suggested common relationships with the criterion phenotype.

More relevant to sociobiology than emotionality and activity is aggressive behavior. Selection of bulls and cocks for fighting has a long history that precedes behavior genetics by centuries. For behavior geneticists mice are more suitable subjects for laboratory experiments. Ebert and Hyde (1976) selected wild female mice (*Mus musculus*) for the degree of isolation-induced aggression using a 5-level scale of intensity based on observable behavior. After 4 generations the high- and low-aggression lines were clearly separated, although considerable individual variability within line remained. Measures of weight and fertility were constant during selection. Defence of the nest (maternal aggression) is highly related to isolation-induced aggression (Hyde & Sawyer, 1979). Nest defense has clear adaptive value, but the authors voice doubts about the contribution of isolation-induced fighting to fitness. It is interesting to note that males in the high- and low-female-aggression lines did not show a correlated response (Hyde & Sawyer, 1980). Perhaps the hormonal and neural bases of male and female aggression are different in important ways.

This small sampling of selection for specific behavior patterns demonstrates that behavior is as genetically manipulable as physical characteristics. In some instances selection affects a relatively broad spectrum of behavior; in others the effect is limited to a single class of behaviors. For most of the experiments cited here the genes whose frequencies must have been altered by selection have not been specified, and it is not clear whether few or many loci were changed in frequency. In the DeFries et al. project an increase in the frequency of the albino allele (c) was shown to account for much of decline of open field activity in the low activity line. In the high activity line the frequency of C increased. There is more to be learned from selection experiments, but they are expensive and time consuming. The evidence we have at present indicates that selection for aspects of behavior is usually successful providing that the parental stock is genetically heterogeneous. It also strengthens the hypothesis that natural selection is the source of variability and change in behavior.

Strain and Gene Variation.   In the course of their research geneticists have produced many highly inbred strains. These strains are useful because their members have identical (or nearly so) genotype except for the sex chromosomes. Inbred strains differ on many aspects of behavior although they have not in general been selected for such traits. A catalog of behavioral differences among these strains would require a volume. An inbred strain is more like a set of replicates of a single individual than a line selected for a character by humans or by nature. Comparing inbred strains is comparable to comparing individuals. The value of inbred strains for geneticists is that the *same* individual can be replicated over and over, and each copy exposed to different environments and experiences. Since members of a strain are genetically identical, differences among its members can be ascribed confidently to the environment. In this section I shall consider two aspects of strain differences in mice: (1) the effect on behavior of varying an allele at a single locus, and (2) the genetics of mating choice.

Henry and Schlesinger (1967) reported on the behavioral effects of placing the albino genotype (cc) and an albino phenotype on C57BL/6J mice that normally carry CC and are jet black. They also replaced in DBA/2J mice the dilute (dd) genotype that produces light brown hair with DD that produces a deep brown color. Compared with standard black C57BLs the albinos were deficient in conditional shock avoidance. They also drank less alcohol and were less active than their pigmented cousins. It is not surprising that albinism would have effects on behavior involving vision, but the wide range of effects shows that a single locus can influence behaviors that seems to have little in common. The D- to dd shift had little effect on behavior, but deep brown mice with a dominant D were more active than standard DBAs. The effects of the albino locus were also studied by Henry and Haythorn (1975) who demonstrated that even a single dose of c that does not reduce pigmentation retards early growth, and impairs hearing. Fuller (1967) found that albino mice in a heterogeneous population were slower to escape from water, less active in an open field, and poorer learners in a water maze. No change was found in a running wheel.

For sociobiologists the effect of genes on mating patterns is of considerable interest. If individuals can evaluate the fitness potential of a prospective mate they might manipulate the prospects for passing on their own genes. Yanai and McClearn (1972) induced estrus in females of two inbred strains, C57BL/1bg and DBA/1bg. An estrous mouse was given an opportunity to choose between two males, one from each line. Females spent more time with males of the opposite strain, and mated more frequently with them. In a second study with a larger number of strains the results were similar, but in some strains female choice was not demonstrated. Female preference failed when the choice was between males of similar ancestry. The preference effect seems to be mediated by a sensory modality, probably olfaction. In a control experiment it was demonstrated that preference was based on the female's avoidance of matching, rather on differential attractiveness of the males. "Neutral" females of heterogeneous genetic background did not show preference, probably because both kinds of males were equally unfamiliar. One could think of this experiment as a demonstration of an incest taboo that reduces the probability of inbreeding.

Natural selection could be influenced if individuals could sense the genotypes of prospective mates, and respond appropriately. Yanai and McClearn (1972) reported that estrous female mice of two inbred strains, when given a choice, preferred males from a different line. They proposed that such a preference is adaptive because it reduces inbreeding. In a second study five strains were tested for female choice of mate (Yanai & McClearn, 1973). When a choice was to be made between males from closely related lines no preference was seen. Females from two of the test lines showed no strain preference. There was no evidence that any type of male had more sex appeal than another. Choice seemed to be based on the discrimination of a male-female genotypic difference rather than to individual attractiveness. Clearly, mice do not mate at random. They may not foresee the results of choice, but choose they do.

A group of immunologists have tested the hypothesis that female selection is based on genes of the major histocompatibility complex (*MHC*) (Andrew & Boyse, 1978; Yamazaki, Yamaguchi, Andrews, Peake, & Boyse, 1978; Yamaguchi, Yamazaki & Boyce, 1978). By using congenic lines that differ only at the *MHC* female's choices could be traced to a known genetic marker. The results of these experiments are too complex to be reviewed here, and I have reservations on the statistical treatment of the data. There was, however, a clear tendency for females to select a mate with a different *MHC*. Some evidence supported the idea that both males and females possess recognition of identity (*Ri*) genes that influence mating choice. Such a system would favor negative assortative mating and increase genetic heterogeneity in a population. One can look forward to additional data on mate choice that is based on genes.

Another study on mating choice involves wild mice (*Mus musculus*) that carry the *t* allele (Lenington, 1983). This gene has the peculiarity of being lethal when homozygous. It persists in natural populations because +/*t* males produce about

90% of t bearing sperm. Females can discriminate between $+/t$ and t/t males and tend to prefer the latter as mates. Females with a $+/t$ genotype are more discriminating than $+/+$ females. This makes good sense as it reduces that probability of the lethal t/t genotypes. Males are more aggressive towards t bearing females and attempt more copulations with t/t females. Lenington suggests that in nature social preferences may lead to mating preferences and thus select mates whose progeny will be of superior quality.

This section makes the point that genes can influence mating patterns, and thus influence evolution. There is an abundant ethological literature on mating behavior and its effect on inbreeding, but little emphasis is given to the genetic base of mating preferences. Preference could, of course, be learned. Probably both genes and experience are involved. To identify genes that might influence the ability to choose mates, it is necessary to have biological markers that can be positively identified. Thus the experiments of Lenington and Boyse and his colleagues are important steps in this direction.

Although I have dealt with mammals in considering the genetics of mate choice, there is an extensive literature on the genetics of mate choice in Drosophila. Ehrman and Parsons (1981) provide a good introduction to the field. There are great differences between humans and mice, and even greater ones between mice and fruit flies, but in all three species it is clear that mate selection is not random.

Genes and the Nervous System.

It seems evident that genes must affect behavior through structures such as the neurosensory and neuromotor systems. Circling and dancing mice have been known for many years, and their breeding has been something of a fad. They have also been of considerable interest to geneticists and neurologists. For behaviorists and evolutionists their stereotyped patterns are less useful, since they are not part of an adaptive species repertoire. The dancing mice survive only because a few scientists and animal fanciers continue to shelter and breed them. A few geneticists have selected animals for more normal aspects of neural structure and its functional correlates. This section describes some examples of the results.

Selection for brain weight in mice is relatively easy and might be expected to have behavioral effects. Differences in brain/body weight ratios between animal species are correlated with their learning ability (Jerison, 1973). Roderick, Wimer, and Wimer (1976) reported the preliminary results of such a selection program. They had three objectives: (1) to demonstrate that neural structure varies among "normal" mice, as well as between the neurological mutants; (2) to determine whether such structural differences have behavioral correlates; and (3) to begin the construction of "a genetic map of the brain that should identify genetically coordinated functional aggregates. . . ." Their program was based on the fact that brain-weight/body-weight ratio varied greatly among inbred strains. The first objective was easily demonstrated. Selection for brain size was effective. Starting with a genetically heterogeneous stock with mean brain weight of 510 mg at maturity, they established a high line, H, with mean brain weight of 620 mg; and a low line, L, with mean brain weight of 380 mg. Percent changes in body weight were much less. The selected lines differed on a number of behavioral tests. H mice were more active than L mice in an open field, and performed better in a water-maze. On a number of other tests no differences were found.

Histological studies showed that inbred lines of mice with a high ratio of hippocampus volume to total brain were low in activity (Wimer, Wimer, & Roderick, 1969). When brains of mice from a genetically heterogeneous stock that had been tested for open-field activity and passive shock avoidance were examined, a correlation was found between test performance and the proportion of hippocampus size to that of the total forebrain (Wimer, Wimer, & Roderick, 1971). In a survey of inbred strains a large variation in the number of granule cells in the *area dentata* of the hippocampus was found (Wimer & Wimer, 1982). These ranged from 270,000 to 450,000. A triple-test cross among three lines showed that the additive genetic component of cell-number variance was .865; and that of environment, .115. After a search of several strains and their hybrids for behavioral correlates a granule cell density in the hippocampus they wrote: "Preliminary analyses indicate that . . . animals with a large granule cell layer tend to be faster learners than those with a smaller layer; the strongest association with behavior is for neuron density in the rostral one-third of this layer." This type of research is just beginning and its eventual outcome can only be imagined at this time. Already it demonstrates that genes affect the details of brain structure, and that these differences have behavioral consequences. I see no reason to believe that the human brain differs from the mouse brain in this respect.

A similar selection program for brain size in mice has found correlated effects on several types of behavior, but has thus far not included detailed anatomical studies (Fuller, 1979). High brain weight mice developed sensorimotor skills more rapidly than control or low line animals. Tests on an unselected heterogeneous line showed small to moderate correlation (.17 to .42) of brain weight with active avoidance and extinction, water-maze learning, and maze-reversal (Jensen & Fuller, 1978).

A somewhat different approach to genetic differences in brain organization is the comparison of effects of brain lesions on a number of strains (Donovick & Burright, 1982). The septal region is considered to have an important role in comparing and processing need states, past experiences, and current sensorimotor information. Using three different lines of mice, a heterogeneous stock, *HET*, and two inbred lines, *C57BL*, and *RF*, the effects of septal lesions in intact and lesioned animals were compared. Strain differences were found in 7 of 16 measures related to emotionality.

It is clear that genetic variation in the nervous system exists in mice, and that this variation has behavioral effects on learning and emotionality. The future of research in this area is promising, and will involve cooperation on a number of behavioral and biological disciplines.

GENES, NEURONS, AND INFORMATION

If I were to give a one sentence answer to "What do genes do?", it would be "They supply information." It would not be a satisfactory reply for a biochemical geneticist, but this volume is directed at psychologists and perhaps sociobiologists. Before continuing let me expose some of my dislikes; some might call them prejudices. I wince when I encounter "a gene for altruism" or "cuckoldry" in pink-footed rabbits. Sociobiologists rationalize such usages as descriptive of behavior that we humans recognize in ourselves, and they usually state that the language does not imply that a specific gene has been located on a chromosome by breeding tests. The biochemist's custom of identifying genes by their action at the chemical level is not appropriate for ethologists and psychologists, though it may be for physicians dealing with behavioral disorders by drugs. One way out is to emphasize genotypes rather than genes, and to ascribe behavior to genic interactions. This is true, but as Dawkins (1982) points out genotypes are not transmitted as a whole in sexual reproduction. Genes are the true replicators that can be passed on for an indefinite number of generations. Of course genes do mutate, but stability is the rule. I am sympathetic to Dawkins' concept of the expanded phenotype, the idea that the influence of a gene goes far beyond its biochemical function to remote physical and behavioral consequences. In the section on empirical studies I referred to a great variety of behaviors that were affected by the albino gene that seem remote from the primary loss of the capacity to synthesize melanin. The weakness of the extended phenotype approach is that as the distance between the gene and a phenotype increases many other genes become involved, and the proportion of variance due to one locus may become so small that it cannot be demonstrated.

We can think of development, behavioral and physical, as an energetic process that is guided by an information system. Behavior results from a flow of information from the external and internal environments to the central nervous system. Neurotransmitters, neuroreceptors, and the body's effectors were all shaped by information carried in the genotype. Genes composed of DNA are the source of information for the development of all living organisms, and changes in DNA have been responsible for the evolution of the myriad species that have inhabited the earth since life began. Some DNA may contains no useful information, and thus be redundant, but this need not concern us here.

In contrast with information transfer, energy transfer is a quantitative process that can be described by the laws of thermodynamics. A strong force always produces more displacement, speed, or heat than a weak one. Energy transfer between systems is never 100% efficient. Only a portion of an animal's caloric intake is utilized for growth and work; the remainder is expended in heat that can be advantageous or detrimental depending on circumstances. Fortunately information transfer is not so restricted. If it were there would be no way for the genetic code to be passed on intact from generation to generation, nor for simpler organisms to evolve into more complex ones through natural selection.

Energy transfer does have implications for sociobiology and natural selection. Such transfers between individuals are constrained by thermodynamics, and are part of the costs of sociality. Examples are lactation in mammals, and nest-feeding of young in passerine birds. The costs of such behavior play an important role in sociobiological theory. These behaviors persist because the parents are programmed by their genes to assign a higher value to the potential immortality of their genes, than to their own immediate welfare. In this sense one might speak of genes for altruism, but the altruistic component is merely a byproduct of a program for nourishing creatures with appropriate characteristics.

For the most part information transfer as studied by psychologists is a two-way process. Individuals exchange information in many ways, by sounds, movements, odors, touch, and any stimulus that can be sensed by the receptors of a target individual. A society is a rich source of information for its members through direct contacts between its members, and through various artefacts. These can range from scent markings in ants and wolves to books and television in humans. Individuals also provide information to a society in the sense that the characteristics of a society change as the composition of its membership changes. The physical environment is also a source of information to individuals, and indirectly to societies. In this case, however, the transfer is limited and not reciprocal. Living organisms from worms to humans can modify their behavior and the environment itself through their activities. They can guide their behavior by observation of their physical environment, and change their environment for their benefit, but they cannot change the physical laws that govern matter, as they can change their social practices. And this ability seems to be limited to a few species, *Homo sapiens* being the best example.

I turn now to genes as bearers of information. Clearly the information coded in an individual's genotype directs development of the sensory, motor, and nervous systems that are involved in behavior. These structures do not, however, convey information back to the genes of that individual nor can they change a genotype by reversing the ontogenetic process and directing changes in DNA. We are stuck with our genes and must adapt for their failings on a somatic rather than a genetic basis. Someday it may be possible to correct inherited deficiencies by gene transfers, but I doubt that these will ever play an important role in human societies. The future of genotechnics is in agriculture, animal breeding, and synthesis of pharmaceuticals. Genes and genotypes will change as they have in the past, through essentially undirected mutation followed by natural selection.

Genes do, of course, exchange information among themselves and the result is an integrated genotype. I shall not attempt to speculate on the specifics of the process, but it is clear that information is passed between genes as a zygote is transformed into an adult organism. My guess is that some of this transfer is reciprocal and some is one-way. More relevant to sociobiology is the exchange of information between organisms. Such exchanges take many forms, gesture, vocalization, secretions, and in humans through artefacts such as the book you are now reading. Humans acquire language, traditions, mannerisms, and specialized skills from social contacts and information exchange. The more complex the social environment, the greater is the possibility of individual variation in acquiring information and making use of it. It is easy to recognize major differences among human societies, but even within the most rigidly organized the experiences of an individual are unique. The uniqueness of individuals stems from both their society and from their genes. The interactions of these two sources of information are the proper study of developmental psychology. Sociobiology deals with the mechanisms through which social behavior has been shaped and constrained by natural selection. It is based on a theory of natural selection in the past, and a calculus of costs and benefits of various forms of sociality. Genotypes have been molded to produce a superior, if not an optimal, behavioral program that will permit members of a species, and their genes, to perpetuate themselves. It is an inferential science with input from observations in nature rather than from designing and carrying out experiments. In contrast, behavior genetics is an experimental science often dealing with artificially selected strains of animals. Its objectives are to determine the degree to which behavioral differences within and between genetically characterized populations are attributable to nature (genes) and to nurture (environmental effects of many kinds).

I shall summarize this discussion of "what genes do" by an analogy. Their role might be likened to that of a machine for constructing a computer out of a supply of components arranged helter-skelter in a bin. The construction program equips the computer with a limited number of built-in functions and, in what we call the higher organisms, with the capacity to acquire new programs as information is fed into it from an outside source. These programs have nothing in common with the program used in the construction of the computer, except that the complexity of that program determines the complexity of the new programs that the computer can handle. Returning to world of organisms we conclude that genes and genotypes are not the physical basis of a program for behavior; they are a program for the production of an organism with a set of receptors, effectors, and nervous system that interact with external stimuli. In animals with simple nervous systems the original construction incorporates a limited set of structures with a limited set of programs. More elaborate systems have extra capacity for adding new programs. Just as the design of a computer places limits on the programs it can accept and run, the gene-based design of an organism limits its behavioral capacities. As behavioral scientists continue to study the relationship of genes and genotypes to behavior, we shall have a better understanding of "*What genes do.*"

ACKNOWLEDGMENT

The preparation of this chapter was aided by a grant from the Harry Frank Guggenheim Foundation.

REFERENCES

Alexander, R. D. (1974). The evolution of social behavior. *Annual Review of Ecology and Systematics, 5,* 325–383.

Andrews, P. W., & Boyse, E. A. (1978). Mapping of an H-2 linked gene that influences mating preference in mice. *Immunogenetics, 6,* 265–268.

Barash, D. P. (1977). *Sociobiology and behavior.* New York: Elsevier.

Bateson, P. (1979). How do sensitive periods arise and what are they for. *Animal Behaviour, 27,* 470–486.

Boice, R. (1977). Burrows of wild and albino rats: Effects of domestication, outdoor raising, age, experience, and maternal state. *Journal of Comparative & Physiological Psychology, 91,* 649–661.

Boice, R. (1981). Behavioral comparability of wild and domesticated rats. *Behavior Genetics, 11,* 543–553.

Britten, R. J., & Davidson, E. H. (1969). Gene regulation for higher cells: A theory. *Science, 165,* 344–357.

Britten, R. J., & Davidson, E. H. (1971). Repetitive and non-repetitive DNA sequences and a speculation on the origins of evolutionary novelty. *Quarterly Review of Biology, 46,* 111–133.

Broadhurst, P. L. (1960). Experiments in psychogenetics: Applications of biometrical genetics to the inheritance of behaviour. In H. J. Eysenck (Ed.), *Experiments in personality* (Vol. 1, pp. 3–102). London: Routledge & Kegan Paul.

Broadhurst, P. L. (1975). The Maudsley reactive and non-reactive strains of rats: A survey. *Behavior Genetics, 5,* 299–319.

Cavalli-Sforza, L. L., & Bodmer, W. F. (1971). *The genetics of human populations.* San Francisco: Freeman.

Clutton-Brock, T., & Harvey, P. H. (1978). *Readings in sociobiology.* San Francisco: Freeman.

Cooke, F., Finney, G. H., & Rockwell, R. F. (1976). Assortative mating in lesser snow geese (*Anser caerulescens*). *Behavior Genetics, 6,* 127–140.

Darwin, C. (1859). *The origin of species by means of natural selection,* 6th ed. Reprinted (1927). New York: Macmillan.

Davidson, E. H., & Britten, R. J. (1973). Organization, transcription, and regulation in the animal genome. *Quarterly Review of Biology, 48,* 565–613.

Dawkins, R. (1976). *The selfish gene.* Oxford: Oxford University Press.

Dawkins, R. (1982). *The extended phenotype.* San Francisco: Freeman.

DeFries, J. C., Gervais, M. C., & Thomas, E. A. (1978). Response to 30 generations of selection for open field activity in laboratory mice. *Behavior Genetics, 8,* 3–13.

DeFries, J. C., Wilson, J. R., & McClearn, G. E. (1970). Open field behavior in mice: Selection response and situational generality. *Behavior Genetics, 1,* 195–211.

Donovick, P. J., & Burright, R. G. (1982). Genetic influences on responses to brain lesions. In I. Lieblich (Ed.), *The genetics of the brain* (pp. 177–205). New York: Elsevier.

Drewek, K. J., & Broadhurst, P. L. (1983). More on heritability of alcohol preference in laboratory mice and rats. *Behavior Genetics, 13,* 123–125.

Ebert, P. D., & Hyde, J. S. (1976). Selection for agonistic behavior in wild female *Mus musculus. Behavior Genetics, 6,* 291–304.

Eckland, B. C. (1968). Theories of mate selection. *Eugenics Quarterly, 15,* 71–74.

Ehrman, L., & Parsons, P. A. (1981). *Behavior genetics and evolution.* New York: McGraw-Hill.

Elston, R. C., & Campbell, M. A. (1970). Schizophrenia: Evidence for the major gene hypothesis. *Behavior Genetics, 1,* 3–10.

Erlenmeyer-Kimling, L. (1972). Gene—environment interactions and the variability of behavior. In L. Ehrman, G. Omenn, & E. Caspari (Eds.), *Genetics, environment and behavior* (pp. 181–208). Orlando, FL: Academic Press.

Erlenmeyer-Kimling, L., & Jarvik, L. F. (1963). Genetics and intelligence: A review. *Science, 142,* 1477–1479.

Feldman, M. C., & Lewontin, R. (1975). The heritability "hangup". *Science, 190,* 1163–1168.

Fieve, R. R., Rosenthal, D., & Brill, H. (1975). *Genetic research in psychiatry.* Baltimore: Johns Hopkins Press.

Fuller, J. L. (1967). Effects of the albino gene upon the behavior of mice. *Animal Behaviour, 15,* 467–470.

Fuller, J. L. (1979a). The taxonomy of psychophenes. In J. R. Royce & L. P. Mos (Eds.), *Theoretical advances in behavior genetics* (pp. 483–304). Alphen aan den Rijn, The Netherlands: Sijthoff & Noorhoff.

Fuller, J. L. (1979b). Fuller BWS lines: History and results. In M. E. Hahn, C. Jensen, & B. C. Dudek (Eds.), *Development and evolution of brain size* (pp. 187–204). Orlando, FL: Academic Press.

Fuller, J. L. (1982). Psychology and genetics: A happy marriage? *Canadian Psychology: Psychologie Canadienne, 23,* 11–21.

Fuller, J. L., Easler, C., & Smith, M. E. (1950). Inheritance of audiogenic seizure susceptibility in the mouse. *Genetics, 35,* 622–632.

Fuller, J. L., & Thompson, W. R. (1960). *Behavior Genetics.* New York: Wiley.

Fuller, J. L., & Thompson, W. R. (1978). *Foundations of behavior genetics.* St. Louis, Mosby.

Gottesman, I. I., & Shields, J. (1972). *Schizophrenia and genetics.* Orlando, FL: Academic Press.

Gould, S. J. (1980). *The panda's thumb.* New York: Norton.

Hale, E. B. (1969). Domestication and the evolution of behaviour. In E. S. E. Hafez (Ed.), *The behaviour of domestic animals* (pp. 22–42). London: Balliere, Tindall & Cassell.

Hay, D. A. (1985). *Essentials of behaviour genetics.* Australia: Blackwell.

Henderson, N. D. (1979). Genetic dominance for low activity in infant mice. *Journal of Comparative and Physiological Psychology, 92,* 118–125.

Henry, K. R., & Haythorn, M. M. (1975). Albinism and auditory function in the laboratory mouse. I. Effect of single gene substitutions on auditory physiology, audiogenic seizures and developmental processes. *Behavior Genetics, 5,* 137–149.

Henry, K. R., & Schlesinger, K. (1967). Effects of the albino and dilute loci on mouse behavior. *Journal of Comparative and Physiological Psychology, 63,* 320–323.

Horowitz, G., & Dudek, B. C. (1983). Behavioral pharmacogenetics. In J. L. Fuller & E. Simmel (Eds.), *Behavior genetics: Principles and applications* (pp. 117–154). Hillsdale, NJ: Lawrence Erlbaum Associates.

Hyde, J. S., & Sawyer, T. F. (1979). Correlated characters in selection for aggressiveness in female mice. II. Maternal aggressiveness *Behavior Genetics, 9,* 571–577.

Hyde, J. S., & Sawyer, T. F. (1980). Selection for agonistic behavior in wild female mice. *Behavior Genetics, 10,* 349–359.

Jensen, C., & Fuller, J. L. (1978). Learning performance varies with brain weight in heterogeneous mouse lines. *Journal of Comparative and Physiological Psychology, 92,* 830–836.

Jerison, H. J. (1973). *Evolution of the brain and intelligence.* Orlando, FL: Academic Press.

Kamin, L. J. (1974). *The science and politics of IQ.* Hillsdale, NJ: Lawrence Erlbaum Associates.

Kidd, K. K., & Cavalli-Sforza, L. L. (1973). An analysis of the genetics of schizophrenia. *Social Biology, 20,* 254–265.

Layzer, D. (1974). Heritability analysis of IQ scores: Science or numerology. *Science, 183,* 1259–1266.

Lenington, S. (1983). Social preferences for partners carrying good genes in wild house mice. *Animal Behaviour, 31,* 325–333.

Lewontin, R. C. (1979). Sociobiology as an adaptionist program. *Behavioral Science, 24,* 5–14.

Mayr, E. (1974). Behavior programs and evolutionary strategies. *American Scientist, 62,* 650–659.

Miller, D. B. (1977). Social displays of mallard ducks (*Anas platyrhyncos*): Effects of domestication. *Journal of Comparative and Physiological Psychology, 91,* 221–232.

Morse, D. H. (1980). *Behavioral mechanisms in ecology.* Cambridge, MA: Harvard University Press.

Motulsky, A. G., & Omenn, G. S. (1975). Biochemical genetics and psychiatry. In R. R. Fieve, D. Rosenthal, & H. Brill, (Eds.), *Genetic research and psychiatry* (pp. 3–14). Baltimore: Johns Hopkins University Press.

Petit, C., & Ehrman, L. (1969). Sexual selection in Drosophila. *Evolutionary Biology, 3,* 177–223.

Plomin, R., DeFries, J. C., & McClearn, G. E. (1980). *Behavioral genetics: A primer.* San Francisco: Freeman.

Price, E. O. (1969). Effect of early outdoor experience on the activity of wild and semi-domestic deermice. *Developmental Psychobiology, 2,* 60–67.

Roderick, T. H., Wimer, R. E., & Wimer, C. C. (1976). Genetic manipulations of neuroanatomical traits. In L. Petrovich & S. McGaugh (Eds.), *Knowing, thinking, and believing* (pp. 143–178). New York: Pergamon.

Scarr, S., & Carter-Saltzman, L. (1983). Genetics and intelligence. In J. L. Fuller & E. C. Simmel (Eds.), *Behavior genetics: Principles and applications* (pp. 217–335). Hillsdale, NJ: Lawrence Erlbaum Associates.

Schneirla, T. C., & Rosenblatt, J. S. (1963). "Critical periods" in the development of behavior. *Science, 139,* 1110–1115.

Scott, J. P. (1962). Critical periods in behavioral development. *Science, 138,* 949–958.

Scott, J. P., & Fuller, J. L. (1965). *Genetics and the social behavior of the dog.* Chicago: Chicago University Press.

Seyfried, T. N., Yu, R. K., & Glazer, G. H. (1980). Genetic analysis of audiogenic seizure susceptibility in C57BL/J × DBA/2J recombinant inbred strains of mice. *Genetics, 94,* 701–718.

Shettleworth, S. J. (1972). Constraints on learning. In D. S. Lehrman, R. A. Hinde, & E. Shaw (Eds.), *Advances in the study of behavior, Vol. 4* (pp. 1–68). Orlando, FL: Academic Press.

Skinner, B. F. (1981). Selection by consequences. *Science, 213,* 501–504.

Streng, J. (1974). Exploration and learning behavior in mice selectively bred for high and low levels of activity. *Behavior Genetics, 4,* 191–204.

Tryon, R. C. (1940). Genetic differences in maze learning in rats. In *39th Yearbook of the National Society for the Study of Education, Part I.* Bloomington, IL: Public School Publishing, pp. 111–119.

Vandenberg, S. C. (1972). Assortative mating, or who marries whom? *Behavior Genetics, 2,* 127–157.

van den Berghe, P. L. (1979). *Human family systems: An evolutionary view.* New York: Elsevier.

Whitney, G., McClearn, G. E., & DeFries, J. C. (1982). Heritability of alcohol preference in laboratory mice and rats: Erroneous estimate. *Behavior Genetics, 12,* 543–546.

Williams, G. C. (1966). *Adaptation and natural selection*. New Jersey: Princeton University Press.

Wilson, E. O. (1975). *Sociobiology*. Cambridge: MA: Harvard University Press.

Wimer, R. E., & Wimer, C. C. (1982). A geneticist's map of the mouse brain. In I. Lieblich (Ed.), *The genetics of the brain* (pp. 395–420). New York: Elsevier.

Wimer, R. E., Wimer, C. C. & Roderick, T. H. (1969). Genetic variability in forebrain structures between inbred strains of mice. *Brain Research, 16,* 257–264.

Wimer, C. C., Wimer, R. E., & Roderick, T. H. (1971). Some behavioral differences associated with relative size of hippocampus in the mouse. *Journal of Comparative and Physiological Psychology, 71,* 57–65.

Yamaguchi, M., Yamazaki, K., & Boyce, E. A. (1978). Mating preference tests with the recombinant congenic strain BALB-HTG. *Immunogenetics, 6,* 261–264.

Yamazaki, K., Yamaguchi, M., Andrews, P. W., Peake, B., & Boyse, E. A. (1978). Mating preference of F2 segregants of crosses between MHC-congenic mouse strains. *Immunogenetics, 6,* 253–257.

Yanai, J., & McClearn, G. E. (1972). Assortative mating in mice. I. Female mating preference. *Behavior Genetics, 2/3,* 173–183.

Yanai, J., & McClearn, G. E. (1973). Assortative mating in mice. II. Strain differences in female mating preference, male preference, and the question of possible sexual selection. *Behavior Genetics, 3,* 65–74.

7 Kin Recognition: Functions and Mediating Mechanisms

Richard H. Porter
George Peabody College of Vanderbilt University

An ability to recognize particular individuals or classes of conspecifics is a fundamental prerequisite for a wide range of social behavior displayed by animals (e.g., Colgan, 1983). In birds and mammals, for example, an initial step in the mating sequence is for an individual to locate a suitable partner, i.e., a conspecific of the opposite sex in the appropriate physiological condition. The likelihood of copulation and fertilization ensuing is enhanced if the latter animal in turn identifies its suitor as an acceptable mate. Complex social organization may similarly be dependent upon discrimination between individuals on the basis of age, sex, or dominance status and the ability to distinguish between members of one's own group and outsiders. As a result of advances in evolutionary biology over the last 2 decades, recognition of genetic kin is currently a topic of considerable interest and research (Beecher, 1982; Fletcher & Michener, in press; Holmes & Sherman, 1982; Sherman & Holmes, 1985). The present chapter focuses primarily upon the issues of *functions* and *mechanisms* of kin recognition and attempts to provide an abbreviated review of relevant research on humans as well as nonhuman species.

The term Kin Recognition refers to discrimination between close genetic relatives and unrelated (or distantly related) conspecifics. Following recent authors (Alexander, 1979; Beecher, 1982; Colgan, 1983; Holmes & Sherman, 1983), kin recognition in the present context is defined as differential interactions among kin as contrasted with nonkin; or selective responsiveness among various classes of relatives. Because kin recognition is inferred from overt behavior, the above definition does not address the issue of cognitive mediation of such recognition, nor does it imply that animals are consciously aware of their relatedness to particular conspecifics. Rather, as is seen below, from an evolutionary perspective it is sufficient that animals behave as though they are aware of their relatedness to others (Alexander, 1979: Holmes & Sherman, 1983).

FUNCTIONS OF KIN RECOGNITION

Evidence of kin recognition has now been documented for numerous vertebrates and invertebrates, including desert isopods (Linsenmair, 1985), honey bees (Getz & Smith, 1983), social wasps (Klahn & Gamboa, 1983), sweat bees (Greenberg, 1979), frog and toad tadpoles (Blaustein & O'Hara, 1982; Waldman, 1981), Coho salmon (Quinn & Busack, 1985), Canade geese (Radesater, 1976), Rhesus and pigtail monkeys (Meikle & Vessey, 1981; Wu, Holmes, Medina, & Sackett, 1980) and several species of rodents (e.g., D'Udine & Partridge, 1981; Gilder & Slater, 1978: Hepper, 1983; Holmes & Sherman, 1982; Grau, 1982; Kareem, 1983; Porter, Wyrick, & Pankey, 1978; Wills, Wesley, Anderson, Sisemore, & Caldwell, 1983). Of what benefit (if any) is such recognition to the individuals involved? That is, do any immediate or long-term genetic advantages accrue to individuals as a function of their ability to recognize close kin? In many instances the adaptive significance of kin recognition is not readily apparent and functional hypotheses are offered without strong empirical support. With the latter caveat in mind, the following discussion concerns what are believed to be two major benefits afforded by kin recognition— i.e., Nepotism and Optimal Mate Choice.

Nepotism

In his landmark series of papers, W. D. Hamilton (1964a, 1964b) pointed out that the overall influence of an individual on the perpetuation of his genes in subsequent generations (i.e., Inclusive Fitness) is an additive function of that individual's own reproductive success (personal fitness) plus his contribution to the reproductive success of his kin, taking into account the degree of genetic relatedness of the latter to the individual in question. Thus, by acting to the benefit of one's kin, an individual can increase the probability of their shared genes being represented in the next (and subsequent) generation(s) in the progeny of those kin. Hamilton further delineates how an ability to recognize relatives would be to one's genetic advantage since it would allow for discriminative investment in kin alone—in other words, *nepotism.*

The best known example of kin recognition and nepotism involves interactions between parents and offspring. Survival of mammalian neonates requires considerable postnatal investment by the lactating mother or, in some instances, the father as well as the mother (Elwood, 1983; Gubernick & Klopfer, 1981). Likewise, in most species of birds, one or both parents incubate the eggs and continue to provide care for the chicks after hatching. Because care of neonates entails substantial costs to parents (Trivers, 1972, 1974) (e.g., metabolic costs involved in the provision of food and warmth; increased risk of predation due to the presence of conspicuous neonates or to limited mobility; decreased opportunity to produce additional offspring), natural selection would favor the evolution of mechanisms to ensure that the caregiver's own offspring (or the offspring of close kin) are the primary beneficiaries of such parental investment. One solution to this problem is for parents to recognize their own offspring and allocate their resources to those young alone. The need to discriminate between own and unrelated infants increases with value of parental care and the potential for making a costly error (Hamilton, 1964b). Accordingly, when a parent's own infants are likely to be found amongst unrelated neonates, as is the case for newly fledged barn swallows (Beecher, Beecher, & Lumpkin, 1981), elephant seals (Petrinovich, 1974), reindeer (Espmark, 1971), and wildebeest (Kruuk, 1972), one often finds evidence of offspring recognition. Parents of these species who might respond *indiscriminately* to their own and alien young would suffer a twofold selective disadvantage through their energy expenditure wasted on unrelated young and the deprivation of necessary resources suffered by their offspring.

On the other hand, if young are born (or hatch) in isolation from other young and remain in the immediate vicinity of the birthplace during their period of dependence upon adult caregivers, there will be little need for the parents to be able to recognize their offspring during that time. Rather, a behavioral rule whereby all neonates at the parental nest or den area are provided with care would effectively restrict parental investment to the parents' offspring. Functionally, therefore, this parental strategy would be equivalent to one based on parental recognition of their own young. In an early test of this hypothesis, Cullen (1957) conducted a series of field experiments with Kittiwakes, a cliff-nesting gull. Unlike ground-nesting gull species, Kittiwakes build their nests on small rocky ledges or outcroppings—"sometimes only four inches wide." Such secluded nest locations appear to be relatively safe from both ground and aerial predators and are physically separate from nest sites of other conspecifics. When Kittiwake chicks were experimentally exchanged between different nests, the parents continued to treat the alien hatchlings in the same manner as they had behaved towards their own chicks (i.e., brooding, preening, or feeding them). The parents did not appear to discriminate between their own and other chicks when exchanged during the first 4 weeks after hatching. Cullen also cites data indicating that parents may attack their own chicks when the latter are encountered outside of the nest area—further suggesting that the young are normally cared for because of their presence in the familiar parental nest. In contrast to Kittiwakes, parents of closely related *colony-nesting* Herring Gulls and Common Gulls begin to recognize their own chicks at about 5-days-of-age, when the chicks begin to wander about and are likely to intrude upon neighboring nests.

It should be pointed out that there are other systems of maternal care that do not require discriminative responding between own and other offspring. For example, mothers and offspring may benefit from communal nursing practiced among related females (e.g., Bertram, 1976; Porter & Laney, 1980; Spencer-Booth, 1970). In such instances it may be more important that the lactating females recognize one another rather than their offspring. By excluding strange females from the nursing group, the communal females ensure that any offspring present were born to members of that group, and are therefore kin. Of course, lack of differential responsiveness to own versus other infants in this context would not necessarily imply that mothers are unable to recognize their own young.

Young mammals and birds are not simply passive recipients of parental care. Aside from responding appropriately to adult-produced signals, offspring effectively communicate their needs to their parents and thereby influence the behavior of the latter (Elwood & McCauley, 1983; Porter, 1983; Trivers, 1974). Neonates may further enhance the share of parental resources that they receive, or otherwise benefit by responding discriminately to their own mother and father. Accordingly, in species where adults reject, react aggressively toward, or even cannibalize strange offspring (see Hausfater & Blaffer Hrdy, 1984, for a recent review), it would certainly be to the neonates' advantage to recognize their own parents and avoid approaching unfamiliar adults.

The literature on human social development indicates that recognition of the mother by the infant has a positive influence on the growth of attachment between the mother and neonate (Bowlby, 1969; Schaffer, 1971). As the infant begins to show evidence of recognizing its mother (e.g., increased smiling, eye contact, or visual following directed towards the mother; reduction in crying when held by the mother as compared with other adults), mothers report more positive feelings towards their baby (Robson & Moss, 1970). In this manner, overt signs of mother-recognition by the infant can accelerate the attachment process and further the likelihood that the mother will exhibit increasing care and investment in that infant. Infants are faced with the immediate problem of locating a source of nurturance and care in the form of a suitable, willing, adult conspecific. From the infant's perspective, the adult need not be a close relative per se providing that it functions as a competent caregiver. Any advantages that accrue to the infant from recognizing and reacting preferentially to its caregiver should be similar regardless of their degree of relatedness to one another. As seen above, however, it is important that the caregiver be more selective in regard to the relatedness of the infant in whom it invests and to whom it becomes attached. It is interesting to note, therefore, that mothers who have recently given birth often report that their infant bears a physical resemblance to a close relative and that this familial resemblance "helped them feel closer to their infant." (Robson & Moss, 1970). The development of mother-infant recognition is discussed further in the section on Mechanisms of Kin Recognition.

Nepotism, as implied by its etymological root (*nepos* = nephew), is not restricted solely to parental investment in offspring, but also includes favoritism shown to other categories of relatives (Sherman, 1980). As previously discussed, individuals can increase their inclusive fitness in two ways: directly, by reproducing and raising viable offspring; and indirectly, through their effect on the survival and reproductive success of kin other than their own offspring. Recent research on nepotism has frequently emphasized interactions between siblings since, genetically, mammalian full siblings are as closely related as are parents and offspring (e.g., Bekoff, 1981). Within each of these classes of relatives, individuals share 50% of their genetic material as a function of direct descent— i.e., their coefficient of relatedness (r) = .50. While this r of .50 is an exact proportion for parents and offspring, it is the mean for full-sibling relatedness.

Because of the considerable difficulties inherent in attempts to study nepotism in nature (e.g., the need for accurate information concerning the degree of relatedness of group members and to be able to observe social interactions over prolonged periods of time), research on sibling interactions has included captive as well as wild populations. Among rhesus monkeys (*Macaca mulatta*) allowed to range freely in a seminatural environment, males tend to join the same group as their older brothers after reaching sexual maturity (Meikle & Vessey, 1981). Brothers also more frequently come to one another's assistance during aggressive encounters than do nonbrothers. Similarly, littermate (full-sibling) spiny mice (*Acomys cahirinus*) are more likely to share limited food resources than are unfamiliar unrelated conspecifics during laboratory tests (Porter, Moore, & White, 1981). Of course, such examples of sibling-directed nepotism must be verified in natural populations before one can convincingly argue that they are of any evolutionary significance.

Holmes and Sherman (1982; Sherman, 1977, 1981) have conducted extensive laboratory and field investigations of kin interactions in Belding's ground squirrels (*Spermophilus beldingi*). Females of this species defend individual territories where they give birth and raise their young. Following weaning, juvenile males move away from their mother's territory while female offspring remain near their birthplace. As a consequence of such sexually dimorphic dispersal patterns, female kin (but not male kin) grow up in close proximity and interact throughout their lifetimes. Observations of free-ranging animals reveal that the frequency of nepotism and cooperation displayed by close kin is positively correlated with their degree of genetic relatedness (Sherman, 1981). Fewer territorial disputes were seen among full-sisters or mothers and daughters compared with more distant kin or unrelated females. Similar cooperation and reduced aggression among sisters and mother-daughter pairs has been reported for Arctic ground squirrels (*Spermophilus parryii*), whose matrilineal social system resembles that of Belding's ground squirrel (McLean, 1982).

Vocalizations elicited by the presence of potential predators (alarm calls) are a striking form of apparent nepotism practiced by several species of ground squirrels. By alerting conspecifics in this manner, the caller concomitantly makes herself conspicuous to the predators and thereby puts herself in considerable danger (Sherman, 1977). Although it is difficult to ascertain the identities of all beneficiaries of alarm calls, field observations suggest that their primary function is to warn mothers, daughters, and littermate sisters (Schwagmeyer, 1980; Sherman, 1977, 1980).

There are numerous examples of species in which individuals either delay their breeding activities or fail to breed altogether. These nonbreeders may nevertheless contribute to the propogation of their genes by aiding the reproductive efforts of close kin. Prior to initiating their own reproductive careers, subadults may enhance their inclusive fitness by remaining with their mother and helping her raise subsequent broods or litters made up of the helper's full- or half-siblings (see Emlen, 1984, for a recent review). Helping behavior by subadult- or young adult-kin, including providing food for the young or the lactating mother, and guarding the den or nest, has recently been documented for mammalian species—e.g., blackbacked jackals (Moehlman, 1979), brown hyenas (Owens & Owens, 1984), and dwarf mongooses (Rood, 1978)--as well as several species of birds (e.g., Emlen, 1984; Woolfenden, 1975). Not all examples of "helpers-at-the-nest" involve close kin of the mother and offspring being assited, however. In these latter cases, helpers are believed to benefit directly through engaging in such activity; possibly by gaining experience that will enhance their own subsequent effectiveness as parents, or by enabling them to exploit resources available on the territory of the parent(s) whom they are helping (Wittenberger, 1981).

The epitome of nest helping is arguably that observed in some of the social Hymenoptera—viz. bees, wasps, and ants. Females display a reproductive division of labor whereby a limited number of individuals (queens) actually lay eggs while the remaining females of the group function as nonreproductive workers or guards. Since female hymenopterans develop from fertilized (diploid) eggs, but males from unfertilized (haploid) eggs, the coefficient of genetic relatedness of females sharing the same set of parents (full sisters) = .75. In contrast, the degree of relatedness of mothers and daughters is .50. Therefore, individual females can gain a greater genetic advantage by helping their mother produce sisters (in a greater proportion than brothers) that may become queens than by producing their own offspring (Hamilton, 1964b; West Eberhard, 1975). During the last 10 years, a number of research reports concerning kin recognition and nepotism in social hymenopterans have been published. Since space does not allow for an adequate review of the literature, only several representative studies are mentioned briefly.

Worker honey bees attack alien queens that are introduced into their colony (Breed, 1981) and, in similar tests, bite half-sisters more frequently than full sisters even if they had all been raised in the same hive (Getz & Smith, 1983). Paper wasps (*Polistes fuscatus*) queens can increase their egg production by establishing a joint nest with a sister (Noonan, 1981). Potential queens (gynes) can distinguish between female nestmates and unrelated females (Shellman & Gamboa, 1982) and a nest-founding queen will allow her sisters to enter her nest but attack other females (Brockmann, 1984). Furthermore, although queens of this same species will accept nests (containing eggs and pupae) of sisters, they tend to destroy or cannibalize nests of nonkin (Klahn & Gamboa, 1983). Entrances to the burrow nests of the sweat bee (*Lasioglossum zephyrum*) are protected by guards who allow nestmates to enter while rejecting other conspecifics or predators (Greenberg, 1979). Since nests are typically made up of several classes of female relatives (e.g., sisters, aunts, nieces), nest guards effectively discriminate between kin and nonkin (Buckle & Greenberg, 1981).

Mate Choice

Sexually reproducing organisms may enhance their production of healthy, viable offspring by favoring or rejecting potential mates based on their degree of genetic relatedness. As an obvious extreme example, wasteful matings with a member of a different species should be avoided—especially if this were to reduce the opportunity for subsequent effective mating with conspecifics. At the opposite end of the continuum, extreme inbreeding (mating among close relatives) can likewise have negative consequences. Data from birds and mammals indicate that close inbreeding often results in high rates of infant and juvenile mortality, reduced litter size, and increased vulnerability to disease and environmental stressors (e.g., Hill, 1974; Ralls, Brugger, & Ballou, 1979).

On a genetic level, populations of inbreeding organisms incur increasing rates of homozygosity at all gene loci. Thus, a deleterious recessive allele that two relatives receive from a common ancestor will, on average, be passed on to three of every four progeny resulting from mating of these kin. Twenty-five percent of the offspring produced by these parents would be homozygous for the recessive allele in question and therefore phenotypically manifest the deleterious trait. An additional 50% of the inbred offspring would be heterozygous for the recessive allele. The accumulation of deleterious recessive alleles in this manner is believed to be the primary basis for reduced fitness of inbred offspring (i.e., inbreeding depression) (Partridge & Halliday, 1984).

In theory, at least, not all of the genetic consequences of inbreeding need be negative. Individuals sharing a local microhabitat may be specifically adapted to that unique environment. Restricting matings to members of that population would perpetuate this adaptation in the offspring and thereby benefit those who remain in the environment of their birth. Inbreeding proffers additional benefits when potential mates are not readily available or when one sex has to compete for mating partners. For further discussion of the costs and benefits of inbreeding, the reader is referred to recent reviews by Partridge (1983) and Bateson (1983).

Organisms for whom inbreeding poses a potential genetic risk would be expected to evolve safeguards against incestuous breeding. Two inbreeding-avoidance mechanisms have been proposed (Maynard Smith, 1978; Partridge & Halliday, 1984): (a) differential dispersion of males and females prior to reaching sexual maturity (which would reduce the likelihood of opposite-sex close kin subsequently encountering one another); and, of more relevance to the present discussion, (b) recognizing close kin and rejecting them as sexual partners.

Accounts of sexual behavior of wild chimpanzees suggest that kin recognition plays a role in the mediation of incest avoidance in this species. Copulation between siblings, or mothers and sons is rarely observed and van Lawick-Goodall (1968) reports that one female "tried to escape the first observed attempts of her two brothers to mount her in a sexual context." With the approach of their first estrous, females shift from associating primarily with closely related males to unfamiliar (presumably more distantly related or unrelated) males (Pusey, 1980). Reduced breeding by sibling pairs in comparison with nonsibling pairs has also been reported for a number of rodents: e.g., gerbils (Agren, 1984), deermice (Dewsbury, 1982), prairie voles (Gavish, Hofmann, & Getz, 1984; McGuire & Getz, 1981), and black-tailed prairie dogs (Hoogland, 1982). Females of this latter species also avoid mating with their sons or father, even when in the same colony.

Bateson (1978, 1983) has hypothesized that instead of simply avoiding the extremes of outbreeding or inbreeding, some animals may display a preference for mating with individuals of intermediate genetic relatedness to themselves. Support for this theory of *optimal outbreeding* (or optimal inbreeding, per Shields, 1983) is provided by laboratory studies of Japanese quail indicating that adults of both sexes respond preferentially to unfamiliar first cousins over familiar and unfamiliar siblings and unrelated birds (Bateson, 1982). The quail in these experiments apparently recognized visually the close kin with whom they were raised and subsequently preferred conspecifics "optimally discrepant" from those familiar birds. In related studies, house mice (*Mus musculus*) have been tested for their responses to odors produced by close relatives as well as by nonrelative mice of the same and different strains (D'Udine & Partridge, 1981; Gilder & Slater, 1978). While the results are not entirely consistent across all strains of mice used in these experiments, they generally support the suggestion that mice prefer odors of opposite-sex conspecifics that are slightly familiar. Females of both the Porton and Steel homozygous normal strains, for example, spent more time investigating bedding material soiled by a nonsibling male of their same strain than bedding from their brothers or from a male of a different strain (Gilder & Slater, 1978). Although results of the above experiments with quail and mice are supportive of the theory of optimal outbreeding, adequate tests of this theory ultimately require data on mate preferences in large, wild-living populations with known genealogies and known social histories during development (Bateson, 1983).

MECHANISMS OF KIN RECOGNITION

The previous discussion has been concerned with the question of *why* organisms have evolved the ability to recognize close kin—i.e., the evolutionary function(s) of kin recognition. We now turn our attention to the proximal mechanisms involved in kin recognition. That is, how are individuals able to identify their kin?

The process of kin recognition is composed of two separable components (Alexander, 1979; Beecher, 1982): (a) the phenotypic *signature* that establishes an individual's identity, or inclusion in a particular class of conspecifics (such as close kin or individuals to be treated preferentially); and (b) recognition of the signature-bearer by kin—in Beecher's words, "recognition proper." The remainder of this chapter is devoted to a further examination of these two constituents of kin recognition.

Phenotypic Signatures

Across species, one would expect individual signatures to involve sensory modalities that are otherwise the most salient for intraspecific communication. Birds, which communicate primarily through visual and auditory signals, employ these same sorts of cues for kin recognition. Japanese quail use visual features to distinguish between first cousins and unrelated conspecifics (Bateson, 1982); mate selection by mallard ducks is influenced by the color of the mother and siblings with whom they were raised (Klint, 1978) and vision appears to be the critical modality for sibling recognition among Canada geese (Radesater, 1976). Bank swallow chicks emit "signature calls" that enable their parents to identify them (Beecher, Beecher, & Hahn, 1981), and young laughing gulls respond discriminately to calls from their own parents (Beer, 1970). In contrast, a number of rodent species seem to rely upon chemical signals for both parent-infant and sibling recognition (e.g., Beach & Jaynes, 1956; Block, Volpe, & Hayes, 1981; D'Udine & Partridge, 1981; Halpin, 1986; Hayashi & Kimura, 1983; Holmes, 1984b; Ostermeyer & Elwood, 1983; Porter, Wyrick, & Pankey, 1978). The coordination of activities within insect societies, including discrimination between nestmate kin and alien conspecifics, likewise depend on the exchange of chemical information (e.g., Barrows, Bell, & Michener, 1975; Breed, 1981; Greenberg, 1979; C. D. Michener, 1974).

Discrimination of kin by visual, auditory, and even olfactory cues has been documented for humans within the first few days after birth. Neonates will work (suck on a nonnutritive nipple) to produce the voice of their mother in preference to that of another woman (DeCasper & Fifer, 1980). Mothers, in turn, recognize their own infant's cries as early as the third day after delivery (Formby, 1967; Morsbach & Bunting, 1979). In a series of tests using the cries of 30-day-old babies, fathers were less accurate than mothers in identifying their own infants (Green & Gustafson, 1983). Nevertheless, 45% of the fathers reliably identified their infant's cries when presented along with cries of three other infants.

At less than 4-days-of-age, infants display an initial preference for their mother's face over the face of a stranger (Field, Cohen, Garcia, & Greenberg, 1984). The authors concluded that although such discrimination of the mother's face is most likely based on visual features, maternal odors could also be implicated. Related experiments on recognition of neonates' faces reveal that mothers can accurately identify their own infants from amongst an array of color photographs of neonates all of the same sex and less than 33 hours old (Porter, Cernoch, & Balogh, 1984).

It is becoming increasingly apparent that olfactory cues may be of greater relevance to the mediation of human social interactions than is generally assumed to be true. Macfarlane (1975), in his pioneering study of infants' responses to maternal odors, found that breastfeeding infants discriminate between a breast-pad worn by their mother and a comparable pad that had been worn by another nursing female. This basic finding that infants recognize and respond preferentially to their own mother's breast odor has been replicated on both sides of the Atlantic since the original report in 1975 (Russell, 1976; Schaal, Montagner, Hertling, Bolzoni, Moyse, & Quichon, 1980). More recent data indicate that recognizable odor signatures of lactating mothers are not restricted solely to the breast region. When breast-feeding infants were simultaneously presented with two gauze pads, one worn in the armpit of their mother and the second worn in the armpit of an unfamiliar lactating female, they oriented preferentially to their own mother's odor (Cernoch & Porter, 1985). In a similar manner, mothers are able to use olfactory cues to identify their infant (in comparison to unfamiliar infants of the same age) beginning as early as the day of birth (Porter, Cernoch, & McLaughlin, 1983; Russell, Mendelson, & Peeke, 1983; Schall et al., 1980).

The ontogenetic history of individual signatures has been the subject of little research. Many morphological features that function as salient cues for kin recognition are obviously genetically mediated—e.g., bird coloration patterns; shape of nose, mouth, and face in humans. Recent investigations of the major histocompatability complex (MHC) in mice provides the most convincing evidence for the control of recognizable phenotypic traits by a specific gene complex. The MHC is a group of linked genes involved in immunological responses, including recognition of an individual's own cells (Marx, 1983; Yamaguchi, Yamazaki, Beauchamp, Bard, Thomas, & Boyse, 1981). Inbred mice respond differently to others of their strain as a function of the genotype of their MHC complex. In particular, males' choice of mate is influenced by females' MHC types (Yamazaki, Boyse, Mike, Thaler, Mathieson, Abbott, Boyse, Zayas, & Thomas, 1976). Individual males differ in their responses to females according to whether the MHC complex of the latter is identical or dissimilar to that of the male. Discrimination of MHC types appears to be based on olfactory cues since males and females can be trained to distinguish between urine from identical-MHC and dissimilar-MHC mice (Yamaguchi et al., 1981).

Phenotypic signatures that are genetically mediated are not necessarily impervious to environmental influences. Thus, although sweat bee and honey bee nestmate recognition appears to be based on "genetically determined" odors (Getz & Smith, 1983; Greenberg, 1979), dietary factors can modify odor signatures in these species (Buckle & Greenberg, 1981; Hölldobler & Michener, 1980). Aggressive interactions between members of different honeybee colonies decrease when all the bees feed on the same diet (i.e., a single species of flower) (Kalmus & Ribbands, 1952). A shared diet presumably results in odor similarity across colonies of honeybees. Maternal pheromone produced by lactating rats (Leon, 1975) and spiny mice (Doane & Porter, 1978) also appears to vary according to the females' diet. Pups of both species respond preferentially to odors from lactating females fed the same diet as the pups' own mothers. It has been suggested that genetically determined chemically complex skin lipids may serve as the basis for unique chemical signatures of individual humans (Nicolaides, 1974). Support for this hypothesis is provided by experiments with tracking dogs. When tested with footprints (Kalmus, 1955) or articles of clothing (Gedda, Casa, & Comparetti, 1980), trained dogs more frequently confused the odors of genetically identical twins than odors of fraternal twins. Human subjects likewise have trouble distinguishing between the odors of identical twins; however, accuracy rates improve significantly when stimulus twins are fed markedly different diets (Wallace, 1977).

A final category of signatures comprises cues that, rather than originating from the signature-bearer's own body, are acquired from external sources. Recognizing kin through acquired labels is somewhat comparable to identifying celebrities by characteristic idiosyncratic items of clothing, such as Napoleon's hat. Among carpenter ants (*Camponotus*), nestmate recognition depends on odors that are produced by the queen and spread throughout the colony (Carlin & Holldobler, 1983). Even workers of different ant species will be accepted into a colony if they possess the label from that colony's queen. Alternatively, workers labeled by a queen of a different species will be rejected by their own genetic sisters. Acquired odor signatures play a similar role in maternal recognition of offspring in goats. While nursing and licking her neonate shortly after birth, the mother goat labels it with a distinctive chemical cue that she uses subsequently to discriminate between her own kid and those labeled by other mothers (Gubernick, Jones & Klopfer, 1979). Females may accept alien kids within a few hours after parturition providing that these kids have not already been labeled by another mother.

Signature Recognition

Regardless of the form and ontogenetic basis of an individual's signature, adaptive responsiveness to the signature-bearer by kin can only occur if that signal is reliably recognized or decoded. A number of recent publications have attempted to elucidate the proximal mechanisms underlying recognition of kin signatures. Based on both empirical data and theoretical considerations, four categories of recognition mechanisms have been proposed (e.g., Alexander, 1979; Blaustein, 1983; Holmes & Sherman, 1982, 1983): spatial location; association/familiarity; recognition alleles; and phenotype matching.

Spatial Location.   According to this mechanism, kin are discerned from nonkin because of the physical location in which they are encountered. If there is a high probability of kin being found only at particular sites, concomitant with little chance of unrelated conspecifics overlapping at those same sites, discriminative kin interactions would be possible without the need to be able to recognize genetic relatives per se. Rather, recognition of the locations where one's kin are to be found, and a behavioral strategy whereby all conspecifics at these sites are treated as if they were kin, would suffice. Birds and mammals that have isolated, well-defined nests or burrows, such as the Kittiwakes discussed previously, may rely upon this mechanism for allocating parental resources during the period that their young are confined to the nest site.

Although the behavioral phenomena that can be attributed to the Spatial Location recognition mechanism are consistent with the definition of kin recognition presented at the beginning of this chapter, this mechanism differs from the other three remaining to be discussed. Specifically, recognition of kin by spatial location is not based on signatures carried by, or emanating from, individual conspecifics. It is not possible, therefore, to discriminate between simultaneously present kin and unrelated conspecifics through this mechanism alone. Accordingly, successful fostering of alien young shortly after birth or hatching can be readily accomplished with species for which offspring recognition is mediated by spatial location. Once the young become independently mobile and likely to roam away from the nest site, however, parents must adopt alternative mechanisms of offspring recognition. As one example, bank swallow parents accept alien chicks up to 15-days-of-age. When the chicks begin to fly (at about 18 days), their begging call is replaced by a signature call that allows parents to discriminate between their own and alien chicks (Beecher, Beecher, & Hahn, 1981).

Association/Familiarity.   Probably the most pervasive yet simple kin recognition mechanism entails becoming familiar with particular kin through direct contact (e.g., Bekoff, 1981). Individuals learn the signatures to which they are exposed and recognize the bearers of those signatures during subsequent encounters. The classic ethological example of kin recognition developing through a process of familiarization is filial imprinting in precocial birds—as first delineated by Lorenz (1937). Chicks normally become attached to their mother by being exposed to either, or both, her visual image and call during a period of optimal sensitivity occurring shortly after hatching.

Since this mechanism is vulnerable to recognition errors (i.e., familiar individuals, regardless of whether or not they are genetically related, are treated as kin), it would be expected to be implicated primarily in contexts where nonkin do not co-occur with kin during the initial phases of the familiarization process. Familiarization is therefore likely to mediate the development of infant-parent recognition, as well as recognition of littermate- or broodmate-siblings; either in a rapid imprinting-like manner, or when young are kept secluded from unrelated conspecifics (as is the case for many birds, mammals, and social insects).

Prior to weaning, altrical rodent species are confined to a nest or burrow where, in many species, social encounters are limited to littermates and their mother. Early contact in this restricted environment results in neonates learning the salient signatures of their close associates and thereby serves as a basis for later discriminative interactions between these same individuals. Familiarization during the natal period has been shown to be one of the mechanisms involved in the development of kin recognition in Richardson's and Belding's ground squirrels. Mothers will accept alien offspring into their individual burrows and treat them as their own if such fostering occurs before the female's own young begin to emerge from underground (Holmes, 1984a; Holmes & Sherman, 1982; G. R. Michener, 1974). After the alien Belding's ground squirrel pups and their foster littermates eventually appear outside of the burrow, they interact like normal biological littermates (Holmes & Sherman, 1982; but see Davis, 1982).

Laboratory experiments with rodents have helped to clarify the role of familiarity in sibling interactions. The degree of mutual investigation and passive bodily contact displayed by mouse siblings as adults was found to be correlated with the length of time that they had lived together prior to being separated (Kareem, 1983). Avoidance of incestuous sibling matings likewise appears to be based on familiarity. Early pairing of *unrelated* males and females results in reduced sexual activity in gerbils (Agren, 1984), prairie deer mice (Hill, 1974), prairie voles (Gavish, Hofmann, & Getz, 1984), and cactus mice (Dewsbury, 1982). It has also been hypothesized that comparable association-based mechanisms may account for outbreeding in avian species (Bateson, 1983) and even the avoidance of incestuous brother-sister sexual activity among humans (Bixler, 1981; Shepher, 1971: Spiro, 1965).

Recognition Alleles. It is theoretically possible for *both* a phenotypic signature, along with the ability to recognize that signature, to be genetically mediated (Hamilton, 1964b). Dawkins (1976) uses the example of a genetically determined green-beard whose bearers would be recognized by that label and treated preferentially by other green-bearded individuals as a direct result of the latter possessing that same gene (or closely-linked gene complex). This mechanism would allow previously *unfamiliar* individuals who share copies of the "recognition allele" to identify one another. Although recognition alleles could, in theory, play a role in the identification of one's relatives, such an allele would actually mediate the recognition of copies of itself—regardless of whether conspecifics who possess that same allele are otherwise close kin (Dawkins, 1982). Recognition alleles therefore would not necessarily discriminate between kin and unrelated conspecifics.

At the present time, there appear to be no data to support unambiguously the recognition allele theory. Furthermore, theoretical arguments against the recognition allele hypothesis have centered upon the complex pleiotropic effects that would be necessitated by this mechanism. As originally pointed out by Hamilton (1964b), a "supergene" would have to influence: (a) the development of the phenotypic signature, (b) recognition of that signature, *and* (c) appropriate social responsiveness to signature bearers. Nonetheless, the above discussed studies of social preferences in mice based on the MHC locus indicate that specific genes mediate the development of recognizable chemical signatures that are discriminated by conspecifics (see Lenington, 1983, for similar data on t-allele discrimination by mice). The mechanisms involved in the recognition of the MHC signature are not understood, however. We return to the topic of recognition alleles in the next section.

Phenotype Matching.   Recognition of relatives by the mechanism of Phenotype Matching involves two steps: An individual first learns the signatures of close kin (or its own signature) and subsequently uses those phenotypic traits as standards against which to compare the signatures of others. Providing that phenotypic similarity is correlated with genotypic similarity, unfamiliar kin can be discriminated based on the degree of correspondence between their phenotypes and the standard signatures (Holmes & Sherman, 1982; Lacy & Sherman, 1983). For instance, an animal might respond selectively to others whose visual or olfactory phenotypes closely match those of familiar kin such as its mother or littermates. As an illustration of self-matching, Dawkins (1982) evokes the image of an animal sampling its own odor and restricting its beneficence to those with similar odors—i.e., the "armpit effect." It should be emphasized that recognition of kin by phenotype-matching does not require that the signatures be genetically determined. Rather, kin signatures that are similar as a result of shared environmental influences could also be employed as phenotypes against which others are assessed. The correlation between phenotype and genotype, *not* the underlying basis for this correlation, is critical.

Findings from several recent experiments are consistent with the phenotype-matching model of kin recognition. Buckle and Greenberg (1981) tested the reactions of sweat bee nest-guards to nonresident bees. Guards raised in nests containing two distinct families equally accepted unfamiliar bees that were their own sisters or the sisters of their unrelated nestmates. The acceptance rate for sisters of unrelated nestmates was greater than that displayed by guards of single-family colonies to unrelated bees. It was concluded that nest guards learn the odor signatures of their nestmates and accept or reject alien bees based on the similarity of aliens' odors to those of the guards' nestmates. On the other hand, there was no evidence to suggest that guards rely upon their own odors as recognition standards. Workers of the social wasp (*Polistes fuscatus*) similarly recognize their sisters; even with no prior exposure to kin as adults (Pfennig, Reeve, & Shellman, 1983). Sister recognition appears to be the result of shared odor cues that are similar to those learned at the natal nest.

Fostering experiments with rodents provide further evidence for recognition among kin that have not been previously exposed to one another. As adults, Richardson's ground squirrel siblings that were reared apart from the day of birth interacted differently than unfamiliar nonsiblings (Davis, 1982). Comparable results have been reported recently for white-footed deermice (*Peromyscus leucopus*) (Grau, 1982), laboratory rats (Hepper, 1983), house mice (Kareem, 1983) and Belding's and Arctic ground squirrels (Holmes & Sherman, 1982). Kin preferences have also been observed in pigtail macaque monkeys that have been removed from their mothers at birth and raised apart from other relatives prior to testing (Wu, Holmes, Medina, & Sackett, 1980). When young monkeys were tested in an apparatus allowing them to approach various stimulus compartments, they displayed significant preferences for unfamiliar half-siblings over unrelated animals and empty cages. It should be pointed out, however, that a recent attempt to replicate these findings with a large sample of older monkeys (i.e., juveniles and young adults) was not successful (Fredrickson & Sackett, 1984).

Familiar conspecifics differing in their degree of genetic relatedness might also be discriminated by assessing similarity of individual phenotypes against a known standard. Taking advantage of a high rate of multiple paternity in Belding's ground squirrel litters, Holmes and Sherman (1982) compared the behavior of littermate full-sisters and maternal half-sisters who had shared the *same* natal burrow and even the same uterine environment. Despite the early association of full- and half-sisters and, presumably, their equal familiarity with one another, full-sisters were less aggressive and more cooperative than were half-sisters as yearlings. It was suggested that the females used themselves as the standard against which to match their littermates, and discriminated between those littermates whom they resembled (full-sisters) and those that were relatively dissimilar (half-sisters).

Two separate research projects have been investigating sibling recognition in toad and frog tadpoles (e.g., Blaustein & O'Hara, 1981, 1982; O'Hara & Blaustein, 1982; Waldman, 1981, 1982; Waldman & Adler, 1979) and newly meta-morphosed frogs (Blaustein, O'Hara, & Olson, 1984). Since tadpole eggs can be easily fertilized in the laboratory, and individual development can occur in isolation from other conspecifics, these amphibians are well-suited for studies of kin recognition. It has been hypothesized that dense social groupings might facilitate the location of food as well as the avoidance of predators (through the release of substances that elicit fleeing in conspecifics) (Blaustein & O'Hara, 1986). To the extent that kin display discriminative aggregations, they could enhance their inclusive fitness by such warning or helping behavior within their own group. In addition, Waldman (1986) suggests that tadpoles may release growth regulating substances that have differential effects on the development of kin and nonkin and could thereby result in benefits for selective schooling with siblings.

As documented in several experiments, tadpoles raised as isolates subsequently discriminate between unfamiliar siblings and unfamiliar nonsiblings (Blaustein & O'Hara, 1981, 1982; Waldman, 1982). Furthermore, isolation-reared Cascades frog tadpoles prefer full-siblings to half-siblings, and half-siblings over nonsiblings (Blaustein & O'Hara, 1982). Isolate-reared American toad tadpoles likewise distinguish between unfamiliar siblings and nonsiblings, and between full-siblings and paternal (but *not* maternal) half-siblings (Waldman, 1981). Waldman concluded that isolated American toad tadpoles recognize siblings through a self-matching process, and the preferential responsiveness to maternal half-siblings over paternal half-siblings was due to the former kin being labeled with ''nonchromosomal contributions from their mother.'' Blaustein & O'Hara (1982) point out, however, that their data on Cascades frog tadpoles ''are consistent with both a phenotypic matching and a genetic recognition system of kin recognition.'' In a later article, Blaustein (1983) stresses that phenotype matching is often cited as the recognition mechanism believed to mediate specific examples of kin recognition even though the empirical data might be equally supportive of the recognition allele hypothesis. This caution would apply to interpretations of the data on rodents and monkeys reared in isolation or apart from kin, as well as evidence of discrimination between familiar half- and full-siblings, referred to earlier in this section. Thus, recognition of kin by animals raised in total social isolation could be mediated by self-matching or through recognition alleles, or even the interaction of these two mechanisms. Unfortunately, as there are no simple manipulations whereby an animal can be deprived of experience with its own phenotype without otherwise disrupting its development, it may not be possible to disprove empirically the phenotype-matching hypothesis (Blaustein, 1983).

Development of Sibling Recognition in Spiny Mice

It should be apparent by now that kin recognition is a complex phenomenon, and documented accounts of kin discrimination within a particular species usually cannot be attributed unambiguously to a single recognition mechanism. To illustrate further the interacting influences of the recognition mechanisms just described, results of investigations into the development of sibling recognition in spiny mice are summarized in this section.

The Egyptian spiny mouse (*Acomys cahirinus*) is a murid rodent indigenous to the Eastern Mediterranean region, and roughly comparable in size to the species of gerbil (*Meriones unguiculatus*) commonly found in pet shops. Like many rodents, young spiny mice maintained in family units in the laboratory spend a great deal of time huddled with their parents and littermates. This observation led to an initial series of experiments (Porter, Wyrick, & Pankey, 1978) to determine whether subadult animals huddle preferentially with familiar littermates over unfamiliar agemates—i.e., do huddling preferences reflect discriminative interactions among close biological kin?

The testing procedure involved placing two pairs of littermate siblings (i.e., a total of four weanlings from two different litters) into a large cage and recording who huddled with whom over a period of 8 days. Littermates had been raised together prior to testing, but weanlings from one litter were unfamiliar with the pair of siblings from the second litter. Across the nine groups of animals tested in this manner, there was a marked tendency for the littermate siblings to pair-up and huddle with one another. In contrast, there were very few instances of dyadic pairing by nonsiblings. Such discriminative pairings by littermates was taken as evidence of sibling recognition among weanling spiny mice. Littermate recognition is based at least in part on olfactory cues since animals rendered anosmic show no evidence of discriminating between littermates and unfamiliar animals. Subsequent experiments using a similar testing paradigm but varying the age of the subjects revealed that littermates and unfamiliar agemates huddle together indiscriminately in groups composed of all four animals in the test cage until they are about 2 weeks old (Porter & Wyrick, 1979). At this age, littermate siblings begin to pair up, and there is a marked decrease in the frequency of indiscriminate group huddling.

The first experimental evidence to suggest that familiarity may be important for discriminative huddling by spiny mouse siblings was provided by an experiment where two pairs of littermates were observed for several days as described above and then all animals were placed individually into separate isolation cages (Porter & Wyrick, 1979). When reunited after either 3 or 5 days of isolation, littermate pairings were once again more frequent than pairings by unrelated weanlings. After 8 days of isolation, however, dyadic pairings of any kind were infrequent—with littermate pairings observed no more than nonlittermate pairs. Eight days of isolation therefore appeared to disrupt sibling recognition among spiny mouse weanlings that had been continually exposed to one another prior to that time. To determine whether sporadic reexposure could possibly perpetuate recognition among separated siblings, littermates that were isolated for 8 days (as in the previous experiment) were reunited for a single 4-hour session on the fifth day of isolation. In tests following the 8-day isolation period, sibling pairings were again more prevalent than nonsibling pairings; indicating that relatively brief reexposure of siblings was sufficient for them to maintain discriminative interactions subsequent to a long period of separation (Porter & Wyrick, 1979).

In the studies reviewed thus far, spiny mouse littermates had been reared together prior to the sibling recognition tests or the beginning of the experimental manipulations. Therefore, animals that were familiar with one another were also close kin (r = .50). To assess directly the relative importance of familiarity versus genetic relatedness on the development of littermate recognition a cross-fostering design was employed (Porter, Tepper, & White, 1981). At the time of fostering, single pups of the same age were exchanged between two unrelated litters, with the family units in each home cage otherwise remaining intact. These pups remained with their foster families with no further manipulations until the beginning of the recognition tests at approximately 30-days-of-age. Individual pups were assigned to one of three conditions that differed according to when fostering took place—i.e., on the day of birth, day 10, or day 20 postpartum.

When observed in groups containing four animals each, pups fostered onto unrelated females (and their offspring) huddled preferentially with their foster littermates over their biological siblings from whom they had been separated. Pairings by separated siblings were as infrequent as pairings by unrelated, un-familiar agemates. This same pattern of results was obtained regardless of the age at which the pups had been fostered (i.e., Day of birth—day 20). These data indicate that littermate recognition results from exposure and recent association in the home cage rather than an inborn ability to recognize one's kin. Familiarity thus appears to be more important than genetic relatedness per se for the develop-ment of sibling recognition in spiny mice.

Related experiments have determined that effective familiarization does not require direct physical contact between individual animals. Unrelated mice that were housed in adjacent cages, and separated only by a wire-mesh partition, later displayed evidence of recognition; viz. they huddled together more frequently than did unrelated animals that had been housed in totally separate cages (Porter, Matochik, & Makin, 1984). The degree of positive social interactions observed among these animals was nevertheless not as great as that by animals allowed complete contact during the familiarization period.

Despite the predominant role of familiarization in the mediation of spiny mouse social discrimination, particularly that involving littermate siblings, addi-tional empirical evidence suggests that other mechanisms could also be impli-cated in kin recognition. Littermates that were separated from each other from the fourth day of life onwards, but who continued to suckle from the same female (their biological mother) at alternating 12-hour intervals, huddled preferentially with one another in tests beginning at 17–21 days (Porter, Tepper, & White, 1981). If nursed by two different females following separation, however, sib-lings show no indication of recognizing one another; thereby demonstrating that the 4 days of exposure in the home cage was not sufficient for long-term recogni-tion. Sharing a mother in common, on the other hand, does appear to be sufficient for the development of discriminative interactions. When unrelated pups with no prior exposure to one another shared the *same* lactating female (but never suckled together at the same time), they subsequently displayed more dyadic pairing than did unfamiliar pups who suckled from *different* females. Young spiny mice presumably recognize their mother's chemical label on agemates and therefore respond preferentially to them. The process through which pups acquire distinctive signatures from their mother is not known, but it may be similar to maternal labeling in goats as discussed previously.

It is not only the mother whose signature may be used as a standard against which animals match unfamiliar agemates. Weanlings may also respond preferentially to unfamiliar individuals whose phenotype is similar to that of the weanlings' familiar littermates. Animals that had an artificial odorant applied directly to themselves alone, or to themselves and the littermates with whom they were housed, subsequently responded discriminatively to unfamiliar animals treated with the same odor (Porter, Matochik, & Makin, 1983). Furthermore, littermate siblings that were separated from one another for 9 days—but each housed with another pup from their same litter during that time—responded preferentially to one another during tests following the separation period. This is in contrast with the lack of discrimination among littermates that have been separated for a comparable period of time but with *no* intervening exposure to other members of their litter. The phenotypes of familiar littermates thus appear to be a significant factor in the development of social preferences. At present, there are no data to suggest that *self-matching* of *natural* phenotypic traits (as opposed to *artificial* odorants) may mediate social recognition in spiny mice.

Within intact suckling litters of spiny mice, maternal influences (viz., labeling of young with maternal chemical cues) may interact with the early direct contact among the young to mediate the development of littermate recognition. While familiarization may be the most powerful mechanism involved in sibling recognition in this species, phenotype matching, based on a common maternal label or other phenotypic traits shared by littermates, also appears to play a significant, if secondary, role. Unlike familiarization, this latter mechanism would allow for kin recognition among animals who have never had direct contact with one another.

HUMAN KIN-RECOGNITION MECHANISMS

Human kin recognition is probably most often simply a matter of being told who one's relatives are and becoming familiarized with their identifiable phenotypic traits. It is obvious, however, that familiarization alone cannot account for all occurrences of kin recognition in our own species (Wells, in press). At least in some instances, unfamiliar individuals can be identified as likely kin because of shared familial characteristics, such as facial features, which may bear a strong resemblance amongst close relatives.

In an attempt to elucidate further the mechanisms involved in the mediation of human kin recognition, recent research in our laboratory has focused on the development of recognition of neonates by visual and olfactory cues. As mentioned previously, mothers are quite accurate in picking out their own infants when presented with photographs of faces of four neonates (Porter, Cernoch, & Balogh, 1984). The mothers tested in this experiment had a mean of only 4.7 hours of postnatal contact with their infant prior to testing—this includes all the time that the infant was in the mother's hospital room, regardless of whether the mother was awake or sleeping. Therefore, a prolonged period of association and familiarization is not necessary for mothers to be able to recognize the face of their neonates.

When asked to comment on how they decided on the photograph they selected as their infant's, one-third of the mothers mentioned that the neonate resembled another family member—typically its father or older siblings. This is consistent with an earlier report by Robson & Moss (1970) that approximately one-half of the mothers whom they interviewed while in the hospital claimed a physical similarity between their infant and a close relative. (See Daly & Wilson, 1982, for similar data from spontaneous comments by mothers shortly after delivery.)

Despite such claims of perceptable resemblance between neonates and close kin, there appears to have been little empirical research to test the validity of this assertion. Therefore, adult subjects were tested for their ability to match photographs of mothers and their newborn infants (Porter, Cernoch, & Balogh, 1984). Each subject was presented with a color photograph of a neonate (less than 40-hours-old) and asked to choose the infant's mother from amongst four photographs of recently parturient women—one of whom was the infant's own mother. Comparable tests were conducted using a mother's photograph as a standard, with subjects asked to guess which of four neonates was the offspring of that particular female. The accuracy rate for matching photographs of mothers and infants, although less than 100%, was significantly greater than chance over the two test series, indicating that infants bear a detectable facial-visual resemblance to their mother as early as the second day of life. In light of these data, one can tentatively conclude that early visual recognition of neonates by their mothers may be mediated through the interaction of rapid familiarization and matching facial features with those of other known relatives, or of the mother herself (i.e., self-matching).

To assess the influence of familiarization on the development of recognition of particular kin, one would ideally like to test individuals with the signatures of relatives with whom there has been no prior association. This is usually not possible when investigating maternal recognition of offspring since contemporary hospital practice encourages immediate postnatal mother-infant contact—at least for mothers of healthy, term infants. Caesarean deliveries, nonetheless, provide an opportunity to assess neonate recognition by mothers who have had limited contact with their babies. Because of the physical trauma associated with the surgical procedure and the concomitant anesthesia and medication, Caesarean-section mothers are less likely to engage in prolonged periods of interaction with their infants during the perinatal period than are vaginal-delivery mothers. Based on this rationale, Porter, Cernoch, and McLaughlin (1983) tested a sample of Caesarean-section mothers on their ability to recognize their newborn babies by olfactory cues alone.

Within the first two days postpartum, each mother was presented with two identical shirts; one that had been worn (and soiled) by her own infant, and another worn by an unfamiliar neonate. To prevent attempts to identify the shirts by visual cues, they were enclosed in individual cardboard containers with a small opening cut into the lid. Mothers were instructed to sniff each shirt through the opening in the containers and guess which one had been worn by their own infant. Although these Caesarean-delivery mothers had a mean of only 2.4 hours of direct contact with their infants prior to the recognition test, a statistically significant proportion correctly identified the shirt worn by their own baby. Similar to the comments by mothers in the earlier experiments on *visual* recognition of neonates, several of the mothers remarked that their infant's odor resembled that of their husband or older child (i.e., the stimulus neonate's father or sibling).

We next turned to the question of whether the odors of close kin are indeed detectably similar. If humans actually have genetically determined biochemical "fingerprints" that serve as a basis for individual odors (most likely in interaction with environmental factors, such as diet), one would expect a correlation between genotypic similarity and odor similarity. As an empirical test of this hypothesis, adult subjects were asked to attempt to match the odors of mothers and their 3- to 8-year-old children (Porter, Cernoch, & Balogh, 1985). The testing procedure was analogous to that described earlier for the mother-infant visual matching experiment, with soiled t-shirts used as the olfactory stimuli. The number of subjects who correctly matched the odors of mothers and children was significantly greater than that expected by chance, indicating that these close relatives share similar detectible odors that could facilitate kin recognition. Although relatives of the mother-child stimulus pairs were not tested in either the odor- or visual-matching experiments, there is no reason to expect that kin would be any less accurate than the unrelated individuals who served as subjects in these studies.

A reasonable question at this point is whether olfactory recognition of kin is of any functional significance for humans. That is, given our greater reliance on visual and auditory cues, and our ability to perceive subtle differences between individuals using these modalities, is there any additional advantage in being able to discriminate kin by their odors? Unfortunately, one can only offer speculative responses to this question.

On the one hand, the ability to recognize kin odors (or the odors of other individuals) may be nothing more than a vestige of a greater reliance on chemical information among our early ancestors. A more intriguing possiblity involves the unique characteristics of odor memory. Numerous authors have commented on the phenomenon whereby vivid memories of distant events are evoked by a brief sample of an odor associated with that occasion. In tests of short-term memory, subjects were more accurate with visual as compared to olfactory stimuli (Engen, 1982). As the length of time between stimulus exposure and the subsequent recognition tests increased to several months, odor cues were recognized at a greater rate than were the visual stimuli. In general, recognition of visual stimuli declined rapidly, while the accuracy level for odor stimuli remained relatively constant over a 12-month period. Therefore, if odor signatures remain relatively invariant over an individual's lifetime, as would be the case if they are in fact genetically mediated, this might allow for more reliable long-term memory of kin odor cues as compared to other forms of signatures. Prolonged memory of kin odors could be of further benefit when assessing kinship by matching unfamiliar individuals' phenotypes with those of known kin with whom one has not had recent contact. For self-matching, however, long-term odor memory offers no obvious advantages over other modalities since the individual's own signature presumably would be readily available for comparison with that of the unfamiliar individual whose kinship is being assessed.

Consistent with the emphasis of the relevant animal behavior literature, empirical studies of human kin recognition have been concerned primarily with the mother-infant dyad. It is hoped, however, that future research will investigate the development and mediating mechanisms of recognition among other classes of human kin. From the limited data reported to date, it cannot be safely assumed that particular recognition mechanisms will be of equal salience across kin categories. Fathers, for example, may differ from mothers on their degree of reliance on association/familiarity as a mechanism involved in offspring recognition. Because males usually cannot be assured of their paternity, preferential investment in neonates based solely on association/familiarity could result in recognition errors and have serious genetic consequences. Fathers might therefore benefit by being more reliant than mothers on self-matching as an offspring recognition mechanism. Perceived similarity between a neonate and the reputed father would increase the likelihood of actual relatedness—assuming that the recognition signatures are genetically influenced. It is interesting, in this regard, that mothers and other relatives more frequently assert paternal- as compared to maternal-resemblance of newborns (Daly & Wilson, 1982). Such allegations of paternal resemblance presumably serve to increase the male's confidence of paternity.

A related issue, also in need of further research, is the development of parental responsiveness and attachment to infants whose phenotypes deviate markedly from those of other family members. Congenital abnormalities or surgical procedures may result in significant alterations in the facial features of infants. Likewise, syndromes arising from inborn errors of metabolism, such as phenyl-ketonuria (PKU) and Maple Syrup Urine Disease, are characterized by distinctive strong body odors (Labows, 1980; Liddell, 1976) that probably do not resemble odors of unafflicted kin. What effect, if any, do these unfamiliar or unanticipated phenotypic features of neonates have on the developing social relationship between parents and such infants? As already mentioned, familial resemblance of neonates appears to have a positive impact on mothers' feelings towards their offspring (Robson & Moss, 1970). Conversely, lack of a readily perceptible phenotypic match between a neonate and close family members might have an adverse effect on the parents' interactions with that child. Similar mismatches are likely to exist between the phenotypes of foster parents and their adopted children or between stepparents and the unrelated children with whom they are living. The probability of successful adoption appears to increase with the perceived similarity between child and foster parent (Daly & Wilson, 1982; Jaffee & Fanshel, 1970). Furthermore, it has been suggested that young children are at a greater risk for abuse by step parents than by biological parents (Daly & Wilson, 1984; Wilson, Daly, & Weghorst, 1980).

CONCLUSIONS

Kin discrimination is a fundamental process in many species that have evolved complex social systems. Once it was ascertained that individuals of a particular species interact differently with kin as compared to nonkin, investigators began to focus on the functions and underlying mechanisms of kin recognition. Although our understanding of these issues has advanced considerably during the last few years, empirical research has not always kept pace with theoretical conceptualizations and hypotheses. Study of the *functions* of kin recognition is especially difficult since it requires long-term observations of free-ranging animals of known genealogies. In addition, there is the problem of measuring the effects of discriminative interactions among kin (e.g., nepotism and incest avoidance) in units of fitness.

The study of kin recognition in animals has provided insights into the selective forces that have shaped analogous phenomena in our own species and has served as an impetus for empirical investigations of human recognition mechanisms. Thus, the recent (albeit limited) literature on human kin recognition has been concerned with the same issues being investigated in a wide range of nonhuman species. Because genetic kinship systems appear to be an important aspect of every known human society (Alexander, 1979); accurate determination of kinship has major legal implications (e.g., for assigning paternity or in inheritance cases); and kin discrimination is a necessary precursor to the development of parent-infant socialization, the mechanisms mediating human kin recognition is a topic worthy of further research efforts.

ACKNOWLEDGMENTS

I am grateful to Andrew R. Blaustein and Warren G. Holmes for their comments on an earlier draft of this paper. Preparation of this chapter was supported in part by grant HD 15051 from the National Institute of Child Health and Human Development.

REFERENCES

Agren, G. (1984). Incest avoidance and bonding between siblings in gerbils. *Behavioral Ecology and Sociobiology, 14*, 161–169.

Alexander, R. D. (1979). *Darwinism and human affairs*. Seattle: University of Washington Press.

Barrows, E. M., Bell, W. J., & Michener, C. D. (1975). Individual odor differences and their social functions in insects. *Proceeding of the National Academy of Science, U.S.A., 72*, 2824–2828.

Bateson, P. (1978). Sexual imprinting and optimal outbreeding. *Nature, 273*, 659–660.

Bateson, P. (1982). Preferences of cousins in Japanese quail. *Nature, 295*, 236–237.

Bateson, P. (1983). Optimal outbreeding. In P. Bateson (Ed.), *Mate choice*, Cambridge: Cambridge University Press.

Beach, F. A., & Jaynes, J. (1956). Studies of maternal retrieving in rats. I. Recognition of young. *Journal of Mammalogy, 37*, 177–180.

Beecher, M. D. (1982). Signature systems and kin recognition. *American Zoologist, 22*, 477–490.

Beecher, M. D., Beecher, I. M., & Hahn, S. (1981). Parent-offspring recognition in bank swallows (*Riparia riparia*): II. Development and acoustic basis. *Animal Behaviour, 29*, 95–101.

Beecher, M. D., Beecher, I. M., & Lumpkin, S. (1981). Parent-offspring recognition in bank swallows (*Riparia riparia*): I. Natural history. *Animal Behaviour, 29*, 86–94.

Beer, C. G. (1970). Individual recognition of voice in the social behaviour of birds. *Advances in the Study of Behavior, 3*, 27–74.

Bekoff, M. (1981). Mammalian sibling interactions: Genes, facilitative environments, and the coefficient of familiarity. In D. J. Gubernick & P. H. Klopfer (Eds.), *Parental care in mammals*. New York: Plenum Press.

Bertram, B. C. R. (1976). Kin selection in lions and in evolution. In P. P. G. Bateson & R. A. Hinde (Eds.), *Growing points in ethology*. Cambridge: Cambridge University Press.

Bixler, R. H. (1981). The incest controversy. *Psychological Reports, 49*, 267–283.

Blaustein, A. R. (1983). Kin recognition mechanisms: Phenotype matching or recognition alleles? *American Naturalist, 121*, 749–754.

Blaustein, A. R., & O'Hara, R. K. (1981). Genetic control for sibling recognition? *Nature, 290*, 246–248.

Blaustein, A. R., & O'Hara, R. K. (1982). Kin recognition in *Rana cascadae* tadpoles: Maternal and paternal effects. *Animal Behaviour, 30*, 1151–1157.

Blaustein, A. R., & O'Hara, R. K. (1986). Kin recognition in tadpoles. *Scientific American, 254*, 108–116.

Blaustein, A. R., O'Hara, R. K., & Olson, D. H. (1984). Kin preference behaviour is present after metamorphosis in *Rana cascadae* frogs. *Animal Behaviour, 32*, 445–450.

Block, M. L., Volpe, L. C., & Hayes, M. J. (1981). Saliva as a chemical cue in the development of social behavior. *Science, 211,* 1062–1064.

Bowlby, J. (1969). *Attachment and loss. Volume 1: Attachment.* New York: Basic Books.

Breed, M. D. (1981). Individual recognition and learning of queen odors by worker honeybees. *Proceedings of the National Academy of Science, U.S.A., 78,* 2635–2637.

Brockmann, H. J. (1984). The evolution of social behaviour in insects. In J. R. Krebs & N. B. Davies (Eds.), *Behavioural ecology: An evolutionary approach* (2nd ed.). Sunderland, MA: Sinauer Associates.

Buckle, G. R., & Greenberg, L. (1981). Nestmate recognition in sweat bees (*Lasioglossum zephyrum*): Does an individual recognize its own odour or only odours of its nestmates? *Animal Behaviour, 29,* 802–809.

Carlin, N. F., & Holldobler, B. (1983). Nestmate and kin recognition in interspecific mixed colonies of ants. *Science, 222,* 1027–1029.

Cernoch, J. M., & Porter, R. H. (1985). Recognition of maternal axillary odors by infants. *Child Development, 56,* 1593–1598.

Colgan, P. (1983). *Comparative social recognition.* New York: John Wiley & Sons.

Cullen, E. (1957). Adaptations in the Kittiwake to cliff-nesting. *Ibis, 99,* 275–302.

Daly, M., & Wilson, M. I. (1982). Whom are newborn babies said to resemble? *Ethology and Sociobiology, 3,* 69–78.

Daly, M., & Wilson, M. (1984). A sociobiology analysis of human infanticide. In G. Hausfater & S. Blaffer Hrdy (Eds.), *Infanticide: Comparative and evolutionary perspectives.* New York: Aldine.

Davis, L. S. (1982). Sibling recognition in Richardson's ground squirrels (*Spermophilus richardsonii*). *Behavioral Ecology and Sociobiology, 11,* 65–70.

Dawkins, R. (1976). *The selfish gene.* Oxford: Oxford University Press.

Dawkins, R. (1982). *The extended phenotype.* San Francisco: Freeman.

DeCasper, A. J., & Fifer, W. P. (1980). Of human bonding: Newborns prefer their mothers' voices. *Science, 208,* 1174–1176.

Dewsbury, D. A. (1982). Avoidance of incestuous breeding in two species of *Peromyscus* mice. *Biology of Behaviour, 7,* 157–169.

Doane, H. M., & Porter, R. H. (1978). The role of diet in mother-infant reciprocity in the spiny mouse. *Developmental Psychobiology, 11,* 271–277.

D'Udine, B., & Partridge, L. (1981). Olfactory preferences of inbred mice (*Mus musculus*) for their own strain and for siblings: Effects of strain, sex and cross-fostering. *Behaviour, 78,* 314–324.

Elwood, R. W. (1983). Paternal care in rodents. In R. W. Elwood (Ed.), *Parental behaviour of rodents.* Chichester, Sussex: Wiley.

Elwood, R. W., & McCauley, P. J. (1983). Communication in rodents: Infants to adults. In R. W. Elwood (Ed.), *Parental behaviour in rodents.* Chichester, Sussex: Wiley.

Emlen, S. T. (1984). Cooperative breeding in birds and mammals. In J. R. Krebs & N. B. Davies (Eds.), *Behavioural ecology: An evolutionary approach* (2nd ed.). Sunderland, MA: Sinauer.

Engen, T. (1982). *The perception of odors.* Orlando, FL: Academic Press.

Espmark, Y. (1971). Individual recognition by voice in reindeer mother-young relationship. Field observations and playback experiments. *Behaviour, 40,* 295–301.

Field, T. M., Cohen, D., Garcia, R., & Greenberg, R. (1984). Mother-stranger face discrimination by the newborn. *Infant Behavior and Development, 7,* 19–25.

Fletcher, D. J. C., & Michener, C. D. (Eds.). (in press). *Kin recognition in animals.* Chicester: Wiley.

Formby, D. (1967). Maternal recognition of infant's cry. *Developmental Medicine and Child Neurology, 9,* 293–298.

Fredrickson, W. T., & Sackett, G. P. (1984). Kin preferences in primates (*Macaca nemestrina*): Relatedness or familiarity? *Journal of Comparative Psychology, 98,* 29–34.

Gavish, L., Hofmann, J. E., & Getz, L. L. (1984). Sibling recognition in the prairie vole, *Microtus ochrogaster*. *Animal Behaviour, 32,* 362–366.

Gedda, L., Casa D., & Comparetti, M. M. (1980). La dignosi di zigotism nei genelli: Esperimenti con cani poliziotti. *Rivista de Biologia, 73,* 95–97.

Getz, W. M., & Smith, K. B. (1983). Genetic kin recognition: Honey bees discriminate between full and half sisters. *Nature, 302,* 147–148.

Gilder, P. M., & Slater, P. J. B. (1978). Interest of mice in conspecific male odours is influenced by degree of kinship. *Nature, 274,* 364–365.

Grau, H. J. (1982). Kin recognition in white-footed deermice (*Peromyscus leucopus*). *Animal Behaviour, 30,* 497–505.

Green, J. A., & Gustafson, G. E. (1983). Individual recognition of human infants on the basis of cries alone. *Developmental Psychobiology, 16,* 485–493.

Greenberg, L. (1979). Genetic component of bee odor in kin recognition. *Science, 206,* 1095–1097.

Gubernick, D. J., Jones, K. C., & Klopfer, P. H. (1979). Maternal "imprinting" in goats? *Animal Behaviour, 27,* 314–315

Gubernick, D. J., & Klopfer, P. H. (1981). *Parental care in mammals.* New York: Plenum Press.

Halpin, Z. T. (1986). Individual odors among mammals: Origins and functions. *Advances in the Study of Behavior, 16,* 39–70.

Hamilton, W. D. (1964a). The genetical evolution of social behaviour. I. *Journal of Theoretical Biology, 7,* 1–16.

Hamilton, W. D. (1964b). The genetical evolution of social behaviour. II. *Journal of Theoretical Biology, 7,* 17–51.

Hausfater, G., & Blaffer Hrdy, S. (1984). *Infanticide: Comparative and evolutionary perspectives.* New York: Aldine.

Hayashi, S., & Kimura, T. (1983). Degree of kinship as a factor regulating preferences among conspecifics in mice. *Animal Behaviour, 31,* 81–85.

Hepper, P. G. (1983). Sibling recognition in the rat. *Animal Behaviour, 31,* 1177–1191.

Hill, J. L. (1974). Peromyscus: Effect of early pairing on reproduction. *Science, 186,* 1042–1044.

Hölldobler, B., & Michener, C. D. (1980). Mechanisms of identification and discrimination in social Hymenoptera. In H. Markl (Ed.), *Evolution of social behavior: Hypotheses and empirical tests.* Weinheim: Verlag Chemie GmbH.

Holmes, W. G. (1984a). Ontogeny of dam-young recognition in captive Belding's ground squirrels (*Spermophilus beldingi*). Journal of Comparative Psychology, 98, 246–256.

Holmes, W. G. (1984b). Sibling recognition in thirteen-lined ground squirrels: Effects of genetic relatedness, rearing association, and olfaction. *Behavioral Ecology and Sociobiology, 14,* 225–233.

Holmes, W. G., & Sherman, P. W. (1982). The ontogeny of kin recognition in two species of ground squirrels. *American Zoologist, 22,* 491–517.

Holmes, W. G., & Sherman, P. W. (1983). Kin recognition in animals. *American Scientist, 71*(Jan.–Feb.), pp. 46–55.

Hoogland, J. L. (1982). Prairie dogs avoid extreme inbreeding. *Science, 215,* 1639–1641.

Jaffee, B., & Fanshel, D. (1970). *How they fared in adoption: A follow-up study.* New York: Columbia University Press.

Kalmus, H. (1955). The discrimination by the nose of the dog of individual human odours and in particular of the odours of twins. *British Journal of Animal Behaviour, 5,* 25–31.

Kalmus, H., & Ribbands, C. R. (1952). The origin of the odours by which honeybees distinguish their companions. *Proceedings of the Royal Society, 140,* 50–59.

Kareem, A. M. (1983). Effect of increasing periods of familiarity on social interactions between male sibling mice. *Animal Behaviour, 31,* 919–926.

Klahn, J. E., & Gamboa, G. J. (1983). Social wasps: Discrimination between kin and nonkin brood. *Science, 221,* 482–484.

Klint, T. (1978). Significance of mother and sibling experience for mating preferences in the mallard (*Anas platyrhynchos*). *Zeitschrift fur Tierpsychologie, 47,* 50–60.

Kruuk, H. (1972). *The Spotted Hyena.* Chicago: University of Chicago Press.

Labows, J. N. (1980). What the nose knows. *The Sciences, Nov.,* 10–13.

Lacy, R. C., & Sherman, P. W. (1983). Kin recognition by phenotype matching. *The American Naturalist, 121,* 489–512.

Lawick-Goodall, J. van (1968). The behaviour of free-living chimpanzees in the Gombe Stream Reserve. *Animal Behaviour Monographs, 1,* 161–311.

Lenington, S. (1983). Social preferences for partners carrying "good genes" in wild house mice. *Animal Behaviour, 31,* 325–333.

Leon, M. (1975). Dietary control of maternal pheromone in the lactating rat. *Physiology and Behavior, 14,* 311–319.

Liddell, K. (1976). Smell as a diagnostic marker. *Postgraduate Medical Journal, 52,* 136–138.

Linsenmair, K. E. (1985). Individual and family recognition in subsocial arthropods, in particular the desert isopod *Hemilepistus reaumuri.* In B. Hölldobler & M. Lindauer (Eds.), *Experimental ecology and sociobiology.* Sunderland, MA: Sinauer.

Lorenz, K. Z. (1937). The companion in the bird's world. *Auk, 54,* 245–273.

Macfarlane, A. (1975). Olfaction in the development of social preferences in the human neonate. In *Parent-Infant interaction,* Ciba Foundation Symposium 33. New York: Elsevier.

Marx, J. L. (1983). A closer look at the genes of the MHC. *Science, 220,* 937–939.

Maynard Smith, J. (1978). *The evolution of sex.* Cambridge: Cambridge University Press.

McGuire, M. R., & Getz, L. L. (1981). Incest taboo between sibling *Microtus ochrogaster. Journal of Mammalogy, 62,* 213–215.

McLean, I. G. (1982). The association of female kin in the Arctic ground squirrel *Spermophilus parryii. Behavioral Ecology and Sociobiology, 10,* 91–99.

Meikle, D. B., & Vessey, S. H. (1981). Nepotism among rhesus monkey brothers. *Nature, 294,* 160–161.

Michener, C. D. (1974). *The social behavior of the bees.* Cambridge, MA. Belknap Press.

Michener, G. R. (1974). Development of adult-young identification in Richardson's ground squirrel. *Developmental Psychobiology, 7,* 375–384.

Moehlman, P. D. (1979). Jackal helpers and pup survival. *Nature, 277,* 382–383.

Morsbach, G., & Bunting, C. (1979). Maternal recognition of their neonates' cries. *Developmental Medicine and Child Neurology, 21,* 178–185.

Nicolaides, N. (1974). Skin lipids: Their biochemical uniqueness. *Science, 186,* 19–26.

Noonan, K. M. (1981). Individual strategies of inclusive-fitness-maximizing in *Polistes fuscatus* foundresses. In R. D. Alexander & D. W. Tinkle (Eds.), *Natural selection and social behavior: Recent research and new theory.* New York: Chiron Press.

O'Hara, R. K., & Blaustein, A. R. (1982). Kin preference behavior in *Bufo boreas* tadpoles. *Behavioral Ecology and Sociobiology, 11,* 43–49.

Ostermeyer, M. C., & Elwood, R. W. (1983). Pup recognition in *Mus musculus:* Parental discrimination between their own and alien young. *Developmental Psychobiology, 16,* 75–82.

Owens, D. D., & Owens, M. J. (1984). Helping behaviour in brown hyenas. *Nature, 308,* 843–845.

Partridge, L. (1983). Non-random mating and offspring fitness. In P. Bateson (Ed.), *Mate choice.* Cambridge: Cambridge University Press.

Partridge, L., & Halliday, T. (1984). Mating patterns and mate choice. In J. R. Krebs & N. B. Davies (Eds.), *Behavioural ecology: An evolutionary approach.* Sunderland, MA: Sinauer.

Petrinovich, L. (1974). Individual recognition of pup vocalization by northern elephant seal mothers. *Z. Tierpsychologie, 34,* 308–312.

Pfennig, D. W., Reeve, H. K., & Shellman, J. S. (1983). Learned component of nestmate discrimination in workers of a social wasp, *Polistes fuscatus* (Hymenoptera: Vespidae). *Animal Behaviour, 31,* 412–416.

Porter, R. H. (1983). Communication in rodents: Adults to infants. In R. W. Elwood (Ed.), *Parental behaviour in rodents.* Chichester, Sussex: Wiley.

Porter, R. H., Cernoch, J. M., & Balogh, R. D. (1984). Recognition of neonates by facial-visual characteristics. *Pediatrics, 74,* 501–504.

Porter, R. H., Cernoch, J. M., & Balogh, R. D. (1985). Odor signatures and kin recognition. *Physiology and Behavior, 34,* 445–448.

Porter, R. H., Cernoch, J. M., & McLaughlin, F. J. (1983). Maternal recognition of neonates through olfactory cues. *Physiology and Behavior, 30,* 151–154.

Porter, R. H., & Laney, M. D. (1980). Attachment theory and the concept of inclusive fitness. *Merrill-Palmer Quarterly, 26,* 35–51.

Porter, R. H., Matochik, J. A., & Makin, J. W. (1983). Evidence for phenotype matching in spiny mice (*Acomys cahirinus*). *Animal Behavior,* 31, 978–984.

Porter, R. H., Matochik, J. A., & Makin, J. W. (1984). The role of familiarity in the development of social preferences in spiny mice. *Behavioural Processes, 9,* 241–254.

Porter, R. H., Moore, J. D., & White, D. M. (1981). Food sharing by sibling vs. nonsibling spiny mice (*Acomys cahirinus*). *Behavioral Ecology and Sociobiology, 8,* 207–212.

Porter, R. H., Tepper, V. J., & White, D. M. (1981). Experiential influences on the development of huddling preferences and "sibling" recognition in spiny mice. *Developmental Psychobiology, 14,* 375–382.

Porter, R. H., & Wyrick, M. (1979). Sibling recognition in spiny mice (*Acomys cahirinus*): Influence of age and isolation. *Animal Behaviour, 27,* 761–766.

Porter, R. H., Wyrick, M., & Pankey, J. (1978). Sibling recognition in spiny mice (*Acomys cahirinus*). *Behavioral Ecology and Sociobiology, 3,* 61–68.

Pusey, A. E. (1980). Inbreeding avoidance in chimpanzees. *Animal Behaviour, 28,* 543–552.

Quinn, T. P., & Busack, G. A. (1985). Chemosensory recognition of siblings in juvenile coho salmon (*Oncorhynchus kisutch*). *Animal Behaviour, 33,* 51–56.

Radesater, T. (1976). Individual sibling recognition in juvenile Canada geese (*Branta canadensis*). *Canadian Journal of Zoology, 54,* 1069–1072.

Ralls, K., Brugger, K., & Ballou, J. (1979). Inbreeding and juvenile mortality in small populations of ungulates. *Science, 206,* 1101–1103.

Robson, K. S., & Moss, H. A. (1970). Patterns and determinants of maternal attachment. *Journal of Pediatrics, 77,* 976–985.

Rood, J. P. (1978). Dwarf mongoose helpers at the den. *Zeitschrift fur Tierpsychologie, 48,* 277–287.

Russell, M. J. (1976). Human olfactory communication. *Nature, 260,* 520–522.

Russell, M. J., Mendelson, T., & Peeke, H. V. S. (1983). Mothers' identification of their infant's odors. *Ethology & Sociobiology, 4,* 29–31.

Schaal, B., Montagner, H., Hertling, E., Bolzoni, D., Moyse, A., & Quichon, R. (1980). Les stimulations olfactives dan les relations entre l'enfant et la mere. Reproduction, Nutrition and Development, 20, 843–858.

Schaffer, H. R. (1971). *The growth of sociability.* Harmondsworth, Middlesex: Penguin Books.

Schwagmeyer, P. L. (1980). Alarm calling behavior of the thirteen-lined ground squirrel *Spermophilus tridecemlineatus. Behavioral Ecology and Sociobiology, 7,* 195–200.

Shellman, J. S., & Gamboa, G. J. (1982). Nestmate discrimination in social wasps: The role of exposure to nest and nestmates. *Behavioral Ecology and Sociobiology, 11,* 51–53.

Shepher, J. (1971). Mate selection among second generation kibbutz adolescents and adults: Incest avoidance and negative imprinting. *Archives of Sexual Behavior, 1,* 293–307.

Sherman, P. W. (1977). Nepotism and the evolution of alarm calls. *Science, 197,* 1246–1253.

Sherman, P. W. (1980). The meaning of nepotism. *American Naturalist, 16,* 604–606.

Sherman, P. W. (1981). Kinship, demography, and Belding's ground squirrel nepotism. *Behavioral Ecology and Sociobiology, 8,* 251–259.

Sherman, P. W., & Holmes, W. G. (1985). Kin recognition: Issues and evidence. In B. Holldobler & M. Lindauer (Eds.), *Experimental behavioral ecology and sociobiology.* Sunderland, MA: Sinauer.

Shields, W. M. (1983). Optimal inbreeding and the evolution of philopatry. In I. R. Swingland & P. J. Greenwood (Eds.), *The ecology of animal movement.* Oxford: Oxford University Press.

Spencer-Booth, Y. (1970). The relationship between mammalian young and conspecifics other than mothers and peers: A review. *Advances in the Study of Behavior, 3,* 119–194.

Spiro, M. E. (1965). *Children of the kibbutz.* New York: Schocken.

Trivers, R. L. (1972). Parental investment and sexual selection. In B. Campbell (Ed.), *Sexual selection and the descent of man* (pp. 136–179). Chicago: Aldine.

Trivers, R. L. (1974). Parent-offspring conflict. *American Zoologist, 14,* 249–264.

Waldman, B. (1981). Sibling recognition in toad tadpoles: The role of experience. *Zeitschrift fur Tierpsychologie, 56,* 341–358.

Waldman, B. (1982). Sibling association among schooling toad tadpoles: Field evidence and implications. *Animal Behaviour, 30,* 700–713.

Waldman, B. (1986). Chemical ecology of kin recognition. In D. Duvall, D. Muller-Schwarze, & R. M. Silverstein (Eds.), *Chemical signals in vertebrates IV: Ecology, evolution, and comparative biology.* New York: Plenum Press.

Waldman, B., & Adler, K. (1979). Toad tadpoles associate preferentially with siblings. *Nature, 282,* 611–613.

Wallace, P. (1977). Individual discrimination of humans by odor. *Physiology and Behavior, 19,* 577–579.

Wells, P. A. (in press). Kin recognition in humans. In D. J. C. Fletcher & C. D. Michener (Eds.), *Kin recognition in animals.* Chichester: Wiley.

West Eberhard, M. J. (1975). The evolution of social behavior by kin selection. *Quarterly Review of Biology, 50,* 1–33.

Wills, G. D., Wesley, A. L., Anderson, H. N., Sisemore, D. A., & Caldwell, J. (1983). Huddling preferences among albino rats. *Psychological Reports, 53,* 183–186.

Wilson, M. I., Daly, M., & Weghorst, S. J. (1980). Household composition and the risk of child abuse and neglect. *Journal of Biosocial Sciences, 12,* 333–340.

Wittenberger, J. F. (1981) *Animal social behavior.* Boston: Duxbury Press.

Woolfenden, G. E. (1975). Florida scrub jay helpers at the nest. *Auk, 92,* 1–15.

Wu, H. M. H., Holmes, W. G., Medina, S. R., & Sackett, G. P. (1980). Kin preferences in infant *Macaca nemestrina. Nature, 285,* 225–227.

Yamaguchi, M., Yamazaki, K., Beauchamp, G. K., Bard, J., Thomas, L., & Boyse, E. A. (1981). Distinctive urinary odors governed by the major histocompatibility locus of the mouse. *Proceedings of the National Academy of Science, U.S.A., 78,* 5817–5820.

Yamazaki, K., Boyse, E. A., Mike, V., Thaler, H. T., Mathieson, B. J., Abbott, J., Boyse, J., Zayas, Z. A., & Thomas, L. (1976). Control of mating preferences in mice by genes in the major histocompatibility complex. *Journal of Experimental Medicine, 144,* 1324–1335.

8 Race, Race Differences, and Race Relations: Perspectives from Psychology and Sociobiology

Irwin Silverman
York University

A sociobiologist evokes much the same responses from his traditional, behavioral science colleagues as would a Marxist in a business school. Both may be tolerated if their ideas are kept in place; small, agrarian societies, perhaps, for the Marxist; bower birds and beavers for the sociobiologist. If they venture beyond, however, they may readily elevate their statuses from minor oddities to dangerous demogogues. The Marxist becomes the usurper of freedom and progress; the evolutionist who casts his eye on humankind risks an array of assignations, including imperialism, colonialism, elitism, sexism, and racism.

Such imputations to Darwinian theory are as old as Darwinian theory (cf. Ruse, 1982; Stepan, 1982), but they have sustained an impassioned revival since the publication of Wilson's (1975) treatise. Replies by sociobiologists have rested, mainly, on the unassailable premise that the products of science cannot be appropriately assessed on the basis of values (Barash, 1982, p. 160; Lumsden & Wilson, 1983, p. 40). The practice obviously detracts from the pursuit of truth and, from a humanitarian standpoint, it is always a two-edged sword. Demogogues have unequivocally favored the merger of scientific and sociopolitical issues; for example, Adolph Hilter said:

> Science is a social phenomenon, and like every other social phenomenon is limited by the injury or benefit it confers on the community. (Rauschning, 1939)

Any further defense might seem superfluous. Nevertheless, there must remain a residue of uneasiness in those, like the author, who use sociobiological constructs in their science, but regard themselves as relatively gentle, tolerant folk. Theories, in themselves, are not racist or sexist or any of the aforementioned;

only the people who propogate them. Thus, though this paper portends to be an academic inquiry, it may be somewhat suffused by the feelings of personal conflict from which it originated. If the reader finds it totally confounded, at least he has been forewarned, and will have the opportunity to view the world from the perspective of the *pro*-sociobiology liberal.

The main focus is the potential scientific applicability of sociobiology to interracial and interethnic attitudes. The arguments of the critics will serve as a frame of reference, but the analyses are not constrained by these. Sociobiology is defined in the broadest sense; not, merely, in terms of the post-1960s synthesis by Wilson and others, but as the interdisciplinary endeavor encompassing the gamut of Darwinian and neo-Darwinian approaches to behavior. This is the same definition implicitly followed, overall, in the critiques.

DETERMINISM

Though the case against sociobiology ranges immensely in substance and specificity, it is held together by a general indictment of something called *genetic* or *biological determinism*. Some representative quotes follow:

> Inherent in the idea of sociobiology . . . is the notion of genetic determinism of individual differences, social differences, the stratification of classes, sexual status and racism.—(Montagu, 1980, p. 12)
> The issue is not universal biology vs. human uniqueness, but biological potentiality vs. biological determinism.—(Gould, 1977, p. 252)
> In place of a social constitution of meanings, it (sociobiology) offers a biological determination of human interaction.—(Sahlins, 1976, p. x)
> Postulating genes to account for human behaviors allows sociobiologists to minimize the difference between the genetically determined biological base and what is learned. They are not worried about their repetition of the errors of the eugenecists, social Darwinists, or racists.—(Washburn, 1978, p. 416)
> Wilson joins the long parade of biological determinists whose work has served to buttress the institutions of their society by exonerating them from responsibility from social problems.—(Letter in the *New York Review of Books*, November 13, 1975, signed by 31 academicians in the Boston area, p. 186)

Genetic or biological determininism are never precisely defined, nor are their meanings apparent. In more formal usage, determinism represents the cornerstone credo of modern science; the assumption that all events are caused. Behavioral scientists who search for causes in the physiological substratum or the phylogenetic record are, by definition, biological or genetic determinists. It is not arguable, nor does it have any critical connotation.

The concept, however, provides cunning propoganda when used to imply a philosophy of life rather than an epistemological strategy. As such, the charge of determinism can be invoked to denigrate anyone's theory and, in fact, has often been similarly applied to decry the social dangers of ultraenvironmentalists. Here the argument has been that the concept of mind as tabula rasa, wholly conditionable, provides the rationale for Orwellian type autocracies (Shultz, 1976, pp. 295–297).

What the critics really mean is evident in their stated alternatives to genetic or biological determinism; for example, *potentiality, learning, change, resolution of social problems.* The actual allegation is that sociobiological theories imply *immutability* of human behavior, which appears to be linked with racism in two different ways. One involves the immutability of racial and ethnic differences on value laden dimensions such as intelligence. The other pertains to the immutability of racism, per se.

Thus, the academic issues harbored in the critiques become more visible. Are there significant race differences in psychological and behavioral dimensions? Are there genetic bases for these? Are genetic factors directly related to racist attitudes and behaviors? What are the natures of these factors and their implications for malleability, both for the cases of race differences and racism?

All of these questions will be considered, but this requires, first, a somewhat more diverse account than that implied in the critiques of the historical and contemporary relationships of behavioral science and racism.

RACE DIFFERENCES

It would be difficult to find an area in the behavioral sciences that has generated as much sustained attention as race and ethnic differences in mental abilities, nor a debate as prolonged and passionate as that between the forces for heritability, with the implication of relative immutability, and those emphasizing environmental origins and individual potential (Richardson & Spears, 1972). Nor does one need to search very far to find the link to racism. Whether cause or effect, the argument for heritability was directly associated with discriminatory immigration policies of the United States in the 1920s (Gould, 1981, p. 232; Snyderman & Herrnstien, 1983).

The association is actually more extensive and current if one includes prejudicial practices of a *de facto* nature; that is, indirect, racist consequences of the mental measurements movement and its implicit assumptions of innate, immutable processes. Governmental bodies in the United States have become concerned of late about violations of antidiscrimination statutes related to the use of standardized, mental tests in a number of areas. The State of California, in 1982, banned the classification and segregation of school children according to Intelligence Quotients, and other states are considering the question. The Federal government, through the *Equal Opportunity Employment Commission,* has imposed stringent limitations on the uses of tests for personnel selection and promotion, and several states have adopted similar legislation. (Anastasi, 1976, p. 62–64). Aroused by a critical study by Ralph Nader, the *Federal Trade Commission* has begun an inquiry into possible discriminatory practices related to college admissions examinations developed by the *Educational Testing Service of Princeton, New Jersey* (Owen, 1983).

A further, broad area of *de facto* discrimination has yet to come under government scrutiny as such. This relates to the abrogation of freedom and civil rights by involuntary mental institutionalization, which many believe is inspired by sociopolitical rather than medical concerns (Ennis, 1972; Silverman, 1983; Szasz, 1970). The so-called serious mental disorders, particularly schizophrenia, rank a close second to IQ in the magnitude of the effort to establish heritability and immutability (Slater & Cowie, 1971). Similar to substandard IQs, the conditions are more frequently found among the economically disadvantaged, who provide an estimated 90% of mental hospital commitments (Szasz, 1970, p. 65), and who are disproportionately comprised of racial and ethnic minorities.

Thus, the assertions appear valid that the historical associations of heritability with both immutability and race differences provided some of the means, if not the impetus, for prejudice. Where the critics seem confused, however, is in their assumptions about where these modes of thought originated and flourished. It is generally implied that it occurred somewhere in the development of evolutionary theory, which is explicated in one source that I encountered. Stepan (1982) attributed it directly to Darwin:

> At the heart of Darwin's argument for evolution, therefore, was a reliance on the traditional chain of races . . . That argument was one of continuity—continuity seemed essential if he were to prove that man's mental, moral, as well as physical features have risen naturally by slow evolution from animal forms. But the argument for continuity led, almost inevitably, to the use of lower races to fill the gap between animals and man. Later scientists would find it only too easy to interpret Darwin as meaning that the races of man now formed an evolutionary scale. (p. 55)

One of the problems with this history, which may be apparent from Stephan's circuitous phrasing, is that Darwin never said, or necessarily implied, any such thing. Others, in fact, find a polar opposite position in his writings (Gould, 1977, pp. 34–38; Gruber, 1981, pp. 181–182). Gould says:

> . . . the father of evolutionary theory stood almost alone in insisting that organic change led only to increasing adaptation between organisms and their own environment and not to an abstract ideal of progress defined by structural complexity or increasing heterogeneity—never say higher or lower . . . Yet most laymen still equate evolution with progress and define human evolution not simply as change, but as increasing intelligence, increasing height, or some other measure of improvement. (p. 37)

Moreover, the mental measurements and race differences movements in the contemporary behavioral sciences are wholly a-Darwinian, and, for all essential purposes, atheoretical. They comprise an area in the interface of psychology and education that is usually titled in texts, journals, and courses, *Individual Differences* or *Differential Psychology*. The field is exemplified by a collection of readings edited by Anastasi (1965) which is prefaced:

> . . . topics were identified that represented foci of lively contemporary activity in the field. These include: the development and use of tests for the measurement of individual differences; quantitative research on the nature of intelligence through factor analysis and similar statistical techniques; behavior genetics and the heredity-environment problem. . . . (p. vii)

Darwin is briefly mentioned twice in the entire volume, as one of the pioneers of animal research (p. 4) and as an example of creativity (p. 283).

The guiding principle for the methods and conclusions of differential psychology is the saw, rooted in conventional wisdom, that "heredity sets limits; environment determines where the individual falls within these." This is the basis of the equation of heritability and immutability in modern behavioral science, and it has always been the more phylogenetically oriented psychologists who attempted to sway their colleagues from such spurious dichotomies (e.g., Hess, 1962; Lehrman, 1970). In contrast, the premise of sociobiological theory is that infracortical and cortical functions evolved in a complementary manner, and that *learning* is always explicable in terms of its adaptive significance. In this model, immutability is not viewed as a consequence of whether a behavior is attributed to heredity or environment, but whether plasticity contributed to survival in the evolutionary history (Alcock, 1979, pp. 50–98).

The main method of differential psychology, used to establish what kind of behaviors are subject to *genetic limits* and, in the hands of some (e.g., Jensen, 1969), the margins of these limits, is the co-twin study; that is, comparisons of concordance rates or correlations between sets of monozygotic and dizygotic twins. Herein, also, is the main source of artifact in individual and race differences data. A review of lesser publicized co-twin studies than those involving IQ and schizophrenia (Slater & Cowie, 1971, p. 97) suggests that it may be impossible to find a behavioral variable for which the method will *not* show heritability. Large sample, correlational techniques will enhance minute effects (Bakan, 1966) and genetics plays some role in every significant facet of development (Plomin, 1986).

The lack of discriminatory power of the co-twin method, coupled with highly questionable validity of both measures of intelligence (Anastasi, 1976, pp. 326–357; Gould, 1981) and criteria for assigning the label, schizophrenia (Silverman, 1983, pp. 45–63) assured that there was never a possibility of reasonably unconfounded data from these areas of research. Granted that heritability has been established in both cases; there are numerous, diverse, plausible explanations of what is inherited, independent of thinking abilities or mental disorder. Among the variables shown as heritable by the co-twin method which could readily account for the findings with IQ are: nervous tension, self-control, self-confidence, and orderliness. Potential latent factors in the relationships for schizophrenia include: introversion, shyness, social presence, need for affiliation, and nonconformity.

Why would competent scientists persist in the use of these ambiguous and controversial measures as the major consequent variables in exploratory studies of genetic variation? Why continue to compile data that is virtually guarenteed to be uninterpretable by any reasonable scientific standard? Apparently, this line of research in psychology was always guided more by public policy considerations than heuristic value.

Further, how could a field seemingly populated in the majority by prototypic, academic, liberal types find itself at the core of racist, public programs; its instruments subject to restrictive legislation at every governmental level. I have dealt with this question in detail elsewhere (Silverman, 1971, 1981). The essential point is that any behavioral science discipline that seeks a role in the resolution of social issues, as does psychology, enhances its vulnerability to exploitation by *all* segments of the political spectrum.

Sociobiologists, who are devoid of social roles in their professional identities, tend to eschew the topic of human race differences. One probable reason for the lack of scientific interest is that the concept of race has dubious validity in its broadest, biological definition, which was forcefully argued more than 30 years ago by one of the founders of the current sociobiological movement (Wilson & Brown, 1953), and is particularly arbitrary in its applications to humans (Fried, 1968; Gould, 1977, pp. 231–236).

Another is that the evolutionist's principle focus is on ultimate or phylogenetic causation, in contrast to the psychologist's attention to proximate or ontogenetic causation (cf. Symons, 1979, pp. 7–10). The former tends to emphasize universals; the latter differences. For example, psychological research on aggression deals mainly with physiological and experiential variables that render individuals more or less aggressive; sociobiologists are more concerned with the origin and significance of aggression throughout the animal world.

This writer found one research endeavor on race differences in the contemporary sociobiological literature. Freedman and his colleagues (Freedman, 1971, 1974, pp. 145–177; 1979, pp. 141–162) observed differences in the nature and extent of emotional expressiveness and responsiveness to adult interventions among samples of newborns from a number of ethnic and racial groups.

Freedman (1979) labors the point that nothing in his findings could be reasonably construed as injurious, and subtly shows (p. 160) that value judgments based on his data can be as readily reasoned to favor one group as another. Perhaps it is not very easy to generate data with arguable sociopolitical implications unless the research emanated from sociopolitical purposes.

In regard to malleability there is a brief note by Freedman (1979, p. 155) to the effect that counterparts of some of his reported differences have been observed in older children. The question of malleability, in fact, is not one of prime significance for sociobiologists in general. It derives significance from the psychological model, in which heredity and environment are regarded as dichotomous determinants, with immutability ascribed to one and infinite plasticity to the other. Within the evolutionary paradigm, all behavioral patterns and psychological processes emerged from the interaction of phylogenetic dispositions and ontogenetic events. Questions about the nature of this interaction are the main foci of attention, and are prerequisite to concerns about malleability. For example, the sociobiologist would probably not embark upon projects such as the much heralded efforts by psychologists to teach human-like language to chimps. There would be no theoretical framework to accomodate the answers without prior resolution of the questions of why, in the evolutionary histories of chimps and humans, their particular forms of communication developed and how these become manifest in ontogeny.

Thus, the most relevant aspects of Freedman's findings from the standpoint of malleability are the differences he noted between groups in maternal style, which were congruent to differences in infant temperment. Herein may reside clues to the puzzle of how innate tempermental dispositions are mediated by the environment to exert their influences on the developing personality. When this puzzle is solved, it may be possible to pose conceptually fruitful questions about potential for personality change.

INNATE SCHEMATA

We now turn from race differences to racist attitudes and behaviors, and the supposed implications in sociobiological theory that these, too, are innate and immutable. The question, in more precise terms, is whether dispositions toward avoidance or antagonism between genetically disparate groups evolved and are maintained by natural selection; that is, does racism exist because it is adaptive?

One way to conceive adaptive functions of racism was brought into sharp focus by the writings of Konrad Lorenz, in Germany, during the Nazi era (Cloud, 1973). Lorenz invoked the ethological concept of *innate schemata,* which normally referred to conspecific preferences in imprinting, as indicative of instinctive, interracial aversions; that is, he postulated that the same mechanisms that keep species generally isolated from each other operate at the level of human populations, and, on this basis, he supported ongoing Nazi programs of segregation. So odious were these pieces in the context of their time and place that critics are inclined to cite them as proforma proof of the inherent racism of the field. For example, Eisenberg (1972) quotes from the material in no less a venerable source as *Science,* with the sole rationale that, "it is necessary to make overt what is latent in treatises on the innate nature of man" (p. 124).

Nor was Lorenz's impact lost on his fellow ethologists. The phrase, "innate schemata" has virtually disappeared from the literature, despite continued interest in the phenomena to which it originally applied. Suspicions may be raised, as well, about the enthusiastic attentions given to meaningless confirmations of the null hypothesis in the reports of several studies which failed to isolate object preferences in imprinting (Fabricius, 1955; Hess, 1959).

By whatever name, the process of imprinting does entail inherent stimuli preferences which serve to keep the young animal oriented to conspecifics, in general, and parents, in particular (cf. Hinde, 1966, pp. 370–371). The data include carefully controlled, replicable demonstrations of gazing preferences in human neonates to schematics of frontal, human faces (Fantz, 1961; Freedman, 1971; Goren, Sarty, & Wu, 1975). The trend, however, is toward interspecies differences in both form and plasticity of stimuli preferences, which appear to be coherently related to ecological variations. Thus, wood ducks, who nest in holes nearby water, respond to precise calls uttered by parents; mallards, who stay in view of each other, attend to visual cues (cf. Gould, 1982, pp. 266–268; Sluckin, 1965, pp. 23–38).

Beyond Lorenz, the relevance of any of this to human races has been considered in just one study I have found. Kilhem and Klopfer (1968) described data suggesting strain-specific imprinting preferences in chicks, with the conclusion, "For students of behavior, the construct 'race' cannot be ignored" (p. 24).

How did the investigators get so handily from strain to race? The reasoning seems to be contained in the following passage (Kilhem & Klopfer):

> Within a species there may be subgroups between which gene flow is particularly enhanced or retarded because of geographic propinquity, behavioral differences, or, particularly in human beings, social or economic factors. Subgroups of a species may pass under many names: variety is one, race another. (p. 16)

The surmise, then, is that circumstances producing reproductive isolation among human groups may have resulted in selective imprinting mechanisms, similar to the effects of artificially produced reproductive isolation in domestic strains.

There is a critical flaw, however, in extrapolating to natural occurring populations from those created by artificial selection. With the exception of relatively few species where opportunities for exogamic mating are ecologically limited, natural selection appears to favor outbreeding (Bischof, 1975). Two adaptive functions are served; the avoidance of "inbreeding depressions" and the propogation of sufficient diversity within the gene pool to provide plasticity in the face of environmental variations. The latter seems particularly relevant to human evolution and, indeed, there is evidence for a universal mechanism to encourage outbreeding: sexual disdain for those with whom you have been raised in early childhood (Shepher, 1971; van den Berghe, 1983).

History supports this viewpoint in the evidence for miscegenist trends, whether emenating from conquest or migration (Cox, 1948, pp. 353–392; Kitano, 1974, pp. 41–63). This is, of course, one reason for the instability of the race concept in humans; the categories keep changing (Volpe, 1982, pp. 126–127).

The challenge, then, is to explain assortative mating, based on ethnicity, and antimiscegenist movements, though the latter may support the present view in the sense that social and political sanctions do not arise unless there is a significant tendency toward the behavior in question. But why do these phenomena occur at all?

The answer may reside in Bateson's (1978) concept of "optimal outbreeding." This refers to a compromise in sexual object choice, observed in infrahumans, between similarity and dissimilarity to self, which is ascribed to, "opposing evolutionary pressures to be well adapted, on the one hand, and highly adaptable, on the other" (p. 660). Optimal outbreeding may function in much the same way as "optimal clutch size" (Lack, 1954), which pertains to systematic variations in birth rates across generations. These variations are attributable to proximate mechanisms responsive to ecological clues regarding future, available resources. Similarly, proximate mechanisms responsive to clues regarding future, relative advantages of adaptation vs. adaptability may determine variations in mating preferences on the dimension of similarity-dissimilarity. Just as optimal clutch size (Dawkins, 1976, pp. 120–131), the unit of selection can be conceptualized in terms of the individual or the group.

This model may provide researchable propositions about historical and demographic variables associated with trends in mate choices, based on the relative advantages of adaptation to extant, ecological niches as opposed to adaptability to changing conditions. Homo sapiens flourish in a variety of environments with enormous ranges in homogeniety, complexity, and predictability. Though it is left to the reader at this juncture to provide more precise operational definitions, the point here is that such ecological differences may relate to mate choice along the dimension of similarity-dissimilarity. We might also generate hypotheses about inter-individual differences in sexual attraction to similar or dissimilar others, based on differential propensities for being well adapted or highly adaptable.

In all such studies, the similarity-dissimilarity dimension may be conveniently represented in terms of miscegenation. Race, however, would merely serve as a crude operational definition, less preferable to a relative measure, reflecting the actual ranges of diversity afforded individuals and/or groups. Indeed, intuition and experience suggest that there are no intrinsic criteria for approach or avoidant, intergroup, sexual attitudes; they can be aroused as intensely between neighboring villages or descendents of different regions within the same national border as any other human grouping.

INCLUSIVE FITNESS

The concept of "inclusive fitness" (Hamilton, 1964) may also provide conjectures about the adaptive functions of racism. Undoubtably the most heuristic, sociobiological principle of the past two decades, inclusive fitness extends the definition of "individual fitness" from the original, Darwinian sense of fitness to survive and propogate. The new construct applies to fitness to enhance all components and counterparts of one's genotype, including those within other individuals of common descent.

The potential relevance to racism resides in the definition of common descent. If it is absolute, confined to some conventional criterion of relatedness such as third cousins, then the relevance is nil. If, however, it is boundless, so that any two individuals can be compared on a scale of genetic communality, then the means for maximization of inclusive fitness would include preferential treatment of nonfamilial, genotypically similar others. Questions remain regarding the specific bases by which individuals estimate genetic communality (Alexander, 1979, pp. 120–122). Nevertheless, it seems evident in the human case that phenotypic variables, coupled with background information, can provide reliable approximations. A caucasion of Nordic descent can probably assume with confidence that others in that category contain a larger representation of his genotype than, for example, East Indian Sikhs.

But is it in the interest of the individuals' inclusive fitness to maintain different standards of behavior toward these groups. In the initial presentation of the principle, Hamilton (1964) suggested the negative. Describing coefficients of relationship from, "unity for clonal individuals," through, "one-eighth for cousins," he concluded, "and finally zero for all neighbors whose relationship can be considered negligibly small" (p. 8). Eleven years later, however (Hamilton, 1975), he appeared to equivocate, stating that, ". . . the inclusive fitness concept is more general than kin selection," and proposing that "mean intra-group relatedness" can influence cohesiveness at the level of human colonies, such as villages or towns (pp. 141–144). Hamilton's interpreters tend to accept the latter view. Symons (1979) considers that inclusive fitness applies to, "nonrelatives in whom genetic affinity can be recognized" (p. 7). Alexander (1979) refers to "extrafamilial nepotism" (p. 161). Dawkins (1976) says that, "the whole point of Hamilton's argument is that the distinction between family and non-family is not hard and fast, but a matter of mathematical probability" (p. 101). van den Berghe (1981) agrees that, "relatedness is a relative matter," and maintains that inclusive fitness theory provides a "convincing answer" to the question of why ethnicity exists at all (pp. 19–21).

Sociobiological theories of the origins of human warfare bear also on the issue, in that intergroup relatedness is usually regarded as a mitigating factor in primitive tribal conflicts (Alcock, 1979, pp. 449–450). Within the present framework, the question is whether the relatedness factor in primitive warfare, in which direct, familial kinship ties between groups could probably be ascertained, can be extrapolated to the modern condition.

Theorists tend to be uncharacteristically inconsistant or vague about the question. For example, Dawkins (1976) regards racial prejudice as, "an irrational generalization of a kin selected tendency to identify with individuals physically resembling oneself and to be nasty to individuals different in appearance" (p. 108). Based on his own interpretation, noted above, that family and nonfamily represent points on a continuum of genetic relatedness, it is unclear why the generalization is irrational. Wilson (1978) puts modern racism in the class of "hypertrophic modifications," which refer to "culturally nurtured" eggagerations of, "biologically meaningful institutions of hunter-gatherer bands and early tribal states" (p. 92). Barash (1979) regards it as a "woefully maladaptive" vestige, to which evolution will, "catch up and select against" (p. 154).

There appears to be a wide acceptance of the influence of genetic relatedness in modern intergroup conflict, and a strain to detach it from its primitive role. Sociobiologists at the forefront may have become somewhat sensitive to their detractors, who have, in fact, made general references to racist implications of any such parallels (Alper, 1979, p. 208; Stepan, 1982, p. 57).

Conventional wisdom aside, however, it remains an open question as to whether genotypic communality is a determining factor in modern intergroup conflict. Thus, we took a brief, empirical assessment of three, classic means by which one group increases the inclusive fitness of its members at the expense of another; warfare, slavery, and control of food resources.

Kidron and Smith (1983) define war as open, armed conflict, characterized by central organization and some degree of continuity. Their atlas of wars since 1945 showed a total of 279, occurring within the boundaries of all but 27 countries throughout the world. The analyses pertinant to the present issue involve the relationships of the combatants. One hundred ninety-five; 71% of the total, were civil wars, including 54 that were regional, whereby it would seem to be a reasonable assumption that protagonists, for the most part, were from the same ethnic and/or racial population. Those between nations comprised 66 border wars, 12 of a more general nature between neighbors, and 4 between nonneighbors. There appeared to be a decided trend for civil wars to be longer in duration, though there were too many cases in which specific time intervals were uncertain to make quantitative comparisons. Comparative death rates would have also been informative, but these data, the authors noted, were not included because of their general unreliability.

The institution of slavery is probably popularly associated with the African slave trade of about 1450 to 1850, conducted by Europeans, Arabs, East Indians, and Americans, in most of the settled western hemisphere and parts of the east (Davidson, 1961). It may be less well appreciated that slavery was ubiquitous throughout the recorded history of humankind, from the Babylonian Empire of 2000 BC to the present. Most significant for the present issue is the observation that slavery before and after the relatively brief period of the African trade was overwhelmingly "endo-ethnic" (Marsh, 1974), with slavers and slaves from the same racial or ethnic group. In fact, the African trade could not have reached nearly the magnitude it did without thriving endo-ethnic movements to supply the human resource, at its core (Davidson, 1961, pp. 79–162; Marsh, 1974, pp. 88–89; Patterson, 1982, pp. 354–356).

World hunger is undeniably racial in its distribution. (Kidron & Segal, 1981) Again, the conventional view is that inequities are implicitly or explicitly sustained by race politics. For example, Barclay, Kumar, and Simms (1976) introduce a selection of edited papers on this position, as follows:

> No longer is there a need for the white administrator, plantation owner, or entrepreneur. The international system of racial domination and subordination can now reproduce itself without the violence of colonial conquest. In place of conquest is the silent violence of malnutrition, infant mortality and substandard living conditions . . . (p. 369)

The problem with this interpretation, however, is that famines and mass malnutrition appear to be primarily due to internal resource distribution. According to the United Nations Food and Agricultural Organization, food supplies in nations where starvation occurs are sufficient to meet the overall nutritional requirements of their populations. The reason for hunger in the midst of plenty relate to local politics and economics. Eighty-five percent of the world's poor live in rural areas where they either work on large estates for inadequate wages or hold plots of land in feudal systems and pay the majority of their harvests in rent. At the height of the 1974 famines in Bangladesh, for examples, an estimated four million tons of rice remained stored in the country for want of buyers with sufficient funds. The organization CARE tried, in vain, for 4 years prior to the 1984 famine in Ethiopia, to negotiate an agreement with the government of that country that would provide for food distribution with a minimum of theft and corruption. (Articles in the *Toronto Star:* April 2, 1983; June 25, 1983; November 11, 1984).

Thus, intergroup oppression seems to show a pronounced endo-ethnic bias. Within the sociobiological concept of resource competition as the basis for intergroup conflict, it is certainly plausible that such conflicts should predominate among proximate groups. It does, nevertheless, suggest that, from a world view, the role of genetic communality is meager and subordinate to pragmatic considerations, at best.

The alternative perspective is that the influences of genetic communality, at least in homo sapiens, is rigidly bounded by some criterion of family. Beyond these boundaries, interpersonal and intergroup interactions are entirely opportunistic. This viewpoint is congruent to the observations above, and to others. We are a species notable for transient allegiances (Wilson, 1968, pp. 159–164). Ingroup - outgroup compositions are in constant flux, in response to changing contingencies. For example, in American history of just the past 3 decades, her most denigrated enemies in war have become her fondest economic partners; her most downtrodden minority group now has members as mayors of 19 large cities, north and south, and a serious presidential candidate.

Moreover, this view is coherent from the standpoint of natural selection. Much significance is attributed to group alliances in human evolution (Durham, 1976; McEachron & Baer, 1982). It seems plausible that selection would have favored plasticity in these formations, inasmuch as individuals and/or groups with maximal options could achieve the most adaptive arrangements in response to variable situational factors. Racism, here defined as apriori interpersonal affinities beyond direct kin, would, naturally, impose constraints on plasticity and limits to options. In the terms of one prominent paradigm (Maynard-Smith & Price, 1973), racial tolerance, confronted by racial intolerance, would have evolved as the *Evolutionarily Stable Strategy*. Whatever small gains might have accrued to inclusive fitness by fixed responses, based on similarity, to extra-familial others, would have been lost to the advantages of the capacity to form situationally optimal alliances.

Social psychological theories and data are also consistant with his outlook, in that they stress the general, amorphous nature and malleability of social attitudes (Wrightsman, 1972, 291–338). Particularly relevant is "cognitive dissonance theory" (Festinger, 1957), which has revealed the ease and extent by which social attitudes are modified to conform to altered circumstances. There is evidence of this, also, in specific regard to racial attitudes (Campbell, 1958; Silverman & Shaw, 1973).

Thus, racism never would have been adaptive. It would have selected out at the time of the transition, about 10,000 years ago, from small, intra- and interrelated bands to larger, heterogeneous groupings.

What might readily have been adaptive from the perspective of this analysis, however, is the capacity for *racist rationalizations*, a self-deceptive tendency which provides for the preservation of commonly held virtues like fidelity and fairness, in the face of our perennial pursuit of pragmatic ingroup-outgroup formations. Endo-ethnic slave movements throughout history created actual or symbolic distinctions to demark slavers from slaves; for example, shaving heads, excommunicating, or assigning labels connoting separate ethnic origins (Patterson, 1982, pp. 35–76). The modern word, *slave*, in fact, somes from *Slav*, the term used for all bondsman in medieval Germany, irrespective of actual descent and including many Germans (Marsh, 1974, p. 55).

One explanation of the adaptive significance of self-deception is that it enhances deception of others (Alexander, 1975, p. 97). What may be selected for, then, on an individual or group basis, is the capacity to maintain self-images of egalitarianism and loyalty, but have rationalizations at the ready if circumstances favor exploitation or desertion of a former ally. The implication of this is that ethnocentric attitudes are primarily a consequence rather than a cause of intergroup strife, which is antithetical to the sequence underlying most approaches to the topic (Kitano, 1974).

In a sense, van den Berghe (1981, pp. 242–244) argues the opposite position, maintaining that alliances based on "common kinship"; that is, ethnicity, compared to alliances based on "common interests," such as classes, are, "more permenant and more basic." He notes, as illustration, that the taking of American hostages in Iran several years ago was not perceived in the United States as part of a class struggle, but as, "an affront of Iranians against Americans." Within the present framework, it may be assumed that the class nature of the conflict was appreciated by Americans, at some level beneath self-awareness, but mass perception of it as a racial incident justified resolution without compromise to their favored economic status.

The general questions illuminated by the contrasting positions, however, may be better resolved empirically than by posing alternative perspectives on history. As a brief example, I asked groups of students, anonymously, how much more they would pay for various expensive products, manufactured locally rather than in a remote country, given that both were of identical quality in all respects. The mean was about fifty cents; the mode, zero. The reasons given by those who said they would pay more mostly entailed eventual, material benefits to themselves from support of the local economy. In comparative psychology, the strength of a motive is measured by the sacrifice an animal will make for its satisfaction. Applied to this demonstration, the intensity levels of nationalism and ethnocentrism, in the absence of direct, selfish, gain, appear virtually nil. Wilson (1978, p. 164) has made a similar surmise, and these contentions are currently being pursued by the writer in more formal research.

Another implication of the present analysis of racism is that its boundaries and targets will show infinite plasticity, but the phenomenon, though more apparent than real, will be ubiquitous in the presence of intergroup conflict. If this represents a pessimistic note to those who abhor the practice, whatever its function, we must be reminded, again, that the equation of genetics and immutability does not stem from the sociobiological model. Powers of choice emanate from the same biological substratum as the most circumscribed reflex. So, also, is anti-racism as much a product of natural selection as racism.

It does, in fact, appear that our systematic self-deceptions are somewhat frail, or, at least, subject to strong conflict. In specific regard to rationalizations, research has shown that they are relinquished when brought to conscious focus, where they can no longer serve ego-defensive purposes (Katz, Sarnoff, & McClintock, 1956). Thus, to the extent that the present speculations are veridical, the most hopeful course for the alleviation of racism is accurate education based on the unfettered search for ontogenetic and phylogenetic origins.

ACKNOWLEDGMENTS

Gratitude is expressed to Michael Bagby and Irene Bevc for their research assistance. In addition to the Editors, others who read earlier drafts of the manuscript and provided helpful comments were: Daniel Freedman, Christine Littlefield, and Pierre van den Berghe. Aspects of this paper were presented by the author at the 1984 meetings of the Canadian Psychological Association and the 1985 meetings of the European Sociobiological Society.

REFERENCES

Alcock, J. (1979). *Animal behavior* (2nd. Ed.). Sunderland: Sinauer.
Alexander, R. D. (1975). The search for a general theory of behavior. *Behavioral Science, 20,* 77–100.
Alexander, R. D. (1979). *Darwinism and human affairs.* Seattle: University of Washington Press.
Alper, J. S. (1979). Ethical and social implications. In M. S. Gregory, A. Silvers, & D. Sutch (Eds.), *Sociobiology and human nature* (pp. 195–212). San Francisco: Jossey-Bass.
Anastasi, A. (Ed). (1965). *Individual differences.* New York: Wiley.
Anastasi, A. (1976). *Psychological testing* (4th Ed.). New York: Macmillan.
Bakan, D. (1966). The test of significance of psychological research. *Psychological Bulletin, 66,* 423–437.
Barash, D. (1979). *The whisperings within.* New York: Harper & Row.
Barash, D. P. (1982). *Sociobiology and behavior* (2nd Ed.). New York: Elsevier.
Barclay, W., Kumar, K., & Simms, R. P. (Eds.). (1976). *racial conflict, discrimination, and power: Historical & contemporary studies.* New York: AMS Press.
Bateson, P. (1978, June 22). Sexual imprinting and optimal outbreeding. *Nature, 273,* 659–660.
Bischof, N. (1975). Comparative ethology of incest avoidance. In R. Fox (Ed.) *Biosocial anthropology* (pp. 37–67). New York: Halstead.
Campbell, E. Q. (1958). Some social psychological correlates of direction of attitude change. *Social Forces, 36,* 335–340.
Cloud, W. (1973). Winners and sinners: A few recent observations on the awarding of the Nobel Prize. *The Sciences, 13,* 16–21.
Cox, O. C. (1948). *Caste, class, and race.* New York: Doubleday.
Davidson, B. (1961). *The African slave trade.* Boston: Little Brown.
Dawkins, R. (1976). *The selfish gene.* Oxford: Oxford University Press.
Durham, W. H. (1976). Resource competition and human aggression. *Quarterly Review of Biology, 51,* 385–415.
Eisenberg, L. (1972, April 14). The "human" nature of human nature. *Science, 176,* 123–128.
Ennis, B. (1972). *Prisoners of psychiatry.* New York: Harcourt, Brace, Jovanovich.
Fabricius, E. (1955). Experiments on the following response of mallard ducklings. *British Journal of Animal Behaviour, 3,* 122.
Fantz, R. L. (1961). The origin of form perception. *Scientific American, 204,* 66–72.
Festinger, L. (1957). *A theory of cognitive dissonance.* Evanston, IL: Row, Peterson & Co.

Freedman, D. G. (1971). Behavioral assessment in infancy. In G. B. A. Stoeling & J. J. Van Der Weoff Ten Bosch (Eds.), *Normal and abnormal development of brain and behavior* (pp. 92–103). Leiden: Leiden University Press.

Freedman, D. G. (1974). *Human infancy: An evolutionary perspective.* New York: Wiley.

Freedman, D. G. (1979). Human Sociobiology: *A Holistic Approach.* New York: The Free Press.

Fried, M. H. (1968). The need to end the pseudoscientific investigation of race. In M. Mead, T. Dobzhansky, E. Tobach, & R. E. Light (Eds.), *Science and the concept of race* (pp. 121–131). New York: Columbia University Press.

Goren, C. G., Sarty, M., & Wu, P. (1975). Visual following and pattern discrimination of face-like stimuli by newborn infants. *Pediatrics, 56,* 544–549.

Gould, J. L. (1982). *Ethology: The mechanisms and evolution of behavior.* New York: Norton.

Gould, S. J. (1977). *Ever since Darwin: Reflections in natural history.* New York: Norton.

Gould, S. J. (1981). *The mismeasure of man.* New York: Norton.

Gruber, H. E. (1981). *Darwin on man: A psychological study of scientific creativity* (2nd Ed.). Chicago: University of Chicago Press.

Hamilton, W. D. (1964). The genetical theory of social behaviour (I). *Journal of Theoretical Biology, 7,* 1–16.

Hamilton, W. D. (1975). Innate social aptitudes of man: An approach from evolutionary genetics. In R. Fox (Ed.), *Biosocial anthropology* (pp. 135–155). New York: Wiley.

Hess, E. H. (1959). Imprinting. *Science, 130,* 133–141.

Hess, E. (1962). Ethology: An approach toward the complete analysis of behavior. In T. M. Newcomb (Ed.), *New directions in psychology.* New York: Holt, Rinehart & Winston.

Hinde, R. A. (1966). *Animal behaviour.* New York: McGraw-Hill.

Jensen, A. R. (1969). How much can we boost I.Q. and scholastic achievement? *Harvard Educational Review, 39,* 1–123.

Katz, D., Sarnoff, D., & McClintock, C. G. (1956). Ego-defense and attitude change. *Human Relations, 9,* 27–45.

Kidron, M., & Segal, R. (1981). *The state of the world atlas.* New York: Simon & Schuster.

Kidron, M., & Smith, D. (1983). *The war atlas.* New York: Simon & Schuster.

Kilhem, P., & Klopfer, P. H. (1968). The construct race and the innate differential. In M. Mead, T. Dobzhansky, E. Tobach, & R. E. Light (Eds.), *Science and the concept of race* (pp. 16–25). New York: Columbia University Press.

Kitano, H. H. L. (1974). *Race relations.* Englewood Cliffs, NJ: Prentice-Hall.

Lack, D. (1954). *The natural regulation of animal numbers.* Oxford: Clarendon Press.

Lehrman, D. S. (1970). Semantics and conceptual issues in the nature-nurture problem. In L. Aronson, D. Lehrman, & J. Rosenblatt (Eds.), *Development and evolution of behavior.* San Francisco: Freeman.

Lumsden, C. J., & Wilson, E. O. (1983). *Prometheon fire: Reflections on the origin of mind.* Cambridge: Harvard University Press.

Marsh, H. (1974). *Slavery and race.* New York: St. Martin's.

Maynard-Smith, J., & Price, G. T. (1973). The logic of animal conflict. *Nature, 246,* 15–18.

McEachron, D. L., & Baer, D. (1982). A review of selected sociobiological principles: Application to hominid evolution. II. The effects of intergroup conflict. *Journal of Social and Biological Structures, 5,* 121–129.

Montague, A. (1980). *Sociobiology examined,* New York: Oxford University Press.

Owen, D. (1983, May). The last days of ETS. *Harper's, 266,* 21–37.

Patterson, O. (1982). *Slavery and Social Death: A Comparative Study.* Cambridge: Harvard University Press.

Plomin, R. (1986). *Development, Genetics, and Psychology.* Hillsdale, NJ: Lawrence Erlbaum Associates.

Rauschning, H. (1939). *Hitler speaks: A series of political conversations with Adolph Hitler on his real aims*. London: Butterworth.

Richardson, K., & Spears, D. (Eds.). (1972). *Race and intelligence*. Baltimore: Penguin.

Ruse, M. (1982). *Darwinism defended: A guide to the evolution controversies*. Reading, MA: Addison-Wesley.

Sahlins, M. (1976). *The use and abuse of biology: An anthropological critique of sociobiology*. Ann Arbor: University of Michigan Press.

Shepher, J. (1971). Mate selection among second generation kibbutz adolescents and adults: Incest avoidance and negative imprinting. *Archives of Sexual Behavior, 1,* 293–307.

Shultz, D. (1976). *Theories of personality*. Belmont, CA: Wadsworth.

Silverman, I. (1971). Crisis in social psychology: The relevance of relevance. *American Psychologist, 26,* 583–584.

Silverman, I. (1981). Psychology: The unwanted science. *New Directions for methodology in social and behavioral science, 8,* 81–87.

Silverman, I. (1983). *Pure types are rare: Myths and meanings of madness*. New York: Praeger.

Silverman, I., & Shaw, M. E. (1973). Effects of sudden, mass, school desegregation of interracial interaction and attitudes in one southern city. *Journal of Social Issues, 29,* 133–142.

Slater, E., & Cowie, V. (1971). *The genetics of mental disorder*. London: University of Oxford Press.

Sluckin, W. (1965). *Imprinting and early learning*. Chicago: Aldine.

Snyderman, M., & Herrnstein, R. (1983). Intelligence tests and the Immigration Act of 1924. *American Psychologist, 38,* 986–996.

Stepan, N. (1982). *The idea of race in science, 1800–1960*. Hamden: Archon.

Symons, D. (1979). The evolution of Human Sexuality. New York: Oxford University Press.

Szasz, T. S. (1970). The manufacture of madness. New York: Harper & Row.

van den Berghe, P. L. (1981). The ethnic phenomenon. New York: Elsevier.

van den Berghe, P. L. (1983). Human inbreeding avoidance: Culture in nature. The Behavioral and Brain Sciences, 6, 91–123.

Volpe, E. P. (1982). *Understanding evolution* (4th Ed.). Dubuque, IA: W. C. Brown.

Washburn, S. L. (1978). Human behavior and the behavior of other animals. *American Psychologist, 33,* 405–418.

Wilson, E. O. (1975). *Sociobiology: The new synthesis*. Cambridge, MA: Harvard University Press.

Wilson, E. O. (1978). *On human nature*. Cambridge, MA: Harvard University Press.

Wilson, E. O., & Brown, W. L. (1953, September). The subspecies concept and its taxonomic application. *Systematic Zoology, 2,* 97–11.

Wrightsman, L. S. (1972). *Social psychology in the seventies*. Monterey, CA: Brooks-Cole.

III

APPLICATIONS

Sociobiology has a wide variety of applications that may be of interest to psychologists. The nine chapters in the final section of the book illustrate how a variety of researchers are currently using sociobiology to help them understand human behavior. The first two chapters, by Martin Smith, a developmental psychologist, and Robert Fagen, a mathematical biologist, provide insights into how modern evolutionary thinking might illuminate our understanding of human development.

Sociobiology may provide some insights into the sources of human conflict and violence as well as suggesting some methods of dealing with them. Two psychologists, Martin Daly and Margo Wilson, examine the evolutionary significance of family violence in Chapter 12. Randy Thornhill, an entomologist, and Nancy Thornhill, an anthropologist, ask whether human rape could have been adaptive in ancestral human populations, and combine their skills in discussing the strengths of the evolutionary perspective for answering the question. Suicide and self-destructive behavior have always been something of a paradox for those taking an evolutionary perspective. Denys de Catanzaro focuses the attention of a biopsychologist on this question in Chapter 13.

The concluding three chapters deal with several aspects of human mating. David Buss uses Darwin's theory of sexual selection to fashion a systematic view of some aspects of sex differences in human mate selection criteria. Incest, its costs, benefits and taboos, has fascinated poets, philosophers and scientists since they began deliberating on the human condition. The final two chapters bring the insights provided by evolutionary theory to this subject. Sociologist Pierre Van Den Berghe, examines the adaptive aspects of incest taboos in the practices of four African societies. Nancy and Randy Thornhill discuss the evolutionary significance of rules of mating and marriage pertaining to affinal and consanguineal relatives. They argue that these rules are not focused on close relatives, that they are focused on inbreeding and adultery and therefore that they enhance the fitness of powerful male rulemakers.

Finally, Martin Smith discusses issues facing evolutionary psychologists and suggests directions for future enquiry. He notes the waning of the polemical criticisms of sociobiology and emphasizes the need for more empirical research designed to test hypotheses derived from evolutionary theory. He also emphasizes that human sociobiology, although grounded in biology, is an interdisciplinary enterprise requiring contributions from anthropology, psychology and sociology and encourages psychologists to become involved in sociobiological research.

9

Evolution and Developmental Psychology: Toward a Sociobiology of Human Development

Martin S. Smith
Brock University

It has long been obvious that human ontogeny is the product of millions of years of biological evolution. Indeed, some observers credit Charles Darwin with founding child psychology, among that gentleman's other accomplishments (Kessen, 1965). However what has not been obvious is the nature of the relationship between our evolution as a species and our development as individual human beings. A number of early psychological researchers such G. S. Hall (1904) and J. M. Baldwin (1894) viewed human development in terms of its evolutionary significance, but, while providing some insights into the function of children's behavior, these attempts did not provide a satisfactory and complete answer to the question of why natural selection shaped the human lifespan as it did.

Recent developmental theorists have generally not dealt with the influence of evolution on development in much detail (e.g., Bandura, 1977; Kohlberg, 1969) or have proposed a model of evolutionary processes that conflicts with the consensus of contemporary evolutionary biologists (Piaget, 1978). The recent covergence of biological disciplines known as sociobiology, however, provides some ideas that have proved useful in understanding human development. In this chapter I summarize some sociobiological thinking relevant to human development, review research that has applied an evolutionary perspective to topics in human development, and discuss obstacles to the creation of a sociobiology of human development.

SOCIOBIOLOGICAL CONCEPTS AND THEIR
RELEVANCE TO HUMAN DEVELOPMENT

Life History Strategies

It is easy to think of evolution as producing the adult form of an organism and to ignore the fact that what actually evolved was an ontogeny, or life history. Presumably infancy and adolescence were shaped by natural selection to the same degree as adulthood. Evolution designed a program for guiding humans through a specific range of environments during a restricted time period, in order to achieve the goal of optimal reproduction.

From an evolutionary perspective, the human lifespan is a strategy programmed by the thousands of genes that constitute individual humans, aimed at replicating themselves in the next generation of humans. Natural selection has selected those genes that have best worked together with other genes in order to produce a developmental program that efficiently produces copies of those genes. In this perspective, ontogenies can be viewed as the way genes program individuals to make copies of themselves.

Of course, the evolution of the human lifespan was constrained by a number of factors, referred to by Wilson (1975) as phylogenetic inertia. This means that as a result of our genetic heritage as primates, it would be difficult for evolution to alter some basic aspects of human development such as sexual reproduction, internal fertilization of females, a prolonged period of immaturity, and extensive parental investment. It is unlikely that there is enough genetic variability or structural flexibility to select for humans who produced offspring by cloning, for instance, or to produce humans who could give birth at the age of four.

But within these broad constraints, evolution could, and did act to select a life history that constituted the most efficient design for replicating genes. That design, of course, is the human life span as we know it, with features including a 9-month gestation period, an infancy stage of extreme helplessness (by primate standards), rapid and continuous physical, cognitive, linguistic and social development during childhood, sexual maturity at 10 to 18 years, with a decline in reproductive capability beginning at 30 to 40 years, followed by a postreproductive phase of senescence, and then death. Other characteristics of the human life history include singleton births, usually, and extensive parental nurturance, particularly from the female parent.

Ecologists refer to the general category of life-history strategy exemplified by humans as a K-selected strategy: long life span, relatively few offspring, considerable parental investment in each offspring (MacArthur & Wilson, 1967). This contrasts with the r-selected strategy demonstrated by animals such as mice and mosquitoes: short life spans, many offspring and little parental investment. Obviously this characterization is relative. A mouse is K-selected compared to a mosquito, but r-selected compared to humans. Although researchers have questioned the ultimate validity of categorizing life-histories in terms of r and K selection (Daly & Wilson, 1983; Stearns, 1977), it remains a useful heuristic for comparing ontogenies.

There have been repeated calls over the last 20 years for developmental psychology to increase its analytic power and generalizability, by becoming more developmental (McCall, 1977), ecologically valid (Bronfenbrenner, 1979), sensitive to historical context (Riegel & Meacham, 1976), cross-cultural (Laboratory of Comparative Human Cognition, 1979) and biological (Scarr, 1979). Integrating a contemporary evolutionary perspective into thinking about development may help the field respond to these injunctions. Evolutionary theorists would heartily applaud the suggestion that developmental psychology should become more concerned with the entire human life span, but would add that a truly longitudinal perspective would take into account the biological evolution of the life span. An evolutionary perspective is by nature cross-cultural; it focuses on behavior in a natural context, and it is concerned with the historical context of development in the broadest sense.

One of the values of viewing the lifespan as an evolved strategy is that it illuminates some nonobvious relationships among seemingly disparate aspects of development. For instance Gould (1977a) provides an evolutionary explanation for the pronounced helplessness of human infants compared to the newborns of other primate species. He suggests that the large size of the human brain at birth, combined with the bipedal, upright human anatomy made it impossible for women to deliver babies with craniums any larger than that of an embryo at 9 months postconception. This perspective suggests that newborn infants may be embryos who have been prematurely expelled from the womb before they are physically able to cope with the world, because the cognitive hardware necessary for later survival is too large for later safe passage. Viewing infancy in this perspective casts a new light on the newborn's abilities and limitations, one that might well produce specific hypotheses regarding developmental patterns and problems.

A social scientist who has some knowledge of the evolution of the human life span is in a position similar to a doctor who has the medical history of a patient. Such knowledge provides extra information regarding the origins of a particular phenomenon, and although that information will not always be relevant to a specific problem, it will often be helpful and will sometimes be essential in the search for a solution.

Inclusive Fitness and Kin Investment

Darwin (1859) stated that evolution selects organisms to accomplish two goals: to survive and to reproduce. In 1964, W. D. Hamilton extended Darwin's reasoning by pointing out that evolution should not only favor the reproduction of offspring, but under some conditions should also select for altruism toward individuals other than direct descendants, particularly collateral relatives such as siblings, nephews, and nieces. Inclusive fitness is a measure of reproductive success that includes the effects of an individual's behavior on the reproduction of nondescendant relatives, as well as descendant relatives such as offspring (Grafen, 1982; Hamilton, 1964; Noonan, this volume). The concept of inclusive fitness greatly stimulated thinking about the evolution of social behavior because it provided a theoretical explanation for the evolution of social behavior other than sex and parenting.

In 1972 Robert Trivers contributed another key sociobiological concept. Parental investment is anything that a parent does to help her offspring survive and reproduce, at the expense of not helping another offspring. Parental investment can include feeding, protecting, and teaching offspring, and any of a variety of physiological and behavioral mechanisms that parents evolved in order to aid the survival and reproduction of offspring. However, as mentioned earlier, under certain circumstances individuals can increase their inclusive fitness by aiding kin other than their offspring, and parental investment can therefore be viewed as being subsumed by the broader category of kin investment, which includes anything an individual does to help a relative survive and reproduce.

The concepts of inclusive fitness and kin investment are relevant to developmentalists because, like most advances in scientific theory, they suggest relationships among phenomena that were not previously considered, or were not considered in enough depth. The concept of inclusive fitness suggests that evolution will have favored behaviors that aid survival and reproduction of offspring and other relatives. Furthermore, evolution should not have selected behavior for any other reason. Therefore we can assume that many aspects of human development evolved because of their contribution to inclusive fitness. While it is relatively easy to conceive of the contribution of such behaviors as language and reasoning to survival and reproduction, the logic of modern evolutionary theory suggests that other universal aspects of development such as play also confer an evolutionary advantage (see Fagen, this volume).

The concept of kin investment is important to developmentalists because it suggests that behaviors that we think of as being quite distinct—such as breastfeeding, working at paid employment outside the home, and teaching offspring how to spell—can all be conceived of as influenced by evolved dispositions to help our children survive and reproduce. These activities can be viewed as aspects of kin investment, or more specifically in these examples, parental investment. Viewing family interactions in terms of kin investment provides a currency for analyzing the strategic decisions family members must make regarding where to allot their finite investment energy and resources. For instance, parents must decide whether to invest more in some of their offspring than in others; and children have to make decisions regarding when to forgo investment in siblings and to start producing and investing in children themselves. Kin investment provides a new perspective for viewing familiar phenomena such as preferential parenting, sibling rivalry, and parent-offspring conflict. It points to some previously unsuspected relationships among these events, leading to testable research hypotheses.

Evolutionarily Stable Strategies

A basic principle of modern evolutionary theory is that natural selection will tend to select traits that maximize the inclusive fitness of the individuals displaying them. However the traits that result from evolutionary tradeoffs are not always the best imaginable mechanisms for aiding the individual's survival and reproduction. Rather they represent an optimum compromise resulting from conflicting selection pressures molding an ancestral phenotype. For example, selection for speed may necessitate a decrease in strength; and selection for large brains may produce increased postnatal infant mortality because of the relatively helpless nature of human infants resulting from their abbreviated gestation period, as discussed above.

Aspects of the environment such as food sources, predators, and climate obviously play a major role in shaping the evolution of animal behavior. It is not quite so obvious that the behavior of other members of an individual's species is also an important selective force. The idea of an evolutionarily stable strategy (ESS) provides a rigorous way of conceptualizing the effect of social pressures on the evolution of behavior (Maynard Smith, 1982). As elaborated by Crawford (this volume), an ESS is an individual trait (or *strategy*) which, if adopted by all members of a population, will not be replaced by an alternative trait as long as the species' ecology remains similar to the conditions when the ESS originated.

ESS modeling generally involves simplified models where the assumptions do not exactly represent conditions in any real species. Nevertheless this kind of modeling illustrates how selection pressures are expected to shape social behavior and field workers have reported that a number of diverse animal species do appear to behave in a way that conforms to predictions from ESS model (e.g., wasps: Brockmann, Grafen, & Dawkins, 1979; crickets: Cade, 1981; sunfish: Gross & Charnov, 1980).

Although ESS models have often been applied to analyze the evolution of animal conflict, they are also useful in understanding the evolution of prosocial behavior such as cooperation. Axelrod and Hamilton (1981; Axelrod, 1984) presented a particularly interesting approach to the evolution of cooperation between unrelated conspecifics that utilizes the game theory methodology underlying the ESS models. Their model provides some insight on the conditions that may have led to the evolution of cooperation in humans.

ESS models may not be directly applicable to human development, although evolutionary theorist George C. Williams (1984) has predicted that ''game theory with fitness payoffs will soon be standard practice in such fields [as the biological foundations for the behavioral sciences]'' (p. 117). Nevertheless ESS thinking has some indirect implications for developmentalists. For one thing, the view of the human life span as an evolved strategy for replicating genes, presented in the previous section, converges with ESS thinking. To quote Richard Dawkins (1980):

> In principle one could regard longer developmental times as strategies in the same sense. 'Life-history strategies' (Gadgil & Bossert, 1970) are just like dungfly courtship strategies, but on a time scale of months or years rather than minutes. (I suggest, by the way, that we should learn to think about evolutionarily stable life-history strategies—Charlesworth & Leon, 1976.) The phenotype of an individual is produced by a complicated interplay of rates (at which developmental processes occur) or time (elapsing between various stages of embryonic development). Genes act on phenotypes by controlling these rates and times (Gould 1977b). The genes that survive down the ages are those that are good at controlling developmental rates and intervals, in such a way that bodies are produced which are good at preserving and propogating those same genes. (p. 353)

Viewed in the way suggested by Dawkins, the genes that influence human development are the survivors of a continuing contest over thousands of years in which sets of genes tried to *beat* other sets of genes, by programming slightly different rates of development. The winners, of course, were those genes that programmed the rate of development that led to the most surviving offspring.

Another central implication of ESS thinking is that the strategy adopted by an individual may depend on the strategy utilized by others around him. Current developmental theories generally have a hard time explaining the development of extreme individual differences within families and small communities. The emphasis in ESS thinking on the adaptiveness of behavioral differences within populations might supply a basis for explaining the development of some individual differences. (For an evolutionary perspective on individual differences in personality, see Buss, 1984, this volume).

Recently theorists have pointed out that differences in ESS's themselves may not be genetic in origin. Rather what may be inherited are evolutionarily stable learning rules (Dawkins, 1980; Harley, 1981; Maynard Smith, 1982, 1984). It is with this kind of suggestion that sociobiology and learning theory are beginning a fruitful interchange (e.g., commentary on Maynard Smith, 1984). This synthesis is of interest to developmentalists inasmuch as it involves the origins of specific developmentally expressed dispositions to learn.

SOCIOBIOLOGY AND HUMAN DEVELOPMENT: AN OVERVIEW OF RESEARCH

Family Structure

Sociobiology suggests that two evolved dispositions are the foundation of the human family: dispositions to mate and to favor kin. Families generally consist of related individuals whose inclusive fitness is sometimes enhanced by each other's survival and reproduction. The only two family members who usually are not related to each other are, of course, the mother and the father, and sociobiologists assume that their role in the family is contingent on each parent's inclusive fitness benefitting more from a partnership to create and raise children than from most alternative strategies, such as raising children alone or abandoning the family. Sociobiologists contend that we are genetically disposed to form families that display several common features. These include monogamous or polygynous marriage systems (rather than polyandrous mating); a tendency for women to marry men with the greatest possible resource-holding capabilities; considerable (by primate standards) male parental investment; greater female than male investment in child care; differential parental investment in offspring according to their projected reproductive potential; and a number of other features reviewed in Alexander (1979), van den Berghe (1979) and Daly and Wilson (1983).

As part of a rich and detailed discussion of evolution and human behavior, Alexander (1979) presents a number of predictions regarding human family behavior that he derived from evolutionary theory. Among them:

> When genetic relationships of potential recipients of nepotistic benefits to the potential giver of benefits are equal, then relatives with the greater ability to translate benefits into reproduction will be favored . . .
> Relatives of the same degree are likely to be distinguished, nomenclaturally and otherwise, only when their abilities to translate benefits into reproduction are consistently different. (Thus, uncles and aunts are usually distinguished from nephews and nieces . . .)
> The boundary of effective nepotism may be clarified by drawing some relatives at the boundary inward, nomenclaturally and otherwise, and by pushing others outward (hence, as already noted, some of the apparent inconsistencies in kin nomenclature) . . .
> Men are physically more powerful than women, hence more likely to have their way in conflicts of interest; rules of kinship and marriage may be expected to reflect that difference. (pp. 157–159)

Alexander believes that the most valid test of these predictions involves surveying family patterns across many cultures, and such ethnographic evidence strongly supports the predictions:

> While some of these predictions are trivial, taken individually, and some may be faulted as circular because our immersion in the human system of sociality already tells us they are true, collectively they are significant, and the larger the list the more important it becomes. Over one hundred such predictions, in one form or another, can be located in this book. (p. 156)

Sociobiology provides straightforward explanations for both the cooperation and conflict that are universal aspects of family life. Cooperation is expected within families because family members share a number of genes by common descent, and therefore aiding a relative may increase an individual's inclusive fitness. However, conflict is also expected because even close relatives, such as siblings, do not share all of their genes, and it is possible to increase one's inclusive fitness at the expense of a sibling. Crawford (this volume) and Noonan (this volume) summarize sociobiological explanations of parent-offspring conflict and sibling rivalry.

There are some significant differences between the sociobiological view of the family and more traditional psychological and sociological perspectives. One such difference, of course, is that sociobiologists view the family as a mechanism that evolved in order to benefit the inclusive fitness of family members, whereas social scientists have generally ignored the question of evolutionary origins and function in analyzing family behavior. Psychologists and sociologists tend to look at family structure as determined by historical and economic factors, whereas sociobiologists agree that such factors can influence family patterns, but argue that evolution has produced a basic blueprint for family behavior that culture elaborates upon. Families are seen as responding to short-term historical and cultural influences, as well as to longer term evolutionary pressures. In spite of focusing on different levels of explanation, sociobiology may be reconcilable with some traditional psychological and sociological approaches to the family, insofar as it provides broad and parsimonious explanations of dispositions toward certain patterns of family behavior that are complemented by narrower micro-theories of psychology and sociology.

Some social scientists object to the view of the family as an evolved matrix of commitments and dispositions designed to further the genetic interests of its members (e.g., Harris, 1979; Livingstone, 1983; Sahlins, 1976). One reason for their disagreement is that the variety of different family systems appears to argue against universal evolved dispositions as the foundation of family structure. Why is it that in modern Western middle-class society the nuclear family is the norm, whereas group marriage with several male and female cospouses comprising a single extended family is an acceptable alternative in parts of Northern India (van den Berghe, 1979)? How can sociobiologists claim that common species-specific dispositions underly the diversity of family types?

Sociobiologists do not contend that the structure of the human family is immutably determined by an inflexible genetic program; rather, they contend that evolution has provided a set of dispositions regarding mating and kin behavior, and these interact with differing social environments to produce a variety of family systems. Indeed it is possible that strong cultural pressures can override evolved dispositions toward caring for kin, leading to parents turning in their children for alleged religious or political crime as in Nazi Germany or contemporary Iran.

Sociobiologists acknowledge that the ecological and cultural environment are major influences on family structure and that the normative family type in a given society is a product of an interaction between evolutionary and environmental influences. Van den Berghe (1979) illustrates how different family systems can be viewed as adaptive variations on a basic evolutionary theme. He compared the family systems of six widely differing societies and comments that:

> Specific types of kinship and marriage organization are not the gratuitous and fortuitous products of human invention, but become fully comprehensible only within the framework of evolutionary theory. Human social organization is, indeed, in good part a cultural creation, but it is an *adaptive*, not a random creation. . . . As human societies become larger, more differentiated, more technologically complex, and more politically centralized, their kinship and marriage systems evolve from the highly flexible models of hunters and gatherers, to the highly structured systems of agrarian societies, to the, once again, extremely flexible family institutions of industrial societies. . . . The very fact that the contemporary industrial family shares so much with that of hunters and gatherers suggests that there is an irreducible minimum of human mating and reproductive systems without which we would not be fully human. (pp. 130–132)

Of course, family systems vary not only between societies; they also vary within societies, and Mildren Dickemann (1979a, 1979b, 1981) has suggested that some differences in mating strategies and family structure between upper and lower classes in stratified agrarian societies may derive from basic differences in the reproductive role of the males and females. In a recent paper, Dickemann (1983) speculates that the female-centered nature of many poor black urban families may result partly from a tendency for females to control resources and mating at the bottom of stratified societies. Dickemann differentiates three categories of family structure within the Black ghetto, based on the degree of male involvement with the family, and suggests that "early socialization of the poverty-class male prepares him for entry into any one of three life histories: that of the stably employed family man, that of marginally employed, loosely bonded male, and that of the largely celibate street corner man" (p. 1). An evolved disposition for women to choose mates based on their ability to contribute to the rearing of offspring influences the family structure of such groups. "To find a women, a man must have a job: the stability of his relationship with her will be determined by the reliability and size of his income" (Dickemann, 1983, p. 11).

Van den Berghe and Dickemann provide evidence that the apparent diversity of family types does not argue against an evolutionary view of family behavior. Such diversity can be understood as the product of the inevitable interaction between evolved dispositions and specific social environments.

Parenting and Other Kin-Directed Behavior

Few developmental researchers would quarrel with the suggestion that humans evolved to nurture their offspring. However, that observation is too general to be relevant to most research questions in human development. Modern sociobiology suggests that dispositions to love and nourish offspring are conditional, and that human parents evolved to carefuly monitor the environment, and distribute parental investment in a way that best maximizes their inclusive fitness in a given environment. More specifically, inclusive fitness theory also implies that:

> Cooperativeness and competitiveness between particular sets of relatives, such as full siblings, may vary across essentially the entire spectrum of possibilities, depending on their appropriateness and needs to use the same resources (e.g., parental care or mates) and the value to each of having a cooperative individual available. (Thus, the phrase *sibling rivalry* simultaneously connotes a high level of competitiveness and implies that it has an unusual or surprising aspect.) . . .
> Older offspring are likely in many circumstances to be reproductively more valuable than younger offspring, and to serve their parents' interests better in the course of serving their own interests because of their typical age and dependency relationships to their siblings (leading to primogeniture). Younger dependent offspring, on the other hand, may be given full attention with fewer reservations because of the diminished likelihood of additional dependent young (hence, may be *spoiled*) . . .
> Offspring that are abandoned or destroyed are likely to have been of low reproductive value, either because of their phenotypic attributes or because of the timing or the circumstances of their appearance . . .
> Nondescendant relatives may sometimes be better avenues of reproduction than descendant relatives (leading in some cases to adaptive celibacy). (Alexander, 1979, pp. 157–158)

From this perspective, humans are viewed as intelligent, flexible reproductive strategists. We have evolved to search for mates who will help us foster our inclusive fitness. We are genetically disposed to make strategic decisions regarding the number and spacing of our offspring; what is optimal in one culture or social stratum may not be optimal in another. As children mature, parents must allocate resources to each child in the form of parental investment, and the eventual reproductive value of each child must be estimated in order to guide these investment decisions. From the perspective of sociobiology, parents are expected not only to attempt to influence their children to conform to the rules and customs of their society, but also to attempt to mold children to best serve the inclusive fitness interests of the parents—which might not always be in the best inclusive fitness interests of the child. This aspect of parent-child interaction is labeled "parental manipulation" (Alexander, 1974), and it has been invoked as a possible explanation for biologically puzzling aspects of development such as homosexuality. Briefly, the suggestion is that parents may unconsciously socialize offspring to become homosexual in the expectation that instead of having children of their own, homosexual offspring will direct their kin investment toward their siblings' children, and that under some circumstances this may be advantageous to the parents' inclusive fitness (Ruse, 1982; Trivers, 1974). There are a number of problems with invoking parental manipulation as an explanation of homosexuality, but the point is that the possibility leads to viewing the development of homosexuality in a new way, and also leads to a different perspective regarding parental socialization practices.

Another example of the way that evolutionary theory can be used to gain insights into the parent-child relationship comes from the work of Martin Daly and Margo Wilson (1980, 1981a, 1981b, this volume) on discriminative parental solicitude, particularly its relationship to child abuse. These researchers suggest that if parents did evolve to favor offspring who would most likely increase their inclusive fitness, humans might have evolved to discriminate against unrelated household members. If this were the case, stepparents would be expected to be less nurturant and more abusive toward their stepchildren than natural parents, on the average. The data appear to confirm this prediction; Daly and Wilson (1980) found that, "the risk of abuse and neglect is likely to be exacerbated where substitute individuals fill the roles of biological parents" (p. 282).

Although Daly and Wilson's data do not establish that stepparents are influenced by an evolved disposition to discriminate against unrelated children, they are consistent with such a conclusion. Sociobiologists do not claim that such evolved dispositions are the major cause of child abuse (they probably are not). Rather, they claim that researchers interested in the determinants of parenting behavior should attend to the possibility that individuals may be less strongly disposed to nurture their stepchildren than their biological children.

In traditional perspectives on socialization, parents are presumed to be more or less aware of the goals toward which they are socializing their children. In Western culture, these goals often involve producing polite, active, law-abiding adults who will have the skills to secure fulfilling, lucrative employment and a similarly socialized spouse. An evolutionary perspective views these end-points of socialization as intermediate steps in achieving the real goal of parenting: the maximization of inclusive fitness through the maximal production of grandchildren. It is not that sociobiologists believe that stepparents consciously decide to be abusive because their stepchildren do not contribute to their inclusive fitness. Rather it is suggested that stepparents lack some of the inhibitions that biological parents develop that constrain parents from abusing children during stressful periods, and it is this relative lack of inhibitions against abuse that mediates the hypothesized evolved disposition. There is no reason to postulate that stepparents are aware that their anger at a crying baby has anything to do with maximizing their inclusive fitness, anymore than they would have to be aware of the role of perspiration in thermoregulation in order to sweat while playing tennis. The possibility that complex and serious parenting decisions can be influenced by factors that are not conscious or cultural, is not readily acknowledged by most approaches to socialization. It is interesting, however, that a number of recent reports on differences among siblings (e.g., Daniels & Plomin, 1985; Rowe & Plomin, 1981; Scarr & Grajek, 1982; Zajonc, 1983) suggest siblings are often exposed to quite different environments within the same family. This finding agrees quite well with the sociobiological contention that human parents are disposed to discriminate among their offspring and to apportion parental investment in a way that maximizes their inclusive fitness.

Cognitive Development

As the title of the discipline implies, sociobiology is probably more relevant to the study of social development than to the study of cognitive development. Nevertheless, the evolution of cognitive dispositions has received attention from sociobiologists, most prominently Charles Lumsden and E. O. Wilson (1981, 1982, 1983; Lumsden, 1983). These researchers state that, "Contrary to an impression widely held among biologists and social scientists, most and possibly all forms of human culture and psychological development are sustained by gene-culture transmission rather than by pure cultural transmission" (Lumsden, 1983, p. 126). They suggest that humans have evolved dispositions toward learning particular ideas and behavior, and that the human cultural environment has played an essential role in shaping these cognitive dispositions (labeled "epigenetic rules" by Lumsden and Wilson). Suggested examples of such epigenetic rules include the infantile preference for normally composed facial features, biases in classification of color, and tendencies to develop phobias toward some objects and not toward others (Lumsden & Wilson, 1982).

Although the Lumsden and Wilson model has been criticized (e.g., Lumsden & Wilson, 1982: Commentary; Maynard Smith & Warren, 1982), it remains the most detailed attempt to analyze human cognitive development in terms of the evolutionary pressures that led to the development of the human mind. Lumsden (1983) suggests that human sociobiology "must be unified with cognitive science and the principles of cognitive-developmental theory" (p. 160). Symons (this volume) also argues that an evolutionary perspective is of central importance in understanding the mechanisms of the human mind.

Social Learning

There has also been some interest in integrating sociobiological and social learning approaches to development, most notably with regard to altruism. MacDonald (1984) presents a model that attempts to explain altruism in terms of both its evolutionary origins and more proximal developmental determinants. MacDonald concludes that:

> The data indicate that human altruism comprises a highly flexible behavioral system that is influenced strongly by affectively salient stimuli present during development . . . The affective system is viewed as a biologically based system resulting from selection for the affective consequences of social stimulation during development. As in the case of attachment, the altruism system is seen as affected by a

variety of perceptual and cognitive processes as well as biological predispositions. (p. 106)

Pulliam and Dunford (1980) have also looked at observational learning as an adaptive process that evolved in order to provide complex organisms with a means of ontogenetically acquiring information about the environment to augment the genetically transmitted information manifested in innate dispositions. These researchers discuss some avenues for understanding the relationships among biological evolution, cultural evolution, learning mechanisms, and cognitive processes in producing the vast range of cultural diversity that is so apparent in human history.

Moral Development and Equity

Moral development and equity are topics that have recently been analyzed in terms of evolutionary antecedents. Alexander (1979, 1982) points out that human moral codes largely grew out of recurring conflicts among individuals that were closely connected to their reproductive interests. He contends that Kohlberg's stages of moral development can be viewed as reflecting the development of attributes necessary to promote one's inclusive fitness. For instance, Kohlberg's first stage is seen as concerned only with the biological survival of the self (selfish or *amoral* stage). In subsequent stages the individual develops a sense of reciprocity that may ultimately benefit reproduction. "Eventually the individual also begins to forego personal (somatic) rewards in favor of unreciprocated rewards to others (nepotism)" (Alexander, 1982, p. 390). Alexander points out that equity theories in the social sciences are invariably incomplete because they do not deal with the currency that ultimately motivates human behavior: inclusive fitness:

> In other words, these theories provide no means of defining human interests in a general or complete sense, therefore no means of dealing generally with the intensities and direction of individual efforts . . . A theory of interests is a theory of lifetimes, what they are about and how their goals are achieved. A growing body of information from biology now provides a reasonable and testable answer; lifetimes have been molded by natural selection to yield the greatest likelihood of survival of the individuals's genetic materials. This likelihood is maximized by success in reproduction, which includes producing offspring, and assisting both descendant and non-descendant relatives. The 'deep and intimate' interactions causing difficulty to equity theorists are actually those most directly involving reproduction-those occurring between mates, potential mates and relatives. The currencies that mold the proximate mechanisms of altruism in these interactions are genetic, not a matter of returned goods or services, and this is the reason the payoffs have not been apparent to investigators outside biology. Even the investments and returns of reciprocity (exchange, equity) are ultimately comprehensible only in terms of their

eventual effects on the 'deep and intimate' interactions of mates and relatives. Included are wealth, status, good will and innumerable other items. (Alexander, 1982, pp. 389–390)

This view of moral development as involving the acquisition of cognitive and affective sets necessary to achieve reproductively relevant resources represents a provocative departure from more orthodox views, and is a promising direction for future inquiry.

Other Research

A number of other researchers have recently analyzed developmental topics from an evolutionary perspective (e.g., general reviews: Blurton-Jones, 1982; Konner, 1981; Smith, 1983a, 1983b; Strayer, 1984; Weisfeld, 1982; infancy: Freedman, 1974; attachment: Lamb, Thompson, Gardner, & Charnov & Estes, 1984; Porter & Laney, 1980; parental behavior: Draper & Harpending, 1982; Konner, 1982; parental bereavement: Littlefield & Rushton, in press; birth spacing: Blurton-Jones, 1983; Blurton-Jones & Sibly, 1978; kin and phenotype recognition: Porter, this volume; Rushton, Russell, & Wells, 1984, 1985; incest avoidance: Shepher, 1983; van den Berghe, this volume; in-law interactions: Carlisle, 1981; children's conflicts: Wiegel, 1984; adolescence: Weisfeld & Berger 1983), but the examples discussed above should suffice to outline the general form of a sociobiology of human development. Let us turn now to problems involved in developing such a subdiscipline.

OBSTACLES TO A SYNTHESIS OF SOCIOBIOLOGY AND DEVELOPMENTAL THEORY

Evolutionary thinking has not had a major impact on mainstream developmental research. This may be partly because developmental researchers appear to have some misconceptions regarding the nature of sociobiological explanation. However there are also some more substantive problems regarding the assumptions of sociobiology and the relevance of evolutionary theory to current developmental questions. A number of the issues discussed here also hamper communication between sociobiology and other social sciences such as social psychology, sociology and anthropology, but I will concentrate on problems that are particularly acute for developmental research.

Obstacle 1. A feeling among developmentalists that a consideration of evolutionary pressures tells us little about contemporary human development

A form of this misunderstanding involves the claim that an evolutionary analysis can add little to our understanding of development, other than post-hoc, largely speculative accounts of the selection pressures that may have produced a particular behavior. Thus, it is claimed that sociobiology cannot produce testable predictions regarding behavior that might add to our knowledge, but can only attempt to explain the evolutionary history of already recognized patterns of development and behavior.

This is a misunderstanding because sociobiological models can generate many predictions regarding the way human behavior should have evolved, if specified selection pressures were indeed active. The preceding section of this chapter reviewed a number of such predictions. Many of these predictions are quite obviously correct, insofar as they predict patterns that have long been apparent. Sociobiologists can hardly be criticized for predicting that evolution should have produced people that behave in the way that people obviously do, although the discpline would not be terribly useful if it merely predicted the obvious. But a number of predictions do not involve such obvious behaviors, or are even counterintuitive. Sociobiological predictions will necessarily involve patterns of behavior that humans should have displayed, in some form, throughout history, since they would be part of our legacy as a species. However, in many cases, these patterns of behavior may have gone unreported, or viewed as some kind of aberration because of prevailing religious, cultural or scientific beliefs.

It should be noted that an individual prediction or set of predictions deriving from a particular model of selection pressures may prove to be incorrect, without invalidating evolutionary theory as a source of ideas for understanding human development. Similarly, the fact that some fundamental assumptions of modern sociobiology, such as inclusive fitness maximization, are relatively impervious to empirical disconfirmation, should not lead social scientists to ignore evolutionary theory as a fertile source of ideas and explanations about human development.

Obstacle 2. A feeling that evolutionary explanations of human development are incompatible with explanations based on more traditional theoretical perspectives such as learning, cognitive or psychodynamic theory

It is not impossible that a sociobiological explanation of a particular behavioral phenomenon—say, sex differences in aggression—may indeed be incompatible with a learning or cognitive explanation, and that one of the explanations is wrong (see Symons, this volume). However, sociobiology generally deals with a different level of explanation than do the more traditional theories. Sociobiologists focus on the ultimate determinants of behavior, whereas other developmental perspectives deal with more proximal causes. So that it is entirely possible to agree, for instance, that young children may learn to be aggressive in the way outlined by social learning theorists such as Bandura (1977), while also maintaining that males may be evolutionarily disposed to be more susceptible to learning aggression observationally.

This potential compatibility notwithstanding, there are some obvious differences in perspective between sociobiology and conventional developmental psychology. The things that sociobiologists think are important, like mating and having babies, are not emphasized in traditional developmental theories, and the things that engross psychologists, like cognitive strategies and schedules of reinforcement, are taken for granted by sociobiologists as proximal mechanisms that evolved to help the individual toward greater fitness. The idea of genetic dispositions that are flexible and contingent on environmental cues is evidently rather foreign to some developmentalists, whereas the rational motivations that appear to influence human behavior are sometimes slighted by sociobiologists.

There are also differences in the temporal and comparative foci of sociobiology and developmental psychology. Developmental psychologists have been exhorted to be more developmental in their research (McCall, 1977), and to examine change over the full life span, rather than concentrate on only one or two age ranges (Baltes & Schaie, 1973). In contrast, the temporal context for sociobiological theorizing is thousands of years; a longitudinal study in evolutionary terms looks at fitness over generations, rather than ontogenetic change over a lifetime. Similarly the comparative perspective of sociobiology is far broader than that of developmental psychology. Developmental psychologists have been criticized for focusing primarily on middle-class, Western, industrialized populations, while neglecting to compare the results of such studies with development in non-Western cultures. In contrast, sociobiological analysis is inherently comparative, viewing human development in the context of the life history strategies of thousands of different animal species.

One of the most heuristic benefits of any new approach to a topic is that familiar phenomena are categorized in novel and, hopefully, illuminating ways. An example of this involves the sociobiological hypotheses that human paternal uncertainty may have lead to:

1. human males being genetically less disposed to invest in putative offspring than females (Barash, 1982)
2. mothers of newborns exaggerating the degree to which newborns resemble the father (Daly & Wilson, 1982)
3. a strong avuncular relationship with sister's children in societies where paternal uncertainty is significant (Alexander, 1979)
4. grandparents favoring daughter's children over son's children (Smith, 1986).

In this example, the sociobiological concept of paternal uncertainty is used to predict and explain four quite different patterns of behavior: differences in male and female parenting patterns; parental communication regarding neonatal appearrance; cross-cultural differences in avuncular behavior; and variations in grandparenting behavior. Whether or not research ultimately determines that these behavioral patterns are influenced by paternal uncertainty, the suggestion that these distinct phenomena might be influenced by the same biosocial anteced- ent should intrigue developmentalists interested in family behavior and social development.

Ultimately, the use of different concepts and terms need not prevent the integration of sociobiological concepts into developmental theory. Any approach to development that is likely to provide novel insights must, by necessity, utilize explanatory concepts that are different from those already in use. As Robert Irwin (1976) said "Every new idea is obscure at first. It is or it wouldn't be new." Researchers have suggested a number of avenues for integrating so- ciobiology with complementary approaches to development, including social learning theory (MacDonald, 1984; Pulliam & Dunford, 1980), Freudian theory (Leak & Christopher, 1982), cognitive-developmental theory (Alexander, 1982; Lumsden, 1983) and family sociology (van den Berghe, 1979). Some of this research was reviewed in the preceding section of this chapter, but it should be noted here that sociobiology comes to integrate existing developmental theory, not to bury it.

Obstacle 3. The feeling that cognition, learning and culture are far more important for human development than is the case for any other animal, and these processes do not involve evolved dispositions to any significant degree

There is no doubt that humans differ significantly from other animals, most notably in their intelligence, memory, language, and ability to develop cultures. It is likely that evolution selected these traits because they aided survival and reproduction. A number of researchers have speculated about the evolutionary circumstances leading to the selection of these characteristics (Lumsden & Wilson, 1981, 1983; Sagan, 1977). However, because the actual content of learning varies so much between cultures and individuals, it is easy to lose sight of the fact that these complex mechanisms presumably evolved to further one goal—fitness; and that this goal is the same as in all other animal species.

Contemporary developmentalists emphasize change in cognitive structure as the key to understanding human development, and this emphasis is understand- able, given the central role cognition plays in human decision-making. However, the broader view of cognition as a set of adaptive mechanisms that enhance survival and reproduction has been underemphasized in psychology's cognitive revolution. Such a broader view could enrich research in cognitive development (Fishbein, 1976; Lumsden, 1983; Symons, this volume).

Similarly, the fact that human development is greatly shaped by cultural norms does not render irrelevant a consideration of evolutionary influences.

Human behavior is multidetermined, and evolved dispositions undoubtedly interact with cultural forces to produce behavior. More importantly, however, culture itself is an important product of biological evolution; the ability to transmit complex information nongenetically between and among generations was an important evolutionary step, and a cultural environment subsequently became a major selective force in human evolution (Alexander, 1979; Lumsden & Wilson, 1981; Pulliam & Dunford, 1980; Richerson & Boyd, 1978). Biological and cultural evolution have been synergistically working together over the last 100,000 years to produce the human ontogeny that developmentalists study today. Sociobiology reinforces the truism that nature and nurture work together to produce human development, and emphasizes that a consideration of the evolutionary roots of cognition, learning and culture can contribute to our understanding of these processes.

Obstacle 4. The feeling that an evolutionary analysis might help us understand simple, reflexive behaviors, but is not of much use in analyzing more complex learned behaviors

This misunderstanding is related to the previous one, and it probably arises because the link between simple, reflexive behaviors and their evolutionary function is usually quite obvious, whereas the fitness contribution of more complex, variegated sequences of behavior may be more subtle. For instance, most developmentalists would readily agree that suckling is an evolved behavioral pattern that has significantly aided the survival of human infants for thousands of years. However, many would balk at considering a parent spanking a child, or a grandmother drawing up a will in the same terms. Yet, from an evolutionary perspective, both of the latter acts might be motivated by fitness-maximizing dispositions to the same degree as suckling, insofar as they result in increased inclusive fitness for the disciplining parent (perhaps by encouraging the chastised child not to injure his or her sibling) or the testating grandmother (by bequeathing resources to her kin in a manner that will optimize her inclusive fitness).

Because spanking and will-making are not present in all cultures, and usually involve some thinking and personal choice, it is easy to conclude that evolved fitness dispositions do not play a role in their motivation. Yet it is quite possible that evolution has selected human adults to achieve certain adaptive goals, without specifying the specific adaptive routes to be used to achieve these goals. Such a strategy would maximally utilize human flexibility and intelligence in furthering the goal of inclusive fitness. Thus the general programs that evolution may have selected in these examples are "Raise your children so they will have the knowledge, skills, and resources to best increase your inclusive fitness, using whatever socialization techniques are efficient and culturally acceptable" and "Accrue as many reproductively-relevant resources as possible, and distribute them in such a way as to maximize your inclusive fitness, generally by bequeathing them to descendants.''

It might be counterproductive for these programs to be any more specific—if they were, individuals might not be able to capitalize on the fitness opportunities of a particular environment, situation, or culture. It also might be counterproductive for the individual to be aware that his or her behavior might be motivated by these simple programs and goals, thus making adaptive a degree of self-deception regarding personal motivation (Alexander, 1974, 1975; Lockard, 1980; Trivers, 1985). The behavior that individuals work out to achieve these goals (e.g., business careers, socialization and schooling of children) may be far more complex than the fitness program themselves. Social scientists concentrate on unravelling the complex and culturally variable surface-level phenomena that are the most striking aspects of most societies, but in doing so they neglect the common motivations underlying this cross-cultural diversity (Symons, this volume). It is this incongruity between the simple goals postulated by sociobiologists as motivating much human behavior and the complexity and variability of the behaviors that humans develop to achieve these that leads many social scientists to reject an evolutionary view of human behavior as too simplistic. However, as Whitehead claimed, the goal of science may well be to seek the simplest explanation of complex facts. A few simple evolved goals could generate behavior of almost infinite variety, given a complex physiological organism like humans and an equally complicated cultural environment. Complex behavior is not necessarily the product of a complex underlying goal structure. Sociobiology may be even more useful in explaining the ultimate motivation for complex social behaviors as it is for explaining simple reflexive behaviors.

Obstacle 5. The perception that an evolutionary analysis focuses on individual genetic differences in development

Behavior geneticists research genetic differences in development; sociobiologists emphasize genetically encoded behavioral programs that are assumed to be much the same for all humans, with the exception of some genotypic sex differences. This does not mean that all humans are expected to behave in the same way; there will be individual variation and developmental changes in the expression of the universal genotype, insofar as some aspects of the biogram will be expressed during infancy, others at adolescence, and so on.

It is also assumed that many of these evolved, genetically encoded traits are facultative. That is, their expression may systematically change depending on the social circumstances influencing the individual expressing them. For instance, it has been suggested that parents may invest differentially in male and female offspring depending on the parents' socioeconomic circumstances (Hrdy, in press; Smith, Kish, & Crawford, in press; Trivers & Willard, 1973). This is because the inclusive fitness of parents may have benefitted by investing more in sons if the family was wealthy or in a favorable environment; or in daughters if the family was poor or in dire circumstances. The result of such a genetic program would be a population where some parents favored daughters, and some favored sons, but a common facultative genetic program would be assumed to underly these parenting biases.

Of course, sociobiologists generally acknowledge that individual genetic differences influence almost all aspects of human development, but such differences have been investigated more by behavioral geneticists than sociobiologists (Plomin, 1983). The fields of sociobiology and behavior genetics share certain common assumptions and methods (Fuller, 1982, this volume; Plomin, 1981). Indeed, it has been claimed that the field of sociobiology subsumes the study of behavioral genetics (Wilson, 1975), and a productive synthesis of concepts and data from the two areas has been initiated (e.g., Rushton, 1984, 1985). However, in practice, human sociobiologists have tended to focus on behaviors that are assumed to derive from a common human genotype, whereas behavior geneticists have concentrated on individual and group differences in areas like intelligence, schizophrenia, and personality. Sociobiologists have had little to say about such controversial topics as racial differences in intelligence (van den Berghe, 1981; Silverman, this volume) and the identification of the field with such topics is inaccurate.

This is not to say that sociobiology has nothing to say about individual differences in development. Sociobiology deals both with the species-typical developmental function, and with individual differences in development (McCall, 1981). The sociobiological emphasis on evolved life history strategies is relevant to the study of the normative developmental function, and facultative traits that vary according to environmental circumstances would result in differences in individual development. Behavior genetics has been largely concerned with individual differences in behavior, although that approach also provides insight into the normative developmental function (e.g., Scarr, 1981).

Obstacle 6. A feeling that an evolutionary perspective on human development involves a pessimistic attitude toward the usefulness of environmental interventions designed to foster optimal development

"Genetically influenced" does not mean *immutable*. And "adaptive" (in an evolutionary sense) does not mean *good*. Because every trait is influenced somewhat by the environment, it may well be possible to design the environment to influence the development of almost any human trait to some degree. Therefore an evolutionary view is not necessarily pessimistic regarding the possibility of nurturing optimal development through appropriate environmental intervention. It simply contends that some aspects of human behavior are easier to change than others. So although sociobiologists generally agree that a disposition to learn and display aggression under certain circumstances is likely to have evolved, this does not rule out the considerable influence of environmental factors such as aggressive models, reinforcement of aggressive behavior, and societal norms regarding the acceptability of violence. In contrast to the earlier statement of the ethologist Konrad Lorenz (1966), a contemporary evolutionary view does not contend that aggression is inevitable or that it benefits individuals to be aggressive in contemporary societies. Rather, we are likely more disposed by nature to be aggressive than to write a book, because the former act resulted in higher inclusive fitness in our evolutionary past than the latter. Obviously, it is possible to raise children to be better writers than fighters; but children probably find it much easier to learn to punch and kick than to write an essay. There is undoubtedly a genetic component to our literary facility, but it is likely that the selective pressures toward producing facultative aggression were probably greater, and therefore aggression is much easier to learn.

Another source of confusion stems from accepting the naturalistic fallacy: that what is *natural* is necessarily good. To suggest that a trait involves the expression of an evolved disposition does not imply that the trait is helpful or harmful for the short-term well-being of either an individual or a society. All that *adaptive* means, in a biological context, is ''contributing to the survival and reproduction of previous generations.'' In suggesting that behaviors such as aggression, infanticide, suicide, and rape may have evolved (and therefore have been *adaptive* for some of our ancestors), sociobiologists are not condoning these behaviors; they are simply trying to formulate a parsimonious explanation for their existence. And, as mentioned above, the fact that they may have evolved does not imply that they are intractable. Manifestly they are not.

Obstacle 7. The influence of natural selection on human ontogeny may not have been powerful and clear enough to make evolutionary processes very relevant to understanding contemporary human development

Although I have outlined some topics where evolutionary ideas may provide insights, it must be noted that the relationship between evolution and extant patterns of human behavior is far from clear. Sociobiology has only begun to generate sufficient theory and data to make attempts at analyzing human development in evolutionary terms potentially worthwhile. A number of sociobiologists and other evolutionary theorists are skeptical regarding possible relationships between evolution and development. Wilson, for instance, has suggested a need to ''decouple'' the study of evolution from the study of development (1975), although it is unclear exactly what is meant by that statement (Cairns, 1977, 1979). Maynard Smith (1984) has some reservations regarding the relevance of evolutionary game theory to human behavior, although he does suggest a couple of avenues for pursuing such a connection.

One of the basic issues involves the degree to which aspects of human development evolved as responses to specific selection pressures. It is possible that many genetically influenced aspects of human development may not actually represent adaptions to selection pressures, but may in fact be rather arbitrary results of neutral mutations, phylogentic inertia and modifications of ancestral traits. This view is close to the position taken by Gould and Lewontin (1979), who criticize what they see as the *adaptationist program* of sociobiology: an alleged tendency to inappropriately interpret extant behaviors in terms of hypothesized selection pressures. Gould and Lewontin's critique has itself been criticized (Barash, 1982; Dawkins, 1983; Dennett, 1983), and the question of the degree to which the genotypes of contemporary species are direct adaptations to historical selection pressures remains open. This question will not be resolved overnight, but it does not appear reasonable to a priori abandon the idea that a number of aspects of human behavior may indeed have evolved as a response to historical selection pressures. It is most unlikely that every aspect of normative human development reflects an adaptation to evolutionary pressures, but it is even more unlikely that no developmental processes evolved to increase inclusive fitness.

Obstacle 8. Sociobiology assumes that human development is influenced by genetic dispositions, but few gene-to-behavior pathways have been traced in humans

There are probably no topics in the behavioral sciences that are more complex than tracing the pathways from gene-to-behavior, and from brain-to-behavior. There have been no easy answers forthcoming in those areas and it is unlikely that these pathways will be completely illuminated in the near future. Because it is currently impossible to point to the specific physiological pathways through which evolved dispositions influence human behavior, critics sometimes dismiss human sociobiology as impossibly speculative. But the absence of specific physiological mechanisms for hypothesized developmental processes has not blocked the consideration of psychodynamic, learning, and cognitive explanations of development, and there is no reason why the adequacy of sociobiological explanation should be more dependent on the demonstration of such mechanisms than these more traditional explanations. Freudian identification, observational learning and Piagetian assimilation would all require genetic and physiological underpinnings, yet such substrata are assumed, and the adequacy of these explanatory constructs evaluated without reference to them. Surely, sociobiological hypotheses can be similarly offered and evaluated without specifying the particular genetic loci and brain-behavior pathways involved.

However, more than most developmental theorists, sociobiologists do feel that the explanation of behavior must ultimately focus on genetic and physiological determinants, and that hypothesized evolved dispositions must eventually be explained in terms of specific gene-structure-behavior links. Sociobiology, therefore, is reductionist in believing that the explanation of social phenomena in terms of genetic and physiological determinants is potentially more powerful and parsimonious than contemporary explanation. However, until research into the genetics and physiology of behavior has matured, provisional explanations of development utilizing traditional hypothetical constructs can be seen as complementing sociobiological explanations of development, as pointed out in discussing Obstacle 2.

CONCLUSIONS

Sociobiology has been one of the most exciting and productive scientific disciplines of the last twenty years. During that same period, the study of human development has blossomed and matured. There is no reason why the integration of concepts from sociobiology and developmental theory cannot be mutually enriching. Developmental psychology might particularly benefit from such a synthesis, insofar as the complexity of human development necessitates the combined analytic tools of a number of disciplines in order to sustain progress toward understanding the determinants of development. A sociobiology of human development does not currently exist as a distinct area of inquiry, but such a subdiscipline appears to be emerging from the research of biologists, psychologists, and anthropologists inspired by the new synthesis of ideas pertaining to the evolution of behavior. A developmental sociobiology would not replace traditional approaches to development, rather, it would constitute a framework for integrating existing theories, and would provide complementary explanations for developmental phenomena. The integration of evolutionary and developmental theory requires flexibility and patience on the part of sociobiologists and developmentalists, but such efforts will enrich our understanding of human development.

ACKNOWLEDGMENTS

I would like to thank Richard Alexander, Dennis Krebs, and Michele Surbey for their comments and advice on this chapter, and Sue Brooks for her research assistance. Preparation of this chapter was facilitated by grants from the Dean of Social Sciences SSHRCC fund at Brock University, and the Social Sciences and Research Council of Canada.

REFERENCES

Alexander, R. D. (1974). The evolution of social behavior. *Annual Review of Ecology and Systematics, 5,* 325–384.

Alexander, R. D. (1975). The search for a general theory of behavior. *Behavioral Science, 20,* 77–100.

Alexander, R. D. (1979). *Darwinism and human affairs.* Seattle: University of Washington Press.

Alexander, R. D. (1982). Biology and the moral paradoxes. *Journal of Social and Biological Structures, 5,* 389–395.

Axelrod, R. (1984). *The evolution of cooperation.* New York: Basic Books.

Axelrod, R., & Hamilton, W. D. (1981). The evolution of cooperation. *Science, 211,* 1390–1396.

Baldwin, J. M. (1894). *Mental development in the child and the race.* New York: Macmillan. (ref from Broughton, Am. Psych, 1981, p. 405)

Baltes, P. B., & Schaie, K. W. (1973). On life-span developmental research paradigms: retrospects and prospects. In P. B. Baltes & K. W. Schaie (Eds), *Life-span developmental psychology: personality and socialization.* Orlando, FL: Academic Press.

Bandura, A. (1977). *Social learning theory.* Englewood Cliffs, NJ: Prentice-Hall.

Barash, D. P. (1982). *Sociobiology and behavior* (2nd ed.). New York: Elsevier.

Blurton-Jones, N. B. (1982). Origins, functions, development, and motivation: Unity and disunity in the study of behavior. *Journal of Anthropological Research, 38,* 333–349.

Blurton-Jones, N. G. (1983). Two investigations of human behavior guided by evolutionary theory. In G. C. L. Davey (Ed.), *Animal models of human behavior.* New York: Wiley.

Blurton-Jones, N. G., & Sibly, R. M. (1978). Testing adaptiveness of culturally determined behaviour: Do bushman women maximize their reproductive success by spacing births widely and foraging seldom? In N. G. Blurton-Jones & V. Reynolds (Eds.), *Human behaviour and adaptation.* London: Taylor and Francis.

Brockmann, H. J., Grafen, A., & Dawkins, R. (1979). Evolutionarily stable nesting strategy in a digger wasp. *Journal of Theoretical Biology, 77,* 473–496.

Bronfenbrenner, U. (1979). *The ecology of human development: Experiments by nature and design.* Cambridge, MA: Harvard University Press.

Buss, D. M. (1984). Evolutionary biology and personality psychology. *American Psychologist, 39,* 1135–1147.

Cade, W. (1981). Alternative male strategies: Genetic differences in crickets. *Science, 212,* 563–564.

Cairns, R. B. (1977). Sociobiology: A new synthesis or an old cleavage. *Contemporary Psychology, 22,* 1–3.

Cairns, R. B. (1979). *Social development: The origins and plasticity of interchanges.* San Francisco: Freeman.

Carlisle, T. R. (1981). Altruism between in-laws: Some predictions from kin-selection theory. *Behavioral Ecology and Sociobiology, 8,* 157–159.

Charlesworth, D., & Leon, J. A. (1976). The relation of reproductive effort to age. *American Naturalist, 110,* 449–459.

Daly, M., & Wilson, M. (1980). Discriminative parental solicitude: a biological perspective. *Journal of Marriage and the Family, 42,* 277–288.

Daly, M., & Wilson, M. (1981a). Abuse and neglect of children in evolutionary perspective. In R. D. Alexander & D. W. Tinkle (Eds.), *Natural selection and social behavior.* New York: Chiron Press.

Daly, M., & Wilson, M. (1981b). Child maltreatment from a sociobiological perspective. *New Directions for Child Development, 11,* 93–112.

Daly, M., & Wilson, M. (1982). Who are new-born babies said to resemble? *Ethology and Sociobiology, 3,* 69–78.

Daly, M., & Wilson, M. (1983). *Sex, evolution and behavior* (2nd ed.). Boston: Willard Grant Press.

Daniels, D., & Plomin, R. (1985). *Differential experience of siblings within the same family.* Manuscript submitted for publication.

Darwin, C. (1859). *The origin of species.* London: John Murray.

Dawkins, R. (1980). Good strategy or evolutionarily stable strategy? In G. W. Barlow & J. Silverberg (Eds.)., *Sociobiology: Beyond nature/nurture?* Boulder, CO: Westview Press.

Dawkins, R. (1983). Adaptationism was always predictive and needed no defense. *The Behavioral and Brain Sciences, 6,* 360–361.

Dennett, D. C. (1983). Intentional systems in cognitive ethology: The "Panglossian paradigm" defended. *The Behavioral and Brain Sciences, 6,* 343–390.

Dickemann, M. (1979a). Female infanticide, reproductive strategies, and social stratification: a preliminary model. In N. Chagnon & W. Irons (Eds.), *Evolutionary biology and human social behavior: An anthropological perspective.* North Scituate, MA: Duxbury.

Dickemann, M. (1979b). The ecology of mating systems in hypergynous dowry societies. *Social Science Information, 18,* 163–195.

Dickemann, M. (1981). Paternal confidence and dowry competition: a biocultural analysis of purdah. In R. D. Alexander & D. W. Tinkle (Eds.), *Natural selection and social behavior: Recent research and new theory.* New York: Chiron.

Dickemann, M. (1983, May). Female choice, male life histories and male celibacy in U.S. Black ghettos. In R. M. Wiegel & N. G. Blurton Jones (Organizers), *Application of Life History Strategies Models to the study of Human Development.* Workshop conducted at University of California, 1983.

Draper, P., & Harpending, H. (1982). Father absence and reproductive strategy: An evolutionary perspective. *Journal of Anthropological Research, 38,* 255–273.

Fishbein, H. D. (1976). *Evolution, development and children's learning.* Santa Monica, CA.: Goodyear.

Freedman, D. G. (1974). *Human infancy: An evolutionary perspective.* Hillsdale, NJ: Lawrence Erlbaum Associates.

Fuller, J. L. (1982). Sociobiology and behavior genetics. In J. L. Fuller & E. C. Simmel (Eds.). *Behavior genetics: Principles and applications.* Hillsdale, NJ: Lawrence Erlbaum Associates.

Gadgil, M., & Bossert, W. II. (1970). Life historical consequences of natural selection *American Naturalist, 104,* 1–24.

Gould, S. J. (1977a). *Ever since Darwin.* New York: Norton.

Gould, S. J. (1977b). *Ontogeny and phyology.* Cambridge, MA: Harvard University Press.

Gould, S. J., & Lewontin, R. (1979). The spandrels of San Marco and the Panglossian paradigm: A critique of the adaptationist programme. *Proceedings of the Royal Society of London, 205,* 581–598.

Grafen, A. (1982). How not to measure inclusive fitness. *Nature, 298,* 425–426.

Gross, M. R., & Charnov, E. L. (1980). Alternative male histories in bluegill sunfish. *Proceedings of the National Academy of Sciences of the U.S.A., 77,* pp. 6937–6940.

Hall, G. S. (1904). *Adolescence, and its relations to physiology, anthropology, sociology, sex, crime, religion, and education* (p. 60). New York: Appleton-Century-Crofts. (ref in Bornstein, Comp. Meth. p. 60)

Hamilton, W. D. (1964). The genetical evolution of social behaviour: I and II. *Journal of Theoretical Biology, 7,* 1–52.

Harley, C. B. (1981). Learning the evolutionarily stable strategy. *Journal of Theoretical Biology, 89,* 611–633.

Harris, M. (1979). *Cultural materialism.* New York: Vintage.

Hrdy, S. B. (in press). Sex-biased parental investment among primates and other mammals: A critical evaluation of the Trivers-Willard hypothesis. In R. Gelles & J. Lancaster (Eds.), *Offspring abuse and neglect in biosocial perspective.* New York: Aldine.

Irwin, R. (1976, December 29). Interview in *Newsweek.*

Kessen, W. (1965). *The child.* New York: Wiley.

Kohlberg, L. (1969). Stage and sequence: The cognitive-developmental approach to socialization. In D. A. Goslin (Ed.), *Handbook of socialization theory and research.* Chicago: Rand McNally.

Konner, M. J. (1981). Evolution of human behavior development. In R. H. Munroe, R. L. Munroe, & R. B. Whiting (Eds.), *Handbook of cross-cultural human development.* New York: Garland STPM Press.

Konner, M. J. (1982). Biological aspects of the mother-infant bond. In R. N. Emde & R. J. Harmon (Eds.), *The development of attachment and affiliative systems.* New York: Plenum.

Laboratory of Comparative Human Cognition. (1979). *American psychologist, 34,* 827–833.

Lamb, M. E., Thompson, R. A., Gardner, W. P., Charnov, E. L., & Estes D. (1984). Security of infantile attachment as assessed in the "strange situation": Its study and biological interpretation. *The Behavioral and Brain Sciences, 7,* 127–171.

Leak, G. K., & Christopher, S. B. (1982). Freudian psychoanalysis and sociobiology: A synthesis. *American Psychologist, 37,* 313–322.

Littlefield, C., & Rushton, J. P. (in press). When a child dies: The sociobiology of bereavement. *Journal of Personality and Social Psychology.*

Livingstone, F. B. (1983). Do humans maximize their inclusive fitness? *The Behavioral and Brain Sciences, 6,* 110–111.

Lockard, J. S. (1980). Speculations on the adaptive significance of self-deception. In J. S. Lockard (Ed.), *The evolution of human social behavior.* New York: Elsevier.

Lorenz, K. Z. (1966). *On aggression.* New York: Harcourt.

Lumsden, C. J. (1983). Gene-culture linkages and the developing mind. In C. J. Brainerd (Ed.), *Recent advances in cognitive-developmental theory.* New York: Springer-Verlag.

Lumsden, C. J., & Wilson, E. O. (1981). *Genes, mind and culture: The coevolutionary process.* Cambridge, MA: Harvard University Press.

Lumsden, C. J., & Wilson, E. O. (1982). Mind and the linkage between genes and culture: Precis of *Genes, mind and culture. The Behavioral and Brain Sciences, 5,* 1–7.

Lumsden, C. J., & Wilson, E. O. (1983). *Promethean fire: Reflections on the origins of mind.* Cambridge, MA: Harvard University Press.

MacArthur, R. H., & Wilson, E. O. (1967). *The theory of island biogeography.* New Jersey: Princeton University Press.

MacDonald, K. (1984). An ethological-social learning theory of the development of altruism: Implications for human sociobiology. *Ethology and Sociobiology, 5,* 97–110.

Maynard Smith, J. (1982). *Evolution and the theory of games.* New York: Cambridge University Press.

Maynard Smith, J. (1984). Game theory and the evolution of behaviour. *The Behavioral and Brain Sciences, 7,* 95–125.

Maynard Smith, J., & Warren, N. (1982). Models of cultural and genetic change. *Evolution, 36,* 620–627.

McCall, R. B. (1977). Challenges to a science of developmental psychology. *Child Development, 48,* 333–344.

McCall, R. B. (1981). Nature-nurture and the two realms of development: A proposed integration with respect to mental development. *Child Development, 52,* 1–12.

Piaget, J. (1978). *Behavior and evolution.* New York: Pantheon.

Plomin, R. (1981). Ethological behavioral genetics and development. In K. Immelmann, G. W. Barlow, L. Petrinovich, & M. Main (Eds.). *Behavioral development.* New York: Cambridge University Press.

Plomin, R. (Ed.). (1983). Special section on developmental behavioral genetics. *Child Development, 54,* 253–435.

Porter, R. H., & Laney, M. D. (1980). Attachment theory and the concept of inclusive fitness. *Merrill-Palmer Quarterly, 26,* 35–51.

Pulliam, H. R., & Dunford, C. (1980). *Programmed to learn: An essay on the evolution of culture.* New York: Columbia University Press.

Richerson, P. J., & Boyd, R. (1978). A dual inheritance model of the human evolutionary process: I. Basic concepts and a simple model. *Journal of Social and Biological Structures, 1,* 127–154.

Riegel, K. F., & Meacham (Eds.). (1976). *The developing individual in a changing world.* Chicago: Aldine.

Rowe, D. C., & Plomin, R. (1981). The importance of nonshared (E_1) environmental influences in behavioral development. *Developmental Psychology, 17,* 517–531.

Ruse, M. (1982). Are there gay genes? Sociobiology and homosexuality. *Journal of Homosexuality, 6,* 5–34.

Rushton, J. P. (1984). Sociobiology: Toward a theory of individual and group differences in personality and social behavior. In J. R. Royce & L. P. Mos (Eds.), *Annals of theoretical psychology, Volume 2.* New York: Plenum.

Rushton, J. P. (1985). Differential K theory: The sociobiology of individual and group differences. *Personality and Individual Differences, 6,* 441–452.

Rushton, J. P., Russell, R. J. H., & Wells, P. A. (1984). Genetic similarity theory: Beyond kin selection. *Behavior Genetics, 14,* 179–193.

Rushton, J. P., Russell, R. J. H., & Wells, P. A. (1985). Personality and genetic similarity theory. *Journal of Social and Biological Structures, 8,* 63–86.

Sagan, C. (1977). *The dragons of Eden.* New York: Ballantine.

Sahlins, M. D. (1976). *The use and abuse of biology.* Ann Arbor: University of Michigan Press.

Scarr, S. (1979, January). Toward a more biological psychology. In *Frontiers of the social sciences.* Symposium at the meeting of the American Association for the Advancement of Science, Houston.

Scarr, S. (1981). An evolutionary perspective on infant intelligence: Species patterns and individual variations. In Scarr, S. *Race, social class and individual differences in I.Q.* Hillsdale, NJ: Lawrence Erlbaum Associates.

Scarr, S., & Grajek, S. (1982). Similarities and differences among siblings. In M. E. Lamb & B. Sutton-Smith (Eds.), *Sibling relationships.* Hillsdale, NJ: Lawrence Erlabaum Associates.

Shepher, J. (1983). *Incest: A biosocial view.* Orlando, FL: Academic Press.

Smith, M. S. (1986). *Grandparenting as kin investment.* Manuscript in preparation.

Smith, M. S., Kish, B. J., & Crawford, C. B. (in press). *Inheritance of wealth as human kin investment. Ethology and Sociobiology.*

Smith, P. K. (1983a). Biological, psychological, and historical aspects of reproduction and childcare. In G. C. L. Davey (Ed.), *Animal models of human behavior.* New York: Wiley.

Smith, P. K. (1983b). Human sociobiology. In J. Nicholson & B. Foss (Eds.), *Psychology survey 4.* Lancaster: British Psychological Society.

Stearns, S. C. (1977). The evolution of life history traits: a critique of the theory and a review of the data. *Annual Review of Ecology and Systematics, 8,* 145–171.

Strayer, F. F. (1984). Biological approaches to the study of the family. In R. D. Parke (Ed.), *Review of child development research: Vol. 7. The family.* Chicago: University of Chicago Press.

Trivers, R. L. (1972). Parental investment and sexual selection. In B. Campbell (Ed.), *Sexual selection and the descent of man.* Chicago: Aldine.

Trivers, R. L. (1974). Parent-offspring conflict. *American Zoologist, 14,* 249–264.

Trivers, R. L. (1985). *Social evolution.* Menlo Park, CA: Benjamin-Cummings.

van den Berghe, P. L. (1979). *Human family systems: An evolutionary view.* New York: Elsevier.

van den Berghe, P. L. (1981). *The ethnic phenomenon.* New York: Elsevier.

van den Berghe, P. L. (1983). Human inbreeding avoidance: Nature in culture. *The Behavioral and Brain Sciences, 6,* 91–124.

Weigel, R. M. (1984). The application of evolutionary models to the study of decisions made by children during object possession conflicts. *Ethology and Sociobiology, 5,* 229–238.

Weisfeld, G. E. (1982). The nature-nurture issue and the integrating concept of function. In B. Wolman (Ed.), *Handbook of developmental psychology.* Englewood Cliffs, NJ: Prentice-Hall.

Weisfeld, G. E., & Berger, J. M. (1983). Some features of human adolescence viewed in evolutionary perspective. *Human Development, 26,* 121–133.

Williams, G. C. (1984). When does game theory model reality? *The Behavioral and Brain Sciences, 7,* 117.

Wilson, E. O. (1975). *Sociobiology: The new synthesis.* Cambridge, MA: Harvard University Press.

Zajonc, R. M. (1983). Validating the confluence model. *Psychological Bulletin, 93,* 457–480.

10

Play, Games, and Innovation: Sociobiological Findings and Unanswered Questions

Robert Fagen
University of Alaska, Juneau

Play, innovation and related phenomena such as games offer sociobiologists and psychologists rich intellectual fare and much room for dispute. The following pages present current sociobiological views and some new ideas on these topics. Sociobiologists themselves disagree about play—what it is, whether it indeed merits study, and (if in fact play matters) what it means in the lives of animals and especially in human life. I review some major ways in which sociobiologists have looked at animal play behaviors, including human play and games. Much of the following research is based on general sociobiological concepts of individual differences, cooperation, kinship, and altruism, introduced elsewhere in this volume. Biologists' continuing fascination with these classic sociobiological preoccupations serves to focus attention on aspects of play and games that might otherwise have been overlooked.

Systematic scientific study of novel, innovative, and creative behavior from modern biological perspectives is a significant new direction for behavioral research. The biology of creativity, discovery, and innovation is currently receiving considerable attention (Findlay & Lumsden, in press; Kummer & Goodall, 1985). Undisputed causal links between play and behavioral discovery (reviewed by Fagen, 1981a and Findlay & Lumsden, in press) exist in humans, in a highly intelligent minority of nonhuman mammals, and perhaps in a few species of birds. The circumstances seem especially propitious for seeking a rapprochement between play research and sociobiology. Such a synthesis could foster productive interchanges between biological and psychological approaches to human behavior on the common ground of animal play.

253

SCOPE

I shall discuss sociobiological approaches to the topics play, games, and innovation. By sociobiology I mean systematic scientific study of the biological bases of social (including sexual and parental) behaviors, using population biology and evolutionary theory as the chief exploratory tools. Lumsden and Wilson (1983) define sociobiology in essentially this spirit.

The terms play, games, and innovation potentially cover vast tracts of intellectual and empirical ground. To employ them without definition, especially in an interdisciplinary context like the present one, openly invites confusion. Therefore, although precise operational definitions of the three terms are notoriously elusive, for the purposes of the present chapter they are defined as follows:

PLAY of animals (including humans) consists of organized, prolonged action sequences performed by one or more individuals in which behaviors recognizable from functional contexts such as agonistic fighting or resource-consumer interaction are performed in ways that cannot possibly lead to the conventional outcomes of these behaviors. In the paradoxical context of play, skilled actions are recombined, exaggerated, varied, and repeated. To human observers, play is intuitively recognizable, seemingly functionless, and apparently pleasurable.

GAMES are structured versions of social play characterized by repeated interaction, role reversal, and rule-like regularity of spatial relationships between the players themselves or between the players and their physical environment. Human games may have explicit rules that may be treated as objects of verbal discourse.

INNOVATION is a novel behavioral performance that can be repeated by the original performer or by conspecifics. In complex group-living species such as wolves, chimpanzees, or humans, innovation can have important social consequences including changes in social status, development of novel relationships with the biotic and abiotic environments, and even entry into an evolutionarily novel adaptive zone.

For bibliographies on play and games, see Fagen (1981a), Smith (1984), and Sutton-Smith (1976). Innovation is ably discussed and analyzed by Lumsden and Wilson (1983) and by Pulliam and Dunford (1980), among others.

WHY CAN'T SOCIOBIOLOGISTS AGREE ABOUT PLAY?

It is no longer possible to identify a specific sociobiological program. Few investigators would quarrel with a Darwinist perspective, but Darwin was a committed pluralist and his heirs still openly contest one of science's richest legacies. A sociobiological consensus on play cannot be expected. Although some sociobiologists (e.g., Kurland, 1977) offer significant field observations of play, others ignore play in their detailed descriptions and analyses of mammalian social interactions—even in species known to be highly playful. A few commentators (e.g., Partridge & Nunney, 1977) explicitly reject play as a legitimate sociobiological topic, whereas leading sociobiologists (Barash, 1973; Hrdy, 1977; Konner, 1982; Lumsden & Wilson, 1983; Symons, 1978; Wilson, 1971, 1975, 1977) consider play at length in their analyses and discussions.

THEORETICAL MODELS OF PLAY AND INNOVATION

Formal evolutionary models with mathematical underpinnings are sociobiological mainstays. They serve to clarify thinking, they help focus attention on particular questions or phenomena, and they occasionally yield counterintuitive predictions that can be measured against field data or experimental results. In this spirit we explore the consequences of some widely held assumptions about play with the aid of evolutionary theory and mathematics.

Graphical and mathematical model-building is a means to understanding behavior. Social scientists and psychologists familiar with the course of quantification and formal deductive analysis in their own fields will recognize similar trends in the history of sociobiological research. In the earliest phase of quantification, scholars devised numerical measures of behavior and subjected these measures to statistical analysis. Often very elaborate, these studies adapted methods of mathematical psychology, sociology, and engineering to animal behavior. For example, Stuart Altmann (1962) applied methods of information theory and Markov chain models to behavior of nonhuman primates. Altmann successfully quantified and dissected the bewildering perplexity of nonhuman primate social behavior. He further identified specific patterns of social communication and association in rhesus. These patterns furnished early evidence for sociobiological theories of kin selection in primate societies.

Specifically suited (and often specifically designed) for exploratory behavioral research, these statistical methods for detecting nonrandom patterns in animal behavior led in turn to a new set of scientific questions and a different kind of modeling. Statistical features of animal behavior demanded explanation. Starting from simple assumptions about underlying behavioral processes, holistic social structures, ecological prime movers, or evolutionary selection pressures, causal explanations of behavior patterns began to take explicit mathematical and graphical form. As a result, new models designed for prediction, explanation, and insight began to join earlier descriptive models in the sociobiologist's workshop. These newer causal models resemble mathematical models in psychophysics. In these formal analyses, fundamental empirical regularities or theoretical relationships, described by simple parametric equations, become building blocks in models of more complex interactions. For example, in sociobiology's sister discipline, behavioral ecology, Fretwell and Lucas (1969) analyzed the dynamic spatial distribution of animals in heterogeneous environments. They imagined an ideal situation in which animals were free to move among spatial areas that differed in resource availability. In this situation, simple graphical models predict differential habitat use as a joint function of population density and habitat quality. Fretwell and Lucas predict so-called "ideal free" spatial distributions of animals. An individual in an ideal free situation is expected to select the habitat type offering it the maximum amount of a limiting ecological resource. This idealized picture of animals moving freely among habitat types makes sense in situations where the value of a preferred habitat to an individual decreases as more individuals crowd into it. Eventually, less productive but less crowded habitats become as attractive as the habitat that was originally colonized. Ultimately population densities in the several habitat types reach an equilibrium at which the amount of resources available per individual is equal for each individual across habitats. Possible deviations from this condition are absorbed by a kind of negative feedback acting on population densities through individual behavior. Any animal finding itself in a habitat type offering resource rewards which are less than the average reward over all habitats simply exercises its freedom of motion and makes tracks to a more rewarding habitat type. By doing so it increases the population density in the new habitat type entered and decreases resource availability to itself as well as to everyone else there. Likewise, its departure increases the availability of food resource to the animals remaining in the habitat type it vacated. This tendency of animals to seek rewarding habitats ensures a stable equilibrium set of densities. In the language of economics, animals behave so as to settle different habitat types at different densities that result in an equal marginal value for each type.

Two models of play and innovation are discussed here. The first views play as a beneficial, but costly and risky component of the individual life history. This model seeks to explain variation among species, among populations within species, and across ages (in individual ontogeny) in the occurrence of play. The second model treats play as a potential source of beneficial innovation. Analysis of the consequences of this assumption makes it possible to explore the evolution of innovative play in a cultural species where nonplayers can "steal" new discoveries via observational learning. Full mathematical details, chapter-length exposition, and extended discussions of these two models may be found in Chapters 6 and 8, respectively, of Fagen (1981a).

The basic assumptions of the first model may be illustrated very simply by considering a particular instance of play by a single individual—a young equid (member of the horse family) exuberantly running in circles and figure-eights near its mother and herdmates. Such vigorous locomotor activity can occupy a small fraction of the youngster's time (say, 1%–5%) on any given day and an impressive fraction of the animal's total running activity. For example, turning while running at high speed is a form of exercise that is presumably important for physical conditioning and that is also risky due to the extreme torque applied to limb joints. In a band of Shetland and Welsh ponies, this form of exercise occurred virtually exclusively in play (Fagen & George, 1977). Possible consequences of this solo locomotor play for the very young pony include:

1. Physical exercise and consequent training of strength and skill.
2. Display of the animal's current state of physical fitness to others, or to itself.
3. Injury sustained in falls or resulting from twisted limbs.
4. Increased risk of exposure to predators, parasites, or pathogens.
5. Expenditure in play of time, energy, nutrients, and attention that could instead have been devoted to feeding, resting, growth, grooming, or other competing behavioral-physiological processes in the life history.

Some comments on these hypothetical consequences of locomotor play may aid in motivating the assumptions of the model. It is frequently assumed that negative consequences of play affect Darwinian fitness by a shorter and more direct route than positive consequences of play. Another way to put this is that play has relatively direct negative consequences and relatively indirect positive consequences. If a playing animal wanders away from its caregiver and is detected by a predator, its potential survivorship over the next half hour has been decreased by play. But if cumulative effects of play make the animal more likely to flee a predator successfully, potential benefits of that particular bout of play will not be effective until days or weeks later and only if the animal happens to be detected and chased by a predator.

Under the assumptions above, it is possible to formulate and solve a mathematical life-history model that automates the intricate theoretical calculations necessary when hypothetical genetic alleles coding for different levels of play motivation enter a life-historical balance sheet. The model offers the interesting prediction that two populations of animals inhabiting the same kind of environment and sharing the same basic biology may exhibit vast differences in play frequencies. This nonintuitive prediction holds when two extreme life-history strategies convey high fitness, but strategies whose characteristics are intermediate result in low fitness. The case of greatest interest to the present discussion is the case in which one of these strategies involves play at some time in the life-history and the other does not. This situation is quite typical of age-structured life-history models and is especially prevalent in models of animals capable of play. Here, the adaptive landscape for play in the life history features two high-fitness peaks, one corresponding to populations of very playful individuals and the other corresponding to populations of nonplayers.

In a model of this sort, the ultimate state of the population depends on historical circumstances. If the original population exhibits characteristics intermediate between play and nonplay, the extreme strategy that appears first by mutation will rapidly take over. But if a population is initially nonplayful, intermediate levels of play cannot invade. This property of the model raises an interesting issue. Play has only been convincingly demonstrated in mammals and birds, where it occurs in some form in virtually all species. How, then, can high levels of play evolve in an adaptive landscape having multiple peaks if play is in fact influenced by several alleles each having a small quantitative effect? Under this plausible set of assumptions, mutant players in a nonplayful population would only have a few of these hypothetical play alleles, they would exhibit intermediate levels of play, and they would be counterselected. Play alleles could never accumulate in sufficient numbers in the population to shift it to the second adaptive peak. It appears that a changing or variable environment along with genetic drift in small populations would be necessary for play to evolve in this situation. A change in the environment would occasionally favor intermediate levels of play and cause the frequency of genetic determinants of play to increase. When the environment returned to its initial state, animals in the population would be genetically predisposed to play at high frequencies. Intermediate levels of play would again be counterselected. There would then be no tendency for the population to return to its initial, nonplayful state.

A possible example of otherwise-inexplicable between-population variation in play of a particular equid species in a single type of environment has recently been reported for the mountain zebra, *Equus zebra* (Penzhorn, 1984). Joubert (1972a, 1972b) and Klingel (1968) observed regular play in mountain zebra, whereas Penzhorn (1984) found play to be a very rare behavior in the same species. Nutritional, demographic, terrain, and meteorological variables as well as differences between observers may be involved, but none of these factors can fully and convincingly account for the evident differences in prevalence of play found in different populations of the mountain zebra. Historical circumstances in evolutionary time may well be a plausible explanation of these differences, as predicted by the model.

When fitness consequences of a particular animal behavior depend on the overall proportion of animals that perform the behavior in a population, then the genetic bases of that behavioral trait are said to be subject to frequency-dependent natural selection. This form of selection is appropriate for social behavior in which the selective value of a particular phenotype depends on what other phenotypes are doing. The animal's fitness as a result of being able to perform a certain behavior depends on the frequency of performers in the population. For example, the gains from damaging fighting behavior depend on the relative frequency of opponents who fight damagingly and opponents who withdraw without a challenge. Likewise, altruists do well when surrounded by other altruists, but they do less well when present at low frequencies in a population of cheaters. Behavior that is good for the individual but damaging to the species can evolve by frequency-dependent natural selection. These theoretical models exemplify one sociobiological approach to the conflict between individual behavioral tendencies and social welfare. They are therefore of potential interest to those branches of psychology concerned with individual-society conflict. Not surprisingly, sociobiologists approach this problem using models based on game theory (e.g., Maynard Smith, 1982).

Possible frequency-dependent natural selection of tendencies to play is, as pointed out above, not assumed by the life-history model. However, I feel that frequency-dependence may be a plausible assumption in this case. Play is assumed to be a kind of adjunct to growth processes, developing the animal's potential strength and skill. As such, it should obey the same evolutionary rules as growth processes in general. Givnish (1982) and Maynard Smith (1982) model growth in size in plants and in red deer. They argue that the effect of size on the outcome of resource competition is relative. Win-loss probabilities in a contest over resources may depend on the size difference between the competing individuals. This assumption makes sense for plants that compete by crowding or shading each other. Likewise, in red deer dominance in stags appears to depend on relative rather than absolute size, and the biggest stag in a local population of red deer mates with the greatest number of hinds in a given year. His success is due to the fact that he is large relative to his competitors—not to the fact that he is large on a fixed scale of measurement (e.g., the hunter's "trophy" category). Therefore, the evolutionarily "best" size for an individual to be in order to gain the most reproductive success relative to competitors will necessarily depend on the size distribution of that individual's potential competitors. Growth in size then becomes an evolutionary game. The winner grows just enough to be biggest without wasting resources on excess growth.

In such a population, if play contributes to physical training, an animal's competitive ability will depend not only on its size but also on its previous (play) experience. For example, a physically fit 100-pound stag might be able to defeat a physically unfit 120-pound stag. Play that builds physical ability then directly affects a component of Darwinian fitness. It is a behavior contributing to an animal's effective size, and therefore to the animal's competitive ability. It follows from this observation that since size strategies are frequency-dependent, play strategies will be as well. Play experience thus interacts with body size to determine Darwinian fitness. Under these circumstances, natural selection would be frequency-dependent, even in a species whose play was all solo play. Naturally, social play opens up additional possibilities for frequency-dependent selective effects, as suggested by the models in Fagen (1981a, Chapter 8) and by any functional hypothesis about play involving social effects such as assessment or enhancement of cooperative tendencies. Thus, although diversity of play strategies has not yet been shown to evolve by frequency-dependent selection in any mathematical model, there are sound theoretical reasons to expect this result. I would predict that there would exist conditions in such a model that allowed a stable evolutionary equilibrium between playful and nonplayful life histories in different individuals in the same population. In general, alternative life-history strategies are well-understood both in a theoretical sense and in specific empirical contexts other than that of play (Dawkins, 1980; Gross, 1983; Maynard Smith, 1982; Rubenstein, 1980), and it would be very surprising if play proved exceptional in this regard.

As originally formulated (Fagen, 1977), my mathematical model of play in the life history exemplifies the adaptationist paradigm of sociobiology (Lewontin, 1979). Careful scrutiny of this model by a determined skeptic would reveal questionable assumptions highlighted by critics of evolutionary optimization models. A safe return to high ground could be made through pro forma warnings that if play is subject to natural selection at all, then such selection is likely to be frequency-dependent; that additive genetic variance for play has not been demonstrated; that genetic drift in small populations may be more important than natural selection in the evolution of mammalian behavior; that animals that play may not be resource-limited in the conventional sense; and that play as a component of development may even be epiphenomenal. These caveats certainly apply here.

A more speculative theoretical model (Fagen, 1981a, Chapter 8) relates play to innovation and cultural evolution and addresses the evolutionary fate of hypothetical play genes coding for innovative tendencies.

The basic conceptual framework of the model is as follows. In a cultural species, playful animals are hypothesized to invent novel, beneficial behaviors. Such innovative play is assumed to be risky and costly in limiting resources. Only a playful animal can discover a novel behavior on its own, but any animal, whether playful or nonplayful, can acquire the behavior once it exists in the culture, via teaching, imitation, stimulus enhancement, or direct observational learning. Nonplayful animals do not run the risks or pay the costs of playing. They acquire innovations by learning them from others, but do not discover anything themselves. The primitive condition is assumed to be nonplay, with play alleles initially arising at low frequencies by mutation.

When the mathematical machinery necessary to define and analyze this model is put to work, we find that model populations evolve by natural selection to a stable genetically polymorphic equilibrium between players and nonplayers. This outcome is the only possible one in the model. Selection is expected to act on noninnovators so as to sharpen their exploitative abilities. They will evolve so as to better recognize, assimilate and implement novel behavioral performances by others. Such increased ability of the noninnovators to steal and use innovators' discoveries will in turn increase selective pressures on the innovators to be more creative and to find ways to reduce the risks associated with their innovative play. It may also force them to be more secretive about their discoveries or even to leave false leads.

Could innovators and implementers be selected in a coevolutionary game to cooperate rather than to compete? And would such cooperation lead to cultural stagnation or, conversely, could it peacefully strengthen the positive feedback between enhanced creative intelligence on the one side and enhanced engineering ingenuity on the other? Axelrod and Hamilton's (1981) model of the evolution of cooperation through repeated encounters suggests that the answer to the first question just posed may well be "yes," but formal theory has not yet been devised to produce a definitive answer. Theory leading to productive speculation about the second question above remains to be formulated.

The model of circumspect creators and prying mimics formally addresses relationships between creativity and society. Among other things, it offers a plausible biological basis for Kipling's "great game." (See *Kim,* a durable classic, not to be confused with Kipling's overly cited *Just-So Stories.*) Indeed, this model tempts users to analyze human activities ranging from art and science to industrial espionage and college term paper agencies, priesthoods and parishoners, and Pleistocene cave art, to cite just a few potential applications. Sociobiologists nonetheless need to observe the limits of such theoretical explanations, limits long since outlined by perceptive and articulate critics.

APPLICATIONS OF SPECIFIC SOCIOBIOLOGICAL PRINCIPLES

Formal models discussed above explicitly address the evolution of play and innovation in a general sociobiological context. In addition, sociobiologists have productively applied concepts of sexual selection, kinship theory, and altruism to these phenomena. Kinship and sexual selection theory shed much light on the structure of animal play. For example, close kin in primate societies play with each other at frequencies exceeding those expected on a simple random model based on mere playfulness or proximity (Fagen, 1981a; Levy, 1979). Closely related playmates appear to behave so as to preferentially share benefits of play interaction with each other. Theoretically, such behavior would be expected from animals that shared play genes by descent from a common ancestor.

Sex differences in frequency and content are a second feature of social play that has received sociobiological attention. Young male macaques are, as a rule, far more playful than young females. (For practical and definitional reasons, it has proved difficult so far to gather quantitative data on possible sex differences in infant play in free-ranging populations. There are, however, indications from the field that infants may indeed represent an exception to the general pattern of sex differences in macaque play. See, e.g., Mori, 1974.)

Symons (1978) uses a sociobiological hypothesis to explain the general pattern of sex differences in macaque play, with particular reference to his own field studies of rhesus macaques. He supposes that play serves to develop intraspecific fighting ability. This hypothesis is convincingly supported by Symons' detailed film analyses and comparative data. He then argues that male rhesus are likely to reap far greater benefits from a given increase in fighting skill. The breeding season in rhesus is punctuated by violent male-male fights over access to females. Dominance relationships also appear to govern access to mates.

Levy (1979) also observed a greater frequency of play in young male rhesus than in young females. She explains this pattern by means of a second sociobiological hypothesis, one very different from that proposed by Symons. Levy argues as follows. Suppose that young males need to form close, cooperative relationships to a greater extent than do females because males disperse together or join new groups to which their male kin have previously dispersed. Immigrant males must literally fight for their survival when joining a new group, and acceptance appears to be difficult if not impossible unless male kin support each other in their efforts to be accepted by their prospective troopmates. Levy assumes that play develops cooperative relationships between individuals and argues that such bonds are especially important among young males for the reasons stated above. For these reasons, she predicts not only that male rhesus should play more but also that they should play more with other males than expected by chance. Both of these predictions appear to be true for rhesus.

Life-history models of social play offer a third interpretation of sex differences in rhesus social play, and of sex differences in play generally. Female rhesus become sexually mature at age four and may produce their first offspring during their 4th year. Males continue growing and become sexually mature at a later age than do females. Typically, male rhesus do not become fathers until they have emigrated from their natal troop, become established in a new troop, and secured access to estrous females during the breeding season—a process that may take several additional years. In rhesus, as in numerous other species of mammals including elephants, red deer, walrus, brown bears, and humans, females grow up faster. Does their accelerated development place greater resource demands on them than on males as juveniles, leaving less time and energy in the life-history for play and making young females relatively more risk-averse? If so, sex-specific costs of play, rather than the sex-specific benefits hypothesized by Levy and by Symons, could account for sex differences in the amount and perhaps even in the kind of play performed by male and female juveniles.

The study of human games, long the province of folklorists, may well offer additional opportunities for sociobiological analysis. Exemplified by Iona and Peter Opie's classic documentation of the games of British children (Opie & Opie, 1967, 1969), by Brian Sutton-Smith's (1976, 1981) justly celebrated and wide-ranging contributions, and by Hildegarde Sbrzesny's (1976) book-length treatment of !Ko games, the study of games is a high point of modern research on human nature and on cultural history.

Sutton-Smith (1980) distinguishes between two broad categories of human game behavior and interprets their differing evolutionary significance. Games of physical skill, as their name implies, test strength, endurance, and coordination.

They reflect themes familiar to students of nonhuman animal play—wrestling, sparring, chasing and fleeing, mock battles over possession of a contested object or spatial site, and prey capture. Except for details of culture and language, these interactions seem continuous with the stylized "games" observed in complex mammalian societies. Sociobiology can suggest plausible biological bases for games of physical skill, as they appear to be direct elaborations of primate play-fighting and play-chasing behavior, and their major features vary relatively little across cultures. It would be surprising if the biological foundations of these games had undergone major modifications in the millions of years of primate evolution.

Human and nonhuman primate games of physical skill offer a probable example of evolutionary continuity in social behavior of intelligent vertebrates. By contrast, human games of strategy and chance appear to be a new arrival on the evolutionary scene—a uniquely human form of game behavior. Sutton-Smith (1980) correctly observes that these games—rule-governed interaction involving explicit symbolic or random elements, as in dice, chess, roulette, Keno, and computer games—have no obvious antecedents in nonhuman primate behavior. Marked cross-cultural variation in the occurrence and characteristics of these games contrasts strikingly with the relative uniformity of games of physical skill.

In the three cases cited above—kin preference, sex differences, and games— sociobiology offers plausible adaptive explanations of phenomena that might previously have seemed puzzling or unimportant. The biology of games of chance and strategy has, furthermore, been singled out for special attention. Although kin preference and sex differences in animal play have been thoroughly discussed and even debated, sociobiological analysis of the rich natural history of human games has scarcely begun.

Konner (1975) and later other sociobiologists analyzed social play in humans and nonhumans in the light of evolutionary theory. These studies, reviewed and extended in Fagen (1981a), identified contrasts between selfishness and cooperation in social play.

Animal social play is not always the cooperative Arcady that early primatologists envisioned. Indeed, it exhibits elements of exploitation and reflects conflicts of interest between players. For example, one animal can bully or intimidate another under the cover of play. Such rough treatment can lead to (simulated?) screams of pain and to intervention by adults. Or, a real fight can erupt from play. Play can also be used to manipulate another animal's behavior, as, for example, when one animal plays with another until the second animal vacates a defendable resource such as a shady resting place, a toy, or a food item. Then, as soon as the second animal relinquishes control of the resource, the first suddenly breaks off play and occupies the shady spot, takes the toy, or seizes and eats the food.

Play rarely erupts into violent aggression. However, field studies reveal that an outbreak of interpersonal violence in a play interaction (termed "breakdown" or "escalation") may be attributed to one of several causes. First, bullying under the cover of play can (as noted above) result in a fight. Second, and perhaps more typically, animals can, as it were, "disagree" about when, where, how, and with whom to play. Disagreement of this sort can lead to threats or to out-and-out aggression. For example, one animal may solicit play from another. Rather than responding in kind, the second ignores the first or begins to move away from it. The first animal continues to solicit play and the second continues to "refuse." A rejected animal is not always persistent in soliciting play from another, especially when alternative playmates are available. Sometimes, however, the first animal persists, threats are exchanged, and a fight begins.

Sociobiologists view potential conflicts of interest in play as logical consequences of the assumption that each individual needs particular kinds and amounts of play. When two individuals' needs for play differ, conflict can enter their relationship as playmates. Take rhesus macaques, for example. If a male still requires play on a given day but no male playmates or female kin are available, he may solicit play from a female with whom he does not normally play. The female, not needing play herself and under no obligation to cooperate by virtue of kinship or past reciprocity, might then refuse the male. Biologically, it would be in the male's interest to persistently solicit play and in the female's interest to reject him in this situation.

Commentators on social play agree that, despite the ever-present potential for conflict of interest, social play interactions are, by and large, stable and cooperative (Altmann, 1962; Fagen, 1981a). Such elaborate cooperative behavior, particularly among immature animals, represents a focus of current sociobiological theory. These theories of the evolution of cooperation (Axelrod, 1984; Axelrod & Hamilton, 1981) yield new insights (Fagen, 1983, 1984) into the evolution of cooperative social play.

Axelrod and Hamilton's theory, spotlighted by a recent general article (Allman, 1984), shows that two animals will be selected to cooperate in a given type of social interaction, rather than being greedy, if they are likely to have many more opportunities to interact with each other in the same way in the future. Repeated play interaction between the same two individuals is of course typical of social play (Fagen, 1981a, pp. 431–432). In group-living species, in mammalian litters, and in avian clutches, provided that juvenile survivorship is sufficiently high, a family or extended family situation allows thousands of play interactions to occur between the same two companions. Furthermore, Axelrod and Hamilton's theory explains that if players are close kin, their biological relatedness further stabilizes social play. Especially elaborate forms of cooperation may then evolve. Thus, theory appears entirely consistent with the earlier findings of ethologists and primatologists that social play can be especially elaborate, stable, and even gamelike in complex societies among close kin under circumstances favorable to juvenile survival. Indeed, when many repeated interactions between the same two juveniles are not highly likely, as in the weakly structured aggregations formed by giraffes, social play is rare even though solo play occurs regularly. Increased group size alone is not sufficient to produce cooperative social play. Giraffe herds can be as large as many primate troops, but they are not permanent and membership is constantly changing. The key to cooperative social play is persistence of personal relationships. For example, in an imaginary social species that formed large, permanent groups but in which individuals did not recognize each other as individuals, cooperation could not evolve through the mechanisms proposed by Axelrod and Hamilton. Wilson (1971, 1975) points to personal relationships between individuals as a major feature distinguishing complex mammalian societies from the far more sophisticated but wholly impersonal insect societies. The sophistication of insect societies is manifest in division of labor, the presence of sterile worker castes, and fine-tuned cooperation in construction, brood rearing, foraging, and nest defense. When we view this distinction between personal and impersonal social environments in the light of Axelrod and Hamilton's theory of repeated interaction and individual recognition, it is easy to understand why social insects do not exhibit social play—another major difference between higher vertebrate and insect societies (Wilson, 1971).

A fascinating question in general sociobiological theory on cooperation, and one which deserves special attention from theoreticians and field workers alike, is the problem of learning to cooperate. Maynard Smith (1982) discusses Axelrod and Hamilton's theory and raises a disturbing theoretical possibility. Because cooperation is contingent on repeated interaction with a particular individual, learning that it would pay to cooperate with that individual might take more time than anyone had. Thousands of interactions with each individual might be necessary. For example, how could two adults ever learn to share food if they had to try different strategies thousands of times before they discovered they could cooperate? They would probably starve long before they learned.

I proposed (Fagen, 1981b) that social play affords the necessary opportunity to interact repeatedly with the same individual in a simulated cooperative situation and to try out tactics leading to different beneficial or costly consequences. Social play may thus help animals learn that there is such a thing as a cooperative strategy. It may also help them learn to apply this strategy to cooperation with particular individuals in particular contexts such as conflict resolution, hunting in groups, coordinated predator avoidance, male-female bonding, or parental care—all serious cooperative interactions well represented by behavioral rehearsals in the paradoxical context of social play.

PROSPECTS

Social scientists now routinely exchange constructive criticism and new insights with sociobiologists, a dialogue that demonstrably benefits all. I can think of two ways for this dialogue to focus productively on questions of mutual interest involving both play and human nature.

First, there is need for a cultural perspective on play in animals. Species in which younger and older juveniles play together could evolve a youth culture consisting of particular games or styles of play. Younger juveniles would learn to play in particular ways characteristic of their culture through observation of older juveniles and through direct experience in play with older juveniles. Different primate troops, wolf packs, or kin groups (including entire families) could invent and develop different variations of species-specific play patterns. In additional species, parent-offspring play could transmit forms of play from one generation to the next. Indeed, suppose that play has only trifling selective value through long periods of evolutionary time. This pluralistic hypothesis, originally proposed by Darwin (Fagen, 1981a, pp. 481–483), was recently revived by Fagen (ibid.) and by Martin (1984). Play having trifling adaptive value and a genetic basis could still respond to cultural dynamics in the manner outlined by recent analyses of cultural evolution. If play has only trifling or inconsistent selective value, then it may be especially sensitive to cultural contingencies. This approach to play is one that unifies the separate insights of the biologist, cultural anthropologist, and psychologist.

My second suggestion is a logical extension of the first. If variation in play occurs both cross-culturally and down through time, then necessarily changes in play patterns are occurring. What are the sources of novel forms of play and of changes in existing forms of play? Existing field studies of nonhuman primates suggest a few of the things that might be happening. As reviewed by Fagen (1981a, pp. 109, 194–195), animals have occasionally been observed to invent novel play-movements and play-signals. Recently Huffman (1984) described how play with stones became a culturally transmitted but nonadaptive element of the behavioral repertoire of a troop of Japanese macaques, *Macaca fuscata*. A natural history of playful inventions and discoveries, particularly those occurring in free-living animals, would be of tremendous value to contemporary students of creativity and innovation, and would surely benefit from the insights of a variety of disciplines.

REFERENCES

Allman, W. F. (1984). Nice guys finish first. *Science, 84*(8), 24–32.

Altmann, S. A. (1962). Social behavior of anthropoid primates: Analysis of recent concepts. In E. L. Bliss (Ed.), *Roots of behavior* (pp. 277–285). New York: Harper.

Axelrod, R. (1984). *The evolution of cooperation*. New York: Basic Books.

Axelrod, R., & Hamilton, W. D. (1981). The evolution of cooperation. *Science, 211*, 1390–1396.

Barash, D. P. (1973). The social biology of the Olympic marmot. *Animal Behaviour Monographs, 6*, 171–245.

Dawkins, R. (1980). Good strategy or evolutionarily stable strategy? In G. Barlow & J. Silverberg (Eds.), *Sociobiology: Beyond nature/nurture* (pp. 331–367). Boulder, CO: Westview Press.

Fagen, R. (1977). Selection for optimal age-dependent schedules of play behavior. *American Naturalist, 111*, 395–414.

Fagen, R. (1981a). *Animal play behavior.* New York: Oxford University Press.

Fagen R. (1981b). *The evolution of cooperation in social play.* Paper presented to the annual meeting of the Animal Behavior Society, Knoxville, TN.

Fagen, R. (1983). Horseplay and monkeyshines. *Science, 83*(10), 70–76.

Fagen, R. (1984). Play and behavioural flexibility: In P. K. Smith (Ed.), *Play in animals and humans* (pp. 159–173). Oxford: Blackwell.

Fagen, R., & George, T. K. (1977). Play behavior and exercise in young ponies (*Equus caballus* L.). *Behavioural Ecology and Sociobiology, 2,* 267–269.

Findlay, S. & Lumsden, C. (in press). *Journal of Social and Biological Structures.*

Fretwell, S. D., & Lucas, H. L. (1969). On territorial behaviour and other factors influencing habitat distribution in birds. I. Theoretical development. *Acta Biotheoretica, 19,* 16–36.

Givnish, T. J. (1982). On the adaptive significance of leaf height in forest herbs. *American Naturalist, 120,* 353–381.

Gross, M. R. (1983). Sunfish, salmon, and the evolution of alternative reproductive strategies and tactics in fishes: In R. J. Wootton & G. Potts (Eds.), *Fish reproduction: Strategies and tactics* (pp. 1–50). Orlando, FL: Academic Press.

Hrdy, S. B. (1977). *The langurs of Abu.* Cambridge, MA: Harvard University Press.

Huffman, M. A. (1984). Stone-play of *Macaca fuscata* in Arashiyama B troop: Transmission of a non-adaptive behavior. *Journal of Human Evolution, 13,* 725–735.

Joubert, E. (1972a). Activity patterns shown by Hartmann zebra *Equus zebra hartmannae* in South West Africa with reference to climatic factors. *Madoqua, Series, I*(5), 33–52.

Joubert, E. (1972b). The social organization and associated behaviour in the Hartmann zebra *Equus zebra hartmannae. Madoqua, Series I*(6), 17–56.

Klingel, H. (1968). Soziale Organisation und Verhaltensweisen von Hartmann- und Bergzebras (*Equus zebra hartmannae* und *E. z. zebra*). *Zeitschrift fur Tierpsychologie, 25,* 76–88.

Konner, M. J. (1975). Relations among infants and juveniles in comparative perspective. In M. Lewis & L. A. Rosenblum (Eds.), *Friendship and peer relations* (pp. 99–129). New York: Wiley.

Konner, M. J. (1982). *The tangled wing.* New York: Holt, Rinehart & Winston.

Kummer, H., & J. Goodall. (1985). Conditions of innovative behavior in primates. *Phil. Trans. R. Soc. Lond. B, 308,* 203–214.

Kurland, J. A. (1977). Kin selection in the Japanese monkey. *Contributions to Primatology, 12.* Basel: Karger.

Levy, J. (1979). *Play behavior and its decline during development in rhesus monkeys (Macaca mulatta).* Unpublished doctoral dissertation, University of Chicago.

Lewontin, R. C. (1979). Sociobiology as an adaptationist program. *Behavioral Science, 24,* 5–14.

Lumsden, C., & Wilson, E. O. (1983). *Promethean fire.* Cambridge, MA: Harvard University Press.

Martin, P. (1984). The (four) whys and wherefores of play in cats: A review of functional, evolutionary, developmental, and causal issues. In P. K. Smith (Ed.), *Play in animals and humans* (pp. 71–94). Oxford: Blackwell.

Mori, U. (1974). The inter-individual relationships involved in social play of the young Japanese monkeys of the natural troop in Koshima Islet. *J. Anthropol. Soc. Nippon, 82,* 303–318.

Maynard Smith, J. (1982). *Evolution and the theory of games.* Cambridge: Cambridge University Press.

Opie, I., & Opie, P. (1967). *The lore and language of schoolchildren.* Oxford: Oxford University Press.

Opie, I., & Opie, P. (1969). *Children's games in street and playground.* Oxford: Oxford University Press.

Partridge, L., & Nunney, L. (1977). Three-generation family conflict. *Animal Behaviour, 25,* 785–786.

Penzhorn, B. L. (1984). A long-term study of social organisation and behaviour of cape mountain zebras *Equus zebra zebra*. *Zeitschrift für Tierpsychologie, 64,* 97–146.

Pulliam, H. R., & Dunford, C. (1980). *Programmed to learn*. New York: Columbia University Press.

Rubenstein, D. I. (1980). On the evolution of alternative mating strategies. In J. E. R. Staddon (Ed.), *Limits to action* (pp. 65–100). Orlando, FL: Academic Press.

Sbrzesny, H. (1976). *Die Spiele der !Ko-Buschleute*. Munchen: Piper.

Smith, P. K. (Ed.). (1984). *Play in animals and humans*. Oxford: Blackwell.

Sutton-Smith, B. (Ed.). (1976). *Studies in play and games*. (21 vols.). Salem, NY: Ayer Co.

Sutton-Smith, B. (1980, October). *Children's folk games as customs*. Paper presented to the Conference on American Folk Custom, Library of Congress, Washington, D.C.

Sutton-Smith, B. (1981). *A history of children's play: The New Zealand playground, 1840–1950*. Philadelphia: University of Pennsylvania Press.

Symons, D. (1978). *Play and aggression: A study of rhesus monkeys*. New York: Columbia University Press.

Wilson, E. O. (1971). *The insect societies*. Cambridge, MA: Harvard University Press.

Wilson, E. O. (1975). *Sociobiology*. Cambridge, MA: Harvard University Press.

Wilson, E. O. (1977). Animal and human sociobiology: In C. E. Goulden (Ed.), *Changing scenes in natural sciences, 1776–1976* (pp. 273–281). Special Publication 12, Academy of Natural Sciences, Philadelphia.

11

Human Rape: The Strengths of the Evolutionary Perspective

Randy Thornhill
Nancy Wilmsen Thornhill
University of New Mexico, Albuquerque

There is considerable misunderstanding outside biology about the nature and validity of the evolutionary approach, especially as applied to human behavior. The value of the theory of evolution by selection in the study of all living things is beyond question. This theory has achieved eminence because of its logical structure, testability, and utility. The hypothetico-deductive model, the scientific method used productively by evolutionists, is the same model used by scientists in other fields.

Certain features of living things seem, on the surface, contrary to the theory of evolution by selection. Human rape is one such feature, but upon analysis the evolutionary approach promises more understanding of rape and related behavior than any other view. Human rape may be an evolved facultative behavior that is condition dependent in that it is employed by men who are relatively unsuccessful in competition for the resources and status necessary to attract and reproduce successfully with desirable mates (Thornhill & Thornhill, 1983; see also Shields & Shields, 1983). We discuss the derivation of this hypothesis in order to clarify its utility for future studies of human rape. The strengths of this hypothesis lie in the logic of evolutionary theory, the testability of evolutionary hypotheses, and in comparative biology. There is an alternative evolutionary hypothesis that may apply: Human rape may be a maladaptive effect of the general adaptive male mating strategy which includes persistence in copulation attempts (Thornhill & Thornhill, 1983). We feel it is unlikely that nonevolutionary perspectives on rape will provide significant understanding of the behavior.

THE GENERAL THEORY OF LIFE

It is important to keep the distinction between proximate and evolutionary causation in mind because not doing so can lead to futile arguments about causation, but it is critical to realize that the two perspectives are not alternatives.

Proximate explanations for the existence of biological traits deal with genetic, biochemical, physiological, developmental (including learning), social, and other immediate causes leading to the expression of the traits. Evolutionary explanations address causes that operated during evolutionary history to lead to present biological phenomena. The evolutionary approach focuses on the relationship between biological characteristics and the selective forces that produced them—that is, the contribution of traits to differential reproduction of individuals in the environments of evolutionary history. The evolutionary approach is called the ultimate approach because selection accounts for the existence of proximate mechanisms. Thus the two forms of causation are not alternatives in any sense. This means that there is really only one general approach in the study of life: the ultimate one. The theory of evolution by selection is not *a* theory of life, it is *the* unifying theory for studying living things.

We are not saying that the study of proximate causation is unimportant. A complete understanding of any feature of life includes elucidation of both proximate and ultimate causation. We are saying that the theory of evolution by selection provides the best direction for investigating proximate causation. This has been shown repeatedly in investigation of nonhuman organisms, and is being increasingly realized in human biology. A good example from human biology is in the use of evolutionary theory to predict and analyze mechanisms of learning associated with kin recognition (see Alexander, 1979; Dawkins, 1982).

The theory of evolution by selection is the theory of life because of its logical foundation, testability, and its power of explanation and prediction. Charles Darwin did not invent the idea of selection; he discovered the process of selection in nature, as did Alfred R. Wallace independently at about the same time. It seems inevitable that selection has acted continuously on all living things throughout the history of life and continues to do so today. This omnipotence of selection argues that the features of life are what they are because of selection in the past, and thus all features of all living things are expected to ultimately promote reproduction or genetic propagation of individuals in evolutionary relevant environments. This theoretical framework tells the investigator how to proceed in order to gain further understanding of life through experiment, observation, and comparative analysis. Because life is a product of selection, an understanding of this process and how it can be applied to elucidate life provides the life scientist with the best direction and insight, regardless of whether he is interested in molecules, behavior, physiology, morphology, proximate or evolutionary causation, or beetles or human beings.

Adaptations are features of living organisms that are the products of the direct action of selection. Such features may or may not be currently adaptive. Because of evolutionarily novel environments features evolved by selection may be rendered maladaptive at present. We do not discuss how adaptations are recognized. This has been fully treated by Williams (1966) and Curio (1973). But, in this regard, it is important to recognize that an incidental effect of an adaptation may be erroneously viewed as an adaptation. For example, human rape may not be an adaptation, but instead a maladaptive effect of an adaptation (Thornhill & Thornhill, 1983). We feel that this view of rape is probably incorrect (see the section on Evolutionary Analysis), but it should be examined empirically and if found to be correct the best understanding of rape will derive from an analysis of the nature of selection that has led to the adaptation that causes rape to occur as an incidental consequence.

It has been claimed by some that viewing traits in terms of evolutionary causation solely as the product of selection ignores the roles of agents other than selection in shaping them (e.g., Lewontin, 1978). For example, drift and mutation are evolutionary agents. That is, they cause changes in gene frequencies from generation to generation (evolution). But, relative to selection, mutation and drift are impotent evolutionary forces, because they act randomly with regard to fitness and thus cannot bring about directional change, i.e., significant cumulative change (see Alexander, 1979, for detailed discussion). Thus, the chances are small that random forces can yield complex traits. Furthermore, viewing features of life as shaped by selection provides the only feasible working theory. Views based on mutation or drift are completely impervious to test as critics of the selectionist approach admit (Lewontin, 1978).

Selection is best defined as nonrandom differential reproduction of individuals. Some investigators add to this definition: because of genetic differences among them. However, to define selection in terms of genetic variation is inappropriate because it confuses selection (a phenotypic event) with evolution (a genetic event) and leads to the erroneous view that in order to study effects (traits of organisms) or causes of selection one must show that there is genetic variation associated with the effects. Selection only causes evolution when there is relevant genetic variation, but an investigator can study causes and effects of selection without any knowledge of whether there is underlying genetic variation.

Commonly, evolutionists examine predictions from hypotheses about the nature of selection maintaining a trait or about the history of selection that has produced a trait. The validity of this procedure does not rest on demonstrating the presence of genetic variation underlying the trait of interest, or on demonstrating that an identified selection pressure causes changes in gene frequencies. These demonstrations are separate from the study of predictions stemming from selection hypotheses. Testing predictions from hypotheses about selective maintenance involves examining expected fitness differentials of individuals across phenotypic distributions within populations. Hypotheses about the selective history of a trait (e.g., human rape) simply assume relevant genetic variation in evolutionary history; in tests of such hypotheses predictions are examined in relation to patterns expected if selection and evolution have occurred in the manner hypothesized (also see Alexander, 1979; Dawkins, 1982).

In the final analysis, the utility of a scientific theory depends on its ability to yield understanding of the phenomena it purports to explain. Biologists study life, the most complex and diverse phenomenon in the universe. Yet, the success of selection theory in the explanation and prediction of life's vast complexity and diversity is demonstrated in every issue of modern journals in biological science.

Investigators studying life outside the framework provided by selection theory are working in a theoretical vacuum with no promise of general understanding. The futility of scientific investigation without a general theory is beyond question (e.g., Alexander, 1975; Daly & Wilson, 1983; Hempel, 1966; Kuhn, 1962; Popper, 1934; Medawar, 1967, 1969). Only recently have the social sciences begun to use modern evolutionary theory, and it promises to revolutionize the study of human behavior.

At present no limits to the theory of evolution by selection have been identified: The theory applies universally to living organisms. By rigorous application of selection theory (i.e., testing via the hypothetico-deductive model; see below) to anything and everything biological any limitations the theory may have are more likely to be identified. Thus there is value in identifying features of life that seem contrary to evolutionary theory. Apparent exceptions to theory seen in nonhuman organisms are abortion of fetuses in mammals and embryos and fruits in plants, sterility in certain social insects, infanticide of own offspring, highly female-biased sex ratios in certain insects which inbreed, and adoption of unrelated offspring in certain birds, mammals, and fish. These traits are too directly linked to reproduction to be merely incidental effects of adaptive characteristics, and thus are best viewed as adaptations in themselves. These apparent exceptions and others are being studied vigorously, and everything known about them at present indicates they are only apparent exceptions and not actual exceptions. A number of human behavioral traits which seem to be exceptions to biological theory are listed in Alexander (1979). Human rape could be added to this list because rape is apparently a behavior of high risk (injury, inprisonment, etc.), with little or no apparent return benefit. Additionally, reports in the popular media imply that rapists do not discriminate victims on the basis of age, that rapists derive equally from all walks of life, that rapists frequently kill victims, etc; these popular impressions are contrary to expectations from evolutionary theory regardless of whether rape is viewed as an adaptation or an incidental effect of adaptive male sexual behavior. Before discussion of the application of evolutionary theory to human rape we address the scientific method in general. The evolutionary biologist uses the same basic scientific model as any other scientists.

THE GENERAL METHOD OF SCIENCE

The scientific method, the hypothetico-deductive model, consists of the following interactive stages: observation, hypothesis formation, identification of predictions, and testing predictions. One can do science by generation and testing of hypotheses and/or by testing assumptions of hypotheses. These endeavors include locating errors in the observations, hypotheses, and tests of others, and for this reason science is often defined in terms of its repeatability and self-correcting nature (e.g., Simpson, 1964).

An observation in the right hands leads to scientific inquiry. Hypotheses begin with speculation, a hunch about the cause of some effect of interest. Scientists should speculate. Without imaginative speculation there would be no hypotheses and thus no direction for seeking understanding.

Certain critics have argued that evolutionary hypotheses are often ad hoc (only specific to the trait in question and without sufficient generality to allow testing) (Gould, 1978; Lewontin, 1978). If true, this is serious, because ad hoc arguments are not testable. Gould and Lewontin consider evolutionary hypothesizing the art of creating just-so stories just the way Rudyard Kipling did in explaining the leopard's spots, the camel's hump, etc. Ad hoc arguments do not represent valid speculation. The initial speculations of the evolutionist are post hoc not ad hoc, and there is nothing wrong with using post hoc leads for generating true hypotheses that are general enough for testing. Post hoc explanations represent an inevitable first step in any observational science.

For a hypothesis (or theory) to be scientific it must be testable. This means it must be *both* predictive and empirically falsifiable. The requirements for predictions are that they be logically derived from the hypothesis and be statements about the unknown. It has been argued that evolutionary theory is not truly predictive because it focuses on historical causes and not future events (Peters, 1976). But as numerous people have pointed out, prediction of future events is not a requirement of a scientific theory. Prediction of the unknown, whether past, present, or future, is the important issue. A hypothesis that predicts everything imaginable is not within the realm of science because it cannot be falsified. That is, a hypothesis that explains everything explains nothing. The theory of evolution by selection erroneously has been called a nonfalsifiable theory (Popper, 1934). It is puzzling how Popper and others could read Darwin's work and conclude that the theory of evolution is nonfalsifiable. Darwin's writing reveals his care in identifying observations that would falsify his theory (for discussion see Ghiselin, 1969; Alexander, 1977). Popper (1934) is usually credited for recognizing that in order for an idea to be considered scientific it must be falsifiable (the criterion of demarcation), but, as we have implied the use of this procedure is apparent throughout Darwin's work. It is also seen in the research of other early scientists using hypothetico-deductive analysis (e.g., Mendel, Newton, Pascal, Pasteur).

One view of the value of the criterion of demarcation is in terms of what logicians call the fallacy of affirming the consequent. Consider some hypothesis and its derived predictions. Assume that the predictions are found to be true. Now consider the following argument: If the hypothesis is true, then the predictions must also be true; the predictions are true. Therefore, the hypothesis is true. According to logicians the conclusion is not valid even if the hypothesis is correct. If the predictions of a hypothesis are confirmed, it is logically invalid to conclude that the hypothesis is correct, because some other hypothesis(es) might yield the same predictions. Thus, the logicians maintain that attempts to falsify hypotheses avoid this fallacy. It is logical to conclude that a hypothesis is false when its predictions are false.

But the major value of the criterion of demarcation is simply that it causes scientists to consider predictions that potentially can eliminate a given hypothesis rather than only evaluating predictions that, regardless of their veracity, will support the hypothesis or multiple hypotheses. The importance of falsification of hypotheses in the advance of science was eloquently stated by Darwin (1874): ". . . false views, if supported by some evidence do little harm, for every one takes a salutary pleasure in proving their falseness; and when this is done, one path towards error is closed and the road to truth is often at the same time opened" (p. 606). Envisioning empirical observations that could disprove hypotheses is vital for scientific advance.

Strict applications of Popperian philosophy and the fallacy of affirming the consequent in scientific endeavors are inappropriate because they deny the significance of positive results in the achievement of understanding and promote the erroneous view that knowledge is an illusion. The notion that knowledge is an illusion and nothing can be known with certainty stems from the Popperian philosophy of science (e.g., Harris, 1982). A strict Popperian accepts only negative results. With this view only falsified hypotheses are valuable; positive results do not count and certainly do not imply understanding, because to accept positive evidence commits the fallacy of affirming the consequent. This is where the actual practice of good scientists deviates from a Popperian perspective. Although one cannot actually prove a hypothesis to be true in the sense of *logical proof,* science can lead to proof of a hypothesis in the sense of meaningful understanding, even certainty, about natural phenomena. For example, we certainly know that insulin is produced in the isles of Langerhans, that bacteria and viruses can cause disease, that natural selection acts incessantly, and that chromosomes house genes. These facts were once hypotheses. The list of what we know assuredly is long and is growing.

The strongest test of a hypothesis involves identification of competing hypotheses that predict mutually exclusive empirically falsifiable outcomes. Such a test in its strongest form supports one hypothesis and falsifies the alternative hypotheses (for further discussion see Platt, 1964). Another aspect of strong scientific testing is that predictions be precise, which increases the likelihood of falsifying the hypothesis generating the predictions. A hypothesis that has passed many crucial tests involving precise mutually exclusive predictions from alternative hypotheses can be said to be corroborated. The number of tests is not the important factor for evaluating the reliability of a hypothesis. Instead, it is the number of severe or crucial tests that determines confidence in a hypothesis. Confirmed hypotheses vary in the degree to which they are corroborated, and, as mentioned earlier, science can achieve a degree of corroboration appropriately labeled certainty.

The use of alternative causal hypotheses also avoids the natural tendency of investigators to become attached to a pet hypothesis. Of course, one can favor a pet hypothesis by setting up weak alternatives that have no chance of matching observation. But this will fail ultimately given the self-correcting nature of science.

The hypothetico-deductive model may be applied in four ways: lab experiments, field experiments, observational analysis, and comparative analysis. In a separate paper the pros and cons of these four methods and the value of each in evolutionary analysis are discussed. The methods are very different in terms of their underlying assumptions, and the four methods are equally valid for examining cause and effect (Thornhill, 1984a).

We discuss the application of the scientific method to human rape after we explain the derivation and foundation of an evolutionary view of rape.

DERIVATION OF AN EVOLUTIONARY HYPOTHESIS FOR RAPE

We have argued that human rape is an evolved facultative behavior that is condition dependent in that it is employed by men who are unable to compete for resources and status necessary to attract and reproduce successfully with desirable mates (Thornhill & Thornhill, 1983; also see Shields & Shields, 1983). This hypothesis is based on the comparative biology of forced copulation, the evolution of intraspecific phenotypic variation, and the general sex difference across organisms in reproductive strategy.

Research on forced copulation in scorpionflies of the genus *Panorpa* has helped clarify the way in which selection has acted in the evolution of forced copulation (Thornhill, 1979, 1980, 1981, 1984b).

Male *Panorpa* exhibit three alternative forms of mating behavior which are present within the behavioral repertoire of each individual male. Two alternatives employed by males to obtain copulations involve nuptial feeding, i.e., the male presents a food item to the female during courtship and the female feeds on it throughout copulation. In one case a male feeds a female a salivary mass that he secretes. After saliva secretion, males stand near their salivary mass and disperse sex pheromone. A female attracted by the pheromone feeds on the saliva during copulation. Alternatively, a male may feed a female a dead arthropod during copulation. In this case a male locates a dead arthropod, feeds on it briefly, and then disperses sex attractant while standing adjacent to the dead arthropod. The third behavior employed by males is forced copulation. A forced copulation attempt involves a male without a nuptial offering (i.e., dead insect or salivary mass) rushing toward a passing female and lashing out his mobile abdomen at her. (Males engaging in forced copulation do not release pheromone.) If such a male successfully grasps a leg or wing of the female with his genital claspers, he then attempts to reposition her so as to secure the anterior edge of the female's right forewing in his dorsal clamp. When the female's wing is secured, the male attempts to grasp the genitalia of the female with his genital claspers. The male retains hold of the female's wing with the dorsal clamp throughout copulation. Forced copulation in *Panorpa* is in no way an abnormal or *aberrant* behavior. It is an aspect of the evolved behavioral repertoire of individual males that is widespread among species of the genus *Panorpa* (Thornhill, 1979, 1980, 1981, 1984b).

The behavior of females toward males with and without a nuptial offering is distinctly different. Females flee from males that approach them without a nuptial offering; however, females approach males with nuptial offerings and exhibit coy behavior toward them. Also, females struggle to escape from the grasp of forceful males, but females do not resist copulation with resource-providing males.

It has been shown in studies involving several species of *Panorpa* that the extent of use of each of the three behavioral alternatives by males is related to the availability of dead arthropods in the habitat, which is determined by absolute abundance of arthropods and by male-male competition for the arthropods. Individual males prefer to adopt the three alternatives in the following sequence: dead arthropod > salivary mass > forced copulation. That is, when males are excluded from dead arthropods via male-male competition, they secrete saliva if they can (a male's ability to secrete saliva is determined by his recent history of obtaining food), and males only adopt forced copulation when the other two alternatives cannot be adopted. A male's body size influences his ability in male-male competition and thus which alternatives are adopted most frequently. Large males tend to adopt the use of dead arthropods as nuptial gifts. Medium-sized males most frequently use saliva. Forced copulation is adopted most frequently by small males.

The behavioral alternatives contribute differently to male fitness. First, the preference of alternatives employed by males is consistent with female choice and thus male mating success. Females prefer males with arthropods over males with salivary secretions and actively attempt to avoid force copulating males. Second, the alternatives appear to be associated with different male mortality probabilities. Relative to large and medium-sized males, small males tend to lose in the competition for food, and thus are forced to feed on dead arthropods in the webs of web-building spiders, which results in high mortality. Third, force copulators have relatively low fitness compared to resource-providing males because females lay few eggs following forced copulation. Finally, whereas resource-providing males always transfer full ejaculates to females, force copulators only transfer sperm in 50% of forced matings (Thornhill, 1980, 1981, 1984b).

Forced copulation in *Panorpa* clearly circumvents female choice. In terms of the fitness interests of female *Panorpa,* it is disadvantageous for them to engage in forced copulation relative to unforced copulations. Females experiencing forced copulation lay few eggs and apparently experience higher mortality as a result of the need to feed on their own. As mentioned earlier, feeding is a risky endeavor in these insects because of exposure to web-building spiders. Selection has operated on female *Panorpa* to result in their ability to: (1) often escape forced copulation attempts (females successfully escape about 85% of the time), (2) avoid insemination in 50% of forced copulations, and (3) resume sexual receptivity quicker after forced compared to unforced copulation. Points 2 and 3 require brief explanation. The lower probability of insemination during forced copulation is apparently the result of the female's ability to prevent sperm transfer rather than some inadequacy on the part of males attempting forced insemination. After unforced copulation females become nonreceptive for a couple of days during which they lay eggs and do not feed. Oviposition and nonreceptivity is controlled proximately by a factor in the semen. During the period of nonreceptivity females will lay eggs fertilized by the male who fed them. A female who experiences forced copulation must find food on her own and feeding is risky. Selection has favored females that return to sexual receptivity soon after forced copulation and in so doing they may obtain food from males rather than from spider webs (Thornhill, 1980, 1981, 1984b).

Conflict between the sexes (in terms of each sex's evolved reproductive interests) in *Panorpa* is extreme in the context of forced copulation. Forced copulation is detrimental to the female because it circumvents female choice, a major route to fitness maximization for female organisms in general (see following). And when a male is dominated socially, forced copulation may represent his only route to successful reproduction despite the low fitness payoffs associated with forced compared to unforced copulation (Thornhill 1980, 1981, 1984b).

Based on understanding the selection that has operated on male *Panorpa* in the context of sexual competition for females, it can be hypothesized that forced copulation as an alternative male behavior frequently will have evolved in resource-based polygynous mating systems. When female mate choice is based importantly on resources and male striving for resources produces losers and winners, forced copulation may be a viable alternative for losers. There is increasing evidence outside humans that forced copulation often has evolved in resource-based polygynous systems (see references in Shields & Shields, 1983; Thornhill & Alcock, 1983; Thornhill & Thornhill, 1983).

Is it valid to apply this hypothesis to humans? Do humans exhibit the appropriate mating system? Below we discuss aspects of human biology which demonstrate the validity of applying this rape hypothesis to humans.

We emphasize that our work on human rape *is not an extrapolation* from nonhuman to human animals. Extrapolation means to infer (i.e., logically deduce and conclude) the unknown by extending or projecting known information. We are not saying that since males of certain nonhuman animals rape so must humans. Nor are we saying that since the selection has been identified that apparently led to forced copulation behavior in *Panorpa*, the same selection has acted in human evolutionary history. The study of *Panorpa* mating systems in itself says nothing definitive about humans. Any insight gained from the study of a particular biological system must be tested elsewhere in order to determine its value outside that system. Furthermore our approach does not involve an "animal model" as some social scientists have suggested to us. Instead, we use an evolutionary model based on an interpretation of how selection should act in the context of sexual competition among males in polygynous systems.

Polygyny is a breeding system in which fewer males than females contribute genetically to each generation. Said differently, polygyny is characterized by greater variance in the reproductive success of males than of females, which stems from greater competition among males than among females for resources and/or status attractive to the opposite sex. As the degree of polygyny increases it becomes increasingly more difficult for individual males to reproduce because fewer and fewer males obtain all the mating opportunities. (See Thornhill & Alcock, 1983, for detailed discussion of types of animal mating systems.)

Humans have morphological, developmental, sex ratio, mortality, senescence, parental, and general behavioral correlates of an evolutionary history of polygyny shown by other polygynous mammals (Alexander et al., 1979; also Daly & Wilson, 1983). Furthermore, most human societies show sanctioned or permitted harem polygyny (Alexander, 1979; Betzig, 1986; Borgia, 1980; Daly & Wilson, 1983; Murdock, 1967). In harem polygynous human societies some men have more than one mate, most men have one mate at a time and there is a pool of bachelors. Studies of harem polygynous preindustrial societies have demonstrated that variance in numbers of offspring attributable to men is much higher than variance in numbers born to women (Chagnon, 1979; Irons, 1979a). The same pattern is suggested by studies of preindustrial harem polygynous societies generally (see Alexander, 1979; Betzig, 1986; Chagnon & Irons, 1979; Daly & Wilson, 1983; Dickemann, 1979a, 1979b, 1981; Low, 1979; van den Berghe, 1979). As expected from mating systems theory (Borgia, 1979; Bradbury & Vehrencamp, 1977; Emlen & Oring, 1977; Trivers, 1972), the important factor explaining the degree of polygyny in preindustrial societies appears to be variation among men in resource holdings and status; there appears to be a positive relationship between the amount of a male's resource holdings and/or status and the number of wives and offspring he has (see especially Chagnon, 1979; Irons, 1979a; Betzig, 1986).

In the relatively few human societies in which polygynous marriages are not permitted, variances in male and female reproduction are more similar than under harem polygyny, but that of males is still greater (see Thornhill & Thornhill, 1983). Thus, all human societies exhibit some degree of polygyny, even those in which monogamous marriage is socially imposed. Human polygyny creates a situation of greater competition among men for women (or resources or status attractive to women) than vice versa. Thus, the evolutionary history of humans was apparently one of polygyny and modern humans exhibit polygynous mating systems. These considerations suggest that it is appropriate to apply our hypothesis for rape to humans.

Some social scientists might point out here that humans are "cultural animals" and this implies that we cannot examine human behavior in light of evolutionary theory. First, humans are not the only animal species that exhibits cultural behavior (for examples see Lumsden & Wilson, 1981). Second, cultural behavior occurs via learning processes, which are themselves products of selection. In order to connect evolutionary theory with cultural behavior we must first discuss the evolution of behavioral variation in general.

Biology has provided a foundation for understanding intrapopulation variation in behavior. Intrapopulational behavioral alternatives are of three general types (Cade, 1980; Dawkins, 1980; West-Eberhard, 1979). First, individuals may have different pure alternative strategies as a result of an evolutionary stable polymorphism in the population. The alternatives stem from genetic differences between individuals exhibiting them. Second, individuals may have a single mixed strategy with two or more alternatives and spend a fixed percentage of time in one alternative and then automatically adopt another. Here, all individuals carry the genes coding for all alternatives each of which is adopted for a fixed portion of time. Last, a single conditional strategy consisting of two or more alternatives may exist within an individual, but adoption of alternatives is condition-dependent and the alternatives are associated with different reproductive returns. All individuals in the population carry genes for all alternatives comprising a conditional strategy.

Conditional strategies are likely to represent the most common form of intrapopulation variation in social behavior of human and nonhuman animals. Selection should typically favor a condition-dependent switch from one alternative to another because a "big-winner" alternative will usually exist that will be more reproductively profitable than other alternatives (for detailed discussion see West-Eberhard, 1979).

The behavioral variants comprising a conditional strategy are best viewed as alternatives because reproductive effort (proportion of an organism's total resources devoted to reproduction) is finite. This is not to say that humans (or other organisms) cannot simultaneously employ multiple alternatives of a conditional strategy. But because reproductive effort is finite, any effort expended in pursuit of one alternative limits that which can be directed into other alternatives.

Conditions causing *Panorpa* males to shift from one alternative behavior to another are understood (see above). Conditions causing people to shift from one alternative behavioral pattern to another have been recognized and are under investigation. Socioeconomic status and correlated income appear to be important determinants of facultative shifts in aspects of sexual behavior (Weinrich, 1977). Patterns of wealth and other ecological factors influence the inheritance patterns adopted, the mating system, and the nature and extent of nepotism and reciprocity (Alexander, 1974, 1979; Burley & Symanski, 1981; Chagnon & Irons, 1979; Dickemann, 1979a, 1979b, 1981; Hartung, 1976; Silk, 1980). Social factors influencing male reliability of parentage (i.e., probability that a putative offspring is a genetic offspring) cause shifts in the nature of male reproductive effort expenditure (Alexander, 1974, 1979; Flinn, 1981; Hartung, 1976; Irons, 1979b; Kurland, 1979). We have argued that social circumstances are important conditions influencing the switch from other reproductive alternatives to forced copulation by men (Thornhill & Thornhill, 1983).

Thus, in all likelihood it seems that differences in behavior among human societies or among individuals within a society probably do not reflect underlying genetic differences, but instead reflect only a single general genetic program very indirectly related to behavioral differences via the influence of differences in the developmental or general social environment. This means there need not be a fixed genetic programming for a given behavior of humans (or scorpionflies) but only a general genetic program whose influence on the phenotype depends on conditions encountered.

During human evolutionary history selection has favored a flexible behavioral phenotype. Genes in interaction with environments produce a set of neural mechanisms associated with perception and decision making and these mechanisms cause social behavior. According to the theory of evolution by selection, perception of alternative behaviors includes unconscious evaluation of benefits and costs to reproduction, which affects decisions about use of alternatives (for detailed discussions of evolutionary perspectives on perception and decision making in humans see Alexander, 1979; Lumsden & Wilson, 1981; Symons, 1979).

Clearly, the cultural behavior of humans does not mean that evolutionary analysis is inappropriate or that we must reconsider the ideas of social science that restrict explanation to humans. Restrictive theories are suspect in themselves (e.g., Rosenberg, 1980). But beyond the logical problems associated with any restrictive theory, the ideas of social science have failed. The social sciences have been unable to provide anything that deserves the title theory, and the superficial levels of explanation and prediction achieved in the social sciences are not impressive to the biologist familiar with the success of the theory of evolution by selection.

Modern biology argues that the sexes differ in reproductive strategy because of anisogamy. This is not an incompletely thought out notion, but one that has proved valuable in its degree of explanation and prediction of sex differences in behavior and other phenotypic traits in humans, nonhuman animals, and plants (Symons, 1979; Thornhill & Alcock, 1983; Trivers, 1972; Wilson & Burley, 1983). A disparity in reproductive interests of the sexes stems from the evolution of the male and female phenomenon. This disparity leads to sexual conflict as was seen in the *Panorpa* scorpionflies discussed earlier. Conflict between the sexes may occur in many contexts (Hrdy, 1981; Parker, 1979; Symons, 1979; Trivers, 1972). Sexual conflict includes those circumstances in which males reduce female ability to choose mates freely or choose the most adaptive schedule of maternal care, which may be to the detriment of female fitness because it appears that control of reproduction, especially mate choice, is a major avenue for maximization of reproductive success by females (Alexander & Borgia, 1979; Thornhill, 1983). Certain males, by preventing or limiting female interaction with other males, may reduce maximum freedom of female mate choice. Also, males may circumvent female choice by forcefully inseminating an unwilling female—that is, rape.

Our definition of human rape incorporates components we feel to be important for an evolutionary view of rape. Rape is forced copulation of a female by a male. By forced copulation we mean copulation without the female's explicit or implicit consent; it need not involve physical force. Males will always strive to control female reproductive behavior and as already mentioned this may result in a conflict of male and female reproductive interests. Any male activity that prevents a female from exercising choice as to copulatory partner or in any other way reduces a female's ability to control her own reproduction may adversely influence female fitness. Rape is a form of behavior in the general behavioral category of sexual conflict involving males reducing female ability to choose mates or choose mates optimally. From an evolutionary perspective, rape occurs when a male circumvents female choice by forced copulation. Thus from the standpoint of the victim's evolutionary interests rape entails two related factors: (1) the ability of the female to choose her sexual partner is circumvented, and (2) the female's option of exchanging sexual favors for social position or material gain is denied. Although we emphasize the relationship between rape and circumvention of female mate choice, rape may sometime primarily circumvent a female's ability to time offspring production optimally.

By considering rape as a category of sexual conflict, we place the behavior squarely in comparative biology and evolutionary theory. All knowledge of sexual differences in reproductive strategy and associated conflict indicates that the above view of human rape is reasonable.

Present understanding of general sexual differences in reproductive strategy in organisms also allows us to place the striving of human males in biological perspective. Human males compete with each other for relative status, including wealth and prestige, which by its nature is always limited (Alexander, 1979; Betzig, 1986; Borgia, 1980). Relative advantage brings with it the resources necessary to successfully rear offspring and thereby brings access to desirable females. Emerging from this competition are males graded by success. At the top of this continuum are the big winners—those males who have achieved high rank (the wealthiest, most prestigious men). These males are represented by men with multiple wives in preindustrial human societies and by the highest executives in large corporations, powerful politicians, leading scholars, and outstanding athletes and entertainers in many industrial societies. Then there are those males who emerge from the competition with enough resources to enable them to rear offspring and gain access to a limited number of desirable females. These males are represented by most males on the face of the earth, i.e., most monogamous males in industrial and all monogamous males in preindustrial societies. Then there are the big losers: those men who are excluded from a share in the wealth, prestige, and resources, and thus access to desirable mates.

The hypothesis that human rape is an evolved mating tactic argues that it is those human males who have the greatest difficulty climbing the social ladder who are most likely to rape. Such males are expected to employ rape as the only behavioral alternative, or depending on their relative social status, they may incorporate rape into a repertoire of other behavioral patterns including low commital pairbonding with one or more females and/or investing any available resources toward sisters or offspring of sisters (the avunculate).

The avunculate seems to be associated with social circumstances causing low reliability of paternity: under the avunculate system, the dispenser of resources is related to beneficiaries by at least ⅛ (when half-sibs are involved) (Alexander, 1977, 1979; Flinn, 1981; Gaulin & Schlegel, 1980; Kurland, 1979; van den Berghe, 1979). If reliability of paternity is low in general, a man's brothers are also likely to have reduced paternity reliability and therefore represent less appropriate recipients of potentially reproductive benefits than a man's sisters.

In humans the benefits to reproduction associated with rape are small because of the small probability of conception following a single copulation or brief episode of copulation; this is the case even in societies without modern methods of birth control and it probably was the case in human evolutionary history. We feel that the important factor influencing costs and benefits associated with human rape, and thus the factor that allows an exploration of this behavior from an evolutionary perspective, is the likelihood of success via other alternatives (also see Shields & Shields, 1983). We have argued that when pairbonding is likely to be an unsuccessful male alternative because of paucity of resources needed to successfully acquire a fit mate and rear offspring and/or because of low reliability of male parentage, rape is more likely to be adopted by a man. Low parental resource levels and probably low reliability of paternity are associated closely with inability to climb the social ladder. Similarly when the avunculate is unlikely to be successful, because of family composition and especially low reproductive value of sister or sisters' offspring, rape is more likely to be used as an alternative (Thornhill & Thornhill, 1983).

Whether human rape currently represents a maladaptive expression of adaptation in the past—rape occurs under conditions similar to those that account for its evolution but it is not currently adaptive in that costs to reproduction exceed benefits when rape is employed—or is currently contextually adaptive is an important consideration but one beyond the scope of this work. In order to obtain insight into the present adaptive significance of rape, a detailed analysis of costs and benefits to reproduction of rape behavior is necessary. A complete analysis of costs and benefits of rape would be difficult in any human society, even in a preindustrial society with relatively simple social structure and uniform punishment for rape and without widespread use of modern conception prophylaxis. Instead, in our work on human rape we have focused on testing predictions pertaining to whether or not societal rules regarding rape and the behavior of rapists and rape victims reflect patterns indicative of an evolutionary history in which rape was contextually adaptive for men.

In considering this evolutionary view of rape, it is important to keep in mind that very small consistent differences in fitness among individuals may have large long-term effects. A small difference in fitness between men who raped when other avenues of reproduction were closed compared to men who did not rape in this context during human evolutionary history would be expected to lead to major evolutionary change.

HUMAN RAPE: SOCIAL SCIENCE HYPOTHESES

Although the social science literature dealing with human rape rarely identifies hypotheses and testable predictions, one can extract views from this literature in an attempt to scientifically test them. There are two general views of rape identifiable in the social science literature: (1) rape is a social pathology which stems from the complexity of modern industrial societies, and (2) rape is an act used by men to dominate women. The first hypothesis stems from sociology and areas of psychiatry (see Rada, 1978, for a review). The second derives from feminist ideology (e.g., Brownmiller, 1975). These hypotheses only address possible proximate causation and are not alternatives to an evolutionary approach. However, if they are correct an evolutionary approach to human rape would be questionable, because they are not derived from, or consistent with any biological view of behavior. Let's assume for the moment that there is some logic behind these hypotheses and it has escaped us. By so doing, we can derive consequences (predictions) that will be met if these hypotheses are applicable.

The social pathology hypothesis primarily restricts rape to industrial societies. This prediction is false. Rape is probably a cross-cultural universal. Its prevalence varies across societies, and the variation seems explicable only in terms of evolutionary theory (Thornhill & Thornhill, 1983). The feminist hypothesis seems to predict that men will rape powerful, older women (but see Ellis &

Beattie, 1983). This is false. Rape is directed primarily at young poor women (Thornhill & Thornhill, 1983). The feminist view would also predict that rapists will derive equally from all walks of life and adult age categories. This appears to be false in all human societies for which there are data. Rapists primarily are young, poor men (Thornhill & Thornhill, 1983).

We conclude that the social pathology and feminist hypotheses are probably wrong, and that investigators studying rape and related behavior would benefit by consideration of the evolutionary perspective.

EVOLUTIONARY ANALYSIS

From the hypothesis that human rape is an evolved facultative behavior we derived 18 predictions (Thornhill & Thornhill, 1983). The predictions that one derives from any hypothesis vary in strength in direct relation to their ability to address alternative hypotheses. This is the case with our 18 predictions. For example, one prediction states that fighting back will deter rape. This is consistent with the hypothesis as well as with any model of behavior in which the currency is reduction of cost or maximization of pleasure to the individual. On the other hand, some of our predictions arise *de novo* from an evolutionary perspective on rape. One prediction states that rapists will find potential victims of maximum fertility (high probability of successful present reproduction) most desirable, whereas other men *and rapists* will find young women at maximum reproductive value (high future reproductive potential) most desirable for long-term pairbonding purposes. A female of maximal reproductive value has her whole reproductive life ahead, which her mate will be able to capitalize on. However, for purposes of successful immediate reproduction (e.g., rape events, casual affairs) males are expected to find females of peak fertility most attractive.

This prediction is also very useful because it is quantitative rather than qualitative. That is, it does not only say that young women will be overrepresented in the rape victim population (a qualitative prediction), but instead it also says that rapists will primarily rape women of high fertility rather than high reproductive value (a quantitative prediction).

For clarity we discuss the derivation and analysis of this prediction (see Thornhill & Thornhill, 1983, for data and detailed discussion). According to evolutionary theory (Symons, 1979; Williams, 1975) human male standards of beauty are expected to reflect correlates of high reproductive value and high fertility. Men who concentrated their reproductive effort toward females outside the age categories of high reproductive capability in human evolutionary history are no one's ancestors. Rapists and nonrapists are expected to prefer nubile women. Rapists in particular are expected to unconsciously evaluate fertility of potential victims to a greater degree than reproductive value because fertility is most closely related to the probability that a copulation will lead to conception and successful gestation and live birth. Female reproductive value peaks at midteens and fertility in early 20s in U.S. women.

We compared the ages of rape victims with ages of females in the general population of the U.S. Statistically, young women are greatly overrepresented and older women are greatly underrepresented in the data on victims of rape. The peak in rape victims in relation to age corresponded with ages of high reproductive capacity. We also examined all major data sets on ages of rape victims in the U.S. The same pattern is revealed by all data sets: Young females of high reproductive capacity are raped most often.

A possible factor contributing to this pattern might be a recent cultural change in attitudes in the U.S. about rape reporting due to wide publicity regarding the more sensitive treatment of victims. Any such change could have conceivably had more of an influence on younger than older women, but if such a report bias exists, which may be the case (Hindelang, 1977), it is unlikely to account for the magnitude of the age effect in rape victimization in the U.S. Furthermore, some of the data we used were compiled in 1958 and 1960 prior to this possible shift in attitude (see Amir, 1971, and references therein). Finally, data from industrial societies other than the U.S. reveal the same pattern as U.S. data.

We examined the distribution of rape victims across age categories in relation to calculated values of reproductive value and fertility. These comparisons were made for each of the two largest sets of rape victim data from the U.S. It is interesting that ages of rape victims seem to follow fertility distributions to a greater extent than reproductive value distributions.

Clearly our prediction about female age in relation to rape victimization was supported, and there is suggestion that fertility of females is more important than reproductive value in rape victimization. As far as present data allow comparisons of ages of rape victims with ages of female victims of other crimes, it appears that only rape is primarily directed at young females of high reproductive capacity. But we emphasize that more testing is needed on the question of ages of rape victims, especially in relation to ages of female victims of other crimes and biases in age-related rape report data. Hindelang's (1977) work suggests a slightly greater tendency to report rape in young compared to older women. Our prediction is that when all biases are understood and eliminated, the age-dependent pattern we have discussed will remain significant in probability of rape victimization.

Another prediction from the hypothesis that human rape represents an evolved facultative behavior is that most of the unexplained variance in patterns predicted by the hypothesis (i.e., the exceptions to predictions) is the result of psychotic mentality (see Thornhill & Thornhill, 1983). The behavior of psychotics is not expected to fit an evolutionary model. For example, we expect that largely it is psychotic men who rape prereproductive and postreproductive females. Present data do not allow separation of the behavior of psychotic and nonpsychotic rapists.

A third prediction from the hypothesis is that rapists, compared to nonrapists, will tend to lack reproductive sisters to serve as recipients of collateral investment. The avunculate was explained in the previous section. The avunculate is less costly than rape and may represent a viable alternative to rape when men cannot compete successfully. (See Thornhill and Thornhill, 1983, for detailed discussion of this prediction and how it could be tested.) Our prediction about the relationship between the avunculate and rape, like the previous predictions, is difficult to derive from views of human behavior outside evolutionary theory and thus is of considerable value for examining the evolutionary perspective on human rape.

There is an evolutionary hypothesis for human rape that is an alternative to the evolutionary view of rape we have emphasized here. It is a possibility that human rape is an inevitable outcome of an evolutionary history in which males were selected to persist in their attempts to copulate and females were selected to discriminate among males and often refuse copulation. In this view, human rape is a maladaptive consequence of an adaptive general mating strategy of men (Thornhill & Thornhill, 1983). This hypothesis is as evolutionary as the notion that human rape represents an evolved facultative behavior. The maladaptive consequence hypothesis views rape as an incidental effect of an evolved adaptation whereas the other hypothesis views rape as molded directly by selection. If the incidental effect hypothesis is correct an understanding of the evolutionary history of the basic adaptive mating strategy of men should yield more understanding of rape and related topics than can be obtained in any other way.

We feel that the maladaptive consequence hypothesis is probably incorrect for two reasons. The first pertains to the costs that we envision to have historically been associated with human rape. At the point in human evolutionary history when retribution from society and/or the victim's kin or mate (see Thornhill & Thornhill, 1983; Shields & Shields, 1983) became a component of the cost/benefit in male decision making about rape as an alternative, those who persisted in copulation attempts to the point of rape when costs exceeded benefits would have been outreproduced by males who adopted rape adaptively. Thus we envision selection acting on human males in evolutionary history in the context of their persistence and forcefulness in copulation attempts. Second, the idea that rape is a maladaptive outcome of an adaptive male mating strategy lacks a foundation in comparative biology which we feel is a major strength of the view that rape is an evolved facultative mating tactic of males. Yet the maladaptive consequence hypothesis remains viable, because available data on human rape do not rigorously discriminate between the two hypotheses. The third prediction discussed immediately above appears to derive solely from the hypothesis that human rape is a facultative mating tactic, and thus if met may falsify the hypothesis that rape is an incidental consequence of adaptive male sexual behavior.

Thus more data are required to examine the two evolutionary rape hypotheses. Our guess is that the notion that rape is an incidental effect will fail and that the view of rape as an evolved facultative behavior will lead to significant under-standing of rape and related topics. We stress that it does not matter which hypothesis is most successful, or whether they are both wrong. What does matter is that investigators identify the best hypothesis, i.e., the one that achieves the most understanding of rape. We have emphasized the hypothesis that rape is an evolved facultative mating behavior in hopes of showing that it is a straight forward logical view from biology, and that it is worth further consideration and refinement.

We have outlined only three predictions in this section in an attempt to clarify our approach. Our other predictions deal with various aspects of the behavior of rape victims and offenders and with rape laws and tabus. All tests of our predic-tions to date support the evolutionary view of rape (Thornhill & Thornhill, 1983). This view of human rape renders intelligible a diversity of behavioral phenomena (rape laws and tabus, the behavior of offenders and victims, etc.) via successful prediction, explanation, and direction for future research. The general conclusion that emerges is that evolutionary theory is very relevant to any at-tempt to understand rape and any of its ramifications (also see Shields & Shields, 1983). In fact, it appears that significant understanding of rape will derive primarily from the evolutionary approach.

SUMMARY

Evolution by selection is the unifying theory of life. This theory has achieved eminence because of its logical foundation, testability, and power of explanation and predictability. But the nature and value of selection theory is poorly under-stood in the social sciences.

We outline the hypothetico-deductive model, the method used by evolu-tionists and other scientists. We then discuss how we used evolutionary theory to direct our investigation of human rape via the scientific method. Human rape has defied explanation by psychiatry and the social sciences. Human rape can be classed with certain other behaviors which seem to be contrary to evolutionary theory.

We have hypothesized that human rape is an evolved facultative behavior that is condition dependent in that it is employed by men who lack other viable reproductive alternatives. The foundation of this hypothesis lies in evolutionary theory and the comparative biology of forced copulation outside humans, sex differences in reproductive strategy, and alternative tactics within populations. The nature of selection responsible for the evolution of forced copulation as an alternative male tactic is best understood in *Panorpa* scorpionflies. The view that human rape is an alternative male mating tactic is not an extrapolation from insect behavior, but instead is a hypothesis about humans based on an interpreta-tion of the selection that apparently is responsible for the evolution of forced copulation across animal species. However, human rape may be a maladaptive consequence of an adaptive general sexual strategy of men. This is an alternative evolutionary hypothesis for human rape. The evolutionary view of rape promises significant understanding of rape and related topics by explanation and prediction of the behavior of rape offenders, victims, and laws and tabus. We discuss the derivation of certain predictions and identify one prediction that may be useful in discriminating between the two evolutionary hypotheses for human rape.

We examine the views of rape in the social science and feminist literature. We conclude that they are probably incorrect and that all future research on human rape should include an evolutionary perspective.

ACKNOWLEDGMENTS

The scorpionfly research discussed has been supported by grants to Randy Thornhill from the National Science Foundation (BNS-7912208, DEB-7910293, BSR-8219810).

REFERENCES

Alexander, R. D. (1974). The evolution of social behavior. *Annual Review of Ecology and Systematics, 5,* 325–383.

Alexander, R. D. (1975). The search for general theory of behavior. *Behavioral Science, 20,* 77–100.

Alexander, R. D. (1977). The changing scenes in the natural sciences, 1776–1976. *Academy of Natural Sciences* (Special Pub. 12), pp. 283–337.

Alexander, R. D. (1979). *Darwinism and human affairs.* Seattle: University of Washington Press.

Alexander, R. D., & Borgia, G. (1979). On the origin and basis of the male-female phenomenon. In M. S. Blum & N. Blum (Eds.), *Sexual selection and reproductive competition in insects* (pp. 417–440). Orlando, FL: Academic Press.

Alexander, R. D., Hoogland, J. L., Howard, R. D., Noonan, K. M., & Sherman, P. W. (1979). Sexual dimorphism and breeding systems in pinnipeds, ungulates, primates and humans. In N. A. Chagnon & W. G. Irons (Eds.), *Evolutionary biology and human social behaviour: An anthropological perspective* (pp. 402–425). North Scituate, MA: Duxbury Press.

Amir, M. (1971). *Patterns in forcible rape.* Chicago: University of Chicago Press.

Betzig, L. L. (1986). *Despotism and differential reproduction: a darwinian view of history.* New York: Aldine.

Borgia, G. (1979). Sexual selection and the evolution of mating systems. In M. S. Blum & N. A. Blum (Eds.), *Sexual selection and reproductive competition in insects* (pp. 19–80). Orlando, FL: Academic Press.

Borgia, G. (1980). Human aggression as a biological adaptation. In J. S. Lockard (Ed.), *The evolution of human social behavior* (pp. 150–185). New York: Elsevier.

Bradbury, J. W., & Vehrencamp, S. L. (1977). Social organization and foraging in emballonurid bats. II. Mating systems. *Behavioral Ecology and Sociobiology, 2,* 1–17.

Brownmiller, S. (1975). *Against our will: Men, women, and rape.* New York: Bantam Books.

Burley, N., & Symanski, R. (1981). Women without: An evolutionary and cross-cultural perspective on prostitution. In R. Symanski (Ed.), *The immoral landscape: Female prostitution in western societies* (pp. 250–271). Toronto: Butterworth.

Cade, W. (1980). Alternative male reproductive behaviors. *Florida Entomologist, 63,* 30–42.

Chagnon, N. A. (1979). Is reproductive success equal in egalitarian societies? In N. A. Chagnon & W. G. Irons (Eds.), *Evolutionary biology and human social behavior: An anthropological perspective* (pp. 374–401). North Scituate, MA: Duxbury Press.

Chagnon, N. A., & Irons, W. G. (Eds.). (1979). *Evolutionary biology and human social behavior: An anthropological perspective.* North Scituate, MA: Duxbury Press.

Curio, E. (1973). Towards a methodology of teleonomy. *Experientia, 29,* 1045–1058.

Darwin, C. (1874). *The descent of man and selection in relation to sex* (2nd ed.), New York: A. L. Burt Co.

Dawkins, R. (1980). Good strategy or evolutionarily stable strategy? In G. W. Barlow & J. Silverburg (Eds.), *Sociobiology: Beyond nature/nurture?* (pp. 331–370). Boulder, CO: Westview Press.

Dawkins, R. (1982). *The extended phenotype.* Oxford: Freeman.

Daly, M., & Wilson, M. (1983). *Sex, evolution and behavior* (2nd ed.). North Scituate, MA: Duxbury Press.

Dickemann, M. (1979a). Female infanticide, reproductive strategies, and social stratification: A preliminary model. In N. A. Chagnon & W. G. Irons (Eds.), *Evolutionary biology and human social behavior: An anthropological perspective* (pp. 321–368). North Scituate, MA: Duxbury Press.

Dickemann, M. (1979b). The ecology of mating systems in hypergynous dowry societies. *Biology and social life, 18,* 163–195.

Dickemann, M. (1981). Paternal confidence and dowry competition: A biocultural analysis of purdah. In R. Alexander & D. Tinkle (Eds.), (417–438). New York: Chiron Press.

Ellis, L., & Beattie, C. (1983). The feminist explanation for rape: An empirical test. *The Journal of Sex Research, 19,* 74–93.

Emlen, S. T., & Oring, L. W. (1977). Ecology, sexual selection, and the evolution of mating systems. *Science, 197,* 215–223.

Flinn, M. A. (1981). Uterine vs. agnatic kinship variability and associated cousin marriage preferences: An evolutionary biological analysis. In R. Alexander and D. Tinkle (Eds.). *Natural selection and social behavior.* New York: Chiron Press.

Gaulin, S. J. C., & Schlegel, A. (1980). Paternal confidence and paternal investment: A cross cultural test of a sociobiological hypothesis. *Ethology and Sociobiology, 1,* 301–309.

Ghiselin, M. T. (1969). *The triumph of the Darwinism method.* Berkeley: University of California Press.

Gould, S. J. (1978). Sociobiology: The art of story telling. *New Scientist, 80,* 530–533.

Harris, C. L. (1982). *Evolution: Genesis and revelations.* Albany: State University of New York Press.

Hartung, J. (1976). On natural selection and the inheritance of wealth. *Current Anthropology, 17,* 607–622.

Hempel, C. G. (1966). *Philosophy of natural science.* Englewood Cliffs, NJ: Prentice-Hall.

Hindelang, M. J. (1977). *Criminal victimization in eight American cities: A descriptive analysis of common theft and assault.* Cambridge, MA: Ballinger.

Hrdy, S. B. (1981). *The woman that never evolved.* Cambridge, MA: Harvard University Press.

Irons, W. (1979a). Cultural and biological success. In N. A. Chagnon & W. G. Irons (Eds.), *Evolutionary biology and human social behavior: An anthropological perspective* (pp. 257–272). North Scituate, MA: Duxbury Press.

Irons, W. (1979b). Investment and primary social dyads. In N. A. Chagnon & W. G. Irons (Eds.), *Evolutionary biology and human social behavior: An anthropological perspective* (pp. 181–212). North Scituate, MA: Duxbury Press.

Kurland, J. A. (1979). Paternity, mother's brother and human sociality. In *Evolutionary biology and human social behavior: An anthropological perspective* (pp. 145–180). North Scituate, MA: Duxbury Press.

Kuhn, T. S. (1962). *The structure of scientific revolutions.* Chicago: The University of Chicago Press.

Lewontin, R. C. (1978). Adaptation. *Scientific American, 239*(3), 156–169.

Low, B. S. (1979). Sexual selection and human ornamentation. In N. A. Chagnon & W. G. Irons (Eds.), *Evolutionary biology and human social behavior: An anthropological perspective* (pp. 462–487). North Scituate, MA: Duxbury Press.

Lumsden, C. J., & Wilson, E. O. (1981). *Genes, mind and culture: The coevolutionary process.* Cambridge, MA: Harvard University Press.

Medawar, P. B. (1967). *The art of the soluble.* Methuen, London.

Medawar, P. B. (1969). *Induction and intuition in scientific thought.* American Philosophical Society, Philadelphia.

Murdock, G. P. (1967). *Ethnographic atlas.* Pittsburgh: University of Pittsburgh Press.

Parker, G. A. (1979). Sexual selection and sexual conflict. In M. S. Blum and N. A. Blum (Eds.), *Sexual selection and reproductive competition in insects* (pp. 123–166). New York: Academic Press.

Peters, R. H. (1976). Tautology in evolution and ecology. *American Naturalist, 110,* 1–12.

Platt, J. R. (1964). Strong inference. *Science, 146,* 347–353.

Popper, K. R. (1934). The logic of scientific discovery (English edition). (1959). Hutchinson: London.

Rada, R. T. (Ed.). (1978). *Clinical aspects of the rapist.* New York: Grune and Stratton.

Rosenberg, R. (1980). *Sociobiology and the preemption of social sciences.* Baltimore: Johns Hopkins University Press.

Shields, W. M., & Shields, L. M. (1983). Forcible rape: An evolutionary perspective. *Ethology and Sociobiology, 4,* 115–136.

Silk, J. B. (1980). Adoption and kinship in Oceania. *American Anthropologist, 82,* 799–820.

Simpson, G. G. (1964). *This view of life.* New York: Harcourt, Brace, and World.

Symons, D. (1979). *The evolution of human sexuality.* Oxford: Oxford University Press.

Thornhill, R. (1979). Male and female sexual selection and the evolution of mating strategies in insects. In M. S. Blum and N. A. Blum (Eds.), *Sexual selection and reproductive competition in insects* (pp. 81–121). Orlando, FL: Academic Press.

Thornhill, R. (1980). Rape in *Panorpa* scorpionflies and a general rape hypothesis. *Animal Behavior, 28,* 52–59.

Thornhill, R. (1981). *Panorpa* (Mecoptera: Panorpidae) scorpionflies: Systems for understanding resource defense polygyny and alternative male reproductive efforts. *Annual Review of Ecology and Systematics, 12,* 355–386.

Thornhill, R. (1983). Cryptic female choice in the scorpionfly *Harpobittacus nigriceps* and its implications. *American Naturalist, 122,* 765–788.

Thornhill, R. (1984a). Scientific methodology in entomology. *Florida Entomologist, 67,* 74–96.

Thornhill, R. (1984b). Alternative hypotheses for traits presumed to have evolved by sperm competition. In R. L. Smith (Ed.), *Sperm competition and the evolution of animal mating systems* (pp. 151–178). Orlando, FL: Academic Press.

Thornhill, R., & Alcock, J. (1983). *The evolution of insect mating systems.* Cambridge, MA: Harvard University Press.

Thornhill, R., & Thornhill, N. W. (1983). Human rape: An evolutionary analysis. *Ethology and Sociobiology, 4,* 137–173.

Trivers, R. L. (1972). Parental investment and sexual selection. In B. Campbell (Ed.), *Sexual selection and the descent of man* (pp. 136–179). Chicago: Aldine.

van den Berghe, P. L. (1979). *Human family systems.* New York: Elsevier.

West-Eberhard, M. J. (1979). Sexual selection, social competition and evolution. *Proceedings of the Philosophical Society of America, 123,* 222–234.

Weinrich, J. D. (1977). Human sociobiology: Pairbonding and resource predictability (effects of social class and race). *Behavioral Ecology and Sociobiology, 2,* 91–118.

Williams, G. C. (1966). *Adaptation and natural selection.* New Jersey: Princeton University Press.

Williams, G. C. (1975). *Sex and evolution.* New Jersey: Princeton University Press.

Willson, M., & Burley, N. A. (1983). *Female choice in plants.* Princeton University Press Monograph in Population Biology, Princeton, NJ.

12 Evolutionary Psychology and Family Violence

Martin Daly
Margo Wilson
McMaster University

According to modern Darwinian theory, organisms have evolved to be effective nepotists. Attacks upon relatives are therefore surprising. Can the concept of evolutionary adaptation shed any light upon family violence? In this chapter, we intend to show that it can.

The evident adaptive design of organisms once constituted the most powerful argument for the intervention of deity in the natural world. Darwin (1859) destroyed that argument by identifying a natural source of adaptation: the historical process of differential survival and reproduction that he called "natural selection." In so doing, Darwin also showed that all evolved traits, whatever their immediate adaptive functions (food detection, mate attraction, predator evasion, and so forth) must contribute to the single ultimate function of reproductive fitness if they are to be naturally selected. The evolved traits of an organism can thus be considered the "tactics" of its reproductive "strategy."

We seek to understand evolved traits by understanding how they contribute to fitness. This is the "adaptationist program" that has guided most progress in the biological sciences (Mayr, 1983). Adaptationist approaches are relatively straightforward when the attributes under study are morphological structures: A first question about a newly discovered organ or skeletal structure is "What is it *for?*" But an adaptationist approach to behavioral control mechanisms ("psyche") engenders controversy, partly for the good reason that there is no consensual structural description of the mechanisms to be explained, but also partly because behavioral scientists have misunderstood adaptationism. An adaptationist "explanation" of a behavioral trait is not an hypothesis about gene action (nor indeed about any developmental process). Neither is it a motivational theory.

It complements rather than competes with the ontogenetic and motivational explanations favored by psychologists. If we analogize the behaving organism to a machine, then psychologists are typically concerned with structural descriptions of how the machine works (perhaps a reductionist neuroanatomical account, for example, or perhaps one employing more abstract intervening variables). They are also concerned with accounts of dynamic changes in that structure. In other words, psychologists study motivation and development. The evolutionary biologist subsumes the psychologist's concerns (as well as those of geneticists, developmental biologists and physiologists) under the rubric of "proximate causation" and poses the additional question of "ultimate causation": *Why* is the machine designed like this? What is the adaptive value of this design that has selectively favored its constituents over their alternatives?

Though ultimate and proximate causal analyses are distinct, the former are not without implications for the latter. Consideration of the fitness-promoting functions of normal motives, for example, might help the motivational theorist avoid implausible constructs such as death instincts. Similarly, an understanding of natural selection should arouse skepticism about any theory that treats society as an agent with interests of its own: The fundamentally competitive nature of the natural selective process suggests that the individual is a more basic node of unitary self-interest than is the larger society, and hence that appeals to society's interests may often be self-serving smokescreens. We might expect, incidentally, that psychologists, more than most social scientists, will find the individualistic focus of modern evolutionary theory congenial.

Evolutionary theory does not imply, however, that social behavior should be a free-for-all without alliances. Evolutionary biologists were long content to conceptualize fitness, the currency of natural selection, as equivalent to personal reproductive success. Hamilton (1964) upset that particular applecart by emphasizing that offspring are not the sole vehicles of fitness. Selection favors those traits that contribute to their bearers' "inclusive fitness," that is to the proliferation of the bearer's particular complement of alleles. Inclusive fitness may be advanced not only by personal reproduction, but also by contributions to the reproductive success of nondescendant carriers of the same genotypes, that is to say contributions to collateral kin. Hamilton thus broadened our conception of the organism from a reproductive strategist to a nepotistic strategist.

Kinship creates common cause: The more closely related are two individuals, the more coincident their interests. From a Darwinian perspective, an organism's "interests" reduce to inclusive fitness: You and I have a commonality of interest insofar as that which enhances my inclusive fitness also enhances yours, a conflict of interest insofar as that which enhances mine damages yours. Genetically identical individuals have identical fitness interests, and in general, the degree of relatedness is an index of common cause. How then to explain violence within the family?

FAILURES OF PARENTAL SOLICITUDE AND INFANTICIDE

Parental solicitude toward own offspring might seem a foregone conclusion. However, every offspring raised in an intensively parental species such as our own demands a huge investment of time and energy that might have earned the parents higher fitness returns elsewhere. The evolved mechanisms of parental motivation are therefore unlikely to be indiscriminate: Natural selection will have favored the allocation of parental effort where it contributes most to the actors' fitness. We might then predict that parental inclination to care for a particular child will vary as a function of the child's own "reproductive value," that is its own expected fitness.

A young organism's reproductive value increases as it approaches maturity, simply by virtue of having survived longer: The expected fitness of a pubertal individual exceeds that of an infant because the infant is likelier to die before reproducing. We thus predict that *parental motivation will have evolved so that parents will appear to value offspring increasingly with offspring age.* (In an expanding population, older offspring are more valuable than younger for a second reason too: They contribute more to parental fitness not only because they are likelier to reproduce but also because they do so earlier.) Test of this prediction is complicated by the fact that the offspring's needs also change with age. If parents feed older offspring more, for example, that is hardly evidence that they value them more. Conversely, if a mother preferentially assists her *younger* offspring, that may be because the older is better able to fend for itself.

Despite these complications, the prediction of greater parental valuation of older offspring has been tested and widely confirmed (Andersson, Wiklund, & Rundgren, 1980; Barash, 1975: Greig-Smith, 1980; Pressley, 1981). The basic test situation is one in which parents with nest-bound offspring of different ages are compared with respect to the degree of risk to self that the parents will accept in order to defend the young against a potential predator. In a typical result, Pressley (1981) found that male sticklebacks (small, freshwater fish) guarding nests full of eggs became increasingly likely to attack, rather than to flee from, a model predator that was dangerous to both the eggs and themselves as the eggs aged and approached hatching.

People, like other creatures, behave as if they value older dependent children more highly than younger ones. This claim may appear controversial: We all know parents who support their younger children in sibling disputes, and we're all familiar with spoiled last-borns. But these are not really counterexamples. It is an expected consequence of familial patterns of relatedness that one will often observe siblings competing for familial resources while the parents strive to even out the results of that competition (Trivers, 1974). Typically, parental imposition of equity will involve supporting the weaker, younger competitor. The situation in which differential parental valuation of offspring comes clearest is the classic conundrum, "Which do you save when one must be sacrificed?"

Daly & Wilson (1984) reviewed anthropologists' characterizations of circumstances in which infanticide is reported to occur, examining a sample of 60 human societies. (The Human Relations Area Files "Probability Sample," an allegedly representative sample of the world's cultures: see Lagacé, 1974.) In 11 of these societies, it was reported that a newborn might be killed at birth if it arrived too soon after the last child or if the mother had too many children already. Not surprisingly, there were no societies in which the normative response to maternal overburdening was reported to be the sacrifice of an older child. (Indeed, such a report would be hardly credible and it is enlightening to contemplate why: Dramatic cultural variability notwithstanding, the most fundamental motives of people in exotic societies are not alien to us. The extreme cultural relativist claim that one man's good is another man's evil is exaggerated. If one says "of course" when told that the mother sacrifices the infant to save the toddler, this reaction merely illustrates that one takes for granted a human tendency to value offspring increasingly with time. That the tendency seems intuitively obvious does not detract from its importance as evidence for the model of people as evolved reproductive strategists.)

Maternal Bonding

This adaptationist view of parental valuation of offspring has implications for the controversial topic of mother-infant bonding. Beginning with the pioneering work of Klaus et al. (1972), a series of studies in a number of different countries have indicated consequences of the amount of immediate postnatal mother-infant contact upon subsequent maternal behavior and child development (e.g., Ali & Lowry 1981; Carlsson et al., 1978; de Chateau & Wiberg, 1977a, 1977b; Hales, Lozoff, Soza, & Kennell, 1977; Kennell et al., 1974; Klaus et al., 1972; O'Connor et al., 1979; Sosa, Kennell, Klaus, & Urrutia, 1976). The basic design of these studies is that new mothers in hospital are randomly assigned to either a "hospital-routine" group in which the baby is removed from the mother at birth and returned periodically for brief feedings or an "extra-contact" group with a few hours of additional mother-infant contact before hospital discharge. Measures which have been considered to reflect maternal bonding to the child in question and which have differed between groups in such studies include duration of breastfeeding, maternal gazing at the child, complexity and frequency of maternal speech to the child during subsequent home visits, and even physical abuse of the children.

The bonding studies have provided much ammunition for the proponents of more natural birth practices. But they have recently provoked considerable criticism as well (e.g., Herbert, Sluckin, & Sluckin, 1982; Lamb & Hwang, 1982; Svejda, Campos, & Emde, 1980). Several much-cited studies have suffered from methodological flaws such as confounded variables and a lack of appropriate blind procedures. Many measures have sometimes been scanned to produce a few significant effects. There have been some failures to replicate, and even the positive results are not always consistent. Enthusiasts have sometimes wildly exaggerated the prognostic implications.

There is indeed much to criticize, then, but the critics threaten to throw out the baby with the bathwater. Attributing sporadic effects to chance cannot explain their directional consistency. Nor can appeals to inferential caution and methodological rigor justify asserting the null hypothesis, as several critics have done. Lamb & Hwang (1982), for example, shrug off a methodologically sound study in which ten hospital-routine infants suffered abuse or nonorganic failure to thrive in comparison to two extra-contact infants (O'Connor et al. 1979; Vietze, O'Connor, Falsey, & Altemeier, 1978) as a "modest effect"; cite Siegal et al. (1980) as a "failure to replicate" (without mentioning that these authors obtained a nonsignificant difference in the same direction); then conclude "we feel comfortable asserting that extended contact appears to have no demonstrable effect on maternal behavior" (Lamb & Hwang, 1982, p. 27)!

The bonding literature is increasingly polemical. Critics of the concept cite evidence that factors such as involvement of the father, economic circumstance, or whether the pregnancy was planned influence the quality of maternal care, and imply that these complications constitute a disconfirmation of "the bonding hypothesis." The hypothesis that is under attack is apparently that the recently parturient female is a hormonally primed automaton in a unique state of readiness to "attach" maternally to the first appropriate stimulus encountered and is oblivious to situational variables: If neonatal contact, then bond, if not, then disaster.

The version of the "bonding hypothesis" that critics have chosen to attack is largely, though not entirely, a straw man. Nobody has maintained that bonding is an invariant reflex. One point raised by several critics (e.g., Herbert et al. 1982) with some justice, however, is that bonding theorists such as Klaus & Kennell go beyond the evidence in asserting the unique quality of *early* postnatal contact, borrowing the dubious ethological concept of "critical periods" during which an experience must occur if normal development is not to be permanently derailed. The hospital studies certainly provide no grounds for the conclusion that early mother-infant separation produces some sort of irreversible deficit.

An adaptationist perspective suggests a compromise viewpoint that is entirely consistent with present evidence: Maternal bonding is likely to entail at least three distinct processes proceeding over different time-courses and is likely to be influenced both by mother-infant interaction and by situational factors. The first process is an assessment of the quality of the child and of the reproductive episode: Mothers are unlikely to be so insensitive to offspring defects or to bad situations as to jeopardize their own fitness in a hopeless cause. The second process is a discriminative attachment to *own* child, as special and unique, established soon after birth. The third expected process of maternal bonding is a gradual deepening of love and commitment to the child, perhaps proceeding over several years. This latter process is to be expected from considerations of the increasing reproductive value of maturing young, as discussed above. The earlier discriminative bonding process has a distinct adaptive function: the channelling of parental investment toward own as opposed to alien young.

Consider the situation of a new mother confronting the mixed blessing of a child-rearing episode of several years' duration. When the offspring's fitness prospects are poor, then we might expect that the establishment of maternal commitment will fail: A parental psychology that abandons lost causes would be selected over one that damages the parent's future reproductive prospects by squandering resources on children of low fitness potential. Such low potential may be an intrinsic matter of poor offspring quality or an extrinsic matter of inauspicious circumstances for a successful rearing. These two categories encompass virtually all the rationales for parentally instigated infanticide encountered in Daly & Wilson's (1984) ethnographic review. Deformed babies were reported to be abandoned or killed at birth in 21 of 36 societies in which infanticidal circumstances were described. Rationales in terms of circumstantial incapacity to rear the child included unwed status of the mother (14 societies) or lack of paternal acknowledgement and acceptance of obligation (6), overburdening due to twins (14), short birth intervals or too many children (11), poverty (3) and death of the mother in childbirth (6), among others.

Reviewing ethnographies, Daly & Wilson (1984) found these and other typological descriptions of the circumstances in which infanticide is allegedly normal practice in the societies in question, but there was little information on either its prevalence or specific cases. In the modern west, by contrast, infanticide is societally condemned in all circumstances, but it occurs nonetheless, and public bodies collect case information. Daly & Wilson (1984) analyzed recent Canadian data on infanticide events, and found several parallels with the ethnographic accounts. Infanticidal Canadian mothers, for example, were mostly unwed: 88.3% of women giving birth in Canada between 1977 and 1979 were legally married, compared to just 39.5% of new mothers committing infanticide during that period.

We suggested earlier that the child's fitness prospects should be a powerful determinant of initial maternal inclination to embark on a childrearing episode, and the data on maternally instigated infanticide are supportive. But what of the second aspect of maternal bonding, namely the *individualized* attachment. In this regard, it is unfortunate that comparative psychologists seized upon the convenient domestic rat as the organism in which to study mechanisms of maternal motivation. Rat studies have given rise to a concept of a generalized maternal *state* in which the newly parturient female is responsive to stimuli characteristic of conspecific infants (e.g., Peters & Kristal, 1983). But rats cannot be taken as prototypical mammals in these matters. Rats will readily care for fostered pups, and experimenters have exploited this willingness in order to standardize stimuli, to measure maternalness as a function of hormonal state, to separate effects of pup age from those of postpartum duration, and so forth. All of this research depends on the rat's insensitivity to the distinction between own and alien offspring. Yet most animals that exhibit parental care are highly sensitive to this distinction. A goat or seal nursing her own infant will attack a like-aged strange youngster who attempts to suckle. A crow or a gull will cannibalize an absent neighbor's chicks while caring for its own. Had these been the animals of study, the concept of a generalized maternal state might never have arisen. The rat is a burrow-dwelling, altricial species in which there is apparently no risk of a mother giving suck to unrelated young in nature. Loss of milk to unrelated intruders is a genuine risk however, for a gregarious, precocious animal like a goat. In general, discriminative solicitude toward own but not alien offspring develops in different species at different postnatal ages, usually at about that stage of development at which mixups and misdirected parental care become an imminent risk (reviewed by Daly & Wilson, 1980: Holmes & Sherman, 1983).

What then of people? We are not goats. Babies are not so precocious as to make sneak raids on lactating women (though older toddlers may be!). But we aren't rats either. Hominids have presumably long lived in social groups containing more than one potentially reproductive woman, a situation where the nursing effort of an indiscriminate mother might be exploited by others. (That wet-nursing has been a paid service testifies to human recognition that a woman's lactational capacity is a resource of value.) And indeed the human maternal bond appears to have a strongly individualistic component from a very early stage. Many new mothers report an initial feeling of "indifference" to their babies (perhaps reflecting the initial "assessment" stage as well as the lack of individuation), but very few feel the same way by one week postpartum (Robson & Kumar, 1980). After having had close contact with their infants over the first few days, mothers commonly report developing a feeling that their baby is uniquely wonderful (Kennell, Trause, & Klaus, 1975; Klaus & Kennell, 1976). Human mothers are highly sensitive to the distinctive features of their babies, recognizing them by voice (Morsbach, 1980; Rothgänger, 1981) and by smell (Porter et al., 1983) within a day or two of birth. Some mothers find their own babies' feces tolerable yet are nauseated by those of other babies. These phenomena suggest that there is indeed a relatively rapid individualization of maternal response preceding the much more gradual deepening of parental love.

If the parental psyche has evolved to value own offspring increasingly with age, then the drastic failure of parental solicitude that is represented by maternal infanticide may be expected to occur primarily very soon after birth. Maternal homicide of own offspring is indeed concentrated upon infants: In Canada between 1974 and 1983, for example, 87 infants were killed by their mothers compared to just 26 1-year-olds, and the numbers continued to decline with the child's age (Fig. 12.1). The pattern of victimization by nonrelatives, whose "valuation" of children is not expected to follow parental patterns, was very

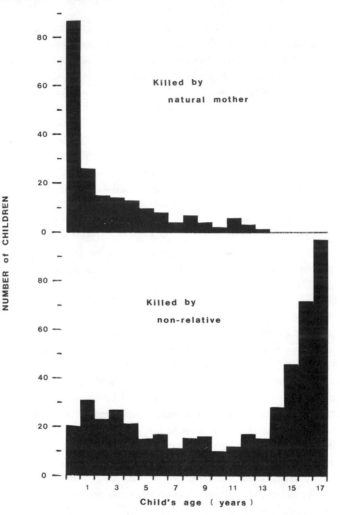

FIGURE 12.1.   Children as victims of homicide in Canada, 1974–1983; age distributions for victims of natural mother (N = 200) versus victims of nonrelatives (N = 493). Mothers, unlike nonrelatives, are decreasingly likely to kill older children.

different, showing no such initial decline and increasing rapidly in adolescence, when parental homicides have virtually disappeared. In part, of course, this difference must be attributable to increasing access of nonrelatives to older children, and by adolescence, adult-like conflicts with nonrelatives are common. But the two histograms in Fig. 12.1 differ dramatically even if one attends only to infant and 1-year-old victims, mothers being far likelier to kill the infant than the older baby, while nonrelatives actually killed more 1-year-olds.

Included among the maternal homicides in Fig. 12.1 are 11 cases in which the mother also committed suicide. Murder/suicides are apparently a rather different matter from nonsuicidal cases. Such mothers often leave notes indicating that they perceive the homicide as compassionate and part of the suicide: Having decided that life is unbearable, they have resolved to save their loved ones by killing them. Thirty-three percent of 15 mothers who killed 2 or more children also committed suicide, compared to 4.1% of 146 who killed a single child. (Interestingly, no woman killed husband and child, though many men killed wife and child; see Daly & Wilson, 1984.) Whatever one makes of these cases, they are clearly different from those in which a woman who intends to go on living disposes of an unwanted child. Suicides constituted an increasing proportion of maternal homicides with increasing child age: 2% of infanticides, 8% of maternal homicides of toddlers aged 1–4, 28% of maternal homicides of school-age children. (The same was not true of nonrelative homicides.) So with the exception of murder/suicides, which are evidently an altogether different phenomenon from the disposal of an unwanted child, it was extremely rare for a Canadian mother to kill her child beyond its infancy. Our reading of the homicide literature suggests that this is true the world 'round.

Child Abuse

Nonfatal abuse of children can also be analyzed from an adaptationist perspective (Daly & Wilson, 1981a, 1981b: Lenington, 1981). If physical abuse of children by parents or parent substitutes is in part the result of lapses of parental solicitude and resentment of parental obligation, then child abuse, like infanticide, should prove especially frequent when parents are confronted with predictors of low offspring contribution to parental fitness. Thus, for example, deformed children, who are likely candidates for infanticide in many societies, incur high risks of abandonment and physical abuse in the modern west.

Lenington (1981), while finding support for this and other adaptationist predictions about child abuse, advocates caution:

> . . . although it is possible to present very plausible arguments for the adaptive significance of child abuse, it has not been possible, and would be extraordinarily difficult, to show that individuals who abuse their children are, in fact, increasing their reproductive success. The entire sociobiological argument, in this case, rests on plausibility. (p. 26)

This is a straw man. An adaptationist analysis does not require that every class of behavior defined by researchers (e.g., child abuse) must enhance the fitness of the actors or else be abandoned to "alternative" explanatory models. Rather, we postulate that *on average,* the consequences of evolved behavioral control mechanisms ("psyche"), operating in environments that do not differ in any critical way from those in which the mechanisms evolved, will be fitness-promoting. It is not in behavioral categories such as *abuse,* but at the more abstract psychological level of parental motivation that adaptation is to be discerned.

Child abuse certainly does not present the aspect of "an adaptation" (ignoring, for the moment, the dubious reification of this phrase): Abusive parents, rather than discretely terminating investment in a poor fitness prospect, vacillate between inflicting damage upon their children and investing their resources in them. It is therefore most *un*likely that "individuals who abuse their children are, in fact, increasing their reproductive success." Contra Lenington, child abuse *per se* may be maladaptive (damaging to the actor's fitness), and nevertheless be better understood as a result of evolutionary theoretical insights, as for example, the prediction of increasing maternal solicitude with increasing maternal age.

INTRAFAMILIAL HOMICIDE

If the human psyche has evolved to be effectively nepotistic, then violence against relatives remains a surprise. We have argued above that the majority of maternal homicides of own offspring, though not necessarily adaptive in modern circumstances, reflect what Alexander (1974) has called "parental manipulation": the allocation of parental investment in the interest of *parental* fitness at the expense of particular offspring. But a substantial proportion of homicides involves relatives other than mother and infant. Why?

It must first be remarked that criminologists have rarely distinguished relationship by blood from relationship by marriage. (Indeed, relatives have typically been lumped together with close friends and lovers as "primary contacts"; e.g., Wolfgang, 1958.) In fact, most murdered relatives are spouses, and a substantial proportion of the remainder are relatives by marriage too. In Daly & Wilson's (1982a) study of homicide in Detroit, for example, victim and offender were "relatives" in 25% of solved cases, but 63% of these "relatives" were spouses, a further 12% were in-laws and step-relations, and only 25% (hence just 6% of all victims in solved homicides) were blood relatives.

More importantly, the Detroit study revealed a lesser *risk* of homicide in blood than in other relationships: though the average adult Detroiter dwelt with 2.3 blood relatives and only 0.7 other persons, within-household homicides included just 22 victims related by blood versus 76 other persons. This difference was not due simply to the high risk of spousal homicide: The risk of homicide at the hands of an unrelated (by blood) adult member of one's household was elevated similarly both for spouses and for other unrelated cohabitants (roommates and in-laws), in both cases exceeding *eleven times* the risk from cohabitant blood kin (Daly & Wilson, 1982a).

An adaptationist analysis of kinship does not, of course, deny the reality of conflict among blood relatives. On the contrary, the absence of perfect genetic identity *guarantees* that individual fitness interests will not be perfectly congruent and hence that relatives will experience conflict (Trivers, 1974). What the adaptationist analysis suggests is that blood relationship mitigates conflict, other things being equal, and there is plenty of evidence in the homicide literature that this is indeed the case (Daly & Wilson, 1982a).

The sort of conflicts that lead a person to kill a blood relative are to some degree predictable. Intense sibling rivalry, for example, is an expected though ironic consequence of kin solidarity, for it is precisely because property is generally held and inherited familially that brothers so often compete for limited resources. A much larger proportion of fratricides than of other homicides derive from property issues. Fratricides are virtually unheard of in property-less societies, but constitute a large proportion of total homicides in societies where there is significant inheritance, especially if the heritable property is, like the family farm, not customarily partitioned (Daly & Wilson, 1982a). Another prevalent category of kin slayings in many societies is that in which juveniles defend their abused mothers by killing their abusive fathers.

So it is by no means the case that the murder of a blood relative must represent a maladaptive collapse of the normal nepotistic thrust of human motives. Yet certain cases demand that we appeal to concepts of psychopathology. Some killers suffer from delusions, according to which the family and friends who are their natural and genuine allies are transformed into enemies. Such a killer is mad, and an evolutionary theoretical approach to the definition of what is normal can provide some insight into criteria of madness (McGuire & Essock-Vitale, 1982). We say someone has lost his reason when he no longer seems to recognize where his self-interest lies or no longer cares to pursue it, and evolutionary theory identifies the bedrock of self-interest as inclusive fitness. As it happens, people who kill blood relatives *are* much likelier to be judged insane than are people who kill nonrelatives (e.g., Gillies, 1976: Guttmacher, 1955: Wong & Singer, 1973). Perhaps the nature of the act itself inspires the diagnosis, which would tell us more about the psychiatrists than the killers. Or perhaps, as the psychiatrists making these judgments would surely insist, there are objective, diagnostic criteria of insanity, distinct from the homicidal act, that happen to be more prevalent among those who kill relatives. *Either* possibility suggests that the state that is called *sanity* is characterized by the intelligible pursuit of nepotistic self-interest and that *insanity* is the forswearing of that pursuit.

THE MALE'S PROBLEM: UNCERTAIN PATERNITY

The basic thesis of this chapter is a straightforward application of Hamilton's (1964) theory. We postulate that the probability of a conflict's being resolved by dangerous means is in part a function of the mutual "valuation" of the antagonists. We expect that natural selection will have shaped A's valuation of B so that it reflects B's expected contribution to A's inclusive fitness. That expected contribution equals RV_B x r_{AB} (the product of B's reproductive value and B's degree of relatedness to A). Archival data on real acts of violence are probably too "noisy" to ever test the precise fit of A's valuation of B to this multiplicative model. However, there is ample evidence, reviewed above, that A is sensitive to both components, RV and r. (Scaling of paper-and-pencil evaluations might be an interesting approach for more precise tests of this multiplicative model, but social desirability effects and other biases threaten validity. Homicide reports, with all their attendant difficulties of analysis, represent genuine, drastic action.)

A complication arises from the fact that genetic relationship is mistakeable. The risk of mistake is of course asymmetrical: Only paternal links are likely to be misattributed. The male who invests substantially in offspring not his own loses fitness that his rivals gain, and it follows that natural selection should have favored a male psyche inclined to adulterous yearnings (e.g., Symons, 1979), to jealous sequestering of own spouse (e.g., Daly, Wilson, & Weghorst, 1982), and to assessment of the probability that putative paternity is genuine (e.g., Daly & Wilson, 1982b).

Men's efforts to dominate and control women can therefore be interpreted as deriving from male reproductive competition. It is not a trivial observation that men in all societies are deeply concerned with the control of female *sexuality*. Male sexual jealousy is the leading motive in spousal homicides in North America and, it would appear, everywhere else. It is also far and away the most cited precipitating factor in nonfatal wife-beating. Though several anthropologists have suggested that there are societies in which female sexual liberty is limited only by incest prohibitions, the ethnographies explicitly contradict this claim. The restriction of female sexual freedom by the use and threat of male violence appears to be cross-culturally universal. The evidence on these points is reviewed by Daly, Wilson, & Weghorst (1982).

The relevance of male sexual rivalry to human violence, including family violence, is amply documented (see also Chagnon, 1968; Hart & Pilling, 1960; Meggitt, 1962; Safilios-Rothschild, 1969). The relevance of paternity assessment to violence has received much less attention. Certainly the revelation of nonpaternity can be a stimulus to violence against both wife and child, and manifest nonpaternity was offered as a justification for routine infanticide in 20 societies in Daly & Wilson's (1984) ethnographic review.

Pseudoparental obligation to clearly unrelated children is a situation with great potential for violent resentment, as witness the overrepresentation of step-fathers among "parental" homicides (Daly & Wilson, 1985, in press; Scott, 1973) and child abusers (Wilson & Daly, in press; Wilson, Daly, & Weghorst, 1980). (Whether stepfather households are more dangerous to children than stepmother households remains unknown.) But we would furthermore expect that men would be increasingly likely to behave violently toward putative *own* offspring, the more phenotypically dissimilar those children to themselves; by way of comparison, phenotypic resemblance to self would not be expected to influence mothers. To the best of our knowledge, this prediction has yet to be tested.

Some Concluding Remarks about Sociobiology and Psychology

If organisms have evolved by natural selection, then species-characteristic behavioral control mechanisms should manifest evident "design" for the promotion of inclusive fitness. We agree with Symons (in press; this volume) that this adaptive design is best sought at more abstract psychological levels rather than in behavioral outcomes. Guns and condoms and automobiles and baby bottles are novelties on an evolutionary time scale; though our inventions may reveal much about our motives, there is no reason to suppose that we will achieve fitness in our uses of them. Fitness is a distal end far removed from the goals that subserve it. If men were simply selected to crave copulation, for example, they might well be unaffected by the thwarting of procreative consequences through contraceptive technology.

An adaptationist view suggests a number of likely psychological phenomena that can be tested for and further analyzed. We have discussed several in this paper: that the valuation of offspring will vary with available indicators of probable contribution to parental fitness, that the sexes will differ in their manifestations of sexual jealousy, that kinship will soften conflict. We expect to find psychological mechanisms subserving the adaptive functions of sexual competition, parental discrimination, nepotistic solicitude for collateral kin, and so forth, but these are merely general guidelines for research. Just *what* these mechanisms will be is an open question. Inbreeding avoidance, for example, might be achieved by sexual disinterest in those one was raised with, or by prepubertal dispersal, or by sexual disinterest in those who smell too much like oneself. It so happens that the first alternative appears to be the human one (e.g., van den Berghe, 1983). Adaptationist considerations alert us to the likelihood that there will be mechanisms functioning to prevent close inbreeding, but they do not tell us what those mechanisms will be. (Which is not to deny that further adaptationist analysis may often clarify why one mechanism has been favored over another.)

The proposition that the psyche has an evolved species-typical structure is sometimes vilified as "genetic determinism." The accusation is doubly misplaced. Adaptationist theories are no more "genetic" than anything else in the life sciences, though both sociobiologists and their critics often imagine otherwise. Genes are an essential part of the causation of all biological phenomena, but gene action is as remote from the level of analysis of sociobiology as it is from that of psychology. The reason that genes appear in sociobiological writings is not because of their role in the proximate causation of biological phenomena, but because their replication provides a currency of fitness and hence of adaptation. Sociobiologists use the proposition that organismic attributes have been designed by natural selection to replicate genes as metatheory organizing their study of those attributes, but they do not therefore study genetics.

The accusation of "determinism" is equally inept (Caplan, 1980). In doing science, we are all committed to a belief in causality. To maintain that behavior is not causally determined (hence is "free") is to reject behavioral science in general. Such a stance is no more congenial to nonevolutionary theorists who attribute behavior to "learning" (see, e.g., Skinner, 1971) than to evolutionists. Scientists strive to improve our understanding of human behavior by the cumulative reduction of "unexplained variance." If we succeed too well in this deterministic quest, will we lose the capacity to believe in individual moral responsibility? This dilemma confronts *all* scientific approaches to behavior.

ACKNOWLEDGMENTS

We thank the Harry Frank Guggenheim Foundation and Health & Welfare Canada for financial support; Deputy Chief Dr. James Bannon and Inspector Robert Hislop of the Detroit police department for access to Detroit homicide files; Dr. Marie Wilt Swanson for the use of her Detroit data; Joanne Lacroix, Craig McKie, Bryan Reingold and Bob Blais of Statistics Canada for the provision of Canadian homicide data.

The data analyses and literature review in this chapter were completed in late 1984. Minor changes in Canadian homicide data for 1974–1983 are possible as a result of the continuous updating of Canadian homicide records by Statistics Canada.

REFERENCES

Alexander, R. D. (1974). The evolution of social behavior. *Annual Review of Ecology & Systematics, 5*, 325–383.

Ali, Z., & Lowry M. (1981). Early maternal-child contact: Effects on later behaviour. *Developmental Medicine and Child Neurology, 23*, 337–345.

Andersson, M., Wiklund, C. G., & Rundgren, H. (1980). Parental defence of offspring: A model and an example. *Animal Behaviour, 28*, 536–542.

Barash, D. P. (1975). Evolutionary aspects of parental behavior: The distraction display of the Alpine accentor, *Prunella collaris*. *Wilson Bulletin, 87*, 367–373.

Caplan, A. L. (1980). A critical examination of current sociobiological theory: adequacy and implications. In G. W. Barlow & J. Silverberg (Eds.), *Sociobiology: Beyond nature/nurture?* Boulder, CO: Westview press.

Carlsson, S. G., Fagerberg, H., Horneman, G., Hwang, C.-P., Larsson, K., Rodholm, M., Schaller, J., Danielsson, B., & Gundewall, C. (1978). Effects of amount of contact between mother and child on the mother's nursing behavior. *Developmental Psychobiology, 11*, 143–150.

Chagnon, N. A. (1968). *Yanomamo: The fierce people*. New York: Holt, Rinehart and Winston.

de Chateau, P., & Wiberg, B. (1977a). Long term effect on mother-infant behaviour of extra contact during the first hour post-partum. I. First observations at 36 hours. *Acta Paediatrica scandinavica, 66*, 137–143.

de Chateau, P., & Wiberg, B. (1977b). Long-term effect on mother-infant behaviour of extra contact during the first hour post-partum. II. A follow-up at three months. *Acta Paediatrica scandinavica, 66*, 145–151.

Daly, M., & Wilson, M. (1980). Discriminative parental solicitude: A biological perspective. *Journal of Marriage & the Family, 42*, 277 288.

Daly, M., & Wilson, M. I. (1981a). Child maltreatment from a sociobiological perspective. *New Directions for Child Development, 11*, 93–112.

Daly, M., & Wilson, M. I. (1981b). Abuse and neglect of children in evolutionary perspective. In R. D. Alexander & D. W. Tinkle (Eds.), *Natural selection and social behavior.* New York: Chiron Press.

Daly, M., & Wilson, M. I. (1982a). Homicide and kinship. *American Anthropologist, 84*, 372–378.

Daly, M., & Wilson, M. I. (1982b). Whom are newborn babies said to resemble? *Ethology & Sociobiology, 3*, 69–78.

Daly, M., Wilson, M., Weghorst, S. J. (1982). Male sexual jealousy. *Ethology & Sociobiology, 3*, 11–27.

Daly, M., & Wilson, M. (1984). A sociobiological analysis of human infanticide. In G. Hausfater & S. B. Hrdy (Eds.), *Infanticide: Comparative and evolutionary perspectives.* New York: Aldine.

Daly, M., & Wilson, M. (1985). Child abuse and other risks of not living with both parents. *Ethology & Sociobiology, 6*, 197–210.

Daly, M., & Wilson, M. (in press). Children as homicide victims. In R. Gelles & J. Lancaster (Eds.), *Biosocial perspectives on child abuse.* New York: Aldine.

Darwin, C. (1859). *On the origin of species by means of natural selection.* London: Murray.

Gillies, H. (1976). Homicide in the west of Scotland. *British Journal of Psychiatry. 128*, 105–127.

Greig-Smith, P. W. (1980). Parental investment in nest defence by stonechats (*Saxicola torquata*). *Animal Behaviour, 28*, 604–619.

Guttmacher, M. S. (1955). Criminal responsibility in certain homicide case involving family members. In P. H. Hoch & J. Zubin, (Eds.), *Psychiatry and the law.* New York: Grune & Stratton.

Hales, D. J., Lozoff, B., Sosa, R., Kennell, J. H. (1977). Defining the limits of the maternal sensitive period. *Developmental Medicine and Child Neurology, 19*, 454–461.

Hamilton, W. D. (1964). The genetical evolution of social behaviour I. and II. *Journal of Theoretical Biology, 7*, 1–52.

Hart, C. W. M., & Pilling, A. R. (1960). *The Tiwi of North Australia.* New York: Holt, Rinehart & Winston.

Herbert, M., Sluckin, W., & Sluckin, A. (1982). Mother-to-infant "bonding"? *Journal Child Psychology and Psychiatry, 23*(3), 205–221.

Holmes, W. G., & Sherman, P. W. (1983). Kin recognition in animals. *American Scientist, 71*, 46–55.

Kennell, J. H., Jerauld, R., Wolfe, H., Chesler, D., Kreger, N. C., McAlpine, W., Steffa, M., & Klaus, M. H. (1974). Maternal behavior one year after early and extended post-partum contact. *Developmental Medicine and Child Neurology, 16*, 172–179.

Kennell, J. H., Trause, M. A., & Klaus, M. H. (1975). Evidence for a sensitive period in the human mother. In *CIBA Foundation Symposium No. 33. Parent-infant Interaction.* Amsterdam: Elsevier-Excerpta Medica-North Holland.

Klaus, M. H., & Kennell, J. H. (1976). *Maternal-infant bonding.* St. Louis: C. V. Mosby.

Klaus, M. H., Jerauld, R., Kreger, N. C., McAlpine, W., Steffa, M., & Kennell, J. H. (1972). Maternal attachment. Importance of the first post-partum days. *New England Journal of Medicine,* *286,* 460–463.

Lagacé, R. O. (1974). *Nature and use of the HRAF files.* New Haven: HRAF.

Lamb, M. E., & Hwang, C.-P. (1982). Maternal attachment and mother-neonate bonding: a critical review. In M. E. Lamb & A. L. Brown (Eds.), *Advances in developmental psychology* (Vol. 2). Hillsdale NJ: Lawrence Erlbaum Associates.

Lenington, S. (1981). Child abuse: The limits of sociobiology. *Ethology and Sociobiology, 2,* 17–29.

Mayr, E. (1983). How to carry out the adaptationist program? *American Naturalist, 121,* 324–334.

McGuire, M. T., & Essock-Vitale, S. M. (1982). Psychiatric disorders in the context of evolutionary biology. *Journal of Nervous and Mental Disease, 170,* 9–20.

Meggitt, M. J. (1962). *Desert People: A study of the Wilbiri aborigines of central Australia,* Sydney: Angus & Robertson.

Morsbach, G. (1980). Maternal recognition of neonates' cries in Japan. *Psychologia: An International Journal of Psychology in the Orient. 23,* 63–69.

O'Connor, S., Vietze, P. M., Sherrod, K. B., Sandler, H. M., & Altemeier, W. A. (1979). *Reduced incidence of parenting disorders following rooming-in.* Unpublished manuscript. Vanderbilt University.

Porter, R. H., Cernoch, J. M., & McLaughlin, F. J. (1983). Maternal recognition of neonates through olfactory cues. *Physiology & Behavior, 30,* 151–154.

Peters, L. C., & Kristal, M. B. (1983). Suppression of infanticide in mother rats. *Journal of Comparative Psychology, 97,* 167–177.

Pressley, P. H. (1981). Parental effort and the evolution of nest-guarding tactics in the threespine stickleback, *Gasterosteus aculeatus L. Evolution, 35,* 282–295.

Robson, K. M., & Kumar, R. (1980). Delayed onset of maternal affection after childbirth. *British Journal of Psychiatry, 136,* 347–353.

Rothgänger, H. (1981). Akustisches Wiedererkennen des Säuglingsschreies durch die Mutter. *Zeitschrift für ärztliche Fartbildungen (Jena), 75,* 441–446.

Safilios-Rothschild, C. (1969). 'Honor' crimes in contempory Greece. *British Journal of Sociology, 20,* 205–218.

Scott, P. D. (1973). Fatal battered baby cases. *Medicine, Science and the Law, 13,* 197–206.

Siegal, E., Bauman, K. E., Schaefer, E. S., Saunders, M. M., & Ingram, D. D. (1980). Hospital and home support during infancy: Impact on maternal attachment, child abuse and neglect, and health care utilization. *Pediatrics, 66,* 183–190.

Skinner, B. F. (1971). *Beyond freedom and dignity,* New York: A. A. Knopf.

Sosa, R., Kennell, J. H., Klaus, M., & Urrutia, J. J. (1976). The effect of early mother-infant contact on breastfeeding, infection and growth. In *Breastfeeding and the mother. CIBA Foundation Symposium No. 45.* Amsterdam: Elsevier.

Svejda, M. J., Campos, J. J., & Emde, R. N. (1980). Mother-infant ''bonding'': failure to generalize. *Child Development, 51,* 775–779.

Symons, D. (1979). *The evolution of human sexuality,* New York: Oxford University Press.

Symons, D. (in press). The evolutionary approach: Can Darwin's view of life shed light on human sexuality? In W. O'Donohue & J. Geer (Eds.), *Theories and paradigms of human sexuality.*

Trivers, R. L. (1974). Parent-offspring conflict. *American Zoologist, 14,* 249–264.

van den Berghe, P. L. (1983). Human inbreeding avoidance: Culture in nature. *Behavioral and Brain Sciences, 6,* 91–123.

Vietze, P. M., O'Connor, S., Falsey, S., & Altemeier, W. A. (1978). *Effects of rooming-in on maternal behavior directed towards infants.* Paper presented at 86th annual convention of the American Psychological Association, Toronto, Ontario.

Wilson, M. I., Daly, M., & Weghorst, S. J. (1980). Household composition and the risk of child abuse and neglect. *Journal of Biosocial Science, 12,* 333–340.

Wilson, M., & Daly, M. (in press). Risk of maltreatment of children living with step-parents. In R. Gelles & J. Lancaster (Eds.), *Biosocial perspectives on child abuse*. New York: Aldine.

Wolfgang, M. E. (1958). *Patterns in criminal homicide*. Philadelphia: University of Pennsylvania Press.

Wong, M., & Singer, K. (1973). Abnormal homicide in Hong Kong. *British Journal of Psychiatry, 123*, 295–298.

13 Evolutionary Pressures and Limitations to Self-preservation

Denys de Catanzaro
McMaster University

It is obvious that individual members of any species generally behave in manners conducive to self-perpetuation. The seeking of food, water, and physical comfort are fundamental drives in all behaving organisms and clearly act toward self-preservation. Also, behaving organisms normally actively escape from or avoid perceptible stimuli that threaten their continued existence. Principles of natural selection easily account for such self-preserving tendencies. Individuals that behave in a self-preserving manner are far more likely to propagate than those that do not; hence, over generations, any predispositions toward self-preservation with a genetic basis are passed on, whereas any contrary predispositions are likely to be rapidly eliminated.

Nevertheless, I would like to argue that the tendency to behave in self-perpetuating manners is not unqualified, but rather is conditional on various life circumstances. This chapter summarizes and extends previous discussions of an evolutionary (both biological and cultural) perspective toward human suicide (de Catanzaro, 1980, 1981). I would like here to consider the question more globally than in previous work, arguing that a conditional nature of self-preservation may be reflected in diverse behavioral phenomena. The major examples are primarily drawn from human behavior, however in theory many of the principles that are discussed could also be reflected in nonhuman behavior. First, evidence that several aspects of self-preservation are innate is discussed, which indicates both the strength and heritable nature of the normal tendency to preserve oneself. Subsequently, known forms of self-destructive behavior, which are antithetical to self-preservation, are briefly surveyed. Various theoretical conditions under which evolutionary pressures would not be expected to favor a self-preserving orientation of behavior are then outlined. It is argued that it is largely in such conditions that we in fact do observe self-destructive behavior. Various biological and cultural mechanisms are suggested to account for this correspondence and deviations from it. It is posited that synergistic interactions of these mechanisms can explain self-destructive behavior.

EVOLVED PHYSIOLOGICAL MECHANISMS OF SELF-PRESERVATION

There is solid reason to believe that many of the basic motivational processes favoring self-preservation were shaped by natural selection. For example, numerous neural mechanisms subserve pain perception and avoidance, including free nerve endings, believed to generate pain messages, which pass through spinal tracts to the thalamus in the brain (see Melzack, 1973; Pomerantz, 1973; Pourier, Bouvier, Olivier, & Boucher, 1968). Recent evidence suggests that chemicals known as endorphins modulate pain perception (Goldstein, 1978). Basic appetitive behavior also clearly involves evolved physiological mechanisms. A perusal of any modern text on physiological psychology (e.g., Carlson, 1981) indicates that feeding, drinking, sleep, and temperature regulation have bases in complex interactions of hormonal and neural processes. Such processes are stereotyped across individuals and it seems extremely unlikely that they are a product of experience alone, although there may be modulating roles of conditioning processes. There is evidence that even specific tastes such as sweet preference (Pfaffmann, 1977) and regulation of salt balance (Krieckhaus & Wolf, 1968; Nachman, 1962) are products of natural selection. The process of reinforcement may similarly depend on evolved mechanisms. Rats press levers at dramatically high rates to receive electrical brain stimulation, which many researchers believe involves a tapping of reinforcement mechanisms (Olds & Milner, 1954; Routtenberg, 1978), while pharmacological studies suggest that specific neurochemical systems may subserve reinforcement (Mogenson & Phillips, 1976; Stein, 1978). Recently, it has been demonstrated that 3-day-old rat pups will engage in such intracranial self-stimulation (Moran, Lew, & Blass, 1981).

Emotion is also not exclusively a function of cognition, but has a "hardwired" physiological basis and can be understood in an evolutionary framework (see also Panksepp, 1982, and various chapters in Plutchik & Kellerman, 1980). The sympathetic nervous system is known to produce rapid changes in heart and respiration rate, blood pressure, focus of blood flow, and availability of energy during subjective states of fear, anger, and even elation, allowing rapid coping with immediate threats or demands. Fear and anxiety responses are also believed to be subserved by a variety of central mechanisms, including the septo-hippocampal system (Gray, 1982). In many mammals, including primates, it is possible to elicit rage and attack sequences through electrical brain stimulation at specific sites (e.g., Delgado, 1969; Flynn, Venegas, Foote, & Edwards, 1970; Panksepp, 1971). Consider also that artificial subjective states of euphoria and dysphoria can readily be induced by a variety of drugs (Goodwin & Bunney, 1971; Iverson & Iverson, 1975); such stereotyped pharmacological manipulability suggests physiological underpinnings of this emotional dimension. This notion is reinforced by behavioral genetic evidence that individual differences in temperament may in part be genetically mediated (Gershon, Bunney, Leckman, Van Eerdewegh, & DeBauche, 1976; Fuller & Thompson, 1978). Moreover, a convergent argument for an innate basis of some emotional variables can be made on the basis of ethological evidence. As first suggested by Darwin (1872), various facial expressions and bodily postures may characterize emotional conditions within species and show similarities across related species.

In summary, the notion that man is motivationally and behaviorally a *tabula rasa* at birth is rapidly eroding in the face of physiological and ethological evidence. It would not be premature to conclude that there are motivational processes, conditioned by evolutionary pressures, that normally orient an individual's behavior toward self-preservation. This does not mean that motivational processes are immalleable or free of influence by cognitive and experiential variables. Learned and cultural processes also support self-preservation. For example, parents routinely teach their children not to eat toxic substances or to run into traffic, which, parenthetically, may relate to novel technologies for which there could not yet have evolved specific defensive mechanisms. Another illustration is the fact that modern religions teach self-preservation. Christianity generally upholds the value of individual life and both it and Islam condemn suicide (see de Catanzaro, 1981, chapter 11). These cultural influences notwithstanding, it is increasingly clear that human dispositions toward self-preservation are a product of a long history of selection pressures.

THE EXTENT OF SELF-DESTRUCTIVENESS

Despite this highly ingrained nature, self-preservation has clear limitations in human behavior. The strongest example is suicide, which is much more common than many people assume it to be. It has been estimated that discrete acts of suicide account for at least 1–2% of all deaths in modern cultures (Choron, 1972; de Catanzaro, 1981), and this may well be an underestimate because of equivocal circumstances surrounding many deaths and biases in reporting (Douglas, 1967). Suicide occurs in virtually every culture in which a careful survey has been conducted, although there is variance in gross rate. Historical evidence suggests that it was not uncommon in the classical civilizations (Rosen, 1971) and in ancient India (Thakur, 1963) and the Orient (Iga & Tatai, 1975). It is also particularly significant that suicide has been observed in a variety of less technologically developed or "primitive" cultures. This has been clear since the early reviews of Steinmetz (1894) and Westermarck (1908). Such cultures include those of Africa (Bohannan, 1960), the South Pacific (Firth, 1961; Malinowski, 1926), aboriginal India (Elwin, 1943), and aboriginal North (Devereux, 1961; Leighton & Hughes, 1955; Rasmussen, 1931; Weyer, 1932) and South (de Cieza de León, 1959) America. There are regions, such as western Nigeria, studied by Asuni (1962), where suicide occurs but is infrequent. However, the evidence overwhelmingly indicates that suicide has long occurred at appreciable rates in a large number of cultures.

There are also numerous unsuccessful suicide attempts (Stengel, 1973), or parasuicides (Kreitman, 1977). Many parasuicides apparently involve little intent to die and may be motivated by benefits experienced in surviving, and are hence not really self-destructive (Kreitman, 1977; Maris, 1981; Stengel, 1973). Nevertheless, those cases involving high lethality methods and intent to die extend estimates of the incidence of human self-destructiveness. As well as discrete suicidal acts, there are untold numbers of cases where individuals bring about or hasten their own deaths through excessive risk-taking or "accidents." Taking risks can be adaptive, of course, since major gains not otherwise available may accrue through risking death. Nevertheless, researchers have long suspected that many accidents may be hidden suicides, and that other individuals with subsuicidal motives may simply be careless (Mellinger, 1978; Menninger, 1938; Shneidman, 1968; Tabachnick, 1973). We must also consider the various ways in which some individuals engage in "chronic suicide," for example through chronic drug abuse (see de Catanzaro, 1981, chapter 15), although undoubtedly many motives unrelated to self-destructiveness can be involved in such behavior.

Among individuals classified as mentally retarded, as autistic, or under various other psychiatric categories are found cases of chronic self-injurious behavior (Bachman, 1972; Carr, 1977; de Catanzaro, 1978). Such behavior includes head-banging, fist-to-head movements, self-scratching, and self-biting. In the more serious cases, such behavior could easily produce death through concussion or hemorrhage were it not for the fact that such individuals are generally protected from themselves in institutions. Some individuals show multiple forms of self-injurious behavior, and such behavior can comprise the greater part of their behavioral repertoire. Self-injurious behavior is inversely correlated with intellectual level, being most common among the severely and profoundly retarded (van Velzen, 1975).

It is much more difficult to identify cases of self-destructive behavior among other species (for more complete discussions see de Catanzaro, 1981, chapter 4; Hamilton, 1980). The clearest instances of nonhuman suicides are found in social Hymenopteran insects, where members of sterile castes may not uncommonly sacrifice their lives in defense of the colony (see Wilson, 1971). Such altruistic self-destruction is exemplified by bees that die in consequence to stinging or termites with exploding abdomens used in colony defense. A second relatively clear instance is the self-injurious behavior occasionally observed in various nonhuman primates, usually chimpanzees or rhesus monkeys that have been held in captivity or experimentally reared in conditions of social isolation. This self-injurious behavior is very similar in form and intensity to that observed among retarded and psychotic humans, and includes head-banging, head-hitting, self-scratching, and self-biting (Cross & Harlow, 1965; Erwin, Mitchell, & Maple, 1973; Frieh, 1942; Gluck & Sackett, 1974; Mason & Sponholz, 1963).

Otherwise, there are few clear ethological or experimental indications that members of other species "commit suicide." The popular media have probably presented a distorted view of mortality incidental to population dispersion in lemmings, and little is known about the causation of phenomena such as beaching in whales. Other possible instances could have been obscured by inadequate sampling or difficulties in discriminating between self-induced and other forms of death. Human suicides are identifiable because of technologies used in implementing them, detailed knowledge of circumstances, and the individuals' verbalizations, and such clues are likely to be absent in our observations of other species. It remains conceivable that individuals of other species occasionally fail to eat or to avoid predators, thus hastening their own deaths, but a human observer might attribute this to illness rather than to psychologically induced failure of self-preservation. However, the theoretical conditions under which natural selection allows an erosion of self-preservation and the expression of self-destructiveness, as discussed below, possibly occur to an exceptional extent in highly social species where genetically related individuals are very interdependent.

The frequency of self-destructiveness presents a challenge to behavioral and evolutionary theory. Suicidal behavior clearly is the antithesis of most other behavior. I would now like to argue that self-destructive motivation is actually not entirely divorced from the general orientation of behavior if we adopt a more sophisticated conception of that orientation derived from sociobiological theory. Indeed, I suggest that there are theoretical limitations to "instincts" of self-preservation, or conditions under which natural selection would not have favored their expression. It should be made clear first, however, that self-destructive behavior is diverse, complex, and undoubtedly multicausal, and that any explanation must account for synergistic causation and some heterogeneity of causation across cases. It should also be emphasized that, although the biological evolution of behavioral dispositions are discussed at length, culture and learning are also clearly important in the causation of human self-destructive behavior.

THEORETICAL LIMITATIONS TO SELF-PRESERVATION

The concept of "inclusive fitness" (Hamilton, 1964), as thoroughly discussed in other chapters of this volume, has been central to the discipline of sociobiology. The idea that evolution favors behavior oriented toward the individual's inclusive fitness is especially fruitful for psychology. Indeed, it explains the "purpose" or "why" of behavior in a manner that is unprecedented among general theories of behavior. The flow or replication of genes over generations determines which behavioral and motivational predispositions are passed on, and hence, in an evolutionary sense, behavior should be somewhat subservient to genetic replication. This is true insofar as the genetics of any new generation come from those who have been successful in propagating, and thus any heritable behavioral traits favoring success in propagation are passed on, whereas other traits are not. Over numerous generations this should ensure that individuals are generally structured to seek replication of their genes. Self-preservation, at least until all possible reproductive opportunities are exploited, is usually an essential component of maintaining and advancing the representation of ones genes in the population gene pool.

Therefore, we can view self-preservation as the usual reflection of a larger process. Self-preservation can be construed as a means toward the greater end of propagation of one's genetic constitution. Accordingly, if we wish to define circumstances under which self-preservation might break down, we should ask whether there are conditions under which it impedes the individual's inclusive fitness or the representation of his genes in future generations.

Clearly, reproductive status is critical in defining such conditions. Generally, individuals should be expected to preserve themselves at least until they have matured and acted sexually and, in the case of females, until they have successfully born offspring. The amount of nurturance of offspring and the relative contributions of the sexes vary considerably across species, but where nurturance is required, the parent's continued existence is obviously of high value for its inclusive fitness until the process is complete. In many species (those that are semelparous; see Wilson, 1975), adults die shortly after reproduction. However, in other (iteroparous) species successfully reproducing on one occasion leaves the possibility of subsequent reproduction, justifying further self-preservation. This may be constrained by senescence, or a gradual erosion of physical vitality with age and by any cost to vitality that reproduction itself brings. It would also be constrained by season in many species that lay eggs prior to adverse and unsurvivable seasonal conditions. Life expectancy, intergenerational length, and average number and temporal distribution of offspring all vary considerably across species, and in any particular species these factors probably reach a balance that is more or less optimal for the specific ecological conditions (see discussions on aging and senescence by Comfort, 1964; Hamilton, 1966; Medawar, 1957; Williams, 1957). In any event, it could be predicted that once an individual is postreproductive or otherwise excluded from reproduction, and has no further role to play in nurturance of its progeny, self-preservation is of little or no value for the individual's inclusive fitness.

Any genetic predispositions favoring a self-preserving orientation of behavior, when expressed prior to or during reproductive (including nurturant) phases of the life cycle, would confer a strong selective advantage for the individual. However, expression of such predispositions after all reproductive opportunities had passed would have no positive reproductive consequences. In fact, to the extent that postreproductive or nonreproductive individuals consumed resources that otherwise would be available to potentially reproducing kin, their self-preservation could actually have adverse effects upon their inclusive fitnesses. Consider the fate of a hypothetical, randomly arising mutation that directly or indirectly induced self-destructive behavior. Such a mutation would be rapidly eliminated from the gene pool if it were expressed prior to reproductive ages. It would be highly disadvantageous to anyone possessing it in whom it was expressed during reproductive ages, the extent of disadvantage depending on how many offspring it prevented the individual from producing. We would expect such a disadvantage to keep its frequency in the gene pool quite low or to eliminate it over generations. However, if through pleiotropy, such a gene expressed itself only postreproductively or after future reproductive prospects were quite diminished for any other reason at any other age, this gene would be immune to selection and not eliminated from the gene pool. Indeed, it is conceivable that many such genetic factors indirectly favoring self-destructiveness expressed in such limited circumstances could have arisen and accumulated over generations in the population gene-pool.

We must further qualify this by considering the individual's residual capacity to behave productively in any manner that might benefit his inclusive fitness. Even if an individual is permanently nonreproductive, he can nonetheless promote his inclusive fitness by working toward the benefit of potentially reproducing kin, such as his siblings' children, who share his genes by common descent. A capacity to do so would therefore protect the value of his continued existence for his inclusive fitness, and favor the expression of self-preservation in him.

Interdependency of kin can surely strengthen pressures eroding self-preservation. Such interdependency occurs in any species with altricial young and parental care, but even more elaborately in humans, the more social of other mammalian species, and social Hymenopteran insects. Wherever the continued existence of one individual impedes the reproduction of close kin, as summated and weighted through coefficients of relationship, more than it enhances the reproduction of the individual himself, self-destructiveness is at least theoretically possible.

In fact, a theoretical function (ψ) defining an optimal continuum of self-preservation and self-destruction, varying across individuals and within any individual over time, is given by the formula:

$$\psi_i = \rho_i + \sum_k b_k \rho_k r_k$$

where ρ_i = total remaining reproductive potential of the focal individual (i), measured in probable future number of offspring not inclusive of those already realized.

ρ_k = total remaining reproductive potential of each kinship member k interdependent with the focal individual, measured as is ρ_i.

r_k = the coefficient of relationship, according to Wright (1922), for each interdependent relative (k), which gives a sibling or child ½, a grandchild or nephew or niece ¼, a first cousin ⅛, and so forth.

b_k = the coefficient of benefit (or cost) conferred upon kinship member k by the continued existence of the focal individual i. This coefficient is often measurable or at least estimable, and limits are definable such that $-1<b<1$. Wherever k is entirely dependent on i, as an infant is upon its mother, b = 1. Wherever k is entirely independent of i, b = 0. If i is burdensome toward k, by competing for resources, otherwise impeding k's reproduction, or in the extreme case killing him or her, b can vary to a value as low as -1.

For many purposes, ρ_i (and similarly ρ_k) could be equated, on a basis of age, to v_a, which is Fisher's (1958) "reproductive value," or to w_a, Hamilton's (1966) "expected reproduction beyond age a," both of which can be defined and measured from actuarial statistics. However, this uses only age as a predictor, whereas ρ, an individual's residual reproductive ability, can also vary substantially with social dominance, physical vitality, and other factors as well as age. The issues bearing on the definition of ρ, and a more complete exposition of this mathematical model are given in de Catanzaro (1986).

The second term of the equation could also be written $\sum_k \delta\rho_k r_k$, where $\delta\rho_k$ is a single term representing the increment or decrement in residual reproductive potential for each k provided by the continued existence of i. This alternative formulation makes the equation directly analogous to Hamilton's (1964) inclusive fitness formula. However, it is distinct in that the concept of residual reproductive potential (ρ) is not the same as fitness and not found in Hamilton (1964), while Hamilton (1966) surprisingly did not consider his w_a statistic within an inclusive fitness framework. The first formula for ψ given above clearly has advantages in that both the general characteristics of ρ_k and the scaling of b_k can be defined.

Note that several interesting conclusions follow from this model. For nonsocial species, $\psi_i = \rho_i$ and $\psi \geq 0$, because $\Sigma b_k = 0$. In such circumstances, self-preservation is predicted according to the theory of senescence as advanced by Medawar (1957), Williams (1957) and Hamilton (1966), such that weakening support of self-preserving attributes occurs with decreasing ρ_i and if $\rho_i = v_a$ or w_a, as a function of increasing age. ψ can assume values < 0 only in social species, which might entail the possibility of overt self-destructiveness, as opposed to a mere diminishing of self-preservation as ψ approaches 0 but assumes positive values. Note that the impact of negative values of b_k will be diminished by increasing values of ρ_i, and that as $\rho_i \to 0$, if $\Sigma b_k \rho_k r_k < 0$, self-destructiveness can be favored. This model accounts better for the survival of postreproductive but nurturant individuals, such as postmenopausal women, than do the discussions of Medawar, Williams, and Hamilton, as well as allowing the prediction of outright self-destructiveness (see also de Catanzaro, 1986).

CORRESPONDENCE OF OBSERVED AND THEORETICAL CONDITIONS FAVORING SELF-DESTRUCTIVENESS

I would now like to suggest, in accordance with arguments made in detail elsewhere (de Catanzaro, 1981), that there is a general correspondence between these theoretical conditions for failures in self-preservation and the actual circumstances in which such failure is observed. The argument will first be made on the basis of archival data concerning completed human acts of suicide, since as discussed above these represent the most unequivocal forms of self-destructiveness. Essentially, without for the moment making any suggestions as to what causal mechanisms might account for the relationship, it is suggested that suicide typically occurs among individuals whose residual capacity to promote inclusive fitness is seriously impaired. In a general, qualitative manner, it is clear that suicide is related to diminished reproductive potential, absence of or unfavorable relations to kin and social group, and coping failure. Examination of the more precise quantitative approach just outlined is in progress and is not reported here.

First, it is clear that suicidal motivation bears a very strong relationship to protracted coping difficulties. One of the best predictors of true suicidal intent is believed to be "hopelessness" or "desperation" (Beck, Kovacs, & Weissman, 1975; Bogard, 1971, Farber, 1968). Beck et al. (1975) have found hopelessness to be a better predictor than "depression," which is a more transitory state. True desperation occurs not only where an individual has difficulty in coping with his present condition, but where he also anticipates that he will never overcome this difficulty. According to our assumption of what coping behavior involves, desperation would mean that an individual finds himself presently and potentially incapable of engaging in reproductive and productive behavior that would promote his inclusive fitness. An examination of certain high risk populations also supports this notion. Suicide is very common in the terminally ill and those with permanently debilitating handicaps (Dorpat, Anderson, & Ripley, 1968; Weiss, 1968); such individuals are relatively incapable of engaging in future reproductive and productive behavior. Suicide is also very common in the chronically unemployed and others with severe economic difficulties (McCulloch & Philip, 1972); such difficulties may engender problems in attracting a mate and supporting offspring, rendering the individual incapable of reproducing, and may preclude other activity that indirectly advances the individual's inclusive fitness.

Social isolation also appears to bear a strong relationship to suicide (Breed, 1972; Ganzler, 1967; Stengel, 1973; Worden, 1976). Indeed, it has been argued that the suicide rate in a population varies inversely with the strength of the relational systems of its members (Henry & Short, 1954). Also, what Durkheim (1897) classified as ''egoistic'' suicide occurred when an individual had insufficient ties to society. An individual that is socially isolated, including isolation from the opposite sex, would have difficulty reproducing. An isolated individual would also be relatively incapable of engaging in productive activity that would benefit others sharing his genes; this may be particularly true if he is separated from kin.

Suicide rate also increases as a function of age, particularly in men (Diggory, 1976; Linden & Breed, 1976). Although many remain productive late in life, the proportion of men that are capable of both productive and reproductive activity may decrease with increasing age. Suicide is very rare in children under 14 (Diggory, 1976; Shaffer, 1974), or before competition and differentiation in reproductive and productive status. In adolescence and early adulthood, when such differentiation is rampant, suicide is a major cause of death; those with relative reproductive and productive difficulties apparently are those most prone to suicide (see Jacobs, 1971; Hendin, 1976; Seiden, 1966). Greater rates of suicide in males than females may relate to differences in reproductive and nurturance strategies; for example, females of any age may be more likely than males to engage in nurturance activities (see Daly & Wilson, 1978).

Suicide also bears a marked relationship to reproductive status. Rates tend to be low among those with stable marriages but quite high in the widowed, divorced, single, and those with unstable marriages (Diggory, 1976; Dublin, 1963; Durkheim, 1897; McCulloch & Philip, 1972). Rates may be especially low among those with dependent children (Breed, 1966; Dublin & Bunzel, 1933). Furthermore, recent divorce or other difficulty with members of the opposite sex is very often a proximate antecedent of suicide (McCulloch & Philip, 1972).

As has been discussed elsewhere (de Catanzaro, 1981), available evidence suggests that suicide in less technologically developed cultures similarly relates to coping failures and diminished reproductive ability. For example, if we examine information on the circumstances of suicide among the Soga tribes in Uganda presented by Fallers and Fallers (1960), a role of coping failures and reproductive status is quite clear. The frequency of associations of suicide with impotence, venereal disease, death or desertion of spouse, old age, general ill health, and social ostracism attests to this. Similar factors are found to be associated with suicide in a wide variety of nondeveloped or primitive cultures (see, for example, Asuni, 1962; Bohannan, 1960; Elwin, 1943; Firth, 1961; Leighton & Hughes, 1955; Westermarck, 1908) as well as ancient civilizations (see Dublin, 1963; Farberow, 1972; Rosen, 1971; Westermarck, 1908).

Recently (de Catanzaro, 1984), I have conducted a survey of samples of several hundred individuals from the general Ontario population as well as several hundred university students. Questions were asked concerning the individuals' previous and perceived future reproductive success, contact with and ability to aid kin, interactions with the opposite sex, and ability to engage in work benefiting community. Other items concerned suicidal ideation and rating of the value the respondents' attached to their own life. The assumptions were that a small percentage of respondents would have seriously contemplated suicide, and that such contemplation would bear a relationship to actual suicide potential. The results clearly indicated that respondents reporting greater suicidal ideation had perceptions that family would be better off without them and were less likely to believe that they could contribute to the welfare of kin in future. Such individuals also more frequently reported fewer and less stable heterosexual relationships, poorer health, and lesser perceived capacities to contribute to community.

It could also be argued that other forms of self-destructive behavior tend to be most frequent among those with poorer reproductive prospects and less contact with kin. The self-injurious behavior of retarded and psychotic individuals tends to occur especially among those with the most severe mental handicaps, who are usually also isolated from kin and meaningful social contact in institutions (see de Catanzaro, 1978, 1981, chapter 16). Alcohol and drug abuse also tend to correlate with protracted coping difficulties, unstable heterosexual relationships, and social isolation, whereas risk-taking is known to be much more common among those without stable heterosexual relationships (see references in de Catanzaro, 1981, chapter 15). Again I must emphasize that no particular causality underlying such correlations is being suggested at this point, and undoubtedly such diverse behavioral patterns derive from many complex interactions of factors that could have little direct relationship to evolutionary heritage. The point here is simply that such behavior patterns apparently are much more frequent in social-ecological conditions that would involve a reduced capacity to promote inclusive fitness.

Another phenomenon, one that is not behavioral so much as physiological, may indicate that in diverse species, self-preservation erodes in chronic coping difficulty that we might interpret as involving a reduced residual capacity to contribute to inclusive fitness. This is what has been called "sudden death" (Engel, 1971; Hughes & Lynch, 1978; Lefcourt, 1976; Pruitt, 1974; Wintrob, 1973). This term has been applied to many different forms of death, in most cases involving death that is unpredicted with an immediate onset. Undoubtedly, the diverse forms of death to which the term is applied have similarly diverse causes, but a large number of these apparently involve a loss of life maintenance when the individual's future prospects are very bleak or hopeless. Cannon (1942) and Lex (1974) have described "voodoo death" in some primitive cultures, where death is induced by spells that give individuals the belief that they are hopelessly entrapped. Richter (1955) and others (e.g., Binik, Theriault, & Shustack, 1977; Griffiths, 1960; Lynch & Katcher, 1974) have investigated a "sudden death" phenomenon in laboratory animals. When these animals are placed in an experimental setting where death is inevitable but would normally take some time to occur, they suddenly die long before there is any obvious physiological reason. Other forms of sudden death have been noted in humans with various chronic medical problems, with sudden death apparently being associated with a psychological state of hopelessness (Hughes & Lynch, 1978).

It is also known that, in humans that are severely depressed or experiencing psychological states of helplessness or hopelessness, various forms of normal self-maintaining behavior tend to break down (Beck, 1967; Seligman, 1975). Such individuals tend to become lethargic and show disruptions in appetite, loss of interest in sex, sleep disruptions, and a failure to engage in normal grooming and work habits. To the extent that such depression and hopelessness reflect concrete and objective coping difficulties and stresses, this may further indicate how normal self-preservation is eroded when the individual's coping abilities are diminished.

In summary, the general ecological positions of documented self-destructive behavior and loss of self-preservation are similar to those predictable through evolutionary theory. Such behavior most frequently occurs where its selective impact is relatively limited and where self-preservation is not of high value for the individual's inclusive fitness. This does not account for all instances and dimensions of self-destructiveness, however, and we can refine the explanation by considering other conditions inducing self-preservation failures.

PATHOLOGY AND GENE EXPRESSION IN NOVEL ENVIRONMENTS

Not all cases and forms of self-destructiveness occur where future prospects for reproductive and kin-solicitous behavior are poor. One would think, for example, that in at least some of the many modern human cases of suicide among young adults, the individuals' coping difficulties would be potentially transitory. Other theoretical conditions could help to explain deviations from self-preservation. These can be related to the notions of "pathology" and "stress."

First, we must consider that processes of natural selection do not perfectly prepare all individuals for the environments that they encounter. Earthly existence is much more dynamic than that. The composition of any species' environment can change considerably over generations, due to continued competition among and within species and changing climatic and geological conditions. Accordingly, traits that have been selected in previous generations may not perfectly adapt to the ecological conditions of later generations. Furthermore, genetic recombination is such that each individual can represent a novel configuration of traits; some such recombinations may be inappropriate for the circumstances that they confront. An example is the surfacing of recessive lethal genes, such as in Tay-Sachs disease or phenylketonuria. Consider also the situation in r-selectionist species (see Wilson, 1975), in which the majority of each new generation succumbs to predation and competition from other species, shifts in environmental conditions, and inappropriate recombination.

Therefore, we must ask to what extent observed cases of self-destructiveness simply represent novel maladaptive recombinations of traits or expression of otherwise adaptive traits in novel circumstances for which they are not prepared. There can be little doubt that these factors do figure in many cases of human self-destructiveness. Perhaps the clearest example is the self-injurious behavior of psychotic and retarded children (see de Catanzaro, 1978, 1981, chapter 16). Individuals displaying such behavior are generally malformed due to genetic or chromosomal aberrations, congenital factors, and/or extremely abnormal rearing conditions (Korten, Van Dorp, Hustinx, Scheres, & Rutten, 1975; Lesch & Nyhan, 1964; Maisto, Baumeister, & Maisto, 1978; Singh & Pulman, 1979; van Velzen, 1975). There is good reason to believe that this self-injurious behavior could be directly facilitated by neurological malformation or damage, which might lessen pain sensitivity, motor control, and the capacity to inhibit motor responses with aversive consequences (see de Catanzaro, 1981, chapter 16). In various laboratory studies of mammals, physiological and environmental abnormalities such as decerebration (Hendrick, 1950), temporal lobe lesions (Kluver & Bucy, 1939), intervention in the caudate nucleus (Korten et al., 1975), middle ear infection (Harkness & Wagner, 1975), dorsal rhizotomy in a forelimb (Dennis & Melzack, 1979), treatment with high doses of catecholamine stimulants (Randrup & Munkvad, 1969), and rearing in social isolation (Cross & Harlow, 1965) have been reported to induce self-injurious or self-mutilative behavior.

There are several respects in which these principles are also relevant to human suicide. First, suicide is known to be more frequent among individuals with psychiatric histories and disorders such as schizophrenia (e.g., Sletten, Brown, Evenson, & Altman, 1972; Temoche, Pugh, & MacMahon, 1964). However, psychiatric diagnostic criteria are not well standardized, with individuals to whom labels such as "schizophrenic" are applied being very heterogeneous in personality and symptoms (Davison & Neale, 1978), and it is conceivable that the correlation of psychopathology with suicide is in part due to the fact that evidence of suicidal ideation causes clinicians to diagnose psychopathology. Furthermore, there are many researchers who believe that the majority of suicides occur among those without histories of psychopathology (e.g., Stengel, 1973). In any event, it is difficult to relate, in any precise manner, clinical diagnoses of psychopathology to biological conditions allowing maladaptive behavior.

More relevant to suicide is the consideration of how modern human environments deviate from those for which individuals are biologically prepared. Consider the many modern technologies through which individuals can readily implement their own deaths. Automobiles, guns, and various poisons now surround the individual in abundance and constitute novel evolutionary factors for which individuals could not conceivably be biologically prepared. The availability of such technologies facilitates impulsive and truly maladaptive acts of suicide (maladaptive in this context means occurring where there is residual ability to promote inclusive fitness). Consider how in previous historical circumstances, innate physiological pain mechanisms would keep an individual from harming himself, and of course in most modern circumstances they still do. However, the modern availability of barbiturates, which induce painless death, allows circumvention of such mechanisms. This factor helps to explain some imperfection in the relationship of suicide to diminished fitness promotion ability in modern cultures. It must be tempered by consideration of the fact that suicide occurs in high rates in many technologically less advanced cultures, as discussed above. Also, there are comparative data on suicide rates and methods in the 19th and 20th centuries from England and Wales, indicating that overall rates of suicide have remained remarkably constant despite technological changes. However, the frequency of suicide through simpler methods of hanging and drowning has declined, being supplanted by suicide through drugs, firearms, and gassing (cf. Littlejohn, 1910–1911; Stengel, 1973).

Similarly, there are other respects in which humans are somewhat out of evolutionary context in modern cultures due to rapid technological and social transitions. Throughout most of human evolution, individuals probably lived in close-knit groups consisting of people related by multiple kinship ties. Modern geographic mobility and the erosion of extended (and even nuclear) family ties have meant greater isolation from kin and more interaction with individuals from diverse genetic backgrounds. This may be relevant to the well-established fact that socially isolated individuals are at high risk for suicide, as discussed above. Also, there is increased occupational diversity and stratification in modern societies, which may enhance competition and subject many individuals to evolutionarily novel stresses. Such factors again may undermine the normal adaptiveness of behavior, because such behavior occurs in situations for which it has not been selected.

LEARNING, CULTURE, COGNITION, AND EMANCIPATION FROM STRICT BIOLOGICAL CONTROL

Another factor could account for some human cases of self-destructiveness. The unique human capacities for learning, cognition, and culture mean that individuals' behavior can often develop somewhat independently of biological constraints. There are few forms of specific behavior in humans that are not at least in part learned. My position is that general motivational and emotional dimensions of human conduct, which are known to relate to nonassociative neural and hormonal processes, express evolved dispositions, but that specific behaviors and associations involve the development of these dispositions in particular environments. It is quite conceivable that this behavioral flexibility may some times engender conduct that is biologically maladaptive, even to the extent of producing suicide.

It is well established (e.g., Hankoff, 1961; Phillips, 1974) that instances of suicidal behavior in modern cultures are sometimes imitated. This is evidenced, for example, by increased frequencies of suicide through specific methods and in specific locations following reports of similar suicides in the news media. This must, of course, be a very selective form of imitation, since only an extremely small proportion of those exposed to information on others' suicides would imitate them. Accordingly, as argued elsewhere (de Catanzaro, 1981), imitation may be involved more in determining the method and temporal and physical location of suicide than the motivation. Other evidence of an involvement of vicarious learning or imitation in some suicidal behavior comes from cases of massed suicides, which have occurred on several occasions in history, most recently in Jonestown, Guyana. We must also consider that many of the methods involved in suicide, especially those in modern technologically advanced cultures, absolutely require learning to be used. It is inconceivable that methods involving guns, drugs, and automobiles would not involve vicarious learning.

Human cognitive ability furthermore allows individuals to contrive novel acts as well as to imitate acts of others. It is possible therefore that some cases of suicide are independently invented as means of dealing with various life predicaments. These "inventions" may be influenced in varying degrees by learning about suicides of others, death in general, and any alternative coping strategies. It is well established that suicide is frequently preceded by prolonged contemplation (Levenson, 1974; Neuringer, 1976; Shneidman, 1957; Tripodes, 1976), although this does not in itself support any particular causation of the behavior. It is conceivable that human suicide may be contrived and/or imitated for various potential impacts on the individual's life goals. For example, a person may suicide in anticipation of insurance benefits for kin, to avert pain when slow death is inevitable, to relieve kin of ones dependence on them, or to escape various intolerable situations. Individuals are basically structured motivationally to promote their inclusive fitness, and such cognitively and imitatively induced behavior may naturally reflect this general fitness orientation. Accordingly, at least some of the correspondence of the social ecology of suicide to biological limits of self-preservation may be mediated by learned, cognitive, and cultural processes. The behavior *per se* involved in suicide may well be learned and cultural, but facilitated by relatively innate motivational variables. Insofar as such cognitive and learned factors usually produce suicide where its negative impact on the individual's inclusive fitness is limited, these factors and the suicidal behavior may recur over generations unimpeded by natural selection.

EVOLUTION, SYNERGIES, AND HUMAN SELF-DESTRUCTIVE BEHAVIOR

A tentative integration of the various principles discussed above might invoke a synergistic biocultural coevolution that has allowed human self-destructive behavior to recur at substantial rates over generations. This assumes variation among individual cases in the nature of the synergy, since any single-factor explanation could not account for the diversity and complexity of this behavior.

As detailed above, selective pressures do not favor an unconditional self-preservation "instinct." Several heritable aspects of such self-preservation were outlined, and it is presumably these very aspects whose limits we should observe under the specified conditions. Briefly, those conditions conducive to a breakdown in self-preservation were serious and potentially permanent impediments to both future reproductive ability and the ability to behave solicitously toward kin. Such pressures are not necessarily unique to humans, and hence we might observe reflections of them in other species, especially those in which there is strong interdependency among kin. Perhaps this would not be evident so much in overt suicide, but rather in phenomena such as sudden death, the facilitation of disease processes and the hastening of senescence, and failure to eat, drink, and avoid predation when residual reproductive and kin-solicitous abilities are diminished.

One process that is probably quite relevant to considerations of innate substrates of human self-destructiveness is emotional variation. It is well established that dysphoria, despondency, depression, desperation, and/or hopelessness are strongly related to human suicidal behavior (Beck et al., 1975; Farber, 1968; Maris, 1981). Common subjective experience surely suggests that dysphoria is a concomitant of failure and blocked aspirations whereas euphoria accompanies success and achievement, and that most individuals can vary on this emotional continuum contingent upon experiences. Also, behavioral-genetic evidence cited above indicates that individual differences in depression are in part due to inheritance, and an innate component of affective variation is further supported by an apparent relationship to brain monoamines (references cited above, see also de Catanzaro, 1981, chapter 10). Recent evidence also suggests that suicidal individuals show relatively low levels of serotonin in the cerebrospinal fluid and brain (Beskow, Gottfries, Roos, & Winblad, 1976; Bourne, Bunney, Colburn, Davis, Davis, Shaw, & Coppen, 1968; Cochran, Robins, & Grote, 1976; Lloyd, Farley, Deck, & Hornykiewicz, 1974; Pare, Yeung, Price, & Stacey, 1969; Shaw, Camps, & Eccleston, 1967), although more research along these lines is needed.

Some biological preparation for self-destructive behavior could therefore be as old in evolutionary terms as is severe negative affect that impedes optimal striving for self-maintenance and advancement. Apparent variation from euphoria to dysphoria is observed in other primates, and in its most extreme form can involve severe despondency like that observed in humans (Harlow, 1974), and self-injurious behavior (Cross & Harlow, 1965; Erwin et al., 1973; Mason & Sponholz, 1963). Goodall (1979) has cited one chimpanzee case of failure to eat and death in apparent despondency. Despite any degree to which heritable affective conditions have favored a breakdown in self-preserving tendencies, they could recur over generations unimpeded by pressures of natural selection, so long as they have accompanied only life circumstances involving a diminished residual capacity to promote inclusive fitness. As well as affective variation, pain perception and avoidance may also constitute heritable and variable factors bearing on the probability of self-preservation and self-destructiveness (see de Catanzaro, 1981, chapter 10).

I am uncertain as to the extent that such factors would have been sufficient in the absence of cultural developments to produce outright suicidal behavior. Clearly, it is demonstrable that certain cultural developments have facilitated and altered suicidal behavior. Consider technology and suicide. Methods such as self-drowning, jumping from high places, and abstinence from food and water must always have been available to man. By far the most widespread method in the world, especially considering less technologically developed cultures, is self-hanging (see de Catanzaro, 1981). This method may always have been available through the use of vines and perhaps even ones own hair, but would be facilitated by the presence of various forms of clothing and, later, ropes. Poisonous plants and animal venoms may also have been discovered early in some regions in human prehistory. The development of weaponry for hunting and warfare must surely have further facilitated suicidal behavior, and methods such as self-stabbing are quite common in accounts from classical civilizations (Rosen, 1971). In modern times, there has been a proliferation of technologies for effecting ones own death, including automobiles, guns, and drugs, such that most individuals have means available at any time for quick, relatively painless death. As was discussed above, this makes impulsive acts of suicide much more likely, and probably increases the frequency of the act and its maladaptiveness.

An involvement of cultural factors, especially imitative learning, must be considered as having contributed to the diffusion of suicidal behavior through human culture. A critical question in suicide research is the extent to which learning about suicidal behavior of others is necessary for one to display the behavior. I would not attempt to answer this question prematurely, and believe that we are badly in need of research investigating the degree to which individuals committing suicide have been influenced by similar actions of others. Vicarious learning alone would seem insufficient to account for the emotional concomitants and social ecology of suicide. In some complex manner, self-destructive behavior has come to occur among those who are extremely thwarted in pursuing normal life goals and who are experiencing dysphoria. If suicide has been transmitted via observational learning, we must somehow explain why it is differentially imitated in this particular social and emotional ecology.

Human cognition, in conjunction with affective variables, could possibly help to explain this selective imitation. We might assume that our inherited structure molds the general way in which we respond, motivationally and emotionally, to biologically critical events such as birth and death of kin, intimate interaction with the opposite sex, threats to personal health and welfare and those of kin, and other factors closely related to inclusive fitness. Through observation of self and the motives and actions of others, individuals gain some cognitive representation of essential life goals that roughly corresponds to inclusive fitness dimensions. Conceptions of the nature of life goals can undoubtedly vary, sometimes deviating from strict correspondence to biological life goals, as for example in the case of an artist who stakes all of his sense of self-worth on the success or failure of his work. However, most people obviously value their family, interaction with the opposite sex, the welfare of children and grandchildren, and other matters of inclusive fitness very highly. If an individual is thwarted in attempting to achieve life goals and perceives little chance of future improvement, dysphoria and despondency are likely, as is a cognitive search for strategies to escape this coping impasse. Under such circumstances, due to perceptions of hopelessness, burdensomeness toward kin, or pain or futility of future existence, there may be imitation or contrivance of suicidal behavior. These relationships may, however, be distorted or otherwise modified by the existence of various pathological, stressful, or novel conditions.

Determining how evolved motivations and specific experiences interact to produce suicidal behavior presents a challenge to suicide research and theory. Suicidal ideation and imitative behavior clearly occur in an emotional and genetic context. An individual's emotional structure may facilitate (or, conversely, inhibit) his contemplation and imitation of suicidal behavior. Such behavior may therefore occur only when certain biological and cultural factors coalesce. In any event, so long as this coalescence occurs (and has occurred) in the ecological conditions detailed earlier in this paper, it will remain unimpeded by evolutionary pressures and can therefore recur at substantial rates over generations. Cultural developments must to a large extent be constrained by their selective consequences, such that those that detract from fitness decline in frequency over generations, whereas those that enhance fitness proliferate. Therefore, even if specific suicidal forms of behavior were largely cultural in origin, so long as these occurred in ecological contexts where they did not eliminate much residual reproductive and productive ability, they could recur over generations.

In summary, motivational and ecological aspects of suicidal behavior may be part of our evolutionary heritage, although these can also be influenced by pathological and novel conditions, but the specific behavior involved in suicide may, at least to some extent, be imitated, contrived, or otherwise culturally transmitted.

REFERENCES

Asuni, T. (1962). Suicide in Western Nigeria. *British Medical Journal, 2,* 1091–1097.

Bachman, J. (1972). Self-injurious behavior: A behavioral analysis. *Journal of Abnormal Psychology, 80,* 211–224.

Beck, A. T. (1967). *Depression: Clinical, experimental and theoretical aspects.* New York: Harper & Row.

Beck, A. T., Kovacs, M., & Weissman, A. (1975). Hopelessness and suicidal behavior: An overview. *Journal of the American Medical Association, 234,* 1146–1149.

Beskow, J., Gottfries, C. G., Roos, B. E., & Winblad, B. (1976). Determination of monoamine and monoamine metabolites in the human brain: Post mortem studies in a group of suicides and in a control group. *Acta Psychiatrica Scandinavica, 53,* 7–20.

Binik, Y. M., Theriault, G., & Shustack, B. (1977). Sudden death in the laboratory rat: Cardiac function, sensory, and experiential factors in swimming deaths. *Psychosomatic Medicine, 39,* 82–92.

Bogard, H. M. (1971). Collected thoughts of a suicidologist. In D. B. Anderson & L. J. McClean (Eds.), *Identifying suicide potential.* New York: Behavioral Publications.

Bohannan, P. (Ed.). (1960). *African homicide and suicide.* New Jersey: Princeton University Press.

Bourne, H. R., Bunney, W. E., Jr., Colburn, R. W., Davis, J. M., Davis, J. N., Shaw, D. M., & Coppen, A. J. (1968). Noradrenaline, 5-hydroxytryptamine, and 5-hydroxyindoleacetic acid in hindbrains of suicidal patients. *Lancet, II,* 805–808.

Breed, W. (1966). Suicide, migration, and race. *Journal of Social Issues, 22,* 30–43.

Breed, W. (1972). Five components of a basic suicide syndrome. *Life-Threatening Behavior, 2,* 3–18.

Cannon, W. B. (1942). "Voodoo" death. *American Anthropologist, 44,* 469–481.

Carlson, N. R. (1981). *Physiology of behavior,* 2nd edition. Boston: Allyn and Bacon.

Carr, E. G. (1977). The motivation of self-injurious behavior: A review of some hypotheses. *Psychological Bulletin, 84,* 800–816.

Choron, J. (1972). *Suicide* New York: Charles Scribner's Sons.

Cochran, E., Robins, E., & Grote, S. (1976). Regional serotonin levels in brain: A comparison of depressive suicides and alcoholic suicides with controls. *Biological Psychiatry, 11,* 283–294.

Comfort, A. (1964). *Ageing: The biology of senescence.* New York: Holt, Rinehart, and Winston.

Cross, H. A., & Harlow, H. F. (1965). Prolonged and progressive effects of partial isolation on the behavior of Macaque monkeys. *Journal of Experimental Research in Personality, 1,* 39–49.

Daly, M., & Wilson, M. (1978). *Sex, evolution, and behavior.* North Scitiate, MA: Duxbury Press.

Darwin, C. (1872). *Expression of the emotions in man and animals.* London: Murray.

Davison, G. C., & Neale, J. M. (1978). *Abnormal psychology.* New York: Wiley.

de Catanzaro, D. (1978). Self-injurious behavior: A biological analysis. *Motivation and Emotion, 2,* 45–65.

de Catanzaro, D. (1980). Human suicide: A biological perspective. *The Behavioral and Brain Sciences, 3,* 265–290.

de Catanzaro, D. (1981). *Suicide and self-damaging behavior: A sociobiological perspective.* New York: Academic Press.

de Catanzaro, D. (1984). Suicidal ideation and the residual capacity to promote inclusive fitness: A survey. *Suicide and life-threatening behavior, 14,* 75–87.

de Catanzaro, D. (1986). A mathematical model of evolutionary pressures regulating self-preservation and self-destruction. *Suicide and life-threatening behavior, 16,* 84–99.

de Cieza de León, P. (1959). *The Incas.* Translated by H. de Onis. Norman: University of Oklahoma Press.

Delgado, J. M. R. (1969). *Physical control of the mind.* New York: Harper & Row.

Dennis, S. G., & Melzack, R. (1979). Self-mutilation after dorsal rhizotomy in rats: Effects of prior pain and pattern of root lesions. *Experimental Neurology, 65,* 412–421.

Devereux, G. (1961). *Mohave ethnopsychiatry and suicide: The psychiatric knowledge and the psychic disturbances of an Indian tribe.* Washington, D.C.: Smithsonian Institution.

Diggory, J. C. (1976). United States suicide rates, 1933–1968: An analysis of some trends. In E. S. Shneidman (Ed.), *Suicidology: Contemporary developments.* New York: Grune & Stratton.

Dorpat, T. L., Anderson, W. F., & Ripley, H. S. (1968). The relationship of physical illness to suicide. In H. L. P. Resnik (Ed.), *Suicidal behaviors.* Boston: Little Brown.

Douglas, J. D. (1967). *The social meanings of suicide.* New Jersey: Princeton University Press.

Dublin, L. (1963). *Suicide.* New York: Ronald.

Dublin, L., & Bunzel, B. (1933). *To be or not to be.* New York: Harrison Smith and Robert Haas.

Durkheim, E. (1951). *Suicide.* Glencoe, IL: Free Press. (Originally published in 1897).

Elwin, V. (1943). *Maria murder and suicide.* London: Oxford University Press.

Engel, G. L. (1971). Sudden and rapid death during psychological stress. *Annals of Internal Medicine, 74,* 771–782.

Erwin, J., Mitchell, G., & Maple, T. (1973). Abnormal behavior in non-isolate-reared rhesus monkeys. *Psychological Reports, 33,* 515–523.

Fallers, L. A., & Fallers, M. C. (1960). Homicide and suicide in Busoga. In P. Bohannan (Ed.), *African homicide and suicide.* New Jersey: Princeton University Press.

Farber, M. L. (1968). *Theory of suicide.* New York: Funk & Wagnalls.

Farberow, N. L. (1972). Cultural history of suicide. In J. Waldenstrom, T. Larsson, & N. Ljungstedt (Eds.), *Suicide and attempted suicide.* Stockholm: Nordiska Bokhandelns Forlag.

Firth, R. (1961). Suicide and risk-taking in Tikopia society. *Psychiatry, 24,* 1–17.

Fisher, R. A. (1958). *The genetical theory of natural selection.* New York: Dover.

Flynn, J., Vanegas, H., Foote, W., & Edwards, S. (1970). Neural mechanisms involved in a cat's attack on a rat. In R. F. Whalen, M. Thompson, M. Verzeano, & N. Weinberger (Eds.), *The neural control of behavior.* Orlando, FL: Academic Press.

Frieh, G. (1942). Chimpanzee frustration responses. *Psychosomatic Medicine, 4,* 233–251.

Fuller, J. L., & Thompson, W. R. (1978). *Foundations of behavior genetics.* Saint Louis: Mosby.

Ganzler, S. (1967). Some interpersonal and social dimensions of suicidal behavior. *Dissertation Abstracts, 28B,* 1192–1193.

Gershon, E. S., Bunney, W. E., Jr., Leckman, J. F., Van Eerdewegh, M., & DeBauche, B. A. (1976). The inheritance of affective disorders: A review of data and of hypotheses. *Behavior Genetics, 6,* 227–261.

Gluck, J. P., & Sackett, G. P. (1974). Frustration and self-aggression in social-isolate rhesus monkeys. *Journal of Abnormal Psychology, 83,* 331–334.

Goldstein, A. (1978). Opiate receptors and opioid peptides: a ten-year overview. In M. A. Lipton, A. DiMascio, & K. F. Killam (Eds.), *Psychopharmacology: A generation of progress.* New York: Raven Press.

Goodall, J. (1970). Life and death at Gombe. *National Geographic, 155,* 592–621.

Goodwin, F. K., & Bunney, W. E., Jr. (1971). Depressions following reserpine: A reevaluation. *Seminars in Psychiatry, 3,* 435–447.

Gray, J. A. (1982). *The neuropsychology of anxiety: An enquiry into the functions of the septo-hippocampal system.* Oxford: Oxford University Press.

Griffiths, W. J. (1960). Responses of wild and domestic rats to forced swimming. *Psychological Reports, 6,* 39–49.

Hamilton, W. D. (1964). The genetical evolution of social behavior. *Journal of Theoretical Biology, 7,* 1–16.

Hamilton, W. D. (1966). The moulding of senescence by natural selection. *Journal of Theoretical Biology, 12,* 12–45.

Hamilton, W. J. (1980). Do nonhuman animals commit suicide? *The Behavioral and Brain Sciences, 3,* 287–279.

Hankoff, L. D. (1961). An epidemic of attempted suicide. *Comprehensive Psychiatry, 2,* 294–298.

Harkness, J. E., & Wagner, J. E. (1975). Self-mutilation in mice associated with otitis media. *Laboratory Animal Science, 25,* 315–318.

Harlow, H. F. (1974). Induction and alleviation of depressive states in monkeys. In N. F. White (Ed.), *Ethology and psychiatry.* Toronto: University of Toronto Press.

Hendin, W. (1976). Growing up dead: Student suicide. In E. S. Shneidman (Ed.), *Suicidology: Contemporary developments.* New York: Grune & Stratton.

Hendrick, I. (1950). *Facts and theories of psychoanalysis.* New York: Knopf.

Henry, A. F., & Short, J. F. (1954). *Suicide and homicide.* New York: Free Press.

Hughes, C. W., & Lynch, J. J. (1978). A reconsideration of psychological precursors of sudden death in infrahuman animals. *American Psychologist, 33,* 419–429.

Iga, M., & Tatai, K. (1975). Characteristics of suicides and attitudes toward suicide in Japan. In N. L. Farberow. (Ed.), *Suicide in different cultures.* Baltimore, MD: University Park Press.

Iverson, S. D., & Iverson, I. I. (1975). *Behavioral pharmacology.* New York: Oxford University Press.

Jacobs, J. (1971). *Adolescent suicide.* New York: Wiley.

Kluver, H., & Bucy, P. C. (1939). Preliminary analysis of functions of the temporal lobe in monkeys. *Archives of Neurology and Psychiatry, 42,* 979–1000.

Korten J. J., Van Dorp, A., Hustinx, Th. W. J., Scheres, J. M. J., & Rutten, F. J. (1975). Self-mutilation in a case of 49, XXXXY chromosomal constitution. *Journal of Mental Deficiency Research, 19,* 63–71.

Kreitman, N. (Ed.). (1977). *Parasuicide.* New York: Wiley.

Krieckhaus, E. E., & Wolf, G. (1968). Acquisition of sodium by rats: Interaction of innate mechanisms and latent learning. *Journal of Comparative and Physiological Psychology, 65,* 197–201.

Lefcourt, H. M. (1976). *Locus of control.* Hillsdale, NJ: Lawrence Erlbaum Associates.

Leighton, A. H., & Hughes, C. C. (1955). Notes on Eskimo patterns of suicide. *Southwestern Journal of Anthropology, 11,* 327–338.

Lesch, M., & Nyhan, W. L. (1964). A familial disorder of uric acid metabolism and central nervous system function. *American Journal of Medicine, 36,* 561.

Levenson, M. (1974). Cognitive correlates of suicidal risk. In C. Neuringer (Ed.), *Psychological assessment of suicidal risk.* Springfield, IL: C. C. Thomas.

Lex, B. W. (1974). Voodoo death: New thoughts on an old explanation. *American Anthropologist, 76,* 818–823.

Linden, L. L., & Breed, W. (1976). The demographic epidemiology of suicide. In E. S. Shneidman (Ed.), *Suicidology: Contemporary developments.* New York: Grune & Stratton.

Littlejohn, H. H. (1910–1911). Suicide. In *Encyclopedia Britannia,* 11th edition.

Lloyd, K. G., Farley, I. J., Deck, J. H. N., & Hornykiewicz, O. (1974). *Biochemical Psychopharmacology, 11,* 387–398.

Lynch, J. J., & Katcher, A. H. (1974). Human handling and sudden death in laboratory rats. *Journal of Nervous and Mental Disease, 159,* 362–365.

Maisto, C. R., Baumeister, A. A., & Maisto, A. A. (1978). An analysis of variables related to self-injurious behaviour among institutionalized retarded persons. *Journal of Mental Deficiency Research, 22,* 27–36.

Malinowski, B. (1926). *Crime and custom in savage society.* London: Routledge & Kegan Paul.

Maris, R. W. (1981). *Pathways to suicide: A survey of self-destructive behaviors.* Baltimore: Johns Hopkins University Press.

Mason, W. A., & Sponholz, R. R. (1963). Behavior of rhesus monkeys raised in social isolation. *Journal of Psychiatric Research, 1,* 299–306.

McCulloch, J. W., & Philip, A. E. (1972). *Suicidal behavior.* New York: Pergamon.

Medawar, P. B. (1957). *The uniqueness of the individual*. London: Methuen.

Mellinger, G. D. (1978). Use of licit drugs and other coping alternatives: Some personal observations on the hazards of living. In D. J. Lettieri (Ed.), *Drugs and suicide*. London: Sage Publications.

Melzack, R. (1973). *The puzzle of pain*. Harmondsworth, Eng.: Penguin.

Menninger, K. (1938). *Man against himself*. New York: Harcourt, Brace, and World.

Mogenson, G. J., & Phillips, A. G. (1976). Motivation: A psychological construct in search of a physiological substrate. In *Progress in psychobiology and physiological psychology* (Vol. 6). Orlando, FL: Academic Press.

Moran, T. H., Lew, M. F., & Blass, E. M. (1981). Intracranial self-stimulation in 3-day-old rat pups. *Science, 214,* 1366–1368.

Nachman, M. (1962). Taste preference for sodium salts by adrenalectomized rats. *Journal of Comparative and Physiological Psychology, 55,* 1124–1129.

Neuringer, C. (1976). Current developments in the study of suicidal thinking. In E. S. Shneidman (Ed.), *Suicidology: Contemporary developments*. New York: Grune & Stratton.

Olds, J., & Milner, P. (1954). Positive reinforcement produced by electrical stimulation of septal area and other regions of rat brain. *Journal of Comparative and Physiological Psychology, 47,* 419–427.

Panksepp, J. (1971). Aggression elicited by electrical stimulation of the hypothalamus in albino rats. *Physiology and Behavior, 6,* 321–329.

Panksepp, J. (1982). Toward a general psychobiological theory of emotions. *The Behavioral and Brain Sciences, 5,* 407–467.

Pare, C. M. B., Yeung, D. P. H., Price, K., & Stacey, R. S. (1969). 5-Hydroxytryptamine, noradrenaline and dopamine in brainstem, hypothalamus, and caudate nucleus of controls and patients committing suicide by coal-gas poisoning. *Lancet, II,* 133–135.

Pfaffmann, C. (1977). Biological and behavioral substrates of the sweet tooth. In J. M. Weiffenbach (Ed.), *Taste and development*. Bethesda, MD: U.S. Department of Health, Education and Welfare.

Phillips, D. P. (1974). The influence of suggestion on suicide: Substantive and theoretical implications of the Werther effect. *American Sociological Review, 39,* 340–354.

Plutchik, R., & Kellerman, H. (Eds.). (1980). *Emotion: Theory, research, and experience* (Vols. 1 & 2). Orlando, FL: Academic Press.

Pomerantz, B. (1973). Specific nociceptive fibers projecting from spinal cord neurons to the brain: A possible pathway for pain. *Brain Research, 50,* 447–451.

Pourier, L. J., Bouvier, G., Olivier, A., & Boucher, R. (1968). Subcortical structures related to pain. In A. Soulairac, J. Cahn, & J. Charpentier (Eds.), *Pain*. Orlando, FL: Academic Press.

Pruitt, R. D. (1974). Death as an expression of functional disease. *Mayo Clinic Proceedings, 49,* 627–634.

Randrup, A., & Munkvad, I. (1969). Relation of brain catecholamines to aggression and other forms of behavioural excitation. In S. Garattini & E. B. Sigg (Eds.), *Aggressive behaviour*. Amsterdam: Excerpta Medica Foundation.

Rasmussen, K. (1931). *The Netsilik Eskimos*. Copenhagen: Report of The Fifth Thule Expedition, vol. 8.

Richter, C. P. (1955). Phenomenon of sudden death in man and animals. *Science, 121,* 624.

Rosen, G. (1971). History in the study of suicide. *Psychological Medicine, 1,* 267–285.

Routtenberg, A. (1978). The reward system of the brain. *Scientific American, 239,* 154–164.

Seiden, R. H. (1966). Campus tragedy: A story of student suicide. *Journal of Abnormal and Social Psychology, 71,* 389–399.

Seligman, M. E. P. (1975). *Helplessness*. San Francisco: Freeman.

Shaffer, D. (1974). Suicide in childhood and early adolescence. *Journal of Child Psychology and Psychiatry, 15,* 275–291.

Shaw, D. M., Camps, F. E., & Eccleston, E. G. (1967). 5-Hydroxytryptamine in the hind-brain of depressive suicides. *British Journal of Psychiatry, 113,* 1407–1411.

Shneidman, E. S. (1957). The logic of suicide. In E. S. Shneidman & N. L. Farberow (Eds.), *Clues to suicide.* New York: McGraw-Hill.

Shneidman, E. S. (1968). Classifications of suicidal phenomena. *Bulletin of Suicidology, 2,* 1–9.

Singh, N. H., & Pulman, R. M. (1979). Self-injury in the DeLange Syndrome. *Journal of Mental Deficiency Research, 23,* 79–84.

Sletten, I., Brown, M., Evenson, R., & Altman, H. (1972). Suicide in mental hospital patients. *Disease of the Nervous System, 33,* 328–334.

Stein, L. (1978). Reward transmitters: Catecholamines and opioid peptides. In M. A. Lipton, A. DiMascio, & K. F. Killman (Eds.), *Psychopharmacology: A generation of progress.* New York: Raven Press.

Steinmetz, S. R. (1894). Suicide among primitive peoples. *American Anthropologist, 7,* 53–60.

Stengel, E. (1973). Suicide and attempted suicide. Harmondsworth, Eng.: Penguin.

Tabachnick, N. (1973). *Accident or suicide? Destruction by automobile.* Springfield, IL: C. C. Thomas.

Temoche, A., Pugh, T. F., & MacMahon, B. (1964). Suicide rates among current and former mental institution patients. *Journal of Nervous and Mental Disorders, 138,* 124–130.

Thakur, U. (1963). *The history of suicide in India.* Nai Sarak, India: Munshi Ram Monohar Lal.

Tripodes, P. (1976). Reasoning patterns in suicide notes. In E. S. Shneidman (Ed.), *Suicidology: Contemporary developments.* New York: Grune & Stratton.

van Velzen, W. J. (1975). Autoplexy or self-destructive behavior in mental retardation. In D. A. A. Primrose (Ed.), *Proceedings of the Third Congress of the International Association for the Scientific Study of Mental Deficiency.* Warsaw: Polish Medical Publishers.

Weiss, J. M. A. (1968). Suicide in the aged. In H. L. P. Resnik (Ed.), *Suicidal behaviors.* Boston: Little Brown.

Westermarck, E. (1908). Suicide: A chapter in comparative ethics. *Sociological Review, 1,* 12–33.

Weyer, E. C. (1932). *The Eskimos.* New Haven: Yale University Press.

Williams, G. C. (1957). Pleiotropy, natural selection, and the evolution of senescence. *Evolution, 11,* 398–411.

Wilson, E. O. (1971). *The insect societies.* Cambridge, MA: Belknap.

Wilson, E. O. (1975). *Sociobiology.* Cambridge, MA: Belknap.

Wintrob, R. M. (1973). The influence of others: Witchcraft and rootwork as explanations of behavior disturbance. *Journal of Nervous and Mental Disease, 156,* 318–326.

Worden, J. W. (1976). Lethality factors and the suicide attempt. In E. S. Shneidman (Ed.), *Suicidology: Contemporary developments.* New York: Grune & Stratton.

Wright, S. (1922). Coefficients of interbreeding and relationship. *American Naturalist, 56,* 330–339.

14 Sex Differences in Human Mate Selection Criteria: An Evolutionary Perspective

David M. Buss
University of Michigan

> *The value, if any, of female beauty for male reproductive success is obscure.*
>
> —Trivers, 1972, p. 172

The application of evolutionary theory to understanding human psychological phenomena is one of the most intriguing, yet frustratingly problematic, scientific enterprises today. Few psychologists doubt that our species has evolved, that we share some attributes with ancestral species, and that prior selection pressures have left their mark on human behavior. But beyond general acceptance of this view, the nature of more specific insights to be gained by the application of evolutionary theory remains stridently disputed by a few and largely ignored by many (cf. Campbell, 1975; Caplan, 1978).

Among the valuable attributes of any psychological theory are the power to array known and sometimes disparate observations in an orderly and coherent fashion; to generate clear predictions about phenomena not yet discovered; and to render sensible otherwise anomalous or incomprehensible findings. Evolutionary theory carries the promise of possessing these valuable attributes. Psychologists, however, have remained skeptical about the large-scale relevance of evolutionary theory to psychological phenomena, in part because the generation of specific evolutionary predictions can be difficult, because we lack precise knowledge about the environmental conditions under which we evolved, and because alternative evolutionary accounts are often easy to generate but difficult to differentially falsify.

Despite these difficulties, anchoring psychology in evolutionary biology offers the promise of transcending disciplinary isolation. By acquiring knowledge about the ultimate (historical) origins of psychological dispositions, evolutionary theory can guide research on human behavior toward identifying the proximal paths through which reproductive ends are achieved (Williams, 1966). For these reasons, the application of evolutionary theory to psychological phenomena remains attractive in spite of its difficulties (Alexander, 1979; Buss, 1984, 1986; Campbell, 1975; Cunningham, 1981; Freedman, 1979; Rushton, 1984a, 1984b).

It is reasonable to suppose that evolutionary theory will carry greater explanatory power and heuristic value in some areas than in others (Symons, in press). In particular, as the core of evolutionary theory may be traced to differential gene replication, evolutionary theorizing should be most relevant to those psychological processes surrounding reproductive behavior. If evolutionary theory affords few specific predictions, little understanding of know facts, and no clear guides to phenomena relevant to human reproduction, then its applicability to psychological phenomena distant from reproduction will be doubtful.

This chapter focuses on one crucial aspect of human reproduction—mate selection. Specifically, the ways in which males and females differ in their mate selection criteria are examined from an evolutionary perspective. Evolutionary accounts of mate selection criteria are traced back to Darwin's (1871) theory of sexual selection, are through more recent extensions in Fisher's (1930) theory of runaway selection and "sexy sons," Trivers' (1972) theory of parental investment and sexual selection, and Symons' (1979) account of human sexuality. Specific predictions about sex differences in selection criteria are generated by these approaches, and the empirical findings are examined in light of these predictions. The discussion outlines several consequences of sex differentiated selection criteria for the broader matrix of reproductively relevant behavior patterns.

DARWIN'S THEORY OF SEXUAL SELECTION

While writing *On the Origin of Species* . . . in 1859, Darwin became dissatisfied with natural selection as the sole mechanism for evolutionary change. Natural selection or "survival selection" was driven by what Darwin termed the "hostile forces of nature," which included climate, weather, food shortages, predators, and parasites. Naturally selected characteristics were those that increased the chances of survival in the struggle for existence. Some characteristics such as the brilliantly colored plumage of peacocks, however, seemed to defy explanation by reference to natural selection in the sense of "survival of the fittest." Darwin developed the concept of sexual selection to account for adaptations that he was unable to attribute to the process of natural selection.

Sexual selection describes differential reproductive success arising when individuals of one sex acquire an advantage over same-sex others in obtaining mates.

Darwin proposed two primary paths through which sexual selection could proceed. The first, *intrasexual selection,* was defined by Darwin as competition among members of one sex (typically males) for access to members of the opposite sex (typically females). In contrast, *intersexual selection* was defined as the differential preference of members of one sex for those of the opposite sex possessing valued characteristics. Darwin called intersexual selection ''female choice'' because he observed that, throughout the animal world, females tended to be more ''choosy'' or discriminating about their mating partners.

Darwin believed that sexual selection was one important cause of sex differences (although natural selection could account for many). For example, the larger size and aggressiveness of males, as well as various organs of offense and defense (e.g., horns, antlers) were believed to have evolved through selection driven by intrasexual male competition. Extremes of male sexual display (e.g., length and vigor of courtship, gaudy display) were believed to have evolved through female choice. Thus, sexually selected sex differences could evolve in the service of competitive advantage over members of the same sex, or in the service of attracting members of the opposite sex.

It is now widely recognized that most or all selection processes can be reduced to differential gene replication (Hamilton, 1964: Williams, 1966). The reproduction of genes is thus the ultimate criterion of selection, and from this perspective, sexual selection does not differ from natural selection. Nonetheless, some evolutionary biologists call attention to certain conceptual advantages to maintaining the distinction between natural and sexual selection because evolutionary vectors can oppose one another (Mayr, 1972). Brightly colored physical features, for example, may attract mates (increasing fitness) as well as predators (decreasing fitness). The intra- and intersexual aspects of sexual selection provide important proximal paths through which differential gene replication is achieved.

The intersexual component of sexual selection initially caused controversy because Darwin simply *assumed* that females have preferences for certain male characteristics, without documenting (a) how such preferences might have arisen, or (b) how they might be maintained in the population (Halliday, 1978). Fisher (1930) provided a partial answer by elucidating how female preferences could be maintained and evolve further, once an initial consensual preference had come into existence.

FISHER'S THEORY OF RUNAWAY SELECTION
AND ''SEXY SONS''

In order for a preference to evolve, there must be some selective advantage accruing to individuals expressing the preference. The selective advantage to the individuals possessing preferred characteristics is clear—they differentially attract mates and therefore have more offspring. But what advantage would accrue to individuals exerting this preference? Fisher's (1930) answer was that females who mate with males who are attractive to females *in general* will, if variation in the preferred characteristic is partially heritable, have more attractive or "sexy" sons. These more attractive sons, in turn, will be preferentially selected by females and will produce more offspring. Therefore, females selecting males who are generally attractive to females will have more grandchildren, and in this way the female preference will evolve or become increasingly pronounced in subsequent gene pools. The female preference and the male characteristics that are preferred will evolve concurrently. Evolution will favor stronger preferences as the preferred characteristics become more extreme.

This process of the coevolution of preferences along with preferred characteristics, called runaway selection, is posited by Fisher (1930) to continue at an accelerating pace until it is checked by an opposing evolutionary vector (e.g., if larger and more colorful display features begin to impede flight and defense, and therefore reduce odds of survival to reproductive age). Selection based on female choice must occur by a *relative* criterion (favoring one extreme of the distribution) rather than an *absolute* criterion in order to produce continuous change in the male (selected) character (Trivers, 1972).

Fisher's (1930) theory of runaway selection can account for the evolution of sexual selection criteria once there exists (for whatever reason) some consensus among females about preferred relative criteria. But what could account for the origin of such preferences? Some preferred characteristics may initially have fitness value in the survival sense. In principle, however, incidental, neutral, or even otherwise dysfunctional male attributes could evolve through female sexual choice. The task was left for Trivers (1972) to provide the next important breakthrough by identifying the specific *functional* male attributes that compose female selection criteria, thus elucidating how preferences can initially arise.

TRIVERS' THEORY OF PARENTAL INVESTMENT AND SEXUAL SELECTION

In a seminal paper, Trivers (1972) proposed that sexual selection is driven by relative parental investment of males and females in their offspring. Parental investment is defined as "any investment by the parent in an individual offspring that increases the offspring's chance of surviving (and hence reproductive success) at the cost of the parent's ability to invest in other offspring" (Trivers, 1972, p. 139). Investments include food, shelter, time, energy, protection, and other resources. Because parental resources are limited, a selective advantage will accrue to those who expend and distribute investments wisely. Parental investment is postulated to be a valuable resource over which intense competition occurs.

Males and females typically differ in their *initial* parental investment. Male sex cells are small compared to female sex cells, and indeed, this size difference defines which organism is male and which is female. Male investment at the moment of conception is smaller than female investment because the large female ovum provides the lion's share of key nutrients for early development. In many species, fertilization occurs internally within females, and this compounds the male-female investment differences. In our species, for example, a male copulation that is trivial in terms of investment can produce a 9-month investment by the female that is substantial in time, energy, and foreclosed alternatives. Because of this imbalance, termination of parental investment at birth or thereafter would usually be more costly for females than for males. Sex differences in investment tend to be self-perpetuating, although other selection factors can favor later male parental investment that equals or exceeds female parental investment (Trivers, 1972).

According to Trivers, competition between members of the same sex for more mates will occur more intensely in the sex that invests least in offspring (see also, Bateman, 1948). In contrast, the sex that invests most in offspring should be selected to be maximally choosy, or to impose more discriminating criteria in selecting mating partners. Where the investment of the sexes is approximately equal, discriminating criteria imposed on potential partners should be about equal for the sexes. Thus, sex differences in parental investment generally will produce sexual selection in the form of intrasexual competition in the sex investing least and intersexual "choice" in the sex investing most. This dichotomy, however, should not be drawn too sharply. Intersexual choice often implies intrasexual competition within members of the same sex.

Trivers (1972) outlines several important characteristics that females should seek in males that compose theoretical criteria for female choice: (1) ability of the male to fertilize eggs (e.g., sexual competence), (2) quality of male genes, including survival and reproductive potential, and (3) quality and quantity of parental care—the willingness and ability of the male to invest resources in offspring (which may be partly heritable). Such resources can provide (a) immediate material advantage to offspring, (b) enhanced reproductive advantage for offspring through acquired social and economic advantages, and (c) genetic reproductive advantage for offspring if variation in the qualities that contribute to resource acquisition are partly based on genetic variation.

Specific predictions about sexual selection criteria can be derived from Trivers' theory. For example, the sex investing most in offspring (typically females) should be more resistant to, and discriminating about, sexual overtures prior to mate selection. The sex investing less in offspring (typically males) should be more indiscriminate and wanton in sexual conduct. These predictions appear to be supported solidly by human data (Symons, 1979, 1980, in press) and are not discussed further here. Instead, the remainder of this paper focuses on the predictions and data on the *different qualitative selection criteria* displayed by human males and females. The specific predictions are drawn from Darwin (1871),

Trivers (1972), Symons (1979), and Buss and Barnes (1986), and center around two clusters of sex differences in mate selection criteria: (1) male resource potential, and (2) female physical cues to reproductive value.

SPECIFIC PREDICTIONS ABOUT MATE SELECTION CRITERIA

Male promiscuity is often highlighted in evolutionary accounts of human sexuality (Symons, 1979) because of its presumed value for male reproductive success. But it is also clear that in our species, male parental investment is often substantial. Trivers (1972) suggests that where male parental care is involved, females should choose males at least partly on the basis of their ability to contribute parental care. In many species, females compete among themselves for males with good territories, and copulate only with males bearing gifts of food (Calder, 1967; Lack, 1940). Territories and food are resources that females presumably can convert into gene copies. Since human females have stringent limitations on the number of offspring they can produce, selection should favor those females who are able to secure maximal resources to be invested in each child. And because offspring are the currency of evolutionary success, acquisition of these resources becomes closely linked with gene replication.

In humans, resources can take many forms and there are diverse phenotypic characteristics that provide proximate correlative cues to resource possession and acquisition potential. Among the most obvious characteristics are income, occupational and social status, possessions, networks of alliance, and family background. Personality characteristics such as hard-working, ambitious, energetic, industrious, and persevering also appear to be correlated with achievement potential (Barron, 1963; Willerman, 1979). If Trivers' theory is correct, female mate criteria should reflect these cues to resource acquisition. Thus, the following specific predictions may be advanced.

Prediction 1: Females, more than males, should value attributes in potential mates that signify possession, or likely acquisition, of resources.

In contrast to females, for whom access to resources for offspring imposes the limiting factor, the main reproductive limitation imposed on males is access to reproductively capable females. According to Trivers (1972), "there is no reason to suppose that males do not compete with each other to pair with females whose breeding potential appears to be high" (p. 171). In spite of this trenchant observation, Trivers did not take the next step to examine the attributes in human females that would provide cues to reproductive value or high fertility.

Reproductive value may be defined in units of expected future reproduction—the extent to which persons of a given age and sex (and other features) will contribute, on the average, to the ancestry of future generations (Fisher, 1930).

Female reproductive value can be expected to increase as sexual maturity approaches, and to decrease as the reproductive years pass. A woman of 35 has a lower reproductive value than a woman of 25 because the average number of future offspring is lower for the woman of 35. Reproductive value must be distinguished from *fertility,* which refers to age-specific birth-rate. Fertility reflects immediate probability of reproduction, while reproductive value reflects long-term probability of reproduction.

Male preferences, from an evolutionary perspective, can be expected to differ depending on whether a long-term mate or a short-term sex partner is sought (Symons, 1979; Thornhill & Thornhill, 1983). For a temporary sex partner, males should seek females possessing the highest fertility (in the early 20s in the United States); for a long-term mate, males should seek females possessing the highest reproductive value (mid-teens in the United States) (Thornhill & Thornhill, 1983). The crucial issue, therefore, concerns which phenotypic female characteristics provide the best cues to fertility and to reproductive value.

Although further research is required to fully delineate these cues, in humans, two strong cues to reproductive capability in females are age and health (Symons, 1979; Thornhill & Thornhill, 1983). In our evolutionary past prior to the development of counting systems, however, age was not a characteristic that could be evaluated directly. Instead, cues that correlated with age and health could be used by males to identify reproductively capable females. Physical appearance probably provides the strongest set of cues, and these include features such as clear, smooth, and unblemished skin, lustrous hair, white teeth, clear eyes, and full lips (Symons, 1979). Behavioral cues such as spritely gait and high activity level also provide cues to youth.

According to this evolutionary argument, males should come to value and view as attractive those physical and behavioral cues in potential mates that correlate with female reproductive capability. Males failing to prefer females possessing these attributes would, on the average, mate with less reproductively capable females. Consequently, such males would tend to leave fewer offspring, and would be selected against. In sum, male mate preferences and standards of female beauty should evolve to reflect the physical and behavioral cues that signify female reproductive capability.

Given the previous arguments that suggest that males generally compete for more matings, what circumstances would tend to favor *male* choosiness for quality females of high reproductive value? The general answer is that males should become more choosy under circumstances that make matings more costly and limited. Where mating systems tend toward monogamy, where females enforce male resource investment prior to mating, and where females enforce prolonged courtship prior to mating, individual matings become more costly to males. Thus, a selective advantage should accrue to those males who successfully discriminate among females of differing reproductive value and mate with females of greatest reproductive value.

In contrast, the strong links between age, physical attractiveness, and reproductive value should not hold for males. Age does not provide a strong cue to male's ability to fertilize eggs, so females need not place as much value on the physical appearance cues that correlate with age. These sex differences in the importance of physical appearance cues as indicators of reproductive capability lead to the second prediction.

Prediction 2: Males, more than females, will value physical appearance in potential mates because appearance in females, especially what is considered attractive, correlates strongly with age and health, which provide powerful cues to reproductive value.

The following corollary predictions are made: (a) judgments of female physical attractiveness will correspond in females closely to the age of maximum reproductive value or fertility, which peak in the mid-teens and early 20s, respectively, and drop off sharply in the late 30s; (b) because male reproductive value is not similarly age linked, judgments of male physical attractiveness will not show the sharp decline in the late 30s; (c) holding age constant, females possessing characteristics that are associated with older age (e.g., wrinkles, skin spots, and perhaps small visible portion of eyes, thin lips, and facial hair) and poorer health (e.g., jaundiced eyes, blotchy skin, poor complexion) will be considered less attractive; and (d) males will value physical attractiveness in potential mates more than will females.

The essential features of Prediction 2 are shown graphically in Fig. 14.1. Four types of relations are depicted in this figure. First are the hypothesized relations among the cues listed down the center column (A). In particular, the physical features (e.g., full lips, clear skin) are hypothesized to be positively correlated with age and health. Second, male standards of attractiveness are hypothesized to have evolved to correlate with these cues (B) because of their presumed correlations with female reproductive capability (C). Finally, male evaluations of female attractiveness are hypothesized to correlate directly with female reproductive value (D). All hypothesized links are probabilistic because phenotypic characteristics rarely are invariantly diagnostic of qualities such as age, health, and reproductive value.

Prediction 3: Because males and females impose different mate selection criteria, their "market value" will be based on different characteristics; cross-character assortment (Buss, 1985) will occur between attractive females and high-resource males.

The specific corollaries of this hypothesis are: (a) high-status males will be married to more attractive females than will lower-status males, and (b) hypergyny (the tendency for females to marry upward in socioeconomic status) will be stronger for physically attractive females than for less attractive females.

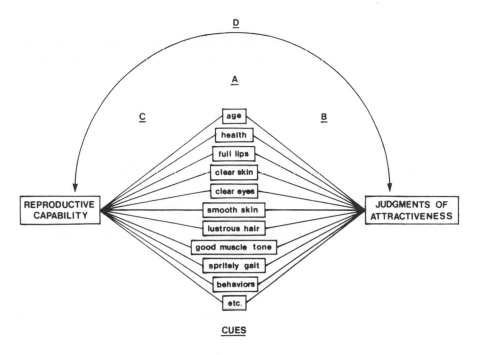

A = Relations between cues, especially between physical cues and age and health.

B = Relations between cues and judgments of female attractiveness.

C = Relations between cues and reproductive capability.

D = Relation between judgments of attractiveness and female reproductive capability.

FIGURE 14.1. Hypothesized links between female attractiveness, cues, and reproductive capability. (An application of Brunswik's (1943) lens model.)

These hypothesized sex differences in mate election criteria must be qualified in several important respects. Most important is that they are predictions about *relative* sex differences, other things being equal. In circumstances where females can provide many material resources and where male reproductive success can be enhanced by acquiring those females and resources, males may be expected to favor resource-holding females.

Similarly, there are conditions that favor female valuation of male physical attractiveness and relative youth. Physical attractiveness in both sexes, for example, may signal low parasite load (Hamilton, 1986) and thus may be favored by both sexes. And males who are *too* old may be poor protectors and providers. *Ceteris paribus,* however, female youth and beauty provide strong cues to female reproductive value and are hypothesized to be relatively more valued by males. *Ceteris paribus,* male characteristics that signal possession or likely acquisition of resources provide strong cues for females of male ability to protect and provide for offspring, and hence should be relatively more valued by females.

SEX DIFFERENCES IN MATE SELECTION CRITERIA:
THE FINDINGS

This section presents three sets of findings that are directly relevant to these specific evolutionary predictions: (1) evidence bearing on the greater emphasis by females on criteria associated with resources acquisition; (2) data relevant to the prediction that males place greater emphasis on physical appearance (attractiveness) as a mate selection criterion; and (3) findings relevant to cross-character assortment between male resources and female beauty.

Table 14.1 shows the results of seven studies bearing on sex differences in the valuation of mate selection criteria associated with resource acquisition. Using a simple nomination procedure, Langhorne and Secord (1955) had college students list the characteristics they wanted in a potential mate or marriage partner. Females, more than males, listed the characteristics of getting ahead, high-status profession, good provider, wealth, and enjoyment of working. Using a questionnaire developed in the 1930s, Hill (1945), McGinnis (1958), and Hudson and Henze (1969) found clear sex differences in the criteria of ambition and industriousness, good financial prospect, and favorable social status. More recently, Buss (1985) and Buss and Barnes (1986), using diverse samples of married and unmarried subjects from different geographical regions of the United States, found striking sex differences in emphasis on the criteria of good earning capacity, ambitious and career oriented, and possession of a college or professional degree. All studies showed greater valuation among females expressed for mate criteria closely linked with resource acquisition.

Table 14.1 also summarizes results from seven studies bearing on the mate criteria related to physical appearance. Using somewhat different procedures, all studies across these decades showed the same large sex difference: males placed greater importance on the mate criterion of physical attractiveness, whether this is worded as good looking, good looks, physically attractive, or physical attractiveness. (Buss, 1985; Buss & Barnes, 1986; Hill, 1945; Hudson & Henze, 1969; Langhorne & Secord, 1955; McGinnis, 1958). This sex difference does not appear to be a transient generational phenomenon, and the magnitude of this sex difference does not appear to have changed over the past 40 years.

Documentation of large and consistent sex differences in mate selection criteria is an important first step in testing the specific evolutionary predictions outlined above. The findings are so consistent across studies that they qualify as among the most robust and consistently replicated psychological findings that have been documented across several generations. Symons (1979) emphasizes

TABLE 14.1
Summary Findings of Sex Differences in Mate Selection Criteria

Authors	Year	Sample Size	Method	Females Value More	Males Value More
Hill	1945	600	ratings	ambition & industrious; good financial prospect	good looking
Langhorne & Secord	1955	5000	nominations	getting ahead; ambitious; enjoys work; high-status profession; good provider; wealth	physical attractiveness
McGinnis	1958	120	ratings	ambition & industrious; favorable social status; good financial prospect	good looks
Hudson & Henze	1969	566	ratings	ambition & industrious; favorable social status; good financial prospect	good looks
Buss	1985	162	rankings	good earning capacity	physical attractiveness
Buss & Barnes[a]	1986	186	ratings	good earning capacity; ambitious & career-oriented	good looking physically attractive
Buss & Barnes	1986	100	rankings	good earning capacity	physically attractive

[a]This sample was composed of married couples between the ages of 20 and 42.

that it is precisely in this domain—that of values and desires—that evolutionary predictions will carry the greatest force. But values and desires are only important, from an evolutionary perspective, if they had or still have clear reproductive consequences, which implies a behavioral medium. From this perspective, a crucial research task is to examine whether expressed sex differences in mate selection criteria affect actual mate choice. Since males and females differ in their selection criteria, it follows that they will differ in the characteristics that lead to high "market value." Thus, it can be predicted that similarly valued individuals will become coupled, in this case attractive females with males possessing resources.

Two large-scale studies were found in the sociological literature bearing directly on these links. The first, a cross-sectional study by Taylor and Glenn (1976), correlated physical attractiveness of females with the occupational prestige of their husbands. For different groups, the correlations were all positive and ranged between $+.23$ and $+.37$. These correlations, although not strikingly large, should probably be viewed as lower-bound estimates because only a single (female) rater was used to assess physical attractiveness. Unreliability of attractiveness ratings would seriously attenuate the obtained correlations. Unfortunately, correction for attenuation is not possible since no reliability estimates were made on the attractiveness ratings. Obtained correlations, however, present at least suggestive evidence that attractive females become mated with males acquiring resources.

Because cross-sectional studies carry certain methodological constraints, longitudinal studies provide a better base from which to test the hypothesized female attractiveness-male resource link. Such a study was conducted by Elder (1969) as part of a broader longitudinal study at the Institute of Human Development in Berkeley, California. Physical attractiveness ratings were made of then unmarried females during adolescence by staff members, with interrater reliabilities above $+.90$. This sample was followed up in adulthood subsequent to marriage, and the occupational status of the acquired husbands was assessed.

Results were examined separately for working class and middle class females. The correlations between female attractiveness and husband's occupational status was $+.46$ for females with working class backgrounds, and $+.35$ for females of middle class backgrounds, statistically significant in both cases. For the sample as a whole, female attractiveness was more strongly correlated with husband's status ($+.43$) than were the female variables of class origin ($r = +.27$) or IQ ($r = +.14$). Thus, attractiveness appears to be an important path to upward mobility for females, and males with high occupational status appear capable of obtaining attractive wives.

Together, these studies provide suggestive evidence that the sex differences in mate selection criteria are enacted in actual marital choices. Males possessing resources and females who are physically attractive are able to command one another in the marriage market. These data suggest that sex differences in mate choice criteria can affect actual choice of a mate, although prospective studies that assess both expressed preferences and subsequent mate choice are needed to corroborate this link.

The next logical question is: Are males who chose attractive females, and females who choose males with greater resources, currently more reproductively successful? There is some evidence, contrary to popular beliefs, that men with higher incomes have wives with more offspring (Daly & Wilson, 1983, pp. 333–334). However, two types of data are still lacking: (1) data on male reproductive success that includes extramarital offspring, and (2) data on reproductive variation associated with variation in female physical attractiveness. Empirical data on these issues are needed to differentiate between the hypothesis that psychological preferences are currently relevant to reproductive success, and the hypothesis that such sex differentiated preferences represent reproductively irrelevant residues that were adaptive only in our evolutionary past.

It is important to place these data sets within a broader interpretive context. They are clearly limited, foremost by the single culture within which the data were collected. Cross-cultural studies are needed to gauge the generality of these sex differences, and such studies are currently underway (Buss, in progress). A second important qualification is that the present framework undoubtedly oversimplies the complex processes that contribute to mate selection. Characteristics other than female attractiveness and male resources are clearly crucial (e.g., kindness, intelligence). Neither earning power nor attractiveness emerge as the most important criteria for either sex (Buss & Barnes, 1986), even though these are the characteristics that show the largest sex differences in preferences. A third qualification is that, in spite of significant sex differences in selection criteria, there is considerable overlap in the preference distributions of males and females. And although mean differences between the sexes have been emphasized here, individual variation within each sex remains an important topic for study (see Buss & Barnes, 1986).

With these qualifications in mind, the data support three specific predictions derived from evolutionary considerations: (1) females, more than males, value and desire mates with resources and resource acquisition potential; (2) males, more than females, value and desire mates who are physically attractive; and as a consequence (3) physically attractive females tend to marry high-status males who have access to resources.

These basic findings must be considered within the broader network of relations that must hold if an evolutionary interpretation of sex differences in mate selection criteria is tenable. Because alternative evolutionary interpretations are easy to generate and difficult to differentially falsify, it is crucial to specify conditions for falsification. If any of the following testable results obtains, the specific evolutionary hypothesis concerning male preference for female attractiveness would be seriously jeopardized:

1. If the standards of female beauty do not correspond closely to the age at which reproductive value or fertility is the highest;

2. if males do not prefer females who are in the age range for which their reproductive capability is the highest;

3. if the cues to female beauty (e.g., smooth skin, clear eyes, full lips, luxuriant hair) do not correlate with female health, age, and reproductive value;

4. holding age constant, if female characteristics that are associated with

older age (e.g., stressed skin, midbody bulge, diminished lips, gray hair) are not viewed as less attractive than those associated with youth.

Data supporting any of these empirical statements would weaken the evolutionary hypothesis based on female appearance and reproductive value.

DISCUSSION AND SPECULATION

I have argued that psychological phenomena closely entwined with reproduction should be most amenable to hypotheses anchored in evolutionary theory. Based on Darwin's theory of sexual selection, on Trivers' theory of the links between parental investment and sexual selection, and finally on Symons' account of human sexuality, clear predictions can be derived about the different mate selection criteria imposed by males and females. Females, typically showing large parental investment and biological constraints on number of offspring, should select mates most capable of investing resources in their children. Males, typically investing less in offspring but being limited in access to reproductively capable females, should seek in females those qualities closely correlated with reproductive value or fertility. In humans, this can be reduced largely to valuation of the correlated features of earning power, status, and ambition in males and physical attractiveness as a surrogate for age, health, and reproductive value in females. The data show strongly that males and females differentially value these attributes in potential mates. Furthermore, attractive females and high-status males appear to command one another on the marriage market.

It is interesting to turn the issue around and speculate about what would happen if males expressed no preference for physical appearance cues that correlate with female reproductive capability, and instead directed their mating efforts randomly. Some males would, by chance variation, choose females outside reproductive age, and these males would become no one's ancestors (Thornhill & Thornhill, 1983). Given a random distribution of physical attribute preferences, if such variation had even a slight basis in genetic variation, then over time male preferences for physical correlates of age, health, and hence reproductive value would be likely to evolve. The same logic applies to female preference for males with resource acquisition potential, although conversion of resources into gene copies requires a larger number of intermediate causal links. Given the powerful reproductive consequences that follow from selecting an appropriate mate, it would be surprising if strong mate preferences had not evolved.

This chapter has focused primarily on one component of Darwin's sexual selection, that of sex differences in mate selection criteria. It is useful to broaden the discussion to examine the links between mate choice and intrasexual competition. These two components of sexual selection can be regarded as interlocking and mutually dependent forces. Males can be expected to compete with one another to embody precisely those attributes on which females base their choice. And females can be expected to compete with one another along criteria imposed by males. Thus, male and female mate selection criteria can drive intrasexual competition. This leads to another set of specific predictions, about which much anecdotal, but little empirical data seem to exist (but see Alexander, 1979; Chagnon & Irons, 1979; Thornhill & Thornhill, 1983): (1) males, more than females, will compete with one another for access to resources (e.g., high paying jobs, prestige, wealth), and will diminish each other's resource acquisition where possible (barring nepotism, reciprocal altruism, and mutually beneficial cooperation); (2) females, more than males, will try to enhance their own appearance, especially along youthful and healthful lines, relative to the appearance of other female competitors.

These predictions lead to the suggestion that males not only compete directly for reproductively capable females, but also that they compete among each other for resources and status that ultimately increase the probability of gaining access to such females. Status and resources are correlated qualities, and elevation in one generally leads to elevation in the other. Acquisition of valuable resources generally elevates status, which in turn leads to more resources.

Interestingly, status and resource holdings, like female reproductive value, often can not be evaluated directly, but instead must be inferred from correlated cues. In humans, the ornamentation adorning persons and their places often is used for this evaluative purpose. Low (1979) suggests that ornaments often function as signals to both sexes of (1) genetic ability to produce robust and successful offspring, and (2) abundance of resources that could be directed toward parental investment. Although speculative, this leads to the hypothesis that males seek attractive females not simply for the *direct* reproductive purposes they could serve. Attractive females also could function as male ornamentation that signals status and fitness to same-sex competitors and to additional potential mates

If these highly speculative notions about attractive females as male ornamentation have any merit, they suggest that there are two evolutionary forces operating in the same direction. Attractiveness in females is valued by males not only for its *direct* reproductive value, but also for the auxiliary reproductive value gained through the acquisition of status-signifying ornamentation. Langhorne and Secord (1955) present suggestive evidence that males are particularly concerned about the impression that a prospective mate would make on their business colleagues and friends, while females tend not to express these concerns. Future studies that confirm this sex difference would support the ornamentation hypothesis.

A network of relations has been hypothesized that starts with sex differences in mate criteria, and moves to a theory of female beauty, to some hypotheses about intrasexual competition, and finally to some speculations about status and ornamentation. Only a few links in the network, such as the sex differences in expressed mate selection criteria and the upward mobility of attractive females, have received empirical attention. Some links in the network will undoubtedly require revision or modification as the precise nature of the proximate and distal connections emerge empirically. Direct research efforts must now be directed toward these intricate links between status, beauty, selection, competition, and reproduction.

ACKNOWLEDGMENTS

The author thanks the following individuals for insightful comments on earlier drafts of this chapter: Kenneth H. Craik, Charles Crawford, Warren Holmes, Anne McGuire, Dan Ozer, Carolyn Phinney, Barb Smuts, Bob Smuts, Don Symons, Nancy Thornhill, and Randy Thornhill.

REFERENCES

Alexander, R. D. (1979). *Darwinism and human affairs.* Seattle: University of Washington Press.

Barron, F. (1963). *Creativity and psychological health.* New York: Van Nostrand.

Bateman, A. J. (1948). Intra-sexual selection in *Drosophila. Heredity, 2,* 349–368.

Brunswik, E. (1943). Organismic achievement and environmental probability. *Psychological Review, 50,* 255–272.

Buss, D. M. (1984). Evolutionary biology and personality psychology: Toward a conception of human nature and individual differences. *American Psychologist, 39,* 1135–1147.

Buss, D. M. (1985). Human mate selection. *American Scientist, 73,* 47–51.

Buss, D. M. (1986). Can social science be anchored in evolutionary biology? Four problems and a strategic solution. *Revue Europeene des Sciences Sociales, 24,* 41–50.

Buss, D. M. (in progress). *The International Mate Selection Project (IMSP).*

Buss, D. M., & Barnes, M. F. (1986). Preferences in human mate selection. *Journal of Personality and Social Psychology, 50,* 559–570.

Calder, C. (1967). Breeding behavior of the Roadrunner, *Geococcyx californianus. Aux. 84.,* 597–598.

Campbell, D. T. (1975). On the conflicts between biological and social evolution and between psychology and moral tradition. *American Psychologist, 30,* 1103–1126.

Caplan, A. L. (Ed.). (1978). *The sociobiology debate.* New York: Harper & Row.

Chagnon, N. A., & Irons, W. (Eds.). (1979). *Evolutionary biology and human social behavior.* North Scituate, MA: Duxbury Press.

Cunningham, M. R. (1981). Sociobiology as a supplementary paradigm for social psychological research. In L. Wheeler (Ed.), *Review of personality and social psychology* (pp. 69–106). Beverly Hills, CA: Sage.

Daly, M., & Wilson, M. (1983). *Sex, evolution, and behavior.* Boston: Willard Grant Press.

Darwin, C. (1859). *On the origin of the species by means of natural selection, or, preservation of favoured races in the struggle for life.* London, England: Murray.

Darwin, C. (1871). *The descent of man and selection in relation to sex.* London, England: Murray.

Elder, G. H., Jr. (1969). Appearance and education in marriage mobility. *American Sociological Review, 34,* 519–533.

Fisher, R. A. (1930). *The genetical theory of natural selection.* Oxford: Clarendon Press.

Freedman, D. G. (1979). *Human sociobiology: A holistic approach*. New York: Free Press.

Halliday, T. R. (1978). Sexual selection and mate choice. In J. R. Krebs & N. B. Davies (Eds.), *Behavioral ecology: An evolutionary approach* (pp. 180–213). Oxford: Blackwell Scientific Publications.

Hamilton, W. D. (1964). The genetical evolution of social behavior. *Journal of Theoretical Biology, 7*, 1–52.

Hamilton, W. D. (1986, April 18). *Personal communication*.

Hill, R. (1945). Campus values in mate selection. *Journal of Home Economics, 37*, 554–558.

Hudson, J. W., & Henze, L. F. (1969). Campus values in mate selection: A replication. *Journal of Marriage and the Family, 31*, 772–775.

Lack, D. (1940). Pair-formation in birds. *Condor, 42*, 269–286.

Langhorne, M. C., & Secord, P. F. (1955). Variations in marital needs with age, sex, marital status, and regional location. *Journal of Social Psychology, 41*, 19–37.

Low, B. S. (1979). Sexual selection and human ornamentation. In N. A. Chagnon & W. Irons (Eds.), *Evolutionary biology and human social behavior: An anthropological perspective* (pp. 462–487). North Scituate, MA: Duxbury.

Mayr, E. (1972). Sexual selection and natural selection. In B. Campbell (Ed.), *Sexual selection and the descent of man: 1871–1971* (pp. 87–104). Chicago: Aldine.

McGinnis, R. (1958). Campus values in mate selection. *Social Forces, 36*, 368–373.

Rushton, J. P. (1984a). Sociobiology: Towards a theory of individuals and group differences in personality and social behavior. In J. R. Royce & L. P. Mos (Eds.), *Annals of theoretical psychology, Vol. 2*. New York: Plenum Press.

Rushton, J. P. (1984b). Genetic similarity theory: Beyond kin selection. *Behavior Genetics, 14*, 179–193.

Symons, D. (1979). *The evolution of human sexuality*. New York: Oxford University Press.

Symons, D. (1980). Precis of *The Evolution of Human Sexuality*. *The Behavioral and Brain Sciences, 3*, 171–181.

Symons, D. (in press). The evolutionary approach: Can Darwin's view of life shed light on human sexuality? In J. Geer & W. O'Donohue (Eds.), *Theories and paradigms in human sexuality*. New York: Plenum Press.

Taylor, P. A., & Glenn, N. D. (1976). The utility of education and attractiveness for females' status attainment through marriage. *American Sociological Review, 41*, 484–498.

Thornhill, R., & Thornhill, N. W. (1983). Human rape: An evolutionary perspective. *Ethology and Sociobiology, 4*, 63–99.

Trivers, R. L. (1972). Parental investment and sexual selection. In B. Campbell (Ed.), *Sexual selection and the descent of man: 1871–1971*. Chicago: Aldine.

Willerman, L. (1979). *The psychology of individual and group differences*. San Francisco: Freeman.

Williams, G. C. (1966). *Adaptation and natural selection: A critique of some current evolutionary thought*. New Jersey: Princeton University Press.

15 Incest Taboos and Avoidance: Some African Applications

Pierre L. van den Berghe
University of Washington

A purely cultural explanation of inbreeding avoidance is no longer tenable in the face of a large body of evidence that many other animals, including nonhuman primates (who are presumably cultureless), have low mating frequencies between close kin. The primate evidence is especially striking (Fedigan, 1982; Itoigawa et al., 1981; Sade, 1968; van Lawick-Goodall, 1971). Both under wild or semiwild, and under experimental conditions, matings between primate mothers and sons, and indeed other familiar close kin are exceptional. Fedigan (1982) reports, for example, that "out of a total of more than 1000 matings, we have never observed a mother-son copulation, only one brother-sister mating, and one grandmother-grandson mating" in an isolated troop of Japanese macaques where all the males remain in their natal troop and thus have ample opportunity for inbreeding.

The human evidence on inbreeding avoidance is voluminous, and several extensive and recent reviews and critical discussions of it are readily available, obviating the need for repetition here (Bixler, 1981; Shepher, 1983; Thornhill & Thornhill, this volume, van den Berghe, 1983). Perhaps the safest conclusion one can draw from a cross-cultural examination of human inbreeding avoidance is that incest behavior and other cultural norms of sexual behavior can only be fully understood as operating within the matrix of the human reproductive system, which, in turn, evolved by natural as well as by cultural selection. Indeed, any attempt to dissociate culture from nature founders on the unshakable reality that man is both a cultural and a natural animal.

The aim of this paper is fairly narrow, namely to shed light on the old and hotly debated questions of the basis of incest taboos; their relationship, if any, to biological predispositions to avoid inbreeding; and the reasons for cross-cultural variability in the strength of incest taboos. Two towering historical protagonists still cast their shadow on practically every discussion of these topics: Freud (1950, first published in 1913) and Westermarck (1891).

In *The Red Lamp of Incest,* Robin Fox (1980) valiantly attempts an at least partial rehabilitation of Freud's notion of the incest taboo.[1] For Freud, incest taboos are necessary to counteract a natural sexual attraction within the nuclear family. On the face of it, Freud's view of incest seems to contradict Edward Westermarck's (1891) notion that close childhood association dulls sexual attraction. Much evidence suggests that, among both humans and other species, close intimacy in early development is the proximate evolutionary mechanism making for avoidance of close inbreeding among warm-blooded vertebrates with heavy parental investment (Bischof, 1975; Bixler, 1981; Packer, 1979; Shepher, 1971, 1983; van den Berghe, 1983; Wolf and Huang, 1980).

Fox (1980) suggests that perhaps Freud and Westermarck could be reconciled, in that Westermarck hit on the more general phenomenon, while Freud dealt with the special case. If it is indeed close early childhood association (apparently between ages 2 and 6) which breeds nonbreeding, and if the "immunizing" kind of contact includes nudity, intimate touching, cuddling and exploratory sex play, as seems to be the case, then those cultures that are sexually permissive (especially of prepubertal sexuality), and that rear boys and girls together are the ones that least *need* incest taboos. Conversely, sexually repressive, sex-segregated societies, which thereby interfere with "natural immunity" to incest, will resort to strong taboos backed up by punitive sanctions to prevent incest.

In short, sexually permissive, relaxed, unsegregated societies foster natural immunity to incest through intimate childhood association between siblings and parents and offspring of opposite sex, and therefore need not taboo and punish that which is unlikely to occur. Repressive, segregated cultures, by leaving open the possibility of sexual attraction between close kin through lack of childhood intimacy, have to fall back on strong taboos and heavy sanctions. It is presumably the latter kind of culture in which Freud grew and which led him to his formulation. From the special case of puritanical turn-of-the-century Vienna, he erected his general theory of the Oedipus complex.

Here I propose to subject the Fox hypothesis to at least a preliminary test based on African data. For this purpose, I picked four contrasting societies, with the full realization that such a small, nonrandom sample does not constitute definitive proof.

---

[1]For another attempt to reconcile Freud and Westermarck on incest, see Spain (1984). It also incorporates a critique of van den Berghe (1983).

TALLENSI

The Tallensi of Northern Ghana, studied by Meyer Fortes, have exogamous patriclans. All references that follow are to Fortes' 1949 classic, *The Web of Kinship Among the Tallensi*. Fortes, like many anthropologists extends the label "incest" to cover all rules of exogamy, and all prohibitions against sex with affines, but he is a good enough ethnographer to note that "the Tallensi have no name for it," and, furthermore, that they distinguish clearly between having sex with wives of agnates which they condemn because it disrupts relations between kinsmen in the lineage, and sex between close kin which they regard as abnormal behavior.

Fortes (1949) writes:

> The feeling of close, personal intimacy in the relationship of uterine kin is best brought out in the native attitude about sexual relations between *saaret*. It is incestuous if the couple knows they are *saaret*, however distant the uterine connection. It is like incest between own brother and sister. . . . Tallensi think of it with disgust rather than horror. Sexual desire for a known *soog* relative is so utterly inconsistent with the general attitude of uterine kin toward each other that it is unthinkable in a decent person. It is a taboo which normal persons take for granted. There are no ritual or jural sanctions against incest with a *soog*, and Tallensi would say there is no need for them. At no point are the relations of uterine kin subject to sanctions: "I will not refuse him, I will not deny him anything," says the native of a *soog*, thinking of this as an axiomatic feature of *soog* kinship."(p.38)

In contrast, sex with wives of agnates threatens lineage solidarity, and relations between kinsmen. Fortes writes that there is a strong (and graduated) prohibition of sexual relations with wives of agnates. It is strongest with a daughter-in-law.

> For a man to have sexual relations with, or even sit on the same mat as, his daughter-in-law is a sin of the first magnitude. . . . that is an extreme taboo say the natives, with every sign of repugnance. It is a sin that can never be wholly atoned for. Sooner or later the culprits will be slain by the ancestor spirits, for, like incest with a father's wife of which it is the counterpart, it destroys irreparably the moral and religious bonds of the father and son.(p.96)

Between distant agnates, the prohibition is mitigated. Says Fortes:

> By contrast, sex relations with the wife of a member of the same lineage or clan outside the range of the inner lineage is a wrong. It is not incest, but the most reprehensible form of adultery. It does not bear the same moral stigma as the corresponding form of incest, nor does it carry religious penalties for the adulterer. (p. 116)

The rationale for this graduated prohibition is clearly based on lineage solidarity, not simply in Fortes' "etic" categories, but in "emic" terms as well. Fortes states:

> The Tallensi explain that such acts are so severely reprobated because they cause deep and irreconcilable "enmity' (*diun*) between father and son, brother and brother, and this is a mortal blow to the solidarity of the family and the lineage. They arouse the wrath of the ancestors. If the injured father, brother, or son does not bring the matter up before the elders of his medial lineage or maximal lineage, he will be struck down by the ancestors. If he does, he must be ritually reconciled with his offending son, brother, or father. But in spite of such a formal reconciliation, "the enmity remains within." (p. 113)

All this is in sharp contrast with sex between kin. In fact, one might well argue that the only connections between the two are the fact of sexual intercourse and the label of "incest" applied to both by Fortes. Incest between close kin, especially between uterine siblings and between father and daughter, is considered *abnormal,* but *less reprehensible* than with the wife of an agnate. Says Fortes:

> We can see, now, why sexual relations with a sister or a daughter are so much less reprehensible than incest with a wife of the lineage. Incest with a sister or daughter does not destroy the solidarity of the males of the nuclear lineage for it does not imply rivalry between them. . . .
> The gratification of lust, contemptible as it is in these circumstances, does not shatter the moral unity or injure the common interests of the lineage as does the usurpation of procreative rights over a wife. It does not, like the latter, destroy a father's authority over his son or a son's filial piety toward his father; for though it is a perversion of the social role of father or brother, it is not a usurpation of critical rights."(p.114)

As with the prohibition against agnates' wives, prohibition against agnates are graduated by closeness of relationship. Fortes writes:

> What has been said of the nuclear lineage applies in only slightly lesser degree to the inner lineage - the widest corporate unit responsibly concerned with the marriages of its members. Beyond the range of the inner lineage but within that of the medial lineage there is some doubt as to whether intercourse with a woman member is incestuous or not. Feeling varies according to the span of the unit and the number of segments it includes. Beyond the range of the medial lineage it is not uncommon for men to have affairs with women of their own maximal lineage or clan. The attitude towards incest with a sister or daughter is stretched to the point of complete tolerance. Sexual relations with a distant clan-sister do not clash with the habits, morals, and organization of family life nor with those of lineage or clan relationships. Indeed, the structure of the society practically compels a man who

TABLE 15.1
Summary of Evidence on Sex and Incest Taboos
in Four African Societies

Society and Location	Attitudes to Sex and Child-Rearing Practices	Attitudes to Incest
Tallensi (Northern Ghana)	Sex a "normal and natural appetite." Sex play tolerated in children. Few sexual prohibitions. Brother and sister are initimate childhood associates.	Incest is abnormal behavior, but neither a crime nor a sin. No penal sanctions against it. No special word for it.
Ashanti (Central Ghana)	Many strong sexual taboos with harsh punishments (e.g. death penalty for intercourse during menstruation). Harsh, repressive treatment of children past infancy. Brothers and sisters separated after weaning.	A heinous crime traditionally punishable by death or expulsion from clan (after British rule, by heavy fine and ostracism).
Ibo (South-Eastern Nigeria)	Many sexual taboos (e.g., on menstruation, post-partum). Emphasis on premarital virginity. Clitoridectomy. Brothers and sisters segregated after 5. Sex play repressed. Masturbation punished.	Incest an abomination. Contaminates the earth. Death penalty.
Zande (Southern Sudan and North-Eastern Zaire)	Sexually permissive. Incest between agnatic half-siblings permitted in nobility. Much adultery. Premarital sex. Open homosexuality. Bawdy sexual bantering. Brothers and sisters intimate until 6. No repression of sex play.	Permitted between half siblings and fathers and daughters in aristocracy. Among commoners, elicits "feelings of shame," but no strong sanctions against it.

357

wants a lover to seek for one among his own clanswomen. Any woman not genealogically related to him is someone he is allowed to marry. His sexual interest in her is an interest in her for the sake of offspring. The Tallensi attach so much importance to marriage that they think it absurd and despicable for a man to desire only a sexual liaison with a woman he can legitimately marry. . . .

A distant clanswoman is in a different position. One cannot marry her, but at the same time she is not so closely identified with one or so familiar as a sister. She is not felt to belong to oneself as one's sister or daughter is. Her genealogical and social identification with one's clan seems to be merely a formal usage and this is enhanced by the knowledge that she will marry out. She is the unmarriageable stranger. One can desire her and enjoy her for sexual gratification without an interest in her reproductive powers and without prejudice to her later legitimate marriage. (pp. 114-115)

Let us summarize the Tallensi evidence. In our terms (and I would suggest, in the Tallensi's own view), prohibition against wives of agnates is not incest at all, but protection of lineage solidarity, and of individual rights of husbands over the reproductive powers of their wives. Adultery with the wife of a kinsman is much worse than adultery with a nonaffine, because it threatens the solidarity of agnates on which lineage organization rests. Logically, the closer the kinship is, the worse the threat. The Tallensi do recognize, however, that sexual attraction to agnates' wives is within the range of normalcy, and does occur, reprehensible though it is. True incest, by contrast, is regarded as abnormal. Fortes states:

Tallensi explain that a normal man does not even have sexual desire for a sister or a daughter. This is the standard, conscious, sexual attitude to a sister and it is in keeping with the conscious attitude about incest with a sister or daughter. Such an act is spoken of as tabooed, but it is neither a crime or a sin. It is simply despicable conduct that the culprits ought to be ashamed of as unworthy of grown persons. Even children talk of copulation with a sibling as something beneath contempt.

Incest with one's own mother the natives regard as a thing of such monstrous iniquity that it is ridiculous to conceive of anyone who is not mentally deranged committing it. Incest with a father's wife, other than one's own mother, or a brother's or son's wife is almost as heinous a sin and is regarded with little less horror; but it is known to happen sometimes. (pp.111-112)

We also know that Tallensi incest taboos (in the restricted sense) are relatively mild. There is no special word for it; it is not explicitly taught; and there are not sanctions against infringement other than contempt and ridicule. In Fortes' words:

Incest occurs occasionally in every Tale community. Such an act soon leaks out, and is remembered with contempt for many years. . . .

There are no penal sanctions against any form of incest, nor are the culprits believed to be subject to automatic mystical retribution. Incest is so incompatible with the pattern of co-operation and the structure of disciplinary and affective relations in the family that this itself serves to banish it from the field of family relationships. Though incest taboos are never deliberately inculcated, the habits, attitudes, and organization of family life (to put the native expressions into sociological language) create internal barriers against incest, in the normal person. This applies particularly to incest with a sister or daughter, whether it is a single impulsive act or a more lasting liaison. (p.111)

Our theory would predict that such relatively mild incest taboos would be associated with a relaxed attitude toward sex, relative absence of sex segregation during childhood, permissiveness of sex play among children, and intimacy between siblings of the opposite sex. All these conditions are present among the Tallensi. Of general sexual attitudes, Fortes writes:

> . . . the Tallensi have a thoroughly matter of fact attitude about sex. They regard sex as a normal and natural appetite. Any aspect of the generative function can be discussed without circumlocution in the presence of men, women or children. . . . The Tallensi take it for granted that children will indulge in sex play, and attach no value to prenuptial chastity. (p. 100)
> Incidentally, there are no taboos on conversation on sex matters among the Tallensi. Men, women and children are all outspoken about sexual matters, though young women are apt to use euphemisms and to talk more circumspectly than men. Some men also say that it is embarrassing to talk about sexual subjects in front of young wives or female relatives-in-law. But no native hesitates to discuss these subjects in the presence of his sister. (p. 251)

Not only is sex play widely tolerated in young children, but sexual partners are typically close agnates. Fortes states:

> . . . it is common knowledge that up to the age of about 8 or 9 boys often try to have sexual intercourse with a small girl playmate in their play and for the most part playmates are close lineage siblings. Adults reprove the children if they discover them in this kind of play, but dismiss it as due to childish irresponsibility. This indeed, is the essence of the general attitude toward incest with a sister or daughter. It is disreputable, because it does not conform to the accepted standards of responsible adult conduct. (p.112)
> . . . the natives are the first to point out that sexual play in childhood generally begin with a classificatory sibling. Family play is a regular thing in the under-9 play-groups; and the final realistic touch is for the "husband" and "wife" to pretend to have coitus. This is common knowledge, and adults laugh at it. A standing joke is to tease a small boy about his so-called sweethearts. As we have seen, Tallensi say that small children "have no sense," and therefore it is not a breach of propriety or morals for them to play at coitus with a sibling. Every man I questioned on the subject told me, with a grin of amusement, that his first sweetheart was a "sister," sometimes of the same extended family, more often of the

same inner or medial lineage. "We were very small and didn't know better," they said.(p.250)

To be sure, the Tallensi, draw the line in their permissiveness of sex play at siblings, yet, it is clear that even siblings are raised in such intimacy, that sex play between them does occur (Fortes, 1949):

> But Tallensi maintain stoutly that even small boys of 6 or 7 do not play at coitus with their *soog* sisters or half-sisters. There are exceptions, of course, they readily admit. There are stupid children, precocious children, and badly brought up children. Among such children instances of brothers copulating with sisters are bound to occur. It has been known to happen even with adolescents, who are presumed to "have sense." If it is found out, the culprits are given a severe thrashing and are taunted for months afterwards by their fellows.

Of the brother-sister relationship, especially between full sibs, Fortes stresses its closeness and intimacy:

> These ties of mutual affection and devotion between *soog* siblings last throughout list and are extended to their children too. One sees this most dramatically in the grief people show, and especially women, over the death of a *soog* sibling. Tallensi say that very often the loss of a full brother is a greater shock to a woman than the death of her husband. A husband is replaceable, a full brother not, they add. (pp. 250–251)

Though unlikely to have read Westermarck, the Tallensi give a similar interpretation of the relationship between siblings: They are *not* sexually attracted toward each other *because* they have been reared so closely and intimately together. It is not punishment which prevents sex between siblings, states Fortes:

> It is because of the intimacy, the closeness to each other in daily life, of brother and sister. Children do not need to be told that it is wrong to copulate with a sibling of the same joint family; they know it themselves. And, in fact, children from the age of 6 or 7 and upwards always say, with an expression of disgust, that sexual play with one's own siblings is wrong. Moreover, though they are not taught it as an avoidance, they are well aware of the conventional attitudes on the subject from listening to adult conversation. (p.251)

And again:

> As has been previously mentioned, Tallensi do not designate incest between brother and sister as sinful. When they say it is forbidden (*kih*), as they sometimes do, they mean it rather in a sense that it is disgraceful, scandalous, and unnatural rather than in the narrower ritual sense. If they are asked why then it is so uncommon, considering the many opportunities and temptations that surely offer, they explain

it by the intimacy of siblings in childhood and adolescence. They deny that the temptation exists. "Look," said Sinkawol, arguing this point with me, "my sister, is she not marriageable? And here am I, however attractive she is, I do not even notice it; I am never aware that she has a vagina; she is just my sister and someone will one day come and marry her and I will give her to him and get my cows. You and your sister grow up together, you quarrel and make it up, how can you desire to have intercourse with ther?" This is a stock argument with the Tallensi.(p.250)

There we have it: The stock Tallensi argument is that they are not aware that their sisters have vaginas, because they are reared closely together. Their incest taboos are almost gratuitous. Sex play is regarded as normal among young children. It is punished if it persists between siblings beyond age six or so, because it is then regarded as unnatural. Such a view, incidentally is remarkably consistent with the *Kibbutz* and Taiwanese evidence as to the critical age period for the establishment of negative sexual imprinting on close childhood associates.

ASHANTI

A few hundred kilometers south of the Tallensi live the state-organized, matrilineal Ashanti, extensively studied by Rattray, Field, Busia, Fortes and others. They provide an interesting contrast to the Tallensi on the issue of incest. The Ashanti, too, have clan exogamy, and the concept of incest (*mogyadie,* literally "the eating up of one's own blood") extended to all members of the matriclan, but instead of the mild sanctions prevalent among the Tallensi, *mogyadie* traditionally entail the death penalty for both parties. (Fortes, 1950, p. 257; Rattray, 1929, p. 304). In Rattray's words:

Mogyadie: Incest (literally "the eating up of one's own blood") has, in Ashanti, a much wider range of meaning than that word implies in our own language. It included sexual intercourse with anyone of the same blood or clan, however remote the connection, and even cases where it would not be possible to trace direct descent. The bearing of a common clan name was considered as conclusive evidence pointing to the existence of a common female ancestress. Perhaps no other sin was regarded with greater horror among the Ashanti. Both parties to the offense were killed. Had such an act been allowed to pass unpunished, then, in the words of my informants, "hunters would have ceased to kill the animals in the forest, the crops would have refused to bear fruit, children would have ceased to be born, the 'Samanfo (spirits of the dead ancestors) would have been infuriated, the gods would have been angered, *abusua* (clans) would have ceased to exist, and all would have been chaos (*basa basa*) in the world. (p.304)

Rattray goes on to note that despite this "incest" prohibition, the Ashanti practice preferential matrilateral cross-cousin marriage, in the hallowed anthropological tradition of confusing incest avoidance and exogamy. He also mentions that even though the death penalty for incest could not longer be imposed under British rule, it was still punished by a fine of 25 pounds, two sheep, a case of gin and 12 yards of calico.

Rattray (pp. 305–306) also mentions another wider category of sexual offences, known as *atwebenefie* (literally "sex with a vagina near the dwelling house") which included *mogyadie,* but is not limited to it. From the perspective of a male ego, *atwebenefie* prohibits sexual relations with all of the following: an agnatic half-sister, any woman of the matriclan, a father's brother's daughter, a brother's wife, a son's wife, a wife's mother, an uncle's wife, a father's wife, a wife's sister, a fellow guild member's wife, and one's own slave's wife. The penalty for infringement was death or expulsion from the clan. The intent of *atwebenefie* prohibition was clearly to avoid sexual conflict between kin, both uterine and agnatic, and between close neighbors.

From the extensiveness of the prohibitions and the severity of the penalties we would predict a punitive, puritanical and sexually restrictive society, where siblings are sex-segregated early in life. The Ashanti do indeed show these characteristics.

Children are indulgently treated as babies, but harshly treated when older, especially boys. Field (1960) writes:

> But one of the most striking features in the African attitude to the child is the contrast between the lavish affection meted out to infants and toddlers and the harsh disregard which is the lot of most older children. The adored small child has to suffer the trauma of growing into an object of contempt - even in the eyes of its father. "Small boy" is an opprobrious epithet. A child of either sex is still sometimes sent to live with relatives or others to whom the parent is under special obligation and is there made to work virtually as a little slave. A proverbs runs, "It is unpleasant to be a child." Particularly it is unpleasant in the matter of food. Any food which fills the belly is considered good enough for children. (p.28)

A story quoted by Rattray (1929) confirms this stringent treatment of children:

> There is a well-known story in Ashanti of a mother who handed over a bad child to King Kwaku Dua I to be trained. When she returned later to inquire after it, she was informed by the King, "I ordered the executioners to kill the child." "But," exclaimed the mother, "I sent you my child to be trained." "Yes," said the King, "that is how I train children." (pp.13-14

Furthermore, there is evidence that punishment is centered around excretory and sex organs, and functions connected with them. Children just weaned are severely ridiculed for bed wetting, so much so that "sometimes a child who has not a strong *sunsum* (spirit) will die after such ridicule." (Rattray, 1929, p. 12).

Theft by a boy is punished "by having red peppers put up his anus." (Rattray, 1929, p. 12).

As for sexual puritanism, the Ashanti have a remarkably wide range of prohibitions, certainly by coastal West African standards. Rattray (1929, p. 298) tells us that it was considered "murder" for any man (other than the husband) to have intercourse with a pregnant woman, or with a girl before her first menses. Women were considered unclean during their menses and lived in an isolation hut for six days (Busia, 1951, p. 72) Before returning to her house she had to wash all her clothes, utensils and stools in the river. The penalty for intercourse during menstruation was death for both parties (Rattray, 1929, p. 306).

Finally, there was considerable sex segregation of siblings. After weaning, daughters remained with their mothers "to be reared and trained under her more immediate supervision." (Rattray, 1929, p. 16). Boys, however, left their mother's direct supervision after weaning. Rattray states: "A male child will sleep with his father as soon as he ceases to be suckled" (p. 3). Though he does not specify the age further, it was presumably around 2 to 3 years of age, i.e. around the beginning of the probably critical period for negative sexual imprinting. Some boys also went to their mother's brother who, under a matrilineal system, had jural authority over them. In either case, siblings of opposite sex were separated during the critical period during which natural sexual aversion could be developed. Fortes (1950) states that "about half of the children under 15 live with their fathers . . . and the other half live in households presided over by their mothers' brothers" (p. 262). He also states that "only about a third of all married women reside with their husbands." As noted by Fortes (1950), there was considerable "underlying hostility in the sibling relationship" (p. 275), which he attributes to the tensions between a man's feelings for his own children and obligations to his uterine nephews.

IBO

The several million Ibo-speaking people of South Eastern Nigeria belong to a number of largely stateless societies, studied *inter alia* by Green (1964), H. K. Henderson (1980), R. N. Henderson (1966), Meek (1937), and Ottenberg (1968). Most Ibo groups are patrilineal, though the Afikpo Ibo have double descent (Ottenberg, 1968).

Without question, the Ibo fall in the category of the peoples with strong incest taboos. As is common in the literature, lineage exogamy (which is fairly strictly practiced) is treated as an extension of incest avoidance with close kin. From the ethnographic context, it is, once more, evident that the two are not the same. Meek (1937) writes for example, of the Nsukka Ibo:

> The Amokwa kindred might almost be described as a small "clan." It is an
> exogamous unit. . . . It is noteworthy, moreover, that, although intermarriage

between the various extended-families of the kindred is forbidden, it is not an offense if sexual relations occur between two unmarried members of different families of the kindred, provided those families are not too closely related. . . . No deep sense of incest or pollution, therefore, is attached to the idea of marital relations between the extended-families of the Amokwa kindred. But the idea of marital or sexual relations of any kind between members of the same extended-family is utterly abhorrent. (p. 145)

Incest with close kin is both abhorrent and severely punished. Of the Onitsha Ibo, Henderson (1980) writes: "Prohibitions against incest are strong, however, and it is said that 'the touch of the sibling stings'" (p. 300). Meek (1937) concurs: "It was forbidden, and in fact an 'abominable' thing, to have sexual relations with any close relative, and it is said that breaches of this law were almost unknown. If a case did occur both the culprits were killed or sold" (pp. 223–226). Any breech of incest, writes Green (1964) about the Umueke Ibo, "is a contamination of the earth." He continues:

And in the old days the offenders would have been buried alive in the central Agbaja market place. . . . This burying of them would purify and appease Ala. It was maintained that even now if such an offence were known to have taken place people would go secretly at night and cut a hole through the mud wall into the man's house and kill him. He would then be placed at the foot of a palm tree, from which passers-by would imagine him to have fallen to his death. (pp. 155–156)

In sum, lineage exogamy is the rule, but in urban areas like Owerri (Green, 1964) it is said to break down, and the taboo against sexual relations between distant agnates is not nearly as strong as against violations of incest taboos between close kin, which, still today are said to be subject to the death penalty (p. 156)

In keeping with our hypothesis, Ibo society tends to be sexually repressive and sex segregated, at least by West African standards. Aside from prohibitions of incest and exogamy, sex among the Ibo is subject to a number of other taboos. "Menstrual blood is believed to be a source of danger and intercourse during this period is an abomination," writes Henderson (1980, p. 148). There is a postpartum sex taboo of 2 to 3 years' duration as intercourse is supposed to affect the milk and sicken the baby. It was an "abomination" for a woman to conceive before her last child was weaned. (Henderson, 1980, pp. 147, 150, 194; Ottenberg, 1968, p. 181; Meek, 1937, p. 224). Uncircumcized boys were supposed to abstain from sex "as it was believed that intercourse could weaken an uncircumcized boy," says Ottenberg (1968, p. 66). A man is supposed to abstain from sexual relations after certain religious rites (Henderson, 1980, p. 223). Premarital virginity is valued, in a girl, and its loss is regarded as a family humiliation. Virginity is tested by the prospective groom with a white cloth (Henderson,

1980, p. 138). The Owerri Ibo observe abstinence during the planting or harvesting of yams (Okere, 1981, p. 136).

Intercourse between the *Osu* pariah group and the other Ibo is not only taboo but "the idea fills him with horror." (Green, 1964, pp. 24, 158). Owerri Ibo widows are expected to abstain from sex for a year after the death of their husband (Meek, 1937, p. 311). For good measure, girls are clitoridectomized and pregnancy before clitoridectomy among the Afikpo Ibo "was considered a terrible abomination, a disgrace to the major patrilineage. In some cases the girl was killed and her parents' houses destroyed or damaged" says Ottenberg (1968, p. 66).

"Throughout the Ibo speaking area, it is an abomination against the land to have sexual intercourse while lying directly on the earth without at least a mat intervening" writes Henderson (1980, p. 168). In short, many aspects and forms of sex are considered dangerous, polluting or debilitating, and punishments for infractions are severe.

In keeping with our hypothesis, we would expect a puritanical, sex-segregated upbringing. Indeed, this is what we find. First, the postpartum sex taboo tends to create a minimum interval of three years between siblings, who therefore belong to different age sets and have different playmates (Henderson & Henderson, 1966). Second, the general pattern of child rearing is one of close association with the mother during the two to three years of lactation, followed by increasing independence and sex segregation (Henderson & Henderson, 1966).

Henderson (1980) writes:

> There is supposed to be strong affection between brothers and sisters, but a boy is taught to regard his sisters as he would a male and also to view the body of "cross-sex siblings" as "pricking like thorns." Thus sex play within the village is openly disapproved of in the few years before puberty, and definitely forbidden after puberty. (p. 109)

Brother-sister relations are characterized by sexual shame. They sleep together until age 8, but not later. A woman feels "great shame" if she sees her classificatory brother urinating, and, in Owerri, brothers and sisters (even classificatory) may not wash in the same place of the river (Green, 1964, p. 157). A similar taboo applies to father-daughter relations. Fathers and daughters in Umueke may not see each other washing, nor talk of sexual matters. After puberty a daughter will leave her mother's house when her father sleeps there (Green, 1964, p. 157).

While siblings under the age of 8 have some contact with each other, it is clear that sex play is strongly discouraged, increasingly so with age. A weaned child observed by his parents to play with his genitals will be told to stop, and will be teased by older children (Henderson & Henderson, 1966, p. 28). After age 3, masturbation is subject to threats: " 'Stop! The (dead) will come and cut off your penis.' Or the mother may threaten to do it herself.'' (p. 28). Toilet training is rather severe. ''A child of 3½ may be slapped for defecating in the house. After age 3 a child might be whipped for urinating in bed. . .'' By age 4 or 5, enuresis is punished by tying a dead snake around the waist. (Henderson & Henderson, 1966, pp. 27, 37).

Until age 5, ''boys and girls play together relatively free of parental restraint but under the observation of the mothers of associated compounds.'' (Henderson & Henderson, 1966, p. 30). From age 4, boys begin to be drawn into the men's world of the masquerade, from which women are excluded, and which is, in fact, the principal symbolic expression of male superiority and vehicle for deriding women in Ibo society. By age 5 to 7, boys join the *mbekwe* (a mask society), where they are disciplined by ''flogging by the leader, intensive group ridicule and the direct threat of future penis loss.'' (Henderson & Henderson, 1966, p. 31). Around the same age, some sex play make take place between lineage mates, which the parents do not consider serious offences between children are below the age of ''sense,'' but

> ''if parents discover such play they will warn the children to stop, reminding them that ''the body of (cross-sex) sibling pricks (like thorns)!'' Children who do this and are discovered by their comrades fear revelation and beg their playmates not to inform their parents.'' (p. 36).

Also around age 5 to 7, girls are taught sexual propriety and restraints. They are ''strictly warned against sitting or standing in positions which expose their genitalia, a firm rule which rationalizes many of the taboos underlying the sexual division of labour'' (Henderson & Henderson, 1966, p. 36). Girls continue to sleep with their mothers while boys move out onto the verandah of the house (Henderson & Henderson, 1966, p. 37). The closer girls move toward puberty, the more closely watched they are by their mothers ''because her reputation will be stained if the girl's hymen is not intact when she goes to her husband'' (Henderson & Henderson, 1966, p. 36).

The onset of menstruation is a momentous and dramatic event as the Hendersons' account (1966) reveals:

> Onitsha people recall no elaborate initiation processes for girls at the time of puberty, but a girl is expected to be frightened at her first menstruation because mothers never speak about sexuality to their daughters until this time. The girl runs frightened to her mother when her first menstruation begins, and the mother warns strictly against further sexual play, pointing out that premarital pregnancy is an abomination (*alu*) and then places her in strict isolation in a hut near the escape door of the house for the duration of the menstrual period. Menstrual blood is regarded as very dangerous to men and should not be shed in the house.
>
> At the time of puberty and menstruation girls have their heads shaved clean and when the hair grows out it is plaited in a new fashion. . . . (p. 41)

In conclusion, although there is considerable cross-sex play among Ibo children until age 5 or 6, child-spacing through postpartum sex taboos minimizes the probability of siblings being close age mates. The upbringing is at least moderately puritanical and punitive on sexual and excretory functions, and sexual segregation begins at the relatively early age of 5 and becomes increasingly rigid as children approach puberty. Even in early infancy, erotic behavior, whether in the form of masturbation or heterosexual sex play is discouraged. The men's masquerade is symptomatic of a sexually repressed society with a lot of antagonism along sex lines. All these conditions are congruent with severely punitive incest taboos.

ZANDE

The stratified, patrilineal Zande of the Southern Sudan and Northeastern Zaire, whose principal ethnographer is Evans-Pritchard, are one of a dozen or so African societies where father-daughter and brother-sister (especially between agnatic half-sibs) incest was allowed and practiced by aristocrats; in this case, by the members of the ruling Avongara clan (DeSchlippe, 1956, p. 12; Lagae, 1926, p. 15; Seligman, 1932, pp. 501, 515). The other clans are exogamous, and thus also avoid incest with nuclear family relatives. There are no strong sanctions against incest, but rather feelings of shame (Seligman, 1932, pp. 501, 509; Evans-Pritchard, 1929, p. 206). Similarly, there is evidence that even though exogamy was practiced in commoner clans, sexual relations between agnates were known to occur. Seligman (1932) writes:

> A woman's relatives, her clansmen . . . should in theory be above suspicion of desiring her sexually. . . . Actually sexual relations do occasionally take place between those to whom marriage is forbidden, but such lapses are considered shameful and cases are known where a husband has sued his wife's brother for adultery.'' (p. 501)

The sanctions against incest thus seem no stronger than those against adultery. Adultery, especially with wives of high status men, was a serious offense, and punishments were severe. "This act is reputedly so serious that formerly the husband could with impunity kill the intruder whom he surprised in this flagrant offence" (Lagae, 1926, p. 77).

> If a man was caught committing adultery he could be and often was ferociously mutilated, his genitals, ears, upper lip, or both hands being cut off, while if he escaped this penalty he would have to pay an indemnity of a woman and twenty spears, or failing a woman thirty spears, to the husband. Nor did the woman go

free; on the slightest suspicion a woman would be flogged, cut with knives, bound
and tortured to make her confess the name of her lover.'' (Seligman, 1932, p. 516).

Yet, it is clear that the severe sanctions against adultery were not due to sexual
puritanism, but to protection of the jural rights of the husband. Husbands were
quite free to have affairs with single women, and ''simple fornication by an
unmarried man with an unmarried woman presents no serious problem in the
eyes of the Azande.'' (Lagae, 1926, p. 77). De Schlippe (1956) explicitly states:
''Sexual morality is based only on the husband's right to his wife. An adulterous
wife and her lover are punishable, but a husband is not bound to fidelity to his
wife'' (p. 16).

By almost any criterion, the Zande must be one of the world's least sexually
repressed societies. They not only practiced incest among the nobility and premarital sex, but also both male and female homosexuality. There was somewhat
a double standard in that male homosexuality (practiced mostly as pederasty) was
totally accepted, both at the court as a supplement to polygyny, and among
commoners as a substitute for wives.

> Azande do not regard it as at all improper, indeed as very sensible, for a man to
> sleep with boys when women are not available or are taboo, and, . . . in the past
> this was a regular practice at court. Some princes may even have preferred boys to
> women, when both were available. (Evans-Pritchard, 1971, p. 183).

Lesbianism was widely practiced, especially among the women of the large
polygynous households. Mutual masturbation ''using bananas or manioc, sweet
potato roots shaped with a knife into a phallus'' was common, according to
Evans-Pritchard (1929, p. 595). Such behavior was, however, punished by death
in royal households, by thrashing among commoners. ''The husband's anger is
due to his fear of the unlucky consequences that may ensue from such practices,'' writes Evans-Pritchard (1937, p. 684). Once more, the punishment of
lesbianism is not so much a matter of morality, as of infringement of the husband's marital rights.

In keeping with a tolerant sexual morality, at least for men, the Zande are
quite bawdy. ''Obscene extremes of abuse are common among the A-Zande . . .
as aids to vituperation. . . . These women tear off their grass covering from
over the genitals and rush naked after the intruder, shouting obscene insults at
him and making licentious gestures'' (Evans-Pritchard, 1929, p. 320). Women
expose their genitals and, even worse, their anus to men as ''the last argument of
a woman in a prolonged family quarrel'' (Evans-Pritchard, 1929, pp. 175–176).

The general picture of Zande sexuality is thus clearly one of widespread
licentiousness restricted principally by husbands' watchful attempts to keep a
sexual monopoly over their wives. ''It is truly remarkable how close a watch
Zande nobles and wealthy commoners keep on their wives. They spy on their
every movement,'' writes Evans-Pritchard (1937, p. 515). Yet, ''neither the

men nor the women are particularly faithful to one another, and absence from one another for more than five or six days puts a great strain on their powers of self-control'' (Reynolds, 1904, p. 241). This paradox created, of course, tremendous tensions between men, exacerbated by extensive polygyny among the nobility and the wealthy. This forced young men ''to choose between adultery or continence. Formerly a man up to the age of 30 to 35 was in the main deprived of access to women. . .'' (Seligman, 1932, p. 516). Military service delayed marriage among commoners, and pederasty alleviated the problem somewhat, but ''the enormous size of the chiefs' harems and those of their sons made a serious inroad on the supply of young Zande girls. . .'' (Seligman, 1932, p. 507).

Information on child rearing practices is somewhat scanty, but from brief accounts one can reconstruct the general pattern of sex segregation and upbringing of siblings. There is no evidence of sexual repressiveness in child rearing practices. Lagoe (1926) tell us:

> Until the age of six, only the mother occupies herself with the child. She is extremely devoted. In the beginning she covers the child with caresses. The father also fondles the child from time to time, but this is rare, since the mother lives largely apart in her own dwelling. The entire early education is left to the mother. (p. 174)

Seligman (1932) remarks: ''The brother-sister relationship is close: as children they have been comrades, though during adolescence their respective occupations tend to keep them apart and their acquire the usual attitude of commoners toward incest.'' (p. 509) Baster and Butt (1953) state:

> The child, suckled and petted until it is three or four, is then trained to help with little household chores and encouraged to be a help rather than an encumbrance to its mother. Between six and seven a boy will gradually leave his mother's protection and come under the tutelage of his father. (p. 47)

From these statements we can conclude that full sibs were in intimate contact with each other until age 6, and that gradual sex segregation set in after that. It is interesting to note that aristocratic incest does not contradict the Westermarck hypothesis. ''Almost invariably'' according to Seligman (1932, p. 515) it was practiced between agnatic half-sibs, who were raised in separate houses by their respective mothers, and who were thus in much less intimate contact with each other than full sibs.

CONCLUSIONS

Obviously, four cases does not constitute proof. They were not even randomly chosen. I picked the Tallensi because I remembered that Fortes was good on sex, and the Zande because I knew them to have practiced royal incest, and because I remembered Evans-Pritchard's account of Zande pederasty. In search of two contrasting cases of sexually repressive cultures, I simply picked the next two societies in the HRAF drawers, after the Tallensi, on which there was sufficient information: these turned out to be the Ashanti and the Ibo. I did not reject any cases that did not fit my hypothesis.

By chance, two of my four societies, the Ashanti and the Tallensi, have, over a quarter century ago, been contrasted by Goody (1956) who was also concerned with the comparative study of incest and other sexual prohibitions, and their relationship to social structure. Although he does not consider the biological bases of inbreeding avoidance, he concurs with me (van den Berghe, 1979; 1980) in the necessity to differentiate clearly between incest and exogamy. He interprets rules of exogamy (and sanctions against adultery) as cultural rules linked with the structure of unilineal descent (either patrilineal or matrilineal). He does not attempt, of course, to reduce kinship structure to a model of individual inclusive fitness maximization, yet his analysis is compatible with mine, though at a different level.

This preliminary test needs to be extended to a greater number of societies. I believe, however, that more extensive statistical tests of hypotheses, while complementary to the present kind of exercise, are no substitute for a detailed examination of primary sources on a few cases.

The ultimate test of the sociobiological paradigm will have to come, not from the kind of "salvage ethnography" of which the present paper is an example, but from fresh field data specifically collected to test hypotheses generated from the theory. For all of its limitations, however, the existing body of ethnography is a mine of retrievable information which offers at least one advantage: the evidence is not suspect on the ground of observer bias in favor of sociobiology.

REFERENCES

Baxter, P. T. W. & Butt, A. (1953). The Azande. In D. Forde (Ed.), *Ethnographic survey of Africa* Part 9. London: International African Institute.

Bischof, N. (1975). Comparative ethology of incest avoidance. In R. Fox (Ed.), *Biosocial anthropology* (pp. 37–67). New York: Wiley.

Bixler, R. H. (1981). Incest avoidance as a function of environment *and* heredity. *Current anthropology, 22,* 639–643.

Busia, K. A. (1951). *The position of the chief in the modern political system of Ashanti.* London: Oxford University Press.

De Schlippe, P. (1956). *Shifting cultication in Africa.* London: Routledge and Kegan Paul.

Evans-Pritchard, E. E. (1929) Witchcraft (Mangu) among the A-Zande. *Sudan notes and records, 12,* 163–249.

Evans-Pritchard, E. E. (1937). *Witchcraft, oracles and magic among the Azande.* Oxford: Clarendon Press.

Evans-Pritchard, E. E. (1971). *The Azande, history and political institutions.* Oxford: Clarendon Press.

Fedigan, L. M. (1982). *Primate paradigms: Sex roles and social bonds.* Montreal: Enden Press.

Field, M. J. (1960). *Search for security.* New York: Norton.

Fortes, M. (1949). *The web of kinship among the Tallensi.* Oxford: Oxford University Press.

Fortes, M. (1950). Kinship and marriage among the Ashanti. In A. R. Radcliffe-Brown & D. Forde (Eds.), *African systems of kinship and marriage.* London: Oxford University Press.

Fox, R. (1980). *The red lamp of incest.* New York: Dutton.

Freud, S. (1950). *Totem and taboo.* New York: Norton.

Goody, J. (1956). A comparative approach to incest and adultery, *British Journal of Sociology, 7,* 286–305.

Green, M. (1964). *Ibo village affairs.* New York: Praeger.

Henderson, H. K. (1980). *Ritual roles of women in Onitsha Ibo society.* Doctoral dissertation, Berkeley: University of California.

Henderson, R. N. & Henderson, H. K. (1966). *An outline of traditional Onitsha Ibo socialization.* Ibadan: Univrsity of Ibadan Institute of Education. Occasional Publication No. 5.

Itoigawa, N., K. Negayama, & K. Kondo (1981). Experimental study on sexual behavior between mother and son in Japanese monkeys (*Macaca Fuscata*). *Primates, 22,* 494–502.

Lagae, C. R. (1926). *Les Azande ou Niam-Niam.* Brussels: Vromant.

Meek, C. K. (1937). *Law and authority in a Nigerian tribe.* London: Oxford University Press.

Okere, L. C. (1981). *Socio-economic and cultural aspects of food and food habits in rural Igboland.* Doctoral dissertation, Buffalo: State University of New York.

Ottenberg, S. (1968). *Double descent in an African society.* Seattle: University of Washington Press.

Rattray, R. S. (1929). *Ashanti law and constitution.* Oxford: Clarendon Press.

Reynolds, H. (1904). Notes on the Azande tribe of the Congo. *Journal of the African Society, 3,* 238–246.

Sade, D. S. (1968). Inhibition of son-mother mating among free-ranging Rhesus monkeys. *Science and Psychoanalysis, 12,* 18–38.

Seligman, C. G., & Seligman, B. Z. (1932). *Pagan tribes of the Nilotic Sudan.* London: George Routledge.

Shepher, J. (1971). Mate selection among second generation kibbutz adolescents and adults. *Archives of Sexual Behavior, 1,* 293–307.

Shepher, J. (1983). *Incest: A biosocial view.* Orlando, FL: Academic Press.

Spain, D. H. (1984). *When titans slash: A reconsideration of Freud and Westermarck on incest.* Unpublished paper, University of Washington, Seattle.

van den Berghe, P. L. (1979). *Human family systems.* New York: Elsevier.

van den Berghe, P. L. (1980). Incest and exogamy, a sociobiological reconsideration. *Ethology and Sociobiology, 1,* 151–162.

van den Berghe, P. L. (1983). Human incest avoidance: Culture in nature. *The Behavioral and Brain Science, 6,* 91–102.

van Lawick-Goodall, J. (1971). *In the shadow of man.* Boston: Houghton Mifflin.

Westermarck, E. A. (1891). *The history of human marriage.* London: Macmillan.

Wolf, A. P., & Huang, C. (1980). *Marriage and adoption in China, 1845–1945.* Stanford: Stanford University Press.

16 Evolutionary Theory and Rules of Mating and Marriage Pertaining to Relatives

Nancy Wilmsen Thornhill
Randy Thornhill
University of New Mexico, Albuquerque

INTRODUCTION

The most preposterous attempts have been made to account for this horror of incest. . .
—Freud, 1922, p. 177

No unitary theory of incest taboos appears capable of accounting for all aspects of the phenomenon of incest avoidance.
—Murdock, 1949, p. 292

. . . the prohibition of incest would then clearly be the only case of the natural sciences being asked to account for the existence of a rule sanctioned by human authority . . . [but] how could rules be analysed and interpreted if ethnology should confess its helplessness before the one pre-eminent and universal rule which assures culture's hold over nature?
—Levi Strauss 1969, p. 24

If this is so important to avoid . . . then why the need for a strict taboo . . . ? A phenomenon as important as inbreeding depression will be noticed and steps will be taken to avoid behavior leading to the variety of diseases and mental deficiencies related to crosses between close relatives. I can't see that . . . the sociobiologists make any but a case that can be described as a 'just so story'.
—Levington, 1983, p. 434

The confusion that has surrounded most of the research on incest leads us to the conviction that the wrong questions have been asked both by ethnographers

373

during field work and by investigators doing literature searches. Part of the problem in incest research stems from the use of an inappropriate theory of human behavior. In general, this research is based on a basic misunderstanding about human motivations. The theory of evolution by natural selection purports that individuals typically will not behave contrary to their own reproductive interests, for instance, by engaging in sexual liaisons which will end in production of inferior offspring. Yet this is exactly what many anthropologists, psychologists, and sociologists argue with regard to incest. The various traditional hypotheses from the social sciences lead to the anomalous conclusion that, no matter how devastating, incest is the favored form of mating in humans because of a desire which originated with our remote ancestors and which has been maintained throughout our history (Freud, 1922; Malinowski, 1927; Murdock, 1949; Parsons, 1954; Seligman, 1929). Moreover, the social sciences generally assume that rules against incest have been erected to keep us all from ruining ourselves, our offspring, our families, and our social organizations. These ideas are basic to all incest research up to the most recent (but see Westermarck, 1891); they are entirely unsatisfactory to us, because they imply that human behavior has not evolved by selection. (See Shepher, 1983, for discussion of the history of ideas pertaining to incest avoidance.)

Apart from the inappropriate questions and the absence of appropriate theory to explain human behavior, incest research has been hampered by failure to recognize the qualitative differences in behavior which have been labeled incest by ethnographers. Since the turn of the century, many anthropologists have doggedly pursued the "incest avoidance does not include exogamy" concept (Fox, 1980; Goody, 1956; McLennan, 1896; Schneider, 1976). As a result, incest has often been confined to mating and exogamy to marriage. Whereas the latter is by definition true, the former, it seems, is often defined by idealogical beliefs specific to each observer. We will show that what is referred to as incest by many social scientists is not confined to mating, and that incest rules do sometimes include marriage rules. Furthermore, it is essential to clarify the distinction between close kin mating and mating and marriage between less closely related individuals. To this end, we divide the behaviors referred to as incest in the literature into three parts. The first part, incest, is sexual relations between closely related individuals (see Shields, 1982; Shepher, 1983); individuals whose relatedness by descent (r) is greater than or equal to $\frac{1}{4}$, for example, parents and offspring, siblings, and half siblings. We delineate this as the incest boundary because this form of mating apparently leads to a high probability of inferior offspring due to exposure of deleterious genetic effects (Adams & Neel, 1967; Schull & Neel, 1965; Wright, 1933; but see Shields, 1982). The second part, inbreeding, is sexual relations between individuals related by $r < \frac{1}{4}$, for example, various degrees of cousins. This form of mating can lead to family or lineage solidarity and wealth concentration which may threaten those individuals in power. The third part is a special kind of adultery;

these relationships (still referred to as incestuous in the literature) occur between individuals who may or may not be genetically related, for example, a man and his son's wife or a man and his brother's wife. This form of mating might occur in societies which practice patrilocal residence (a married couple lives with the husband's male relatives) and can threaten paternity or negatively affect cooperation among family members.

We will focus on evolutionary hypotheses for "incest" rules. We propose the hypotheses to ask why rules regulating mating between close kin exist and why they are so diversified. Why incest rules exist is an important question (but see Shepher, 1983). It seems that they shouldn't given the increasingly well recognized, proximate developmental mechanism which promotes voluntary incest (r $\geq$ ¼) avoidance: the Westermarck effect (Alexander, 1979; Lumsden & Wilson, 1981; Shepher, 1971, 1983; Spiro, 1958; van den Berghe, 1980, 1982; Westermarck, 1891). Why incest rules are so diverse across social systems is also an important question because of the apparent arbitrary application of mating and marriage rules. For example, severity of punishment for incest varies across societies (Brown, 1952; Goody, 1956; Minturn, Grosse, & Haider, 1969) from little or no punishment in the Vedda and the Andamanese (Radcliffe-Brown, 1922; Seligman, 1911) to exile in the Tallensi (Fortes, 1936) or torture and death in the ancient Chinese and Romans and perhaps the Zulu (Gluckman, 1950; Morgan, 1826; Weinberg, 1955). And mating and marriage rules are almost never directed only at close consanguineal kin (r $\geq$ ¼, Murdock, 1949; Shepher, 1983; van den Berghe, 1980, this volume). Before examining incest rules we discuss social rules in general.

The Nature of Social Rules

Social rules are made to modify and control behavior. That is, only when it is necessary to curb the desires of individuals, and when those desires conflict with the desires of powerful individuals or are, in egalitarian societies (a societal category in which there is no disparity in wealth), contrary to the desires of many individuals, are rules made (Alexander, 1978, Betzig, 1982; Borgia, 1980; Dizinno, 1983; Thornhill & Thornhill, 1983).

It is men rather than women who have the greatest influence on rule making, and powerful men have more influence in shaping rules than men without power (Alexander, 1978, 1979; Chagnon, 1982). As Alexander (1974, 1979) has pointed out, men who rule attempt to control the reproductive behavior of other men. Thus the degree of disparity in wealth and status among men across societies influences social rules. In societies in which men are less capable of controlling one another (because of little opportunity for one man or a few men to gain a preponderance of power) the rules are expected to be less harsh and, when broken, less frequently punished. Conversely, as societies become more dominated by a few men, rules promoting fitness of rule makers are expected to become more strict and punishment for their infraction more harsh. This is because as some men are afforded greater opportunity to gain power (through resource control, polygyny, exceptional hunting or warring skill, etc.) they will translate this power into increasing reproductive success (descendent and non-descendent kin), which by its nature reduces the reproductive success of other men in the society (Betzig, 1986). Because of the way selection acts, we expect the evolved concern among men for maintenance of high levels of reproduction; thus rules are generated which control the abilities of other men to gain power and thereby gain reproductive success.

In nonstratified preindustrial societies rules act to increase paternity confidence (Daly, Wilson, & Weghorst, 1982; Kurland, 1979) and to some extent promote lineage solidarity (van den Berghe, this volume). In industrial and preindustrial stratified societies rules increase paternity confidence as well but also preserve, via group solidarity, the society in order to better deal with aggression from outside the society (Alexander, 1978, 1979, 1981) and decrease the likelihood of overthrow of those in power by factions within the society (see the section on *Cousin Marriage*).

Incest Rules

Are these concerns relevant to incest rules? We suggest that rules against actual incest ($r \geq \frac{1}{4}$) which are allegedly almost ubiquitous (e.g., Schneider, 1976), primarily will be found under special circumstances. We also propose that most rules which are generally called incest rules in ethnographies are actually inbreeding and adultery rules (as defined earlier). That is, rules against mating and marriage are not usually focused on close kin ($r \geq \frac{1}{4}$) because close relatives are unlikely to mate. The rules are more often directed at more distant kin and nonkin who, if they mate, or marry, threaten the reproductive interests of rule-making men. We expect mating and marriage rules to be predictable given mating system, descent, and extent of social stratification in a society. The components judged important by the rule makers in a given society should include paternity confidence, lineage solidarity, and concentration of wealth. Our approach can be divided into three interrelated hypotheses, which are discussed presently. These hypotheses yield a number of predictions which are exclusive of predictions generated by earlier anthropological and sociological hypotheses.

The assumptions underlying most work on incest are: (1) that humans prefer to mate with close relatives, or (2) that incest must be socially controlled, to a greater or lesser extent, to preserve the society, or the kinship group, or to avoid detrimental fitness effects to individuals as a result of inbreeding depression. Shepher (1983) has written a comprehensive review of the traditional hypotheses and one recent hypothesis for rules against incest and for incest avoidance and finds no strong support for them. Shepher (1983; also Alexander, 1979; Lumsden & Wilson, 1981; van den Berghe, 1980, 1982; Westermarck, 1891) proposes an evolutionary hypothesis which states that, as a result of natural selection, humans do not desire incestuous mating and do avoid incest. He argues that the evolved proximate mechanism facilitating the avoidance is the Westermarck effect. The Westermarck effect (Westermarck, 1891) is a mechanism of social learning of incest avoidance. Close physical association between individuals activates the mechanism. Shepher (1971, 1983) feels that the Westermarck effect will not be triggered unless interacting individuals are between 2- and 6-years-of-age. We disagree and suggest that a more parsimonious hypothesis is that cosocialization of an individual of any age with a child who is experiencing the sensitive stage, should lead to sexual aversion between them. This eliminates the need for hypothesizing complex mechanisms of mother/son and father/daughter incest avoidance (see Thornhill & Thornhill, 1984). When cosocialization does not occur during the sensitive stage it appears that the mechanism for avoiding close inbreeding is not learned, and incest might occur (van den Berghe, 1982). There is some evidence for a greater number of rules against incest in a few societies which have features inconsistent with promotion of the Westermarck effect (see below and van den Berghe, this volume). Shepher (1983) argues that rules against actual incest are made because the critical learning stage is sometimes missed and rule makers recognize the inevitability of a low frequency of incestuous mating mistakes.

HYPOTHESES, PREDICTIONS, AND ETHNOGRAPHIC EVIDENCE

The approach we propose, which stems from an evolutionary perspective on incest, mating, and marriage, is best considered as three interrelated hypotheses. Individuals are only rarely incestuous (mating with kin with whom they share $\geq$ ¼ of their genes) and:

A. Rules are made to (1) ensure that females are kept sexually isolated from those men (excluding their own husbands) with whom they are in frequent social contact as a result of social organization, and (2) to prevent sexual interactions within lineages and thereby to promote their solidarity in the interests of rule makers.

B. Rules are made to prevent relatives from concentrating wealth and/or power by intermarrying and thus becoming a powerful family force, which might pose a threat to the social status of leaders (also see Alexander, 1981).

C. When men are unable to enforce A (i.e., rules which promote paternity reliability and lineage solidarity) they will concentrate on a modified form of B which is directed at prevention of resource and/or kin concentration.

These rule categories or hypotheses can be viewed in relation to mating system, descent, and social stratification (Table 16.1). Social stratification can be strong as in caste societies, Ancient Romans, Egyptians, and Chinese. Stratification was so extreme in these societies that a few powerful men made the rules and extracted large reproductive benefits from them. In some societies such as the Nyakyusa, Yanomamö, Tallensi, and Nuer there is a more equitable division of power and (except perhaps for the Nuer; see Gough, 1971) no apparent

TABLE 16.1
Expected Rules Pertaining to Mating and Marriage of Consanguineal
and Affinal Kin and Expected Extent of Punishment
for Breaking Rules in Relation to Mating System,
Descent, and Extent of Social Stratification.

Stratification, Mating System, and Descent	Examples	Rule Categories and Punishment		
		A	B	C
Patrilineal/ Highly Polygynous/ Stratified	Ashanti Caste Societies Zulu Ancient Egypt	Harsh	Harsh	----
Bilateral/ Socially Imposed Monogamous/ Stratified	Ancient Rome Ancient Greece U.S.A.	Harsh	Harsh	----
Patrilineal/ Moderately Polygynous/ Nonstratified	Tiwi Nyakyusa Yanomamo	Moderate	----	----
Patrilineal/ Mildly Polygynous/ Nonstratified	Nuer Tallensi	Mild	----	----
Matrilineal/ Monogamous/ Nonstratified	Plateau Tonga Cewa Lamba Yao	----	----	Mild
Bilateral/ Ecologically Imposed Monogamous/ Nonstratified	!Kung San Some Eskimo Vedda	----	----	Mild

A–C refer to rule categories described in text. ---- indicates no rule is expected. Enforcement of rules should be thought of as relative, e.g., moderately polygynous societies are expected to have less harsh rule enforcement than highly polygynous societies but more harsh than mildly polygynous societies.

stratification by wealth, but still some men are capable of controlling women and other men to their own reproductive advantage. Lastly there may be little or no disparity in power between men as in the Vedda, Plateau Tonga, some Eskimo groups, and many Micronesian societies. In these societies men have little or no control over each other and reduced control over women.

The extent of control and associated reproductive benefits can be judged by the level of polygyny exhibited in a society (Betzig, 1986). Polygyny is characterized by greater variance in male than female reproductive success, which stems from greater competition among males than among females for resources and/or status attractive to the opposite sex. All human societies probably show some degree of polygyny. In more monogamous societies variance in reproductive success among males is reduced but still present. As the extent of polygyny increases it becomes increasingly more difficult for individual men to reproduce because fewer and fewer men obtain all the available women (see Thornhill & Thornhill, 1983 for detailed discussion).

Rules under A. (above) differ from typical adultery rules in that they (a) apply to marriage rules as well as rules for nonmarital sexual behavior, and (b) that the potential perpetrators are usually readily available to one another because of clan or household composition. For example, incest (as labeled by ethnographers) and adultery are sometimes the same. The difference between them is often a functional one and often is recognized as such in human societies. The term incest is not generally applied to these behaviors (except by ethnographers) but a term indicative of grave sexual offense generally is. Adultery may not threaten lineage solidarity, "incest" may (also see Goody, 1956; Leach, 1961). Also in the absence of rules, incest in the form of mating with an affinally related individual, for instance a man and his son's wife, may be easier to accomplish under patrilocal residence, because of proximity, than adultery may be. Additionally, many marriage rules treated as incest by ethnographers are best viewed as rules to prevent concentration of wealth and/or power via inbreeding, B. (above).

Thus, we feel it is misleading to mass a variety of behaviors into a category-"incest"—and view them from the perspective which is connoted by the word (i.e., sexual behavior involving close genetic relatives). Many of these behaviors are inbreeding and adultery. Rules regarding these behaviors are best called rules of mating and marriage pertaining to relatives rather than incest rules. Here we discuss the derivation of seven predictions from our evolutionary view (also see Table 16.1), and outline some ethnographic evidence. Although the predictions are testable, the observations we use to examine the predictions come from selected ethnographies and thus do not represent tests. The purpose of this section is to examine feasibility. Here we are looking generally at the ethnographic literature to see if the hypotheses are at all tenable.

Prediction 1. Under patrilineal systems of descent, rules of mating and marriage should be applied to a greater number of both consanguines and affines than under matrilineal systems of descent. This prediction stems from the greater concern with paternity and the greater degree of polygyny in patrilineal than in matrilineal systems. Paternity is of greater concern to males under patriliny than under matriliny because matriliny is characterized by avuncular nepotism rather than, as in patriliny, paternal nepotism (Alexander, 1974, 1979; Flinn, 1981; Gaulin & Schlegel, 1980). Under polygyny the higher reproductive success of some males is associated with social domination of other, less successful males as well as with control (sometimes extreme) of female sexual behavior. Success allows winners to generate self-benefitting rules.

The Nuer are an East African, patrilineal, and segmentary society. A segmentary society is one in which the lineages are divided into groups (segments), each of which can trace descent from a common male ancestor. The segments become increasingly large in ascending generations, ultimately to incorporate all lineages of a clan into descent from one common ancestor (Evans-Pritchard, 1940). The lineages differ in prestige but evidently not enough to make this a highly polygynous system (Evans-Pritchard, 1940; but see Gough, 1971).

The rules of mating and marriage (incest rules according to Evans-Pritchard) in the Nuer are quite extensive. Forbidden by these rules are sexual relationships between a man and the wives of his father, brothers, sons, or maternal uncles, and between a man and his maternal and paternal aunts or with the wives of his affines (e.g., a man's wife's brother's wife) (Evans-Pritchard, 1949). Clearly these rules do not apply only to incest, but are also adultery rules.

The Zulu, a patrilineal, patrilocal people do not allow sexual relationships between any member of the patriline or matriline nor with two people who share a common grandparent (Gluckman, 1950). The Zulu are a stratified society. We discuss them at greater length below (Prediction 4).

In matrilineal societies the rules of incest are almost always confined to within the matrilineage (e.g., Plateau Tonga—Colson 1958; Yap—Labby, 1976). Mating and marriage rules in matrilineal societies are discussed more fully in connection with prediction 7.

Prediction 2.   In ecologically imposed monogamous societies (i.e., societies in which men are unable to accumulate enough resources to provide for more than one woman and her offspring, see Alexander et al., 1979) there should be few or no rules regarding mating and marriage between affines and consanguines. This prediction stems from two considerations. The first is related to benefits females may achieve via extra pairbond copulation. Females are expected to copulate with men other than their pair-bond mates only when benefits (material, genetic) exceed the costs (an undesired pregnancy, risk of injury by mate, loss of mate's investment) (Benshoof & Thornhill, 1979; Symons, 1979). Under systems of scarce ecological resources material benefits to be gained by female infidelity will be negligible. Conditions of scarce ecological resources in humans do not appear to include protein shortages (Lee, 1969). This is important given that, under conditions of protein stress, there may be an advantage to females of extrabond copulation (i.e., in trade for protein). The second factor important in the derivation of this prediction is that although under unilineal inheritance (through only one sex—e.g., father to son) even relatively small amounts of resource could be concentrated by an endogamous lineage, ecologically imposed monogamous societies are characterized by scarce and ephemeral resources *and* by bilateral inheritance (Alexander, 1979; van den Berghe, 1979). Thus, the probability of families concentrating and controlling large amounts of reproductive resources is low in ecologically imposed monogamous societies.

Some Eskimo groups, many of which are ecologically imposed monogamous societies (Alexander et al., 1979), reputedly have at least the concept of incest in their folklore (Hennigh, 1966). However, the ethnographer was unable to find any actual instance of "incestuous" sexual behavior either in the present or in the memories of his informants or even of any believable event of sexual behavior in the folklore (e.g., a female was ravaged by a polar bear, and apparently Hennigh interpreted this as incest by a father figure). Although it is never clearly stated, it seems that there are no incest taboos in the Eskimo societies studied by Hennigh, and certainly nothing which qualifies as a control of the behavior (but Hennigh thinks the folk tales serve as such).

The Veddas of Ceylon also exhibit ecologically imposed monogamy (Alexander et al., 1979). They are bilaterally inheriting (Seligman, 1911) and seem to be almost devoid of an incest concept. The nearest reference to incest by Seligman is with regard to parallel cousin marriages. (The preferred form of marriage is allegedly between cross cousins, either matrilateral or patrilateral. See the section on *Cousin Marriage* for description of cousin types.) The incident which led Seligman to describe parallel cousin marriage as incest had occurred 50 to 60 years prior to his field work, and is the only mention of incest in his 463 page ethnography. Because of the classificatory kinship terminology Seligman defined this incident as brother/sister incest. Seligman observed that the marriage of "brother and sister" had been greeted with "horror" and the "brother" and "sister" were either exiled or killed, but no further mention is made of taboos or methods of prevention.

Worth noting is that in the Eskimo folktales and the Vedda history the incest inferred by the investigator is sexual relationships between fathers and daughters or brothers and sisters. That is, incest as we use the term in this paper, if indeed they describe incest at all. It may be that the folklore or historical account is an attempt, by the people in the societies, to explain why they feel adverse to mating with close relatives.

The Andamanese are another example of an ecologically imposed monogamous society. In this society there are no rules of inheritance and no real wealth. There also are no incest restrictions at all (Radcliffe-Brown, 1922).

These ethnographies suggest that prediction 2 may be worth pursuing. However, there is a complicating factor. In ecologically imposed monogamous societies there are, in general, few rules, at least no endemically enforced ones (Alexander, 1979; Hoebel, 1954). Thus, predicting that there should be no incest rules or inbreeding and adultery rules may not be a strong device for testing our view of rules of mating and marriage among affinal and consanguineal kin.

Prediction 3.   Sexual intercourse between close kin (incest) primarily should be ruled against in preindustrial societies in which warring involves frequent, long periods of male absence (also see van den Berghe, this volume). In such societies there may be a high potential for missed periods of development (between men and their daughters, younger sisters, or nieces) critical to incest avoidance.

The Nayar are the warring caste of a number of other castes which live in Kerala, India. Most young men of the Nayar subcastes (commoner, "retainer," royal, etc.) are given military training and were traditionally often away at war (Gough, 1961; Irons, 1979). The Nayar are matrilineal and matrilocal. The household is divided into separate areas for males and females. From the time of puberty a girl is not allowed into the boys' section nor vice versa (Mencher, 1956). Although Nayar men could be more free in their behavior with older female relatives they could not show the same freedom with younger related females after these girls had reached puberty. Specifically avoided were younger sisters and sisters' daughters. The Nayar recognize this avoidance as a deterrent to possible incest (e.g., "they might otherwise commit incest") (Mencher 1956, p. 183). Interestingly, the relationship between a Nayar man and his younger sister next to him in age was ". . . fairly close, particularly if they were not too far apart in age and had played together as small children" (Mencher 1956, p. 183). The Westermarck effect probably operates under this circumstance. Whether or not a man's avoidance of younger sisters and sisters' daughters constitutes a rule is an open question, but the Nayar claim that it is "bad" for brothers and sisters to have "relations" (Mencher, 1956). Gough (1961) states that sexual relations within a clan were forbidden, but she gives no further indication of what this entails. Thus the Nayar claim that incest may happen and behavior aimed at it's avoidance is prescribed. Whether or not this behavior is enforced by explicit rules is not clear.

There are reasons for making rules against sexual intercourse between very close kin that complicate prediction 3. One such reason is that these incest rules may reinforce rules against adultery and inbreeding (mating and marriage among affines and more distant consanguines), because by calling a behavior (e.g., inbreeding or adultery) incest the behavior is associated with the unpleasant images of actual incest (Alexander, 1979). Another reason may stem from the recognition of the relationship between close inbreeding and reduced offspring viability. Leaders in state societies have often placed a premium on large population size, especially the production of large numbers of soldiers (e.g., the ancient Hebrews, Greeks, Romans, and recently in Russia and Nazi Germany). Thus it seems that rules were made discouraging behaviors which reduced fertility (abortion, contraception, infanticide) and encouraging behaviors that promoted family stability and associated high levels of parental care (strict monogamy, outlaw of adultery and divorce, etc.) (see Lewinsohn, 1958). Actual incest can reduce fertility in humans and it is conceivable that legislation against it in some state societies may stem in part from attempts by leaders to prevent close inbreeding because of knowledge of its detrimental effects in domestic plants and animals and its occurrence in royal lines in some societies. For example, the ancient Hebrew leaders may have outlawed sexual intercourse between close relatives because it was known to occur in Egyptian royal lines. Even though people (Hebrews in this example) may only rarely engage in incest, leaders have knowledge of its occurrence and its detrimental effects and for these reasons may institute a rule or law against incest as a hedge against possible population depletion and the associated increase in vulnerability of the nation to outside aggression.

Prediction 4. In highly stratified societies rules of mating and marriage should be harshest and most stringently enforced, as well as extensive in their application (number of included individuals). This prediction stems from the disparity in wealth and status in such societies. Rule makers in highly stratified societies (men with great power) have increased ability to enforce rules as a result of greater control over necessary and desirable resources. Under highly stratified systems it is often in the rulers' best interest to inhibit any form of lineage or family endogamy. This is because there may be great potential for a moderately wealthy family to concentrate wealth by preferential marriage of relatives, increase its power substantially, and usurp the leaders' position in the society.

The discussion here deals only with the Ancient Chinese and Romans, the Ashanti, and the Zulus.

The Ancient Chinese were patrilineal and extremely stratified. Marriage was prohibited with any relative to the 5th degree of consanguinity ($r = \frac{1}{32}$). Additionally forbidden to marry were any persons sharing the same surname (e.g., a man and his father's brother's offspring or his brother's offspring) and any widow of a relative to the 4th degree. Infractions of these rules were punished by decapitation or strangulation (Weinberg, 1955; Westermarck, 1891). Any sexual relationship between relatives more distantly related than the 5th degree were punished by 100 blows to the male and banishment for both parties (Weinberg, 1955).

These rules are harsh, and one consequence appears to be the prevention of accumulation of wealth by anyone other than the rule makers. As a specific example of this, the levirate (marriage of a man to his brother's widow) was outlawed in Ancient China, but the sororate (marriage of a man to his deceased wife's sister) was not. Under patrilineal inheritance a man may divide his wealth between his sons (and ultimately his grandsons). By the marriage of two brothers to one woman, a father's entire accumulation of wealth may go to one set of grandchildren (i.e., wealth would concentrate rather than divide). The Chinese emperors by making and strictly enforcing specific marriage rules may have been attempting to prevent this.

The Ancient Romans afford a fascinating view of incest laws. It appears that these laws changed depending on how strong and unified the empire was. It remained constant, though, that *incestus jure genitum* (sexual relations between ascending and descending kin whether by blood or adoption *ad infinitum*) was enforced. The fluctuations came in the *incestus jure civile* (sexual relations between other people, nondescendent kin or nonkin). At varying times the *j. civile* included relatives to the 6th degree inclusive ($r = \frac{1}{64}$), fathers and step-daughters, fathers and daughters-in-law, a man's stepmother and mother-in-law, the wife of a deceased brother, a deceased wife's sister or an illegitimate sister. The punishment for breaking the *j. civile* was the same as that for adultery; both parties were hurled from the Tarpenian Rock (presumably a high place). If they lived they were either thrown off again or banished from the Empire (Corbett, 1930). The Romans were bilaterally inheriting (Morgan, 1826; Weinberg, 1955) and this may explain the laws excluding from marriage such affinal relatives as a wife's sister. If women inherit property, sisters, by marrying the same man, can concentrate rather than divide wealth. The children resulting from sisters sharing a husband would receive more than they otherwise would.

The Ashanti historically have been classified as matrilineal. This classification seems anomalous given that until 1903, with the advent of British rule, Ashanti was a highly stratified kingdom (Fortes, 1950), and the degree of polygyny was great (Betzig, 1982). The rules regarding incest have been recorded (Rattray, 1929) and analyzed (Goody, 1956; van den Berghe, this volume). These rules are harsh and extensive. Before discussing these rules we offer evidence in support of the contention that Ashanti were not matrilineal throughout the strata of society but instead were primarily patrilineal in the upper portions of class hierarchy and primarily matrilineal in the lower (also see Betzig, 1982).

First it should be stressed that fathers invested in their offspring despite Rattray's (1929) insistence that paternal involvement was minimal. The avunculate was operable but, Rattray notes, that when a father was wealthy the maternal uncle had little involvement with his sister's children. Rattray further notes that there exists an inconsistency with regard to choosing marriage partners for children. Sometimes he found that maternal uncles chose marriage partners for their sister's offspring, but other times he found that fathers chose the husbands and wives of their offspring. The confusion was probably due to failure to recognize different reproductive strategies in different strata. Rattray also found that wives were viewed as property of their husbands and the most undesirable form of marriage was one in which the man did not buy his wife and thus did not have some (large?) degree of control over her behavior, and her place of residence. All of these considerations are in opposition to what is known to be common to matrilineal inheritance (see Flinn, 1981).

Ashanti incest rules indicate a greater degree of male control than is generally found in matrilineal societies. The rules encompassed all matrilineal kin, and also included (for a man) agnatic half siblings, patrilateral parallel cousins, a brother's wife, a son's wife, a wife's mother, an uncle's wife, the wife of a man of the same company or guild, the wife of anyone of the same trade, the wife of one's own slave, father's wives, and a man's wife's sisters (the latter only applied to commoners). All of these rules, if broken were punishable by execution. The Ashanti, as evidenced by the different terminology applied to these rules, recognized the difference between making rules against matrilineal kin mating and those against men mating with wives of various other men. The intrigues with various wives were sometimes seen by the Ashanti as easier to accomplish under patrilocal residence than other forms of adultery. In addition to protecting paternity these rules seem to be directed at preventing accumulation of wealth and power by those other than the king's own lineage.

Other Ashanti laws support the view of a high degree of male control at the highest (at least) strata. These include laws of treason, murder, and rape (see Rattray, 1929).

The Zulu were a polygynous, patrilineal, stratified, African society. Inheritance was via primogeniture. The Zulu practiced the levirate, the sororate, and sororal polygyny. The rules of incest encompass any member of a father's clan, any member of a mother's clan, anyone who shares a common grandparent, anyone of the same "sib" (a group of clans who share a common ancestor via patrilineal descent), or anyone of a mother's sib (Gluckman, 1950; Krige, 1977). These rules may be directed at promotion of lineage solidarity by reducing competition within clans. They may also function to discourage inbreeding and thereby prevent wealth accumulation by families other than those in power.

We were unable to find any direct information on the punishment for breach of incest rules for the Zulu. Adultery, however, was punished severely (Gluckman, 1950). It is reasonable to assume that the punishment for incest may have been equally as harsh or harsher. Additionally, the Zulu had other restrictions on behavior which may have served to dissuade potential incest participants. These are discussed under prediction 6.

Of note is the difference between strata in application of incest laws. For example, although it was a capital crime the emperor Claudius married his brother's daughter, after changing the rule (Morgan, 1826). As with the Romans, the Zulu royal families seemed immune to incest rules. Krige (1977) relates that if a member of a royal sib was attracted to a girl within it he would fission the sib thereby eliminating the marriage constraint (see Betzig, 1986, for discussion of other rule following differences between strata).

These examples leave the impression that there is certainly more to incest rules than an attempt to maintain a healthy level of genetic outbreeding or an attempt at controlling deep incestuous desires.

Prediction 5.   In polygynous, nonstratified societies the rules of mating and marriage pertaining to affines and consanguines should be *mainly* directed at males and females who by virtue of their affinal ties and residence pose an easily realized threat to the paternity of the rule makers, for example, women who live virilocally (with their husbands) and men who, patrilocally (with their fathers), share this residence (other than husband). In stratified societies these rules sometimes may not need to be made because of other rules and actions regarding female sexual behavior (e.g., claustration and veiling, genital modification, eunuch guards, etc; Dickemann, 1981; Lewinsohn, 1958) and harsh punishment for adultery. The rules in nonstratified, polygynous societies probably serve the interests of many men, because of the more equitable nature of male status in these societies. This results in a more equal distribution of power and degree of polygyny among men compared to the situation in stratified societies. Thus, men face a greater difficulty controlling each other and controlling women and, as a result, suffer a loss in reliability of paternity. Also because of the lower disparity in power in polygynous, nonstratified societies, rules of mating and marriage between affinal and consanguineal relatives should be less harsh than under highly stratified systems. In addition to these rules, other societal pressures should be employed (see next prediction).

The Tallensi are an African, nonstratified partrilineal and patrilocal group. They regard as "incestuous and repugnant" sexual relations between a man and his son's wife, his brother's wife, father's wife, and any two men (related or not) having intercourse with the same woman (Fortes, 1936). It is not surprising then that women marrying into the patriclans (i.e., wives of the patriline members) are termed objects of inbreeding and adultery, if men are motivated by a desire to know who they have fathered.

The Nuer (discussed above, see prediction 1) have a social and residential organization similar to the Tallensi and have extensive rules regarding adulterous relations with affines (Evans-Pritchard, 1949). Wives of brothers, fathers, and sons as well as wives of brothers-in-law, and uncle's wives are all included in this category of rules. Wives of dead relatives are excluded because the Nuer practice the levirate.

Women who are forbidden via rules of mating and marriage sometimes become legal wives upon the death of a father (in the case of widow inheritance) or brother (in the case of the levirate). Zulu are an example of the former, Nuer, Zande, and Nyakyusa, the latter.

In many cases the rules against mating with close kin are nonexistent while rules such as the above (directed at nonkin—a special kind of adultery rule) are quite prevalent. For example the Tallensi view sex with a mother as incomprehensible, the idea is considered laughable (Fortes, 1936). The Nuer consider sexual relations with a mother, daughter or sister an unbelievable phenomenon which "never occurs" (Evans-Pritchard, 1949).

Prediction 6.   In polygynous, nonstratified and stratified societies there should be a high incidence of classificatory kinship terminology of affinal kin as well as female avoidance of male affines. Polygynous societies are typically patrilocal (Flinn, 1981; Murdock, 1949) which increases the opportunity for adultery among affines (see Prediction 5). Classificatory kinship terminology may be one way of controlling adultery. Classificatory kinship terminology may also reduce factioning within the lineage by preventing mating and marriage within it. By classifying all lineage members as close kin (even those who are not genetically related, e.g., affines) expectations of social reciprocity are reinforced. Social unity within a lineage is often critical in patrilineal societies, especially if they are warring (Chagnon, 1979, 1982). The practice of avoiding male in-laws by females may also reduce adultery.

The Lozi are a society originally patrilineal in descent and of patrilocal residence (Gluckman, 1950). The Lozi traditionally were the dominant tribe of an African kingdom (Jensen, 1932) but did not appear so when Gluckman studied them. They have a fairly elaborate form of kinship terminology. All cousins are classed as brothers and sisters, a man calls the wife of any brother-in-law "my sister," a woman calls the brother of her co-wife "my brother" and a woman calls her father-in-law, "father," and grand-father-in-law, "grandfather," all of the brothers and sisters of a woman's father are called "my father" and all mother's sisters and brothers are called "my mother." It seems that all of these individuals are said not to marry but Gluckman indicates that they do at least sometimes marry one another.

The Lozi also practice some in-law avoidance. A woman must cover her body while in the presence of her senior male affines. A man avoids his mother-in-law, but not as strictly as a woman avoids her father-in-law. Interestingly, the avoidance between a woman and her male affines relaxes as she bears children. A woman's reproductive value and her attractiveness to men may decline with each child she bears as well as with age.

The Zulu were stratified, patrilocal, patrilineal, and polygynous (Gluckman, 1950). The Zulu also had an elaborate kinship terminology. Father's brothers were called father and father's brothers children were called brother and sister. Brothers of father's father and of mother's father were called grandparent. Mother's mother, sister's daughter, mother's father's sister's daughter (i.e., second cousin) and wives' of father were all called mother. These people were all forbidden to marry as were all cross-cousins (Krige, 1977). Additionally, in the Zulu a married woman practiced in-law avoidance. She "shuns through bashfulness" her father-in-law, all of his brothers and her elder brothers-in-law. In their presence she had to wear a garment which completely covered her body and a covering over her eyes (Krige, 1977).

The Nyakyusa are an African chieftainship organized by age-sets (cohorts of same-aged males) and patrilineal descent (Wilson, 1950). They are moderately polygynous, it appears, and patrilocal. It is a peculiar form of patrilocality because residences consist of young men (all the same age and childhood neighbors of one another, and often times related) all living in a quasi-neolocal neighborhood right next to that of their fathers.

The Nyakyusa have an elaborate system of in-law avoidance by women (Wilson, 1950). A woman may never look at her husband's father, enter his house, meet him on a path, nor may she mention his name, or words that sound like his name. This avoidance is extended to the brothers, half-brothers and male cousins of her father-in-law. A woman also avoids, though less strictly, her mother-in-law's brothers, half brothers and the husbands of her own full sisters. In fact, all men who are kin to a bride's father-in-law and are of his generation are avoided by a wife. Wilson (1950) writes "And any familiarity whatever between father-in-law and daughter-in-law savours of incest or indecency to the Nyakyusa" (p. 128). It appears that the reason behind the peculiar form of patrilocality, given by the Nyakyusa themselves, is the necessity for father-in-law avoidance.

Prediction 7.   Rules against mating and marriage between consanguineal and affinal kin in matrilineal/avuncular societies should be concentrated almost exclusively within the matriline. We expect rules directed at preventing adultery between affinal kin to be of less concern relative to rules directed at mating and marriage behavior of matriline members.

Matrilineal societies are characterized by scarce resources relative to patrilineal societies. Men in matrilineal societies have great difficulty controlling what few resources do exist and thus have reduced ability to make and enforce self-benefitting rules. When men are unable to enforce rules that aid paternity reliability it will be in the interest of *most* men to maintain more or less even distribution of status and resources. Mating and/or marriage between matriline members (e.g., a man and his matrilateral parallel cousin) may not only concentrate wealth but, additionally, increase the number of relatives in a matriline (Fig. 16.1). In preindustrial societies (especially patrilineal nonstratified and matrilineal) an important measure of wealth and status is number of kin (Alexander, 1979; Chagnon, 1979, 1982).

Richards (1950) discusses some Bantu societies with regard to their social structure. These societies are all matrilineal and include the Cewa, Ila, and Lamba. These groups of people have exogamous matriclans, and practice exogamy with regard to the matrilineage as well. A possible exception is the Cewa whose clan exogamy is not known, but it is true that the Cewa marry outside the matriline (Richards, 1950). Murdock (1949) classifies all of these groups as

A   B

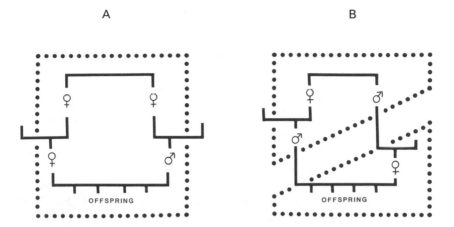

FIGURE 16.1.   In Matriline A marriage of matrilateral parallel cousins increases members in the matriline by incorporating a man's children into his matriline. In Matriline B marriage of matrilateral cross cousins (this would also apply to unrelated individuals) disperses kin because a man's children are incorporated into the matriline of his wife. Dotted lines enclose matrilines.

having "normal matrilineal extension" of incest tabus and "non-extension of incest tabus" patrilincally. That is, the incest tabus are confined to within the martriline.

The Plateau Tonga, another matrilineal group of African people, studied extensively by Colson (1958) view "incest" with "horror," "incest" being sexual relations between members of a matrilineage. Kin who are paternally related can and do indulge in sexual liaisons and this is virtually ignored (Colson, 1958). The list of matrilineal societies which confine incest rules to within the matriline is a long one and includes the Ndembu (Turner, 1965), the Yao (Mitchell, 1956), and the Yap (Labby, 1976).

The general conclusion from the evidence reviewed with regard to our predictions is that future research is called for in light of the view we have advanced. This research is now in progress and includes cross-cultural tests of the predictions outlined here as well as other predictions. It appears that the recognition of incest rules as something much more extensive than rules against close kin mating—instead as mating and marriage rules pertaining to various categories of relatives by consanguinity and affinity—will provide a fruitful avenue of research toward understanding a variety of behaviors and social features.

In the following two sections we discuss two recent hypotheses which address specific aspects of the incest question, namely royal sibling incest and cousin marriage.

Royal Incest

Institutionalized incest has occurred only in royal lines of highly stratified social systems (van den Berghe & Mesher, 1980). In highly stratified societies women in the top stratum may be unable to acquire suitable mates because of the hypergynous nature of such societies (Dickemann, 1979). Since men take wives from the lower strata one alternative is to kill female offspring in the royal or highest stratum (Dickemann, 1979, 1981), thereby removing the difficulty of whom they will marry once they reach adulthood. The probability that a royal female will be used for alliance may be low because the number of powerful strata are limited. None-the-less, this possibility does exist. In some societies (e.g., the royal Brahman caste of Kerala, India) a family will marry one son to a woman of equal rank and all other sons will take concubines from lower strata (Mencher, 1956). In this system, then, high ranking females are of some value for alliance. However, if a high ranking daughter has no opportunity to reproduce due to lack of appropriate alliances and due to the hypergynous nature of a society, she represents a waste of parental effort, especially since her value in directing nepotism to her brothers' children is low.

If a high ranking woman has no chance of reproducing with an unrelated equal or higher ranking man, one alternative is to marry a brother. Van den Berghe and Mesher (1980) have treated the subject of royal incest and point out that the cost of close inbreeding approaches zero for a man whose wives of no relatedness to him number in the hundreds. At most he wastes some time and energy; at best he gains a son of high relatedness to him who will in turn become highly polygynous (see van den Berghe & Mesher, 1980 for discussion).

This argument assumes that royal sibling incest means royal sibling copulation, not simply royal sibling marriage. Moreover, critical to van den Berghe and Mesher's hypothesis is the inheritance of rank and throne by the highly related son produced by royal sibling incest. This is an assumption of the hypothesis which may be invalid. Bixler (1982) found only one instance of succession by an offspring of incestuous parents in Ptolemaic Egypt and none in Pharaonic Egypt or Hawaii.

An alternative to van den Berghe and Mesher's hypothesis for the existence of royal incest is as follows. A wealthy man is required to pay large dowries for the marriage of his daughters. It seems to be the case in highly stratified societies that the wealthier a man is, the greater the dowry amount he is required to pay for his daughter's marriage (Dickemann, 1981). In a highly stratified society, the dowry associated with the marriage of a daughter results in loss of wealth and thus power and status. This loss may not be compensated for by the marriage of sons who are obtaining brides from lower strata. It may sometimes be a good strategy to retain (rather than kill) female offspring because of the possibility of alliance formation. When the alliance is impossible or undesirable an alternative may be to marry them to their brothers (who are at the same time married to many other women). Thus no loss of wealth and power via large dowries is suffered. Additionally a father could choose a suitable sire (perhaps a cousin or other relative) for the offspring of his daughter. These offspring could then inherit wealth from their uncle, their mother's brother (who may claim paternity). With this system both a woman's father and her brother would have increased relatedness to offspring of their daughter/sister and gain relatives and heirs with no loss of wealth or prestige.

We have not located evidence pertaining to this hypothesis as yet. It is true however that Ancient Egyptian high-ranking men sometimes adopted boys who were without familial ties and married them to their "sisters" (i.e., daughter of the adoptive father) (Brinton, Christopher, & Wolff, 1955). It should further be kept in mind that Egyptian kinship terminology is unclear. For instance the terms "lover," "beloved," "husband," and "wife" appear to have applied to cousins and not always to brother and sister (Bardis, 1967), and classificatory kinship terminology may confuse matters in some of the African kingdoms that van den Berghe and Mesher cite as well (Lancaster, 1983).

Cousin Marriage

Anthropologists have defined four categories of cousins (Fig. 16.2). Matrilateral cousins are related through the mother: patrilateral cousins related through the father. Parallel cousins are related through *same* sexed parental siblings (the offspring of two brothers or two sisters). Cross cousins are related through *opposite* sexed parental siblings (the offspring of a man and those of his sister or a woman and those of her brother).

Alexander (1977, 1979) has hypothesized that incest avoidance is the reason that cross cousin marriages are favored over parallel cousin marriages in some societies. He argues that there will be a preference for cross-cousin marriages when parallel cousins are more closely related than $\frac{1}{8}$. This can occur under sororal polygyny (one man married to a group of sisters), and the sororate (a man marries the sister of his deceased wife). Additionally, he suggests that in these systems cousins should be treated differently and identified by different terms depending on how they are related to an individual. Alexander found that 95% of sororally polygynous societies do distinguish between cross and parallel cousins. Under sororal polygyny offspring of sisters have an average relatedness of $\frac{3}{8}$, because they are half siblings through their father ($r = \frac{1}{4}$) and first cousins through their mothers ($r = \frac{1}{8}$). Alexander reasons that by distinguishing between parallel and cross cousins and by preferring the latter as marriage partners, inbreeding at a damaging level (incest, $r \geq \frac{1}{4}$) is successfully avoided.

Although he argues that this hypothesis explains rules about cousin marriage in terms of optimal outbreeding, what Alexander has discovered is differential *treatment* (in terms of nepotism) of cousins, not *rules* regarding their nepotistic behavior or marriage patterns.

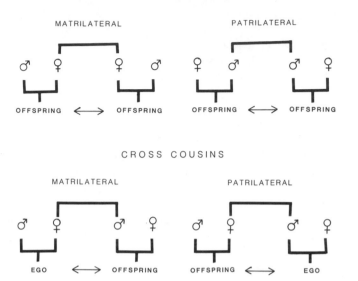

FIGURE 16.2. Types of cousins related by various kinship ties (see text). Lines above symbols indicate siblings, lines below indicate marriage. Arrows point to sibling groups that are cousins to one another.

Matrilateral parallel cousins (mother's sister's offspring) under sororal polygyny are often raised together in the same house (sororal polygyny is characterized by wives living in one house and nonsororal polygyny by wives maintaining separate households with their offspring; Murdock, 1949). Therefore such cousins may behave toward each other as siblings. Consequently rules regarding their sexual behavior with one another would be minimal or absent because the Westermarck effect should operate (Westermarck, 1891). Likewise, differential treatment of cousins would be predicted for a society such as the Turkmen (Irons, 1979) in which offspring of brothers by different women (patrilateral parallel cousins, $r = \frac{1}{8}$) live in the same house and offspring of sisters (matrilateral parallel, $r = \frac{1}{8}$) live separately (i.e., the opposite of the situation described above). In this case there is no asymmetry in genetic concentration but there is a residential difference, which we predict would affect cousin (in this case patrilateral parallel) treatment via the Westmarck effect, but again not rules about marriage and sexual behavior.

We have found evidence in support of this prediction in the residence and marriage patterns among the people of Vellore, South India. A group of brothers live, together with their wives and offspring, in their father's house. The children are ". . . all brothers and sisters to each other . . . None . . . will marry each other." (Centerwall & Centerwall, 1966, p. 1160). There is no indication of a rule in this society regarding parallel cousin marriage. There is a preference for cross cousin marriage.

Again, cousin marriage comes in four forms: offspring of same sex siblings marry (matrilateral or patrilateral parallel) or offspring of different sex siblings marry (matrilateral or patrilateral cross) (Fig. 16.2). Parallel cousin marriage is quite rare. When it does occur, it is most often patrilateral and usually found in strongly male dominated societies (Alexander, 1977, 1979). Cross-cousin marriage occurs in many societies (van den Berghe, 1979, 1980) and is preferred in some societies (Alexander, 1979; van den Berghe, 1979, 1980). Inbreeding depression at the level of first cousin (r = ⅛) is difficult to assess. Some investigators think it is slight (Lenz, 1970; Hughes, 1982); others think it is large (Schull & Neel, 1965). The negative effects of first cousin marriage may be more than negligible. Even so, people do it regularly, and it is the preferred mating pattern in many societies. Thus, the positive effects of first cousin marriage must outweigh the costs.

The positive effects of cousin marriage may be to (1) promote family alliance and concentrate wealth, or (2), in avuncular societies, to maintain control of both wives and sisters and increase paternity confidence. The first effect was recognized long ago by Westermarck (1891) and has subsequently been discussed by anthropologists (for further discussion and references see Murdock, 1949). The second effect, although in different form, has been discussed by Richards (1950).

Nondispersal of wealth is facilitated by first cousin marriage, especially with regard to brideprice payments. Brideprice is paid by a prospective groom to the father of his intended wife. In patrilineal systems patrilateral parallel cousin marriage could concentrate wealth because by marrying a patrilateral parallel cousin under patriliny the bridewealth payment remains within the patriline. This would not be the case for patrilateral cross cousin marriage because the brideprice would become the property of another patriline (Fig. 16.3A). But under patrilateral parallel cousin marriage a few individuals can maintain possession of the wealth, namely those within the patriline enclosed by dotted lines in Fig. 16.3B. This concentration of wealth could quickly lead to large disparities between patrilines. This sort of system could only be maintained in the most single-family dominated societies or societies in which large disparities cannot be realized, as a result of the nature of resources (see Alexander, 1979).

An alternative to patrilateral parallel cousin marriage is patrilateral cross-cousin marriage (Fig. 16.3A), which appears to be the alternative chosen (van den Berghe, 1979) in many polygynous, nonstratified societies. In this way brideprice at least remains within the hands of consanguinal relatives, and each generation of cross-cousin marriage increases relatedness, and possibly nepotism, between uncles and aunts and their nieces and nephews. The other thing cousin marriage of any sort does is increase the number of kin that a family can potentially control.

A   B

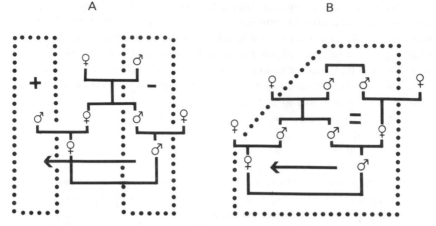

FIGURE 16.3. Dispersal of brideprice (indicated by arrow) in patrilateral cross (A) and patrilateral parallel (B) cousin marriages. Dotted
lines enclose partrilineages. = no loss of wealth, − loss of wealth, +
gain in wealth.

Under matriliny considerations about cousin marriage are somewhat different
from those above. Matriliny is characterized by avuncular nepotism and by
matrilocal residence (Flinn, 1981; van den Berghe, 1979). Under these conditions a husband has relatively little control over his wife because she lives with
her (protective) relatives. At the same time, if he lives with his wife, he cannot
also be living with his matrilineal kin and concerning himself with the affairs of
his sisters and their offspring. This has been termed the ''matrilineal puzzle'' by
Richards (1950). One solution, which is recognized and preferred by many
individuals in matrilineal societies (Radcliffe-Brown & Forde, 1950; Schneider
& Gough, 1961), is the marriage of a man to his mother's brother's daughter
(matrilateral cross cousin). Two things can be accomplished by this: (1) men are
more likely to remain with their own matrilines (at least with their mother's
brother) as they simultaneously live with their wives, and (2) there is a somewhat
greater concentration of brideprice, because under avuncular investment a man
furnishes the brideprice for his sister's sons.

For a man, matrilateral cross cousin marriage may be the best of both worlds
because he can maintain his investment in his nephews as well as having a
greater likelihood of living with, thereby limiting the activities of, his wife—
(especially if the cousin marriage system has proceeded for a number of generations) (Fig. 16.4). This could happen if a man, who lives with his wife, also has
his sister's son living with him as his daughter's husband. Each generation a man
lives with his matrilineal kin (at least his mother's brother) and his wife. This
marriage form also increases the number of individuals a man (the uncle in each
generation) can manipulate. This system may also serve to increase the reliability
of paternity of men who marry their matrilateral cross cousin.

Matrilateral cross-cousin marriage, however, limits the options for females. It decreases female ability to form sexual ties with men of their choice both before marriage (if she is expected to marry her cousin) and after marriage (if she is under the watchful eyes of her husband, his matriline and her own matriline) (Fig. 16.4). It makes sense that cross-cousin marriage preference is largely found in matrilineal societies (van den Berghe, 1980) given male concerns, but since men seem to be less able to gain the strong leading edge in intersexual conflicts in matrilineal societies compared to patrilineal societies, a prediction is that cross-cousin marriage should be less often realized in matrilineal societies that prefer it than in patrilineal societies that do.

van den Berghe (1980) lists data on societies that prefer or disapprove of cousin marriages by descent system. He found that 50.8% (N = 216) of patrilineal societies disapproved of all cousins marrying. Thirty eight percent of patrilineal societies preferred cross-cousin marriage and 5.6% preferred parallel cousin marriage. Of matrilineal societies 46.5% (N = 71) disapproved of any cousins marrying, 51% preferred cross-cousin marriage and 0 preferred parallel cousin marriage. These data suggest that matrilineal societies prefer cross-cousin marriages more often than patrilineal societies do (51% and 38% respectively), but the prediction can only be supported anecdotally. From the matrilineal ethnographic literature it appears that, although preferred, cross-cousin marriage rarely occurs. Turner (1965) found that among the Ndembu less than 10% of all marriages were between cross cousins, and this system of marriage is preferred in this society. Colson (1958) found among the Plateau Tonga less than 5% of

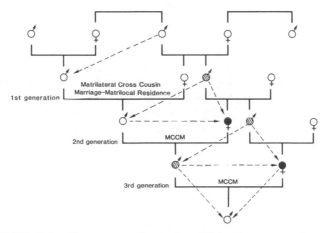

FIGURE 16.4. Three generations of matrilateral cross cousin marriage and matrilocal residence (MCCM). Dashed arrows indicate direction of male investment.
♂ = males who benefit by controlling nephew (son-in-law), daughter, and grandnephew (grandson).
♀ = females controlled by husband and 2 matrilines.

marriages are between preferred cousins and a small percentage of the Lakeside Tonga actually practice preferred cousin marriage (van Velsen, 1964). In patrilineal societies the expectation is that the preferred form of marriage should more often be the actual form, but we have no information with which to address this as yet.

Cousin marriage may be discouraged or outlawed in state societies in order to prevent concentration of wealth within a family. This is complementary to Alexander's (1981) hypothesis regarding the outlawing of cousin marriage. Alexander argues that marriages among cousins would create factioning to the detriment of whole group unity which is especially desired by leaders in large, warring, state societies. The hypothesis that we envision is that cousin marriage is discouraged or outlawed by rule makers whose concern is protection of their ruling positions from uprisings of, and possible overthrow by, powerful groups within their nations. An effect of cousin marriage is concentration of wealth. When large amounts of wealth or large pieces of land are involved the advantage of cousin marriage may be considerable. The benefit of cousin marriage in state societies is maximized when the families participating in this marriage have little to gain by marrying out: (a) there is no advantage in alliance formation with potential competitors, (b) most or all of the local wealth or resource is owned or controlled by a few powerful families (because if not, the advantage of alliance with nonkin may be real), and (c) the wealth must be of a nature which allows maximum benefit by concentration (e.g., land).

SUMMARY

Incest has captured the attentions of researchers from many fields. Yet little understanding of incest and related behavior has been achieved. Researchers generally have assumed that close inbreeding (between relatives whose relatedness (r) is high, e.g., fathers and daughters, brothers and sisters, etc.) should be common except that incest rules are made to keep populations free of the deleterious effects of close kin matings (defective offspring). The problem with this assumption is that it neglects consideration of the operation of selection. If a behavior seriously detracts from the reproductive potential of individuals, selection should act against it. Close inbreeding can have serious effects on offspring viability. In humans, selection has resulted in the evolution of the proximate mechanism involving cosocialization of close relatives during development which promotes incest avoidance (the Westermarck effect). Additionally, recent evidence indicates that incest between close kin rarely occurs (van den Berghe, 1982).

We feel it is imperative to divide behaviors usually lumped under the heading of incest into three categories. The first, incest, involves mating between individuals with $r \geq \frac{1}{4}$ (e.g. parents and offspring, siblings, and half-siblings); the second, inbreeding, involves mating between relatives with r < ¼ (cousins of various degree). The third category is best thought of as a special category of adultery since the participants in the sexual encounters which are ruled against (and still called incestuous in the literature) may share no genes by descent. They are often related by affinity rather than by consanguinity.

This paper examines rules regarding inbreeding and adultery pertaining to relatives by consanguinity and affinity. The view we propose is as follows. Individuals are rarely incestuous. Rules are not focused on close relatives; instead they are focused on inbreeding and adultery and are made to enhance the fitness of powerful men, the rule makers. These rules can function in any of three categories: (1) to ensure that females are kept as sexually isolated as possible from men (excluding their own husbands) with whom they are in frequent contact. (2) to prevent sexual interactions within lineages and thereby to promote lineage solidarity, and (3) to prevent relatives from concentrating wealth and/or power by intermarrying. The category of rules that is most important in a given society depends on mating system, residence pattern, degree of social stratification, and ecological circumstances influencing resource accumulation.

ACKNOWLEDGMENTS

We thank Martin Daly, Henry Harpending, William Kuipers, Gene Mesher, Pierre van den Berghe, Margo Wilson and Bruce Woodward for comments on the manuscript. Also, we thank P.A.R. Thornhill and A. R. Thornhill for their patience.

REFERENCES

Adams, M., & Neel, J. V., (1967). Children of incest. *Pediatrics, 40,* 55–61.

Alexander, R. D. (1974). The evolution of social behavior. *Annual Review of Ecology and Systematics, 5,* 325–383.

Alexander, R. D. (1977). Natural selection and the analysis of human sociality. In *The changing scenes in natural sciences 1776–1976* (pp. 283–337). Academy of Natural Science, Special Publication, 12.

Alexander, R. D. (1978). Natural selection and societal laws. In T. Englehardt & D. Callahan (Eds.), *The foundations of ethics and its relationship to science* (Vol. 3), Morals, science and society. Hastings-on-Hudson, NY: Hastings Institute.

Alexander, R. D. (1979). *Darwinism and human affairs.* Seattle, WA: University of Washington Press.

Alexander, R. D. (1981). Evolution, culture, and human behavior: Some general considerations. In R. D. Alexander & D. W. Tinkle (Eds.), *Natural selection and social behavior: Recent research and new theory* (pp. 509–520). New York: Chiron Press.

Alexander, R. D., Hoogland, J. L., Howard, R. D., Noonan, K. M., & Sherman, P. W., (1979). Sexual dimorphisms and breeding systems in pinnipeds, ungulates, primates and humans. In N. A. Chagnon & W. G. Irons (Eds.), *Evolutionary biology and human social behavior: An anthropological perspective* (pp. 402–435). North Scituate, MA: Duxbury Press.

Bardis, P. D. (1967). Incest in ancient Egypt. *Indian Journal of History of Medicine, 12,* 14–20.

Benshoof, L. & Thornhill, R., (1979). The evolution of monogamy and concealed ovulation in humans. *Journal of Social and Biological Structures, 2,* 95–106.

Betzig, L. L. (1982). Despotism and differential reproduction: A cross-cultural correlation of conflict asymmetry, hierarchy, and degree of polygyny. *Ethology and Sociobiology, 3,* 209–221.

Betzig, L. L. (1986). *Despotism and differential reproduction: A Darwinian view of history.* New York: Aldine.

Bixler, R. H. (1982). Sibling incest in the royal families of Egypt, Peru, and Hawaii. *Journal of Sex Research, 18,* 264–281.

Brinton, C., Christopher, J. B., & Wolff, R. L., (1955). *A history of civilization.* Englewood Cliffs, NJ: Prentice-Hall, Inc.

Borgia, G. (1980). Human aggression as a biological adaptation. In J. S. Lockard (Ed.), *The evolution of human social behavior* (pp. 166–191). New York: Elsevier.

Brown, J. S. (1952). A comparative study of deviations from sexual mores. *American Sociological Review, 17,* 135–146.

Centerwall, W. R., & Centerwall, S. A., (1966). Consanguinity and congenital anomalies in South India: A pilot study. *Indian Journal of Medical Research, 54,* 1160–1167.

Chagnon, N. A. (1979). Is reproductive success equal in egalitarian societies? In N. A. Chagnon & W. G. Irons (Eds.), *Evolutionary biology and human social behavior: An anthropological perspective* (pp. 374–402). North Scituate, MA: Duxbury Press.

Chagnon, N. A. (1982). Sociodemographic attributes of nepotism in tribal populations: Man the rule breaker. In Kings College Sociobiology Group (Eds.), *Current problems in sociobiology* (pp. 291–319). Cambridge: Cambridge University Press.

Colson, E. (1958). *Marriage and the family among the Plateau Tonga.* Manchester: Manchester University Press.

Corbett, P. E. (1930). *The Roman law of marriage.* Oxford: Clarendon Press.

Daly, M., Wilson, M. & Weghorst, S. J., (1982). Male sexual jealousy. *Ethology and Sociobiology, 3,* 11–27.

Dickemann, M. (1979). Female infanticide, reproductive strategies, and social stratification: A preliminary model. In N. A. Chagnon & W. G. Irons (Eds.), *Evolutionary biology and human social behavior: An anthropological perspective* (pp. 321–368). North Scituate, MA: Duxbury Press.

Dickemann, M. (1981). Paternal confidence and dowry competition: A biocultural analysis of purdah. In R. D. Alexander & D. W. Tinkle (Eds.), *Natural selection and social behavior: Recent research and new theory* (pp. 417–437). New York: Chiron Press.

Dizinno, G. A. (1983). *Male homosexual behavior: An evolutionary analysis.* Doctoral dissertation, Florida State University, Tallahassee, FL.

Evans-Pritchard, E. E. (1940). *The Nuer, the modes of livelihood and political institutions of a Nilotic people.* Oxford: Clarendon Press.

Evans-Pritchard, E. E. (1949). Nuer rules of exogamy and incest. In Meyer Fortes (Ed.), *Social structure studies presented to A. R. Radcliffe-Brown.* Oxford: Clarendon Press.

Flinn, M. (1981). Uterine vs. agnatic kinship variability and associated cousin marriage preferences: An evolutionary biological analysis. In R. D. Alexander & D. W. Tinkle (Eds.), *Natural selection and social behavior recent research and new theory* (pp. 439–475). New York: Chiron Press.

Fortes, M. (1936). Kinship, incest and exogamy of the northern territories of the Gold Coast. In L. H. D. Buxton (Ed.), *Custom is king.* London: Hutchinson.

Fortes, M. (1950). Kinship and marriage among the Ashanti. In A. R. Radcliffe-Brown & D. Forde

(Eds.), *African systems of kinship and marriage* (pp. 252–284). London: Oxford University Press.

Fox, R. (1980). *The red lamp of incest*. New York: E. P. Dutton.

Freud, S. (1922). *Lectures on psychoanalysis*. London: Allen and Unwin.

Gaulin, S. J. C., & Schlegel, A. (1980). Paternal confidence and paternal investment: A cross cultural test of a sociobiological hypothesis. *Ethology and Sociobiology, 1*, 301–309.

Gluckman, M. (1950). Kinship and marriage among the Lozi of Northern Rhodesia and the Zulu of Natal. In A. R. Radcliffe-Brown & D. Forde (Eds.), *African systems of kinship and marriage* (pp. 166–206). London: Oxford University Press.

Goody, J. (1956). A comparative approach to incest and adultery. *British Journal of Sociology, 7*, 286–305.

Gough, K. (1961). Nayar: Central Kerala. In D. M. Schneider & K. Gough (Eds.), *Matrilineal kinship* (pp. 298–384). Berkeley: University of California Press.

Gough, K. (1971). Neur kinship: A re-examination. In T. O. Beidelman (Ed.), *The translation of culture: Essays to E. E. Evans-Pritchard* (pp. 79–122). London: Tavistock.

Hennigh, L. (1966). Control of incest in Eskimo folktales. *Journal of American folklore, 79*, 356–369.

Hoebel, E. A. (1954). *The law of primitive man: A study of comparative legal dynamics*. Cambridge: Harvard University Press.

Hughes, A. (1982). Preferential first-cousin marriage and inclusive fitness. *Ethology and Sociobiology, 1*, 311–318.

Irons, W. (1979). Investment and primary social dyads. In N. A. Chagnon & W. G. Irons (Eds.), *Evolutionary biology and human social behavior: An anthropological perspective* (pp. 181–212). North Scituate, MA: Duxbury Press.

Jensen, A. E. (1932). The political organization and the historical traditions of the Barotze on the upper Zambezi (english translation by F. Shultze). [Württenbergisher verein für Handelsgeographie E. V., Museum für Länder-und Völkerkunds.] Jahrelsbericht: Linden Museum, Stuttgart.

Krige, E. J. (1977). *The social system of the Zulus*. Pietermaritzburg: Shuter and Shooter.

Kurland, J. (1979). Paternity, mother's brother and human sociality. In N. A. Chagnon & W. G. Irons (Eds.), *Evolutionary biology and human social behavior: An anthropological perspective* (pp. 145–180). North Scituate, MA: Duxbury Press.

Labby, D. (1976). The Yapese concept of incest. *The Journal of the Polynesian Society, 85*, 171–180.

Lancaster, C. S. (1983). Sexual rivalry in human inbreeding or adaptive cooperation. *The Behavioral and Brain Sciences, 6*, 109–110.

Leach, E. R. (1961). *Rethinking anthropology*. London: Athlone Press.

Lee, R. B. (1969). !Kung Bushmen subsistence: An input-output analysis. In A. P. Vayda (Ed.), *Environment and cultural behavior*. Austin: University of Texas Press.

Lenz, W. (1970). *Medical genetics*. Chicago: University of Chicago Press.

Levington, J. S. (1983). Darwinism: love it or leave it. *Evolution, 37*, 432–435.

Levi-Strauss, C. (1969). *The elementary structures of kinship*. Boston: Beacon.

Lewinsohn, R. (1958). *A history of sexual customs*. New York: Harper and Brothers.

Lumsden, C. J., & Wilson, E. O. (1981). *Genes, mind and culture*. Cambridge, MA: Harvard University Press.

Malinowski, B. (1927). *Sex and repression in savage society*. New York: Meridian.

McLennan, J. F. (1896). *An inquiry into the origin of exogamy*. London: Macmillan.

Mencher, J. P. (1956). The Nayars of South Malabar. In M. F. Nimkoff (Ed.), *Comparative family systems* (pp. 163–191). Boston: Houghton Mifflin.

Minturn, L., Grosse, M., & Haider, S. (1969). Cultural patterning of sexual beliefs and behavior. *Ethnology, 8*, 301–318.

Mitchell, K. (1956). *The Yao village, a study in the social structure of a Malawian people*. Manchester: Manchester University Press.

Morgan, H. D. (1826). *The doctrine and law of marriage, adultery and divorce*. (Vol. I). Oxford: W. Baxter.

Murdock, G. P. (1949). *Social structure*. New York: MacMillen.

Parsons, T. (1954). The incest taboo in relation to social structure and the socialization of the child. *British Journal of Sociology, 5*, 101–107.

Radcliffe-Brown, A. R. (1922). *The Andaman islanders*. Cambridge: Cambridge University Press.

Radcliffe-Brown, A. R., & Forde, D. (Eds.). (1950). *African systems of kinship and marriage*. London: Oxford University Press.

Rattray, R. S. (1929). *Ashanti law and constitution*. Oxford: Clarendon Press.

Richards, A. I. (1950). Some types of family structure amongst the Central Bantu. In A. R. Radcliffe-Brown & D. Forde (Eds.), *African systems of kinship and marriage* (pp. 207–251). London: Oxford University Press.

Schneider, D. M. (1976). The meaning of incest. *The Journal of Polynesian Society, 85*, 149–170.

Schneider, D. M., & Gough, K. (Eds.). (1961). *Matrilineal kinship*. Berkeley: University of California Press.

Schull, W. J., & Neel, J. V. (1965). *The effects of inbreeding on Japanese children*. New York: Harper and Row.

Seligman, B. A. (1929). Incest and descent: Their influence on social organization. *Journal of the Royal Anthropological Institute, 59*, 231–272.

Seligman, C. G. (1911). *The Veddas*. Cambridge: Cambridge University Press.

Shepher, J. (1971). *Self imposed incest avoidance and exogamy in second generation kibbutz adults*. Xerox Monograph Series Nos. 72–871, Ann Arbor, MI.

Shepher, J. (1983). *Incest: A biosocial view*. New York: Academic Press.

Shields, W. M. (1982). *Philopatry, inbreeding and the evolution of sex*. Albany: State University of New York.

Spiro, M. E. (1958). *Children of the kibbutz*. Cambridge: Harvard University Press.

Symons, D. (1979). *The evolution of human sexuality*. Oxford: Oxford University Press.

Thornhill, N. W., & Thornhill, R. (1984). Review of Joseph Shepher, 1983. Incest: A biosocial view. *Ethology and Sociobiology, 5*, 211–214.

Thornhill, R., & Thornhill, N. W. (1983). Human rape: An evolutionary analysis. *Ethology and Sociobiology, 4*, 137–173.

Turner, R. E. (1965). *Schism and continuity in an east African pastoralist society*. Manchester: Manchester University Press.

van den Berghe, P. L. (1979). *Human family systems*. New York: Elsevier.

van den Berghe, P. L. (1980). Incest and exogamy: A sociobiological reconsideration. *Ethology and Sociobiology, 1*, 151–162.

van den Berghe, P. L. (1982). Human inbreeding avoidance: Culture in nature. *Behavioral and Brain Sciences, 6*, 91–124.

van den Berghe, P. L. & Mesher, G. (1980). Royal incest and inclusive fitness. *American Ethnologist, 7*, 300–317.

van Velsen, J. (1964). *The politics of kinship*. Manchester: Manchester University Press.

Weinberg, S. K. (1955). *Incest behavior*. New York: Citadel Press.

Westermarck, E. A. (1891). *The history of human marriage*. London: MacMillen.

Wilson, M. (1950). Nyakyusa kinship. In A. R. Radcliffe-Brown & D. Forde (Eds.), *African systems of kinship and marriage* (pp. 111–139). London: Oxford University Press.

Wright, S. (1933). Inbreeding and homozygosis. *Proceedings of the National Academy of Sciences, 79*, 411–420.

lutionary perspective is its
gists, no less than other
disciplinary ruts that may
rizes important scientific
ry perspective among her
plinary endeavour that is
and that also draws upon
complementary theory.
gists, psychologists, so-
he contributors. Donald
at progress in the social
rs to specialize in rela-
them toward separate,
thinking should be an
the social sciences. A
heory is a focus which
groups that might not
family sociologists,
s.

vestigations of human
of the field that was
epistemological cri-
ment of any area of
ance our understand-
will continue to see
future discussions of
also to be hoped that
rspective will feel a
ning or evidence to
stitute professional
that there is neces-
ary political views.
An agenda for the
hypotheses derived
ready been carried
olved dispositions
ed by examining a
ded in a detailed
useful in this re-
sed on evolution-
pectives, such as
is no reason to
se of other per-

volume is considerable:
apparent that researchers
only to provide a general
testable research hypoth-
earch studies. It is not yet
role in influencing each of
lume, but the first steps in
ented in these chapters. We
tend and correct the prelimi-

is volume is that a full under-
sideration of the evolutionary
thoughts and feelings today
owever, it should be noted that
onary psychologists, and this is
a that involves the synthesis of
sciplines. Is evolutionary theory
tive phenomena? To what degree
ological evolution? Are evolution-
he structures of a society or in the
nong the least substantive but most
involves what label should be at-
an sociobiology? Evolutionary psy-
lack of absorbing issues for evolu-
future.

the most salutary aspects of an evo
ciplinary nature. Academic psychol
ientific researchers, are apt to fall into
the breadth of vision that often characte
. A psychologist who includes an evolutiona
tools involves herself in an explicitly interdisc
on a foundation of biological theory and research,
hropology, sociology and psychology for data and
This volume neatly illustrates this synthesis, with biolo
ciologists and anthropologists all represented among t
Campbell (1969) presented the intriguing suggestion th
sciences would be facilitated by encouraging researche
tively unique interdisciplines, rather than channelling
rather ethnocentric disciplines. Expertise in evolutionar
important component of developing interdisciplines in
shared interest in the explanatory value of evolutionary
encourages the exchange of ideas and findings among
otherwise say much to each other: for instance, amon
developmental psychologists, and cultural anthropologist

Another encouraging aspect of recent evolutionary in
behavior is the waning of the type of polemical criticism
occasionally voiced several years ago. Methodological an
tiques are an expected and necessary part of the develop
inquiry, but ideologically motivated attacks do little to adv
ing of the determinants of behavior. It is to be hoped that w
less ideological heat and more empirically based light in
evolutionary influences on human behavior. However, it is
social scientists analyzing behavior from an evolutionary p
special responsibility to protest the use of evolutionary reas
support inhumane social policies. To fail to do so might co
irresponsibility, and could give comfort to those who allege
sary link between an evolutionary perspective and reaction

In what directions might evolutionary psychology proceed
future might include more empirical studies aimed at testing
from evolutionary models. A number of such studies have a
out, as reviewed in this volume, but the degree to which ev
continue to influence our activities will ultimately be determin
body of carefully designed empirical research that is groun
knowledge of contemporary evolutionary models. Particularly
gard would be studies that attempted to contrast predictions ba
ary theory with others derived from other psychological pers
social learning or psychodynamic perspectives. Although ther
expect that evolutionary predictions will always contradict th

spectives (the approaches could well be complementary regarding many topics, the testing of some competing hypotheses might well advance our understanding of human motivation.

Other avenues for progress involve the continuing integration of evolutionary thinking into frontier areas of psychological investigation. For instance, some cognitive biases in human judgement presented in the seminal work of Tversky and Kahnemann (1974) likely reflect selection pressures in our evolutionary history. A thorough consideration of evolutionary factors might help resolve some contemporary issues regarding the structure and function of even more basic cognitive architecture (Anderson, 1983; Pylyshyn, 1984). Another active area that might benefit from an infusion of evolutionary thinking is behavioral economics, and a start in this direction has been made by Becker (1981). Although this volume surveys a wide range of topics, there are a great many more that might be illuminated by evolutionary analysis. Darwin (1872/1979; p. 222) truly said "In the future I see open fields for far more important researches. Psychology will be securely based . . . [on an evolutionary] foundation, that of the necessary acquirement of each mental power and capacity by gradation. Much light will be thrown on the origin of man and his history. . . . There is grandeur in this view of life."

REFERENCES

Anderson, J. R. (1983). *The architecture of cognition*. Cambridge, MA: Harvard University Press.
Becker, G. S. (1981). *A treatise on the family*. Cambridge, MA: Harvard University Press.
Campbell, D. T. (1969). Ethnocentrism of disciplines and the fish-scale model of omniscience. In M. Sherif & C. W. Sherif (Eds.), *Interdisciplinary relationships in the social sciences*. Chicago: Aldine.
Darwin, C. D. (1979). *The origin of species* (6th ed.). In R. E. Leakey (Ed.), *The illustrated origin of species*. New York: Hill and Wang. (Original work published 1881).
Pylyshyn, Z. M. (1984). *Computation and cognition: Toward a foundation for cognitive science*. Cambridge, MA: MIT Press.
Tversky, A., & Kahnemann, D. (1974). Judgement under uncertainty: Heuristics and biases. *Science, 185*, 1124–1131.

Author Index

A

Abbot, J., 184, *203*
Ackerman, P., 108, 111, *114*
Adams, M., 374, *397*
Adler, K., 190, *203*
Agren, G., 182, 187, *198*
Albon, H. D., 18, *27*
Alcock, J., 4, 20, 24, *26, 29*, 32, *56*, 209, *215*, 277, 278, 281, *290*
Allen, V. L., 100, *113*
Allen, J., 5, *26*
Allen, E., 63, 64, 65, *77*
Alexander, R. D., 4, 14, 18, *26*, 31, 32, 34, 39, 40, 41, 43, 45, 46, 47, 49, 50, 51, 52, 53, 54, 55, *56, 57, 58, 66, 77*, 84, 85, 90, 97, 98, *113*, 123, 124, 136, *144*, 175, 176, 183, 186, 197, *198*, 214, 218, *219*, 231, 234, 237, 240, 241, 242, 243, *248*, 270, 271, 273, 278, 280, 282, *288*, 302, *306*, 336, 349, *350*, 375, 376, 377, 380, 381, 382, 388, 391, 393, 396, *397*
Allison, A. C., 35, *57*
Allman, W. F., 264, *266*
Ali, Z., 296, *306*
Alper, J. S., 215, *19*
Altemeier, W. A., 297, *308*

Altman, H., 323, *333*
Altmann, S. A., 255, 264, *266*
Amir, M., 285, *288*
Anastasi, A., 207, 209, *219*
Anderson, H. N., 176, *203*
Anderson, J. R., 403, *403*
Anderson, W. F., 319, *330*
Andersson, M., 295, *306*
Andrews, P. W., 165, *171, 174*
Appley, M., 103, *114*
Ardrey, R., 99, *113*
Aronfreed, J., 104, 105, *113, 114*
Asuni, T., 314, 320, *329*
Axelrod, R., 4, *26*, 45, 57, 85, *86, 98, 114*, 229, *248*, 261, 264, *266*
Ayala, F., 63, *77*

B

Bachman, J., 314, *329*
Baer, D., 217, *220*
Baer, R., 99, *114*
Bailey, R. C., 101, *115*
Baldwin, J. M., 225, *248*
Ballou, J., 181, *202*
Balogh, R. D., 184, 194, 195, *202*

405

Subject Index

A

Adaptation, 6, 37, 270–273
  conditional strategies, 20, 138–139
  constraints on, 124–125
  and function, 121–124
  and morality, 245
  and psychological mechanisms, 126–130
  specificity of, 139–140
  See also Natural selection
Adaptationist program
  and behavioral science, 293
  of sociobiology, 246
Adaptation and phenotypic resemblance, 197
Adultery, 368, 374–375
  incestuous, 374–375
  in Zande, 368
Age,
  and mate selection, 341–343
  of rape victims, 284
  and suicide, 320
Aggressive behavior,
  genetics of, 163, 245
Alarm calls,
  in nepotism, 179
Albinism, behavioral effects in mice, 164
Allele, 33
Altruism,
  evolution of, in humans, 96–102, 109–113
  and evolutionary theory, 43–45, 82–102

and incidental helping. 84
individual, 83
parameters of, 81–82
and psychology, 102–113
reciprocity, 84–86
and socialization, 236
and sympathy, 109
See also Helping behavior, Inclusive fitness,
  Nepotism, Kin selection, Reciprocal
  altruism
Amphibians, sibling recognition by, 189–190
Ancient China, incest rules in, 383
Ancient Egypt, royal incest in, 391
Ancient Rome, incest rules in, 384
Andamanese, incest rules in, 381
Anisogamy, 280
Ants, carpenter (*Camponotus*)
  kin recognition in, 85
Anxiety and self-preservation, 312
Appetitive behavior and self preservation,
  312
Artificial selection, 162–164
Ashanti, incest avoidance in, 361–363
Assortative mating,
  behavioral consequences of, 158
  in humans, 101
Audiogenic seizures, 157
Avunculate,
  and paternity uncertainty, 282
  in Ashanti, 384

419

Hippocampus,
  artificial selection in mice, 167
Hitler, Adolf
  and biological determinism, 64
  and science, 205
  and Social Darwinism, 5
Homicide, 302–303
Homology, 9
Homosexuality,
  and parental investment, 234
  and sociobiology, 65
  in Zande, 368
Hopelessness, 319, 326
Human nature, 141–144
Human sexuality,
  and evolution, 49
Hume, David
  and epistemology, 75
Hypergyny,
  and mate selection, 342
Hypothetico-deductive model,
  and evolutionary theory, 273–275

I

Ibo,
  incest avoidance in, 363–367
Id,
  evolutionary relevance of, 55
Ideology,
  critique of its application
      to sociobiology, 63–64
  feminist, and rape, 283–284
Imprinting,
  and kin recognition, 187
  and race, in humans, 212
  and species recognition, 212
Impulsive behavior,
      and suicide, 324–327
Inbred strains,
  in behavior genetics, 164
Inbreeding, 374
  avoidance, 181
  benefits of, 181
  See also Incest, Incest avoidance
Incest, 374
Incest avoidance,
  and familiarity, 187
  in humans, 373–397
Incest rules, 376–377
  evolutionary hypothesis, 66, 377–379

evolutionary predictions, 379–391
  and Westermarck theory, 354
Incest taboo,
  See also Inbreeding, Incest avoidance, In-
      cest rules
Inclusive fitness, 12, 44, 49, 232
  and family violence, 294
  and human development, 228
  and kin selection, 214
  and race in humans, 214
  and self preservation, 315–319
  and suicide, 319–322
  See also Kin selection, Kin recognition,
      Nepotism
Industrialization,
  and suicide, 320
Infanticide,
  causation of, 138–140, 295–301
  and congenitial defects, 298
  in mice, 20
  by mother vs non-relatives, 299–301
  and parental incapacity, 298
  and parental investment, 295
Information, 168–171
Ingroups,
  in evolution of human altruism, 100
In-law relatives,
  and family violence, 302
  and incest avoidance, 355–356
  and mating rules, 373–397
Innate schemata, 211
Innovation, 254–261
Intelligence,
  heritability of, 156–157
  and innate cognitive structures, 128
  See also Mind, Cognition, I.Q.
Interdisciplines,
  and social science, 402
Intersexual selection, 16, 337
Intrasexual selection, 16, 337, 348
I.Q.
  heritability of, 210
  in social policy, 207–208
Iran,
  conflict with America, 218
  cultural pressures on family, 232

J

Japanese quail
  optimal outbreeding in, 182